Cognitive Science

Cognitive Science

An Introduction

Second Edition

*Neil A. Stillings, Steven E. Weisler, Christopher H. Chase,
Mark H. Feinstein, Jay L. Garfield, and Edwina L. Rissland*

A Bradford Book
The MIT Press
Cambridge, Massachusetts
London, England

This book was set in Palatino by Asco Trade Typesetting Ltd., Hong Kong and was printed and bound in the United States of America.

Library of Congress Cataloging-in-Publication Data

Cognitive science : an introduction / Neil A. Stillings ... [et al.].
 — 2nd ed.
   p.   cm.
"A Bradford book."
Includes bibliographical references.
ISBN 0-262-19353-1
1. Cognition. 2. Cognitive science. I. Stillings, Neil A.
BF311.C5523   1995
153—dc20   94-29553
                                                                                      CIP

To our parents

Contents

List of Authors

Neil A. Stillings
Ph.D. in psychology, Stanford University. Professor of Psychology in the School of Communications and Cognitive Science, Hampshire College. A founding member of Hampshire's cognitive science program with over twenty years of teaching experience. Organizer of the 1986 national workshop on teaching cognitive science, funded by the Sloan Foundation, and the 1993 national workshop on undergraduate cognitive science, funded by the National Science Foundation. Coeditor of the entire textbook and primary author of chapters 1, 2, 3, and 12.

Steven E. Weisler
Ph.D. in linguistics, Stanford University. Associate Professor of Linguistics in the School of Communications and Cognitive Science, Hampshire College. Research and publications in syntax and semantics. Coorganizer of the 1993 national workshop on undergraduate cognitive science, funded by the National Science Foundation. Coeditor of the entire textbook, primary author of chapter 9, and coauthor of chapters 6 and 10.

Christopher H. Chase
Ph.D. in neuroscience, University of California at San Diego. Associate Professor of Cognitive Science in the School of Communications and Cognitive Science, Hampshire College. Research and publications in cognitive neuroscience, particularly reading development and developmental dyslexia. Primary author of chapter 7.

Mark H. Feinstein
Ph.D. in linguistics, City University of New York. Professor of Linguistics in the School of Communications and Cognitive Science, Hampshire College. Member of the Hampshire faculty since 1976. Research and publications in phonology, mammalian vocalization, animal cognition, and evolution of cognition and behavior. Primary author of chapter 11 and coauthor of chapter 6.

Jay L. Garfield
Ph.D. in philosophy, University of Pittsburgh. Professor of Philosophy in the School of Communications and Cognitive Science, Hampshire College. Research and publications in foundations of cognitive science, philosophy of mind, philosophy of language, metaphysics, epistemology, and Buddhist philosophy. Directs Hampshire's exchange program with the Tibetan universities in exile in India. Author of *Belief In Psychology* (MIT Press) and author or editor of other books. Primary author of chapter 8 and coauthor of chapter 10.

Edwina L. Rissland
Ph.D. in mathematics, MIT. Professor of Computer Science, University of Massachusetts at Amherst and Lecturer on Law, Harvard University Law School. Research and publications on knowledge representation, case-based reasoning, artificial intelligence and the law, and machine learning. Fellow of the American Association for Artificial Intelligence and Vice President of the International Association for Artificial Intelligence and Law. Primary author of chapters 4 and 5.

Preface to the Second Edition

The second edition of *Cognitive Science: An Introduction* retains the organizational format and the level of presentation of the first edition. Many chapters of the book have been substantially revised, however, and several new chapter sections have been added. The changes are detailed in the Note to the Teacher. The team of authors who wrote the first edition remains largely unchanged. David Rosenbaum and Lynne Baker-Ward have gone on to other pursuits. We have particularly missed David's colleagueship and his ability to put his love of the field into words. Fortunately, Christopher Chase joined the Hampshire College faculty at just the right time and volunteered to take over the chapter on neuroscience.

One or two people were primarily responsible for each chapter: Stillings, chapters 1, 2, 3, 12, and several passages on neural computation in chapter 7; Rissland, chapters 4 and 5; Feinstein and Weisler, chapter 6; Chase, chapter 7; Garfield, chapter 8; Weisler, chapter 9; Garfield and Weisler, chapter 10; and Feinstein, chapter 11. Neil Stillings and Steven Weisler edited the entire manuscript.

Many people deserve our thanks for helping with the preparation of the second edition. The authors are part of the cognitive science community in the five-college area centered in Amherst, Massachusetts. It is impossible to mention all of the colleagues and students who contributed to our work, but we thank them for their help. We appreciate the suggestions and corrections of people who wrote to us about the first edition. Patricia Churchland, Richard Thompson, Lee Spector, Jamie Callan, Paul Utgoff, and Jody Daniels reviewed parts of the manuscript for the second edition and made many helpful suggestions. Conversations with Gary Marcus, Sean Stromsten, Sean Hill, Andy Barto, and Richard Yee were also very helpful. Rebecca Neimark prepared the new figures with admirable patience and professionalism. Michael Zenner, Michael Patterson, and Stacey Guess helped with references and with the computerized scanning of the first edition. Leni Bowen helped with permissions, typing, and editing at several crucial points, and she kept Hampshire College's cognitive science program on an even keel throughout our work.

We could not have seen this revision through without Betty Stanton's generosity, faith, and friendly persistence and Teri Mendelsohn's professionalism and unfailing good cheer. The copy editors, Anne Mark and David Anderson, caught our lapses in clarity and our stylistic imperfections with almost frightening accuracy, and they even corrected our antiquated Beethoven scholarship.

Katherine Pfister and Monica and Tim Stillings deserve special thanks for their support for Neil Stillings during the preparation of this edition.

Preface to the First Edition

The seven authors of this book have worked together for many years in the cognitive science community that has grown up in the five-college area surrounding Amherst, Massachusetts. Six of us (Stillings, Feinstein, Garfield, Rosenbaum, Weisler, and Baker-Ward) teach in Hampshire College's School of Communications and Cognitive Science (Baker-Ward recently moved to North Carolina State University). The seventh, Edwina Rissland, is a member of the Computer and Information Science Department at the University of Massachusetts. We have all also been members of the interdepartmental graduate program in cognitive science at the University of Massachusetts.

The cognitive science program at Hampshire College is a unique educational experiment. Hampshire was planned during the 1960s as an experimenting college, and cognitive science was one of the innovative programs it offered when it opened its doors in 1970. In 1972 a single academic department (then called the School of Language and Communication) was formed to house the cognitive science faculty along with faculty members in computer science and communications. The authors would like to thank the college and its leadership for allowing us to develop our commitment to the idea that cognitive science could be an exciting area of undergraduate study. We would also like to thank William Marsh, who was the co-founder and for many years the leader of the program.

Although we worked jointly to lay out the book and rework the manuscript, one or two people were primarily responsible for each chapter: Stillings, chapters 1, 2, 3, and 12; Rissland, chapters 4 and 5; Feinstein and Weisler, chapter 6; Rosenbaum, chapter 7; Garfield, chapter 8; Weisler, chapter 9; Garfield and Weisler, chapter 10; Feinstein, chapter 11; and Baker-Ward, the cognitive development section of chapter 3. Neil Stillings edited the entire manuscript.

Because seven people contributed to the book and because it is rooted in fifteen years of curricular experimentation and development at Hampshire College and the University of Massachusetts, it is impossible to mention everyone who contributed to its development. We thank all of the friends and colleagues who helped bring the book into existence.

The first draft of the book was written with the support of a faculty development grant to the authors from the Charles A. Dana foundation. The completion of the book would have been impossible without the enthusiastic support of Betty Stanton of The MIT Press.

The following people reviewed various parts of the manuscript at various points in its preparation. Gary Dell, Stevan Harnad, Keith Holyoak, and Zenon Pylyshyn deserve particular thanks for reading large chunks of the manuscript. Michael Arbib, Kevin Ashley, Robert Berwick, Charles Briggs, Carol Christensen, Charles Clifton, Bo Dahlbohm, Willem DeVries, Michael Gazzaniga, Allen Hanson, Norbert Hornstein,

John Haugeland, Haym Hirsch, David Kelley, Judith Kroll, David LeBeaux, Wendy Lehnert, Ken Livingston, Dan Lloyd, Lynn Nadel, Marty Ringle, Penni Sibun, Catherine Sophian, Devika Subramaniam, Paul Utgoff, Marie Vaughn, Robert Wall, Thomas Wasow, Sandy Waxman, and Bonnie Webber all read one or more chapters. All of these people exercised their professional expertise with care, and in addition many of them shared their thoughts on the nature of cognitive science and the challenge of teaching it to undergraduates.

We owe a great debt to Anne Mark, who served as manuscript editor. Her sense of expository and organizational clarity and her eye for both conceptual and typographical error are staggering. Nelda Jansen turned our ideas for figures into finished art work with efficiency and unfailing good humor. Erik Antelman and John Gunther also provided invaluable assistance in preparing the figures.

David Rosenbaum's preparation of chapter 7 was partially supported by a Research Career Development Award from the National Institute of Neurological and Communicative Disorders and Stroke (1 K04 NS00942-01) and by a grant from the National Science Foundation (BNS-8408634). The preparation of chapter 12 was partially supported by a grant from the National Science Foundation (SER-8163019) to Neil Stillings.

Ruth Hammen and Leni Bowen kept the School of Communications and Cognitive Science at Hampshire College running smoothly throughout the preparation of the book and lent a hand at several crucial points. The family members and friends of the authors helped with the special stresses of textbook writing. Katherine Pfister deserves special thanks for her steadfast support and good advice while Neil Stillings was editing the manuscript.

Note to the Teacher

We wrote *Cognitive Science: An Introduction* because we believe that undergraduate cognitive science programs ought to be offered to students and that an introductory course ought to be part of the cognitive science curriculum. At the undergraduate level, we feel that cognitive science is best conceived of as a broad interdisciplinary field that draws primarily on psychology, artificial intelligence, linguistics, philosophy, and neuroscience. The disciplines are to some extent distinct in their methods, theories, and results, yet they are strikingly unified by the convergence of their core questions and by the emergence in each of them of a computational, or information processing, view. In this text we try to maintain a consistent computational viewpoint, while honoring the distinctive contributions of each of the disciplines.

In our view the claim that cognitive science is distinguished by a computational or information-processing approach should not be taken too narrowly. The term *computational* should not be taken to mean that artificial intelligence ought to be the central or dominant discipline in cognitive science rather than an equal partner. The term *information processing* should not be restricted to a particular kind of process modeling that has been popular in cognitive psychology. As explained in chapters 1 and 2, we use these terms to refer to any research that concerns cognitive phenomena, such as perception, thought, or language, and that includes abstract levels of analysis that are designed to explain the functional significance of the inner workings of intelligent systems. In this book linguistic competence theories, production systems, parallel distributed processing models, the analysis of functional neural pathways in perceptual systems, and a wide range of other research is all considered computational.

Chapters 2 through 8 have explicit disciplinary origins. The reasons for maintaining some degree of disciplinary identity are both theoretical and practical. On the theoretical side, there is not yet a unified view of cognitive science that is widely accepted and that erases disciplinary boundaries. We feel that students deserve early exposure to the actual diversity and theoretical ferment in cognitive science. We have tried to write a book that is not a polemic for a premature and unstable unification of the field. On the practical side, the institutional structure of cognitive science continues to reflect its origins in the contributing disciplines. Most cognitive science programs are interdepartmental. Most faculty members hold degrees in one of the contributing disciplines. Many students gravitate toward cognitive science after an initial interest in one of the disciplines and go on to graduate study in disciplinary departments. For the time being, then, most teaching staffs and students are comfortable with an introductory course that contains some clear disciplinary signposts. Cognitive science groups should find it easy to build their locally developed emphases and syntheses into a course by emphasizing certain chapters in the text over others, stressing selected issues in lectures, and possibly including some supplementary reading.

The twelve chapters of the book reflect two useful themes for course planning. First, emphasizing the disciplines that contribute to cognitive science, the book consists of an introductory chapter, followed by seven chapters with disciplinary orientations, followed by four chapters on interdisciplinary research topics. Second, emphasizing the core topics of cognitive science, chapters 1 through 5 present a unified introduction to representation and thought, chapters 6, 9, 10, and 11 treat language, chapter 12 treats vision, and chapters 7 and 8 treat the neural and philosophical foundations of the field. A course that emphasized topics might cluster the chapters on language and also shift chapters 7, 8, or 12 out of order. The following remarks about the chapters can be used as an initial guide to course planning. The varying lengths of the chapters should be taken into account in deciding how much time to devote to them.

Instructors who are familiar with the first edition of the book should pay particular attention to the changes that have been made for the second edition. The new edition is about twenty percent longer than the previous one. Although the organizational format of the first edition has been retained, significant revisions, noted in the remarks below, have been made in most chapters.

1. "What Is Cognitive Science?" The concepts of representation and formal system are briefly introduced. The notion of levels of analysis is covered more thoroughly than in the first edition. The role of computers in cognitive science is discussed. The interdisciplinary nature of cognitive science is outlined (although the example analyzing the word *the* has been dropped from this edition). The material introduced in this chapter is expanded and reviewed throughout the book.

2. "Cognitive Psychology: The Architecture of the Mind" This chapter was substantially revised for the second edition. The classical view of the cognitive architecture, organized around the concept of physical symbol systems, is explicitly compared to the connectionist, or parallel distributed processing, view, of the cognitive architecture. The foundational material in chapter 1 is deepened considerably in sections 2.3 and 2.10, which are new to this edition. In the context of the classical view, propositional networks, schemas, working memory, imagery, and skill acquisition are introduced in some depth. The presentation is similar to the first edition. Section 2.10 introduces both the mechanics of connectionist networks and the controversy over the relation between connectionism and the classical view. Chapters 1 and 2 constitute an introduction to the foundations of cognitive science and should be covered in sequence at the beginning of the course.

3. "Cognitive Psychology: Further Explorations" In this chapter the classical and connectionist notions of cognitive architecture developed in chapter 2 are applied to the study of concepts, memory, reasoning, and problem solving. The treatment in the first edition has been substantially revised to reflect connectionist research and other new developments. The chapter can be taught out of order, and the sections within it are largely independent of each other. Unfortunately, the section on cognitive development had to be dropped from this edition to hold down the length of the book.

4. "Artificial Intelligence: Knowledge Representation" The chapter begins with several case studies of AI programs, which give beginning students a feel for AI. Several approaches to knowledge representation are then introduced and

compared, building on chapter 2. Semantic networks, frames and scripts, production rules, and formal logic are covered. The presentation is largely the same as that in the first edition.

5. "Artificial Intelligence: Search, Control, and Learning" This chapter continues the exploration of AI, beginning with an introduction to search and control. Search algorithms are covered in some detail in order to introduce beginning students to algorithmic thinking. Symbolic approaches to learning are treated in some detail, establishing a useful contrast with the material in section 2.10. The first five chapters can be taught as a unified introduction to central cognitive representations and processes.

6. "Linguistics: The Representation of Language" Linguistic competence theories are introduced as theories of linguistic representation. The section on phonology has been substantially revised to reflect recent developments. The material on syntax is largely unchanged, although the presentation has been strengthened in various ways. The final section on linguistic universals has been expanded and deepened. One or more of chapters 9, 10, and 11 can be read immediately following this chapter.

7. "Neuroscience: Brain and Cognition" This chapter has been entirely rewritten. The introductory material on neuroscience has been expanded, reflecting our view that it is increasingly important for cognitive science students to be familiar with basic concepts in neuroscience. We decided to put more emphasis on fundamental knowledge than on the very latest developments, although the treatment of neural representation and computation and of neuropsychology has been deepened considerably as well. The chapter should be assigned after chapters 1 and 2 and before chapter 12.

8. "Philosophy: Foundations of Cognitive Science" The chapter begins with a review and extension of the foundational concepts introduced in chapters 1 and 2 and goes on to cover philosophical issues concerning functionalism, propositional attitudes, qualia, and knowledge representation. The presentation is largely the same as that in the first edition, although several passages on philosophical issues raised by connectionism have been added. The chapter should be assigned after chapters 1 and 2.

9. "Language Acquisition" A description of the stages of language acquisition is followed by an introduction to the theoretical perspectives that have arisen out of linguistic innateness theories and recent formal work on learnability and parsing. The chapter has been revised and expanded to include more recent research.

10. "Semantics" This chapter is a relatively informal introduction to formal semantics as it is studied by linguists and philosophers. It begins with a treatment of quantifiers, names, tense, and scope. Possible worlds and their application to the analysis of necessity and propositional attitudes are then introduced. The chapter closes with a revised section on the role of formal semantics in psychology and AI. Although the chapter is self-contained, many of the basic ideas in it are introduced in chapters 1 through 4 and chapter 6.

11. "Natural Language Processing" The roles of grammar, discourse, and general knowledge in human and machine language understanding are discussed. The chapter also includes new sections on connectionist models and on language production.

12. "Vision" The format of this chapter is unchanged. Low-, intermediate-, and high-level vision are all covered in some depth. The perspectives of AI, psychology, and neuroscience are integrated. Although most of the material from the first edition has been retained, several recent lines of research have been added. The final section of the chapter on the architecture of visual computation has been completely rewritten to reflect new results in neuroscience and connectionism.

We believe that the introductory course in cognitive science should be offered to students in their first or second year of college-level study. The course will typically contain a mix of beginning students and older students who have some experience with one (or possibly more) of the contributing disciplines. We have tried to make the book accessible to committed first-year students. We have also included material that is challenging to these students and at the same time holds the interest of older, more sophisticated students. Lectures, discussions, and assignments should also be geared toward a range of intellectual sophistication, covering the fundamentals as well as pushing into more difficult material.

We also believe that an introductory course is a useful component of graduate programs in cognitive science. Because it provides a quick introduction to the multiple theories, results, and methods of cognitive science, this book should be useful in graduate courses, particularly when it is supplemented by more advanced readings.

Although the initial investment of time can be substantial, planning and teaching a cognitive science course can be an intellectually exciting experience that involves reflecting on the foundations of one's field, learning some new areas, and working closely with colleagues. The field of cognitive science depends on the strength of its introductory courses. We urge our colleagues around the world to make the necessary investment in undergraduate instruction.

Writing the second edition of this text has been an even more humbling experience than writing the first. Cognitive science has changed at a dazzling rate in recent years. Please write to the first author at the address below with your comments and suggestions. You can also request a copy of the National Science Foundation sponsored report on undergraduate cognitive science.

Neil Stillings
nstillings@hamp.hampshire.edu

School of Communications and Cognitive Science
Hampshire College
Amherst, MA 01002

Chapter 1

What Is Cognitive Science?

One of the most important intellectual developments of the past few decades has been the birth of an exciting new interdisciplinary field called *cognitive science*. Researchers in psychology, linguistics, computer science, philosophy, and neuroscience realized that they were asking many of the same questions about the nature of the human mind and that they had developed complementary and potentially synergistic methods of investigation. The word *cognitive* refers to perceiving and knowing. Thus, cognitive science is the science of mind. Cognitive scientists seek to understand perceiving, thinking, remembering, understanding language, learning, and other mental phenomena. Their research is remarkably diverse. It includes, for example, observing children, programming computers to do complex problem solving, analyzing the nature of meaning, and studying the principles of neural circuitry in the brain.

1.1 The Cognitive View

Like all intellectual disciplines, cognitive science involves the adoption of a definite perspective. Cognitive scientists view the human mind as a complex system that receives, stores, retrieves, transforms, and transmits information. These operations on information are called *computations* or *information processes*, and the view of the mind is called the *computational* or *information-processing* view.

The perspective of cognitive science, although it is necessarily partial, provides a unique and rich set of insights into human nature and the human potential, including our potential to develop more powerful information technologies. The cognitive view arose from some quite natural puzzles that fascinate all of us at one time or another. One historical origin of cognitive science was the Greek philosophers' interest in deductive reasoning, the process by which one assumes some information to be true and derives further information that follows logically from the assumptions. For example, from the premises *All dogs have fleas* and *Fido is a dog*, one can logically derive the conclusion *Fido has fleas*. In his theory of syllogistic reasoning, Aristotle showed that deductively valid arguments often take one of a small number of general forms. Learning to reason deductively, then, can be viewed as learning an information process by which valid forms of argument can be recognized and produced. By the seventeenth century the philosophers Leibniz and Hobbes were arguing that all thought was a kind of calculation with nonnumerical information. Today, as we will see in the chapters that follow, linguists and philosophers continue to study the logical properties of language, cognitive psychologists compare people's actual reasoning processes to the idealized systems devised by philosophers and mathematicians, and researchers in artificial intelligence write computer programs to do logical reasoning.

To take another example, consider Louis Armstrong's brilliant improvised solo on his 1927 recording of "Potato Head Blues," which was a landmark in his decisive contribution to the development of jazz. We could adopt many different perspectives on this event. A physicist and biologist might collaborate to study how Armstrong shaped his notes in terms of the production of an air stream by certain complex muscle contractions and the physical properties of the vibrating trumpet. A musicologist might study how the African-American community in New Orleans combined properties of African and European music during the late nineteenth and early twentieth centuries. A music theorist might study how jazz improvisation is governed by the harmonic structure, or chord "changes," of a tune. But the music theorist's analysis raises fascinating questions about human information processing. How was Armstrong able to learn the rules and creative possibilities of harmony without any formal training in music theory? In his improvisation he was essentially composing music while he played. How could he possibly create compositions of great structural elegance so quickly? Part of the answer must be that the human mind has general characteristics that make it possible to learn the rules of improvisation and to apply them with great facility. Recent research on skill acquisition, described in chapter 2, has uncovered some of these characteristics. The results of the research could be used to help design new methods to teach musicians to improvise.

Many other examples could be given of the naturalness of the information-processing view. Whatever else people are doing, they are always taking in, storing, retrieving, transforming, transmitting, and acting on the basis of information. Our knowledge of the general characteristics of human information processing always provides one interesting perspective on human activity. This knowledge is equally relevant as we confront the intellectual potential of computers, wondering what their special strengths and limitations might be.

1.2 Some Fundamental Concepts

Understanding how the computational, or information-processing, view of the mind has led to a significant body of scientific research requires a more detailed understanding of what it means to say that something is a computational system. To set the stage for the following chapters, we will begin to explain and illustrate some fundamental concepts here. We will illustrate these concepts with the example of a familiar information process, doing arithmetic. Specifically, we will analyze the multiplication of non-negative whole numbers.

Information Processes Are Contentful and Purposeful

The first concept is that an important part of understanding an information process is understanding its significance, or the purpose that it serves. An information process typically allows an organism or system to make systematic responses to some range of environmental conditions. The responses are typically adaptive or goal oriented. The information process has a quality of meaningfulness about it. That is, we think of the information in the system as being *about* the world, as having content, significance, or meaning. Such contentful qualities are also sometimes called *semantic*, or intentional, qualities. We find it natural to ascribe understanding, beliefs, or knowledge to any system that acts adaptively in response to information that it takes in from its environment. An understanding of an information process (or information-processing system) will thus include an account of the content of the information it deals with as well as an account of its *competence* to employ that information in the service of certain goals.

Let us consider a simple, but instructive, example, whole-number multiplication. Without philosophical pause, we will stipulate that there is a world of numbers and relations among them that exists independently of any organism or device that carries out numerical computations. The product of two numbers is a third number that is determined by a function, or mapping, from pairs of numbers onto single numbers. This function, call it $\cdot$, is defined by the following characteristics, which must hold for all numbers x, y, and z: $x \cdot 0 = 0$; $x \cdot 1 = x$; $x \cdot y = y \cdot x$; $x \cdot (y \cdot z) = (x \cdot y) \cdot z$; and if $z > 0$ and $x > y$, then $x \cdot z > y \cdot z$. Also, the multiplication and addition functions are related. If we call addition $+$, then for all x, y, and z, $x \cdot (y + z) = x \cdot y + x \cdot z$.

For a device to qualify as a multiplier it must possess *representations* or *symbols* that stand for numbers. It must be able to accept and produce these symbols, and it must be able to transform them in a way that faithfully represents the product function as it was just defined. That is, when the device is fed two symbols, representing two numbers, it must produce the symbol that represents the product of the two numbers. Notice that by focusing on the purpose of a process, on the competence that it has to display, we have achieved a certain kind of purity. We have specified what a multiplier must do (its response function or input-output behavior) without specifying *how* it might do it, beyond requiring that it possess some kind of representation of numbers.

An analysis concerned with the structure of a system's environment, with the information that the system has at its disposal, and with the goals it can satisfy through its deployment of that information, can be called a semantic analysis, a competence theory, a knowledge-level analysis, or an ecological theory (if there is a special emphasis on an analysis of the environment and adaptiveness to it). We all use this kind of explanation in our everyday lives. We make assumptions about what people know and what their goals are, and we assume that they can, for the most part, use their knowledge rationally to meet their goals. This *folk psychology* is quite successful. It is a crucial part of our lives that we are able to predict and explain our own and others' behavior at the knowledge level much of the time.

Given our conscious awareness of our own beliefs and goals, and our everyday methods of discovering other people's, it might be imagined that analyzing the human mind at the knowledge level is not a significant scientific problem. However, cognitive scientists have found that in several important areas our awareness of the information we possess is limited and even misleading. An example of the limitations of awareness is our judgment of the distance from us of an object in our visual field. We know that we possess depth perception. In scientific research on vision, however, it becomes important to know just how accurate depth judgments are, whether they are affected by the familiarity of the object, whether they depend on the presence of other objects in the scene or on the visibility of the ground, and so on. We cannot answer such questions just by consulting our visual awareness. Careful laboratory studies as well as careful studies of the visual environment are required. By studying the environment, we might find that the presence of other objects in a scene can provide information about depth. For example, a nearer object can partly occlude the visibility of a more distant object because it blocks the light reflected from part of that object. Occlusion is thus a possible cue to depth. We could then study in the laboratory whether our depth judgments make use of occlusion information, and, if so, how that information interacts with other information about depth.

An example of how awareness can be misleading is our feeling that we have a uniformly vivid impression of the visual world that is nearly 180 degrees wide. It is rather easy to demonstrate that this impression is an illusion and that we are not able, for example, to perceive much detail in the periphery of the visual field without moving our eyes. Given that our awareness is a poor guide to the information that is immediately available in different parts of the visual field, careful laboratory research is again the only route to discovering our visual competence. In line with these examples from vision, it will be shown in chapter 6 that we are largely unaware of our competence with the sound and grammatical structures of our native languages.

If, rather than trying to understand an existing system, we are trying to *construct* a system to carry out a process, it is obviously also very helpful to begin with a clear understanding of what we are trying to accomplish. It would be unfortunate, for example, if the designers of an electronic calculator did not fully understand the correct behavior of the arithmetic functions that their machine was supposed to calculate. For this reason, a surprising amount of the research in artificial intelligence involves trying to figure out just what knowledge is involved in certain types of intelligent behavior.

Information Processes are Representational
To characterize an analysis at the knowledge level, we have already invoked our second key concept, *representation*. The information that figures in a computation must be represented in some way. Further understanding of a computation requires an understanding of how the information is represented. Returning to the example of multiplication, we have so far said that a multiplier must represent numbers, but we have not said how. To develop more detail, let us suppose that the representation is the familiar decimal place-value notation. In this notation there are ten digit symbols, "0," "1," "2," ... "9," which represent the numbers 0 through 9. Notice that we distinguish here between symbols, such as "5," which are part of the representation, and numbers, such as 5, which are being represented, by placing quotation marks around the symbols. The distinction can be brought out more clearly by recalling the Roman notation system, in which "V" is the symbol for 5, there is no single digit symbol for the number 2, there is a single digit symbol for the number 50, namely, "L," and so on. In decimal notation numbers larger than 9 are represented by *concatenating* the digit symbols into *strings*, such as "65," which is a string of length 2 with "5" in the first position and "6" in the second position. The assignment of a number to a symbolic string is determined systematically by the decimal place-value function, in which the contribution of each digit symbol to the assignment is determined jointly by its basic assignment and its position in the string. For example, knowing that the basic assignments of "6" and "5" are 6 and 5 and knowing the place-value function, one can determine that the assignment of "65" is $6 \cdot 10^1 + 5 \cdot 10^0$, which equals $60 + 5$, or 65. The decimal place-value function establishes a one-to-one correspondence, or mapping, between digit strings and numbers. Note that although the Roman system also uses strings of digit symbols to represent numbers, the mapping between strings and numbers cannot be defined as a place-value function (consider, for example, the significance of the digit symbol "I" in the left position of the strings "II" and "IV").

Place-value representation illustrates some properties that can give representations generality and power. First, a potentially infinite set of symbols can be constructed by beginning with a relatively small stock of basic symbols and using one or more rules of construction, or *syntax*, to build new, complex symbols. In the case of whole numbers the ten digit symbols are the basic symbols, and concatenation is the sole syntactic rule. Allowing strings of digits to be of unlimited length produces a potentially infinite stock of symbols. Representational schemes that include rules for building complex symbolic structures out of simpler ones are called *combinatorial, generative*, or *productive*. Second, the meaning, or *semantic interpretation*, of a complex symbol is built up from the meanings of the syntactic parts of the symbol. Typically, each basic symbol has a fixed meaning, and each syntactic rule is associated with a semantic rule that contributes to the interpretation of the complex symbol. For whole numbers, the numbers 0 through 9 are the fixed interpretations of the ten basic digit symbols "0" through "9." The syntactic rule of concatenation is associated with the place-value rule of interpretation. For example, if we already have a digit string *"xyz,"* and we concatenate "5" onto it to make *"5xyz,"* then the place-value rule says that the numerical interpretation of *"5xyz"* is $5 \cdot 10^3$ (or 5,000) plus the numerical interpretation of *"xyz."* Representational schemes in which the interpretation of complex symbolic structures is determined by the interpretations of their syntactic parts are said to have a *compositional semantics*. Third, information processes that transform symbolic input structures into symbolic outputs can be defined in terms of syntactic structures of the inputs and outputs. Such information processes analyze the syntactic structures of inputs and build syntactically structured outputs. Such information processes are also called *algorithms*. Because the meanings of symbolic structures are a function of their syntax, information processes that operate on syntax can produce meaningful results and represent meaningful operations in the domain that is represented.

These properties of algorithms can be illustrated by the example of multiplication. We have to define a process that operates syntactically on decimal place-value representation in such a way that the process succeeds in representing the multiplication function, ·. The well-known process for multiplying numbers with paper and pencil, call it ⊗, will serve our purposes. It is illustrated in the following example:

$$
\begin{array}{r}
65 \\
\otimes\ 32 \\
\hline
130 \\
195 \\
\hline
2080
\end{array}
$$

The decimal multiplication algorithm is a fairly complicated information process. It requires, among other things, a memory for the products of all of the pairs of digits (e.g., "2" ⊗ "3" yields "6"), an ability to process columns in concatenation order starting with the "ones" column, an ability to "carry," an ability to save partial results until all columns are processed, and an ability to carry out paper-and-pencil decimal addition.

As we said in the previous section, the algorithm can be said to represent the product function if it operates in such a way that the representational mapping between symbols and numbers is maintained. Let us explore this in more detail by looking at the example above. The representation assigns the string "65" to the number 65, "32" to 32, and "2,080" to 2,080. The product of 65 and 32 is 2080. Therefore, when the longhand decimal multiplication algorithm is applied to "65" and "32," the output must be "2,080." More generally, if we map any two input numbers onto digit strings, apply the algorithm, and map the resulting string back to a number, that number must be the product of the input numbers. If the algorithm always mimics the operation in the world, we say that they have the same structure, or are *isomorphic*. Notice, again, that it is critical to distinguish between the operation on symbols and the operation in the domain of numbers that it represents. Many different algorithms could be used to represent multiplication. For example, repeated addition is a possible algorithm for multiplication. To multiply "65" by "32" using this approach, we would apply an algorithm for addition to 32 copies of "65."

Information Processes Can Be Described Formally
The third basic concept results from further attention to the notion of algorithm that was just developed. An algorithm is defined completely in terms of processes that operate on a representation. The processes do not operate on the domain being represented. They are not even defined in terms of the meaning of the representation, which is carried separately by the semantic mapping from the representation to the domain. An algorithm is a *formal* procedure or system, because it is defined in terms of the form of the representation rather than its meaning. It is purely a matter of manipulating patterns in the representation.

The algorithm for paper-and-pencil decimal multiplication, for example, is entirely a matter of manipulating strings of digit symbols according to certain rules. A person with no knowledge that the strings stand for numbers could be taught to carry out the rules correctly. In fact, most of us probably carry out these rules without thinking about why they lead to correct results. Why, for example, does carrying the 1 when multiplying 65 by 2 lead to a correct result? Exactly why is the 195 placed one space to the left before adding it to the 130? Answering these questions requires referring to the place-value mapping that determines the meaning of decimal notation. But one need not know about the place-value mapping to carry out the process. The process is meaningful, but it acquires its meaning indirectly.

An appreciation of the formal nature of information processes brings out two further points. First, since algorithms can be carried out without any higher knowledge about their meanings, they can be carried out by physical systems, which can be biological or engineered. This insight is one of the intellectual foundations for computer science and for the belief that a scientific understanding of mind can be achieved. Second, a formal analysis of an information process provides a particularly convincing demonstration that we understand its inner workings. Because it makes no reference to the meaning of a process, an algorithmic analysis of a process shows exactly how it is done without leaning on our understanding of its meaning.

In summary, the cognitive scientist approaches information processes by distinguishing between formal operations on symbols and the representational relations between symbols and what they stand for. The realization that an organism or machine can produce meaningful behavior by performing formal operations on symbolic structures that bear a representational relationship to the world is a key insight of cognitive science.

Our choice of example should not be taken to mean that cognitive science is easy. Cases like the multiplication algorithm or typical computer programs are good illustrations, because they show that the strategy of cognitive science makes sense. A computer program that multiplies numbers or does database management is obviously performing formal operations on information that has a well-defined representational relationship to a particular domain. Just as obviously, the success of the programs is due entirely to the fact that the formal operations preserve the representational relationship. No inaccessible form of intelligence or understanding is present. Things are not so simple with biological organisms, however. The human mind was not built by a team of engineers and programmers who can just hand over the blueprints and programs. The information processes and representational relationships required for human intelligence are extremely complex, and they can only be discovered by careful and creative research.

Cognitive Science Is a Basic Science

A fourth point about the information-processing view is that the concepts just introduced are employed by cognitive scientists in the pursuit of basic scientific knowledge. Cognitive scientists seek to discover highly general and explanatory fundamental principles of information processing. This goal collides with the tremendous variability that we see in human thought and behavior. We might doubt that any principles of human information processing can be found that hold across all cultures and historical epochs. Certainly we will have to dig deeper than our simple example of the decimal multiplication algorithm, which is a relatively recent human invention that is spottily distributed among the world's people and may slowly disappear from human cognition as electronic calculators become more common. To take another example that is explored in detail in chapters 6 and 9, although people seem to communicate by making noises with their vocal tracts in all of the world's societies, languages show tremendous variation. Do the formal structures and processes of all of the world's languages have anything in common? Research suggests that important *linguistic universals* do indeed exist and that they play an important role in children's acquisition of their native languages. Of course, the hypothesized universals must also explain how the great surface variety in the world's languages is possible.

1.3 Information Processes Can Be Analyzed at Several Levels

The distinction between studying the competence or knowledge of a system and studying its formal information processes can be thought of as a distinction between levels of analysis. The formal analysis is at a *lower* level, providing an account of the information processes that *underlie* the competence that is visible at a *higher*, behavioral level. The analysis of the semantic mapping from the formal representations to the domain can be thought of as a bridge between the formal and knowledge levels. It explains why a formal system is a successful implementation of a particular competence. Although the formal analysis can be thought of as deeper than a knowledge-level analysis, it does not replace it. Each level of analysis contributes its own insights to the overall picture. Without the knowledge-level analysis, including the understanding of the representational mapping, we wouldn't have an understanding of what the algorithm accomplishes, and we wouldn't be able to capture the fact that two different algorithms with different representations both compute the same function. Without the formal analysis we would know what a system does but not how it does it. Reviewing the example of decimal multiplication, the abstract competence analysis $(x \cdot 0 = 0$, etc.) tells us what the product function is, the representational analysis shows that decimal notation systematically represents numbers, and the formal analysis fully specifies the mechanics of the algorithm. If we ignore a level of analysis, we miss an important part of the picture.

The use of multiple levels of analysis to study intelligent systems is one of the hallmarks of cognitive science. Research on a topic can be focused on one or another level of analysis at a given time, depending on the most promising avenues of study, and findings at one level can influence understanding at other levels. The goal is to develop an ever more insightful and complete picture of cognition at all levels of analysis.

Information Processes Must Be Physically Implemented
The analysis of systems at the knowledge level and the formal level, and the use of the concept of representation to tie these levels together, distinguish cognitive science (including computer science) from other sciences. To a surprising extent information processes can be studied at the knowledge and formal levels independently of their physical implementations. This is somewhat remarkable because an information process cannot actually occur unless it is implemented in some physical medium. For any actual information-processing system there obviously are physical levels of analysis aimed at uncovering its biology or physics. Further, there must be some relationship between the physical and formal levels of analysis, because the ability of a physical system to carry out a formal information process depends completely on its physical construction. Just as biologists concluded in the nineteenth century that life arises from particular organizations of matter and energy and not from a special life force, so cognitive scientists proceed from the assumption that cognition arises from material structure and processes and not from any mysterious extraphysical powers. These considerations raise the question of what role physical levels of analysis should play in cognitive science.

The answer to the question must proceed from an understanding of the relationship between the formal and physical levels. Just as a representational mapping ties the knowledge and formal levels of analysis together, so the formal and physical levels are tied together by an *implementational* mapping. The formally defined representations and processes must be mapped onto arrangements of some physical medium and transformations of that medium. The mapping must establish an isomorphism between the formal and physical levels, so that the states and changes in the physical medium faithfully preserve all of the informational relationships in the formal system. To return to our multiplication example, any physical system that implements the standard decimal multiplication algorithm must bear a precise correspondence to the algorithm. Consider the state of having a multiplicand of "65." A human being with pencil and paper physically implements this state by inscribing certain two-dimensional shapes in a particular left-to-right order in a particular position on the paper. In an electronic calculator a multiplicand of "65" might be implemented by the distribution of electrical charge in certain circuit components. In both cases there is a precise correspondence between physical states and transformations in the computing system and the formal structure of the algorithm.

The Necessity of Higher Levels of Analysis
We might imagine that our ultimate goal is to understand the physical workings of an information-processing system and that having a physical understanding would render the understanding at the formal and knowledge levels unnecessary. Consider an electronic calculator that can multiply as an example. There is a sense in which its behavior can be completely understood in terms of the movement of electrical current through

circuits made up of conductors and semiconductors. The physical analysis would make use of the circuit diagram, laws governing electrical circuits (e.g., Ohm's and Kirchhoff's laws), and perhaps some more detailed electron physics needed to understand the behavior of the semiconductors.

The most immediate problem with sticking with the physical analysis is that, by dispensing with the knowledge level, we lose any account of the significance of the calculator's behavior. The physical description does not capture the fact that the calculator is a multiplier. This loss of meaning has many consequences. A mistake in the circuit design, for example, would not be reflected in the physical description, since the circuit laws give equally nice descriptions of useful and useless circuits. Further, at the physical level we could not express the fact that two calculators of different design both multiply, because their physical descriptions could be arbitrarily different (e.g., an electronic calculator and an old-fashioned mechanical adding machine). This kind of inadequacy is generally referred to as the failure of a level of analysis to capture a generalization. The knowledge level is needed to capture generalizations that involve the significance or purpose of an information process or the content of its representations. The physical level of analysis obviously captures other generalizations that cannot be expressed at the knowledge level, such as Ohm's law.

Acknowledging the need for the knowledge level, we might still hope to dispense with the formal level of description. Given that we have a representational mapping from the world to the formal system and an implementational mapping from the formal system to a physical medium, we could imagine bypassing the formal level and working with a single direct map from the world to the physical medium. For example, we could map the world of numbers and the product function directly onto charge distributions and their fluctuations in the circuits of an electronic calculator without bothering with the formal analysis of place-value notation and the multiplication algorithm defined over it. Once again, however, the formal level captures generalizations that cannot be expressed on either the knowledge level or the physical level. In this case the generalizations have to do with the algorithms a system is using. Physical descriptions are full of physical detail that is irrelevant to the algorithm in question, and, worse, they cannot express the fact that two systems of different physical construction compute the same algorithm (e.g., a person and an electronic calculator both doing decimal multiplication). Algorithmic concerns also cannot be expressed at the knowledge level, because the knowledge level abstracts away from the formal detail of computation in order to lump together processes that have the same semantics in spite of having different algorithms. The generalizations that can be captured at the formal level are profound, forming a good part of the discipline of computer science. We will see in section 5.1, for good example, that it is possible to define and compare different algorithms for searching through large sets of alternatives without any consideration of either the semantics or the physical implementation of the alternatives.

Each level of analysis, then, has its own focus and descriptive vocabulary, allowing a conceptually clear explanation of some aspect of computational systems that is obscured or even lost at other levels of description. The concepts at each level express different generalizations and impose different categorizations on information-processing systems.

In addition to this conceptual reason for maintaining higher levels of analysis, there are methodological reasons as well. It is obvious that the design of engineered computational systems can be profitably guided by high-level decisions about what sorts of algorithms they must compute and what parts of the world they will have to deal with. It is perhaps not so obvious, but equally important, that our attempts to understand biological information-processing systems, such as the human mind/brain, at the physical level can be guided by understanding at the knowledge and formal levels. Physically, the brain is enormously complex. We can get a much better idea of what to look at in the brain and how to look at it if we have a good idea of what the brain is computing and what algorithms it is using to do the computations. In particular, a theory of some mental process at the formal level is a source of hypotheses about the implementational mapping from formal representations and processes to nervous tissue. We will see in chapter 7, for example, that analysis of auditory localization in the barn owl at the behavioral and formal levels guided a systematic and successful search for the neural circuits that compute the direction of an environmental sound from the acoustic input to the ears.

The Importance of the Physical Level of Analysis
The fact that the knowledge and formal levels capture unique generalizations and that a particular formal system can be physically implemented in any number of ways suggests the possibility that cognitive science could be pursued without regard to the physical level of analysis, which could be left to biologists and engineers. Although it is true that the higher levels of analysis are the distinctive province of cognitive science and that much research in the field takes place exclusively at these levels, the physical level cannot be ignored, largely for practical reasons.

Understanding the physical implementation of information processes is obviously a crucial piece of an overall understanding of cognition, since all cognition occurs in some physical medium. Researching mappings between the higher levels of analysis and the physical level is greatly facilitated by an understanding of both levels. It is therefore not a good idea to enforce a complete division of scientific labor between people who work at the knowledge and formal levels and people who work at the physical level.

In general, results at one level of analysis can always potentially affect research at other levels, because the levels are mutually constraining. We have already pointed out that a formal theory of an information process constrains its physical implementation, because the physical implementation has to be a faithful instantiation of the formal process. The constraints run in the other direction as well. Discoveries about the physical structure of the brain can strongly suggest that it is computing certain kinds of algorithms and not others or that it represents knowledge in certain ways and not others. We will see in chapter 2, for example, that in recent years relatively simple facts about the brain, such as the speed with which neural cells can generate signals and the way in which the cells are interconnected, have been used by some researchers to draw far-reaching conclusions about the representations and algorithms that characterize cognition in biological organisms. In the realm of technology the availability of a particular kind of hardware can spur research into new representations and algorithms that are particularly suited to that hardware. For example, in recent years it has become feasible to build computers that have thousands of interconnected, active processors rather than just one. This possibility triggered a wave of research on parallel algorithms that could take advantage of many simultaneously active processors.

Ideally, research on cognition should occur at all levels of analysis, and all fruitful interactions among levels should be encouraged. Building bridges between the higher levels of analysis and the physical level has been, and continues to be, the most difficult problem in the cognitive and neural sciences. In recent years, however, it has also been one of the most active areas of new research.

1.4 Computers in Cognitive Science

It should be clear from the discussion so far that a number of concepts and distinctions that are important in computer science are part of the underlying assumptions of cognitive science. More generally, the growth of computer science has greatly accelerated the development of cognitive science. Computers thus have a tendency to become a metaphor for all information processing. The metaphor is often useful, but it is potentially misleading as well.

The rough outline of the analogy between computers and the human mind should already be apparent. Our stress on the independence of an information process from its physical implementation is akin to the common distinction between software and hardware in the computer world. For example, when we see the same word-processing program running on two different brands of computers, it is obvious that an information process can be rigorously defined as a formal process without reference to any particular physical device. Current computer software also makes it clear that formal information processes can be powerful and flexible. Highly complex information, ranging from documents to personnel records to satellite photographs, can be represented and stored in computers. Programming languages allow finite sets of simple instructions to be flexibly combined to define complex operations on the stored information. Today's computers and computer software are concrete examples of information processors and processes that make it easier to understand what cognitive science is about.

On the other hand, computers are very far from exhibiting some of the most impressive, yet mundane, aspects of human cognition, such as learning a language, identifying the objects in a naturally occurring visual scene, or solving simple problems via analogies with other situations. Therefore, it is misleading to take the computer metaphor to mean that current computer programs, programming languages, and hardware are good models for human cognition. The usefulness for cognitive science of any current piece of computer science or technology is a matter of research, not prior stipulation. Research is now under way on new "generations" of computer software and hardware that many workers in the field think will be needed to advance computer intelligence.

This research includes the part of computer science called *artificial intelligence, or AI,* which overlaps considerably with cognitive science. Many researchers in AI try to model their computer programs after human intelligence, and they derive inspiration from insights into human information processing that come from other disciplines in cognitive science, such as psychology and linguistics. The insights also flow in the other direction. Attempts by AI researchers to program systems that can understand language, see, or solve problems have led to new, testable hypotheses about human cognition. In its interplay with the other cognitive science disciplines AI provides a powerful alternative methodology for exploring and testing theories of cognition that supplements the empirical methods of psychology and linguistics. Chapters 4 and 5 of this book are about AI.

The technique of expressing a cognitive theory as a computer program and then running the program to explore the ramifications of the theory is now an important tool throughout cognitive science. Many theories are complicated enough that it is impossible to figure out what their predictions are without simulating them on computers. There are differences of emphasis between AI and the computer simulation of theories of human cognition. Much AI research is oriented toward practical results. A program that is too slow, for example, might be of no use. On the other hand, a useful AI program might not use the same algorithms as a human being solving the same problem. Researchers oriented toward simulation have complementary goals. Their measure of success is whether their programs work the same way as human (or animal) cognitive processes. It doesn't matter to them if the computer simulation is impractically slow, or slower than the biological process it simulates, as long as it makes the right predictions. In spite of these differences there is no absolute line between AI and simulation research. Any AI program might turn out to be a good theory of human cognition, and any simulation program might prove to have practical applications.

1.5 Applied Cognitive Science

Cognitive scientific theories are leading increasingly to practical applications. Many of the applications are in the domain of education and learning. As cognitive psychologists have come to understand the information processes involved in reading, for example, they have begun to develop new ways of diagnosing and treating children's reading difficulties. Linguistic theory has led to much more precise knowledge of the speech impairments that follow strokes in the left hemisphere of the brain. This new knowledge promises to be useful in designing appropriate speech therapy and computer-driven linguistic prostheses for stroke victims.

Other applications of cognitive science are more surprising. Contemporary theories of human memory have been applied to the question of the reliability of legal witnesses. This research has already led to important changes in the role of eyewitness testimony in the legal process. Another example is the application of new psychological theories of skill acquisition and visual-motor imagination to the design of training programs for athletes.

Artificial intelligence research is leading to applications in expert systems and robotics. Expert systems have been developed to aid in configuring computer systems, exploring for oil, establishing the structure of complex organic compounds, and diagnosing diseases.

These developing applications are exciting, particularly to those within the field or thinking of going into it. The excitement should be tempered, however, by an awareness of the moral and political questions raised by applied cognitive science. Just as physicists must confront the implications of nuclear technology, and biologists the implications of genetic engineering, so cognitive scientists must confront the implications of knowledge technology. The potentially controversial applications of cognitive science research range from the possible development of a new generation of intelligence tests, which might be misused, to the large-scale introduction of intelligent robots in manufacturing industries, which might cause a massive loss or displacement of jobs. As in other sciences, the less and the more controversial applications often flow from the same underlying theoretical research. For example, results in computer vision might be used to design either a visual prosthesis for the blind or the control system of a cruise missile carrying a nuclear warhead. We hope that this book will provide the basic understanding of cognitive scientific theory that is needed to think about the policy issues posed by new information-processing technologies. We also strongly recommend the study of relevant aspects of history, social science, and the humanities, because the perspective of cognitive science, although crucial, must be supplemented by other perspectives.

1.6 The Interdisciplinary Nature of Cognitive Science

The Five Disciplines

As noted earlier, cognitive science is an interdisciplinary field that has arisen from the convergence on a common set of questions by psychology, linguistics, computer science, philosophy, and neuroscience. The five contributing disciplines will undoubtedly retain their separate identities, because each of them involves a much larger set of concerns than the focus on a basic science of cognition. A more interesting question is whether cognitive science will become a distinct academic discipline in its own right, within which the contributions of the five converging disciplines become so thoroughly intermingled and transformed that they are no longer identifiable. This book presents cognitive science in its current form. The distinctive contributions of each of the five disciplines are highlighted, particularly in chapters 2 through 8. The topics selected for discussion, however, are those where the disciplines have shared the most common ground. Chapters 9 through 12 present several examples of research areas in which the interdisciplinary collaboration has been particularly close and has begun to obscure some of the differences among disciplines.

Obviously, no one of the five contributing disciplines encompasses the entire subject matter of cognitive science, and each discipline brings to the field a focus on particular areas. Neuroscientists are primarily concerned with the organization of the nervous system. Linguists are concerned with the structure of human language and the nature of language acquisition. Philosophers are concerned with logic and meaning, and with clarifying the fundamental concepts of cognitive science, such as information and knowledge. Psychologists are concerned with general human mental capacities, such as attention and memory. Computer scientists are concerned with the possibilities for AI. Cognitive science encompasses all of these concerns. Cognitive scientists, although they usually specialize in one or two of the contributing disciplines, benefit greatly from the cross-fertilization of all of them.

The most important differences among the five disciplines are in the research methods that they use to address the nature of mind. Psychologists emphasize controlled laboratory experiments and detailed, systematic observations of naturally occurring behaviors. Linguists test hypotheses about grammatical structure by analyzing speakers' intuitions about grammatical and ungrammatical sentences or by observing children's errors in speech. Researchers in AI test their theories by writing programs that exhibit intelligent behavior and observing where they break down. Philosophers probe the conceptual coherence of cognitive scientific theories and formulate general constraints that good theories must satisfy. Neuroscientists study the physiological basis of information processing in the brain.

The Study and Practice of Cognitive Science

From the student's point of view one of the main attractions of cognitive science is the diversity of its methods. The field accommodates a wide variety of personal intellectual styles and preferences. Those who are attracted to laboratory work can pursue experimental psychology or neuroscience. Those who dislike laboratory work but who like abstract problems and careful logical analysis can pursue philosophy. Those who love the challenge of writing computer programs can pursue AI, and those who love thinking about language can pursue linguistics. Those who are fascinated by the development of children can pursue cognitive development. This list could go on, but the general point is that cognitive science needs researchers who are motivated by many different kinds of curiosity and who like to do many different kinds of work. The field thrives on the presence of people who ask the widest possible variety of questions about the mind.

Your own intellectual tastes will probably lead you to prefer some of the chapters in this book over others. It is natural to pick a specialty, but we urge you not to let your preferences lead you to neglect other chapters. Cognitive science depends on a continuing dialogue among its various specialties, and the intelligence of the dialogue requires people with a good grounding in the fundamentals of the contributing disciplines. Today, a new generation of cognitive scientists is learning these fundamentals as undergraduates and beginning graduate students. The resulting increase in mutual understanding will enhance the collaborative research of the future.

Suggested Readings

The material in this chapter is covered from a similar point of view and at a somewhat more advanced level in chapter 2 of Newell's *Unified Theories of Cognition* (1990). An advanced treatment is given in the first four chapters of Pylyshyn's *Computation and Cognition: Toward a Foundation for Cognitive Science* (1984). Chapters 8 and 9 of Churchland's *Neurophilosophy: Toward a Unified Science of the Mind/Brain* (1986) present a case for the cooperative pursuit of research at different levels of analysis as well as a case for giving neuroscience the guiding role. Gardner's *The Mind's New Science: A History of the Cognitive Revolution* (1985) presents a history of cognitive science.

References

Churchland, P. S. (1986). *Neurophilosophy: Toward a unified science of the mind/brain.* Cambridge, Mass.: MIT Press.

Gardner, H. (1985). *The mind's new science: A history of the cognitive revolution.* New York: Basic Books.

Newell, A. (1990). *Unified theories of cognition.* Cambridge, Mass.: Harvard University Press.

Pylyshyn, Z. W. (1984). *Computation and cognition: Toward a foundation for cognitive science.* Cambridge, Mass.: MIT Press.

Chapter 2

Cognitive Psychology: The Architecture of the Mind

2.1 The Nature of Cognitive Psychology

Psychologists formulate and test theories about the human mind and behavior. Cognitive psychology concerns human cognition, our capacities for sensory perception, memory, thinking, problem solving, and learning. The cognitive psychologist who is oriented toward cognitive science views the human mind as a remarkable information-processing system that is extraordinarily powerful in most circumstances and yet surprisingly limited in others. As you read this paragraph, the meaning of each word is effortlessly activated within a mental dictionary of tens of thousands of words. But you probably do not remember the names of the six coauthors of this book. A book-reading computer, using current technology, would have a much easier time remembering names than deploying meanings.

We begin this book with cognitive psychology for two reasons. First, cognitive psychology focuses on the human mind. In order to fully appreciate work in artificial intelligence (AI), it is necessary to have some familiarity with theories of human intelligence. Second, in keeping with the emphasis on basic science within cognitive science, cognitive psychologists have tried to develop theories of highly general cognitive capacities. They have asked what sort of general information-processing capacities a mind must have in order to do the many things it does. That is, they have tried to figure out what the overall design, or architecture, of the mind is. It is a good idea to begin the study of cognitive science by confronting some of the most basic questions about how it is possible for the mind to work as it does.

In order to maintain the focus on the most general cognitive capacities, we will delay discussion of two of the more specialized information-processing subsystems of the mind. Language will be extensively discussed in chapters 6, 9, 10, and 11. Vision will be discussed in chapter 12. Linguistic and visual information processing have many specific characteristics that require extensive and interdisciplinary investigation.

Along with the distinctive focus on the general properties of the human mind, cognitive psychology has contributed a particular method of investigation to cognitive science. Cognitive psychologists specialize in testing theories by making systematic, precise observations of human behavior, often under laboratory conditions. Several discussions in the chapter include detailed examples of laboratory experiments. In learning to think like a cognitive psychologist, you should do more than simply absorb the theory of cognitive architecture that is being presented. You should also consider and try to evaluate the experimental evidence discussed. When the evidence for a theory seems weak to cognitive scientists, they try to devise a further experiment that will either support the theory or weaken it in favor of some alternative. Cognitive psychology depends on the interplay of theory and systematic empirical evidence.

2.2 The Notion of Cognitive Architecture

A fundamental view in cognitive science is that an intelligent system is not completely homogeneous. It must consist of a number of functional subsystems, or modules, that cooperate to achieve intelligent information processing and behavior. This view is supported by results in cognitive psychology, some of which are presented in this chapter and the next, and by discoveries that animal brains contain numerous specialized regions, some of which will be described in chapter 7. It is also supported by attempts to build intelligent devices. Computer designers and AI researchers have found that they have to impose a great deal of structure on their machines and programs in order to achieve powerful information processing.

Our particular concern in this chapter is a kind of structure called *cognitive architecture*. Cognitive architecture refers to information-processing capacities and mechanisms of a system that are built in. The architecture of a system may or may not give it the potential to acquire information-processing capacities that are not specifically built in. For example, the architecture of the simplest electronic calculators fixes their mathematical capacities, whereas the architecture of programmable calculators allows them to acquire new capacities by being programmed. Although the new capacities are not functional until the programs are loaded into the machine's memory, the potential for them is inherent in its architecture. If we understand the architecture, we understand not only what the machine does now but the range of things it can potentially do and how it is able to do them. Given the responsiveness of human cognition to experience, the desire to understand the human cognitive architecture makes sense. To the extent that we understand it, we understand not just what some individual or group is capable of at a particular time and place but rather the human cognitive potential.

Since most adult cognitive abilities depend on extensive learning experiences, it is difficult to uncover the contribution of the cognitive architecture to these abilities and separate it from the contribution of specific experiences. The high degree of flexibility of human cognition requires that we think of much of the human cognitive architecture not as determining specific thoughts and behaviors but as an abstract set of mechanisms that potentiates a vast range of capabilities. We must get underneath people's behavior in particular circumstances to discover the basic information-processing capacities that allow adaptive responses to a wide range of situations.

Individual Differences in Cognitive Architecture

It should be noted that we make the simplifying assumption here that the human cognitive architecture is uniform across individuals. In fact, there is some architectural variation across individuals. The nervous system is subject to genetic variation, its early development can be altered by various kinds of nutritional or experiential deprivation, it can deteriorate with age, and it can be injured. In principle, variations can be qualitative or quantitative. Qualitatively different architectures have different information-processing components or structures. For example, a person who is totally deaf and a hearing person do not have the same cognitive architecture. The cognitive architecture of the hearing person includes a subsystem that provides acoustic input. That subsystem is functionally absent in the deaf person. In other respects the two people may have the same cognitive-architectural structures. In fact, enough of the deaf person's auditory architecture may be intact to allow considerable auditory cognition, even though the person cannot respond to sound. A case in point is Ludwig van

Beethoven, who composed his late works after going deaf. So-called color blindness is a more subtle example of a structural difference. A person with normal human color vision possesses three visual input channels for daylight vision, which have peak sensitivities in three different regions of the visible spectrum. A color-blind person might be missing one of these input channels and therefore be unable to make as many color discriminations as the person with three channels (Nathans 1989). An example of a quantitative difference in cognitive architecture is the deterioration of night vision with age. Owing to aging processes that are universal and currently irreversible, older people cannot see as well as younger people in the dark. The part of their visual architecture that is responsible for night vision operates qualitatively in the same fashion as that of younger people, but they are much less sensitive at low illumination levels and much slower to adapt to sudden changes in illumination.

We bypass variations in the architecture across individuals for two reasons. First, most human beings appear to have structurally very similar architectures. The variation is mostly quantitative. Once a structure is well understood, its quantitative variations tend to be easy to understand. Second, understanding what might be called the generic human architecture is a good way to begin to discover and try to understand the qualitative variations that do exist. Of course, there are cases where the observation of a structural variation can lead to new insights about cognitive architecture. Studies of so-called split-brain patients (introduced in chapter 7) are one such case.

The tendency of cognitive scientists to focus on the fundamental structure of the cognitive architecture tends to surprise students whose initial interest in human cognition arises from curiosity about cognitive differences among people. Different people have different abilities and different styles of thinking. It is natural to be curious about possible inborn differences that facilitate the development of unusual cognitive abilities, in the arts, sciences, practical affairs, and so on. In complex societies, which contain many demanding and competitive environments, such differences are also of practical importance. To cognitive scientists, however, the question of inborn human uniformity is deeper and more fascinating. A key contribution of cognitive science has been to bring out the interest and scientific importance of what we tend to take for granted: that almost all people have remarkably similar cognitive potential and even remarkably similar developed cognitive capacities. Nearly everyone is able to negotiate the visual world with great success, learn a natural language, and acquire a vast store of knowledge that can be deployed flexibly to meet the demands of an ever changing environment. Although we do not yet know everything we would like to about the limits and variability of human skill acquisition, it is also safe to say that with suitable practice nearly everyone could become competent at a wide range of cognitive and sensory-motor skills, from baseball, to cooking, to managing a preschool classroom, to solving physics problems, to leading a nomadic life in the desert.

This perspective on human cognition also leads toward a perspective on human differences that does not overemphasize genetic variability. To a very large extent the differences in people's cognitive abilities are the result of differing goals and experiences. It is no doubt true that if environment and experience could be held constant, people's achievements would vary, in part because of inborn cognitive differences, but these variations can be seen as the wrinkles in the rich and never completed tapestry of human accomplishment that is woven from the interaction between the basic cognitive architecture and the variety of human environments.

In a sense, the root problem of cognitive science is to understand how the cognitive architecture makes mundane human competence possible. An analogy with the history of chemistry is useful here. The alchemists did not make much progress when they focused their attention on exotic problems such as transmuting lead into gold. Chemistry advanced when thinkers began to focus on the underlying architecture of all matter. From this point of view mundane substances such as table salt and water are as interesting as gold, and understanding ordinary chemical reactions, such as the burning of a candle, holds the key to progress. Following this lead, we will concentrate on the ordinary in cognition.

2.3 A Global View of the Cognitive Architecture

In order to focus our discussion in this chapter, our first task is to break the cognitive architecture into subsystems. Everyday intuition, evidence about the brain, and evidence from laboratory studies in cognitive science are in good agreement about at least some of the major components of cognition. Human beings can receive information through their senses, think, and take physical action through voluntary muscular movement. As it is depicted in figure 2.1, then, we can initially conceive of the human information processor as consisting of a central thinking system that receives information about the world from sensory systems and issues movement commands to the motor system. In addition, language plays a large and biologically unique role in human cognition. It is shown as a specialized subsystem of the central cognitive processor in figure 2.1. Central processes are the subject of this chapter. The linguistic component of the cognitive architecture is treated in chapters 6, 9, and 11. In chapter 12 we take up vision as an example sensory system. Chapter 7 concerns the neural implementation of the architecture.

The decomposition of the human information-processing system shown in figure 2.1 should be taken as illustrative and provisional at this point. The senses (vision, audition, and so on) could be represented as separate subsystems, raising questions about whether they intercommunicate directly or only via the central system. Evidence might lead us to split the central system up into a number of components with distinctive channels of interaction. On the other hand, it must be recognized that the

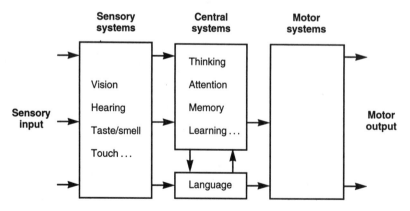

Figure 2.1
A global view of the cognitive architecture. (Used with the permission of Neil Stillings.)

boundaries between modules and the channels of communication may not be so clear-cut. The separation between central processes and the sensory and motor systems, for example, is not as sharp as the figure indicates. After sensory information is initially registered, it is operated on and transformed successively, making it difficult to identify where sensory or perceptual processing stops and central processing begins, or what portion of the transformation from sensory input to motor output is to be designated central. Similarly, the boundaries between the linguistic system and sensory, motor, and other central systems is not completely clear. Some of the fuzziness will probably be resolved by future research, but it may also be necessary to recognize that any simple partitioning of the cognitive architecture is partly an intellectual convenience that obscures some of the complexities of human information processing.

Input and Output Systems

Each major component of the cognitive architecture has particular functions. The first job of a sensory system is the *transduction* of some form of physical energy impinging on the body into a form that usable by cognitive processes. At the physical level of analysis, the incoming physical energy is transduced into electrochemical activity in specialized nerve cells called *receptors*. At the formal level of analysis this electrochemical activity can be looked at as a complex signal or code that represents information contained in the incoming physical energy. Typically the initial encoding must be transformed in various ways to produce a clear representation of the most useful information. Sensory systems have elaborate architectures to accomplish the initial transduction and further processing of sensory input. In the visual system, for example, the retinas at the backs of the two eyes contain millions of *photoreceptor* cells. The initial encoding delivered by the photoreceptors is processed extensively by several other layers of retinal cells and by many specialized regions in the brain.

The specialization of sensory systems is one source of evidence for the *modularity* thesis concerning the cognitive architecture (Fodor 1983). A prominent feature of this thesis is that sensory systems are *informationally encapsulated*. That is, a sensory system transforms a class of environmental inputs into outputs that are useful to central processes, but the computation of its output is not affected by central processes. Input systems are thought to have evolved to rapidly deliver reliable information to central processes, and their structure and operation is argued to be genetically determined and not substantially modifiable. The modularity thesis amounts to a claim that some of the boundaries among the major components of the cognitive architecture in figure 2.1 can be drawn in a principled way using a combination of computational and biological criteria.

Fodor (1983) argues that the initial processing of spoken linguistic input is also modular. Given the intimate connection that we sense between language and thought, it seems strange at first to think that the processing of linguistic input could be informationally encapsulated. Knowledge and expectations that are available centrally might well affect the perception of language. There is considerable debate about this issue, but regardless of the outcome of that debate later chapters will make clear that there is much that is biologically and computationally special about language.

Similar points could be made about the motor system. It also involves transduction. In order for actual movement to occur, neural codes must cause muscular contraction. This transformation is accomplished by neurochemical events at a specialized type of connection between motor nerve cells and muscle cells called a *neuromuscular junction*. As with sensory systems, several parts of the brain are specialized for motor control.

Central Systems

Our primary job in this chapter and the next is to characterize the architecture of the central information processes. We will assume that the sensory and linguistic systems can deliver meaningful input to the central processes. For example, we assume that the visual system can reliably deliver the spatial locations, shapes, colors, and identities of common objects in the visual field. And we assume that the linguistic system can reliably identify the words and the grammatical structure of incoming sentences. We assume that the motor system responds reliably to motor command sequences issued by central processes by moving the body in the appropriate ways. The execution of motor commands includes moving the muscles of the vocal tract to produce speech. So, given that the central system has appropriate inputs and outputs, we ask how it is organized to accomplish the aspects of cognition that we associate distinctively with it.

Everyday terms for some of the capabilities of central cognition are listed in figure 2.1. First and foremost, we can think. That is, we can reason from known facts to novel conclusions, we can solve problems, we can plan our activities and evaluate alternative plans, and so on. Furthermore, our thinking capacity is remarkably flexible. It is often not controlled by immediate sensory input or the need for immediate action. There is no obvious limit to our thinking, in the sense that we draw new conclusions, make new plans, and solve new problems in remarkably diverse domains every day. Thinking is usually characterized by a focus of attention. The positive side of attention is that it seems to maintain the goal-directedness of thought. The negative side is that our attentional capacity seems to be limited and is sometimes overwhelmed. In addition to drawing on current perceptual input, thought also takes inputs from memory. Human memory, though far from infallible, seems relatively unlimited both in capacity and in ability to yield up information that is relevant to current thought processes. Finally, there is our capacity to learn. We acquire the knowledge that resides in our memories, and we are able to acquire many cognitive and sensory-motor skills during our lifetimes.

It is apparent that central processes must have a rather complex architecture of their own. In the 1980s a view of the architecture of cognition came to a kind of maturity after a long period of development that began in earnest in the 1950s. We will refer to this view, perhaps a bit too grandly, as the *classical* view (Fodor and Pylyshyn 1988). In truth, it would be more accurate to call it a family of views, since there have been a number of somewhat different architectures proposed that are all recognizably classical (Anderson 1983; Newell 1990; Simon 1990 are examples). Much of this chapter will be devoted to developing a generic version of the classical view. The chapter will also introduce a significant critique of the classical view and a family of new proposals about cognitive architecture that have arisen over the last ten years. These views go under a number of names, including *connectionism, parallel distributed processing,* and *artificial neural networks.*

Physical Symbol Systems

A key hypothesis in the classical view of the cognitive architecture is that the central processes of the human mind constitute, among other things, a general-purpose computational system, or *physical symbol system* (Newell 1980; Newell, Rosenbloom, and Laird 1989). The hypothesis includes the framework developed in chapter 1. That is, it is assumed that cognition can be analyzed as formal symbol manipulation processes, which can be given a semantic interpretation that accounts for their meaningfulness and adaptiveness to the environment. The symbol system is physical because the formal processes are implemented in a particular physical medium, the brain. The additional content of the hypothesis has to do with the range of symbolic processes that are made possible by the cognitive architecture. The idea is that the architecture contains built-in structures and operations that make central cognitive processes programmable. The architecture contains a set of built-in information-processing facilities that endow it with the potential to acquire an unlimited range of further information processes.

Universal Machines   Research in computer science and allied mathematical fields has led to an understanding of properties that a flexible programmable system seems to require. The system must have a memory in which symbols can be stored and from which they can be retrieved. Maximum flexibility requires that the size of the memory be arbitrarily extendible, since there is no limit to the amount of stored information that a task might require. Extendibility is made possible in computers through the provision for adding ever more or larger mass storage units, such as disk and tape drives. Human memory is extendible through external storage media such as handwritten notes, books, tapes, and computerized records. The storage capacity of the human brain is also extremely large, so that its limits are not exceeded for many tasks.

The processor must be able to store symbols in memory and retrieve them. Moreover, symbolic processing requires that what is stored in memory can depend on what has recently been retrieved. This allows the processor to systematically produce new symbolic structures in response to those already in memory or to transform structures already in memory. For example, a calculator might be able to retrieve a pair of symbols from memory and produce a third symbol according to an algorithm that represents addition.

A truly flexible system is able to acquire new information-processing procedures. In conventional programmable systems some of what is retrieved from memory functions as instructions to perform certain operations rather than merely as data to be fed into operations. For example, a programmable calculator might be able to retrieve a triple of symbols from memory and treat the first symbol as an instruction to perform some arithmetic operation on the second two symbols. In computer science, the process of treating information stored in memory as instructions is often referred to as *interpretation*, since the system is, in a sense, interpreting the information as instructions. This sense of interpretation is obviously different from the kind of semantic interpretation discussed in chapter 1. The interpretation function inside the machine establishes a relation between formal symbols and formal operations, whereas semantic interpretation establishes a relation between formal symbols and operations and some significant domain external to the system.

In the 1930s Turing (1937), an early computation theorist, gave one of the first general characterizations of the class of symbolic transformations that can be computed by formal processes. He defined a class of devices, now called *Turing machines* (described in more detail in chapter 8), each of which computed some input-output function. He called the entire class of functions computable by Turing machines the *computable functions*. (He also proved the existence of functions that are not computable.) The argument (known as *Church's thesis, Turing's thesis*, or the *Church-Turing thesis*) that the computable functions are a natural class has stood the test of time in the sense that all other proposed universal characterizations of computation have been shown to define the same class of functions. A device capable of computing any computable function is known as a *universal machine*. Turing defined a universal Turing machine, for example, that could mimic the computations of any other Turing machine. The mimicry of another machine was accomplished by storing a description of it on the universal machine's memory tape and interpreting the description. The description of the other machine is essentially a program. A consequence of Turing's results is that if a system has a memory and the ability to interpret the contents of its memory as instructions to perform operations, the repertoire of built-in operations needed for universality is extremely simple.

The universal Turing machine, although a convenient mathematical fiction, is not suitable for practical computation and hence has never been built. Its extremely inefficient memory retrieval scheme requires scanning serially through arbitrarily long sections of its memory tape to locate needed information or to find the correct cells to write in. Its primitive operations are so simple that considerable programming is required to build up operations such as addition or comparing two strings of symbols for equality. Because of the inefficiency of memory storage and retrieval, these relatively elementary operations would be extremely inefficient, making complex programs that depended on them fatally slow.

From the late 1940s through the present the *von Neumann architecture*, named after the mathematician John von Neumann, has been employed in most practical general-purpose computers. The hallmark of a von Neumann machine is a large *random-access memory*. Each cell in the memory has a unique numerical address, which can be used to access or replace the contents of that cell in a single step. In addition to its ability to address memory locations directly, a von Neumann machine also has a central processing unit (the *CPU*) that possesses a special working memory (*register memory*) for holding data that are being operated on and a set of built-in operations that is rich in comparison with the Turing machine. The exact design of the central processor varies considerably, but typically includes operations such as adding two binary integers, or branching to another part of a program if the binary integer in some register is equal to zero (so-called *conditional branching*). The CPU can interpret information retrieved from memory either as instructions to perform particular operations or as data to apply the current operation to. Thus, a portion of memory can contain a sequence of instructions, called a *program*, and another portion of memory can contain the data to be operated on by the program. The CPU repeatedly goes through a *fetch-execute* cycle, in which the next operation and its arguments are retrieved from memory and the operation is applied to the arguments. Although it computes the same class of functions as a universal Turing machine, a von Neumann machine runs efficiently because of its random-access memory and because its architecture can be implemented in electronic circuitry that makes its basic operations extremely fast (currently from millions to tens of millions of instructions per second in desktop computers).

Although it is immensely practical, a von Neumann machine, like the universal Turing machine, might be called an immaculate universal device. It has the potential to do anything, but as it comes out of its shipping carton it actually can do nothing—until a program is loaded into its memory. The noncommittal purity of von Neumann machines is a major source of their economic success. The machines are engineered precisely to be bendable to the demands of any information-processing task and therefore have the widest possible market. The manufacturer wastes no money building in functions that many users would not want. The flexibility of a von Neumann machine, however, can only be realized by an intelligent programmer. It is a tool, perfectly adapted to an environment of programmers but lacking any innate autonomy. The clean separation between hardware and software, where the responsibility of the hardware is to provide efficient and cost-effective computational potential via programmability, has been a spectacularly successful technological strategy.

This strategy obviously would not suffice for biological success. Organisms must be innately endowed with specific computational capacities that are dedicated to tasks necessary for their survival. In addition, more intelligent organisms, including humans, can acquire new information-processing abilities by interacting with their environments. They can, in a sense, be programmed by a sequence of goal-oriented experiences in their environments. Neither dedicated computational capacity nor learning from experience is typical of physical symbol systems as they have been developed technologically. The fact that physical symbol systems need have no built-in active survival mechanisms demonstrates that symbol-systemhood is not a sufficient condition for intelligence. One claim of the classical view, however, is that being a physical symbol system is a necessary condition for intelligence at the human level. At the heart of this claim is the notion that the extraordinary behavioral flexibility demonstrated by human beings can only be achieved by a physical symbol system.

It seems clear that nervous systems that function as full symbol systems are not widespread in the biological world. Solutions to particular computational problems abound in evolution, for example, the frog's visual prey-detection system, the bat's sonar localization system, the electric signaling system of the electric fish, the housefly's flight-control system, or the song-acquisition mechanisms of various species of songbirds, but only the human nervous system seems to be a full symbol system. Newell (1990) refers to the shift from dedicated hardware for specific computational functions to a general-purpose physical symbol system as the *great move*. It is not clear just why humans exhibit so much more cognitive flexibility than other intelligent animals, such as the other primates. Their cognitive architectures are probably both qualitatively and quantitatively different from ours, but the details of the differences are far from clear. Just how human cognitive flexibility emerged from evolution's generally more focused ways is also not clear. Given the differences between biological information processing and computing technology as it has developed so far, we cannot look to the details of the von Neumann architecture for insight into the architecture of the human central processor. There is no evidence, for example, that human memory consists of discrete, numerically addressable locations or that the primitive, built-in operations of human thought are the same as those of a von Neumann machine. It is a matter of empirical research to discover how a physical symbol system is implemented in the human mind and brain. The physical symbol system hypothesis makes no prior commitment about the details.

Computation in Symbol Systems   The hypothesis that the mind is (among other things) a physical symbol system is highly abstract. There has been considerable discussion about just how it constrains theories of cognition. A basic requirement is that the cognitive system be able to compose new functions or transformations over its representations. Newell (1990) has pointed out that there are many ways that this capacity might be implemented. The von Neumann solution of using the same medium for representing both data and instructions is elegant but only one option. Another option might be to implement new functions directly in reconfigurable hardware, essentially building special-purpose subsystems to compute new functions as needed. The notion of interpretation would shift quite radically in such a system. Instructions, in some sense, would be needed to build the special-purpose subsystem, but once built the subsystem would run directly, without the interpretation of instructions retrieved from a memory. Some points about the classical architecture made below can be seen as a claim that human cognition includes both von Neumann–style interpretation and a mechanism for constructing new functions that operate without interpretation.

The memory retrieval processes in a symbol system allow what Newell (1990) calls *distal access* to symbols. Formally, what this means is that the processing of one symbol or symbolic structure can reliably evoke the processing of other symbolic structures that are needed in the current computation. A common example is when a single symbol serves as an index or pointer to a larger symbol structure with which it is associated and which can be brought into the computation. In standard computer programming languages when the name of a procedure or subroutine is encountered during a computation, it triggers the application of the entire subroutine. In human language understanding the occurrence of any well-understood content word potentially triggers the processing of extensive symbol structures that represent the meaning of the word. Newell argues that the need for distal access reflects a constraint on the physics of computational devices. The physical implementation of any information-processing system imposes a limit on the amount of information that can be involved in a computation at any moment. The limit can be overcome by passively storing large amounts of symbolic structure in regions of the system that are physically distinct from the regions that are actively supporting the computation and by arranging a mechanism that allows the passive structures to be brought into the computation when needed.

The ability of a symbol system to maintain internal representations of the world, to access them, and to transform them with processes that are not immediately driven by sensory input or tied directly to motor output is crucial to its flexibility. The physical symbol system hypothesis is motivated in part by the human capacities for planning, problem solving, and reasoning that are not driven by the immediate sensory input and that make novel use of large stores of knowledge.

Symbol systems' ability to process syntactically structured symbols is also widely considered to be crucial to their flexibility and power. Although facilities for handling complex syntactic structure are not transparently built into the simplest universal architectures, such as the Turing machine, or even into standard von Neumann computers, programs for building, recognizing, and transforming symbolic structure can be built up from the primitive operations in such architectures. Universal computational capacity seems to require such facilities. Fodor and Pylyshyn (1988) argue that structured symbols and *structure-sensitive* computation are defining characteristics of human cognitive processes. The human cognitive architecture, they argue, has an intrinsic capacity to build up complex symbols out of simpler ones, to identify the parts of complex symbols and their arrangement, and to carry out computations that depend on symbolic structure. These capacities are very apparent in natural languages. English noun phrases, such as *the old man*, are a convenient example. *The old man* is itself a complex symbol, as can be seen from related structures, such as *the man* or *the young man*. It can also serve as a unitary part of larger structures such as *The old man kicked the uncooperative donkey*, as can be seen from related structures such as *Irving kicked the uncooperative donkey, The uncooperative donkey kicked the old man,* or *The donkey who the old man kicked was uncooperative.* The structure-sensitivity of natural language processing is brought out in these examples by the fact that who did the kicking and who was kicked cannot be determined without identifying the grammatical structure of the sentences. *Kick, man,* and *donkey* are present in three of the sentences, but the kicker and the kickee are not the same in all three. (The structure of natural languages is taken up in detail in chapter 6.)

Structure-based computation makes possible the *productivity* and *systematicity* of symbolic computation. Complex symbols are built up and processed according to sets of rules or constraints. The rules can be applied repeatedly to produce or analyze ever more complex symbolic structures. To return to the example in chapter 1, a system that contains rules for dealing with arithmetic expressions can deal not only with expressions, such as $3 + 2$, but also with arbitrarily complicated expressions, such as $(3 \cdot (5 + 7)) + (6 \cdot 9)$, in which the order of application of the arithmetic operations depends on the structure of the expression. Similarly, the rules in natural languages for forming noun phrases and combining them with other types of phrases allow for the generation and processing of an unlimited stock of novel sentences, which can be arbitrarily complex. Claims about the productivity of a system are somewhat abstract, because the ability of a system to apply a set of rules or constraints is limited by its finite computational resources. For example, a calculator with 64,000 memory cells and no auxiliary storage might not be able to process an arithmetic expression containing 100,000 symbols. Similarly, the grammatical rules for English allow for sentences that would be too long to produce or process in a lifetime, and even some relatively short sentences, such as *The old man who the uncooperative donkey that the circus trainer sold kicked died,* raise interesting questions about limits on the capacity of natural language processing. In spite of these limits, it can be argued that in domains such as natural language or musical composition within a style human cognition is spectacularly productive.

Structure-based computation is also systematic. Information processes operate on representations in terms of their structure, guaranteeing that representations with similar structures will be processed in the same way. A system that employs the rules of arithmetic will not deal correctly with $3 \cdot (5 + 7)$ but balk at $7 \cdot (5 + 3)$ or $(3 + 2) \cdot (5 + 7)$, for example. Similarly, a person who knows English vocabulary and grammar easily understands novel sentences, such as *John kissed the skunk,* and, having understood a sentence of a particular form, will rarely fail to understand other utterances with the same syntactic form, such as *The skunk kissed John.* Even nonsense utterances that contain cues to grammatical structure, such as *The wug scrogged the blap,* receive considerable processing relative to syntactically unstructured strings such as *wug scrog blap.*

As we pointed out in chapter 1, the meanings of structured representations can be specified in terms of their syntactic structure. The semantic mapping from *John kissed the skunk,* for example, requires that the person specified by the grammatical subject of the sentence must have a certain relationship to a skunk in the world. The required relationship is reversed in *The skunk kissed John.* This type of *compositional* semantics is hypothesized to be characteristic of human language and thought.

In recent years the physical symbol system hypothesis has become controversial in cognitive science. A particular subject of attack has been the detailed claim that rule-governed processing of syntactically structured representations is central to human cognition. In the rest of this chapter we will first develop the classical view further and then sketch the alternative views that have arisen under the name of *connectionism* or *parallel distributed processing*.

2.4 Propositional Representation

The Language of Thought

Preliminary Arguments for Propositional Representation   We begin our further exploration of the classical view of the cognitive architecture with one of the fundamental questions that has occupied its proponents. What "language" is our factual, or *declarative*, knowledge represented in? In writing a computer program, the programmer specifies a representational format for the data structures. For example, in an employee information system the facts about each employee might be stored as a record, containing slots for name, address, phone number, title, monthly salary, number of dependents, seniority, and so on. The format for a record is an abstract minilanguage for specifying the information about the employee. What, then, can we say about the much more general ability of the human mind to represent an unlimited variety of facts in an unlimited variety of subject areas?

One possibility is that facts are represented solely in the thinker's native *natural language*, for example, English or Chinese. This possibility is attractive. For one thing, we clearly do possess linguistic representations, since we produce and understand them all the time. And natural languages are clearly powerful enough to represent an unlimited variety of facts, unlike artificially restricted personnel record languages and the like. Introspectively, it often seems that we think in our native languages as well. We will not embrace this theory, however. Instead, we will assume that facts are also and primarily represented in a still more powerful internal *propositional* representation that is largely unconscious and that is translated into natural language when we talk.

Although it is difficult to fully justify this fundamental assumption in advance, there are some introspective arguments and experimental evidence that justify adopting it at least provisionally. Much of the material in the rest of the chapter can also be seen as further support for it, although that point will not be emphasized (see also Fodor 1975).

The theory of an underlying propositional representation corresponds to the frequent introspective sense of a distinction between having an idea and putting it into words. The distinction emerges behaviorally in the tip-of-the-tongue phenomenon, where we have a concept clearly in mind but experience a delay in retrieving the appropriate word for it. Furthermore, even in cases where we easily generate the English name for a concept (*dog, chair,* and so on), we often are not very good at giving its English definition. When asked to define even the most familiar concepts, we often find ourselves laboring. This phenomenon suggests that the definitions are expressed in an internal representation that is associated with an English word. We retrieve the word effortlessly, but a full translation of the definition into English is not immediately available and requires considerable mental effort. A final reason for at least initially adopting the internal representation theory is that it explains how young children can begin acquiring concepts in spite of the fact that they are not born knowing a natural language. Whatever we might think of adults' abilities to define concepts in their native languages, children seem easily able to learn concepts that they will be completely unable to explain until they have been talking for quite some time.

Experimental Evidence for Propositional Representation   A now classic experiment by Sachs (1967) is an example of the kind of laboratory evidence that supports the theory of an underlying propositional representation. In the experiment subjects listened to paragraphs on various topics, such as Galileo's work on the telescope. The passages were interrupted, and subjects were given a *recognition memory* test for a sentence that had occurred 0, 40, or 80 syllables earlier in the passage. In the test the subject was presented with a sentence and asked to judge whether it was the same as a sentence in the passage or changed. For the Galileo passage the subject could be presented with any one of the following four sentences. The actual sentence was sentence (1).

(1)   He sent a letter about it to Galileo, the great Italian scientist.

(2)   He sent Galileo, the great Italian scientist, a letter about it.

(3)   A letter about it was sent to Galileo, the great Italian scientist.

(4)   Galileo, the great Italian scientist, sent him a letter about it.

Notice that sentences (2) and (3) have the same meaning as sentence (1), although they have different grammatical forms. Sentence (4) has a different meaning. At a delay of 80 syllables (20–25 seconds) subjects rarely made the error of thinking that sentence (4) had occurred in the passage. However, they frequently and mistakenly thought they remembered sentence (2) or sentence (3). Thus, under the conditions of Sachs's experiment subjects were able to remember the meaning of a sentence without remembering its linguistic form. A reasonable explanation of the finding is that the meaning was represented in an underlying nonlinguistic form that could be translated into a variety of linguistic paraphrases, which subjects confused in the recognition test. The finding actually accords well with our frequent feeling that we can remember the gist of what someone has said but not the exact words. The experiment demonstrates quantitatively that the representation of exact wording can be lost remarkably quickly under quite normal listening conditions. We will return to the analysis of memory experiments in chapter 3, but it should be pointed out here that linguistic representation obviously can be remembered. One does not sing paraphrases of "The Star-Spangled Banner," for example.

Propositional Form   If we adopt a theory of underlying propositional representation, we take on the imposing problem of figuring out in detail what the formal structures of propositions are. We will propose only the most rudimentary structures here, because the experimental methods of the cognitive psychologist are not the best tools to apply to the detailed analysis of the problem, initially. As a starting point, we assume that propositions are the simplest complete units of thought. They are complete in the sense that they can have a truth-value; that is, they can be true or false. Anything simpler seems incomplete in this sense. For example, *Mary* is not a complete proposition, nor is *likes*, but *Mary likes John* is because it seems to express a complete thought that can be either true or false.

Propositions typically capture relations, such as *liking*, that hold between arguments, such as *John* and *Mary*. *Like* is a two-place relation, or predicate, that requires two arguments to form a proposition. The arguments are not interchangeable: *Mary likes*

John and *John likes Mary* are distinct propositions. We can distinguish among the arguments of a predicate by noting the roles that they play in the proposition. *Mary* is the subject and *John* the object of *Mary likes John*. There are predicates with one place, such as *red*, predicates with three places, such as *give*, and so on. Two or more propositions that share arguments can often be expressed in a single sentence: for example, "Mary likes the teacher who gave her an apple," which is built out of a *liking* proposition and a *giving* proposition.

Propositions and their parts were placed in italics above to distinguish them from linguistic representation. Theorists usually also adopt special formal notations for propositions that allow them to be processed by formal procedures and that allow a formal theory of meaning to be specified. We will informally introduce a simple version of *propositional network* notation, which involves the theoretical commitments that are most important in cognitive psychology. Figure 2.2 shows propositional network notations for the propositions just discussed.

In this notation each proposition is a unique structural unit built around a *propositional node*, which is symbolized by a circle with a number inside it. The value of the number has no meaning other than to distinguish the proposition from other propositions. The propositional node is connected to its *constituent* nodes by *links*, or *pointers*, which are symbolized by arrows. Each link has a label that specifies the role that its target plays in the proposition. Every propositional node must have a link to a relation node, which is symbolized by a word in capital letters. The propositional node must also have the right number of links to nodes for the arguments of the relation. Argument nodes are symbolized by small letters when they represent particular individual entities in the world, such as the particular person, Mary. In some cases a previously anonymous entity must be assigned a name, such as *a* for the apple that John gave to Mary. Argument nodes are symbolized by capital letters when they represent general concepts for objects, or categories that objects belong to. *APPLE* and *TEACHER* are examples in the figure. The relation *IS-A* is used for propositions, such as *John is a teacher*, that assert that a particular entity falls in a certain category.

In the four propositions in part (*a*) of figure 2.2 some of the argument nodes occur more than once. For example, the node *john* occurs in three of the propositions. Part (*b*) of the figure displays the interconnections among the propositions more clearly by displaying each node once. Here, we see immediately that *john* is a structurally central node in the total network, because it is immediately connected to three of the four propositions. Note that the diagram of a proposition can be rearranged at will as long as the links still connect the same nodes. The differences between part (*a*) and part (*b*) of the figure demonstrate this point. Since our primary interest will be in the interconnections among propositions, rather than in their internal structure, the labels on the pointers have been suppressed in part (*b*). Readers interested in pursuing questions about the use of networks to represent the internal details of propositions should consult Johnson-Laird, Herrmann, and Chaffin (1984). We give a more formal analysis of propositions in chapter 10.

Experimental Evidence for Simple Propositional Units   There is good experimental evidence that propositions are important functional units in cognitive processing. One preliminary example is an experiment by Kintsch and Glass (1974). They compared memory for sentences that expressed a single proposition with memory for sentences with the same number of content words that expressed more than one proposition. For

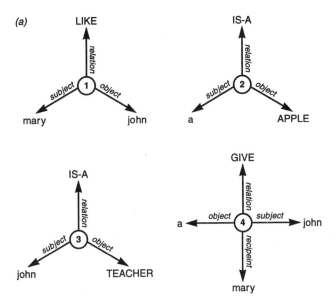

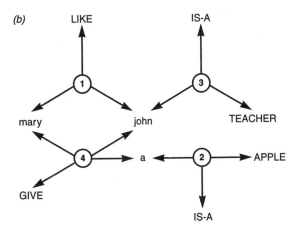

Figure 2.2
Network notation for propositions. (*a*) Notation for four propositions with all links labeled. (*b*) The four propositions combined into a single network. The link labels are suppressed.

example, sentence (5) is constructed from one proposition, involving the three-place relation *BUILD*, whereas sentence (6) is constructed from three propositions, involving the three one-place relations *CROWDED, SQUIRM,* and *UNCOMFORTABLE*:

(5)   The settler built the cabin by hand.

(6)   The crowded passengers squirmed uncomfortably.

Subjects tended to recall the first kind of sentence better than the second. This indicates that it had more unity in an underlying representation that determined the subjects' memory performance.

Propositional Networks as Associative Networks

A number of further assumptions must be introduced to make propositional networks a full-fledged theory, or *model*, for long-term declarative memory. *Long-term memory* refers to cases where a piece of information remains out of the immediate sphere of consciousness for some reasonable length of time (from minutes to years) and then is *retrieved*, or brought back into conscious attention, when it is relevant to some ongoing thought process. The basic assumption of the theory is that at each moment in time each node in a network is at some level of *activation* and that activation spreads among nodes along the links. If the level of activation reaches a high enough value in some portion of the network, that portion of the network is accessible to conscious attention. The links are therefore *associative* connections that determine the tendency of one item of information to lead to another in thought.

Our experience of the stream of consciousness in everyday life supports this notion of *spreading activation*. If we relax our attention to current goals, one idea seems to lead to another with no effort, and the connections among the ideas, although meaningful, are much looser than would be dictated by a rationally controlled and goal-directed process. The flow of ideas seems to reflect a rich network of associations among facts and experiences stored in long-term memory. Virginia Woolf captured this mode of experience in her novels, and psychoanalysts use it to try to uncover associations that are thought to be suppressed by the ego's mechanisms of defense. In more goal-directed thought we are able to pick and choose from the activated material the information that is relevant to our goal, and we are able to increase and maintain the activation of this material by attending to it.

Although the theory of association of ideas goes back to Aristotle and was developed vigorously by nineteenth-century philosophers and psychologists, the information-processing approach has made possible the development of versions of the theory that make novel qualitative and quantitative predictions. Most versions of the theory make several assumptions in addition to the assumption that activation spreads through a network along the links. First, it is assumed that activation spreads simultaneously, in *parallel*, to all of the links leading from a node, and that it can spread in either direction along the links. Second, it is assumed that the activation at a node fades rapidly with time. Third, it is sometimes assumed that the total activation at a node is divided among the links that lead from it. Thus, as activation spreads through the network, it is weakened by successive divisions as it reaches successive nodes. The second and third assumptions prevent a single thought from rapidly activating the entire long-term memory permanently, throwing it into a state of permanent confusion. That is, the usefulness of spreading activation depends on some relevant nodes being in a higher state of activation than the other nodes in a network. Fourth, it is often assumed that nodes and links can have different activation capacities. For example, links might be assumed to differ in the proportion of the available activation they receive, where the higher-capacity links are the ones that have been more frequently activated in the past. Quantitative predictions become possible when concrete assumptions are made about how rapidly activation spreads, how rapidly it decays, and so on (Anderson 1983; Ratcliff and McKoon 1981).

Propositional networks are examples of richly interconnected information structures that can be processed in parallel. The spreading activation mechanism is parallel because the activation process affects many parts of a network simultaneously. The theory is one proposal for a very simple parallel computational mechanism that can efficiently make parts of a network available for further processing. It agrees with our intuitions from the stream of consciousness and also with overwhelming evidence that the nervous system is designed on the physical level for highly parallel information processing. The connectionist approach to the cognitive architecture, which will be discussed later in this chapter, arose in part from a desire to explore the properties of parallel computation in networks more generally.

Experimental Evidence for Propositional Networks   The kind of evidence that has been obtained in the laboratory for propositional network structure is well illustrated by the work of McKoon and Ratcliff (1980). They exploited a prediction of spreading activation theory that is not obvious at first sight. Activation spreading from a source proposition raises the level of activation of other propositions. This should *prime* them for participation in later information processes. Consider the network in figure 2.2. Thinking about Mary, even just reading the word "Mary," should spread some activation to the *john* node, which will make it easier for this node to reach a level of activation sufficient for conscious processing. For example, the prior activation of the *mary* node might make it easier to read the word "John" or to answer the question "Is John a teacher?"

On each study-test sequence of McKoon and Ratcliff's experiment the subjects read two short paragraphs with simple propositional structures, which were presented on a computer screen. They were then given an immediate recognition memory test. Thirty-six test words appeared on the screen, one at a time. For each word the subjects responded as quickly as possible by pressing a "Yes" key if they thought the word had appeared in one of the stories or a "No" key if they thought it had not. On *primed* trials the test word was preceded by a test word from the same story. On *unprimed control* trials the test word was preceded by a test word from the other story. There were also "No" trials in which the test word had appeared in neither of the stories. Response times on primed trials were faster than response times on unprimed trials. The network theory predicts this finding, because there was always some associative pathway between any two words in a story. Associative pathways between two words from different stories would have to have been established prior to the experiment and would not be consistent enough across subjects to show up in the data.

McKoon and Ratcliff also constructed their stories to allow quite detailed predictions of the relative sizes of priming effects within stories. Here is one of their paragraphs:

> The businessman gestured to a waiter. The waiter brought coffee. The coffee stained the napkins. The napkins protected the tablecloth. The businessman flourished documents. The documents explained a contract. The contract satisfied the client.

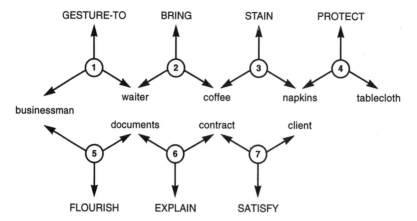

Figure 2.3
Propositional network for a paragraph. Prime-test pairs were *waiter-documents*, *coffee-contract*, and *napkins-client*. (Adapted from McKoon and Ratcliff 1980.)

This is a boring story with an exciting propositional structure, which is diagrammed in figure 2.3. (Note that for simplicity we have used some shorthand, for example, *waiter* rather than an *IS-A* proposition linking the concept WAITER with a name *w*.) In the story the following pairs of nouns are all exactly the same number of sentences apart: *waiter-documents*, *coffee-contract*, and *napkins-client*. The second word of each pair was primed by the first during the experiment. If the subject remembered the story word for word, the priming effect would be the same for all pairs. In the network structure, however, the distances between the pairs are quite different. There are four links and three nodes between *waiter* and *documents*. There are eight links and seven nodes between *coffee* and *contract*, and there are twelve links and eleven nodes between *napkins* and *client*.

The priming effect of *waiter* on *documents* should be quite strong, because activation is split up among pathways only a few times. It should be successively weaker for the other two pairs, because of the increasing dilution of the spreading activation along the longer pathways. The results were as predicted. The response time to *documents* was 736 milliseconds unprimed and 665 milliseconds when primed with *waiter*, giving a 71-millisecond priming effect. The priming effects for *contract* and *client* were 47 milliseconds and 30 milliseconds, respectively. (Actually, the response times are averages over forty-eight different paragraphs with the same propositional structure; the use of different paragraphs ensures that the results are due to the structure and not to peculiarities of the content of a particular paragraph.) In a second experiment McKoon and Ratcliff showed that similar priming effects could be obtained with more complex and realistic prose passages.

2.5 Schematic Representation

Conceptual Schemas
The theory that declarative knowledge is a network of propositions is incomplete as it has been developed so far in this chapter. The most serious gap is that although a representation for specific facts has been developed, no account has been given of the

general knowledge that allows the system to formulate or understand such facts in the first place. For example, in figure 2.2 we represented the fact that a certain object was an apple by storing an *IS-A* relation between *APPLE* and *a*. But this proposition is useful only because the mind also possesses general information about apples; that is, it has a general *concept* of apple. People know that an apple is an edible fruit that grows on a tree, has a roundish shape, is often but not necessarily red when ripe, and so on. Part of a theory of the architecture of the mind must be an account of such general knowledge.

Our initial hypothesis about the general knowledge for basic concepts is that it is represented in the propositional network. The network can easily contain general propositions, such as one asserting *ROUND* of *APPLE*, as well as propositions about particular objects, such as our example linking *APPLE* and *a*. The cluster of general propositions attached to a concept node forms a conceptual *schema* for the concept. We will use the term *schema* (plural is either *schemas* or *schemata*) for any cognitive structure that specifies the general properties of a type of object or event and leaves out any specification of details that are irrelevant to the type. A schema is an *abstraction* that allows particular objects or events to be assigned to general *categories*. General knowledge of the category can then be applied to the particular case.

The conceptual schema for apples specifies general information about fruithood, shape, color, and so on, but it leaves out many characteristics of individual apples, such as the precise details of their coloring, whether they fell or were picked, the supermarket where they were purchased, and so on. The schema *abstracts away* from the details in order to allow categorization and further thought and action based on the categorization. Some form of schematization is essential to intelligent information processing. Since every concrete object has an infinite number of characteristics, if we tried to deal with each object in all of its individuality, we would be permanently paralyzed and bewildered. Categorization also obviously has pitfalls, as well. Apples picked from the tree are less likely to be bruised, and those sold by certain supermarkets are more likely to be fresh. Allowing one's attention to be captured and held by the precise coloring of an apple can be the stuff of poetry, even though it prolongs the shopping trip and provokes stares from busy passersby. In chapter 3 we will explore further the nature of the information contained in conceptual schemas.

Complex Schemas

Our general knowledge seems to go considerably beyond concepts for discrete objects and events, such as *apple* or *give*. Some examples that have been investigated in cognitive psychology and AI are (1) schemas, or *frames*, for complex visual scenes, such as what a room looks like (Minsky 1977), (2) schemas, or *scripts*, for complex activities, such as going to a restaurant (Schank and Abelson 1977), and (3) schemas for people's personalities, including one's own self (Cantor and Mischel 1979; Markus 1980). We will look at research on scripts, person schemas, and the self-schema.

Scripts   Cognitive scientists use the term *script* or *activity schema* to refer to a declarative knowledge structure that captures general information about a routine series of events or a recurrent type of social event, such as eating in a restaurant or visiting the doctor. Schank and Abelson (1977) and other script theorists have hypothesized that scripts contain the following sorts of information: an identifying name or theme (such as *eating in a restaurant*), typical roles (*customer, waiter, cook, ...*), entry conditions (*customer is hungry and has money*), a sequence of goal-directed scenes (*entering and getting a table, ordering, eating, paying bill and leaving*), a sequence of actions within each scene (in the ordering scene *customer gets menu, customer reads menu, customer decides on order, customer gives order to waiter, . . .*).

Pursuing our strategy of building schemas into propositional networks, it is clear that the kind of information listed above can be captured as a set of propositions connected to a script or activity node. Some theorists have felt that assumptions must be added to propositional network theory to handle the seemingly highly organized structure of scripts. First, scripts are difficult to encode as a tangle of propositions. The script for eating in a restaurant contains a sequence of subactivities (entering, finding a table, and so on) that must be evoked in the correct order. And each subactivity (such as the ordering scene) has, in a sense, its own subscript. Furthermore, introspection suggests that entire scripts seem to be activated as units without interference from stray propositions that happen to be associated with parts of the script. Second, if scripts have any real validity as cognitive structures, we ought to be able to say more about these structures in general than that they are a cluster of interrelated propositions. That is, the scripts for different activities ought to have the same general structure: a theme, roles, entry conditions, a sequence of scenes, and so forth.

On the other hand, some theorists have pointed out that if scripts are hypothesized to be large, rigidly organized structures, it is hard to explain how they are learned from experience and how they can be flexibly retrieved and employed in situations that depart from the standard. Discussions of the theoretical issues raised by complex knowledge structures can be found in Rumelhart and Ortony 1976, Schank 1982, Anderson 1983, and Kolodner 1983. We will also return to these theoretical issues in chapter 4, since the research methods of AI are an excellent means for exploring the properties of various proposals for knowledge structure.

Without attempting to resolve these issues here, we will assume that scripts and other complex schemas can be effectively activated as units and that they exert strong influences on the way that information in the current situation is processed. We will also assume that there can be associations between complex schemas and representations of particular events that were categorized under the schema. For example, just as there can be associations between the conceptual schema for *apple* and knowledge about particular apples, so there can be associations between the restaurant script and knowledge about particular visits to restaurants.

Experimental Evidence for Scripts   Bower, Black, and Turner (1979) investigated the influence of scripts on information processing by having subjects read and later try to remember brief stories about events that were instances of scripts. For example:

> The Doctor
> John was feeling bad today so he decided to go see the family doctor. He checked in with the doctor's receptionist, and then looked through several medical magazines that were on the table by his chair. Finally the nurse came and asked him to take off his clothes. The doctor was very nice to him. He eventually prescribed some pills for John. Then John left the doctor's office and headed home.

Although this story is easily understandable, it does not explicitly mention a number of the typical elements of the script for a visit to a doctor, such as arriving at and entering the office, or getting weighed and having one's blood pressure checked. Script theorists hypothesize that when we hear or read about a scripted event, our knowledge of the entire script is activated, which allows us to fill in, or infer, the scenes and actions that are not explicitly mentioned. Because of this ability the story above could be told in an entirely different way, perhaps beginning as follows:

> John was feeling bad today. It seemed like forever before he finally arrived at the doctor's office. He looked around at the various health posters on the wall. Finally, the nurse came and checked his blood pressure and weight....

Bower, Black, and Turner hypothesized that, when trying to remember stories, subjects would tend to confuse material that they had actually read with material that they had filled in on the basis of their script knowledge. Their prediction was borne out in two experiments. In a *recall* experiment subjects read eighteen brief stories like the one just given about different people in different scripted settings and later tried to write down exactly what they had read. Subjects showed a significant tendency to recall actions that were part of the script but were not stated in the story. For example, in recalling "The Doctor," the subject might incorrectly recall reading that the nurse checked John's blood pressure and weight. The subjects showed a much smaller tendency to incorrectly recall actions that were not part of relevant scripts. A second, *recognition* memory experiment confirmed this tendency. In this experiment a different group of subjects read the same eighteen stories. They were then presented with a series of sentences and asked to rate on a 7-point scale how sure they were that they had read the sentence, from 1 ("very sure I did not read it") to 7 ("very sure I did read it"). Some of the sentences were from the stories, some were script actions that were not stated in the stories, and some were plausible actions that were neither stated in the stories nor typical script events. Subjects showed a significantly greater tendency to falsely recognize unstated script events than unstated nonscript events. These memory experiments suggest that script knowledge is used in understanding stories and that the activation of a script and its use to fill in gaps in the story leave memory traces that can become confused with the memory traces for what was actually read or heard. We will return to the study of the influences of schematization on memory in chapter 3.

Person Schemas   Psychologists who study personality and social behavior have proposed that schemas exist for types of people. For example, it is plausible that we have schematic concepts for the extroverted person or the mature person. Such schemas might influence our impressions of people and our predictions of how they will behave in various situations. Cantor and Mischel (1979) showed that people agree on the typical characteristics of different personality types and that person schemas influence the initial perception of and later memory for other people. For example, when subjects read a description of an extrovert that explicitly mentioned features that were only moderately typical of extroversion, the subjects apparently inferred or "filled in" the more typical features that were not mentioned. In a later recognition memory test they tended to incorrectly remember the highly typical features as having been mentioned in the original description. Cantor, Mischel, and Schwartz (1982) demonstrated an interaction between schemas for social situations (for instance, a party) and schemas for personality types (for instance, extrovert). Subjects' predictions about how a person would behave were a joint product of the situation and person schemas.

The Self-Schema   One's knowledge of oneself probably occupies a special place in the store of knowledge about people, and psychologists have proposed that the self-concept is a particularly elaborate and influential schema. Markus (1980), for example, has proposed that the self-schema exerts powerful effects on the person's perception, memory, and thought. Information that is consistent with the schema is processed more efficiently and better remembered. Incoming information is hypothesized to be evaluated relative to the schema and resisted if it is inconsistent. Plans and predictions of future behavior are crucially influenced by the schema.

Markus hypothesized that some characteristics will be part of a person's self-schema and that others will not. For example, a person may conceptualize himself or herself in terms of a cluster of attributes that were traditionally considered masculine, such as competitive and ambitious, or in terms of a cluster of attributes that were traditionally considered feminine, such as gentle and sensitive (Markus et al. 1982). Markus termed such people *masculine* and *feminine schematics*. She also hypothesized that there are people who are aschematic with respect to traditional notions of gender in the sense that they do not conceptualize themselves in terms of these traditional clusters of attributes. Using a personality test called the Bem Sex Role Inventory (Bem 1974), she was able to classify her subjects as masculine schematics, feminine schematics, or aschematic with respect to traditional gender schemas. She was then able to show that subjects' behavior on a variety of information-processing tasks was influenced by their gender schematization. For example, Markus et al. (1982) collected response times in a property verification task concerning the self. In this task subjects were presented with adjectives and asked to judge as quickly as possible whether those adjectives were self-descriptive. Masculine schematic subjects answered most quickly for traditionally prototypical masculine adjectives, and feminine schematics answered most quickly for feminine adjectives, whereas aschematics showed the same response times for masculine, feminine, and neutral (for instance, "friendly") adjectives.

Propositions, Schemas, and the Architecture of Cognition

Now that we have examined some evidence for propositions and schemas of various kinds, we can return to the claim that they are part of the cognitive architecture. The claim that propositional representation is part of the cognitive architecture is central to the classical view. Notice that it is the *facility* for propositional representation, not any particular proposition, that is hypothesized to be built into the architecture of cognition. Propositions are simple, and therefore easy to implement physically, but they have the productive syntactic structure required by the classical view. They also have considerable power to represent the world (an issue taken up in more detail in chapter 10). The usefulness of a long-term memory full of propositions depends on distal access. There must be an efficient mechanism for retrieving particular propositions from memory when they are relevant or needed for ongoing cognition. Spreading activation in an associative network has proven to be a fruitful hypothesis about the retrieval mechanism, although other mechanisms have been proposed. The potential hypotheses about the basic scheme for long-term memory retrieval include any efficient *content-addressing* mechanism, that is, any mechanism that takes propositions or fragments of propositions as inputs and locates other propositions in memory with overlapping content.

The classical view is also strongly associated with the claim that mechanisms for organizing propositional knowledge into abstract schemas are built into the biology of cognition. The representational format of schemas and the nature of the abstraction process—that is, the process by which concepts, scripts, and so on, are learned—are matters of current debate and research, some of which will be described in chapter 3.

Cognition requires some mechanism for abstraction, or for assimilating information to known concepts or categories. The idea that conceptual knowledge is structured so that it can be retrieved without interference and used efficiently also makes a great deal of sense. Augmenting propositional representation to do these jobs is a natural elaboration of the classical view.

2.6 Cognitive Processes, Working Memory, and Attention

Before continuing our exploration of cognitive representation, we must consider how representations are processed. So far, propositional-schematic representations have been proposed as a medium for the storage of information in human *long-term memory*. Associative activation has been proposed as a scheme for retrieving that information. In terms of the mechanics of the architecture an item of information counts as retrieved if its activation is above some threshold. (Alternatively we could say the probability of retrieval is some continuous, increasing function of activation giving every proposition in memory some nonzero chance of retrieval at any given moment.) Propositions that are retrieved are available for further processing or for motor output. Earlier, we also associated retrieval with availability to consciousness.

The retrieval mechanism alone obviously does not suffice to account for our thoughts or actions. It delivers an associative stream of information. There have to be further mechanisms that assess retrieved information for relevance to current goals and that can weld pieces of retrieved information into coherent streams of thought that lead to conclusions, decisions, or solutions to problems.

Goal Orientation and Flexibility of Cognitive Processes

In addition to the associative retrieval process, then, we must hypothesize the existence of other processes that serve to transform the information that is active at any given moment. The active information will typically include not only information from long-term memory but also information arising from sensory systems and information about current goals. The processes required are reasoning, planning, or problem-solving processes that can take the available information as inputs and produce conclusions, decisions, or action commands as outputs.

Suppose one had a goal to spend some time reading a book, and the current visual input yielded the information that it was too dark to read. A simple reasoning process might combine these two pieces of information and yield a *subgoal* to increase the level of illumination. This goal might trigger a visual search for a source of electric light, producing visual information that there is a lamp near one's chair, which in turn might lead to a goal of turning on the lamp, triggering a visual search for the switch, yielding visual information that in turn triggers the motor action of reaching for the switch. Suppose that at that point the lamp does not go on. This information might trigger a suspension of the top-level reading goal, which might lead to the retrieval of information that a paper on the material to be read is due in the very near future, which might lead to a restoration of the reading goal. The restored goal might lead to the retrieval of a schema concerning electrical appliances that includes the fact that they usually have to be plugged into an electrical outlet. This fact might trigger the construction of a new subgoal to check whether the lamp is plugged in. This goal might trigger a visual search for the disposition of the plug at the end of the cord or perhaps the production of a request to a friend in the room, "Could you check to see if this lamp is plugged in?" If it turned out that the lamp was plugged in, the schema concerning electrical appliances might again come into play, leading to further troubleshooting plans.

This sort of mundane thought involves a great deal of reasoning that coordinates goals, sensory input, and information retrieved from memory. It requires us to sketch plausible outlines for some additional features of the cognitive architecture, which will be explored further later in this chapter and in the next. The example of the lamp illustrates the assumption of figure 2.1 that the sensory systems must output active representations that can serve as inputs to central processes along with the representations retrieved from long-term memory. For example, the perception of a lamp in the immediate environment must be fed to the reasoning processes in an appropriate representational form. Similarly, active central representations must be capable of functioning as inputs to motor systems so that movements may be effected, for example, the arm movements needed to reach a switch or the eye movements needed to make a visual search. The obvious assumption to make is that the relevant perceptual outputs and motor inputs are in propositional-schematic form.

Goal orientation is a key feature of the lamp example and any similar case of everyday thought. It is plausible to assume that goals are represented in propositional-schematic form. It is an easy matter to translate goals such as *I desire that the lamp be on* into the network notation of figure 2.2 (the proposition node of the *ON* proposition serves as the object of the *DESIRE* proposition). Within the immediate context of cognitive processing, goals can have several origins. They can be retrieved from memory (remembering an intention to read an assignment), generated by cognitive processes that were driven by other earlier or higher goals (generating an intention to turn on a lamp), or in some cases provided relatively directly by sensory input (being asked by a friend to turn on a lamp). (The question of the ultimate origin of one's goals is a larger question.) The ability of goals to direct processing can be explained by our earlier assumptions about the dynamics of activation and by an assumption that cognitive processes tend to require a goal as one of their inputs. The representation of an immediate goal will be kept active by its ongoing involvement in processing. Its activation will be repeatedly refreshed as it is picked up as an input to current processes. Other active representations, arising from memory, sensory input, or previous processes, will serve as effective inputs to current processing only if they prove relevant to the immediate goal, and their activation will fade rapidly if they are irrelevant.

Cognitive processing that can defer an immediate response to sensory input and that can combine this input with goals and retrieved memories achieves great flexibility. This flexibility comes in part from the ability of cognitive processes to produce chains of subgoals. The result is that a simple action, such as turning a light switch, can be triggered by an unlimited variety of higher goals. The immediate superordinate goal, for example, might be to turn the light on, to turn the light off, to acquire a small piece of plastic, to produce a clicking sound, to generate an excuse for getting up from a chair, and so on. Higher up the hierarchy of goals, there are an unlimited number of goals that could be served by increasing or decreasing the illumination in a room. Another aspect of this flexibility is the novel combination of goals with sensory input or items retrieved from long-term memory. For example, the goal of lighting an uncooperative lamp in a friend's apartment can be usefully conjoined with visual information that a friend is present (leading to a request to check the plug) or with a memory of having seen some lightbulbs on a particular kitchen shelf earlier in the day (resulting in a trip to the kitchen to get a fresh bulb). These novel combinations generate great variability in the use of the conceptual or schematic knowledge stored in long-term memory. A small brown part of circular cross section protruding at right angles from the brassy surface of a lamp base generally falls under the concept of light switch, but in the appropriate context it can also fall under the concepts of plastic-thing or thing-that-clicks. Similarly, the information contained in a given schema does not influence cognition in a rigid, uniform way in all contexts. The standard restaurant script does not absolutely dictate our behavior in restaurants, for example, and, as in an old parlor game, we can think of many uses for a brick. The general point is that sensory input does not rigidly determine which schemas affect ongoing cognitive processing and that active schemas do not always affect cognitive processing in exactly the same way.

Basic Cognitive Processes and Interpretive Processing
We have now laid out some of the properties that cognitive processes appear to have, proceeding roughly at the knowledge level but taking advantage of our more formal analysis of propositional representation. This analysis paves the way for a more formal analysis of cognitive processes, which will unfold in the rest of this chapter and much of the next.

We can begin with the point that some processes have to be built into the cognitive architecture. The information in long-term memory would be completely inert without some built-in processes, and the associative retrieval process alone is not enough to drive goal-oriented cognition. Just as a calculator or computer has to have some built-in operations, such as addition, so must the human cognitive architecture. To see what might be required, return to the example of the recalcitrant lamp. Suppose the current active goal is to get the lamp on. Via the associative retrieval process this goal might activate a structure of roughly the form *Turning the switch on an inactive lamp usually causes the lamp to go on*. With a bit of work we could expand our formalism for propositional representation to accommodate this kind of structure, but we will suppress our momentary temptation to do this and assume that such structures can be represented in memory and be activated at appropriate times. The point here is that the mere activation of the structure is not enough. There has to be an additional process that takes the structure and the current goal as inputs and produces a subgoal of getting the switch turned. This process is a component of a larger cognitive ability called *means-ends analysis*, and it may well be built into the cognitive architecture. The general form of the process is to note combinations of an end (i.e., a goal) and a representation that specifies a means to that end and then to set a subgoal of carrying out the means. In chapter 3 the larger significance of means-ends analysis for human cognition will be taken up. The point here is to give a concrete example of the kind of elementary process that might be built into the cognitive architecture. Developing a well-supported theory of fundamental processes made available by the cognitive architecture is one of the most difficult problems in cognitive psychology.

As we saw in the general discussion of universal machines, once a modest stock of processes is built into an intelligent system, it becomes possible to expand the system's processes indefinitely by interpreting data from memory as instructions. Humans pretty clearly have this ability. Following a remembered recipe for chocolate chip cookies, for example, can be seen as retrieving a sequence of instructions, each of which must be interpreted. Interpreting each step, of course, involves a great deal more interpretation, since operations such as *Combine 2 cups of flour, 1 teaspoon of baking soda, and 1 teaspoon of salt in a bowl* are not built into the cognitive architecture. Generally, many cognitive schemas, such as the restaurant script, can be interpreted as recipes for thought or action in appropriate contexts. Problem solving using means-ends analysis may also be thought of as an interpretive process in which the order in which various means are invoked varies considerably depending on current goals and situational conditions.

Finally, it should be noted that processes for storing new representations in long-term memory must be built into the architecture. Most simply, it can be assumed that any new representation constructed by central processes or arising from sensory processes has some probability of being stored in memory. A plausible further assumption is that the longer the new representation remains active in ongoing cognitive processing the greater the probability that it is stored. The associative links of the new representation will be a function of its formal content. Thus, a proposition about apples will be stored with links to the *APPLE* node, and so on. Assumptions similar to these are at the core of most classical theories of long-term memory storage, and they account for a large range of data. The assumptions can be fleshed out in various ways. For example, the relation between processing time and probability of storage can be given a precise mathematical form, or it can be assumed that the nodes and links of a new representation have independent probabilities of storage, allowing the storage of partial representations containing incomplete information and associative pathways.

The storage of new schemas raises more difficult questions. Although it is possible for a schema to be specified directly (as when a teacher tells a student that a regular pentagon has five sides of equal length), most schemas are learned from examples that contain irrelevant details. Some process of abstraction allows representations of specific instances to contribute to the construction, alteration, and strengthening of general schemas. The learning of new schemas is one of the most active areas of research in cognitive science. As we pointed out in our earlier discussion of schemas, ideas about schema learning have implications for schema representation as well. Schemas must be represented in a way that makes them easy to learn by example.

Working Memory and Attention
We have already hypothesized that there is a limit to the amount of information in long-term memory that is active above threshold at any given moment. This limit is hypothesized to arise because activation fades rapidly and possibly because a fixed pool of activation is divided among active associative pathways. There are also limits on the rate at which the sensory systems can deliver representations to central processes. Many of these limits have been extensively studied. For example, it takes about a tenth of a second to recognize a visual object under the best of conditions, and it takes about a quarter of a second to make the eye movement needed to bring an object to be recognized to the center of the visual field, where its detail can be processed. It is generally assumed that representations arising from perception, like those arising from memory, lose their activity rapidly if they are not utilized by ongoing cognitive processes. Finally, it is assumed that new goals and other representations generated by ongoing cognitive processes also lose activation rapidly.

These constraints on activation limit the amount of information that is available for processing at a given moment. The differential availability for immediate processing of a limited amount of information in effect constitutes a short-term memory. The contents of this memory fade rapidly and are re-created from moment to moment, but they are immediately accessible. The properties of long-term memory are complementary: a very large amount of information can be stored relatively permanently, but nearly all of it is in a quiescent state, only potentially available for processing. We will use the term *working memory* for the set of active representations.

In thinking about the design of intelligent systems, the distinction between working and long-term memory is a natural one. It would never be the case that all of a system's knowledge is needed for the computation at hand, so most of it should be kept in a quiescent state of potential availability. In contrast, it makes sense to keep differentially available some stock of knowledge that is likely to be relevant to the ongoing task. Current computers, even though they do not need to be as flexible as an intelligent organism, typically have several memory stores that vary in accessibility, for example, register memory, cache memory, main memory, and disk memory. Easy-access memories can entail costs in physical materials and in the fallibility of guesses about what information is most likely to be needed in a computation. These costs increase as the size of the memory increases, so for a given range of computational tasks, there will be an optimal size for the memory.

Perhaps the most striking thing about human working memory is its very limited capacity. If more than a few subgoals and partial results are involved in a computation, some of them lose their activation, becoming inaccessible. For example, if one tries to multiply two- or three-digit numbers mentally using the standard paper-and-pencil algorithm, the number of partial results that must be maintained during the computation usually overwhelms the capacity of working memory. Difficult problems, such as deciding on a chess move or planning a big party, also often overwhelm working memory, because they generate many subgoals and alternatives that must be held in memory long enough to be compared. The limited capacity of working memory has a profound effect on human cognition. It affects the way we approach any reasonably complex cognitive task.

There are several ways in which the limits on working memory can be at least partially overcome. One is to redesign the task so as to reduce the working-memory load. For example, there are algorithms for mental arithmetic that generate many fewer partial results than the standard algorithms. A second approach is to use an external storage medium, such as writing down subgoals, alternatives, and partial results on paper. A third approach, called *chunking*, occurs when a complex representation in long-term memory functions as a single item in working memory. For example, working memory is typically overwhelmed by a novel ten-digit phone number, if it must be represented as ten distinct items plus their serial order. But if the number is 617-500-1776, it can be coded as the Boston area code, followed by five-hundred, followed by the American year of independence. For the person familiar with them, each of these three items has a well-integrated schematic representation in long-term memory and therefore is activated as a single structure. Several lines of evidence point to the conclusion that working memory can hold only about three or four chunks of information at a time (Broadbent 1975).

Given the limited-capacity of working memory, goal-oriented cognition is necessarily associated with a focus of attention. Computationally, the simplest notion of the focus is that many representations active enough to be available for processing actually receive little or none. The senses, associative retrieval from long-term memory, and the cognitive processes themselves produce a steady flow of active representations. Some of the active information is unrelated to current goals and thus fades without further processing. Goals, in the broadest sense, can be said to filter active information. Goals as concrete as looking at a particular region of space and as abstract as wanting to make a lot of money can function, in concert with built-in cognitive processes and the contents of long-term memory, to select active information for further processing. A natural question is whether attentional selection can operate directly to prevent the formation of representations that do not meet some criterion. When one is attending to the bass player, for example, to what degree is the processing of the other instruments attenuated? The existence of *early filtering* is a matter of some dispute, but our assumption here is that perceptual systems produce high-level representations independently of current goals and that the filtering comes after the representations have been produced. There are obviously some exceptions to this: eye movements are in large part under goal-oriented control, for example. Similarly, although associative memory retrieval is heavily influenced by currently active material, irrelevant associative pathways cannot be selectively turned off by current goals.

The contents of working memory and the focus of attention roughly coincide with the contents of consciousness. Most of what has been said here reflects our conscious experience. We are aware of the need to focus our attention. We try to avoid distraction when engaged in important tasks and do not attempt to do two or more difficult tasks simultaneously. We know that our working memories are fairly easily overloaded and try to arrange everyday tasks to reduce or avoid overload. Theories of memory and attention, however, must still ultimately be based on the results from the laboratory, where it is possible to make highly sensitive measures of whether a particular piece of information has affected cognitive processing. There are any number of reasons why we might fail to be able to report that some bit of information was present in working memory. The primary one is that if we try to remember what was present in working memory even a few moments ago, much of its contents will have lost activation and thus not be directly retrievable. Yet, if we try to introspectively monitor and report the contents of working memory during cognition, our performance on the primary task will be affected by the additional monitoring task.

The severe limit on the capacity of human working memory is puzzling in the context of modern life, where circumstances that tax the limit arise rather frequently. Given that the expansion of working memory must be associated with physical costs (in circuit complexity, energy expenditure, and so on), it may be that a modest working memory was optimally adaptive for most of the course of human evolution, when the tasks of living may have been less complex (though perhaps no less challenging in other ways). On the other hand, it may be that the capacity of working memory is more broadly optimal. A larger working memory might have a high probability of containing much irrelevant information and incompatible goals, which would require fancy management processes to prevent distraction and to filter inconsistent results (such as decisions to move left and right at the same time). The issue is complicated further by the fact that with repeated encounters with a given type of situation the limitations of working memory can be overcome by chunking and by skill formation, which will be described below.

2.7 Mental Images

We now have the outlines of an architecture for central cognition: a format for representing information, a sense of the processes required for manipulating the information, and a theory of long-term and working memory. We could accept these outlines and proceed to try to supply more detail. However, considerable research suggests that our sketch omits important features of both cognitive representation and cognitive processes. Consider first the matter of representation.

The discussion of representation so far has not considered one of the most striking features of conscious thought. Thinking sometimes seems to take the form of seeing things in the "mind's eye," even though the things are not actually present. Our theory has not made any distinction between thoughts that are accompanied by this *visual imagery* and thoughts that are not. Visual imagery seems to be evoked by particular kinds of thinking tasks. For example, if someone asks you how many pennies a dime is worth, you will probably not experience any visual imagery in retrieving the answer "Ten." On the other hand, if someone asks you to describe in detail exactly what the two sides of a penny look like without pulling one out of your coin purse, you will probably find yourself looking at pennies in your mind's eye. A good way to honestly undertake to answer this question is to try to draw pictures of the two sides of a penny (this is a difficult task; see Nickerson and Adams 1979).

Theory of Visual Images

The Nature of Visual Images   Research on visual imagery centers on the hypothesis that imagery is a special-purpose component of the cognitive architecture containing representations and processes that are dedicated to processing certain kinds of visual information and that are distinct from the aspects of the architecture that support propositional representations. It is important to realize that the compelling subjective distinction between visual and nonvisual thought does not constitute very good evidence for the hypothesis. Propositional-schematic representations predict qualitatively different subjective experiences arising from different representational content. Activating propositions about love can give rise to warm, loving feelings; activating propositions about one's dental appointment can make one wince; and activating propositions containing information about visual appearance might give rise to feelings of seeing. As always, the cognitive psychologist must move beyond the intuitions that initially motivate a hypothesis and attempt to construct precise, experimentally testable theories. Attempts to get at the nature of visual image representation and processing have produced some of the liveliest debates in cognitive science.

The claim that visual imagery is a distinct component of the cognitive architecture places a strong requirement on the researcher. It must be shown that the visual representations we experience as images have obligatory characteristics that are not easily alterable as a function of beliefs. The propositional-schematic system already outlined is clearly capable of representing a wide variety of information. Pylyshyn (1984) has proposed the *cognitive penetrability* criterion as a test for when a representation or process is biologically built into the architecture. Roughly, this criterion means that if imagery is part of the architecture, then it should always operate in the same way and not be affected by changes in one's beliefs or knowledge concerning vision or the visual world. For example, experiments have produced evidence that mental images can be scanned in a way analogous to the way actual scenes are scanned. The scanning operation might be cognitively penetrable, however. Subjects in experiments might scan their mental images just because they know that they would scan a real visual scene. Under other circumstances it might turn out that they can shift attention between or answer questions about two locations in an image without scanning. In that case it might be argued that image scanning is neither built into the architecture nor an obligatory component process in performing certain tasks. Instead, it might be that subjects can optionally employ it in order to mimic their perceptual experience but discard it if they think that perceptual mimicry is not called for. Cognitive penetration is difficult to assess because subjects may not be aware of the knowledge that they are bringing to bear on a task. They may strive to perform an imagery task in a way that is natural and feels like seeing without being able to articulate how they did it. In such cases subjects are said to be using *tacit* knowledge. Experimenters try to uncover the influence of tacit knowledge by altering the situation in a way that either influences subjects to alter their beliefs or that makes it impossible for the beliefs to influence their performance.

Although intuition is a poor source of evidence, it is one source of hypotheses for constructing a theory of imagery. Images do seem to be constrained in ways that differ from both actual perceptual experience and propositional representation. A rather abstract verbal description of an object can easily be encoded propositionally and remembered. However, when the object is imagined, it seems that a number of properties must be added to the description. Yet these properties fall far short of all those that would be present in an actual visual scene. Following Simon (1972), if someone tells you that you will have to search in a box of toy blocks for a three-inch cube that has two adjacent blue sides, you can remember that description with no trouble. Now, if the person tells you to imagine the cube in your mind's eye, certain information that was not in the original description will be present in your image. The cube will have a particular orientation relative to a point of view: for example, the front, top, and right sides might be visible, and the back, bottom, and left sides might be invisible. Two particular sides will be blue: perhaps the top and right sides. None of this information was specified in the original description, and none of it was required to form and remember a representation of that description. But the information must be specified in order to form a mental image of the cube. On the other hand, an actual scene of a cube would contain much more information: the other visible side would have a color, all sides would have texture, the cube would probably have some visible means of support, the illumination would cause shading on the cube's surfaces and cast shadows on nearby surfaces, and so on. One can optionally begin to add all this detail to one's image, but it does not obligatorily have to be present, and one's imaging capacity is quickly overloaded if too many details are added. Notice also that imaginal representations do not seem to contain information that would not be available during actual visual perception. So, for example, in an image of a cube it seems that its sides must be oriented relative to a viewpoint and that there can be no representation of the back of the cube that does not involve "seeing through" the sides that hide it. It would be possible to design a detailed spatial representation that represented all the surfaces of an object equally, without reference to a viewpoint, but human spatial imagination does not seem to have such a representation available.

The intuition that visual imagination mimics visual perception suggests the hypothesis that imagery makes use of representations and processes that are specific to the visual system. Active propositional-schematic representations must be able to evoke the construction and processing of representations in the visual system. The assumption, implicit in figure 2.1, that sensory systems feed into central systems but that central systems do not feed back must altered. If the hypothesis is correct, arrows will have to be added to the figure running from the central systems to the sensory systems. Kosslyn and his associates (Kosslyn 1980; Kosslyn and Koenig 1992) have developed a detailed theory that visual imagery involves the visual system. Their view is that visual imagery involves unique representational formats and dedicated processes, which also operate during visual perception. They propose that visual imagery is the immediate result of an active representation in a short-term *visual buffer*, which must be generated from an underlying long-term representation and which fades rapidly unless it is constantly refreshed.

The claim that visual imagery involves the visual system does not automatically resolve the question of just how the representations involved in imagery are different from propositional-schematic representation. After all, two systems that make use of different physical resources could still employ the same type of representation. The claim here, however, is that the propositional and imaginal representations of the same content, namely, objects in space, differ in crucial ways. There is a systematic difference in *what* information is represented explicitly, and this difference makes it possible to define processes that operate specifically on this information. An image of a cube contains much orientation-specific information. The schematic concept of a cube does not contain any such information, but it might well contain the information that all cubes have six sides, which is not explicitly represented in an image.

It is helpful to think of the visual buffer in analogy to a block of memory in a computer that is organized to be read out directly onto the computer's monitor screen (a *bit-mapped* memory). Each cell in the memory represents a point (or *pixel* for *picture element*) in the two-dimensional picture displayed on the monitor. The cell therefore has many two-dimensional geometric properties: a position (which can be represented as an x, y coordinate value), adjacent neighbor cells, a distance from every other cell (defined by analytic geometry), and so on. Other cells in the computer's memory do not have these spatial properties. Geometric, or graphics, procedures can be programmed to operate on the cells in terms of their geometric properties, to draw lines between points, move points around, and so on. A spatially organized area of memory plus a set of graphics routines constitute a specialized subsystem in computers with graphics facilities. It is important to realize that the geometric character of a memory cell is not necessarily determined by its physical location on a memory chip. For example, two cells that represent neighboring points in the image might be on different memory chips, separated by several millimeters. They are neighbor cells because the values loaded into them always represent neighboring points in the image, and because the routines that operate on the cells always treat them as representing neighboring spatial points.

The human visual buffer is hypothesized to be a similar specialized subsystem. The buffer is a short-term memory structure with intrinsic two-dimensional spatial properties. It is used in both visual perception and imagery. During imagery, it is operated on by a rich set of procedures that can load it, refresh it, and perform various transformations on it. The buffer is hypothesized to have a number of characteristics that current computer graphics systems do not have. For example, in vision and imagery, the center of the visual buffer has the highest resolution, and there is a spatial focus of attention that can be moved around within the buffer, directing processing to a particular location. The computer analogy can be used to understand the significance of the claim that the buffer and the associated processes for manipulating it are part of the cognitive architecture. In some computers the graphics subsystem is not a fixed part of the architecture of the computer. The memory cells whose values are displayed on the screen are just a part of the general main memory. They behave geometrically because programs have been written for the machine that treat them that way. However, different programs could be written that operated on the same memory cells in a completely different way. For example, the memory cells could be loaded with baseball statistics, and the programs could compute lifetime batting averages, and so on. When the graphics software is running, the graphics subsystem can be said to be part of the *virtual* architecture of the system, but it is not part of the underlying, hardwired architecture. In a computer with a dedicated graphics system the memory and the graphics routines can be wired into the hardware in such a way that they are not reprogrammable. The memory can only be manipulated by this fixed set of primitive graphics routines, which are intrinsically spatial. For example, a command to draw a line between two points would be wired into the system and would fill the memory cells that represent the points lying between the two target points. Such primitive commands would not be terribly useful for calculating batting averages. The visual system is a dedicated system. To the extent that visual imagination uses the resources of the visual system, imagery is like a dedicated graphics processor. Its spatial characteristics are built in and not easily reprogrammable by experience or changes in tacit knowledge.

The Functions of Visual Imagery   The clear reason for the existence of visual imagery is to make the computational resources of the visual system available for reasoning about the shapes and spatial arrangement of objects in the absence of visual input. It is useful to be able to plan a route before walking it or to consider possible rearrangements of the furniture in a room before beginning the heavy lifting. Such problem-solving processes typically originate in ordinary goal-oriented thought that draws on propositional-schematic long-term memory. Although long-term memory contains information about routes, rooms, and so on, this information does not include the explicit spatial detail contained in images. The built-in central processes are also not designed to process detailed spatial information. The result is that when spatial reasoning is required, long-term propositional representations are used to construct images, which contain the needed spatial information and which can be operated on by the specialized processes available in the visual system.

The hypothesized distinction between the categorical and rather skeletal information that is present in propositional memory and the additional detail that becomes available in an image is quite clear in our conscious experience. If you are asked for the shape of the faces of a cube, you will probably answer that they are square with little or no experience of imagery. However, if you need to know how many edges a cube has, it is likely that you will answer the question by forming a mental image of a cube and counting the edges by shifting your attention systematically to various locations. Your long-term representation of a cube did not explicitly represent the number of edges. Notice that the image of the cube does not explicitly represent the number of edges either. But it does represent each individual edge, making the count possible. The theory is that processes of visual perception and attention are used on the image of the cube just as they would be in looking at an actual cube. Imaginal perception is made more difficult by the lack of external input to the visual buffer. The image must be continually refreshed, and details of particular surfaces or corners must be generated as attention is shifted. It is difficult to avoid skipping or double-counting some edges. The task is taxing enough that it can lead to a subtle interplay between imagery and reasoning within the propositional system. For example, one might solve the problem by noticing from the image that the cube is like a room. The floor and ceiling each have four edges, making a subtotal of eight, and the walls meet to make four more edges, for a grand total of twelve. Here the image evoked another propositional schema that imposes a grouping on the edges of the cube, probably provides an explicit code for the edges formed by the walls (a room has four "corners"), and allows some simple addition rather than laboriously counting all twelve edges. This kind of interplay seems to be typical of imagery tasks that require conclusions about the geometric structure of complex multipart objects. Propositional knowledge about the structure of the objects and propositional reasoning facilities can be used to minimize the amount of detail that has to be imaged and the number of shifts of attention within the image. There is often a trade-off between the loads on central and imaginal processes, however. For example, the imaginal load of the edge-counting task could be reduced by realizing that a cube is formed by gluing six squares together at their edges in such a way that each edge mates with one other edge. Since it takes a pair of square edges to make each cube edge, the twenty-four edges on the six squares must be reduced by half in forming the cube. If one's cube schema contains the information that a cube has six square faces, this strategy does not require forming a stable image of a cube at all, but it does involve a complicated line of logical-mathematical reasoning.

The limited capacity of visual imagination seems to be a joint product of the limited capacities of central processing and of visual attention. Image processing is usually evoked by ongoing, goal-oriented central processing. Working memory therefore limits the number of goals and schemas that are driving image formation and processing. The processes that are specific to the visual buffer also have a limited capacity. The apparent clarity of ordinary vision tends to blind us to this limitation, but at any moment only a small portion of the visual field receives detailed processing. The capacity of image processing is further reduced by the fact that the visual buffer is not refreshed by external input. The image must be refreshed by central sources of activation. It is not clear whether the central system and the visual system draw on separate pools of activation capacity. There is some evidence for a common resource that must be allocated among all processing demands (Cantor and Engle 1993).

Experiments on Visual Imagery

Mental Scanning   The theory sketched above is plausible, but it must be supported by laboratory evidence. A fruitful approach has been to study whether response times during image manipulation reflect the specialized spatial characteristics that are hypothesized to be characteristic of image representation and processing. When attention is shifted from one region to another in an image, for example, it is assumed that the shift involves a scan across the space represented in the image. If scanning takes place at a constant rate, shifts between regions that are farther apart should take longer. More precisely, a graph that plots scanning time against distance should be a straight line with a positive slope that represents the scanning rate.

Kosslyn, Ball, and Reiser (1978) tested the scanning assumption experimentally. They first had subjects memorize a map of a fictitious island that contained various distinct locations, such as a hut, a well, and a marsh. On each trial the subject was asked to form an image of the map with attention fixed on one of the locations. A word was then presented that named another location on the map, and the subject scanned to the named location and pushed a "Yes" button when it was reached. (The experiment also included "No" trials in which the target location was not on the map.) The results showed that the scanning times were a linear function of the actual distances on the map, supporting the assumption that scanning takes time and follows a straight path between two locations.

This experiment has been criticized (Pylyshyn 1984; Finke 1985) because the results could reflect the subjects' tacit knowledge of visual scanning rather than the operation of a scanning function that is a component of the cognitive architecture. Under the tacit knowledge account, subjects take longer to answer questions about locations that are farther apart because they know that real perceptual scanning takes time. Under other conditions, however, there might be no relation between response times and spatial extent. An experiment by Mitchell and Richman (1980) demonstrated that the map-scanning task does indeed engage subjects' tacit knowledge of the relation between scanning time and distance. Their subjects looked at Kosslyn, Ball, and Reiser's (1978) map and were told about the scanning task. Without actually doing the task, they estimated the scanning times for pairs of locations on the map. Their time estimates were linearly related to distance, just as the actual image-scanning times had been.

One approach to strengthening the evidence for a built-in scanning operation is to try to set up a situation in which subjects have to answer some question about two spatial locations but are not told or even encouraged to mimic visual scanning. If scanning is an obligatory primitive operation, response times should still be affected by distance. Finke and Pinker (1982) conducted an experiment that met these criteria. On each trial a pattern of four dots appeared on a screen, and the subject formed an image of the dots. The pattern was turned off, and after a two-second delay an arrow appeared on the screen in an unexpected position and orientation. The subject's task was to decide as quickly as possible whether the arrow was pointing at one of the previously shown dots. The response times on "Yes" trials increased linearly with increasing distance between the arrow and the dot. This result suggests that subjects were forced to use a scanning operation, even though they were not instructed to scan and the demand of the task was to answer a question as fast as possible. Other, similar experiments have not shown the linear relation between time and distance (Finke and Pinker 1983; Pylyshyn 1981). In these studies the subjects had information about both locations involved in a directional judgment before the judgment was required. This pattern of results poses a challenge for both the tacit knowledge and the architectural theories. The tacit knowledge theorist must explain why the subjects invoke their knowledge of scanning in one version of the task and not in the other. The image theorist must explain why judgments about two spatial locations sometimes invoke the scanning operation and sometimes do not. A possible interpretation of such data within the image theory is that when subjects are given advance information about all relevant spatial locations, they can build directional information into a propositional representation and answer questions without performing the scanning operation on an image held in the visual buffer.

Mental Rotation   Mental rotation provides a second example of the use of response times to study the properties of mental imagery. The term refers to the ability to imagine objects rotating in space. When we need to think about how an object would look from a different orientation, we often experience it rotating to that orientation in our mental image. To illustrate, decide which of the fives in figure 2.4 are backward.

Figure 2.4
Which of these fives are backward?

To come up with the answer, you probably mentally rotated each number. Most people find it difficult to answer the question without doing mental rotations. Mental rotation is hypothesized to be one of the built-in operations that can be applied to visual images. Experimental research on mental rotation was initiated by Shepard (1968) and has been pursued with great ingenuity and detail by him, his associates, and other researchers.

The experience of mental rotation suggests the hypothesis that mental rotation is analogous to physical rotation in the world in the sense that during a mental rotation the representation must pass through intermediate states that correspond to the path of a physical rotation. A further hypothesis, analogous to the scanning case, is that mental rotation occurs at a constant rate. If this is true, then a graph in which degrees of mental rotation are plotted against rotation time should be a straight line with a positive slope equal to the rate of rotation.

Cooper (1975) studied the mental rotation of eight irregular two-dimensional shapes, illustrated in figure 2.5. The eight experimental subjects were first trained to discriminate between each standard form and its reflection at a fixed orientation. After the training four test sessions were conducted. On each test trial a single form appeared, and the subject's task was still to say whether the form was standard or reflected. However, the forms now appeared not only at the training orientation but also at five new orientations. In the new orientations the forms were rotated clockwise 60, 120, 180, 240, and 300 degrees from the training orientation. Example test stimuli are given in figure 2.5. Try to decide whether each test stimulus is standard or reflected. You will probably experience mental rotation during your decisions. The subjects in the experiment reported that they experienced rotating the test stimulus into its training orientation and then checking to see whether it matched their mental representation of the standard or reflected form.

The data from Cooper's subjects conformed to the hypothesis that they made their judgments by doing mental rotations and that mental rotation occurred at a constant rate. The results in figure 2.6 fit a straight line remarkably well. The slope of the line represents 2.1 milliseconds to complete each degree of rotation. Thus, the average subject took 130 milliseconds, a little over one-tenth of a second, to rotate an object 60 degrees, regardless of how far he or she had already rotated it. Notice that all of the response times are about 75 milliseconds longer than what it would take just to do the mental rotation; for example, the average total response time for the 60-degree stimuli was about 884 rather than 130 milliseconds. The reason is that subjects took about 754 milliseconds on each trial to do some other things: for example, before subjects did a mental rotation, they had to decide which of the eight objects involved in the experiment was being displayed, and after determining whether the form was standard or reflected, they had to make a response by pressing one of two buttons.

In another experiment, using the same subjects, Cooper (1976) was able to get strong evidence that mental rotation follows a trajectory that is analogous to a

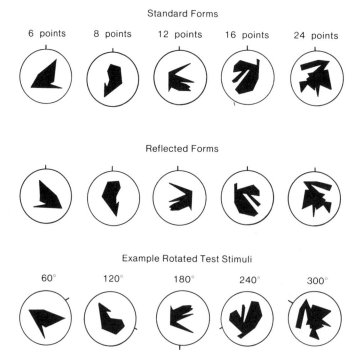

Figure 2.5
In Cooper's (1975) experiment subjects first learned the standard and reflected version of eight forms at fixed orientations, as in the examples above. Test stimuli appeared either at the training orientation or at one of five angular departures from the training orientation. Examples of rotated test stimuli are given in the third row of the figure. In each case the test stimulus is a rotation of either the standard or the reflected form that appears above it. (Adapted from Cooper 1975.)

physical rotation. On each trial the subject was briefly shown one of the standard forms and then given a signal to begin mentally rotating it in a clockwise direction. During the subject's mental rotation a test form appeared. The subject's task was again to determine whether the test form was standard or reflected. Using the data from the previous experiment, Cooper was able to predict how long it would take for the subject to mentally rotate to a certain orientation. On some trials the test form was presented in exactly that orientation (the *expected* trials). On other trials the test form was presented either past or short of that orientation (the *unexpected* trials). The data from the experiment are shown in figure 2.7. On expected trials the response time was constant, indicating that Cooper correctly predicted when the subject's mental image would come into correspondence with the test stimulus. On many of these trials the test stimulus was shown at an orientation that the subject had never seen before, indicating that the mental rotation followed a complete trajectory rather than clicking only among familiar orientations. The unexpected trials showed a linear relation between response time and the degree to which the orientation of the test form departed from the predicted orientation of the subject's image. Subjects were apparently able to either continue or reverse their mental rotations in order to bring their images into correspondence with the test stimulus.

Cooper's experiments provide evidence that mental rotation is a precise *analog* of physical rotation. The mental rotation operation seems to transform the image contin-

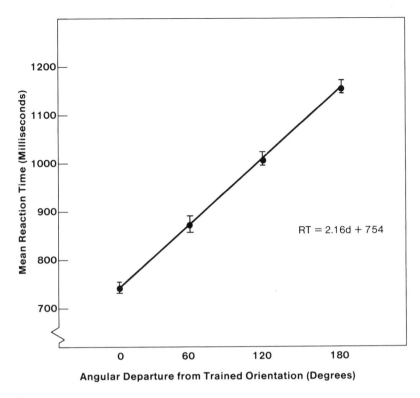

Figure 2.6
Mean reaction time as a function of angular departure from the trained orientation. The equation is for the best-fitting straight line through the four data points. (Adapted from Cooper 1975.)

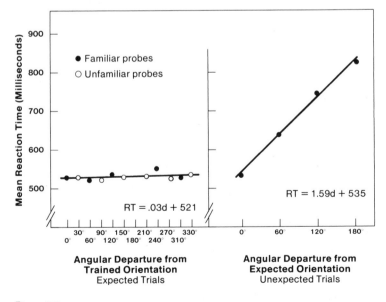

Figure 2.7
Reaction time results from Cooper 1976. (Adapted from Cooper 1976.)

uously and as a whole. The data accord well with the hypothesis that the rotation operation is part of the cognitive architecture and that it operates on a visual buffer. On the other hand, it is difficult to rule out the influence of tacit knowledge in mental rotation experiments. Subjects have a lifetime of experience with seeing physical rotations. One strength of Cooper's method is that subjects are not told to mentally rotate the stimuli; their task is simply to judge whether the target and test forms are the same or different. It can be argued that subjects had every reason to find some quicker and easier way to make the judgments in these experiments but that the nature of the imagery system forced them to rely on a rotation operation that is part of the cognitive architecture.

Other evidence on mental rotation appears to reflect the limited capacity of image processing and the interplay with central processes. Some investigators have found evidence that mental rotation is influenced by structural information that is not thought to be explicitly encoded in the visual buffer. Such information may be present in the long-term schematic representation that is used to generate an image, or it may be developed by pattern recognition processes that operate on the buffer. Hochberg and Gellman (1977) found that patterns that contain easily identifiable "landmark" features are rotated at a faster rate. Pylyshyn (1979) found that the judgment subjects have to make influences the rate of rotation. In his task target and test figures were displayed simultaneously, and the subject had to judge whether the test figure was a subpart of the target figure. As shown in figure 2.8, in some cases the test pattern was a "good" subfigure made up of connected pieces of the whole that did not intersect with other pieces of the whole. In other cases the test pattern was a "poor" subfigure that was disconnected or that intersected with other parts of the whole. The rotation rate was affected by the goodness of the test figure. When the test figure was a good subpart, mental rotation was more rapid. This result demonstrates that a fixed-rate rotation operation was not applied a single time to each of the target figures. One possibility is that the rotation operation applies not to the visual buffer but to more abstract representations that contain considerable structural information. Other interpretations, however, are consistent with the notion that mental rotation is a primitive operation that applies to the visual buffer. The target figures may exceed the capacity of the buffer and the rotation operation, forcing subjects to rotate them piece by piece. The subject may break the target figure into structurally coherent pieces in order to manage the piecemeal rotation process. Matching a poor subfigure might then require more subpart rotations, producing a response-time curve with a higher intercept and steeper slope.

By measuring subjects' eye movements back and forth between different parts of target and test figures, Just and Carpenter (1976) found evidence that subjects do sometimes mentally rotate figures part by part, rather than all at once. They also found evidence that in their experiment subjects rotated objects in 50-degree steps, which apparently conflicts with Cooper's (1976) evidence favoring much smaller steps, or possibly a continuous transformation. It is possible, however, that when the target and test shapes are simultaneously present, as in Just and Carpenter's experiments, mental rotation is facilitated by the additional external input to the visual buffer. Many experimenters have also noted that with practice rotation rates tend to speed up and differences among shapes tend to decrease (Shepard and Cooper 1982; Pylyshyn 1979). The complex web of findings on mental rotation provides a major challenge for any theory. It seems clear that the mental rotation operation has a limited capacity and

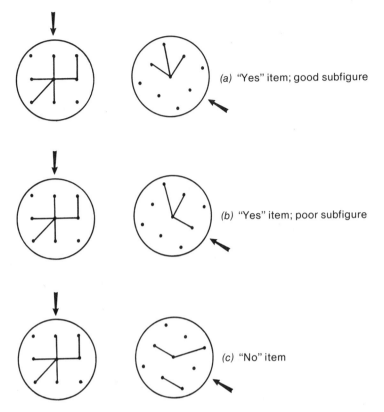

(a) "Yes" item; good subfigure

(b) "Yes" item; poor subfigure

(c) "No" item

Figure. 2.8
Examples of the type of stimuli used in Pylyshyn's (1979) study. The subject mentally rotates the figure on the left until its top coincides with the arrow in the figure on the right. The subject then judges whether the right-hand figure is a subpart of the left-hand figure. The correct answer is "Yes" in (a) and (b), and "No" in (c). The rate of mental rotation is faster when the test item is a good subfigure, as in (a), than when it is a poor subfigure, as in (b). (Adapted from Pylyshyn 1979.)

that subjects can adjust to the limits by breaking a figure into parts or representing only its most distinctive features. It appears that if mental rotation operates on the visual buffer, subjects use propositional or structural representations to decide on which aspects of a figure to load into the buffer before rotating. With practice on a set of figures the subjects might begin to make better decisions about which aspects of the figures to image, leading to fewer false starts and piecemeal rotations on a typical trial and thus lowering the estimated overall rate of rotation.

Converging Evidence concerning Visual Imagery
The literature on visual imagery is perhaps the best available illustration of the difficulty of determining whether a particular process or representation is biologically built into the architecture of cognition. The intuitive sense that there is something special and natural about visual imagery that is fundamentally different from more conceptual and abstract thought has proved to be difficult to back up with strong experimental evidence.

In recent years researchers have combined cognitive studies with physiological methods in a search for converging evidence favoring the theory that visual imagery involves distinctive representations and processes in the visual system (Kosslyn and Koenig 1992). One type of research has made use of two methods capable of measuring relative activity in different brain regions during cognition, positron emission tomography (PET scanning), and Xenon-133 regional cerebral blood flow (rCBF) scanning. This research has shown that imagery tasks, in contrast with cognitive tasks that do not involve imagery, lead to selective activation of several brain areas known to be involved in visual perception: the occipital cortex, the parietal cortex, and the inferior temporal cortex (see chapters 7 and 12 for more information). The involvement of the occipital cortex is particularly interesting because it is the most plausible site for the visual buffer. The occipital cortex is known to explicitly represent space and spatially located primitive features (such as local boundaries) and not to represent higher-order categorical features (such as global shape or object identity). Spatial information is laid out *topographically* on the cortex with adjacent areas in the visual field represented by activity in adjacent areas of the cortex.

Another technique involves *neuropsychology*, the study of cognitive deficits in people who have suffered brain damage from accidents or illness. The pattern of results in this area of research is highly complex, reflecting the complexity of the visual system, the complex relations between central processes and visual processing during imagery, and the tendency for brain damage to affect rather large areas that rarely correspond well to computational functions (an issue taken up further in chapter 7). For example, there is evidence that damage to the right parietal lobe impairs mental rotation. This evidence is consistent with more general findings that the right hemisphere of the brain is specialized for the representation and processing of spatial relations. However, people with left hemisphere damage can also show mental rotation deficits. Within the theory we have been sketching, this initially puzzling finding can be explained by the assumption that mental rotation also involves the use of abstract descriptions of objects to guide the generation of images and to refresh and track the image as it rotates. These processes are consistent with other evidence about the computational capacities of the left hemisphere (Kosslyn and Koenig 1992).

We have now augmented our initial theory of the cognitive architecture. Our initial discussion focused on propositional-schematic representation and central processing constrained by a limited working memory. The sensory input and motor output systems were assumed to be relatively self-contained, with sensory systems delivering active propositional representations of current input for central processing, and motor systems accepting active propositional specifications of desired motor output. Within this picture it could be assumed that the sensory and motor systems might possess specialized representations and processes. The research on visual imagery led to the conclusion that the visual system does indeed possess specialized representations and processes and that these facilities can be recruited by central processes. The same kind of result appears to hold for the other sensory systems and for motor systems as well. For example, central cognitive processes can recruit specialized facilities of the auditory system in the absence of acoustic input or of motor systems without moving. The involvement of sensory and motor representations and processes in thought, even when environmental input and output are absent, means that a theory of central cognition cannot be developed independently of theories of sensory and motor systems.

2.8 Automatic and Controlled Processes

Intuitions about imagery were one source of our decision to develop an account of the architecture of sensory and motor systems and their interplay with central cognition. Another set of intuitions, in this case about attention and working memory, lead to a final expansion of the classical conception of cognitive architecture. We have already mentioned the conscious experience of having one's working-memory capacity overloaded, while doing mental arithmetic or playing chess. But an equally important realization is that some complex cognitive processes do not overload working memory. They seem to occur with very little or no attentional effort. For the experienced driver, driving a car requires little deliberate attention. One can engage in other complex cognitive activities, such as listening to a radio talk show or a sports broadcast, while driving a car. People often report becoming lost in thought while driving and suddenly realizing that they have driven for miles without paying any attention to what they were doing. Listening to a radio show seems to require attention and control, and driving does not. By contrast, think back to the first time you were behind the steering wheel of a car and imagine trying to concentrate on a talk show or a baseball game. Driving required a great deal of attention back then. The distinction between tasks that require much and little attention seems to have less to do with the nature of the task itself and more to do with the prior experience of the person engaging in it. The ability of expert chess players to play many games simultaneously, devoting a few seconds to each move, suggests that even chess, an unusually difficult, purely cognitive task, can become nearly as automatic as driving.

Let us use the term *controlled processing* to refer to cognition that makes heavy demands on the limited resources of working memory and attention and the term *automatic processing* for cognition that reflects reduced demands that are somehow the result of practice. We have already explored the characteristics of controlled processing in some detail. It is goal-oriented and flexible. It draws on both primitive, built-in processes and the ability to interpret representations in long-term memory. It is constrained by the limited capacity of working memory, although to some extent the constraints can be overcome by chunking. We will proceed to develop the contrast with automatic processing and then look at how automatic procedures are acquired.

Automatic Processes

Researchers hypothesize that automatic processes make very small, or possibly no, demands on working memory, so their capacity is very large relative to the controlled processes. They do not operate by interpreting declarative information. Rather, they are like *compiled* programs in computers. That is, they specify information processes directly, rather than having to be interpreted by some other process. We saw above that dialing a ten-digit phone number places a heavy load on working memory if each digit is a single item. The load on working memory is reduced if the number is broken up into three chunks that are stored as schemas in long-term memory. Even in this case, however, the three chunks have to be interpreted by a process (possibly built in) that converts active representations into sequences of motor commands. There are other cases in which dialing a phone number seems to be more automatic. Anecdotes such as the following are fairly common. A professor is trying to place a phone call from her office while simultaneously contributing to an ongoing conversation. She inadvertently dials her home instead of the colleague she intended to reach. A possible analysis of this error is that dialing one's home number can become an automatic procedure that can be carried out while attention is devoted to a concurrent controlled-processing task, in this case holding a conversation. In addition, the load on working memory imposed by the conversation appears to interfere with control by the goal of dialing the colleague's number. In the absence of control the automatic procedure is triggered by the phone-dialing stimuli in the context (for example, having a phone in hand).

This example illustrates two key characteristics of automatic procedures that are emphasized in current theorizing. First, they behave like compiled information processes that run without interpreting declarative knowledge or making demands on working memory. Second, they are automatically triggered by patterns in the currently activated information, which includes sensory input, declarative knowledge that is currently active, and currently active goals. They are often referred to as *data-driven* or *pattern-driven* processes, because they are evoked by patterns in the informational data that the mind currently confronts rather than being selected in a rigid sequence by a hierarchically controlled planning process. Automatic procedures that are triggered by patterns of active information are also often called *productions*.

Experiments on Automatic and Controlled Processing
A simple but flexible experimental task that provides evidence for the limited capacity of controlled processes is the Multiple Frame Attention and Search Task (MFAST), investigated by Shiffrin and Schneider (1977; Schneider and Shiffrin 1977). In one version of the task the subject is given a memory set of from one to four target letters and is told to search for a target letter in a rapid sequence of twenty frames, displayed on the screen of a computer terminal. The subject responds "Yes" if any target letter is present and "No" if no target letters are present. Each frame contains from one to four letters and is exposed for from 40 milliseconds to 800 milliseconds. The target letter on a "Yes" item occurs once in one frame of the sequence of frames. In the varied mapping condition the memory set changes on every trial, and in the consistent mapping condition the memory set is the same on every trial. The experimental procedure is summarized in figure 2.9.

MEMORY SET SIZE = 2
FRAME SIZE = 4

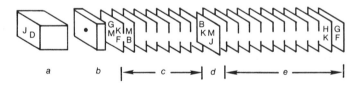

Figure 2.9
An example of a "Yes" trial in one version of the multiple-frame search task, in which the memory set contains two characters and each frame contains four characters. Time moves from left to right in the figure. (*a*) The memory set is presented. (*b*) A fixation dot (which tells the subject where to focus) goes on for 0.5 seconds when the subject starts the trial. (*c*) Some number of distractor frames occur that do not contain a member of the memory set. (*d*) The target frame, which contains one member of the memory set, occurs. (*e*) More frames that do not contain a member of the memory set occur. The duration of each frame is varied in different experiments. (Adapted from Schneider and Shiffrin 1977.)

The varied mapping condition was predicted to show characteristics of controlled processing. Because the memory set changes on every trial, the subject must change the rule relating the alphabet to the "Yes" and "No" responses on every trial. Thus, the flexible nature of controlled processes is required. As the experimenter increases the size of the memory set, increases the number of letters in each frame, and reduces the exposure time on each frame, the load on the controlled process increases. At some point it will reach the limit of its capacity, and the subject will begin to make frequent errors. The data accorded well with this prediction. Subjects were nearly 100 percent correct with a frame time of 120 milliseconds, a memory set size of one, and a frame size of one. When the frame size was increased to four, however, the frame time had to be increased to 400 milliseconds to allow near-perfect performance. When the memory set size was also increased to four, performance fell to 50 percent correct on "Yes" trials at the 400-millisecond frame time. When the frame time was doubled to 800 milliseconds per frame, subjects still detected the target letter only 70 percent of the time. The results were collected after over ten hours of practice, and there was no evidence that the subjects were improving at that point.

The consistent mapping condition was predicted to show the characteristics of automatic processing after adequate practice. Because the memory set and its relation to the "Yes" response remained constant on every trial, the flexibility of controlled processes was not necessary. As predicted, after ten hours of practice subjects' performance did not show evidence of the capacity limitation that was present in the data from the varied mapping condition. Subjects were able to detect over 90 percent of the targets with a memory set of four items and a frame size of four items, even when the frame time was reduced to 120 milliseconds. Performance was still 80 percent correct with a frame time of 80 milliseconds. To appreciate just how impressive this level of performance is, recall that there were twenty frames per trial. Thus, subjects were searching for a single target character amid seventy-nine distractors that appeared within an interval of 1.6 seconds. The evidence supports the theory that after sufficient practice subjects no longer had to devote attention to searching for the target characters.

A truly automatic process should show at least two further characteristics. First, if a task has become largely automated, attentional resources should be freed up to perform another task concurrently. Second, it should be difficult to control the occurrence of an automatic process. Shiffrin and Dumais (1981) reported some informal evidence that the first characteristic is present in the MFAST task. Subjects were often able to carry on conversations while performing the consistent mapping task. In an elegant experiment Schneider and Fisk (1982) were able to test the prediction that subjects can attend to another task while an automatic process is occurring. In an MFAST task subjects simultaneously searched for consistently mapped targets in two corners of a four-character display and for variably mapped targets in the other two corners. When they were told to devote their attention to the variably mapped search, their accuracy on both searches was equal to accuracy in control conditions in which each search task was performed alone. These results supported the theory that subjects are able to detect targets in the consistent mapping task without attention and in parallel with the occurrence of controlled attentional processes.

The second critical prediction is that automatic processes should occur even when people consciously try to prevent them from occurring. Shiffrin and Schneider (1977) were able to test this prediction in yet another elegant application of the MFAST task.

Subjects were first trained in a consistent mapping task with a frame size of four until their performance showed evidence of automatic target detection. They were then transferred to a special version of the variable mapping task with a frame size of four. They were instructed to ignore two positions in diagonally opposite corners of the display and search for the variable targets only in the other two corners. On half of the trials a character that had been a target in the consistent mapping condition appeared in one of the two ignored positions. The prediction was that the automatic response to this character would tend to occur in spite of the subject's attempt to ignore that position in the display. The automatic response would distract the subject from the variable mapping task, thus lowering accuracy. The reason that the automatic process interferes with the controlled process in this situation is that the automatic process redirects attention. In other cases automatic processes would not be predicted to interfere with controlled processes.

The data supported the prediction. When the old consistent mapping target occurred in the same frame as the variable mapping target, accuracy on the variable mapping task dropped from 85 percent to just over 60 percent, indicating that the automatic response to the old consistent mapping target in an ignored position distracted the subject from the search for variable mapping targets. The data indicate that what becomes automatized in the consistent mapping task is the detection of the target and the diversion of attention to it. The automatic attentional response disrupts the ongoing focus of attention on other tasks. Subjects were unable to consciously turn off this automatic shift of attention. Such automatic shifts of attention seem to occur frequently in everyday life. For example, if one is attending to a conversation at a party, one's attention can be involuntarily shifted by the occurrence of one's name in another, ignored conversation.

2.9 The Acquisition of Skill

Most complex cognitive, perceptual, and motor skills are thought to require a mixture of automatic and controlled processing. At the highest level of performance controlled processes are used to maintain goals and to flexibly direct skilled performance to meet novel situations that could not previously have been automatized. The lower-level, more consistent components of the skill are performed automatically. When a person is first beginning to learn a skill, controlled processes are responsible for a much larger share of the performance. It appears that beginners perform skills largely by interpreting declarative knowledge in the manner described earlier. The beginner is like an inexperienced cook working from an unfamiliar recipe. Each line of the recipe must be read and interpreted as an instruction to perform some action. Worse, in many cases there is no explicit recipe for the skill, so the beginner must slowly discover one.

The Stages of Skill Learning

Various theorists have attempted to divide the process of skill learning into stages that characterize the slow transition from dominance by controlled to dominance by automatic processes (Fitts 1964; LaBerge 1976; Anderson 1983). Their conclusions have been remarkably similar across a wide range of skills.

The Interpretive Stage   The first stage, which can be called the *interpretive* stage, is characterized by the discovery of the relevant aspects of the task and the storage of declarative knowledge that can be interpreted by general procedures to perform at the beginner's level. Performance is error prone, both because some of the declarative knowledge may be incomplete or incorrect and because the controlled interpretive process can overload working memory or be speeded beyond its capacity. Consider the task of learning to play "bent" or "blue" notes on the harmonica. The first challenge is to discover by experimentation just what is required to play a bent note. Relevant features turn out to be lowering the position of the tongue, quite a bit for low notes and just a little for high notes, and altering the amount of breath. Soon it is possible to play single bent notes with a fair degree of reliability, and it is time to try to introduce them into phrases. This tends to be extremely difficult at first. A great deal of attention has to be devoted to playing the bent notes correctly: the beginning musician has to anticipate a coming bent note and consciously issue instructions to change the position of the tongue and alter the amount of breath. Since the bent notes cannot be played quickly, the phrases are played slowly and rhythm is disrupted. This exploratory, halting, and often verbalizable phase of performance has been studied in perceptual, motor, and complex problem-solving tasks (see again Fitts 1964; LaBerge 1976; Anderson 1983).

The Compiled Stage   The second stage of skill acquisition can be called the *compiled* stage. During this stage the parts of the skill are chunked, or compiled, into a procedure that is specific to the performance of the skill. Demands on working memory are considerably less, because the skill-specific information does not have to be held in a declarative form while it is being interpreted by a more generalized procedure. Because declarative knowledge is less involved, it also becomes more difficult to verbalize the processes involved in performance. To return to the harmonica example, in the compiled stage there seems to be a single voluntary command to bend the note that is no longer accompanied by an awareness of what is being done with the tongue position or breath.

This compilation, coding, or chunking process has been observed in a wide variety of tasks. LaBerge (1976), for example, argues that it occurs in learning to perceive individual letters. When adult subjects learn a new letterlike form, they must learn to identify a particular configuration of lines and curves as a unit without devoting attention separately to each line or accessing declarative knowledge about the lines (which might be verbalizable as, for example, "It looks like a backward check mark, but the long line is straight up and down"). The process also seems to occur with perceptual category learning, which takes place when we form a single category for a set of separate items. An everyday case is the assignment of any character from the set 1 ... 9 to the category of *digit*. When presented with a 3, we assign it to the digit category without activating the set of all nine digits in working memory and interpretively searching through it for the presence of 3. Shiffrin and Schneider (1977, Experiment 3) studied the acquisition of entirely new categories of letters—such as G, M, F, P—in their MFAST task. Their data confirmed the transition from a slow error-prone identification of category membership that involved a deliberate scan of working memory to a fast and accurate identification with no scan.

A similar progression occurs when learning complex thinking skills, such as solving Euclidean geometry problems. Anderson (1983) shows that students begin their work in geometry by applying highly generalized problem-solving procedures that draw on postulates that are stored in declarative memory or in the textbook itself. With practice, the application of a particular postulate can be compiled into a single production, so that certain kinds of information in a problem will invoke the application of the postulate without requiring that its full statement be brought into working memory and checked for applicability. This kind of problem-solving skill will be discussed more fully in chapter 3.

Once a procedure has been formed, attention is often still required for performance of the skill. Although the subject may not be able to accurately estimate the demand on controlled processing resources at this point, the demand can be measured under controlled experimental conditions. In a task that involved learning to identify new letterlike characters LaBerge (1976) compared an unprimed condition to a primed condition, in which the subject was cued on what to look for in advance of each trial. During the second stage of acquisition, performance in the primed condition was superior because the subject was able to shift attention to the needed identification before the trial.

The Automatic Stage   The final stage of learning can be called the *automatic* stage. Most researchers have observed that performance continues to improve after the subject has acquired procedures that are specific to components of the skill. During this stage the procedures become maximally automatic. The main mechanism of further automatization seems to be simple *strengthening*. The tendency of appropriate inputs to activate a procedure and the tendency of the procedure to run to completion once activated become strong enough that the additional activation that might be available by devoting attentional resources to the procedure produces no further increase in performance. For example, in LaBerge's experiment the difference between primed and unprimed trials eventually disappeared with practice. The interpretation of this finding was that shifting attention to the upcoming identification task produced no benefit because attentional resources were no longer needed for its optimal performance. Schneider and Fisk (1982) also found no improvement in performance when subjects were instructed to devote their primary attention to an automatized task rather than to a concurrent task.

For more complex tasks Anderson (1983) and Rumelhart and Norman (1978) argue that procedures are *tuned* as well as strengthened. With tuning, a procedure comes under the control of the optimal range of inputs. Before tuning, a procedure may be fired too often by an irrelevant situation, or it may fail to be fired by appropriate situations.

Cheng (1985) has proposed a reinterpretation of the data on automatization and the theory of skill acquisition. She argues that the formation of an automatic process does not involve a complete withdrawal of attention and that automatic processes are not qualitatively different from controlled processes. Her theory concentrates on the first two stages of acquisition. The claim is basically that the bulk of improvement in most tasks results from the discovery of the relevant features of the task and the compilation of efficient procedures. She calls these processes *restructuring*. The result, she argues, is a substantially lower but not a zero demand on attentional resources. If there is a third stage of skill acquisition, she would argue that the strengthening of procedures never involves a qualitative shift to a complete withdrawal of processing resources. Rather, strengthening would involve a continued shrinkage of the demand on resources.

What Can and Cannot Be Automated?
Contemporary research on skill acquisition highlights the tremendous plasticity of cognitive processes. Dramatic improvements in performance occur as specialized pro-

cedures are compiled and automatized. It is natural to wonder what the limits of automatization are. Research on the limits of skill development confronts a logical problem: it is always possible that with further appropriate training performance would improve. As a practical matter, controlled experimental observation of skill development in an individual for more than a few months is expensive and difficult, though not impossible (see, for example, Chase and Ericsson 1981). Estimates of the time it takes to reach the known pinnacle of skill in highly demanding, complex activities such as chess (Chase and Simon 1973) and musical composition (Hayes 1981) suggest roughly ten years of devoted practice (Ericsson, Krampe, and Tesch-Römer 1993). This observation has led in recent years to careful studies of experts in particular domains, which will be described further in chapter 3.

At this point generalizations about the limits of automatization and skill development are at least as risky as predictions of the best possible time in the marathon. Nevertheless, some qualitative conclusions can be suggested. It seems that complex skills are typically not completely automatized. Optimal skilled performance seems to balance the speed and high capacity of automatic processes with the goal-directedness and flexibility of controlled processes. A system that acted only by allowing the currently most active automatic procedure to carry through to completion without any influence by goals would be incoherently impulsive, without consciousness as we know it. In addition, the ability to interpret declarative knowledge, albeit with quite limited capacity, seems to be crucial to coping with problems we have never encountered before. It is precisely what is unique and most challenging about a situation that is unlikely to yield to automatized components of a skill, because the past experiences that would be the basis for building the procedure are lacking. And since declarative knowledge is activated by the high-capacity spreading activation process, the limitation is not as great as it might appear to be.

Automatic Processes and the Cognitive Architecture

The capacity for automatization is a highly significant feature of the cognitive architecture. The cognitive processes underlying a person's performance of the same task change dramatically as a function of practice. Our organization of many tutorial activities around the maxim "Practice makes perfect" reflects a basic recognition of this fact. However, both qualitative and quantitative details of the relation of practice to performance are still emerging, and our intuitive understanding of them seems to be imperfect. Improvement in the performance of complex cognitive and sensory-motor skills continues to take place over years and many thousands of hours of practice. Over time the underlying cognitive organization of a skill undergoes qualitative changes. Ericsson, Krampe, and Tesch-Römer (1993) argue that we may often mistakenly attribute the result of superior practice to innate talent. The qualitative differences that appear to be the mark of genius may be just as much or more a mark of a person's dedication. The notion that inborn talent can be easily identified in children is also called into question by the results on skill acquisition. Since the cognitive processes underlying performance at the novice and expert level are different, superior performance at the novice level may not be a good predictor of superior performance at the expert level.

The mastery of a cognitive skill involves the long-term storage of procedures. There are significant questions about how this *procedural knowledge* is represented and whether it is distinct from *declarative knowledge*, which is stored in propositional-schematic format. Some aspects of the evidence favor a strong distinction. New declarative memories are relatively easy to store. They are often acquired in a single exposure. The compilation and automatization of a component of a skill seems to require many exposures. There seem to be many routes to the activation of a declarative memory, but each aspect of a skill seems to be under the control of precise sensory or cognitive conditions. In the early stages of skill acquisition, knowledge of the procedure shows strong signs of propositional storage, such as a high load on working memory, awareness of what has been learned, and an ability not only to perform the skill but also to use the knowledge in other ways, such as to talk about it or analyze it. Late in learning, the load on working memory is reduced dramatically, the details of the skill recede from awareness, and the procedural knowledge is expressible only as a performance.

There is neuropsychological support for the distinction between declarative and procedural knowledge as well (see chapter 7 and Squire 1987). The two types of knowledge can be dissociated by brain damage. People with severe anterograde amnesia are unable to learn new facts, although they are able to learn new sensory-motor and cognitive skills. Their other cognitive abilities, their working memories, and facts that they acquired prior to their injuries are also intact. Apparently, the amnesia damages tissue that is involved in the transfer of active representations in working memory to long-term propositional-schematic memory. This mechanism is apparently not involved in skill acquisition. Examination of the brains of amnesic patients typically reveals damage to specific regions, the medial temporal area or the midline diencephalic area. The dissociation between declarative and procedural storage mechanisms produces some striking behavior. For example, an amnesic can learn a new skill (such as solving the Tower of Hanoi puzzle, described in chapter 5) but fail to remember any of the occasions on which the skill was practiced. The distinction between declarative and procedural knowledge in human cognition may represent an optional design choice that came about during the evolution of cognitive systems and their physical substrates. Skill acquisition seems to be widely distributed and often quite well developed in nonhuman organisms. The skill acquisition mechanism, although it works in the same way regardless of the content of the skill, may also be represented in different cognitive and physiological systems. For example, much of the learning that goes on during the acquisition of a visual-motor skill may occur in visual and motor systems rather than in the central system. The capacity for declarative knowledge may have required the evolution of a specific physiologically localized system in a narrower range of organisms. In a cognitive architecture designed from scratch around classical computational principles, such as that of Newell (1990), a single long-term memory with suitably designed storage and retrieval processes may be sufficient.

Classical theories of skill representation have centered around the notion of productions, which can be symbolized as IF C THEN A, or $C \rightarrow A$. The idea is that when currently active sensory and cognitive representations satisfy certain conditions C, then actions A are triggered. The acquisition of a production has three possibly distinct aspects. First, a direct connection has to be established between the conditions and the action, so that the conditions can evoke the action reliably without the necessity of working-memory intensive and unreliable problem-solving processes. Second, the procedural compilation process is a chunking mechanism that can combine productions involving simple actions into more complex productions that specify sequences or patterns of action. Finally, the C-side of a production also involves chunking. The conditions for the production have to be integrated into a perceptual category or schema that is neither overly specific nor overly general. There are many questions about how productions are formally represented and about what is included in particular condition-action schemas as they are being learned. (The formal aspect of production systems in the context of AI is considered further in chapter 4.) These questions become critically important when the question of *transfer of skill* is addressed. When the demands of a task change, productions that were learned under the old demands may fail to transfer to or even interfere with performance on the new task, depending on what the two tasks have in common and on how the common and distinct aspects are represented in the original productions, if at all. These issues are explored by Singley and Anderson (1989).

2.10 The Connectionist Approach to Cognitive Architecture

The sketch of the cognitive architecture developed above is sometimes called a *classical* picture or is said to express the *symbolic paradigm* in cognitive science. In the 1980s several groups of researchers developed an alternative conception of the architecture. Several terms have been used somewhat interchangeably to designate their approach, including *connectionism, parallel distributed processing, artificial neural networks*, and *the subsymbolic paradigm*. In this section we will introduce the connectionist approach and compare it with the classical approach. The development of what appears to be a radical new approach to a scientific field inevitably raises foundational questions about the nature of the field and the defining commitments of the contrasting research programs. We will sketch the continuing debate about what the important differences between the classical and connectionist approaches are and about whether the two approaches are compatible.

Basic Features of Connectionist Architecture

A connectionist network consists of a number of computationally simple processing *units* that communicate with each other via *connections* that are capable of carrying only extremely simple signals. We will use the term *connectionist architecture* to refer both to particular networks and to general characterizations of networks. Figure 2.10 illustrates a simple connectionist network for computing the Boolean logical function known as *exclusive OR*, or *XOR*. The XOR function is illustrated in part (*a*) of the figure. It maps an input pair of binary digits, each of which can be 0 or 1, onto an output binary digit, which can be 0 or 1. Exclusive OR is equivalent to the English phrase *either A or B but not both*. Thus, the output of the function is 1 when exactly one of the inputs is 1, and the output is 0 when neither or both of the inputs is 1.

First, let us look at the structure of the network, illustrated in part (*b*) of the figure. There are five units in the network, symbolized by circles. They are organized into three layers: an *input layer*, a *hidden layer*, and an *output layer*. The connections among units are symbolized by arrows, which indicate the direction of the connection between two units. Units in the hidden layer are called hidden units because they are isolated from the network's environment. They neither receive input from the environment nor send outputs to the environment. The connections in the network are all between adjacent layers, making it strictly *hierarchical*, and the connections all proceed from the input layer toward the output layer, making it a *feed-forward* network. Networks that also include backward connections and that therefore contain loops are *(a)*   XOR FUNCTION

Input 1	Input 2	Output
0	0	0
1	0	1
0	1	1
1	1	0

(b)   XOR NETWORK

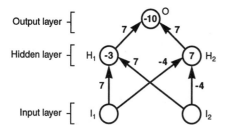

(c)   THRESHOLD ACTIVATION FUNCTION

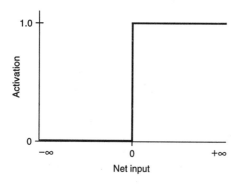

(d)   NETWORK COMPUTATIONS

Input pattern		Net inputs		Activations		Net Input	Activation
		H_1	H_2	H_1	H_2	O	O
0	0	-3	7	0	1	-3	0
1	0	4	3	1	1	4	1
0	1	4	3	1	1	4	1
1	1	11	-1	1	0	-3	0

Figure 2.10
Computing the XOR function with a connectionist network

called *recurrent* networks. Adjacent layers of this network are *fully connected* because each unit at a level is connected to all units at the next higher level.

The processing restrictions on single units in connectionist networks are rather severe. A single connection is not allowed to carry complex symbolic information, as a single wire connecting two computers might. Units are only allowed to transmit simple numerical values, which in the example can be positive, negative, or 0. Each unit in a network is an active processor that takes the numbers arriving at its input connections at a given moment and transforms them into a single output number, which is transmitted along any connections to other units. The transformation between the inputs and the output performed by a single unit is typically restricted to relatively simple mathematical operations. Units are not endowed with the complex logical-processing capacities of electronic microprocessors, for example. The XOR function is an elementary illustration of one of the consequences of this restriction. In the example model, the hidden units are interposed between the input and output units because a single output unit of the kind used in the model cannot compute the XOR function alone.

The input units in the example simply encode the input digits. If an input unit is receiving a 1 (or 0) from the environment, it sends an output value of 1 (or 0) along each of its connections with other units. The operation of the hidden and output units is a bit more complicated. A unit receives input values from other units that feed it. The input values to a unit, i, must be collected into a single value, called the *net input* to i, or net_i. The net input must then be converted into a value that represents the resulting activation of the unit. The output of the unit is the activation value. (In some networks the activation value is converted into an output value by some further transformation.) The output value is sent along any connections to units that are further downstream.

The calculation of the net input for the hidden and output units in the example is typical of connectionist models. Each connection coming into a unit has a numerical weight, which can be thought of as its sensitivity. Typically, weights are allowed to be positive, negative, or 0. The numbers next to the connection links in part (*b*) of the figure are the weights on the connections. To calculate net_i for a unit, the incoming value on each connection is multiplied by the weight on the connection, and the resulting products are added up. The net input to a unit thus involves a *weighted sum* of the output values of the units to which it is connected. In this example, as in many connectionist models, there is also a bias associated with each unit. The biases are shown as numbers inside the circles representing the units. The bias on a unit is simply added into the net input and can be thought of as an intrinsic activation tendency that is independent of inputs that arise from the current environmental stimulation. (A bias can also be thought of as the weight on a connection that receives a constant input of 1.) The net_i to a unit, then, is the weighted sum of the inputs from other units plus the bias. The weighted-sum-plus-a-bias scheme can obviously be extended to units that have any number of connections and weights.

Suppose the input to the XOR net is (1, 1). In that case each input unit will be sending a 1 to each hidden unit. The net_i to the first hidden unit will thus be $(1 \cdot 7) + (1 \cdot 7) + (-3) = 11$. The net_i to the second hidden unit will be $(1 \cdot -4) + (1 \cdot -4) + 7 = -1$. These net input values must be transformed into activation values before they are sent on to the output unit. What is needed is an activation function that specifies an activation value for each possible value of net_i. In this case we use the simple binary threshold function shown in part (*c*) of the figure. As can be seen, if net_i

is less than or equal to 0, activation is 0, and if net_i is greater than 0, activation is 1. Units that compute their net input via a weighted sum and that use a threshold function to map the net input onto one of two activation values are called *linear threshold units*. For the input $(1, 1)$, the activation value of the first hidden unit is 1, and the activation of the second hidden unit is 0. Since the output of a unit is equal to its activation in this model, these values can now be propagated to the output unit. The net_i to the output unit is $(1 \cdot 7) + (0 \cdot 7) - 10 = -3$. Since net_i is less than 0, the activation and hence the output of the unit is 0, which is the correct response to the original input of $(1, 1)$. This series of calculations corresponds to the fourth row of the table in part (d) of the figure, which gives the net_i and activation for the hidden and output units in response to the four possible input patterns.

It is of some interest to explore further why the computation of XOR requires hidden units. To get away without hidden units, we would need to set the two weights on a single output unit so that the weighted sums for the $(0, 0)$ and $(1, 1)$ inputs were less than the weighted sums for the $(1, 0)$ and $(0, 1)$ inputs. If this were possible, we could set the threshold of the activation function to yield 0 for the lower values and 1 for the higher values. However, if we assign weights so that $(0, 1)$ and $(1, 0)$ put the weighted sum over the threshold, $(1, 1)$ also puts it over. The problem is that the set of inputs mapped to 0 is not *linearly separable* from the set of inputs mapped to 1. The geometric significance of linear separability is illustrated in figure 2.11. The four desired outputs are plotted as points in a two-dimensional Cartesian space, which has an axis representing each input value. There is no way of drawing a line through the space so that $(1, 0)$ and $(0, 1)$ are on one side of the line and $(0, 0)$ and $(1, 1)$ are on the other side. Minsky and Papert (1969) showed that networks with a single layer of linear threshold units (historically known as *perceptrons*) cannot compute functions that do not satisfy the linear separability criterion.

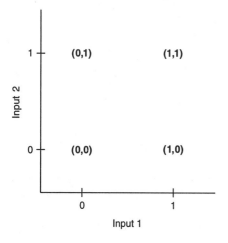

Figure 2.11
The four possible inputs to XOR are plotted as points in two-dimensional Cartesian space. The set of inputs mapped to 0 is not linearly separable from the set of inputs mapped to 1. That is, there is no way of drawing a line through the space so that $(1, 0)$ and $(0, 1)$ are on one side of the line and $(0, 0)$ and $(1, 1)$ are on the other side.

The figure also shows that the separability criterion is met by other simple logic functions. The network computes XOR by converting it into a two-stage combination of logical functions that *can* be computed by linear threshold units. By checking the activation values of the hidden units in part (*d*) of figure 2.10, the reader can verify that the first hidden unit computes *inclusive or* ("either A or B or both") and that the second hidden unit computes *not-and* ("not both"). The output unit then computes the *and* of the outputs of the two hidden units. The output unit thus requires that "A or B or both" and "not both" be true simultaneously, which is simply XOR.

The idea of thinking of the input to the XOR net as a point in two-dimensional space can be generalized. An ordered pair of two numbers specifies a point in two-dimensional space, and an ordered triple of three numbers specifies a point in three-dimensional space. In three-dimensional space the linear separability criterion would be met if we could fit a two-dimensional plane between the classes of input points that map to different output values. In general, an ordered list, or *vector*, of n numbers specifies a point in n-dimensional space (and the linear separability criterion can be extended to the notion of fitting an $(n - 1)$–D hyperplane between two sets of points). Connectionist networks can be thought of as devices for performing mathematical operations on vectors. A large, preexisting body of mathematics concerning vectors can be used directly in describing the behavior of networks (Jordan 1986). For example, in addition to thinking of the input to a net as a vector of values, we can think of the weights on a unit as a vector. The weighted sum for the net input to the unit can then be thought of as the product of the weight vector and the input vector. If we arrange the weight vectors on all of the units in a given layer of a net into rows in a *weight matrix*, then the product of this matrix with the input vector yields the vector of net inputs. The strategy of thinking about networks in terms of mathematical operations on vectors and matrices and of interpreting these operations geometrically has proved very fruitful and is employed extensively in advanced treatments of connectionist models.

The cognitive task that a network performs is determined in part by the arrangement of the units and connections, in part by the representations that are employed at the input and output levels, and in part by the weights on the connections. In the XOR net, for example, the arrangement of the units and connections, and the use of binary representation, dictate that the network computes a function from two binary inputs to one binary output. However, the values of the weights and biases determine *which* function of this type is computed. If we changed the weights in figure 2.10 in various ways, the network would compute other functions. The reader might ponder, for example, the problem of setting the weights and biases so that the network computes NOT-XOR (also known as *if and only if* or IFF), which yields 1 whenever XOR yields 0 and vice versa. There are six weights and three biases, which we could arrange into a nine-valued weight vector. Listing the weights from left to right and bottom to top, followed by the biases in the same order, the vector for figure 2.10 would be $(7, -4, 7, -4, 7, 7, -3, 7, -10)$. Each setting of the nine values can be imagined as a point in a nine-dimensional *weight space*, and each setting is associated with one of the sixteen possible functions from the set $\{(0, 0), (1, 0), (0, 1), (1, 1)\}$ to the set $\{0, 1\}$. In a sense, finding a setting of the weights and biases that computes a particular function, such as NOT-XOR, is a matter of moving around in this nine-dimensional space until one finds an appropriate point.

The fact that changing the weights in a network changes its performance raises the possibility that networks could *learn* to perform tasks by adjusting their own weights on the basis of experience. Learning has indeed been a prominent theme in connectionist research. The challenges facing any learning procedure are daunting. In larger networks the weight space that must be searched for a suitable set of values is enormous. If we increase the number of units in each layer of a three-layer hierarchical network toward 100, for example, the number of connections quickly goes into the hundreds and then the thousands. If the network is going to learn a task from scratch, it needs some systematic procedure for adjusting its weights to improve its performance in response to its experience. Prior knowledge of the function to be computed cannot be used because the network is assumed not to have any such knowledge. Many procedures have now been devised that allow connectionist networks to learn various kinds of tasks under various environmental conditions. In fact, the weights in figure 2.10 are rounded-off versions of values that were actually learned via a procedure known as the *backpropagation* algorithm or the *generalized delta-rule* (Rumelhart, Hinton, and Williams 1986).

The backpropagation algorithm can be used to illustrate some of the characteristics of connectionist learning procedures. It applies in cases where the task of the network is to map a set of inputs onto a set of outputs and was developed specifically to work for networks with at least one layer of hidden units. The network is started with an arbitrary configuration of weights, usually chosen randomly. It is highly unlikely that this initial weight configuration computes the desired function. The problem faced by the network is to move from this initial point in weight space to a satisfactory point by adjusting its weights using information gained from its experience. Clearly, as the network receives inputs and produces outputs, it will need some feedback about whether the outputs it is producing are correct or incorrect. The backpropagation algorithm uses a detailed form of feedback. During training, each time the network receives an input and produces an output, the output is compared with the correct output for that input. The actual output vector is compared with the correct output vector element by element. If there is any error in the value produced by a particular output unit, the weights on the connections coming into that output unit are changed slightly in directions that tend to correct the error. Error signals a e then propagated back through the successive layers of hidden units where error-correcting adjustments to weights are also made.

The notion of a weight space can be used to understand backpropagation geometrically. If a network is being trained to compute a particular function, each setting of the weights produces some amount of error on an input pattern or set of patterns. Thus, there is a function from points in weight space to error values, and the error values can be seen as a defining a surface over the weight space. The error surface has high points, representing large amounts of error, and valleys, whose lowest points represent minimum amounts of error. The lowest point (or points) on the surface, the *global minimum* (or *minima*), represents a setting of the weights where there is the least error, and the network is coming as close to computing the desired function as it can. If the error value at a global minimum is 0, then the network computes the desired function at this setting of the weights.

Although it is not possible to draw a picture of an error surface with many dimensions, it is useful to look at graphical depictions of simple cases. In figure 2.12 a measure of error is graphed with respect to the value of one weight in a hypothetical

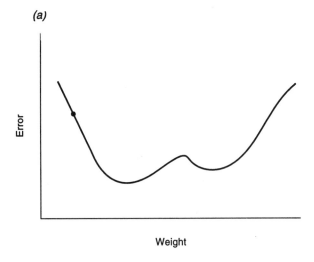

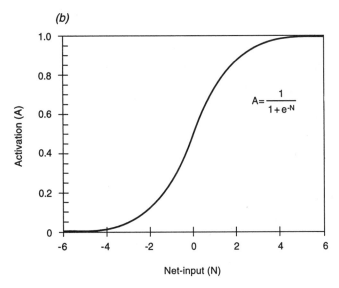

Figure 2.12
(a) A hypothetical error surface with respect to a single weight. The dot represents the current combination of weight and error. Increasing the weight slightly will reduce the error (the point will move down on the curve). A mathematical expression for the slope of error function (the first derivative of the function) can tell us which way to adjust the weight to seek a minimum. If the slope at a point is negative (as it is above), increase the weight; if the slope is positive, decrease the weight. (b) A continuous activation function (the logistic function) that can be used instead of the threshold activation function in figure 2.10.

network. We can imagine this curve as a cross section through a complex error surface, allowing us to look at what happens to the error value when we vary one weight while holding the other weights constant. At a given point in its training the weight in question will have some particular value, marked on the graph. No learning algorithm will be able to see the whole error surface and therefore be able to move to a minimum in a single step. If the algorithm can take small steps downward, however, it will eventually reach a minimum. Imagine a climber with no map or compass who needs to descend a mountain to a valley floor and who is caught in a dense fog that allows only a few feet of visibility. The climber can descend the mountain by taking each step in the locally downward direction. What the algorithm needs to do, then, is to use the error measure at a particular weight setting to determine the local slope of the error surface. The weights can then be adjusted to a point that will be lower on the slope. The steps are typically kept small enough that they rarely jump over a minimum. Complex error surfaces can contain *local* minima, which are lower than their immediate surroundings but higher than the lowest point on the surface, the *global* minimum. There has been research on when local minima that represent unsatisfactory solutions tend to exist as well as on learning algorithms that can find their way out of local minima (e.g., Rumelhart, McClelland, and the PDP Research Group 1986, chapters 7 and 8).

A mathematical expression for the slope of the error surface with respect to a given weight can be derived using the calculus (Rumelhart, McClelland, and the PDP Research Group 1986). The expression involves the slope of the activation function. The linear threshold function of figure 2.10 will not do because its slope is not well defined at its threshold, where it jumps discontinuously. The linear threshold function can be replaced, however, by functions that *are* continuous, such as the logistic activation function, shown in figure 2.12. The logistic function is similar to the threshold function in that it squashes the net input into an activation value between 0 and 1 and makes a rapid transition when the net input is around 0. During learning, the adjustment to a weight on an output unit depends only on the amount of activation coming into the weight and the degree to which the unit's output was in error. The adjustment to a weight on a hidden unit depends on the calculations for the units that it is connected to in the next layer. Thus, error signals have to be computed beginning at the output layer and then propagated backward through the network layer by layer.

The Attractions of Connectionism
Having developed some of the basic features of connectionism, we are now in a position to consider the reasons why researchers have found it attractive. One hope is that the connectionist approach will close the gap between cognitive research and brain research. Thus, some of the attractions of connectionism can be discussed in terms of increasing the *neural plausibility* of theories in cognitive science. At the cognitive level of analysis the connectionist approach to some phenomena is considered by some researchers to be more natural and potentially fruitful than classical approaches.

Neural Plausibility   Connectionist networks are sometimes called artificial neural networks because they resemble the actual networks of neural cells (or *neurons*) in the brain. Abstracting away from physiological detail, a real neuron can be viewed as a simple processing unit that takes a weighted sum of numerical inputs and produces a numerical output that is a simple nonlinear function of that sum. The dense interconnection of neurons suggests that the brain's *computing style* is highly parallel and therefore possibly similar to that of connectionist networks.

This view of the brain is bolstered by the fact that the signaling rate of neurons is extremely slow by the standards of electronic devices. Whereas the electronic components that make up computers commonly cycle millions of times per second, neurons send at most a few hundred discrete electrochemical pulses per second down their output fibers. Given that there is a certain amount of imprecision in the timing of these impulses and in the response of receiving neurons, it is reasonable to hypothesize that, at most, the brain can perform about one hundred serial steps of computation in a second. This limit is known as the *100-step rule* (Feldman and Ballard 1982). Many significant cognitive processes occur in less than a second. Examples are recognizing familiar objects, understanding spoken words in context, and making simple inferences while reading a written passage. All of the available evidence suggests that such processes are computationally complex, involving at least thousands of elementary operations. The brain could not carry them out in less than a second if it relied on strictly serial algorithms, executing a single operation at a time. Therefore, the argument goes, the brain must utilize highly parallel algorithms that allow many operations to be performed simultaneously. Anatomically, the brain appears to be wired up to do just that, and research with artificial neural networks has shown that complex information processes can be carried out in parallel.

Support for the 100-step rule comes from traditional research in AI, where computer programs for vision and language understanding typically went through thousands of steps of computation to perform simple acts of recognition and understanding. Such programs had to be run serially because conventional digital computers execute a single instruction at a time. In many cases even high-speed conventional computers are not fast enough to execute these programs in "real time," that is, at rates comparable to those of the brain. By at least one estimate a serial computer would have to be able to execute at least ten trillion instructions per second to match the computing power of the human brain (Moravec 1988). Current conventional supercomputers are several orders of magnitude below this figure. Such results led AI researchers in some domains to begin designing highly parallel algorithms and to develop parallel hardware on which to run them.

Learning via adjustable weights on connections also has an initially high degree of neural plausibility. It is widely believed that much of the learning in the nervous system is mediated by changes in the efficiency of synapses, the sites of communication between neurons. Some candidate mechanisms for synaptic plasticity are actually under study.

A final argument for the neural plausibility of connectionist models is that they respond to simulated damage in ways that are similar to the changes in cognition that occur with actual brain damage. When the brain is damaged, its performance tends to degrade gracefully. The decrements in performance tend to be proportional to the amount of damage, and, in particular, small insults rarely lead to catastrophic losses of function. *Graceful degradation* is typically not a feature of conventional electronic circuits or computer programs. Removing a single component from a circuit or a single statement from a program will often cause complete malfunction.

Resistance to damage in neural networks is a natural consequence of their highly parallel design. In a network containing many units in each layer, no one unit (or small group of units) is a critical link in a serial chain of computation. Further, the ability to compute the appropriate output for a particular input can be redundantly distributed across many weights on many units. Altering or destroying some of these weights does not destroy the network's ability to compute the output, or something close to it, because no one weight makes an absolutely critical contribution to the representation of the input-output pair. This kind of distributed representation of a computation usually arises when a learning algorithm makes many small adjustments to many weights to improve the overall performance of a network. The result is that each weight makes some small contribution to the computation of many input-output pairs.

Neural plausibility arguments are highly abstract and therefore do not provide strong evidence for connectionist models. Most models are not models of particular neural circuits and are not supported by detailed anatomical or physiological evidence. The models ignore a wealth of known biological detail, and many of them possess features, such as the unit-by-unit error signals of the backpropagation algorithm, that probably do not occur in real nervous systems. These matters are discussed further in chapter 7. In spite of the analogy, then, the units and connections in most models are not intended to represent actual neurons and synapses. The precise neural implementation of the model is usually left open. The units in a model, for example, might map onto groups of neurons, single neurons, or clusters of one or more synapses. Arguments for neural plausibility can be thought of as promissory notes to be redeemed by future research. Such notes have also, of course, been issued in profusion by the classical school. The difference is that the classical models leave the method of payment almost completely open (e.g., "payment will be made by the superior temporal lobe"), whereas connectionist models suggest a number of relatively more detailed methods of payment. By investigating directly how to build cognitive functions out of neuronlike elements, connectionists may inspire neuroscientific research and hasten its convergence with research at the cognitive level.

Cognitive Plausibility   Connectionist models also have a number of features that make them immediately attractive as cognitive models, before any particular cognitive process has been modeled in detail. One of the chief attractions is that connectionist models are specified in terms of a small set of simple mechanisms. Detailed qualitative and quantitative predictions can be generated by writing and running computer programs that simulate the models. Detailed simulations of classical theories have also been developed. However, they typically assume rather complex mechanisms to be part of the cognitive architecture. For example, a classical model of mental imagery might take the operations of zooming, scanning, and rotating as primitive building blocks. A connectionist model would presumably show how these operations could be implemented in networks. It is tempting to assume that the connectionist approach is getting at underlying general principles that might explain a variety of higher-level phenomena. It is sometimes said that connectionism is exploring the *microstructure* of cognition.

In addition to the level of detail at which models are specified, connectionism lends itself to the study of problems that have been somewhat neglected within the classical approach. Classical theories, for example, concentrate on central cognitive processes and do not include detailed accounts of the operation of perceptual and motor systems. Because of their ability to handle large arrays of input or output information in parallel, connectionist models apply naturally to these areas, however. Connectionist learning algorithms also promise to offer a uniform account of change with experience. The study of learning has become somewhat fragmented within the classical approach, with different mechanisms being proposed for the acquisition of declarative and procedural knowledge, for example. In comparison with the classical approach, connectionism promises to yield an account of the entire cognitive system in terms of highly detailed and general principles of learning and information processing.

In the territory where classical theories are strongest, the possible advantages of connectionism can be spelled out in more detail. Classical models often assume the existence of powerful pattern-recognition processes or content-addressed memories. For example, the theories of skill acquisition described above assume that a set of environmental conditions will match the appropriate productions in a production memory. In computer simulations production retrieval is typically accomplished through a serial pattern-matching algorithm that searches memory for productions whose condition parts match the current environmental context. The theoretical assumption, however, is that in the actual cognitive architecture the matching process is done in parallel through some sort of direct content-addressing. The ability of connectionist networks to map input vectors onto output vectors in parallel opens up the possibility of explaining such pattern-recognition and memory-retrieval processes in detail.

Connectionism also offers an approach to a dilemma that has arisen in the classical theory of schematic knowledge. As we saw earlier in this chapter, once one has hypothesized a propositional language of thought, it is natural to assume that general concepts, or schemas, are represented as sets of propositions. In the case of everyday concepts the propositions can be seen as a list of rules, or necessary and sufficient conditions, that must be satisfied by any instance of the concept. The problem is that most of the concepts that we regularly employ do not seem to have definitions of this kind. Instead, there tend to be many relevant features of varying importance: apples, for example, are often roughly round (when intact), are often largely red, tend to have a smooth, shiny skin, have a woody stem of narrow cross section (when present), and so on. Such features are neither necessary nor sufficient for membership in a category, but they do affect the probability of membership. They are *soft* rather than *hard constraints* on the concept. To implement soft constraints within a propositional framework, probabilities must be attached to each proposition, and algorithms must be developed to learn the probabilities and to process them to make decisions about category membership. Because of their ability to pass vectors of values through weighted connections, networks are obviously well suited for this kind of computation. If a vector of input values represents the presence or absence (or likelihood) of a large set of features, and if the weights represent probabilities, or relevance to various possible categorizations, a network can simultaneously assess the evidence for all possible categorizations and select the most appropriate solution. Networks are said to be good at combining soft constraints to achieve the *best fit* to a situation. If certain features are missing, or if the incoming feature vector is unusual, the network will still be able to weigh the evidence and arrive at a decent solution. This capability is a cognitive variant of graceful degradation. An exceptional situation might bring a system governed by hard constraints to a halt, exposing its *brittleness*. Connectionist learning algorithms that adjust the weights in a network essentially allow the network to discover the constraints on a set of concepts through its experience with examples. Behavior that appears to be governed by rules can emerge within this framework when the constraints operating in a domain are indeed hard or close to it. Thus, it is argued that the same mechanisms can handle both rule-governed and probabilistic domains.

This approach to concepts represents a general dissatisfaction in the connectionist community with identifying cognition as the processing of structured symbolic expressions, such as propositions. A proposition, such as GIVE(JOHN, TEACHER, APPLE), is related to a wealth of experience with objects, people, and situations. Connectionists have argued that predicates such as APPLE or GIVE are surface manifestations of a vastly richer microstructure. Even simple concepts, such as APPLE, might on different occasions involve varying levels of activation of thousands of *microfeatures*, many of which cannot be verbalized. Depending on the profile of activation over these features, a somewhat different concept of apple might be constructed in each situation. Our conscious, verbal notion of a stable, well-defined apple might be a convenient fiction, or approximation, that stands for the overlap among all of these situationally specific concepts of apple that are constructed on the fly and that do the real work of apple cognition. In such a system, the concept of apple would be *distributed* over many units, which also participate in computations involving other concepts. No units would be dedicated to the concept of apple, and to a large extent the concept of apple would not be associated with a particular pattern of activation (although our conscious apprehension of the concept and the word might require a particular pattern of activation of some subset of units). The attractions of such a *subsymbolic* view of the essence of cognition have been well articulated by Smolensky (1988).

An Example   A model called NETtalk, developed by Sejnowski and Rosenberg (1987), can serve to illustrate some of the attractions of connectionism as well as what connectionist models look like when they are scaled up to meet the demands of a realistic cognitive task. The goal of NETtalk was to learn the notoriously difficult mapping from English spelling to pronunciation. A phonemic representation was used for speech. For example, a phonemic representation for the text "I could dance" in a certain dialect might be /ay kUd dæns/ (where the phonetic characters, or *phonemes*, are pronounced as shown in table 6.1). This example demonstrates some of the complexities of the mapping from English text to speech. The letter 'c' is pronounced /k/ in 'could' and /s/ in 'dance'. The 'e' in 'dance' isn't pronounced at all, and somehow the sequence 'oul' in 'could' comes out as /U/.

One approach to computing the mapping would be a set of explicit correspondence rules. For example, a rule such as 'X*a*ve#' → /e/ could specify the pronunciation of the letter 'a' when it is preceded by anything (X) and followed by 've' and a space (#). The rule would cover the pronunciation of 'a' in most words ending in 'ave', such as 'gave', 'shave', or 'enclave'. Pesky irregular words, such as 'have', could be handled by word-specific rules, such as '#h*a*ve#' → /æ/. We could treat the rules as production rules and handle the conflicts between the general rules and the exception rules either by always giving more specific rules priority or by storing the exception rules in a special production memory that is always searched first. We could also try to devise a production-learning algorithm that would learn the rules from examples, such as '#have#' − /hæv/, '#gave#' − /gev/, and so on. The algorithm would have to be able to hypothesize rules and adjust their generality based on some record of their success.

Figure 2.13 sketches the alternative approach of NETtalk, a feed-forward network with layers of input, hidden, and output units. The input layer contained 203 units divided into 7 groups, each containing 29 units. Each group could encode a single

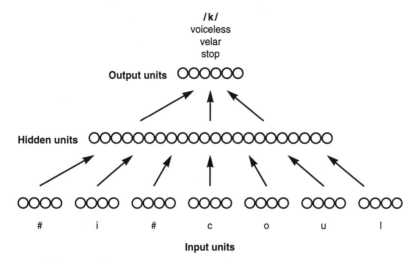

Figure 2.13
The architecture of NETtalk. Only some of the units and connections are shown. The input to the network is a string of seven characters, which can be letters, spaces (#), or punctuation marks. The seven characters are encoded by seven groups of input units. Each group contains 29 units, one for each possible character. The input layer is fully connected to the hidden layer of 80 units. The hidden layer is in turn fully connected to the output layer of 26 units. Each output unit represents a feature of English pronunciation (see text). The goal of the network is to activate the output units that correspond to the correct pronunciation of the center character of the input string. Given the 'c' in the figure, the network should activate the units for *voiceless*, *velar*, and *stop*, which represent the correct phoneme, /k/. (Adapted from Sejnowski and Rosenberg 1987.)

character using a local code. One unit in the group was allotted to each letter of the alphabet, and three additional units were used to encode space and punctuation. In the figure, the space unit would be active in the first group of input units, the 'i' unit would be active in the second group, the space unit in the third group, and so on. Given a seven-character string as an input, the network attempted to compute the pronunciation of the middle letter. The pronunciation of an entire text was computed by moving the text through this seven-letter window one character at a time. If the input text were "I could dance," the input in the figure, '#i#coul', would be followed by 'i#could' with 'o' as the central letter. The architecture of the network is thus based on the assumption that letter-to-sound correspondences can be computed if left and right contexts of three character spaces are available.

A distributed representation was used for the phonemic output. The representation was based on the fact that the sounds of English (and other natural languages) can be represented as sets of features (see tables 6.1 and 6.2). For example, the sound /k/ can be represented by the set of features {voiceless, velar, stop}, where *voiceless* means that the vocal cords are not vibrating, *velar* means articulated at the soft palate, and *stop* means that the airstream is interrupted. Related sounds have similar feature sets; for example, the features for /p/ are {voiceless, bilabial, stop} because /p/ is identical to /k/ except that it is articulated with the lips. The output layer contained 26 units. There was one unit for each possible phonetic feature (the feature set was somewhat smaller than in table 6.2). There was a unit that represented silent characters. There were also several units that represented information about stress and syllable boundaries, which we will ignore here. This is a distributed representation because each feature unit participates in the representation of more than one sound. For example, the feature *stop* is part of the representations of /p/, /b/, /t/, /d/, /k/, and /g/. Each phoneme, then, was represented by a 26-element vector with 1s and 0s in the appropriate slots. For example, the vector for /k/ would have 1s in the slots representing *voiceless*, *velar*, and *stop* and 0s elsewhere. Each of the phoneme vectors can be thought of as a point in 26-dimensional space (each point is a vertex on a 26-dimensional hypercube).

The goal of the network is to produce the vector for the phoneme that is the correct pronunciation of the letter being presented to the center input unit. In the figure, the correct pronunciation of 'c' is /k/, so the network should activate the units for *voiceless*, *velar*, and *stop*. During training the network will miss its targets by some amount. Even after extensive training there will be some error because the output of the logistic activation function lies strictly between 0 and 1. Therefore, some criterion has to be adopted to determine when the network has produced an output vector that is close enough to the target vector in the 26-dimensional feature space. A match criterion would require that the output be, say, .9 or higher on units for which the target value is 1 and .1 or lower on units for which the target value is 0. A distance, or best-guess, criterion would pick the phoneme vector that is closest to the output vector in the 26-dimensional space. If the closest phoneme vector is the target, then the output is considered correct. The distance criterion is weaker than the match criterion because an output that fails to match the target vector can still be closer to the target than it is to any other phoneme vector. Although the distance criterion may seem too weak, it is reasonable in the sense that it is often possible to add recurrent lateral connections within the output layer or another layer of connections to pull output vectors toward the nearest target (Hinton and Shallice 1991).

The hidden layer of the network contained 80 units. The input layer was fully connected to the hidden layer, and the hidden layer was fully connected to the output layer. These connections yield $(203 \cdot 80) + (80 \cdot 26) = 16{,}240 + 2{,}080 = 18{,}320$ weights. The units also had adjustable biases. The network was trained via repeated presentations of correct input-output pairs constructed from a 1,024-word text. The weights were adjusted using the backpropagation learning procedure. After fifty passes through the text, representing about 250,000 training pairs, the network achieved 95 percent correct performance by the best-guess criterion. When the net was then tested, without further training, on a new 439-word text, it was correct 78 percent of the time.

Our focus here is not on NETtalk's precise level of performance or on its suitability as a model of human reading but rather on how it illustrates the attractive characteristics of connectionist models. No assumptions had to be made about the kinds of rules that are needed to map text to phonemes. No special mechanisms had to be set up to handle the distinction between regular aspects of the mapping and exception words. The network learned an internal representation, encoded in the final set of weights, that captured much of the complex mixture of regularity and irregularity that characterizes English spelling. The representation is directly addressed by the input. That is, there is no need for a search through memory to locate the knowledge relevant to the input. The questions about how to construct and revise text-to-phoneme production rules in response to evidence did not have to be dealt with in advance. During training, the current weights represent the network's overall hypothesis about the mapping. The backpropagation algorithm uses the error in the output vector on each training pair to make small weight adjustments that improve the hypothesis.

The network's relatively high level of performance on a new text demonstrates the ability of networks to generalize to novel inputs and to fail gracefully rather than crash when the environment changes. The net automatically maps any input vector onto an output vector, using its weights to evaluate various aspects of the input and combine them to settle on a solution. This capacity is a natural consequence of connectionist principles. To achieve similar capacities in a system containing a large set of rules, we would have to figure out how to search for, evaluate, and apply partially matching rules.

NETtalk also performed well after simulated damage, or *lesions*, to its weights. One form of simulated damage is to randomly alter each weight by an amount lying between $-d$ and $+d$ for some constant d. As d increased, NETtalk's performance fell off gradually. When d was less than 65 percent of the average weight, performance degraded very little. Even after severe damage the network relearned more rapidly than it had learned originally, confirming that the damaged weights retain significant information about the mapping.

The network's resistance to damage suggests that its learned representation of the text-to-phoneme mapping is well distributed across the weights. There is a significant question, however, about just how the mapping is encoded. We might find, for example, that the network actually encodes production rules, of the kind introduced above, in some relatively straightforward way. With over 18,000 weights in the network, it takes a nontrivial investigation to discover how the mapping is accomplished. Sejnowski and Rosenberg's (1987) study of NETtalk's representation revealed that it was moderately distributed. About 15 percent of the hidden units were significantly activated by each input, and all hidden units responded to more than one input. When patterns of activation over the hidden units were studied, they revealed considerable regularity that reflected the regularities of the English spelling and sound systems. For example, the activation patterns for vowels and for consonants formed two distinct clusters. Generally, similar patterns of activation were involved with similar letter-to-phoneme correspondences. For example, activation patterns over the hidden units were very similar for 'c' − /k/ and 'k' − /k/ pairs, or for 'a' − /e/ and 'a' − /æ/ pairs. Patterns of activation for exceptional cases were quite different from those for regular cases and tended to form their own clusters. In effect, NETtalk learned the regularities and then found a way to recognize the exceptions, setting weights in such a way that the standard response was overridden.

Connectionism as a Theory of Cognitive Architecture

Having seen something of how connectionist models work and having sampled some of their attractions, we are now in a position to consider the implications of connectionism for the classical theory of the cognitive architecture. The basic concepts of connectionism (units, connections, activation functions, weights, and so on) are at a lower level of analysis than classical cognitive theories. A connectionist theory of the cognitive architecture must make claims about the representation of cognitive content and about information processing at the cognitive level. One approach to developing a connectionist theory of the cognitive architecture is to adopt many of the classical theory's assumptions about representation and processing. Connectionism is then treated as a lower-level enterprise that explores the possibilities for implementing classical models with parallel algorithms and machines. An alternative, more radical approach is to begin with the basic concepts of connectionism and use the attractive properties of networks discussed above as a guide to building a new theory of the cognitive architecture. Such a theory would be a direct competitor with the classical theory that might challenge many of its key assumptions. Various mixtures of the two research strategies are imaginable, as well.

Connectionism as Implementation of Classical Theory   We can begin by exploring the implementational position a bit further. An analogy with digital computers shows that the position is possible. The classical architecture can be considered analogous to a programming language on a computer. A programming language constitutes a universal computational architecture that makes certain capabilities immediately and transparently available to the programmer. For example, new symbol structures and procedures for operating on them can be directly defined. Several levels of analysis down, however, we can describe the computer as a device constructed by interconnecting a very large number of logic devices, each one of which computes some relatively simple function from an input vector of 0s and 1s to an output vector of 0s and 1s. The example of XOR demonstrates that simple logic functions can be implemented as connectionist networks. By suitably interconnecting many of these little networks, therefore, we could construct a large network that implemented the architecture of a programming language. Analogously, we could construct a classical cognitive architecture in this way.

Knowing that it is possible in principle to build the classical architecture using connectionist machinery is a far cry from knowing exactly how to do it. The implementational view of connectionism begins with the assumption that the classical theory has given us a revealing picture of the fundamental capacities of the mind at a particular level of analysis and seeks to discover how these capacities can be implemented in terms of structures and processes defined at a lower level of analysis. Such a research program is worth undertaking only if it might lead to an expanded understanding of human cognition. Connectionist principles might offer deeper or more general explanations of some cognitive phenomena. The research might lead to discoveries about the neural underpinnings of cognition. It might solve some of the open problems with the classical theory. For example, it might show how semantic networks or production retrieval can actually be implemented. Finally, it might generate new empirical findings. For example, a connectionist theory of production systems that included a novel distributed representation of productions might make new predictions about constraints on skill acquisition, errors in skilled performance, or transfer of skills across tasks.

Some connectionist research has begun to demonstrate how major components of the classical theory can be given connectionist implementations. For example, Shastri and his colleagues (Shastri and Ajjanagadde 1992) have shown how semantic networks and certain aspects of conceptual and propositional reasoning associated with them can be given a connectionist implementation. Touretzky and Hinton (1988) have shown that simple production systems can also be given a connectionist implementation. Although these researchers have not confined their work to the implementational approach, these particular pieces of research demonstrated in detail that significant parts of the classical architecture can be built from connectionist components and that taking classical theory seriously can lead to important insights about how to structure connectionist models. Their work also suggests some revisions of classical ideas.

Classical Critique of the Attractions of Connectionism   In the course of urging implementational connectionism some proponents of the classical approach have developed a critique of the claimed advantages of connectionism (Fodor and Pylyshyn 1988). They have argued first that connectionists have misconceived the necessary properties of classical models and second that much of the critique of classical theory actually concerns issues of implementation.

One illustration of the first argument is that connectionists have put overly restrictive conditions on rules in classical models. Fodor and Pylyshyn, and others, have argued that classical models are not restricted to all-or-nothing rules that fail completely when their conditions are not perfectly matched. It is possible to allow rules to fire with some probability when their conditions are partially matched, for example, or to specify a process that attempts to compute an intermediate course of action when the conditions for more than one rule are partially matched. Classical rules also do not have to be implemented as explicit structured expressions, as is sometimes implied in connectionist critiques. If we consider a conventional computer program as an analogy with a classical model, we see that some of the rules involved in its execution are implemented as explicit expressions and others are not. The program, proper, is indeed a list of expressions stored in memory and retrieved one by one for execution. The processes that interpret the instructions during execution are indeed sensitive to their syntactic structure. However, the interpreter's rules are wired directly into the circuitry of the computer. They are not stored in a memory, and their internal structure cannot be inspected by any other process in the system. A classical system must have at least some implicit processes, because a system that was all data in need of interpretation would never do anything. Computers are designed with a minimal complement of implicit rules, but the human cognitive architecture could have a completely different balance between explicit and implicit rules. The classical approach is more deeply committed to explicit data structures, because most models include processes that can build, store, retrieve, analyze, and decompose syntactically structured representations.

The argument that many connectionist claims concern implementation can be illustrated with the 100-step rule and the issue of graceful degradation with physical damage. The 100-step rule is based on assumptions about neural computation and therefore concerns neural implementation. It decisively favors connectionist models only if there is no way to implement classical models in parallel hardware. But in many classical models significant parallelism is assumed in both basic operations and algorithms. For example, in a speech-understanding system that used production rules to build representations of incoming sentences, the basic operation of production retrieval could operate in parallel, and many rules that dealt with aspects of the sound, syntactic, and semantic structure of the sentence could apply in parallel. Similarly, there is no known barrier to implementing classical models in a way that makes them less brittle in the face of physical damage. The connectionist advantage in the realm of implementation, then, is relative rather than absolute. Since connectionist theories are specified at a lower level of analysis, they specify aspects of implementation that are left open (and are possibly difficult to resolve) in classical models.

The conclusion of the conservative classicist is that connectionism should be pursued as a way of exploring the implementation of classical models. The parallel implementation of classical models is possible, and connectionism offers many concrete ideas about parallel implementation. On the other hand, the claimed cognitive advantages of connectionism are illusory. Needless to say, most connectionist researchers disagree with this limited interpretation of their insights.

Connectionism as an Alternative to Classical Theory   In order for connectionism to be viewed as an alternative to the classical theory, the basic low-level assumptions about networks have to be used to construct a high-level theory that makes novel claims about information representation and processing. Many researchers believe that the attractions of connectionism point in this direction.

As we have learned, classical theory makes a standard set of interlocking assumptions about the nature of cognitive representations and the processes that work on them. Cognitive representations are assumed to be structured. Thus, they exhibit *productivity*: there is a finite set of syntactic rules that can generate an unlimited set of novel expressions. The processes that operate on expressions are *structure-sensitive*. Structured representations and structure-sensitive processing guarantee that cognition is highly *systematic*, because representations that share formal properties are automatically treated uniformly by processes that are sensitive to those properties. The representational mapping from expressions to the world is *compositional;* that is, it is a function of the internal structure of the expressions. Suppose a person reasons from GIVE(MARY, JOHN, BOOK7) to HAVE(JOHN, BOOK7). The claim is that there have to be syntactic processes that can reliably generate two- and three-place predications with standard slots for the predicates and the arguments. There has to be an inference rule relating GIVE and HAVE that can access the second and third arguments of GIVE and generate a HAVE expression with these two arguments placed in the first and second argument slots. The representational mapping from the GIVE expression to the world hinges on the distinction among the three argument slots. That is, GIVE(MARY, JOHN, BOOK7) is true if and only if Mary, John, and a particular book are related in a such a way that Mary was the giver and John the recipient of a particular book. If the expression has a different internal syntactic structure, such as GIVE(JOHN, MARY, BOOK7), then a different relationship has to hold in the world.

As we have seen, one of the main attractions of connectionism is that networks are capable of performing interesting computations without explicitly coded symbolic representations or structure-sensitive rules for processing. Their lack of symbolic processing seems to be critical to some of their most attractive properties, such as graceful degradation, lack of brittleness, ability to exploit soft constraints, and ability to generalize to decent solutions in new contexts. These observations have led to the hypothesis that computation over structured symbolic expressions is not the essence of cognition.

An immediate objection to this hypothesis is that at least some of our thought definitely seems to have the characteristics of symbolic computation. There are two somewhat different ways of answering the objection. One is that the appearance of symbolic computation can emerge from processes that are not symbolic. NETtalk gives some of the flavor of this claim. The network is able to learn regularities such as '#ciX' → /s/ (initial 'c' followed by 'i' is pronounced /s/) without, in any obvious way, constructing and manipulating production rules during learning. The net obeys the production rules. The rules provide a good high-level description of the net's behavior. But there doesn't seem to be any scientific payoff in claiming that the net literally constructed the rules or uses them to produce the behavior. This view of NETtalk suggests the possibility that the concepts of the classical theory might not map onto the lower-level theory, as we would expect in an implementational reduction. Production rules might be said not to exist in roughly the same sense that phlogiston has been said not to exist since Lavoisier developed the modern chemical theory of combustion. Or, perhaps, production rules might be retained only as a useful approximation of the system's global behavior. An analogy here is the case of Newtonian mechanics. Newton's laws provide an excellent description of the macroscopic behavior of many physical systems, even though the laws are strictly false (if twentieth-century physics is accepted), and many Newtonian concepts, such as velocity-independent mass, have no counterpart in modern physics. Churchland (1986) discusses the range of reductionistic relationships that can exist among theories couched at different levels.

The notion that the mechanisms of cognition are not symbolic is plausible for perceptual processes but less so for processes that are less stimulus-bound and more extended in time, such as reasoning and problem solving. Simple inferences, such as inferring A from A & B, seem to depend on being able to break A & B into three parts, the propositions A and B and the logical connective &. Thus, we can infer *wugs eat flib* from *wugs eat flib, and blaps are morf* without knowing the meanings of several terms in the expressions. It is hard to implement this kind of reasoning in a system without relying on structured symbolic representations and structure-sensitive processes. The pattern of inference is completely systematic in the sense that it generalizes over propositions A and B of any length, content, and internal structure (Fodor and Pylyshyn 1988).

The strongest version of the classical position includes the claim that the productivity and systematicity of thought processes at the cognitive level require that the syntactic structures of cognitive representations map onto lower levels in a direct manner. For example, if a system is processing a representation of A & B, there should be distinct physical regions of the system that encode A, &, and B. In a computer A might be represented by the contents of one or more particular memory locations, and so on. There should also be some distinct physical encoding of the syntactic relations among the three symbols. A simple notion of the syntactic relations here is that the three symbols are *concatenated* into a string, that is, A comes before &, which comes before B. In a computer with numerically addressable memory locations, concatenation can be represented by placing adjacent items in adjacent memory locations, or, more generally, by augmenting the representation of each item in the string with the address of the location of the next item of the string. Such addresses, known as *pointers*, facilitate the efficient storage and processing of arbitrarily complicated syntactic structures. Pointers also allow the physical code for an expression to be highly and unpredictably discontinuous. Yet on any particular occasion particular memory locations (which are bits of physical stuff in particular electrical states) are dedicated to encoding the expression. No one has argued that the brain possesses a numerically addressable random-access memory, but arguments for the classical position often appear to include the hypothesis that the physical implementation of cognitive representations in the brain is at least as direct as it is in von Neumann computers. The hypothesis is somewhat open ended because there are few detailed proposals for lower-level implementations of classical models. It is hard to say in advance just what sorts of implementations satisfy the hypothesis.

Some researchers have argued that even the paradigm case of systematic reasoning can be handled by connectionist models that are not straightforward implementations of classical models (van Gelder 1990; Smolensky 1988). One proposal is that distributed representations can possess a rich internal structure without being divisible into parts that correspond to the syntactic structure of a classical representation. Processing in a network might reflect this internal structure even though the structure isn't implemented transparently in the activation values on the units or in the connection weights. For example, expressions of the form *A & B* might be represented as vectors of activation values. However, we might not be able to identify any of the units as representing the constituents *A*, *&*, and *B*, or their relations, because the representation of each of these aspects of the syntactic structure is distributed across the units. Nevertheless, it might be possible to enter such vectors into a network with appropriate weights and reliably produce output vectors that represent the *A* parts of the expressions. This process would implement the rule of inference from expressions of the form *A & B* to *A*, yet there would not be the kind of direct implementation of syntactic structure predicted by many proponents of the classical approach. Even if such highly distributed representations prove to be feasible for systematic reasoning, evidence would then have to be sought that they actually figure in human cognition. The issue could be decided by findings about neural circuitry or by findings about the learning or application of rules that support distributed representations.

The discovery that reasoning rests on distributed representations that are processed as syntactically structured expressions would have uncertain effects on the classical approach. A classical theory might remain the best account of people's reasoning competence as well as of much of the flow of thought. The lower-level connectionist theory would explain the nontransparent implementation of syntactic structure and perhaps certain kinds of reasoning errors and rule-acquisition phenomena. A successful connectionist theory might also explain relationships between cognitive processes that depend on structured representations and perceptual processes that rely more on soft constraints and finding best fits. Smolensky (1988) argues for a particular version of the theoretical balance, distinguishing between the conscious rule interpreter, or symbolic processor, and the intuitive, or subsymbolic, processor. The symbolic processor, although implemented as a connectionist network, is organized to behave at the cognitive level as a universal machine. It accounts for our ability to carry out sequential rule-governed computations over syntactically structured representations. Subsymbolic processing arises from the lower-level, intrinsic characteristics of connectionist networks, such as microfeatural soft constraints and the best-fit principle. Smolensky associates the operation of the symbolic processor with the conscious acquisition and application of culturally transmitted knowledge. Paradigm cases might be long division, or selecting college courses on the basis of the rules for graduation. He argues that intuitive thought does not arise from unconscious symbolic computation, involving unconscious structure-sensitive rules. This claim is incompatible with the many classical proposals for unconscious symbolic representation and computation, particularly in language (see chapters 6, 9, and 11 for details).

The Future   The classical approach remains a fertile source of new cognitive theory and empirically testable hypotheses. Connectionism has also proven to be a viable foundational approach to cognition. The two approaches still appear to be strikingly complementary to each other. They work primarily at different levels of analysis. Phenomena that seem to have natural explanations within one framework tend to challenge the other. At this point the relation between the two approaches remains to be decided by future research. More full-scale connectionist models of cognitive phenomena, as opposed to small-scale demonstrations, must be developed and compared in detail to competing classical models (Coltheart et al. 1993; Hinton and Shallice 1991; Marcus et al. 1992; Van Orden, Pennington, and Stone 1990). Better explanations of *why* connectionist models perform as they do at the cognitive-behavioral level are also needed. Connectionist learning algorithms can serve as a kind of abstract genetic technology that allows researchers to grow systems that compute desired input-output functions without understanding very clearly why the final system is or is not successful (McCloskey 1991; Seidenberg 1993). Although the outcomes of cognitive science research cannot be predicted, it is possible to predict that a fertile and exciting period of investigation lies ahead.

Suggested Readings

Cognitive Psychology and Its Implications (Anderson 1990) covers the entire field of cognitive psychology using general theoretical ideas about cognitive architecture that are similar to those developed in this chapter. *The Architecture of Cognition* (Anderson 1983) presents similar ideas at an advanced level, developing spreading activation theory and the theory of production systems in considerable formal detail. *Computation and Cognition: Toward a Foundation for Cognitive Science* (Pylyshyn 1984) is a rigorous development of a theory of functional architecture. *Connectionism and the Mind: An Introduction to Parallel Processing in Networks* (Bechtel and Abrahamsen 1991) introduces connectionist models and the foundational arguments for connectionism. *Explorations in Parallel Distributed Processing: A Handbook of Models, Programs, and Exercises* (McClelland and Rumelhart 1989) is a text and software package (separate DOS and Macintosh editions) that introduces the computer simulation of connectionist models and allows the student to explore existing models and design and run new ones. *Social Cognition* (Fiske and Taylor 1991) is an excellent resource for readers wishing to follow up on our brief remarks about schemas for the self and other people.

References

Anderson, J. R. (1983). *The architecture of cognition.* Cambridge, Mass.: Harvard University Press.

Anderson, J. R. (1990). *Cognitive psychology and its implications.* 3rd ed. New York: W. H. Freeman.

Bechtel, W., and A. Abrahamsen (1991). *Connectionism and the mind: An introduction to parallel processing in networks.* Cambridge, Mass.: Blackwell.

Bem, S. L. (1974). The measurement of psychological androgyny. *Journal of Consulting and Clinical Psychology* 42, 155–162.

Bower, G. H., J. B. Black, and T. J. Turner (1979). Scripts in memory for text. *Cognitive Psychology* 11, 177–220.

Broadbent, D. A. (1975). The magical number seven after fifteen years. In A. Kennedy and A. Wilkes, eds., *Studies in long-term memory.* New York: Wiley.

Cantor, J., and R. W. Engle (1993). Working-memory capacity as long-term memory activation: An individual-differences approach. *Journal of Experimental Psychology: Learning, Memory, and Cognition* 19, 1101–1114.

Cantor, N., and W. Mischel (1979). Prototypes in person perception. In L. Berkowitz, ed., *Advances in experimental social psychology.* Vol. 12. New York: Academic Press.

Cantor, N., W. Mischel, and J. C. Schwartz (1982). A prototype analysis of psychological situations. *Cognitive Psychology* 14, 45–77.

Chase, W. G., and K. A. Ericsson (1981). Skilled memory. In J. R. Anderson, ed., *Cognitive skills and their acquisition.* Hillsdale, N.J.: Erlbaum.

Chase, W. G., and H. A. Simon (1973). The mind's eye in chess. In W. G. Chase, ed., *Visual information processing*. New York: Academic Press.

Cheng, P. W. (1985). Restructuring versus automaticity: Alternative accounts of skill acquisition. *Psychological Review* 92, 414–423.

Churchland, P. S. (1986). *Neurophilosophy: Toward a unified science of the mind/brain*. Cambridge, Mass.: MIT Press.

Coltheart, M., B. Curtis, P. Atkins, and M. Haller (1993). Models of reading aloud: Dual-route and parallel-distributed-processing approaches. *Psychological Review* 100, 589–608.

Cooper, L. A. (1975). Mental rotation of random two-dimensional shapes. *Cognitive Psychology* 7, 20–43.

Cooper, L. A. (1976). Demonstration of a mental analog of an external rotation. *Perception and Psychophysics* 19, 296–302.

Ericsson, K. A., R. Th. Krampe, and C. Tesch-Römer (1993). The role of deliberate practice in the acquisition of expert performance. *Psychological Review* 100, 363–406.

Feldman, J. A., and D. H. Ballard (1982). Connectionist models and their properties. *Cognitive Science* 6, 205–254.

Finke, R. A. (1985). Theories relating mental imagery to perception. *Psychological Bulletin* 98, 236–259.

Finke, R. A., and S. Pinker (1982). Spontaneous imagery scanning in mental extrapolation. *Journal of Experimental Psychology: Learning, Memory, and Cognition* 8, 142–147.

Finke, R. A., and S. Pinker (1983). Directional scanning of remembered visual patterns. *Journal of Experimental Psychology: Learning, Memory, and Cognition* 9, 398–410.

Fiske, S. T., and S. E. Taylor (1991). *Social cognition*. 2nd ed. New York: McGraw-Hill.

Fitts, P. M. (1964). Perceptual-motor skill learning. In A. W. Melton, ed., *Categories of human learning*. New York: Academic Press.

Fodor, J. A. (1975). *The language of thought*. New York: Thomas Y. Crowell.

Fodor, J. A. (1983). *The modularity of mind*. Cambridge, Mass.: MIT Press.

Fodor, J. A., and Z. W. Pylyshyn (1988). Connectionism and cognitive architecture: A critical analysis. In S. Pinker and J. Mehler, eds., *Connections and symbols*. Cambridge, Mass.: MIT Press.

Hayes, J. R. (1981). *The complete problem solver*. Philadelphia: Franklin Institute Press.

Hinton, G. E., and T. Shallice (1991). Lesioning an attractor network: Investigations of acquired dyslexia. *Psychological Review* 98, 74–95.

Hochberg, J., and L. Gellman (1977). The effect of landmark features on "mental rotation" times. *Memory and Cognition* 5, 23–26.

Johnson-Laird, P. N., D. J. Herrmann, and R. Chaffin (1984). Only connections: A critique of semantic networks. *Psychological Bulletin* 96, 292–315.

Jordan, M. I. (1986). An introduction to linear algebra in parallel distributed processing. In Rumelhart and McClelland 1986.

Just, M. A., and P. A. Carpenter (1976). Eye fixations and cognitive processes. *Cognitive Psychology* 8, 441–480.

Kintsch, W., and G. Glass (1974). Effects of propositional structure upon sentence recall. In W. Kintsch, ed., *The representation of meaning in memory*. Hillsdale, N.J.: Erlbaum.

Kolodner, J. L. (1983). Reconstructive memory: A computer model. *Cognitive Science* 7, 281–328.

Kosslyn, S. M. (1980). *Image and mind*. Cambridge, Mass.: Harvard University Press.

Kosslyn, S. M., T. M. Ball, and B. J. Reiser (1978). Visual images preserve metric spatial information: Evidence from studies of image scanning. *Journal of Experimental Psychology: Human Perception and Performance* 4, 47–60.

Kosslyn, S. M., and O. Koenig (1992). *Wet mind: The new cognitive neuroscience*. New York: The Free Press.

LaBerge, D. (1976). Perceptual learning and attention. In W. K. Estes, ed., *Handbook of learning and cognitive processes*. Vol. 4. Hillsdale, N.J.: Erlbaum.

Marcus, G. F., S. Pinker, M. Ullman, M. Hollander, T. J. Rosen, and F. Xu (1992). Overregularization in language acquisition. *Monographs of the Society for Research in Child Development* 57 (4).

Markus, H. (1980). The self in thought and memory. In D. M. Wegner and R. R. Vallacher, eds., *The self in social psychology*. New York: Oxford University Press.

Markus, H., M. Crane, S. Bernstein, and M. Siladi (1982). Self-schemas and gender. *Journal of Personality and Social Psychology* 42, 38–50.

McClelland, J. L., and D. E. Rumelhart (1989). *Explorations in parallel distributed processing: A handbook of models, programs, and exercises*. Cambridge, Mass.: MIT Press.

McCloskey, M. (1991). Networks and theories: The place of connectionism in cognitive science. *Psychological Science* 2, 387–395.

McKoon, G., and R. Ratcliff (1980). Priming in item recognition: The organization of propositions in memory for text. *Journal of Verbal Learning and Verbal Behavior* 19, 369–386.

Minsky, M. (1977). Frame system theory. In P. N. Johnson-Laird and P. C. Wason, eds., *Thinking: Readings in cognitive science*. Cambridge: Cambridge University Press.

Minsky, M., and S. Papert (1969). *Perceptrons*. Cambridge, Mass.: MIT Press.

Mitchell, D. B., and C. L. Richman (1980). Confirmed reservations: Mental travel. *Journal of Experimental Psychology: Human Perception and Performance* 6, 58–66.

Moravec, H. (1988). *Mind children: The future of robot and human intelligence*. Cambridge, Mass.: Harvard University Press.

Nathans, J. (1989). The genes for color vision. *Scientific American*, February, 42–49.

Newell, A. (1980). Physical symbol systems. *Cognitive Science* 4, 135–183.

Newell, A. (1990). *Unified theories of cognition*. Cambridge, Mass.: Harvard University Press.

Newell, A., P. S. Rosenbloom, and J. E. Laird (1989). Symbolic architectures for cognition. In M. I. Posner, ed., *Foundations of cognitive science*. Cambridge, Mass.: MIT Press.

Nickerson, R. S., and M. J. Adams (1979). Long-term memory for a common object. *Cognitive Psychology* 11, 287–307.

Pylyshyn, Z. W. (1979). The rate of "mental rotation" of images: A test of a holistic analogue hypothesis. *Memory and Cognition* 7, 19–28.

Pylyshyn, Z. W. (1981). The imagery debate: Analogue media versus tacit knowledge. *Psychological Review* 88, 16–45.

Pylyshyn, Z. W. (1984). *Computation and cognition: Toward a foundation for cognitive science*. Cambridge, Mass.: MIT Press.

Ratcliff, R., and G. McKoon (1981). Does activation really spread? *Psychological Review* 88, 454–462.

Rumelhart, D. E., G. E. Hinton, and R. J. Williams (1986). Learning internal representations by error propagation. In Rumelhart and McClelland 1986.

Rumelhart, D. E., J. L. McClelland, and the PDP Research Group (1986). *Parallel distributed processing: Explorations in the microstructure of cognition. Vol. 1: Foundations*. Cambridge, Mass.: MIT Press.

Rumelhart, D. E., and D. A. Norman (1978). Accretion, tuning, and restructuring: Three modes of learning. In J. W. Cotton and R. Klatzky, eds., *Semantic factors in cognition*. Hillsdale, N.J.: Erlbaum.

Rumelhart, D. E., and A. Ortony (1976). The representation of knowledge in memory. In R. C. Anderson, R. J. Spiro, and W. E. Montague, eds., *Schooling and the acquisition of knowledge*. Hillsdale, N.J.: Erlbaum.

Sachs, J. S. (1967). Recognition memory for syntactic and semantic aspects of connected discourse. *Perception and Psychophysics* 2, 437–442.

Schank, R. C. (1982). *Dynamic memory: A theory of reminding and learning in computers and people*. Cambridge: Cambridge University Press.

Schank, R. C., and R. P. Abelson (1977). *Scripts, plans, goals, and understanding: An inquiry into human knowledge structures*. Hillsdale, N.J.: Erlbaum.

Schneider, W., and A. D. Fisk (1982). Concurrent automatic and controlled visual search: Can processing occur without resource cost? *Journal of Experimental Psychology: Learning, Memory, and Cognition* 8, 261–278.

Schneider, W., and R. M. Shiffrin (1977). Controlled and automatic human information processing: I. Detection, search, and attention. *Psychological Review* 84, 1–66.

Seidenberg, M. S. (1993). Connectionist models and cognitive theory. *Psychological Science* 4 (4), 228–235.

Sejnowski, T. J., and C. R. Rosenberg (1987). Parallel networks that learn to pronounce English text. *Complex Systems* 1, 145–168.

Shastri, L., and V. Ajjanagadde (1992). From simple associations to systematic reasoning: A connectionist representation of rules, variables, and dynamic bindings using temporal synchrony. Technical report MS-CIS-90-05, Computer and Information Science Department, University of Pennsylvania, Philadelphia, Penn.

Shepard, R. N. (1968). On turning something over in one's mind: Preliminary proposal for some experiments. In Shepard and Cooper 1982.

Shepard, R. N., and L. A. Cooper (1982). *Mental images and their transformations*. Cambridge, Mass.: MIT Press.

Shiffrin, R. M., and S. T. Dumais (1981). The development of automatism. In J. R. Anderson, ed., *Cognitive skills and their acquisition*. Hillsdale, N.J.: Erlbaum.

Shiffrin, R. M., and W. Schneider (1977). Controlled and automatic human information processing: II. Perceptual learning, automatic attending, and a general theory. *Psychological Review* 84, 127–190.

Simon, H. A. (1972). What is visual imagery? An information processing interpretation. In L. W. Gregg, ed., *Cognition in learning and memory*. New York: Wiley.

Simon, H. A. (1990). Invariants of human behavior. *Annual Review of Psychology* 41, 1–19.

Singley, M. K., and J. R. Anderson (1989). *The transfer of cognitive skill*. Cambridge, Mass.: Harvard University Press.

Smolensky, P. (1988). On the proper treatment of connectionism. *Behavioral and Brain Sciences* 11, 1–74.

Squire, L. R. (1987). *Memory and brain*. New York: Oxford University Press.

Touretzky, D. S., and G. E. Hinton (1988). A distributed connectionist production system. *Cognitive Science* 12, 423–466.

Turing, A. M. (1937). On computable numbers, with an application to the Entscheidungsproblem. *Proceedings of the London Mathematical Society* 42, 230–265.

van Gelder, T. (1990). Compositionality: A connectionist variation on a classical theme. *Cognitive Science* 14, 355–384.

Van Orden, G. C., B. F. Pennington and G. O. Stone (1990). Word identification in reading and the promise of subsymbolic psycholinguistics. *Psychological Review* 97, 488–522.

Chapter 3
Cognitive Psychology: Further Explorations

We have now sketched the classical theory of the human cognitive architecture. We have also seen that the new connectionist approach to cognition offers both challenges to the classical theory and promising avenues for extending it to lower levels of analysis. In this chapter we consider further how the architecture supports several complex cognitive functions: conceptual information processing, memory, reasoning, and problem solving. Our primary strategy will be to ask what the classical theory has to say about these complex functions. At various points we will also mention current connectionist approaches.

3.1 Concepts and Categories

Schemas played an important role in our sketch of the classical theory of the cognitive architecture. We have endowed them with several important properties. Once a schema is activated by some features in the current external or cognitive environment, it exerts effects on the allocation of attention and working-memory resources, serving as a filter that discards irrelevant information and focuses processing on what is relevant. Because it can function as a single chunk in working memory, it can facilitate processing. Because it organizes attention and processing, it can have effects on later memory (these are discussed further later in this chapter). Because a schema represents generalizations about the world, it triggers inferences or predictions that guide thought and action. Schemas act to classify objects and situations, to assign them to categories. Once a classification is made, all the knowledge associated with the relevant category can be brought into play. Finally, we noted that schema-driven cognition can lead to various kinds of error. The dominance of a particular schema can lead us to ignore features of a situation that are actually relevant to current goals or to make inappropriate or incorrect inferences.

Research on schemas is guided by a number of deep issues. There are many questions about how schemas are represented, how they are activated, and how they are learned. In this section we will explore some of these questions further, focusing mostly on concepts for concrete objects.

Theories of Concepts for Concrete Objects

A great deal of psychological research has been devoted to the information content of simple, concrete concepts, such as *dog* or *chair*. One attractive theory of simple conceptual schemas is the *definitional* theory, which has a long history in philosophy and thus is sometimes known as the classical theory of concepts. This theory states that the information content of a concept is a definition that gives the necessary and sufficient conditions that an object must meet to fall under the concept. For example, a reasonable schema for *grandmother* would be a small network of propositions containing the information that a grandmother is a female person, with at least one child who has at least one child. Each proposition, or *feature*, of the schema is necessary for grandmotherhood, and the schema as a whole is sufficient to determine grandmotherhood. The definition is general because many possible attributes of people are not mentioned in it, such as height or favorite ice cream flavor. Even reasonably probable attributes of grandmothers are not mentioned, such as *over forty years old* or *has gray hair*. The power of definitional schemas is that reasoning from a definition to a particular situation is completely reliable, because every property in the definition is true of every instance.

In spite of the attractions of the definitional theory, many psychologists have been impressed with its potential problems. The most immediate problem is that we do not seem to have a very clear sense of the necessary and sufficient conditions for most simple concepts. Many of us, for example, are quite willing to apply the concept *grandmother* to a woman whose only child is an adopted son who has children. Matters are much worse for concepts such as *dog*. Just what makes an object a dog seems to be unknown to most people who use the concept, aside from an occasional professional biologist or breeder. Further, the definitional theory gives no account of our use of characteristics of objects that could not figure in a definition because they are neither necessary nor sufficient. Introspection suggests that our use of most ordinary concepts frequently involves knowledge of properties that are clearly not necessary. Without seeming to register any mental reservations, we blithely assume that grandmothers are over forty and that dogs have four legs (although a dog can lose a leg without ceasing to be a dog). When we think very carefully, we realize such things, but it seems likely that most of the time we opt for more efficient thinking. We classify objects on the basis of features that are available in the current input but that are logically insufficient. An object will be classified as a dog, not on the basis of a careful assessment of its morphology or chromosomes but on the basis of its shape, gait, or bark, although these characteristics might also be true of a movie robot or of some unfamiliar marsupial from an isolated island.

Such intuitions have led cognitive scientists away from the definitional approach toward alternatives that allow a much broader range of characteristics to play a role in conceptual schemas. Such approaches are *probabilistic* in the sense that most of the features or characteristics associated with a concept will have a likelihood that is less than absolute. Predictions based on a categorization decision will be inherently probabilistic. The categorization decision itself also becomes probabilistic. The available features of an object will assign it to a category with some probability rather than absolutely. Some objects will be difficult to classify because the available features do not support any category very strongly or support more than one equally.

Under the probabilistic approach the instances of a concept tend to have a *family resemblance* structure (Wittgenstein 1953; Rosch and Mervis 1975). They tend to resemble each other the way members of a family do. Some members of a conceptual family will be very *typical* because they share many features with many other family members. Some members of a family might, however, be highly *atypical* because they share only a few features with other family members. The robin, for example, is a typical bird in that it is similar to other common birds—for example, it shares the capacity for flight, a length of about nine inches, a tendency to perch in the branches of trees, and the ability to sing. None of these features is necessary for birdhood, but the family resemblance theory assumes that they play a strong role in our concept of bird, nonetheless. The penguin, however, has none of these common features, although it does have feathers and lay eggs, which are closer to being necessary features. The family resemblance theory assumes that the penguin is an atypical bird with many uncommon features and therefore is difficult to view as a bird.

The family resemblance structure of a concept can be captured in various ways. One way is to set up a *probabilistic* schema. Such a schema is an organized representation of the features that are relevant to a concept, but the features are assigned probabilities or weights that indicate how strongly they are associated with the concept. The probabilities can be used by cognitive processes to make categorization decisions about particular exemplars or to reason about them. For example, a probabilistic schema for *dog* could be used to decide whether to categorize a fox as a dog or to predict the likelihood that a fox can howl or that it eats meat. Another type of schema is called a *prototype*. Each feature of a prototype is an average value of that feature over all the examples of the concept that have been encountered. Categorization and prediction are based on some measure of similarity to the prototype.

Some Experimental Research
Rosch and Mervis (1975) found a strong family resemblance structure in six *superordinate* categories: fruit, vegetables, clothing, furniture, vehicles, and weapons. In each category the experimental subjects were given twenty items that were instances of the category and asked to think of features of each of the instances. For example, one of the instances of the furniture category was *chair*, and a particular subject might have written down the features *for sitting on; made by people; used in the home; made of wood, metal, or upholstered; has a seat, a back, and legs (usually four), and sometimes arms.* The features that subjects listed were used to compute a *family resemblance* score for each instance of a superordinate category. To illustrate, the score for *chair* would be the total number of cases where a feature listed for *chair* was also listed for another concept. For example, if *has legs* was also listed for *sofa* and *table*, and if *has a back* was also listed for *sofa*, then the score for *chair* would go up by three. *Chair* got the highest family resemblance score in the furniture category, confirming the intuition that it is a pretty typical item of furniture. *Telephone* got a very low family resemblance score, confirming the sense that it is an atypical item of furniture.

Rosch and Mervis went on to show that the family resemblance scores predicted people's performance on other tasks. One important finding was that the family resemblance scores consistently predict people's immediate intuitions about the typical and atypical instances of categories. When a different group of subjects was asked to directly rate category instances on a 1-to-7 typicality scale, instances that received high, intermediate, and low ratings were in most cases the same as those that received high, intermediate, and low family resemblance scores. Thus, in both the typicality ratings and the family resemblance scores for furniture, chair ranked above rug, which ranked above telephone.

Typicality, and hence family resemblance, has also been shown to affect the basic mental operation of assigning an instance to the category. The typicality rating of an instance predicts how fast it can be assigned to a category (Rips, Shoben, and Smith 1973; Rosch 1973). In one version of the experiment each trial consists of the presentation of a target superordinate concept, such as *bird*, followed by the presentation of a test subordinate concept, such as *robin*. The subject responds as quickly as possible either "Yes" or "No," indicating whether the test concept is an instance of the target concept. In the case of *bird–robin* the correct response would be "Yes," whereas in the case of *bird–rabbit* it would be "No." When the target concept is *bird*, the "Yes" response to *robin* is considerably faster than the "Yes" response to *chicken*. Within the *bird* category *robin* has among the highest scores on typicality and family resemblance, and *chicken* has among the lowest. Birds with intermediate scores, such as *eagle* or *pigeon*, have intermediate response times.

Rosch (1978) also used family resemblance theory to construct a partial account of why we develop the categories we do at various levels of abstraction. She found a high level of similarity within categories in typical use and visual shape, suggesting that characteristics of the visual system and of culture constrain categories. She also proposed that optimally useful categories cut the world up at a *basic* level that most clearly distinguishes categories from each other. The basic level maximizes within-category resemblance while minimizing between-category resemblance. For example, *chair* is a basic-level term because most chairs share a high number of perceptual and functional features that are not shared by contrasting concepts such as *table* or *lamp*. Superordinate concepts, such as *furniture*, are less useful because they lump together many basic concepts, making only a very few features highly predictable, such as *found in the home*. Highly specific *subordinate* concepts, such as *kitchen table*, are also nonoptimal because they are largely redundant with the somewhat more general basic concepts, in this case *table*.

Propositional Network Models for Concepts

Propositional network models of the kind introduced in chapter 2 can be used for representing family resemblance structures (Collins and Loftus 1975). In this context networks are often called *semantic* networks because they represent general knowledge about the semantics, or meaning, of concepts rather than facts about specific objects. A diagram of a little piece of a network for the concepts *vegetable* and *green bean* is shown in figure 3.1. Both concepts are associated with a number of features. The number attached to each featural proposition is its strength, or weight. Various factors are thought to influence the weights (Smith and Medin 1981): for instance, the probability that the feature is true of an instance of the concept, the degree to which the feature uniquely distinguishes the concept from other concepts, and the past usefulness or frequency of the feature in perception and reasoning. Figure 3.1 can be considered part of a vast associative network among concepts. Obviously, much of a typical person's knowledge about vegetables and green beans is not shown. Also, many other concepts associated with the features are missing from the diagram. Many other concepts are associated with *GREEN*, for example.

In the simple categorization task the comparison process begins with the automatic activation of the target and test nodes by the presentation of the target-test pair. Activation spreads in parallel along all associative paths from each of the two nodes. The amount of activation depends on the weights of the paths. Some of the activated paths from the two nodes will intersect, forming activated pathways that connect the two nodes. The controlled process that decides on the response monitors the amount of activation from connected paths and responds "Yes" when some threshold is exceeded. Highly typical items (like vegetable–green bean) will have many strong connected paths, and the threshold value will be exceeded rapidly. Less typical items will have fewer high-strength connected paths and more strength in unconnected paths

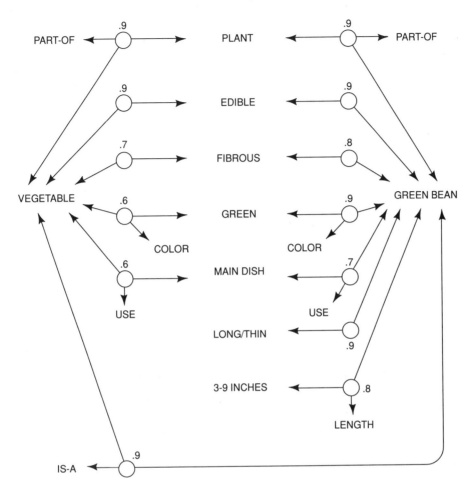

Figure 3.1
A small part of a semantic network

and thus will take longer to reach threshold. Atypical items might even require the controlled process to check the nature of the intersections that are retrieved before making a "Yes" response.

Semantic network models of concepts also predict priming and context effects. Conceptual information processing will be facilitated if a prior context has activated the pathways that are required for the task. Loftus and Cole (1974) gave subjects a superordinate category name and a feature and asked them to produce an instance of the category possessing the feature. For example, when given *vehicle* and *red*, the subject might respond *fire engine*. In some cases the category was presented before the feature, and in other cases the feature was presented before the category. Subjects were able to produce instances faster when the category was presented first; for example, they produced *fire engine* faster in response to *vehicle* followed by *red* than in response to *red* followed by *vehicle*.

The spreading activation model handles this result quite naturally. When activation spreading from the concept and feature nodes intersects at some third node, that third node becomes available as a possible answer. Activation begins spreading first from the term that is presented first, thus priming the network. Priming with a category name, such as *vehicle*, is more efficient because there are fewer links to *vehicle* than there are to very widespread features, such as *red*. Thus, the activation emanating from the feature is diluted among many more paths and rapidly weakens.

Exemplar and Connectionist Models
Although there has been much disagreement about the form of conceptual schemas, the notion of schema has been central to classical theories of cognition. The proponent of schemas, however, shoulders the burden of explaining the relationship between the schema, which is a representation of general knowledge, and specific exemplars that are encountered in experience with a category. The schema must be constructed from experiences with specific exemplars. Propositional-schematic models of mental representation clearly have the power to store both a schema and associated representations of particular examplars, potentially raising a host of questions about whether all exemplars are stored and when and how exemplars contribute to the construction of the schema. One radical solution of schema theory is that exemplars are never stored but just contribute to the schema. If the schema is a prototype, then each exemplar contributes an adjustment to the value of each of the features in the prototype, which represents some sort of average over all the exemplars encountered. If the schema is a network with weights, as in figure 3.1, each exemplar would adjust the weights according to some procedure. The pure prototype theory is obviously too austere for many types of concepts. A prototype for *cow*, for example, would have to list a single color feature, yet it is pretty clear that a person can have general knowledge that cows can be black, brown, or black and white. Network models can clearly handle this kind of complexity, but the price is having to come up with a detailed theory of how the schematic network is built over time.

Some researchers have tried to escape this theoretical burden by proposing that schemas are not constructed at all. Instead, representations of all exemplars are stored in memory, and new objects are categorized by comparing them to all items in memory and computing some measure of fit to each possible category. The degree of fit to a category determines the probability of assigning the object to the category. Imagine a child whose only conceptual categories are *cat* and *dog*. Each time the child encounters a confirmed instance of a cat or a dog a full description of that instance, in the form of a vector of features, is stored in memory with the appropriate label. After a while the child might have ten exemplars of *cat* and ten exemplars of *dog* stored in memory. Now, along comes a novel object that the child wishes to categorize. We might ask, What is the probability that the child will call the object a dog? Exemplar theories use the following kind of calculation (Medin and Schaffer 1978; Nosofsky 1988). First, the vector of features describing the novel object is formed. The similarity between this vector of features and every dog or cat exemplar in memory is then computed. All the dog similarities are then added up to get a total dog-similarity value. All the cat similarities are also added up to get a total cat-similarity value. The probability the child will say "dog" is given by an equation such as the following:

$$P(\text{dog}) = \frac{\text{total dog-similarity}}{\text{total dog-similarity} + \text{total cat-similarity}}$$

This formula nicely pits the new object's similarity to previously seen dogs against its similarity to previously seen cats. If the similarities to dogs and cats are equal, then the probability of saying "dog" will be .5, just what we would expect. If the similarity to previously seen cats is 0, then the probability of saying "dog" will be 1.0, and so on. This type of formula can be extended to handle multiple categories and various other complexities, such as biases favoring or disfavoring particular categorizations. Its use hinges, however, on being able to represent objects as vectors of features and on having a psychologically realistic way of measuring similarity.

Exemplar models have been applied to performance in laboratory concept-learning experiments, in which subjects learn to sort some novel set of objects into two or more categories. In these studies the featural composition of the exemplars is known, so it is possible to compute predicted categorization probabilities using a formula like that above. Often the exemplar models do a better job at predicting subjects' performance than prototype or schema models.

An immediate concern about exemplar models is finding a cognitively realistic mechanism for rapidly computing and adding up large numbers of similarities. It would be nice to do this in parallel. Since each exemplar is represented as a vector of features, it ought to be possible to design a connectionist model that could learn to do the computations from exposure to a set of training pairs. Kruschke (1992) has developed such a model. The architecture of Kruschke's model for a simplified domain is shown in figure 3.2. The two input units are able to represent objects that vary along two

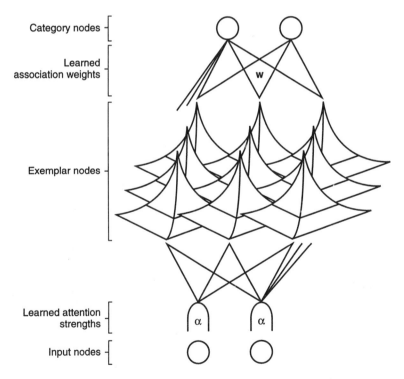

Figure 3.2
The architecture of Kruschke's exemplar-based connectionist model of category learning. The model is known as ALCOVE, for Attention Learning Covering Map. (Adapted with permission from Kruschke 1992.)

dimensions, say, size and brightness. Each exemplar would be represented by a vector of two numbers, representing its perceived size and perceived brightness. The hidden nodes in the network are called exemplar nodes because each node represents an exemplar. When the model is used to simulate a laboratory experiment, there is a hidden node for each exemplar presented in the experiment. The connections from the input nodes to the hidden nodes are set up in such a way that an exemplar node responds maximally when its exemplar is presented. It also responds when other exemplars are presented, but its response decreases from the maximum as a function of the distance from the ideal exemplar in the two-dimensional stimulus space. Suppose the pyramid in the middle of the diagram is the response profile of the hidden unit representing a six-inch, medium-gray object. The highest point on the pyramid is the unit's activation when the six-inch, medium-gray object is presented. The sloping sides of the pyramid illustrate that the response of the unit to other exemplars depends on how similar they are to the six-inch, medium-gray object. A seven-inch, dark-gray object might evoke a fairly strong response from the unit, whereas a one-inch, white object might evoke almost no response. Thus, when an exemplar vector is fed into the model, each hidden exemplar-unit responds with its similarity to the input. The network therefore computes the similarities between the input and the entire set of possible exemplars in parallel.

The hidden nodes are fully connected to the category nodes, with each connection having an adjustable weight. There are two category nodes in the figure because it is assumed that exemplars are to be sorted into two categories. The net input to an output node is a weighted sum of the hidden-node activations, which are similarity values. Thus, the activation of an output node is a total similarity value, just the kind of number needed in the equation above. The activations can be substituted into the equation (or one much like it) to predict the probability that an exmplar will be assigned to a given category (i.e., the activation of the category node divided by the sum of the activations of both category nodes). The network is thus a parallel computer for exemplar-based categorization.

The weights in the network can also be trained using the backpropagation algorithm. Each time an exemplar is presented to the network, the correct categorization is compared to the output values on the category nodes. The error is used to adjust the weights between the hidden and category nodes. The error is also propagated backward to adjust the attention strengths, which are special weights that apply to all connections emanating from an input node. The attention strengths simulate a standard finding in concept-learning experiments that subjects learn to pay more attention to relevant dimensions of the exemplars and to pay less attention to irrelevant dimensions. For example, suppose that in a task that varies size and brightness, the categorization is based completely on size, with all objects smaller than six inches being assigned to category A and all objects larger than six inches being assigned to category B, regardless of brightness. In such a task subjects learn to pay attention to size and to ignore brightness. The attention weights in the model simulate this aspect of concept learning.

One might object to Kruschke's architecture out of a sense that it requires so many hidden nodes, covering the entire input space. As the number of input dimensions grows, the number of hidden exemplar nodes needed grows exponentially. The problem is not so great as it first appears, however. For one thing, the model performs well when hidden nodes are randomly scattered throughout the input space with an appropriate density. It is not necessary that every possible vector of inputs have its own hidden node. Perhaps more important, the hidden nodes are based directly on the input dimensions and therefore reflect perceptual-representational capacities that the organism possesses prior to learning. The nodes do not represent every logically possible way of coding the exemplars.

The last point introduces a difference between the exemplar-based network and standard fully connected three-layer networks, such as NETtalk (described in chapter 2). The exemplar nodes respond only to a restricted region of the input space, and the response in that region is based on similarity. Single exemplar nodes, or groups of them, therefore cannot learn novel representations of the input. In standard back-propagation learning, by contrast, the hidden nodes respond to the entire input space without any prior constraint. During learning they can therefore come to represent interesting structure in the input-output transformation that is being acquired. Thus, NETtalk could treat the letter 'c' as similar to 'k' in contexts where it is pronounced /k/ (as in *cat*), but treat it as similar to 's' in contexts where it is pronounced /s/ (as in *city*). There are many concept-learning situations where the ability to learn new internal representations is important. The text-to-sound mapping in reading may be such a case. Another case, discussed later in this chapter, is the ability of chess masters to "see" a chessboard in terms of strategy and likely moves.

Conceptual Complexity
A bit of reflection will suggest that our discussion of concepts so far has been seriously oversimplified. Even the simplest concepts involve an enormous amount of knowledge. Your knowledge about cucumbers, for example, might include tactile information ("those tiny bumps with tiny little spines growing out of them"), the picking size for several varieties, when and how to plant, type of machinery and labor needed for farm harvest, how to test for bitterness, smell when rotting, use in several of the world's cuisines, next-door neighbors hate them, waxy grocery store surface an unnatural phenomenon, and so on.

Models that represent objects or concepts using vectors of features appear in this light to be clearly useful in describing categorization on the basis of perceptual attributes. They may therefore be good models of learning in perceptual systems or of procedural learning in cases where the conditions that specify a certain action occur repeatedly during training. But the realization that even concepts for simple objects involve complex knowledge immediately makes relevant the whole controversy over connectionist knowledge representation introduced in chapter 2. Our general knowledge of simple concepts can include explicit rules (*don't put rosemary on cucumbers*), arbitrarily complicated propositional content (*the new factory in Black Creek has stopped buying picklers under four inches long*), and features whose relation to perceptual input is mediated by complex knowledge (*unnatural*).

The problems with vectors of features begin to manifest themselves at a fairly elementary level of analysis (Barsalou 1993). For example, listing *black* as a feature of an object fails to represent the fact that black is the color of the object. In traditional terminology, the feature *black* is the value of the attribute *color*. In a feature list representation it is difficult to represent the fact that the value *black* is *bound* to the attribute *color*. Attribute-value relations matter in conceptual learning. Suppose subjects in a laboratory learn a simple classification task in which the black objects fall in one category and the yellow in another. A subject who is then given an intradimensional-shift problem in which categories are also based on *color* (say, *green* vs. *red*) will tend to have an easier time than with an extradimensional shift in which the categories are based on another dimension, such as *size* (*large* vs. *small*). Feature lists also often fail to represent relations among features that are critical to a concept. Listing *wings* as a feature for *bird*, for example, fails to note that the wings are attached to opposite sides of the body. These problems are not necessarily insoluble. Connectionists have pointed out that our verbal labels for features, such as *black* and *wings*, may be a misleading shorthand for a much richer, distributed, microfeatural vector representation. For example, all colors might be distributively coded on a common set of input nodes in a way that would support generalization among tasks for which color was a relevant dimension. Or, the verbal label *wings* might be a convenient stand-in for a complex encoding that does capture the relation of wings to body. As attractive as such ideas are, they are not yet worked out well enough to be applied in the domain of real concepts.

The propositional-schematic theory of declarative knowledge, although it has not lent itself to elegant quantitative theories of concept learning, is clearly equipped to take on the complexities of conceptual knowledge. Still, the wealth of knowledge associated with simple concepts raises questions about the notion that a schema for a concept is a relatively small collection of privileged information. Any bit of knowledge connected with a concept can be relevant if the context is right. What we have been singling out for inclusion in schemas (both in the last chapter and this one) is perhaps only distinguished by the frequency with which it is useful. Putting all of the knowledge about a concept into its schema does not pose a representational problem. All of the relevant propositions can be tied together, and they can even be organized hierarchically by having proposition nodes point to other proposition nodes or by using frame or script structures. Such large structures pose a processing problem, however. It is hard to imagine such a large network being uniformly activated in working memory. In fact, it would be a bad idea, because then the information that is needed in the current context could not be picked out by its differential level of activation. What we need to explain is how the right information associated with a concept is activated at the right time.

A plausible explanation is that the context primes the relevant aspects of a concept. If a concept is presented in isolation, as in the laboratory experiments mentioned so far, only the strongest pathways will receive significant amounts of activation, leading to thoughts about such mundane matters as the greenness of cucumbers. In real-life situations, however, concepts occur in a context that can contribute additional activation to weaker but more relevant associations. If you are thinking of serving your neighbors cucumbers in a salad, the activation of salad concepts and the concept of your neighbors may strongly activate the knowledge that they hate cucumbers, thus saving you from a culinary faux pas.

An experiment by Barsalou (1982) provided a laboratory test of the hypothesis that less central features receive additional activation from relevant contexts. Table 3.1 illustrates four of the item types from the experiment. Subjects perform a *feature verification task*, which can be illustrated by looking at item type 1 in the table. On each trial the subject first saw a sentence with the subject noun underlined, for example, "The *skunk* was under a large willow." The subject then saw a phrase that denoted a possible feature or property of the subject, for example, "has a smell," and had to respond as quickly as possible, by pressing one of two buttons, whether or not the

Table 3.1
Examples of four of the types of items and the average response times in milliseconds from Barsalou's (1982) experiment

Item type	Response time
1. High-weight feature—Neutral context Target: The <u>skunk</u> was under a large willow Test: Has a smell	1113
2. High-weight feature—Relevant context Target: The <u>skunk</u> stunk up the neighborhood Test: Has a smell	1145
3. Low-weight feature—Neutral context Target: The <u>roof</u> had been renovated before the rainy season Test: Can be walked on	1404
4. Low-weight feature—Relevant context Target: The <u>roof</u> creaked under the weight of the repairman Test: Can be walked on	1259

subject had the property. In the example the correct answer is obviously "Yes." Since the sentence appears before the property, any information that occurs in the sentence could potentially prime the property before it appears, thus speeding up the response time to it.

The theory of contextual priming makes an interesting set of predictions for the four types of items. For item types 1 and 2 the feature that is tested has a very high weight and thus will be strongly activated regardless of context. Adding a relevant context in item type 2 should not speed up the response time. For item types 3 and 4 the feature tested has a low weight and thus will not be strongly activated without additional priming. In the neutral context of item type 3 activation should be low, leading to a slow response time. Adding a relevant context in item type 4 should prime the feature, increasing its activation and speeding up its response time. The data in the table confirm the predictions. Context had a small (negative) effect on response times for high-weight features and a large facilitating effect on low-weight features.

This result and many others that also confirm the underlying line of reasoning have led Barsalou (1993) to propose a dynamic theory of concepts. Since only a part of the knowledge relevant to a concept is activated in a context, there is a sense in which the concept that is actually functioning in that context is created at that moment. Although the total base of long-term knowledge may be the same across contexts, one's effective concepts of cucumber during spring planting and while planning an August dinner menu may be quite different. In some respects this theory is strikingly similar to the connectionist claim about the contextual variability of concepts (discussed in chapter 2). It shows that the classical theory of declarative knowledge is not committed to a notion of rigid conceptual schemas that are cross-situationally stable.

Given that the classical theory is able to incorporate a form of contextual variability in concepts, disputes about concept representation may actually hinge more on the role of perceptual representations versus central representations not tied to a sensory modality and on the role of symbols versus subsymbols or microfeatures. Many connectionists lean toward highly distributed representations that are tied to perceptual experience and that are subsymbolic in the sense that even what are normally taken to be primitive features such as *red* or *wings* can only be understood in terms of their basis in a more primitive level of microfeatures. Recently, Barsalou (1993) has begun to develop a theory that challenges both the connectionist and the classical approaches. He rejects vector representations because of the failure so far to demonstrate that they can capture the degree of structure that is clearly required in conceptual representations. But he also favors the role of perceptual representations over the classical emphasis on propositional representations that are not tied to sensory modalities (sometimes called *amodal* representations). The richness and variability of concepts are tied to perceptual representations that are argued to be symbolic, structured, and productive.

The Theoretical Nature of Concepts

Our discussion of concepts and categorization so far has emphasized what might be called a descriptive and statistical approach. Concept learning has been thought of mainly as a matter of gathering data about the observable characteristics of objects, which are stored in the form of exemplars or a summary schema. Categorization decisions can be seen as evaluating hypotheses about the category membership of objects by weighing the observable features against the accumulated knowledge by measuring and summing up similarities. The fact that the learning and decision making can be carried out very efficiently by connectionist networks doesn't change the focus on a statistical characterization of surface characteristics. Our discussion of conceptual complexity admitted a wider range of conceptual knowledge into the picture, but this knowledge was again differentiated only by its tendency to be activated by various contexts.

Conceptual knowledge can have a theoretical character, however, which can alter and even override the influence of observable features, similarity, or frequency of occurrence (Medin 1989). A single observation of the melting point of lead might be trusted because of a theory of the uniformity of chemical elements. A single observation of a Bonduel cucumber being superior to a Black Creek cucumber would not support generalization without more observations and might lead to a rash of alternative causal explanations that would require observations systematically related to the alternatives. When given the information that an object is three inches in diameter and asked whether it is a quarter or a pizza, people judge it a pizza, even though the diameter is more similar to that of the quarters they have seen than to that of the pizzas they have seen (Rips 1989). To some extent this result might be handled by a statistical model that looked at the amount of variability across exemplars, but it is clear that people also have causal and social theories about quarters and pizzas that allow them to predict the range of possible diameters. They know, for example, that as an item of American coinage, the quarter has an officially designated diameter.

Concept acquisition can also be guided by goals, which can include the desire to construct rules or theories that govern a domain. At the simplest level, goals influence which concepts we acquire. We probably miss many interesting patterns in our environments simply because our goals never led us to attend to and process the relevant features. The goal of making sense of a domain can also affect how we process examples, because a current theory of the domain can lead us to attend differentially to various features or to interpret them in a particular way. Theoretical goals even affect which examples we are exposed to, because our ideas might lead us to seek out particular kinds of examples. Dunbar (1993) demonstrated these phenomena in an experiment on scientific reasoning. Some subjects adopted a find-evidence goal, which led them to search for evidence consistent with a current hypothesis, even when they had been exposed to some inconsistent evidence. Upon exposure to the inconsistent evidence, other subjects concluded that the current hypothesis was ruled out and adopted a find-hypothesis goal, which led them to search for a hypothesis that could account for the anomalous features. These two groups of subjects interpreted some features of the evidence differently in setting their goals, and in trying to meet their goals, they attended to and processed different features of the evidence.

It is apparent that a complete theory of concepts will have to take into account both perceptual-statistical factors and factors that are due to the pursuit of goals and the use of rules and theories. The former have a *bottom-up* character, in which concept formation and use are driven by incoming data. The latter have a *top-down* character, because the theories and rules influence the interpretation of the data. Research by Armstrong, Gleitman, and Gleitman (1983) and Landau (1982) suggests that the findings from the two approaches do apply to the same conceptual domains. They employed concepts that have clear classical definitions in terms of necessary and sufficient features, such as *odd number* or *rectangle*. People reason correctly with these definitions in judging whether a particular figure is a rectangle or whether, say, 57 is an odd number. Nevertheless, typicality effects were found in these domains. People rate 3 a more typical odd number than 57, and they rate *square* a more typical geometric figure than *ellipse*. In categorization tasks these ratings predict relative response times. Thus, 3 can be classified as an odd number much more quickly than 57.

The researchers accounted for these results by arguing for a distinction between features that are at the core of a concept and more probabilistic features that are useful in identifying instances or making likely guesses about instances. Rating tasks are likely to activate many useful probabilistic features. Speeded categorization tasks involve perceptual representations and possibly automatized procedures for making rapid, automatic identifications. The frequency and similarity-influenced strength of a representation or procedure will be influential in such tasks. In tasks that allow or require more careful reasoning, however, people are able to differentiate and attend to core features of a concept, which may be necessary by definition or be involved in a theory of the domain. One basic reason for such findings is that core features are often not very useful in identifying instances. For example, it is usually easier to see whether someone is over forty-five years old than it is to see whether that person has grandchildren. Thus, an assessment of a person's age tends to be incorporated into the identification procedure for grandparenthood, although it is not part of the definition.

Because simple concepts are, in a sense, part of the bedrock of cognition, they will no doubt continue to be the focus of active research in all of the cognitive science disciplines.

3.2. Memory

The ability to remember facts and past events when they are needed is one of the most striking aspects of human cognition. We depend on our memories constantly. We assume that we can remember a new phone number for a few seconds without writing it down, that we can recall our own birthdates, that we can remember the three major theories of the origin of World War I during examinations, and so on. Our dependence on memory is often noticed only when memory fails us. Forgetting the name of a new acquaintance, forgetting to buy the milk, or forgetting during a final exam can lead one to wonder how memory works and how it can be improved. In this section the ideas about the architecture of cognition are applied to memory functions. To begin with, the problem area must be delimited somewhat, because the word *memory* is used to refer to just about any way that current behavior can be sensitive to previous experience. We will concentrate on the acquisition of new declarative knowledge that for the most part recombines known concepts into new representations. A representative case would be your memory for the material in this chapter after studying it. For the moment we will not treat procedural knowledge, although it is a form of memory. We speak of remembering how to ride a bicycle, for example. We will also ignore the use of procedural memory to remember facts indirectly. For example, if you do not remember which way you move the shift lever on your bicycle in order to downshift, you might be able to recall it by going through the motions of downshifting. In spite of these simplifications, memory for declarative knowledge is quite a complex topic.

Acquiring New Memories

The Three Stages of the Memory Situation   Memory situations fit a general schema. Cognitive psychologists have a good representation of this schema and use it to analyze memory performance. A complete memory situation is extended in time and consists of three stages. The *acquisition* period is the time when the person acquires the knowledge to be remembered (the *target* knowledge). The *retrieval* situation is a later time at which it would be adaptive for the target knowledge to be activated and utilized by some information process. The *retention interval* is the time period that passes between the acquisition period and the retrieval situation. A theory of memory performance in a particular type of situation potentially requires a careful analysis of the cognitive processes that occur at each of the three stages.

Short-Term and Long-Term Storage   During the acquisition period a representation of the target information must be formed, or *stored*. The stored representation is often called the *memory trace*. The memory trace must be activated and utilized by some ongoing information process in the retrieval situation. One of the most introspectively compelling aspects of memory is the distinction between *long-term* and *short-term* storage. A simple case of the distinction is the difference between one's memory for one's own phone number and one's memory for a new phone number that is remembered only long enough to dial it. The general picture of the cognitive architecture developed so far is nicely consistent with this phenomenon.

When a new fact (such as a phone number) is presented, a cognitive representation of it is constructed. At the moment of construction this representation is in a high state of activation, which will be maintained as long as attention continues to be devoted to it. Obviously, if a retrieval situation arises while the controlled processing is still going on (or within a few moments after it ceases), there will be no problem in retrieving the fact, because it is already either the focus of attention or active enough to become so. Short-term memory, then, refers to the retrieval of a new fact from working memory, which in this context is sometimes called the *short-term store*. An effective strategy for retaining new information in working memory is *rehearsal*. Thinking of an item of information over and over, or repeating it aloud over and over, ensures that it remains in an active state.

In many memory situations, however, the retrieval situation arises from minutes to years after the disappearance of the activation due to the initial encounter with a new fact. In these cases retrieval will occur only if some representation of the fact survives in the network of declarative knowledge. In such cases new propositions and links are established in the propositional network, and it is often said that information has been *transferred* to *long-term storage*. As part of our theory of attention and working memory, we have already assumed that controlled processing of new representations is (at least sometimes) capable of establishing those representations in the declarative network. This fundamental assumption, however, raises the question of what controlled processes, or *encoding strategies*, are best for establishing new knowledge.

An Example Memory Experiment   The contrast between short- and long-term memory and the influence of encoding strategies are well illustrated in an experiment by Bjork and Jongeward (Bjork 1975). They contrasted the effect of two different encoding strategies: *rehearsal*, introduced above, and *elaboration*. On each of the twenty trials in the experiment the subject was asked to quickly study a list of six common, unrelated four-letter nouns. The six words were then removed, and after 20 seconds the subject tried to recall them. On half of the trials the subject was told to try to remember the words using a rehearsal strategy, which involved simply thinking of the words over and over. On the other half of the trials the subject was told to use an elaboration strategy. In this case the subject tried to construct meaningful relationships among the words by making up sentences, stories, or images that involved them. At the end of the experiment, with no advance warning, the subject was asked to try to remember the words from all twenty trials. Half the subjects received a *free recall* test, in which they wrote down as many of the words as they could remember. The other half of the subjects were given an *old-new recognition* test. In such a test the subject is given a list of words that contains both the words from the study trials, called the *target* or *old* words, and other words, called *distractors*, *foils*, or *new* words. The subject is asked to judge whether each word is a target or a distractor.

Rehearsal proved to be the best memory strategy for the initial recall following each trial. When they rehearsed a list, subjects recalled a higher percentage of the words and often recalled them in the same order in which they were presented. The elaboration strategy led to lower initial recall in which the order of presentation was often scrambled. However, elaboration produced much better results in the final performance tests. Recall for words that had been elaborated was about twice as great as recall for words that had been rehearsed. Recognition of elaborated words was also much better than for rehearsed words, although recognition memory for the rehearsed words was still reasonably good.

The results of the experiment demonstrate that the rehearsal strategy is an efficient way to maintain a small amount of information in an active state, allowing excellent short-term memory performance. The results also demonstrate that the elaboration strategy produces much better long-term recall performance and somewhat better long-term recognition performance. One of the main goals of the rest of our discussion of memory is to explain why elaboration produces this pattern of results.

The Effects of Encoding Processes on Memory

Levels of Processing   The encoding processes that occur during acquisition obviously exert a tremendous effect on later memory performance, since they determine the potential existence and the form of the memory trace that will be available to retrieval processes. A major theme in modern research has been the effects on memory of the

Table 3.2
Typical questions and responses used by Craik and Tulving (1975)

Level of processing	Question	Answer	
		Yes	No
Structural	Is the word in capital letters?	TABLE	table
Phonemic	Does the word rhyme with weight?	crate	MARKET
Category	Is the word a type of fish?	SHARK	heaven
Sentence	Would the word fit the sentence: He met a ____ in the street?	FRIEND	cloud

level or *depth* of processing during acquisition. The level of processing is a rather loose notion that has been used to refer to the degree to which a person understands and devotes controlled processes to the meaning of the target information. The theory is that deeper, more meaningful acquisition processing generally leads to better memory performance. Craik and Tulving (1975) conducted a series of experiments that demonstrate this generalization. Subjects were shown a series of English words. Before they saw each word they were given a question to answer about the word. As shown in table 3.2, some questions required superficial processing, and some required deeper processing that involved the meaning of the word. After answering questions for a list of forty or so words, the subjects were given recognition or recall tests for the words. Words that had been subjected to deeper processing were better remembered.

The Role of Intention to Remember   The theory that depth of acquisition processing exerts a decisive influence on later memory has a somewhat surprising corollary: The mere intention to remember should not influence memory performance. The evidence comes from experiments in which two groups of subjects are induced to use the same cognitive processes while studying target material. The subjects in the *intentional learning* group are informed that they will be taking a memory test and therefore have an intention to remember. The subjects in the *incidental learning* group believe that their encounter with the target material is for some other purpose and receive a surprise memory test. The levels-of-processing theory predicts that the memory performance of the two groups will not differ. That is, as long as the cognitive processes engaged in by the two groups are the same, the additional intention to remember in one of the groups will produce no increment in performance.

Experiments by Hyde and Jenkins (1973) and Craik and Tulving (1975) confirmed this prediction. Referring to table 3.2, it is easy to see how Craik and Tulving did their incidental learning experiments. Subjects in incidental conditions were told that the experiment concerned the perception of words and the speed of reaction to the questions, and they were given a surprise memory test. Subjects in intentional conditions were told beforehand that there would be a final memory test and that it was just as important as answering the questions.

Elaboration   As researchers have tried to make the concept of levels of processing more precise, they have tended to replace it with other, related concepts (Cermak and Craik 1979). One of these concepts is *elaboration*. Elaborations are additions to the target information. In response to a single item or proposition in the target information a person may generate any number of related propositions, called elaborations. The elaborations may simply be additions to the target item, but they may also serve to relate the target item to other target items or to previously acquired knowledge. Elaborative processes occur constantly in everyday thinking. Consider a student reading a chapter in a textbook. Appreciating the consequences of each sentence in the chapter, relating the sentences to each other, and relating the chapter to previous knowledge and experience are all elaborative activities that involve the generation of many propositions that do not occur in the text.

Bjork and Jongeward's experiment illustrated that instructions to elaborate on target material can produce strong improvements in memory performance relative to rote rehearsal. Craik and Tulving's basic level-of-processing experiment can also be seen as an example of elaboration. The various questions in table 3.2 lead the subject to form elaborative propositions about the target information concerning its typeface, phonemic structure, conceptual structure, or potential role in an event. Craik and Tulving conducted a further experiment in which the amount of elaboration was varied at the semantic level of processing. During acquisition, subjects answered sentence-frame questions for all words. However, the complexity of the sentence frame varied from low, to medium, to high. For example, for the word *watch* a simple frame was *He dropped the ____*, and a high-complexity frame was *The old man hobbled across the room and picked up the valuable ____ from the mahogany table*. Determining that *watch* fits the high-complexity frame requires more propositions to be processed, leading to a more elaborate memory trace. Recall was indeed considerably higher for words that were presented with high-complexity frames.

Given evidence that elaboration has powerful effects on memory, the critical problem is to explain these effects. Why does elaboration tend to improve memory performance? Anderson and Reder (1979) and Anderson (1983) have shown in more detail how cognitive architectures of the type we have considered can predict the effects of elaboration. The example given in figure 3.3 will be used to illustrate this type of explanation. Imagine a subject participating in a *paired-associate* learning experiment in which the target information is a list of word pairs, such as *dog-chair*. The subject attempts to learn the word pairs by elaborating on each one. The figure shows the subject's elaboration and the resulting network of propositions that could potentially be stored in long-term memory. Note that we have introduced some shorthand into the diagram to cut down on the complexity of the figure. Relation pointers and relation nodes have been suppressed, and the name of the relation for each proposition has been placed inside the proposition node. In this case the shorthand makes no difference, because activation spreading along relation pointers through relation nodes does not affect the memory process.

The memorial advantages of elaboration stem from the fact that elaborations contain a number of propositions with overlapping, or redundant, information. If any part of the elaboration can be retrieved during the memory test, there is a good chance of producing a correct response. Figure 3.3 illustrates the kind of indirect retrieval that can occur. During an attempt to recall, only one proposition becomes active enough to be selected by the controlled process that is directing recall: *The dog loves the masters*. Thus, on this first step *dog* has been retrieved, but *chair* has not. Devoting attention to this proposition, however, primes the elements of the proposition, spreading stronger activation to previously weak elements of the structure. In this case priming *masters* raises the activation level of *The masters possess the chair* enough to make it available to the recall process. This kind of successive repriming of a network by a controlled

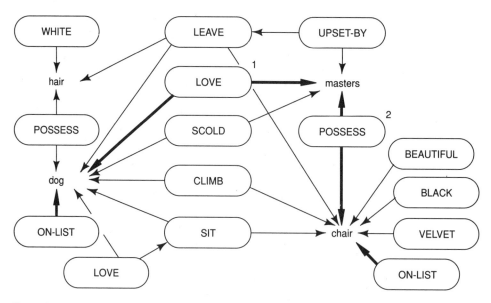

Figure 3.3
An example of elaboration in a memory experiment. One of the items that the subject was instructed to
remember was *dog-chair*. The subject's verbal elaboration for the item was *dog-chair, dog-chair, the dog loved
his masters; he also loved to sit on the chairs; his master had a beautiful black velvet chair; one day he climbed on
it; he left his white hairs all over the chair; his masters were upset by this; they scolded him.* The figure shows a
hypothetical underlying propositional representation of the elaboration. Propositions 1 and 2 in bold lines
are retrieved at test time in that order. Other propositions receive insufficient activation for retrieval.
(Based on Anderson 1976.)

process is called *node refocusing* by Anderson (1983). There are obviously many paths
of activation in the example network that could lead indirectly to retrieval of the target
information.

Note that the network must somehow include the information that *dog* and *chair*
were on the list, if the subject is to avoid incorrect recall of other parts of the elaboration. The example includes simple ON LIST propositions that *tag* an item as target
information. If such propositional tags are not retrievable, the subject might still be
able to respond correctly by detecting that the target items are members of more of
the retrieved propositions. This is an example of a *reconstruction* process, in which the
subject is able to guess the target information intelligently even when it is not retrieved. The redundancy of networks makes other types of reconstruction possible as
well. Suppose that all of the paths to *chair* in the example network received insufficient
activation to allow retrieval. If the information that the dog loved to sit on something
that its masters owned was available, *chair* would be an obvious guess for the missing
information.

The refocusing and reconstruction processes provide a general framework for explaining the effects of elaboration in specific memory situations. For example, some
types of elaborations tend to enhance memory performance more than others (Stein
and Bransford 1979; Bradshaw and Anderson 1982). Bradshaw and Anderson showed
that elaborations of a sentence tend to be more effective if they concern the causes or
effects of the facts described in the sentence. For the following target sentence, study-

ing the irrelevant elaboration would be less effective in promoting later recall than studying either the cause elaboration or the effect elaboration:

Target: Mozart made a long journey from Munich to Paris.

Irrelevant: Mozart felt fruits were unwholesome for children.

Cause: Mozart wanted to leave Munich to avoid a romantic entanglement.

Effect: Mozart was inspired by Parisian musical life.

Bradshaw and Anderson argued that the cause and effect elaborations led to networks with more interconnections than did the irrelevant elaborations. In the example the target and irrelevant sentences might end up having only the *Mozart* node in common. The target and cause sentences will have both the *Mozart* and *Munich* nodes in common, and they might well lead to the production of further interconnected elaborations. For example, a subject might encode the proposition that Paris is far enough from Munich to deter a rejected lover from pursuit via late-eighteenth-century modes of transport.

Effects of Schematic Processing on Memory   The theory of elaboration just sketched predicts that the activation of organized knowledge structures, such as schemas or scripts, during the acquisition of target material should have important effects on memory. The availability of a schema that is relevant to the target information should often make a host of highly interrelated elaborations immediately available.

Owens, Bower, and Black (1979), for example, showed that the recall of a rather general story could be improved by prefacing it with a specific theme. A general story about Nancy's visit to the doctor, for example, contained the following sentences:

> Nancy stepped on the scale and the nurse recorded her weight. The doctor
> entered the room and examined the results. He smiled at Nancy and said,
> "Well, it seems my expectations have been confirmed."

The more specific version was exactly the same except that it began with the information that Nancy had been seeing a college professor and thought she might be pregnant. The assumption is that this theme information activates a rich schema about how unmarried college students cope with unexpected pregnancy. The schema allows many more elaborations than the skeletal script for a visit to the doctor that is activated by the general version of the story. In fact, subjects who studied stories with themes recalled 46 percent more than subjects who studied general stories. In another study Chiesi, Spilich, and Voss (1979) showed that subjects who come to a situation with more complex schematic knowledge are able to generate elaborations that produce a higher level of recall. In this study subjects who were classified independently as having a high level of baseball knowledge recalled more from passages about baseball games.

Errors Induced by Elaboration and Schematic Processing   The elaboration theory predicts various kinds of errors as well as advantages. For figure 3.3 we explained how the correct recall of *chair* could be reconstructed if it or its list tag were unretrievable. But the same processes might lead to the incorrect recall, or *intrusion*, of *masters* or *hair*, which both resulted from the subject's elaboration process.

Elaboration that is guided by a schema compounds the problem. Target information that fits well into the schema will be redundantly encoded. Many of the redundant propositions are highly plausible inferences, however, that may prove difficult to discriminate at test time from information that was actually presented. In chapter 2 we saw that Bower, Black, and Turner (1979) found evidence for exactly this kind of error in both recognition and recall tests. These errors provided strong evidence for the existence of scripts for everyday events and for the role of scripts in story understanding. In their study of the advantages of stories with themes, Owens, Bower, and Black (1979) also found that subjects tended to recall their elaborations as having been part of the story. The additional elaboration connected with the presence of a theme triggered four times more errors of this type than the general stories. In fact, for the thematic stories, after twenty-four hours, subjects recalled one elaboration for every two propositions that actually occurred in the story.

In much of everyday life the retrieval of schema-based inferences is probably adaptive, since the inferences are usually correct. On the other hand, there are occasions when it is important to be able to discriminate the origin and time of storage for items of information in memory. Legal witnesses, for example, are expected to be able to discriminate what they experienced from what they inferred. There is some evidence that eyewitness testimony is contaminated by elaborative and schematic processes. Some of the most interesting evidence comes from the transcripts of the "Watergate" tapes. The tapes were audio recordings of meetings between President Richard Nixon and his advisers, including his counsel John Dean. Dean testified against Nixon before the Senate's Watergate Committee about some of the taped meetings before the tapes were revealed.

Neisser (1981) undertook to compare Dean's testimony about two particular meetings with the transcripts of those meetings. He found evidence for a very high degree of schematic processing. It appeared that Dean's meetings with the president all contributed to a single coherent thematic schema, or knowledge base, about the Watergate affair. Dean had a great deal of trouble reconstructing particular events. Although most of his testimony was true in general, he often attributed statements to people that they never made, that they made on a different day, or that someone else made. His testimony also showed evidence of the influence of his self-schema. Errors in his recall typically revised the facts to be more consistent with his view of himself and his own role in the affair.

Laboratory studies have also found evidence of schematic processing in eyewitness testimony. In an early study by Loftus and Palmer (1974) subjects first viewed a film of an automobile accident and then answered questions about the accident. One group of subjects was asked, "About how fast were the cars going when they smashed into each other?" For a second group of subjects the end of the question was changed to "when they hit each other?" The first group gave much higher estimates of speed. A week later the subjects were called back for further "testimony," and they were all asked, "Did you see any broken glass?" Although there was no broken glass in the film, 32 percent of the subjects who had answered the "smashed" question a week earlier— but only 14 percent of the subjects who had answered the "hit" question—reported having seen broken glass. A likely explanation is that the information about the violence of the collision implied by the first question was incorporated into the representation of the accident, as an elaboration. The report of the broken glass was then generated reconstructively by applying a schema containing the information that automobile smashups typically break glass. Loftus's methodology and theoretical conclusions have been criticized (by McCloskey and Zaragoza 1985, for example). However, studies employing modified methods have continued to find that misleading postevent information can impair memory performance (Lindsay 1990).

Storage versus Retrieval in Memory Performance
Although the above discussion suggests that schema-driven elaboration is very important in human memory, it alone does not determine memory performance. What information gets retrieved at retrieval time depends on the retrieval cues that are present in the external and cognitive environment and on the deliberate retrieval strategies that a person engages in. The retrieved information must then be used to generate a memorial decision or report, which is affected by more or less deliberate reconstructive processes and by decision criteria or goals that are relevant in the retrieval situation.

Semantic elaboration is particularly useful when the retrieval situation is likely to contain cues that are semantically related to the original information and when the goal in the retrieval situation is to recall knowledge that is conceptually related to currently active representations. Many everyday memory situations have this character. Current goals often can be met even if traces of originally experienced material are mixed up with inferences and elaborations that occurred during acquisition or retrieval.

The natural advantage of elaboration can be lessened, however, if the nature of the retrieval situation is changed. For example, a memory test can be made less difficult by providing cues that have the potential to activate less accessible information in memory. The previously mentioned experiments reported by Bjork (1975) demonstrate that on a recognition test memory for unelaborated items can be quite good. The study by Chiesi, Spilich, and Voss (1979) provides another example: subjects who were low in baseball knowledge and who showed poor recall for baseball stories did very well on a recognition test. These results confirm the theory that one of the main advantages of elaboration is to provide multiple potential associative retrieval pathways to each proposition. Recognition testing tends to diminish this advantage because the test item usually directly activates the right region of memory.

Under some retrieval conditions elaboration can be a disadvantage relative to other strategies. In Bjork's experiment the rehearsal strategy was superior to elaboration for the immediate recall condition, probably largely because rehearsal maintains a number of words in working memory, which can be reported on an immediate test. Even the classic level-of-processing results depend on the nature of the memory test employed. Structural and phonemic processing, illustrated in table 3.2, produce superior performance if the memory test requires memory for the physical appearance of a word or for its phonemic properties (Morris, Bransford, and Franks 1977; Stein 1978). A semantic elaboration strategy might not encode these properties directly at all, and the properties would be difficult to reconstruct from the elaborations, since the elaborations are related to meaning and the properties are independent of meaning.

The dependence of memory performance on interactions between acquisition and retrieval conditions has been discussed by Morris, Bransford, and Franks (1977) as the principle of *transfer-appropriate processing* and by Tulving (1983) as the principle of *encoding specificity*. Our discussion so far indicates that classical theories of the cognitive architecture have good resources for explaining these interactions. These resources can be further explored by considering some of the types of memory errors that were discussed above.

Source Monitoring   Many of the errors discussed above can be seen as failures to recall the origin, or source, of information retrieved from declarative memory. When an eyewitness attributes a statement to the wrong person, or when a subject in a memory experiment recalls her own inference as a fact that was stated in a text, a source error has occurred. Johnson (Johnson, Hashtroudi, and Lindsay 1993) and others use the term *source-monitoring* to refer to the processes involved in judgments about the sources of remembered material. As we have seen, the theory of the cognitive architecture predicts the occurrence of source errors. Perhaps the most general explanation of why they occur is that long-term declarative memory and its associated storage and retrieval processes are not set up to keep track of sources with high reliability. There are not separate memory stores for knowledge arising from different sources, nor do declarative structures appear to be automatically indexed by source.

On the other hand, information that is relevant to source will often be contained in an active working-memory representation that is stored in long-term memory. Furthermore, elaborative processing can be deliberately dedicated to creating representations of source information. Subjects who distrust a source of information (Dodd and Bradshaw 1980) or who are warned that they might receive misinformation (Greene, Flynn, and Loftus 1982) show a reduced tendency to confuse information sources in memory. The explanation of these effects in terms of elaboration theory is that subjects generate many more propositions concerning the source and reliability of information than they normally do. At the time of the memory test these propositions have a good chance of being retrieved, both because they were encoded in the first place and hence possibly stored and because they are interrelated with other propositions.

Given that particular information is potentially available in memory, source errors also vary with people's retrieval strategies and with the criteria they set for reporting a memory. In an experiment by Hasher and Griffin (1978), when doubt was raised about the encoding schema at the time of the memory test, subjects made fewer reconstructive intrusions and actually recalled more of the original target information. Subjects in these experiments apparently altered both their retrieval strategies and their decision processes. They did not use the encoding schema to focus their retrieval, and they were more careful not to report information with an uncertain source. In a study of the eyewitness suggestibility effect Lindsay and Johnson (1989) also found evidence that source errors can be reduced when people shift their decision criteria in recognition situations. Subjects saw a picture and then were exposed to misleading postevent verbal information. Half of the subjects then received a standard "Yes"-"No" recognition test in which they saw a series of items and had to judge which items had appeared in the picture and which had not. The other subjects took a source-monitoring test, which required that they judge test items to be new, present in the picture, present in the verbal information, or present in both the picture and the verbal information. Subjects in the standard recognition condition tended to attribute items from the postevent information to the picture, whereas subjects in the source-monitoring condition did not make these errors. Subjects in the recognition condition were not concentrating on the possibility of source errors and probably tended to treat any sense of familiarity with a test item as grounds for a "Yes" (or "Old") response. In the source-monitoring condition, however, subjects had to try to retrieve information that was source relevant and to use information from memory to discriminate among sources. For example, if an item appeared in the picture, one should be able to remember facts about its visual appearance (shape, position, and so on).

Memory and the Cognitive Architecture

The classical theory, as we have developed it so far, includes three types of memory: working memory, long-term declarative memory, and procedural memory. It has been argued that various representations and processes are important for the operation of each type of memory. The framework provided by the classical theory has been remarkably successful in accommodating a wide range of memory phenomena. Nevertheless, there are memory phenomena and ideas about memory that are not so obviously compatible with the classical theory.

Implicit versus Explicit Memory   The term *explicit* memory is sometimes used to refer to the phenomena discussed so far in this section. In explicit retrieval situations the rememberer views the situation as a memory situation and engages in some conscious, attention-demanding, controlled processing to generate a memory decision or report. The report often refers to a particular acquisition situation, as in the cases of recognizing a sentence that appeared in a particular story or recalling what a person said on a particular occasion. Consider the contrast with the procedural memory built up during skill acquisition. Here the typical retrieval situation is the performance of the skill. The measure of procedural acquisition is whether the performace of the skill improves. The performer simply performs the skill as well as possible, without engaging in any of the cognitive processes needed to generate memory reports and without trying to reflect upon any particular prior practice session. Indeed, we have argued that the contents of automatized productions cannot be declaratively accessed at all. In contrast with explicit tests of memory, skilled performance can be referred to as an *implicit* test of memory. The distinction between explicit and implicit memory is rather informal and is largely defined in terms of the characteristics of memory situations rather than characteristics of the memories themselves. Thus, it would be misleading to simply identify declarative memory as explicit memory and procedural memory as implicit memory. Declarative knowledge, for example, is often accessed and processed implicitly during speech, planning, or reasoning without reference to any specific prior acquisition situation and without the operation of the cognitive processes associated with explicit memory reports.

The distinction between the two types of memory has become important because of the discovery that explicit and implicit memory for the same material can be dissociated in both normal and amnesic subjects. For example, many amnesics, when given a list of words to study, show little or no memory for the list on a standard "Yes"-"No" recognition test given, say, two hours later. However, the exposure to the study list does affect performance on a word-completion test. In one version of this test, the amnesic subjects are given three-letter word stems, for example, TAB_____, and asked to complete them to form the first word that comes to mind, for example, TABLE. Subjects tend to complete the fragments to form words that appeared on the study list. The subjects' performance reveals implicit but not explicit memory for the list. This kind of implicit memory phenomenon is called a *repetition priming effect*. The priming here, which can last for hours or days, is not the same as priming via immediate activation in declarative memory (discussed in chapter 2), which lasts at most for seconds and typically for well under a second. Interestingly, when the word-completion task is given to amnesics with explicit-memory instructions to complete the stems with words remembered from the study list, the priming effect disappears. In chapter 2 we saw that there is a dissociation between declarative and procedural memory in amnesia. The amnesic can learn new skills but has a severe, sometimes total, deficit in the ability to acquire new declarative knowledge. Priming studies suggest that a broader generalization might be that explicit and implicit memory are dissociated in amnesia.

A dissociation between explicit and implicit memory has also been established in people without amnesia, though less dramatically. Normal subjects' performance on explicit and implicit tests of memory is differentially affected by different study conditions. For example, subjects' use of a semantic elaboration strategy during the study of a list might improve explicit recall of the list but have little effect on priming. Conversely, shifting from auditory presentation during study to visual presentation during testing might decrease the priming effect considerably but have no effect on explicit memory performance.

This research has led to questions about whether implicit memory requires the postulation of one or more new components in the cognitive architecture (Schacter 1993). The dissociation evidence itself, however, provides only weak support for this view. One reason is that it is possible to produce experimental dissociations among types of explicit or types of implicit memory. Fractionating the cognitive architecture with every dissociation is clearly unwarranted. Further, the dissociation can be accounted for by theories that focus on the kind of storage-retrieval interactions that were introduced above (Roediger, Weldon, and Challis 1989).

Schacter (1993, for example) has suggested that the impasse between structural and processing accounts of implicit memory can be resolved by looking to further neuropsychological evidence. He argues that there is independent evidence for the existence of perceptual representation systems (PRS) that are distinct from declarative, or semantic, memory and that are the site of many priming effects, including the word-stem completion effect. There are neurological patients, for example, whose access to the meanings of words is severely compromised but who have relatively intact access to the perceptual form of words. Petersen and others (Petersen et al. 1988; Petersen et al. 1990) have used the PET-scanning technique on normal subjects to monitor the brain regions that are activated by the processing of the visual form of a printed word and the processing of its meaning. They found evidence that the processing of the visual form of words is associated with posterior areas in the brain and that the processing of meaning is associated with frontal areas.

The PRS theory fits in well with our sketch of the cognitive architecture. The propositional-schematic code of the declarative system is designed to deal with semantic information. It makes sense that it is not involved in processing visual input to identify the visual appearance of a word. The analysis of the visual appearance of a word should be done in the visual system, which would have direct associative links to nodes representing either words or concepts in the declarative system. This is apparently the case, and visual priming effects represent a residue of processing in the visual system. One further possibility is that priming should be looked upon as a procedural knowledge phenomenon. Depending on the study task, it could involve either a temporary sensitization of preexisting procedural representations or a small and unstable modification of procedural knowledge. It will take some time to work out the relative merits of this view versus the view that implicit memory is a distinct phenomenon.

A problem with viewing implicit memory strictly in terms of procedural knowledge embedded in perceptual systems is that declarative knowledge might also be subject to implicit memory effects. It was pointed out above that in everyday speech, planning, and reasoning, declarative knowledge is typically accessed and used implicitly. Declarative memory might be primed, therefore, by acquisition processes that activate propositional-schematic networks. Blaxton (1989) found exactly this effect. In one acquisition condition subjects read words aloud in a neutral context, for example, the display XXX followed by the word METROPOLIS. This is the kind of condition that is thought to prime perceptual representation systems and that typically facilitates implicit tasks such as word completion. In a second acquisition condition subjects had to generate a word given its first letter and a semantically related context word; for example, given CITY−M__, the subject might generate METROPOLIS. This kind of task has been found not to prime word completion. These two study tasks were compared for their ability to prime performance on two different implicit memory tests. One test was a word-fragment completion test; for example, given instructions to complete the fragment M_T___OL_S with the first word that comes to mind, the subject might generate METROPOLIS. As predicted, performance on this test was primed by the neutral context study task relative to the semantic generation study task. In the second implicit memory test the subject attempted to answer general knowledge questions, for example, *In what fictional city did Clark Kent and Lois Lane live?* In this condition the priming relation was reversed. The semantic generation study task primed memory performance relative to the neutral context study task. This result is consistent with the prediction that declarative knowledge should be primed by processes that activate propositional-schematic networks.

Although implicit memory phenomena have become a valuable methodological probe for settling questions about the cognitive architecture, the possible functions of implicit memory, per se, have been less widely discussed. If we view priming effects as temporary elevations of accessibility in the standard processing subsystems of the architecture, however, then it makes sense to view implicit memory as a way of temporarily caching knowledge that has recently been used in particular circumstances on the bet that the knowledge is likely to be needed in similar circumstances in the near future. In von Neumann machines frequently used instructions or data are often cached in a separate memory store. This makes sense given the physical organization of computers. In the brain, which has many specialized processing subsystems and representations, and which seems to rely on the propagation of activation along connections for knowledge retrieval and processing, it would make more sense to accomplish caching via a relatively short-term mechanism for potentiating pathways.

Episodic versus Semantic Memory   The research on source-monitoring and on explicit memory is focused in part on the recollection of particular past occasions. Introspectively, we often feel a difference between remembering a past occasion, which is accompanied by a distinct conscious awareness of a particular moment or event, and remembering a fact. The difference is not just that memory for occasions involves dated, located autobiographical information and that mere factual memory does not, because it seems introspectively that an autobiographical memory can have the character of mere factual memory. Suppose that you remember that you took your first headfirst dive off a board in a neighborhood pool during the summer between the fifth and sixth grades. Although this fact concerns yourself, it might have roughly the same subjective status as remembering that Lincoln was the sixteenth president of the United States. Perhaps this is because you learned it from your mother or sister or worked it out for yourself, reasoning from other autobiographical information. On the other hand, your recollection might have the quality of actually being there, of being transported back to the experience. The term *semantic memory* is sometimes used to refer to memory for facts that is unaccompanied by the recollection of a past personal occasion, and the term *episodic memory* is sometimes used to refer to the conscious recollection of past episodes. Some researchers (Tulving 1983, 1993) have argued that distinct memory structures or processes must be postulated to explain differences between episodic and semantic memory.

As always, although introspection is a fertile source of hypotheses about cognition, it does not get us very far in evaluating them. The evidence for the reconstructive character of recall and the fallibility of source monitoring raises immediate questions about using differences in conscious awareness as evidence for distinct episodic and semantic memory systems. Researchers have documented errors in which a particular personal experience is judged to be the source of remembered information that actually originated in some other experience or in one's own thoughts at some previous time or even during retrieval. The lack of an absolutely reliable subjective criterion for episodic memory has become important in recent years in the context of psycho-therapy, where some clinicians work with patients on the recovery of ,childhood memories. Although many of these memories refer to actual events, others appear to be the result of fallible source-monitoring and reconstruction processes that are in part triggered by the misleading postevent suggestions that arise during therapy (Loftus 1993). This evidence does not strongly disconfirm the possibility of separate episodic and semantic systems. It does, however, suggest that if there are distinct systems, they must be highly interconnected, and they must feed representations into explicit judgment processes without reliable source-tags.

A plausible alternative hypothesis is that there are not separate systems. The declarative memory system as it has been outlined so far clearly contains many resources that might be used to account for differences between semantic and episodic memories. We might hypothesize that retrievable episodic memories have three important properties. First, they contain rich information about one's experience of the scene and the event that transpired. Second, they are well elaborated in terms of the self-schema. Third, they are relatively distinctive, or unique, so as not to suffer interference from the activation of thousands of similar traces. These properties would explain why we feel transported back to incidents like the diving scene but often not to breakfast three days ago. The lack of episodic content in the recall of semantic traces can also be explained by the lack of the same three factors. Why, for example, does remembering that Abraham Lincoln was the sixteenth president of the United States not evoke the memory of any specific event in one's life? Presumably this fact is associated most strongly with other facts about Lincoln and the Civil War period rather than with facts about oneself or facts and images about events during which this fact came up. Further, this fact and other facts about Lincoln may have occurred in hundreds of contexts (sitting in particular classrooms, reading particular books, and so on). To the extent that these contexts are activated at all, the activation will probably be weak and spread across a number of very similar pathways, making retrieval difficult.

Reiser, Black, and Abelson (1985) obtained evidence that the experience of an event is organized in terms of the general schema or script for the everyday activity that is going on. As a result, the episodic memory for the event is associated with the knowledge schema that guided perception and behavior during the event. Reiser, Black, and Abelson showed that people can readily retrieve episodic memories when they are cued with the name of an activity, such as "went to a restaurant." After reading such cues, subjects averaged 2.1 seconds to retrieve a specific episodic memory. These results demonstrate that semantic knowledge, in this case schemas for everyday actions, is richly interconnected with episodic memory. The evidence for such interconnections poses a challenge to the theorist who maintains that semantic and episodic memory are functionally distinct.

A number of researchers have looked to the brain for evidence that would help resolve questions about the episodic-semantic distinction. An experiment by Shimamura and Squire (1987), for example, suggests that there may be distinct deficits in declarative and episodic memory in amnesia. In the acquisition phase of the experiment, amnesic and control subjects studied obscure facts (e.g., "The name of the town through which Lady Godiva supposedly made her famous ride is Coventry"). Later, they were given a factual knowledge test that included the facts previously studied (e.g., "What is the name of the town through which Lady Godiva supposedly made her famous ride?"). This is an implicit memory test that taps declarative knowledge. The amnesic subjects were severely impaired in their ability to recall the studied facts. More precisely, their fact recall after a two-hour delay was equal to that of control subjects who were tested after a seven-day delay. This result is evidence against the notion that amnesia involves a generalized deficit in explicit memory. It favors the notion of a deficit in the formation of new declarative knowledge, whether that knowledge must be used implicitly or explicitly. Shimamura and Squire went on, however, to test explicit source memory in their subjects as well. Whenever patients correctly recalled a previously studied fact (e.g., Coventry), they were asked when they had last heard that fact. Amnesic subjects were much more likely than the seven-day-delay control subjects (who had equal levels of fact recall) to fail to remember that the study session was the last time that they heard the fact. Further, patients with severe source amnesia had about the same level of fact recall as patients with little source amnesia. That is, the severity of a patient's source amnesia could not be predicted from the severity of his or her fact-recall deficit. This dissociation of a deficit in declarative memory and a deficit in explicit memory suggests that there may indeed be something special about episodic memory.

Tulving (1993) describes a single case of amnesia that has a different character from the cases above and may provide even stronger support for the distinctness of episodic memory. In addition to a total source amnesia for recent events, the man in question, K. C., shows no episodic memory for his entire life. He cannot even remember highly distinctive life events, such as his brother's accidental death, or having his jaw wired shut for a week after a traffic accident. Like many other amnesics, however, his intelligence, factual knowledge, and language skills are intact. Although K. C.'s ability to acquire new factual knowledge is severely impaired, Tulving and his colleagues have established experimentally that he can acquire new facts, even though he has a complete source amnesia for those facts. This finding is illustrated by the following anecdote:

> When we drive by ... Toronto's Sky Dome—a structure built after K. C. became amnesic—he is familiar with it in the sense that he knows what it is and what its name is. Of course, when I ask him whether he has ever been inside, he says that he does not know; when I ask him, "When did you drive by here last time," he does not know; when I ask him whether he's ever seen it before, he says, "I guess so," and when I ask him to explain why he guesses so, he says, "Otherwise I would not know its name." (P 68)

There is evidence that source amnesia is related to frontal lobe damage as opposed to the medial temporal and diencephalic damage that is typically found in cases of amnesia. Frontal tissue may be involved in encoding and storing information about the spatial-temporal circumstances or contexts of events in one's life. The possibility that episodic memory involves particular brain tissue does not settle the matter of the distinctiveness of episodic memory at the computational level of analysis, however. It might still be fruitful to view episodic and semantic memory as a single declarative memory system that uses a common set of processes and representations. The fact that the processing or representation of spatial-temporal context is physically instantiated in particular tissue may allow a behaviorally dramatic type of brain lesion, but in itself it establishes very little about the computational details of those processes and representations. The issues at the computational level can only be settled by specifying the episodic-semantic theory more rigorously, so that it makes clear, testable predictions that are distinguishable from an equally well developed unitary model of declarative memory (McKoon, Ratcliff, and Dell 1986).

A particular type of neuropsychological data rarely compensates for the need to develop a theory further. Some of the reasons why data arising from brain scans or brain damage are no easier, and sometimes more difficult, to interpret than ordinary behavioral data are discussed further in chapter 7. Converging evidence from multiple behavioral and neuroscientific domains can be very helpful in sorting out hypotheses, as was seen above in Schacter's development of the PRS idea, but in such cases as well the data must be interpreted in light of a theory. The further progress of research on the episodic-semantic distinction rests, then, both on the development of new sources of evidence and on new theoretical ideas.

Connectionist Models of Memory   If we see human memory as mainly a matter of retrieving or activating knowledge that is relevant to current input, then connectionist networks have a number of attractive properties as models of memory. Their ability to compute complex input-output mappings can be seen as an ability to retrieve the knowledge that is appropriate to a given input. Networks can form interesting internal representations and can store mixtures of specific facts and generalizations. When given partial or noisy input, networks have the ability compute a correct or plausible output.

In spite of these attractions the connectionist approach has not been widely applied to many of the phenomena described in this section. In large part this is because a theory of human memory performance depends on a theory of the entire cognitive architecture. Some account of working memory and attention is necessary, as well as an account of the procedural-declarative distinction. The effects of elaboration cannot be accounted for without a fairly well developed theory of central mental representations and cognitive operations. Given the microstructural level at which connectionist theories are developed, it is not yet possible to model large chunks of the cognitive architecture. The successes of connectionist modeling have so far come in studies of subsystems of the architecture, of the learning of particular mappings that are important in human cognition (e.g., NETtalk, described in chapter 2), and of some of the general properties of networks, such as their ability to generalize and form categories.

The connectionist study of memory has also been set back by the discovery that some of the standard network architectures and learning algorithms are poor models of certain basic phenomena in human memory. Consider a standard three-layer network (containing input, hidden, and output layers) trained with the backpropagation algorithm described in chapter 2. The usual training regime for such networks involves repeated exposures to a set of correct input-output pairs (the training set). If the descent along the error surface (see figure 2.12) is kept reasonably conservative, the network's performance gradually approaches the correct input-output mapping as long as the training set is either equivalent to the ultimate test set or statistically representative of it. These training conditions and the resulting performance improvement might be plausible models for skill acquisition or category learning, but they are not so plausible for declarative memory. People often learn new facts with a single exposure, or perhaps a few exposures. They are able to retain facts over long periods of time without constant retraining or refreshing. The training regime for human declarative memory does not involve continuous cycling through a representative training set with gradual improvement across the entire set. If the backpropagation algorithm is applied in a training regime similar to those of everyday life or laboratory memory experiments, it is likely to produce poor results. In such a training regime, new items are constantly entering the training set, and there are periods of time when certain old items or sets of old items drop out of the training set but still must be retained. However, the algorithm has no way of preserving its knowledge of items that are not currently in the training set. The network's knowledge is contained in its weights, yet it adjusts *all* of its weights to minimize error on the current inputs. We might expect, then, that if some items are not currently being trained, the weight patterns that encoded those items might more or less quickly be destroyed as weights are readjusted to reduce error on new training pairs. That is, we might expect that in this type of network new learning would *interfere* with old learning much more radically than it actually does in human memory.

Several researchers have done computer simulation studies of networks that confirm these expectations (McCloskey and Cohen 1989; Ratcliff 1990). Ratcliff looked at recognition memory in the *encoder* architecture. An encoder network learns to reproduce the input vector after passing it through a layer of hidden units. That is, the network learns to compute the identity mapping, in which the correct output vector for a given input vector is identical to the input vector. Learning is required because the input units are fully connected to a hidden layer, which usually contains a smaller number of units, and which develops an internal representation of the input set. The measure of recognition memory is the similarity between the output vector actually produced by the network and the input vector. Such a similarity measure can be converted into a "Yes"-"No" recognition judgment using some reasonable decision rule. For example, if the similarity is greater than a certain threshold, say "Yes," otherwise say "No." Using networks of various sizes and training conditions similar to those in various types of memory experiments, Ratcliff confirmed the interference problem for the backpropagation algorithm. The networks tended to forget items that had dropped out of the training set and to give responses that reflected acquisition of the items that currently were in the training set. Unlike what happens in human learning, increasing the number of exposures to an item before it dropped out of the training set did not enhance its retention. A number of reasonable modifications of the networks and the algorithm did not change the results.

The unsuitability of the standard backpropagation model and its obvious variants for modeling certain memory phenomena should not be taken as evidence against the connectionist approach generally. Other network architectures and learning algorithms are being developed and explored. Kruschke's (1992) exemplar-based model, for example, does not suffer from catastrophic interference. The learning of particular items only affects the hidden units that respond to them. When training switches to new items, different hidden units are affected, thus preserving the original learning. Ultimately, the failure of a particular class of models can be taken as a sign of success in the sense that the models are specified clearly enough to make disconfirmable predictions. As we noted above in our discussion of the research on the episodic-semantic distinction, progress in research requires that theories and models make clear predictions.

3.3 Reasoning

As pointed out in section 2.6, goal-directed thought involves manipulating information to draw conclusions of various kinds. We decide what to do next, we predict what is likely to happen, we figure out why a certain event occurred, and we solve all manner of problems. In some cases the needed conclusions are directly available in declarative memory or perceptual input. In other cases, however, the conclusions can only be generated by processes that transform currently active representations to produce new information.

Deductive Reasoning

Traditionally, deductive reasoning refers to the use of rules to derive logically valid conclusions from sets of premises. To take a simple example, imagine that you are thinking about taking apart your washing machine. You do not have stored in your declarative knowledge base the proposition "My washing machine can't shock me," but you might arrive at this conclusion by retrieving the first three premises (P1–P3) below and deducing it as a valid conclusion (C2).

P1. If the cord on an electrical appliance is unplugged, then it cannot shock me.
P2. My washing machine is an electrical appliance.
P3. The cord on my washing machine is unplugged.

C1. If the cord on my washing machine is unplugged, then it cannot shock me.
C2. My washing machine cannot shock me.

The first conclusion, C1, is generated by an instantiation, or property inheritance, operation. That is, a washing machine is an instantiation of electrical appliance. The concept *washing machine* inherits the properties of its superordinate concept *electrical appliance*. This is essentially a matter of fitting an instance into a more general schema, a process that we have assumed throughout our discussions of cognitive processes and concepts. But a second, extremely important deductive process is involved as well. The desired conclusion, C2, is derived from C1 and P3 by a rule, or procedure, called *modus ponens*: Given propositions of the form *if P then Q* and *P*, derive *Q*. One of the inputs to modus ponens, then, is a *conditional*, or *if-then*, proposition, such as C1. A conditional consists of an *antecedent*, or if-part, and a *consequent*, or then-part. The other input to modus ponens is a proposition that matches the antecedent of the first input. The output of modus ponens is the consequent of the first input. Thus, since P3 matches the antecedent of C1, modus ponens can be applied, producing the consequent of C1. We are apparently able to make this kind of inferential leap quite effortlessly. The question is, How do we do it?

Deductive Systems   A mechanism for generating deductive inferences would be a system of formal rules, like modus ponens, that could be applied syntactically to propositions regardless of their content. Philosophers and mathematicians have described powerful versions of such systems (e.g., the first-order predicate calculus, discussed in chapter 4). The rules in such systems are completely formal, and they deal only with the logical aspects of propositions, such as the *logical connectives* (*if-then, not, and, or, if-and-only-if*) and *quantifiers* (*every, all, some*). Because of these properties, they are extremely general. Modus ponens is an example. It is purely formal because it applies any time the antecedent of a conditional premise matches another premise. It is general because the antecedent, *P*, and the consequent, *Q*, can be any proposition, regardless of content. Rips (1988) has shown how goal-oriented productions can be used to build a psychologically plausible deductive system. It would seem to be a good thing if an adequate set of deductive rules were either built into the cognitive architecture or acquired naturally during experience. Indeed, modus ponens and rules involving conjunction (e.g., if *P and Q* is a goal, establish *P* and *Q* separately) can be argued to be ubiquitous in human cognition.

Experimental Evidence: The Selection Task   There is evidence, however, that people do not acquire a general deductive system based on formal syntactic rules. Consider the selection task (Wason and Johnson-Laird 1972). The subject is presented with four cards, each bearing a single character.

     E   K   4   7

The subject is told that each card has a number on one side and a letter on the other side and that the following conditional statement is true: If a card has a vowel on one side, then it has an even number on the other side. The subject is then asked to pick exactly the cards that must be turned over in order to figure out whether the conditional statement is true.

A common response is to pick only the card with the vowel. This amounts to applying modus ponens. The *E* satisfies the antecedent of the conditional, so the consequent had better be true, which can be determined by turning over the card. Our hypothetical subject errs, however, in not also picking the card with a 7. To see this, suppose that the card was turned over and found to have an *A* on the other side. The card would violate the conditional. The error is in effect a failure to apply another rule of logic called *modus tollendo tollens*: If a conditional is true, and its consequent is false, then it follows that its antecedent is false. In our first example, if your washing machine shocked you, then it was plugged in.

The high rate of error on the selection task has suggested to many researchers that most people do not possess a fully general formal deductive system. It was discovered early on, however, that making the selection task less abstract by introducing more concrete content into it sometimes improved people's performance. In one such study D'Andrade (1982) asked subjects to imagine that they managed a store in which the following rule was in force: If a purchase exceeds $30, then the receipt must have the manager's signature on the back. The subjects showed considerable insight into the need to check the amounts on receipts with no signature. However, practice on this problem did not improve their performance on abstract versions of the task. A pure deductive-system theory cannot explain this finding. Since formal deductive rules apply to the forms of propositions regardless of their content, changes in content should not affect the operation of a deductive system. The mere introduction of more concrete content, however, does not explain the finding either, since not all concrete versions of the problem produce facilitation. Manktelow and Evans (1979), for example, failed to find facilitation in a version of the task that used the rule, "If I eat haddock, then I drink gin."

Pragmatic Reasoning Schemas   One possible approach to the influence of content is case-based reasoning (Riesbeck and Schank 1989). In this kind of approach reasoning is successful to the extent that the content of the problem evokes a past similar case. Some sort of analogy-finding process is required to map the current case onto the analogous case. Most subjects in the check-cashing study had presumably never had to enforce a check-verification rule, so a case-based explanation would require mapping the situation onto a similar situation, such as experiencing this type of rule as a customer. Case-based reasoning is discussed further in chapters 4 and 5.

Cheng and Holyoak (1985) took a somewhat different approach, proposing a theory of *pragmatic reasoning schemas*. Such schemas differ from formal deductive rules in several respects. They apply to a class of situations rather than to propositions of a given form. Therefore, they are sensitive to context and are not strictly syntactic. Situations involving permission were one class of situations studied. Situations involving obligation and causation are other examples. A pragmatic reasoning schema consists of a set of deductive rules, represented as production rules, that are specific to the relevant class of situations and that are related to goals in that situation. In a permission situation, for example, a person might have a goal of performing a certain action or of avoiding punishment. As a developed knowledge structure that covers a whole class of situations, a pragmatic reasoning schema also differs from the specific cases used in case-based reasoning. In an unfamiliar situation the schema can be directly evoked by features of the situation that fit the schema without the need of an analogy-mapping process.

A familiar permission situation is the common rule that only people over the age of twenty-one may drink alcohol. Cheng and Holyoak propose that in general a permission situation involves a precondition, P (e.g., over twenty-one), that must be satisfied if some action, A (e.g., drinking), is to be taken. The schema will tend to be evoked in situations where a desired action is regulated by some authority. The hypothesized content of the schema is four production rules:

1. If A is to be taken, then P must be satisfied.
2. If A is not to be taken, then P need not be satisfied.
3. If P is satisfied, then A may be taken.
4. If P is not satisfied, then A must not be taken.

Note that the antecedents of the four rules correspond to the four possibilities that are tested in the selection task. Therefore, subjects who have learned the permission schema ought to perform correctly in a selection task that clearly involves permission. The idea is that in repeated encounters with permission situations people learn to recognize them and develop rules for dealing with each of the ways that they present themselves.

The four rules correspond to more general principles of deductive reasoning. In a situation where A is to be taken, rule 1 corresponds to modus ponens. Rule 4 corresponds to modus tollens. Rule 2 blocks an error called denying the antecedent, in which the person incorrectly derives *not Q* from *if P then Q* and *not P*. Rule 3 blocks a related error known as affirming the consequent, in which the person incorrectly derives *P* from *if P then Q* and *Q*. The rules are not equivalent to the general logical rules, however. First, they are evoked by the features of permission situations rather than by the general syntactic form of propositions. Second, they involve the so-called deontic concepts of permission (may) and obligation (must), whereas the general deductive rules involve only the conditional and negation. Rule 3 is not even logically valid if there are two or more preconditions for the action.

In one of their experiments Cheng and Holyoak compared subjects' performance under rules that had a permission rationale with performance under the same rules with no rationales given. For example, in one of the no-rationale conditions subjects were to imagine that they were postal clerks checking letters for compliance with the following rule: if a letter is sealed, then it must carry a 20-cent stamp. The regulatory setting and the use of the deontic term *must* in the rule should have some power to invoke the permission schema, so performance should be better than in completely abstract versions of the problem. In the rationale condition subjects were told that the reason for the rule is to increase profit from personal mail, which is nearly always sealed, and that sealed letters are defined as personal and therefore must carry more postage than unsealed letters. The researchers reasoned that the rationale would make the rule appear less arbitrary and help evoke the permission schema. Performance in the rationale condition was indeed much better than in the no-rationale condition among Michigan college students. The results were very different among Hong Kong students, however. A postal rule much like the one in the experiment had recently been in force in Hong Kong, so the presumption was that the Hong Kong subjects already knew the rationale for such rules. They performed equally well in both conditions. However, when they were given a different rule, with which they were not familiar, the effect of the rationale manipulation was the same as it had been in Michigan. In a second experiment Cheng and Holyoak showed that performance on the abstract version of the task could be improved substantially by stating it in bare-bones permission form. Subjects were asked to imagine that they were authorities checking whether people were obeying regulations of the form, "If one is to take action A, then one must first satisfy precondition P."

Mental Models   One question about Cheng and Holyoak's proposal is whether their results unambiguously support the existence of productions that take the form of deductive rules. Johnson-Laird and his colleagues (Johnson-Laird 1983; Johnson-Laird and Byrne 1991) have argued that people typically do not reason by applying deductive rules, even of the restricted kind proposed in the theory of pragmatic reasoning schemas. Rather, they use the problem description to construct mental models that represent various possibilities and then check the models to see if any of them violate the desired conclusion. A simple conditional, *if P then Q*, is hypothesized to lead most people to set up a rather impoverished mental model, consisting of a case (*P, Q*), which contains both *P* and *Q*, and another possible case (. . .), containing no specified content. In permission versions of the selection problem, knowledge of permission situations or of the meanings of deontic terms is hypothesized to lead the subject to construct more models, such as a complete set of models for a true conditional, (*P, Q*), (*not P, Q*), and (*not P, not Q*), and possibly a model for the situation that renders the conditional false (*P, not Q*). Such a set of models can be successfully compared to the four cards. For example, a card containing *not Q* can be evaluated by looking at the models containing *not Q*. Since one model is satisfactory and the other is not, the card must be turned over. The evaluation of the relative merits of the pragmatic reasoning schema approach and the mental models approach is still proceeding. Many people's deductive reasoning may blend syntactic rules and models, since the cognitive architecture as we have sketched it permits both. A mental model is still a cognitive representation. It just has a different structure than a proposition, and different operations apply to it. Reasoning with mental models is also potentially as powerful as reasoning with rules. As we pointed out in chapter 1, since formal expressions have a representational mapping to their domains (models), meaningful rule-governed operations on those expressions map onto operations in the domain (model). *Mental* models, then, are simply an alternative, somewhat more direct representation of the domain. In spite of their potential generality, however, people rather systematically fail to exploit their full power. Further philosophical and mathematical aspects of the relationship between formal logical expressions and models are taken up in chapter 10.

A somewhat vexing question is why more comprehensive logical reasoning capacities are neither part of the cognitive architecture nor naturally acquired by most people. One possibility is that concrete knowledge is more useful in the practical reasoning situations that human beings typically face. In the washing-machine example reasoning would typically be less a matter of processing the forms of a few propositions than of processing a model that included electric current flowing through wires. Genuinely practical reasoning about the possibility of being shocked requires a rich model that includes notions of insulation and grounding, and of alternative possible sources of power, such as batteries or capacitors. The result may be that natural circumstances rarely arise in which a person's goals and experiences lead to the acquisition of maximally abstract deductive reasoning schemas or procedures. The potential usefulness of formal logic may be further restricted by the severely limited capacity of the controlled processes that might be required to apply logical rules to large sets of premises. The role of formal logic in artificial intelligence (AI) systems, which are not necessarily limited in this way, will be discussed in chapter 4. The AI researcher can explore the question of whether logic would be more useful if more raw computational power were available or whether its limitations are more fundamental.

The theory of deductive reasoning via mental models illustrates three general themes in human reasoning and problem solving. The first is the strong influence of specific knowledge structures on intelligent thought. In the case of deductive logic, highly general formal principles that are independent of any particular context could be part of everyday information processing, but they seem not to be. The second theme is the tension between *normative* or *prescriptive* principles and the actual procedures that people follow. The rules of deductive logic developed by logicians from Aristotle onward are normative in the sense that they can be shown to yield valid inferences. Yet people often violate the normative standard, as in the selection task. The third theme concerns the question of how people manage to get around successfully, if they do not follow normatively correct principles. The answer seems to be that human thought is *heuristic*. That is, people employ procedures that are efficient and that work most of the time, even though they sometimes lead to error.

Reasoning and Connectionism

Reasoning and problem solving pose large challenges for connectionism. They tend to be serially extended in time, to show evidence of structure-sensitive processing, and to resist regimentation into fixed-length input and output formats. In the washing-machine example conclusion C1 is derived first and then is used as a premise in deriving C2. Modus ponens is a structure-sensitive rule that has to be able to isolate the antecedent and consequent of a conditional and match the antecedent against another premise. The antecedent, consequent, and matching premise can have any propositional content, making it impossible to code them directly into fixed-length vectors. Moreover, modus ponens may have to find its two input premises among more than two candidates. None of these problems is insurmountable (at the very least a connectionist implementation could be developed for deductive rules or model-based reasoning), but they make connectionist modeling in this domain more difficult than it is for perception or categorization.

There are good arguments, however, for pursuing connectionist approaches to some aspects of inference. Shastri and Ajjanagadde (1992) have focused on the nearly effortless inferences we make in understanding ordinary situations or stories. In chapter 2 and in sections 3.1 and 3.2 we have already pointed out that the activation of schematic knowledge triggers inferences. When we hear that John sold a book to Mary, we infer that Mary now owns the book. This inference is similar to the washing-machine example.

D1. For all x, y, z: if x sold y to z, then z owns y.
P1. John sold book3 to Mary.

C1. If John sold book3 to Mary, then Mary owns book3.
C2. Mary owns book3.

The general knowledge involved here, D1, can be considered part of the core representation of *sell*. Again, two processes are required to make the inference. First, some process has to map D1 onto the event involving John, Mary, and book3. Here, the process is called *variable binding*: the variables x, y, and z are bound to John, book3, and Mary, respectively, producing C1. The second process is to infer C2. As we did in the examples above, we can see this as an application of modus ponens, inferring C2 from P1 and C1. Within the classical theory of the cognitive architecture, the explanation most ready at hand for this inference involves considerable use of working memory. An active representation of the incoming information P1 would lead, via spreading activation, to the retrieval of the schematic information D1. P1 and D1 together would satisfy the input conditions of a variable-binding process, which would then produce C1, adding it to working memory. P1 and C1 together would satisfy the input conditions of modus ponens, which would produce C2, adding it to working memory.

Shastri and Ajjanagadde argue that these simple, or reflexive, inferences are made with remarkable efficiency. They are made in real time, during the course of conversation, reading, or thought, taking probably a few hundred milliseconds on average. The process just outlined looks suspiciously working-memory intensive from this perspective. Furthermore, as our long-term knowledge base grows, there is no obvious increase in the amount of time such inferences take. This could pose a problem for our classical account, because the activation of the *sell* concept could spill quite a few propositions into working memory in many contexts, triggering an episode of problem solving.

There is an alternative classical account, however, that does not have these defects. All of the processing can be looked upon as the application of a single production rule. The rule would be triggered by the occurrence of a *sell* proposition in working memory. Its action would be to add an *own* proposition with the proper variable bindings to working memory (i.e., the *recipient* of *sell* is bound to the *subject* of *own*, and the *object* of *sell* is bound to the *object* of *own*). Under this account neither the schematic proposition D1 nor its instantiation C1 is ever added to working memory, and the general inference rule modus ponens is never applied. The use of production rules that are specific to particular concepts to reduce the load on working memory and the need for general deductive machinery is a standard idea in classical theories (Winograd 1972, for example, advocated such a procedural semantics). In consonance with our treatment of skill acquisition in chapter 2, this production, and others like it, could arise from the compilation of a frequently occurring, working-memory intensive inference, such as the inference deriving C2 above. Like other productions, these conceptual-inference productions could be accessed and to some extent applied in parallel. Perhaps the major loose end in this proposal is that no computational mechanism is specified for accessing and applying the productions in parallel.

In a connectionist context we could imagine hardwiring such rules into a network or setting up a network that could learn them. The most immediate problem with this proposal is the necessity of variable binding. Each application of such rules requires that any variables in the rule be bound to the specific objects that figure in the current input representation. Variable binding is difficult to implement in connectionist networks (Fodor and Pylyshyn 1988) and has become a major issue in connectionist research (Smolensky 1990). Connections cannot be dedicated to particular bindings, because novel bindings occur all the time. But simply simultaneously activating all the relevant nodes fails to distinguish what is bound to what. In Shastri and Ajjanagadde's model a binding relationship between two nodes is encoded by their synchronized rhythmic firing. Their network is a modified semantic network, which encodes both factual knowledge and the production rules. A part of such a network is schematically illustrated in figure 3.4. As depicted, the network uses local rather than distributed coding, with each node involved in the representation of only one concept. If each node were implemented as an ensemble of units at a lower level, however, nodes could be encoded distributively over the lower-level units. The single nodes for individuals (Mary, John, book3, etc.) are *focal* nodes that would be connected to many other nodes, representing information about those individuals. A number of nodes are required to represent each predicate, although only the argument nodes are shown. The connections between predicates represent production rules. Activation along a set of connections applies the rule with the proper variable binding.

The assumptions about activation are rather different from those for other networks we have looked at. In standard networks, at a given moment, a unit has an activation level, which can be represented as a number. In Shastri and Ajjanagadde's network, once a unit exceeds threshold, it emits pulses rhythmically. In addition to the fact that a unit is firing, the timing of its pulses has representational significance. The binding of an argument node to an entity node is represented by their synchronous (or in-phase) firing. Figure 3.5 illustrates how synchronous firing is used to encode the initial bindings and how the firing of a rule establishes the appropriate new bindings. Although only one rule is shown in the figure, it should be clear that rules can fire in parallel as activation spreads through the network. Since the rules are firing in parallel, the

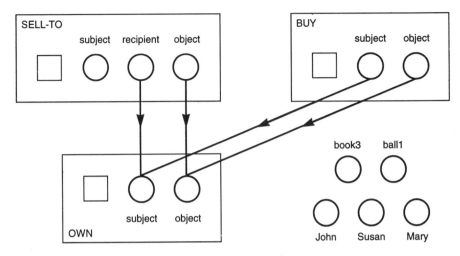

Figure 3.4
A network representing the three predicate concepts SELL-TO, BUY, and OWN, as well as the focal nodes for the representations of five entities: John, Mary, and so on. The arrows from SELL-TO to OWN represent the rule that if x sells y to z, then z owns y. The arrows from BUY to OWN represent the rule that if x buys y, then x owns y. The arrows map argument nodes of antecedent predicates onto the correct argument nodes of consequent predicates. The large rectangles demarcate the nodes involved in the representation of each predicate. The squares represent aspects of predicate representation that are not discussed here. (Adapted with permission from Shastri and Ajjanagadde 1992.)

amount of time needed for an episode of reflexive reasoning is not determined by the number of inferences made but by the length of the longest chain of rules. The main limitation that is apparent from the figure is the number of separate phases that can be maintained. Each entity involved in an episode of reasoning must be assigned a distinct phase. As can be seen from the figure, the number of phases that can be kept distinct depends on the time between pulses and the ability of the system to discriminate small phase differences. This limitation is not severe, however, because reflexive reasoning rarely involves more than a handful of entities. The researchers also show how the inference rules can be made probabilistic and context sensitive.

The use of phase relationships to accomplish dynamic variable binding has considerable neural plausibility. The neurons in the brain fire in rhythmic trains of pulses (see chapter 7 for details), and there is some evidence that synchronous neural firing has representational significance (Gray and Singer 1989). The model as illustrated in figures 3.4 and 3.5 has to be fleshed out in various ways. An input mechanism must be specified that creates the initial phases and phase correspondences. Since the variable bindings and inferences are transient, some mechanism must be developed for storing new facts permanently in the network. A mechanism is needed for learning the productions, and some account must be given of how reflexive inference is related to reasoning or problem solving that is extended in time and working-memory intensive.

Overall, Shastri and Ajjanagadde's research is an example of what appears to be a growing convergence of the classical theory of production systems and connectionist theory (Anderson 1993, for example, presents further ideas about this convergence).

(a)

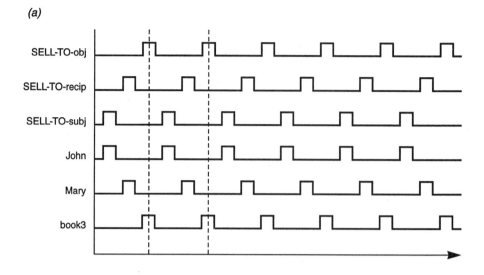

(b)

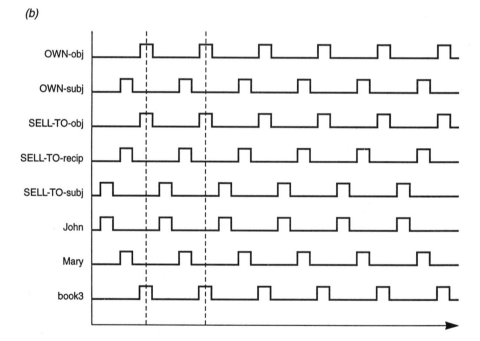

Figure 3.5

Illustration of how synchronous firing represents binding relationships. (*a*) The dynamic encoding of *John sold the book to Mary*. Each horizontal line on the graph represents the pulse train of a unit. Each blip on a line represents a pulse. Notice that the *John*, *Mary*, and *book3* units are firing in different rhythms. They are out of phase. The *John* unit is firing in phase with the subject unit of *sell-to*, representing the dynamic binding of *John* to the subject variable. The *Mary* unit is bound to the recipient unit of *sell-to*. The synchronous firing of these two nodes is highlighted by the two vertical dotted lines. Finally, the *book3* unit is firing in phase with the object unit of *sell-to*. (*b*) Dynamic binding relationships after activation propagates from *sell-to* to *own*, thus applying the rule *if x sells y to z, then z owns y*. The model assumes that when a unit becomes activated, it fires in synchrony with the node that is driving it. The *Mary* unit

Nondeductive Reasoning

As we pointed out in the discussion of deduction, most practical reasoning contains significant nondeductive elements. Even the simplest examples of inference that we explored above were mixtures of deductive and nondeductive reasoning. The application of a rule such as modus ponens, whether it is applied explicitly or assumed in a production rule, is purely deductive. On the other hand, the premises that the rule is applied to are often generated nondeductively on the basis of probabilistic characteristics of categories. The total inferential episode is thus *inductive*, that is, based at least implicitly on empirical hypotheses about the world that could be false. The washing-machine example involved the premise *If the cord on an electrical appliance is unplugged, then it cannot shock me.* This premise might be the result both of a generalization over exemplars of electrical appliances and of a theory or mental model of how appliances work. It is actually false, since some electrical appliances, such as TV sets, contain components that can hold a substantial electrical charge after they are turned off and unplugged.

Inductive Heuristics   Our awareness of the inductive nature of most of our reasoning varies considerably. Simple, schema-based inferences are typically not accompanied by any feeling of coping with uncertainty. They can be seen as simple cases of an availability heuristic (Tversky and Kahneman 1973), a general tendency to reason on the basis of information available in memory or the environment. This heuristic comes out in more extended, effortful cases of inductive reasoning as well. Try, for example, to estimate whether there are more English words that begin with *r* or more that have *r* in the third position. To make this estimate, most people generate cases of both types of words and choose the type for which they find the most cases. The procedures that access the mental dictionary, however, make it much easier to retrieve words in terms of their initial sounds. Thus, most people generate more cases of *r*-initial words and incorrectly estimate that they are more common (Tversky and Kahneman 1973).

Availability has been shown to influence social reasoning and judgment, as well. In a study by Taylor and Fiske (1975) subjects observed conversations between two people and were then asked to judge how influential each actor had been in the conversation. Some observers could see the face of only one actor. These observers thought that the person they could see clearly was more influential, whereas observers who could see both participants equally well judged them to be equally influential. The perceptual availability of one participant's behavior apparently led to more attention to and encoding of that participant's contributions. At the time of judgment easily available recall led to exaggerated judgments of influence. In related experiments a number of researchers have found that nearly any characteristic that makes a person distinctive, or *salient*, in a group interaction will lead to more extreme social judgments about the person (Fiske and Taylor 1991; chap. 9).

The dependence on schematic knowledge structures also leads to another heuristic in probabilistic reasoning, known as the *representativeness* heuristic. Try making the following two probability estimations:

---

is now also firing synchronously with the subject unit of *own*, and the *book3* unit is also firing synchronously with the object unit of *own* (as illustrated by the vertical dotted lines). (Adapted with permission from Shastri and Ajjanagadde 1992.)

1. A group of 100 people contains 70 engineers and 30 lawyers. One person is ch seroat random from the group. What is the probability that the person is an engineer?

2. Now, another person is chosen randomly from the same group, who has been described by a friend as follows:

> Jack is a forty-five-year-old man. He is married and has four children. He is generally conservative, careful, and ambitious. He shows no interest in political and social issues and spends most of his free time on his many hobbies, which include home carpentry, sailing, and mathematical puzzles.

What is the probability that Jack is an engineer?

In a study by Kahneman and Tversky (1973) the average subject gave a .7 probability estimate on the first question and a .9 probability estimate on the second question. In the first case subjects were responding normatively to what decision theorists call the *prior odds* or *base rates* in the population. In the second case they used the information that Jack is typical, or representative, of the class of engineers to revise their estimate.

Kahneman and Tversky were able to show, however, that the revised estimate in the second case does not obey the normative principles of the decision theorist. A second group of subjects answered the same questions as the first group, with one change. The second group was told that the population of 100 people contained 30 engineers and 70 lawyers. The average subject gave a .3 estimate on the first question and a .9 estimate on the second question. This result shows that on the second question subjects were basing their estimates only on the typicality, or representativeness, of the personality description. The estimate was unaffected by the difference in prior odds. Statistical decision theorists have shown, however, that optimal predictions require taking into account both the known evidence and the prior odds. The basic reason for this is that there is some probability that a person who is a lawyer would have Jack's personality description. The chances of sampling such a person are higher in a group having a higher proportion of lawyers. Subjects behaving normatively would have given lower estimates about Jack on the second version of the problem.

The representativeness heuristic is probably successful in much of everyday life. Assigning objects or situations to categories on the basis of typicality seems to be pretty successful much of the time (although the extent to which concept learning actually takes base rates into account is still under study; e.g., Kruschke 1992). It may be that in most situations the evidence is strong enough to overwhelm the prior odds. At times the prior odds of various possibilities may be close enough not to matter, and at other times there would be no way to estimate them anyway. But there are cases where representativeness and availability combine to produce serious practical errors. Chapman and Chapman (1967) studied *illusory correlations* in the use of the Draw-a-Person Test (DAP), which is used in psychiatric and psychological diagnosis. Clinicians believed (and to some extent still believe) that when asked to draw a person, paranoid patients tend to emphasize the eyes, dependent patients the mouth, and so on. Careful statistical studies of the DAP have shown that these correlations do not actually exist. Chapman and Chapman gave a group of college students a set of data, which consisted of randomly paired drawings and psychological symptoms. Although there were no correlations between drawing characteristics and symptoms in the data (because of the random pairing), the subjects "discovered" the same correlations that the clinicians believed in. It seemed likely that subjects devoted more attention and encoding to pairs that were representative of stereotypes that they already held and that these pairs were more available in later memory for the evidence. Chapman and Chapman found evidence supporting this explanation by asking another group of subjects to simply list the body parts that were called to mind by each of the symptoms. The associative connections revealed by this technique predicted the illusory correlations extremely well. Hamilton (1979) has applied a similar analysis to racial stereotyping.

Learning to Apply Normative Rules   In the picture we have developed so far, human reasoning is heavily influenced by the retrieval of situation-relevant productions and schemas (as well as specific cases or sets of exemplars). The success of human reasoning is based in large part on the mind's enormous capacity to store knowledge structures and to retrieve them appropriately. The representativeness and availability heuristics can be seen not so much as consciously applied strategies as the natural outcome of the tendency to go with what memory and the environment deliver. Limited-capacity controlled processes function to fit active representations to current goals.

It is important to note, however, that human beings have been able to overcome the limitations of concrete and heuristic reasoning to develop highly general normative theories. The question of how the great logicians and statisticians were able to come up with their normative theories is beyond our purview at the moment, but questions about how well people can learn these theories and incorporate them into their everyday cognition are more immediately accessible. Given that a normative theory exists, it is not hard to see that people can store the rules of the theory in the declarative knowledge base and develop procedures for interpretively applying them. If the information processes required are too complex, then one can use external aids for memory storage and calculation, such as writing all of one's observations down on a sheet of paper and computing a correlation coefficient with an electronic calculator. Although the research by the Chapmans and others (for instance, Tversky and Kahneman 1971) demonstrates that even trained professionals can unconsciously slip into normatively incorrect heuristic reasoning, some recent research gives more cause for optimism.

Nisbett and his colleagues (Nisbett 1993) have found evidence that people do tend to develop abstract rules for reasoning that are similar to the rules of normative theories. These rules are applied inconsistently, depending on various contextual cues. An inductive example is the *law of large numbers*, which asserts that a large random sample drawn from a variable population is more likely to reveal the characteristics of the population than a small sample. The following problem is adapted from the work of Jepson, Krantz, and Nisbett (1983):

> The registrar's office at a large university has found that there are usually about 100 students in Arts and Sciences who have a perfect academic record (grades of *A* in all courses) at the end of their first term at the university. However, only about 10 to 15 students graduate with a perfect record through all four years. What do you think is the most likely explanation for the fact that there are more students with perfect records after one term than at graduation?

A statistical answer to this question would somehow make the point that many students' performances in a single term will be unrepresentative of their overall performances or abilities. For example, the subject might simply point out that it is much more difficult to be perfect for eight straight terms than for one. Nonstatistical answers would tend to show evidence of the representativeness heuristic, which would fit the problem into a causal theory about student performance. An example noted by the researchers was a response that argued that students tend to work harder when they first come to college than they do near graduation.

The degree to which peoples' reasoning reflects their intuitive conception of the law of large numbers depends on the degree to which a situation has statistical features. The degree to which situations involve factors that are commonly thought to involve chance variation varies considerably, for example, as does the degree to which they involve any sort of repeated sampling that can be systematically summarized. Nisbett and his colleagues deliberately varied these factors in some of their studies and found that the more "statistical" cues were present in a situation, the more likely subjects were to give answers based on the law of large numbers. The academic performace problem above, for example, evoked an intermediate proportion of statistical answers, about one-third. Over 90 percent of the answers to a problem about lung cancer and smoking drew statistical answers. On the other hand, very few statistical answers were given to a problem that asked students to weigh their own personal experience of going to a single meeting of a university course against the results of an opinion poll that surveyed all students who had just completed the course.

The natural occurrence but inconsistent application of abstract rules for reasoning suggests that appropriate training might increase the consistency and accuracy of use. Fong, Krantz, and Nisbett (1986) showed that a single training session on the law of large numbers markedly improved both the frequency with which subjects applied the law and the quality of their reasoning with it. Training sessions that featured a standard formal presentation of the statistical theory and training sessions that featured examples that were analyzed using statistical reasoning both were effective, and an even larger effect was found when the formal and examples training methods were combined. Given the effects of problem content that are common in studies of reasoning, a striking finding of the study was that subjects were able to apply the law to a wide range of problem content, including domains that were not obviously statistical and that were not covered in the training (the academic performance problem above would be an example). In an ingenious second study the researchers showed that the same findings held for students in a standard introductory statistics class. Students were contacted by phone outside of class and asked to participate in a sports opinion survey that included a number of questions that could be answered either statistically or nonstatistically. Students called at the beginning of the course tended to give non-statistical answers, but students called at the end of the course tended to give statistical answers.

The independent effect of examples training suggests that subjects can learn to recognize features in a situation that make statistical reasoning appropriate. The lack of content effects suggests that such features must be quite abstract, however. At this point the precise nature of such features is not known, although the results on expert problem solving discussed in the next section suggest that it is possible to learn to recognize abstract or nonobvious features of situations.

The Complexity of Reasoning
It is apparent that no simple theory of human reasoning will suffice to explain all that is known. Inferences based on a categorization can be the result of unconscious statistical generalization over exemplars. Yet the deliberate application of normative

statistical principles is needed to explain other cases. Reasoning can be based on the recall of a single experience, on the evocation of a pragmatic schema that generalizes across a range of related situations, or on the application of a completely general formal rule, such as modus ponens. The knowledge that enables reasoning can be stored procedurally or declaratively, and episodes of reasoning range from virtually automatic to highly attention demanding. The implications for cognitive science are nicely summed up by Smith, Langston, and Nisbett (1992).

One way of looking at the situation from the point of view of the classical theory of the cognitive architecture is that all aspects of the architecture participate in reasoning (just as we found them to participate in memory). The cognitive architecture could be viewed as a highly intricate inference engine. Goal-directed cognition is largely a matter of arriving at decisions, predictions, conclusions, judgments, and actions, all of which either are inferences or involve inference in some sense. The architecture is structured in such a way that the needed inferences can be delivered on several timescales using a wide range of information.

3.4 Problem Solving

Reasoning and problem solving overlap considerably, and some researchers have attempted to combine theories of the two processes (see, for example, Newell 1980; Stillings 1975). Typically, researchers speak of problem solving, as opposed to reasoning, when the needed principles are more specific to a domain (such as chess, sewing, or physics) and when the information processing needed to reach the desired goal takes place over an extended period of time. Some of the most interesting findings concern the contrast between novice and expert problem solving. The general theory of the acquisition of cognitive skills, sketched in chapter 2, gives a good account of the striking improvements that occur when a person practices solving problems in a particular domain. We will use the two domains of chess and physics problems to illustrate this research.

Novice Problem Solving

In their studies of problem solving Newell and Simon (1972) developed several concepts that characterize human problem solving in relatively unfamiliar domains. The concepts were incorporated in their theory of the *General Problem Solver* (GPS). The processes of subgoaling and means-ends analysis, introduced in section 2.6, are key concepts of GPS. In the GPS theory a person's problem-solving efforts are said to take place within a *problem space*, consisting of potential *states* of knowledge and *operators* that transform one state of knowledge into another.

The Novice Chess Player as a General Problem Solver   In the basic problem space for the game of chess the states are the possible configurations of the pieces on the board, and the operators are the legal moves. On a particular turn the problem that a player faces is to select a move that maximizes the chances of winning the game. The player can search the problem space by imagining various moves, the opponent's possible replies, further moves, and so on. Chess is typical of difficult problems, however, in that it is impossible to search the entire problem space to find the best possible solution. In fact, just to search all possibilities for the next three moves early in a chess game, a player would have to imagine well over 1,000 sequences of moves (if there are more than 10 possible moves on each turn, then there are more than $10^3 = 1,000$ possible sequences). The problem solver is thus forced to use heuristic methods.

The fundamental heuristic method identified by Newell and Simon was means-ends analysis. The problem solver tries to select operators, the means, that will achieve the end, or solution to the problem. The basic principle of operator selection is *difference reduction*; that is, operators are selected that reduce the difference between the current state of the problem and the desired end, or goal. The final goal is often reached by establishing and achieving a series of subgoals that represent partial solutions.

A novice chess player might have the subgoal of keeping the king out of immediate danger. On a certain turn this might lead to a further subgoal of protecting a certain square that could be reached by one of the opponent's bishops. The problem is then to select an operator (move) that will defend that square. If two possible defending moves are discovered, then they must be evaluated in terms of other subgoals, such as keeping control of the center of the board or defending the queen. This kind of strategy is highly heuristic because it drastically cuts down on the possible moves that are actually examined and because it can fail to examine possibilities that are crucial to the ultimate goal of winning (or not losing) the game.

Heuristic search via means-ends analysis is a vast improvement over exhaustive search or trial and error, and it is one of the most typical strengths of human intelligence. Once a person is able to represent the states and operators of a problem, the method can be used. Nevertheless, it is a form of unskilled cognition, slow and error prone. As we saw in chapter 2, means-ends analysis makes heavy demands on controlled processing. The currently relevant subgoals and the possible states of the problem being considered must be maintained in an active state. The operators are stored in declarative memory and must be accessed interpretively by the general means-ends process. Limited working-memory capacity can be quickly overwhelmed by the game of chess. Over twenty different operators can be relevant on a given turn. A number of different heuristics, such as protecting the king and controlling the center, can be active, causing subgoals to be constructed. Each subgoal can lead to the consideration of more than one move. It is not surprising that beginners play rather poor chess.

The Beginning Physics Student as a General Problem Solver   Although solving elementary word problems in introductory physics is very different from playing chess, the beginning physics student uses the same general problem-solving method as the novice chess player. The states and operators are different, of course. The typical beginning physics student operates in what Larkin (1981) has called an *algebraic problem space*. The student has acquired a set of equations that interrelate a number of fundamental physical variables. Figure 3.6 illustrates part of such a set of equations. The student uses the equations as operators: evaluating the algebraic expression on the right side of an equation yields the value of the variable on the left side. A state of knowledge is simply a list of the physical variables that figure in the current problem, some of which have been assigned values and some of which remain to be determined.

To solve a word problem, the student forms a representation of the text of the problem, which consists of variables whose values are given in the problem and variables whose values are the final goal state. The student then works backward from the goal by finding an equation (operator) containing the goal variable, usually on its left side. Finding the values of the other variables in the equation (usually on the right

E1. $v_f = v_0 + at$
E2. $x = v_0 t + .5at^2$
E3. $v_f^2 = v_o^2 + 2ax$
E4. $v_a = (v_o + v_f)/2$
E5. $x = v_a t$

Where:

t is the interval of time from the initial to the final state of a body
x is the distance traveled by the body during the time interval
v_0 is the initial velocity of the body
v_f is the final velocity of the body
v_a is the average velocity of the body
a is the acceleration of the body
      for a body under gravitational force $a = 9.8$ m/s^2

Figure 3.6
Some kinematic equations memorized by a beginning physics student. (Based on Larkin 1981.)

side) is then set as a subgoal. This general heuristic of working backward from the goal can be applied again to subgoals, if necessary, to finally reach equations that can be evaluated in terms of the given variables. Larkin and her associates (Larkin 1981; Larkin et al. 1980) found that beginning physics students used this strategy. Larkin wrote a computer program, called "barely ABLE," that solved problems using the same strategy.

The following problem provides an illustration:

> An object dropped from a balloon descending at 4 meters per second lands on the ground 10 seconds later. What was the altitude of the balloon at the moment the object was dropped?

Figure 3.7 illustrates an inefficient solution to the problem via a means-ends search through the small algebraic problem space defined by figure 3.6. The hypothetical student sets the overall goal by realizing that the height of the balloon when the object was dropped is the total distance traveled by the object, namely, x. The student then selects the operator E5, a nice simple equation with x on the left side. The selection of E5 is confirmed when the student realizes that one of the variables on the right side of E5, t, is given in the problem. A subgoal is set to find the other right-side variable, v_a. This process is followed two more times until E1 is selected, which has no unknown values on its right side. E1 is evaluated, and the result is fed back to the previous subgoal; this subgoal is in turn evaluated, and its result is fed back to the first subgoal. The subgoals must be retrieved from memory and evaluated in the reverse of the order in which they were formed. Thus, they are what is called a *push-down* stack, and during evaluation they are popped off the stack in reverse order to be evaluated. As in chess, keeping track of multiple subgoals imposes a heavy load on working memory, although in this case the student has recourse to external storage using pencil and paper.

This example is particularly compelling, because it is clear that the novice can get solutions with only a vague sense of how to map some of the phrases in word problems onto the variables, even without understanding why the equations are as they are. In fact, it is possible to see that E5 is a poor choice for the first operator. Our

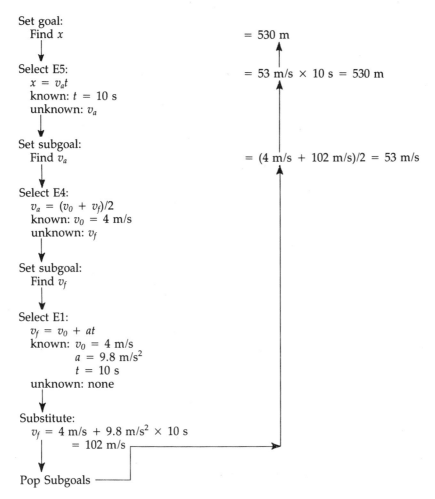

Figure 3.7
Novice solution to the physics problem given in the text

imaginary student selected it partly on the basis of an auxiliary heuristic favoring nice simple equations, but neglected another heuristic favoring equations with all known quantities on the right side.

Expert Problem Solving
Although the general problem-solving strategy described so far is intelligent, it falls far short of the best performance achieved by experts, who have years of practice in a particular domain. Research on expert problem solving confirms the general principles of skill development that were outlined in chapter 2.

The Expert Chess Player The mystique surrounding excellent chess players might suggest the hypothesis that these players use the same kind of problem-solving strategy that novices do but apply the strategy with fantastic speed, allowing many more potential moves to be examined. Early research by de Groot (1965) failed to uncover any evidence that expert players searched more moves, searched farther ahead, or searched faster than ordinary players. The only obvious difference was that the experts chose better moves.

De Groot also explored a second popular hypothesis that expert chess players have spectacular visual imagery ability and near-photographic memories. In one experiment subjects were given from 2 to 10 seconds to view a chess position containing about 25 pieces. They then were given a blank board and a pile of pieces and were asked to try to reconstruct the position from memory. The results showed striking differences among players at different levels: grand masters and master-level players were 93 percent correct, experts 72 percent correct, "A" level players 50 percent correct, and novices 33 percent correct. However, a further experiment by Chase and Simon (1973) showed that these results were not due to generally superior visual memory abilities in the more skilled players. The earlier experiment was repeated with one difference: the 25 pieces were placed randomly on the board rather than being taken from an actual game position. Players at all levels were equally poor in their ability to reconstruct the random positions.

Chase and Simon proposed that this highly chess-specific memory was due to perceptual learning. They hypothesized that chess experts had learned to recognize common configurations of pieces as single perceptual units. When reconstructing a position, the expert would be recalling, say, six or seven of these configurations, or chunks, each containing from three to five pieces. Six or seven items is known to be within the range of normal working memory. On this hypothesis the superior performance of the chess expert is a normal manifestation of skilled perception, exactly comparable to the reader's ability to remember this—*Our daisies took a beating in the thunderstorm*—better than this—*Ora setoaet ntie h nesomud ii sok baignhtudrtr*. The two sequences contain the same letters, but years of practice with reading have established eight perceptual units that are automatically detected in the first sequence.

Chase and Simon (1973) performed a further experiment to test the theory of chunks. They videotaped subjects performing the reconstruction task and then precisely timed the intervals between successive piece placements. These interresponse times showed a pattern that was predictable from the chunking theory. Longer intervals of greater than 2 seconds would be followed by a burst of several short intervals of less than 2 seconds. This is what would be expected if the subject took time to retrieve the next configuration and then reconstructed it on the board from working memory. The pieces that were clustered by interresponse time also turned out to be highly interrelated by standard chess theory.

The agreement of the observed configurations with standard chess-playing theory suggests why they might help in playing the game. The configurations are meaningfully related to possible future moves. Detecting a particular configuration could automatically activate possible relevant moves. Strong informal evidence for such automatic configuration-action productions is provided by the fact that expert (especially master-) level players are able to notice excellent moves after only seconds of looking at a position. In simultaneous chess demonstrations master-level players are able to win many games against lower-level players, taking only a few seconds per move. In an interesting theoretical calculation Simon and Chase (1973) showed that 50,000 configurations would be enough to describe all of the board positions that could arise in normal chess play. This figure is realistic, since skilled adult readers can acquire a vocabulary of 50,000 written words. Interestingly, biographical evidence indicates that

Verbal Statements   *Productions Invoked*

"It's already got a velocity of 4 meters per second
and it accelerates at 9.8 meters per second squared
so its final velocity 10 seconds later, well,

let's say its total additional velocity 10 seconds later   P1. $v_0, a, t \rightarrow v_f$
would be 98 meters per second

and that plus the 4 that it had to start with

would be 102 meters per second

so its average velocity during that period would be   P4. $v_0, v_f \rightarrow v_a$
106 over 2 or 53 meters per second,

and at 10 seconds that would mean it had dropped   P5. $v_a, t \rightarrow x$
530 meters."

Figure 3.8
An expert's solution to the example physics problem. Each production corresponds to an equation in figure 3.6; for example, P1 = E1. (Courtesy of H. Simon.)

it takes about the same amount of time to acquire an extensive chess "vocabulary" as it does to acquire a large reading vocabulary: about ten years, involving 10,000 to 50,000 hours of study.

The Expert Physicist   The general principles of skill acquisition also apply to expertise in physics. Experts do not search the algebraic problem space. In understanding a word problem, experts abstract all the bodies, forces, and energies, often drawing a diagram (or imagining one) to clarify the situation. They work forward, rather than backward, applying principles to develop further information about the situation. Then they solve for the unknown quantity. For example, figure 3.8 shows what a physicist said after reading the example problem about the balloon. There are a number of notable features in this verbal protocol. The expert subject rapidly develops basic information about the situation without attending to the goal. Although computations that are equivalent to equations E1, E4, and E5 are performed, they seem to be in the form of productions. The production P1, for example, works in the following manner: the presence of v_0, a, and t in a problem automatically triggers the computation of v_f by a compiled procedure. There is no evidence of retrieving equations in a declarative form and interpretively substituting values given in the problem into the equation. Compare the following fragment of a protocol from a novice subject who applied equation E2 directly:

> "Now we want x equals v zero times the time plus one-half of.... It's descending at the rate of 4 meters per second ... that equals v zero ...." (H. Simon, personal communication)

Here an equation is retrieved in declarative form, and values given in the problem are interpretively matched with and substituted for variables in the equation.

Note that in the expert solution the three principles represented by equations E1, E4, and E5 end up being invoked in exactly the reverse of the order in which they are invoked in the means-ends search in figure 3.7. The solution is reached directly at the end of the chain without the need to return results to subgoals. Like our hypothetical novice, the expert misses the easy solution of applying equation E2 directly, providing additional evidence that the search was not guided by means-ends analysis. However, the actual novice just quoted, who did use equation E2, still took over four times as long to reach a solution because of the time-consuming process of interpretively mapping the information given in the problem onto the equation.

Like the chess expert, the physicist has learned to recognize many typical physical situations, each of which evokes the application of well-compiled physical principles. Even though the search through the problem space is not guided by strategic goal setting, it is effective for at least two reasons. First, the principles that are evoked invariably lead to valuable information about the situation that will nearly always contribute to any problem posed about the situation. Second, no time is wasted searching for the optimally applicable principle, and no controlled processing capacity is wasted substituting into equations and keeping track of subgoals.

Becoming an Expert   The most challenging question that faces the problem-solving theorist is characterizing exactly how people acquire their expertise in various domains. How does a system that stores operators in a declarative form and uses means-ends search discover meaningful configurations and link them to appropriate actions? Larkin (1981) developed a learning mechanism for the "barely ABLE" program, which allowed the program to bootstrap itself out of means-ends algebraic search into "more ABLE" expertlike behavior. Basically, whenever an equation was applied during a means-ends solution, the learning mechanism attempted to build a corresponding production that could be applied in the future. For example, the application of E1 in figure 3.7 would cause the learning mechanism to attempt to form the production P1 of figure 3.8. Since productions are automatically evoked by configurations of variables in the situation, they gradually come to dominate means-ends search as learning progresses. Before learning, the ABLE program successfully simulated the order in which principles were applied by novices, and after learning the order shifted to fit that of the experts.

The ABLE program, however, does not fully capture the process by which the expert realizes that a physical concept applies to information in a situation. Physical concepts are highly abstract, and it is still not completely understood how the physicist can see the common features among situations that appear rather different on the surface. Chi, Feltovich, and Glaser (1981) found that physics experts could classify physics problems according to underlying physical principles. For example, a problem involving a spring applied to a body would be classified with a problem involving a body sliding down an inclined plane, according to the principle of conservation of energy. Novices did not make these classifications, and current computer programs are not yet able to make them either. People's ability to learn to perceive situations in terms of the principles of an abstract theory may also be involved in the discovery that people can learn to apply normative statistical principles, as discussed in the previous section.

Suggested Readings

Cognitive Psychology and Its Implications (Anderson 1990) and *Cognitive Science: An Overview for Cognitive Scientists* (Barsalou 1992) cover the topics of this chapter more extensively. *Rules of the Mind* (Anderson 1993) is a fascinating treatment of skill acquisition from the standpoint of Anderson's ACT theory of production systems. It includes a computer disk containing programs that simulate the theory.

References

Anderson, J. R. (1976). *Language. memory, and thought.* Hillsdale, N.J.: Erlbaum.

Anderson, J. R. (1983). *The architecture of cognition.* Cambridge, Mass.: Harvard University Press.

Anderson, J. R. (1990). *Cognitive psychology and its implications.* 3rd ed. New York: W. H. Freeman.

Anderson, J. R. (1993). *Rules of the mind.* Hillsdale, N.J.: Erlbaum.

Anderson, J. R., and L. M. Reder (1979). An elaborative processing explanation of depth of processing. In Cermak and Craik 1979.

Armstrong, S. L., L. R. Gleitman, and H. Gleitman (1983). What some concepts might not be. *Cognition* 13, 263–308.

Barsalou, L. W. (1982). Context-independent and context-dependent information in concepts. *Memory and Cognition* 10, 82–93.

Barsalou, L. W. (1992). *Cognitive science: An overview for cognitive scientists.* Hillsdale, N.J.: Erlbaum.

Barsalou, L. W. (1993). Flexibility, structure, and linguistic vagary in concepts: Manifestations of a compositional system of perceptual symbols. In A. F. Collins, S. E. Gathercole, M. A. Conway, and P. E. Morris, eds., *Theories of memory.* Hillsdale, N.J.: Erlbaum.

Bjork, R. A. (1975). Short-term storage: The ordered output of a central processor. In F. Restle, R. M. Shiffrin, N. J. Castellan, H. R. Lindeman, and D. B. Pisoni, eds., *Cognitive theory.* Vol. 1. New York: Wiley.

Blaxton, T. A. (1989). Investigating dissociations among memory measures: Support for a transfer appropriate processing framework. *Journal of Experimental Psychology: Learning, Memory, and Cognition* 15, 657–668.

Bower, G. H., J. B. Black, and T. J. Turner (1979). Scripts in memory for text. *Cognitive Psychology* 11, 177–220.

Bradshaw, G. L., and J. R. Anderson (1982). Elaborative encoding as an explanation of levels of processing. *Journal of Verbal Learning and Verbal Behavior* 21, 165–174.

Cermak, L. S., and F. I. M. Craik, eds. (1979). *Levels of processing in human memory.* Hillsdale, N.J.: Erlbaum.

Chapman, L. J., and J. P. Chapman (1967). Genesis of popular but erroneous diagnostic observations. *Journal of Abnormal Psychology* 72, 193–204.

Chase, W. G., and H. A. Simon (1973). Perception in chess. *Cognitive Psychology* 4, 55–81.

Cheng, P. W., and K. J. Holyoak (1985). Pragmatic reasoning schemas. *Cognitive Psychology* 17, 391–416.

Chi, M. T. H., P. J. Feltovich, and R. Glaser (1981). Categorization and representation of physics problems by experts and novices. *Cognitive Science* 5, 121–152.

Chiesi, H. L., G. J. Spilich, and J. F. Voss (1979). Acquisition of domain-related information in relation to high and low domain knowledge. *Journal of Verbal Learning and Verbal Behavior* 18, 257–274.

Collins, A., and E. F. Loftus (1975). A spreading activation theory of semantic processing. *Psychological Review* 82, 407–428.

Craik, F. I. M., and E. Tulving (1975). Depth of processing and the retention of words in episodic memory. *Journal of Experimental Psychology: General* 104, 268–294.

D'Andrade, R. (1982). Reason versus logic. Paper presented at the Symposium on the Ecology of Cognition: Biological, Cultural, and Historical Perspectives, Greensboro, N.C., April.

de Groot, A. D. (1965). *Thought and choice in chess.* The Hague: Mouton.

Dodd, D. H., and J. M. Bradshaw (1980). Leading questions and memory: Pragmatic constraints. *Journal of Verbal Learning and Verbal Behavior* 19, 695–704.

Dunbar, K. (1993). Concept discovery in a scientific domain. *Cognitive Science* 17, 397–434.

Fiske, S. T., and S. E. Taylor (1991). *Social cognition.* 2nd ed. New York: McGraw-Hill.

Fodor, J. A., and Z. W. Pylyshyn (1988). Connectionism and cognitive architecture: A critical analysis. In S. Pinker and J. Mehler, eds., *Connections and symbols.* Cambridge, Mass.: MIT Press.

Fong, G. T., D. H. Krantz, and R. E. Nisbett (1986). The effects of statistical training on thinking about everyday problems. *Cognitive Psychology* 18, 253–292.

Glass, A. L., and K. J. Holyoak (1986). *Cognition.* 2nd ed. New York: Random House.

Gray, C. M., and W. Singer (1989). Stimulus-specific neuronal oscillations in orientation specific columns of cat visual cortex. *Proceedings of the National Academy of Science* 86, 1698–1702.

Greene, E., M. S. Flynn, and E. F. Loftus (1982). Inducing resistance to misleading information. *Journal of Verbal Learning and Verbal Behavior* 21, 207–219.

Hamilton, D. L. (1979). A cognitive-attributional analysis of stereotyping. In L. Berkowitz, ed., *Advances in experimental social psychology.* Vol. 12. New York: Academic Press.

Hasher, L., and M. Griffin (1978). Reconstructive and reproductive processes in memory. *Journal of Experimental Psychology: Human Learning and Memory* 4, 318–330.

Hyde, T. S., and J. J. Jenkins (1973). Recall for words as a function of semantic, graphic, and syntactic orienting tasks. *Journal of Verbal Learning and Verbal Behavior* 12, 471– 480.

Jepson, D., D. H. Krantz, and R. E. Nisbett (1983). Inductive reasoning: Competence or skill? *Behavioral and Brain Sciences* 6, 494–501.

Johnson, M. K., S. Hashtroudi, and D. S. Lindsay (1993). Source monitoring. *Psychological Bulletin* 114, 3–28.

Johnson, M. K., and C. L. Raye (1981). Reality monitoring. *Psychological Review* 88, 67–85.

Johnson-Laird, P. N. (1983). *Mental models*. Cambridge, Mass.: Harvard University Press.

Johnson-Laird, P. N., and R. M. J. Byrne (1991). *Deduction*. Hillsdale, N.J.: Erlbaum.

Kahneman, D., and A. Tversky (1973). On the psychology of prediction. *Psychological Review* 80, 237– 251.

Kruschke, J. K. (1992). ALCOVE: An exemplar-based connectionist model of category learning. *Psychological Review* 99, 22–44.

Landau, B. (1982). Will the real grandmother please stand up? The psychological reality of dual meaning representations. *Journal of Psycholinguistic Research* 11, 47–62.

Larkin, J. H. (1981). Enriching formal knowledge: A model for learning to solve textbook physics problems. In J. R. Anderson, ed., *Cognitive skills and their acquisition*. Hillsdale, N.J.: Erlbaum.

Larkin, J. H., J. McDermott, D. P. Simon, and H. A. Simon (1980). Expert and novice performance in solving physics problems. *Science* 208, 1335–1342.

Lindsay, D. S. (1990). Misleading suggestions can impair eyewitnesses' ability to remember event details. *Journal of Experimental Psychology: Learning, Memory, and Cognition* 16, 1077–1083.

Lindsay, D. S., and M. K. Johnson (1989). The eyewitness suggestibility effect and memory for source. *Memory and Cognition* 17, 349–358.

Loftus, E. F. (1993). The reality of repressed memories. *American Psychologist* 48 (5), 518–537.

Loftus, E. F., and W. Cole (1974). Retrieving attribute and name information from semantic memory. *Journal of Experimental Psychology* 102, 1116–1122.

Loftus, E. F., and J. C. Palmer (1974). Reconstruction of automobile destruction: An example of the interaction between language and memory. *Journal of Verbal Learning and Verbal Behavior* 13, 585–589.

Manktelow, K. I., and J. S. B. T. Evans (1979). Facilitation of reasoning by realism: Effect or non-effect? *British Journal of Psychology* 70, 477–488.

McCloskey, M., and N. J. Cohen (1989). Catastrophic interference in connectionist networks: The sequential learning problem. In G. H. Bower, ed., *The Psychology of learning and motivation: Advances in research and theory*. San Diego, Calif.: Academic Press.

McCloskey, M., and M. Zaragoza (1985). Misleading postevent information and memory for events: Arguments and evidence against memory impairment hypotheses. *Journal of Experimental Psychology: General* 114, 1–16.

McKoon, G., R. Ratcliff, and G. S. Dell (1986). A critical evaluation of the semantic-episodic distinction. *Journal of Experimental Psychology: Learning, Memory, and Cognition* 12, 295–306.

Medin, D. L. (1989). Concepts and conceptual structure. *American Psychologist* 44 (12), 1469–1481.

Medin, D. L., and M. M. Schaffer (1978). Context theory of classification learning. *Psychological Review* 85, 207–238.

Morris, C. D., . D. JBransford, and J. J. Franks (1977). Levels of processing versus transfer appropriate processing. *Journal of Verbal Learning and Verbal Behavior* 16, 519–533.

Neisser, U. (1981). John Dean's memory: A case study. *Cognition* 9, 1–22.

Nelson, K., and J. Gruendel (1981). Generalized event representations: Basic building blocks of cognitive development. In A. Brown and M. Lamb, eds., *Advances in development psychology*. Vol. 1. Hillsdale, N.J.: Erlbaum.

Newell, A. (1980). Reasoning, problem solving, and decision processes: The problem space as a fundamental category. In R. S. Nickerson, ed., *Attention and performance VIII*. Hillsdale, N.J.: Erlbaum.

Newell, A., and H. A. Simon (1972). *Human problem solving*. Englewood Cliffs, N.J.: Prentice-Hall.

Nisbett, R. E., ed. (1993). *Rules for reasoning*. Hillsdale, N.J.: Erlbaum.

Nosofsky, R. M. (1988). Similarity, frequency, and category representations. *Journal of Experimental Psychology: Learning, Memory, and Cognition* 14, 54–65.

Owens, J., G. H. Bower, and J. B. Black (1979). The "soap-opera" effect in story recall. *Memory and Cognition* 7, 185–191.

Petersen, S. E., P. T. Fox, M. I. Posner, M. Mintun and M. E. Raichle (1988). Positron emission tomographic studies of the cortical anatomy of single-word processing. *Nature* 331, 585–589.

Petersen, S. E., P. T. Fox, A. Z. Snyder, and M. E. Raichle (1990). Activation of extrastriate and frontal cortical areas by visual words and word-like stimuli. *Science* 249, 1041–1044.

Ratcliff, R. (1990). Connectionist models of recognition memory: Constraints imposed by learning and forgetting functions. *Psychological Review* 97, 285–308.

Reiser, B. J., J. B. Black, and R. P. Abelson (1985). Knowledge structures in the organization and retrieval of autobiographical memories. *Cognitive Psychology* 17, 89–137.

Riesbeck, C. K., and R. C. Schank (1989). *Inside case-based reasoning*. Hillsdale, N.J.: Erlbaum.

Rips, L. J. (1988). Deduction. In R. J. Sternberg and E. E. Smith, eds., *The psychology of human thought*. New York: Cambridge University Press.

Rips, L. J. (1989). Similarity, typicality, and categorization. In S. Voisniadou and A. Ortony, eds., *Similarity, analogy, and thought*. New York: Cambridge University Press.

Rips, L. J., E. J. Shoben, and E. E. Smith (1973). Semantic distance and the verification of semantic relations. *Journal of Verbal Learning and Verbal Behavior* 12, 1–20.

Roediger, H. L. I., M. S. Weldon, and B. H. Challis (1989). Explaining dissociations between implicit and explicit measures of retention: A processing account. In H. L. I. Roediger and F. I. M. Craik, eds., *Varieties of memory and consciousness: Essays in honor of Endel Tulving*. Hillsdale, N.J.: Erlbaum.

Rosch, E. (1973). On the internal structure of perceptual and semantic categories. In T. E. Moore, ed., *Cognitive development and the acquisition of language*. New York: Academic Press.

Rosch, E. (1978). Principles of categorization. In E. Rosch and B. B. Lloyd, eds., *Cognition and categorization*. Hillsdale, N.J.: Erlbaum.

Rosch, E., and C. B. Mervis (1975). Family resemblances: Studies in the internal structure of categories. *Cognitive Psychology* 7, 573–605.

Schacter, D. L. (1993). Understanding implicit memory: A cognitive neuroscience approach. In A. F. Collins, S. E. Gathercole, M. A. Conway, and P. E. Morris, eds., *Theories of memory*. Hillsdale, N.J.: Erlbaum.

Shastri, L., and V. Ajjanagadde (1992). From simple associations to systematic reasoning: A connectionist representation of rules, variables, and dynamic bindings using temporal synchrony. Technical report MS-CIS-90-05. Computer and Information Science Department, University of Pennsylvania, Philadelphia, Penn.

Shimamura, A. P., and L. R. Squire (1987). A neuropsychological study of fact memory and source amnesia. *Journal of Experimental Psychology: Learning, Memory, and Cognition* 13, 464–473.

Simon, H. A., and W. G. Chase (1973). Skill in chess. *American Scientist* 61, 394–403.

Smith, E. E., C. Langston, and R. E. Nisbett (1992). The case for rules in reasoning. *Cognitive Science* 16, 1–40.

Smith, E. E., and D. L. Medin (1981). *Categories and concepts*. Cambridge, Mass.: Harvard University Press.

Smolensky, P. (1990). Tensor product variable binding and the representation of symbolic structures in connectionist systems. *Artificial Intelligence* 46, 159–216.

Stein, B. S. (1978). Depth of processing reexamined: The effects of precision of encoding and test appropriateness. *Journal of Verbal Learning and Verbal Behavior* 17, 165–174.

Stein, B. S., and J. D. Bransford (1979). Constraints on effective elaboration: Effects of precision and subject generation. *Journal of Verbal Learning and Verbal Behavior* 18, 769–777.

Stillings, N. A. (1975). Meaning rules and systems of inference for verbs of transfer and possession. *Journal of Verbal Learning and Verbal Behavior* 14, 453–470.

Taylor, S. E., and S. T. Fiske (1975). Point of view and perceptions of causality. *Journal of Personality and Social Psychology* 32, 439–445.

Tulving, E. (1983). *Elements of episodic memory*. Oxford: Clarendon Press.

Tulving, E. (1993). What is episodic memory? *Current Directions in Psychological Science* 2 (3), 67–70.

Tversky, A., and D. Kahneman (1971). Belief in the law of small numbers. *Psychological Bulletin* 76, 105–110.

Tversky, A., and D. Kahneman (1973). Availability: A heuristic for judging frequency and probability. *Cognitive Psychology* 5, 207–232.

Wason, P. C., and P. N. Johnson-Laird (1972). *Psychology of reasoning: Structure and content*. Cambridge, Mass.: Harvard University Press.

Winograd, T. (1972). *Understanding natural language*. New York: Academic Press.

Wittgenstein, L. (1953). *Philosophical investigations* (G. E. M. Anscombe, trans.). New York: Macmillan.

Chapter 4

Artificial Intelligence: Knowledge Representation

4.1 The Nature of Artificial Intelligence

Marvin Minsky, one of the founders of the field of artificial intelligence (AI), has said that AI is the science of making machines do things that would require intelligence if done by humans (1968, v). As cognitive scientists we stress the relationship between human and machine intelligence. We are interested in using AI techniques to enlighten us about how human beings do intelligent tasks and in using knowledge about human intelligence gathered in other disciplines to inform AI research. For instance, in getting a machine to do geometric analogy or integral calculus problems, we are, of course, interested in getting the machine to produce correct solutions, but we are also interested in learning more about the power and flexibility of human problem solving. We will put much less emphasis on the engineering approach to AI, which is concerned with programming computers to do tasks efficiently for the sake of getting them done rather than for the sake of shedding light on human intelligence. Also, we will continue to postpone the consideration of language and vision until later and concentrate on the structures and processes of intelligent thought.

The questions studied in AI are quite similar to those we have already encountered in our study of cognitive psychology. However, the methods of AI are different from those of psychology. The AI researcher attempts to develop and test computer programs that exhibit characteristics of human intelligence. The goal of developing a working computer program requires that the representations and processes of a theory be formalized in detail. As a result, a program's failures can give a fine-grained insight into where the theory needs to be changed. The complete control over the workings of a cognitive process that is possible in AI contrasts with the limited control available in experimental cognitive psychology. The inner workings of a human mind cannot be directly observed or reprogrammed at will by the psychologist, who must use ingenious and very time-consuming observations of human behavior to make inferences about underlying cognitive processes. Each advance in knowledge takes a great deal of work and rests on a chain of inferences about internal processes. AI researchers can systematically tinker with programs and run them with varying inputs and knowledge bases, while looking in complete detail at their internal workings. Nevertheless, the psychologist has the advantage of working directly with the human mind, whereas the AI researcher is always working with an artifact, which is only inferentially related to the human mind and is in many respects a pale substitute for it. Their methods are complementary, and at any point in the development of some area of cognitive science either set of methods might offer the best route toward new ideas.

Ubiquitous Themes in Artificial Intelligence

Following our treatment of cognitive psychology, it should come as no surprise that AI research is deeply concerned with the problem of *knowledge representation* and the processes that intelligently manipulate representations, for instance, by making inferences from them, and the problems of *search* and *control*. Further, we have seen that a major source of power and flexibility in human intelligence is the ability to acquire skill or expertise with experience. Thus, a major research issue in the cognitive science approach to AI is the study of the problem of *learning*. In this chapter we attack these problems afresh, from an AI perspective. We will see in more detail how various types of symbolic representations and processes can be implemented formally. We begin with a brief review of the key problems concerning thought processes, emphasizing aspects of the problems that are most important in AI research.

Knowledge Representation   *Knowledge representation* is the name given to the cluster of issues involving such questions as

1. What is the knowledge involved in the performance of the task, its types, structure, and organization?
2. How is this knowledge to be represented in the computer?
3. What sort of knowledge is made explicit by the representation? What is de-emphasized? What sort of knowledge is it possible to represent?
4. How is the knowledge to be acquired and/or revised?

In asking question 1, we are addressing the fundamentally epistemological issue of isolating and taking stock of the knowledge involved in the task we are trying to get the computer to perform. We are trying to establish how this knowledge can be characterized, perhaps how it can be broken into classes, and what connections exist in it. In asking question 2, we are trying to match up our representational needs with known representation schemes like the ones we discuss in section 4.2. In asking question 3, we are addressing the adequacy and biases of the representation. And in asking question 4, we are trying to determine how our knowledge base can evolve and be maintained. This question is clearly related to questions about learning (for example, how to infer new knowledge, how to support generalization and specialization).

Of course, our answers to such questions depend on our purposes and the task at hand. For instance, representing mathematical knowledge in order to study how novice students solve algebra word problems is different from representing mathematical knowledge to prove theorems with computers. All of these questions involve significant analysis of the domain of knowledge itself. We delve further into these issues in section 4.2.

Search and Control   *Search* is the name given to issues involving the exploration of alternatives, as in a game-playing situation where one considers, "If I move here, then my opponent moves here or here, and then I move here or here or here in response, and then...." *Control* is the name given to issues involving the organization of processes in a system, in particular, questions of what processes should act when and what processes should have access to what information.

There are many well-understood techniques to handle search; we present a few of the best known in chapter 5. Of course, the problem of search is related to that of knowledge representation because what we perceive as alternatives depends on what we represent. Questions to ask when considering search include

1. What are the alternatives, their characteristics, and organization?
2. What are the dangers in pursuing "bad" paths of possibilities and the rewards for finding "good" ones?
3. Will the search in fact find a solution among the possibilities, if one exists?
4. If so, is the solution unique or optimal or "good enough"?

In asking question 1, we are considering issues such as using operators for generating the alternatives (as in the legal moves in a board game), using evaluation functions for assessing the alternatives, and using structures like trees or networks for organizing the alternatives. In asking question 2, we are considering whether certain kinds of information may help eliminate bad search routes and suggest concentrating on good ones, whether it is possible to recover from exploring a bad sequence of alternatives, whether there are penalties for missing fruitful lines of exploration and wasting resources, and whether there are ways to find successful alternatives quickly. In asking questions 3 and 4, we are asking the obvious questions about the possible existence of solutions and about the desirable characteristics of uniqueness and optimality, and barring such computationally desirable solutions whether a solution can be found that is good enough for our purposes.

Control involves coordination of the processes that make up the computer model, communication of information between them, and decisions about what process should do what when. Control and the related issue of program architecture—that is, the design of the system—constitute an extremely important topic for AI systems. Even though we will have little to say about it in this chapter, some questions to consider about control are

1. What kinds of processes are there?
2. How are the processes coordinated and controlled?
3. What processes have access to what information and how do they communicate with one another?
4. How are computational resources allocated?

We touch on such issues in chapter 5.

Learning   The last major theme in AI, *learning*, concerns how a system gets "better" in the sense of knowing more and being able to do more. Sometimes this means "merely" acquiring new facts. Sometimes it means reorganizing the knowledge base or the structure of the program itself. Most frequently it means performing a task better. Learning is a very rich and exceedingly important topic that touches on important issues from psychology and epistemology. Some of the questions about learning from the AI point of view are

1. What primitive capabilities and knowledge does the learning system possess?
2. How are new knowledge and capabilities acquired and melded into those already known to the learning system?
3. What is the role of the teacher (for instance, as critic) in the system's learning?
4. What is the role of examples or experiences presented to the learning system?

Question 1 addresses the baseline of performance that the learning system is to start with. It clearly cannot start with nothing—but how much is enough, and how much is too much? This issue is often the focus of attacks on learning systems ("The system knew it all along"), and there is no simple analysis of it, as any philosopher or AI researcher will attest. Question 2 addresses issues of acquisition and improvement. Once the base for the learning system has been established, how should it go about acquiring new capabilities and improving its performance? Some learning is inductive and based on examples, some proceeds by criticizing a problem-solving performance and then refining it. Question 2 also addresses the integration of new knowledge and performance capabilities into the existing system. Questions 3 and 4 single out two other important issues. Question 3, on the role of the teacher in (or when absent, the self-direction of) the system, has long been recognized, as it has been in psychological studies of learning. Question 4, on the role of examples, has been too long overlooked but is now more consciously addressed. Examples provide grist for the mill of learning, and without them almost all learning systems could not function. These four questions therefore address what could be called the basic learning cycle: start, acquire, revise, improve. Thus, as a group, they address key aspects in what could be called the basic components of a learning system: performance knowledge, learning mechanisms, criticism, selection of new problems.

Case Studies of Artificial Intelligence Programs
Before delving into details about representation, search and control, and learning, we examine three AI programs to give an idea of what such programs can do and to show how the three themes are relevant. The first, called AM, is a program designed to model discovery in mathematics. The second, MYCIN, performs expert-level medical diagnosis of bacterial diseases. The third, HYPO, models certain aspects of legal reasoning with precedent cases.

Mathematical Discovery: The AM Program   AM (Automated Mathematician) is a knowledge-based program that was developed to discover mathematical concepts (Lenat 1977; Davis and Lenat 1982). AM was initially provided with both a rich fund of rules of thumb concerning how to discover and judge the importance of concepts and a good set of basic concepts in set theory. With these it developed concepts in elementary number and set theory, for instance, the concept "prime number." Noteworthy about AM is its use of (1) a rich knowledge base encoded in frames, (2) a large base of discovery rules, and (3) an interesting control mechanism, called an agenda, to focus its attention on things to do. AM's task was to discover new concepts and thereby extend its knowledge base of concepts.

Each concept is represented by a cluster of information, a *frame*, which includes information stored in *slots* with names like NAME, DEFINITION, EXAMPLES, GENERALIZATIONS, SPECIALIZATIONS, and WORTH. A frame can be viewed as a structured index card with the slots as places to enter various aspects of the entity being catalogued.

AM's initial knowledge base contained about 100 frames for basic concepts like "set" and "set union." Knowledge of how to manipulate this stock of concepts was contained in a rule base containing about 250 heuristics. A *heuristic*, from the Greek stem for "discover," is a rule of thumb or a suggestion that usually proves to be useful but is not guaranteed to be so; the fundamentals of heuristic reasoning were extensively explored by the mathematician George Polya in his books on mathematical problem solving (see, for example, Polya 1957). Heuristics are often naturally encoded in what is called a *situation-action* or *if-then* rule: for example, "*If* you are in a situation involving a variable ranging over a set of values, *then* investigate what happens when the variable takes on extreme values." This heuristic of examining extreme cases turned out to be critically important in AM.

At any given time there are many things AM could attempt, such as trying to find examples or generalizations of a concept. However, since it does not have enough resources, in terms of time or computer power, to do them all, it maintains a "wish list" or *agenda* of things to do that is ordered according to such measures as importance, recency, and what Lenat calls *interestingness*—that is, how interesting a concept is. When AM is ready to start working on a new task, it consults this agenda and selects the task with the highest rating.

Creating new concepts, like "prime number," is the principal task for AM. (Note that it is the person running the program who provides a name like "prime number" for a concept. AM itself has no notion that it is discovering a concept with a classic name.) This activity involves creating a new frame for the concept and filling in its slots (for instance, listing some examples $(2, 3, 5)$ of prime numbers in the EXAMPLES slot). Filling in a slot is accomplished by executing a collection of relevant heuristic rules, such as "Try to create extreme examples."

The basic processing cycle in AM is as follows:

1. Choose a task from the agenda.
2. Gather relevant heuristic rules and execute them, where a heuristic rule is deemed relevant if executing it is likely (though not necessarily guaranteed) to bring AM closer to satisfying the task.
3. Place any new tasks spawned in the process of step 2 on the agenda; this involves assigning a measure to rank the new task and perhaps reordering the old agenda. (New tasks are thus not necessarily placed at the top or the bottom of the agenda but rather according to their perceived importance.)

Then the cycle repeats itself.

Heuristics help not only in accomplishing tasks but also in ordering the agenda and hence in determining what to do next. Thus, heuristics guide AM's exploration through a large "space" of possibilities. This is why Lenat calls AM a *heuristic search* model of discovery.

There are only three types of tasks on AM's agenda:

1. *Fill in the slot of a concept*
   A heuristic relevant to filling in the example slot is
   > To fill in examples of X, where X is a kind of Y. Check examples of Y; some of them might be examples of X as well.

   For instance, to fill in examples for the "prime number" concept, AM would consider examples of the "number" concept.
2. *Create a new concept*
   A heuristic relevant to this task is
   > If some (but not most) examples of X are also examples of Y, then create a new concept defined as the intersection of X and Y.

   For instance, some odd numbers are also prime numbers. The intersection concept would be "odd prime number."
3. *Add a new task to the agenda*
   A heuristic relevant to this task is

If very few examples of X are found, then add the following task to the agenda: "Generalize the concept X."

For instance, since there are very few examples of "even prime number" (2 is the only one), then this heuristic would spawn the task "Generalize the concept even prime."

Note that something that sounds so straightforward, like "Generalize the concept X," can be quite complicated and subtle. For instance, in the "even prime number" example two obvious generalization choices are "even number" and "prime number" (both of which are accomplished by dropping a condition); a more aggressive generalization would be "any number." As we will see in chapter 5, generalization is a central task for learning systems.

AM has roughly forty heuristics that deal with the creation of new concepts. Typical heuristics deal with generalization, specialization, and exception handling. Dropping a condition is one generalization technique; another is to change a constant to a variable. We have already seen the generalization-specialization connections between concepts like "number," "prime number," and "even prime number." An example of an exception might be the number 2, which is the only even prime and thus an exception to the statement "All primes are odd."

Figure 4.1 contains an edited segment from the actual episode in which AM discovered the concept "prime." This session was preceded by AM's discovery of concepts for "multiplication" and "division," which led to the concept "divisors of a number." To find examples of the last concept, AM investigated extreme cases, that is, numbers with very few or very many divisors. Numbers with no divisor or only one divisor are essentially nonexistent, so AM does not judge them to be interesting. AM actually discovered "primes" indirectly, then, by first investigating the very interesting concept of numbers with three divisors. Since AM noticed that numbers with three divisors always seem to be squares of numbers with two divisors (that is, primes), this raised the "interestingness" value of the emerging concept of "prime," which AM then explored more thoroughly. AM then used the concept of "prime" in generating various conjectures like "unique factorization" that arise out of the question, "Ask whether the relation between a number and its divisors is a function."

One reason why AM performed so well was that the techniques it could apply to concepts in its knowledge base (like dropping a condition) were semantically meaningful. That is, such formal operations in the program had meaning in the domain of set and elementary number theory. There was a happy match between AM's internal manipulations and those of its domain, mathematics (Lenat and Brown 1983; Ritchie and Hanna 1984).

Medical Diagnosis: The Expert System MYCIN   MYCIN is an expert system, that is, a kind of AI system that performs expert-level reasoning in a typically narrow, yet deep, field of expertise. A very thorough exposition and review of the MYCIN project can be found in Shortliffe 1976 and Buchanan and Shortliffe 1984.

MYCIN can diagnose certain kinds of bacterial infections and recommend administration of appropriate drug therapies. Such an expert system is particularly important because bacterial infections require immediate treatment and because a considerable amount of expertise is involved in their diagnosis and treatment. Since decisions on cases of infection must often be made by a physician who is not an expert on bacterial diseases, consultation with an expert—person or program—can be very valuable. An

Task 65:
Filling in examples of the following concept: "DIVISORS-OF."
3 Reasons:
(1) No known examples for DIVISORS-OF so far.
(2) TIMES, which is related to DIVISORS-OF, is now very interesting.
(3) Focus of attention: AM recently defined DIVISORS-OF.
26 examples found, in 9.2 seconds, e.g.: DIVISORS-OF(6) = {1 2 3 6}

Task 66:
Considering numbers which have very small set of DIVISORS-OF (i.e.,
very few divisors).
2 Reasons:
(1) Worthwhile to look for extreme cases.
(2) Focus of attention: AM recently worked on DIVISORS-OF.

Filling in examples of numbers with 0 divisors.
  0 examples found, in 4.0 seconds.
  Conjecture: no numbers have 0 divisors.

Filling in examples of numbers with 1 divisor.
  1 example found, in 4.0 seconds, e.g.: DIVISORS-OF(1) = {1}.
  Conjecture: 1 is the only number with 1 divisor.

Filling in examples of numbers with 2 divisors.
  24 examples found, in 4.0 seconds, e.g.: DIVISORS-OF(13) = {1 13}
  No obvious conjecture. This kind of number merits more study.
  Creating a new concept: "NUMBERS-WITH-2-DIVISORS."

Filling in examples of numbers with 3 divisors.
  11 examples found, in 4.0 seconds, e.g.: DIVISORS-OF(49) = {1 7 49}
  All numbers with 3 divisors are also Squares. This kind of number
  merits more study.
  Creating a new concept: "NUMBERS-WITH-3-DIVISORS."

Figure 4.1
Trace of how AM discovered the concept of prime number. (From Davis and Lenat 1982.)

expert consultation program for bacterial infections is amenable to an AI approach
because a body of well-understood, circumscribed medical knowledge already exists
about identifying and treating them. Moreover, additional information can be obtained
from standard laboratory tests, and there is a body of expertise in deciding which of
these to perform. Finally, once a diagnosis has been made—or rather, once a list of
possible diagnoses has been rank ordered—the various drug therapies can also be
ordered on the basis of information about the disease and the patient.

MYCIN uses a *rule-based* approach. That is, its expertise is encoded in terms of
if-then production rules like the following (Buchanan and Shortliffe 1984, 71, 122):

IF: 1) The gram stain of the organism is gramneg, and
         2) The morphology of the organism is rod, and
         3) The aerobicity of the organism is anaerobic
THEN: There is suggestive evidence (.6) that the identity of the organism is
         bacteroides.
IF: The identity of the organism is pseudomonas
THEN: I recommend therapy chosen from among the following drugs:

1—colistin (.98)
2—polymyxin (.96)
3—gentamicin (.96)
4—carbenicillin (.65)
5—sulfisoxazole (.64)

The .6 in the conclusion of the first rule is a *certainty factor*, which is the mechanism whereby MYCIN handles degrees of evidence and uncertainty. A certainty factor of $+1$ indicates a fact known to be true, a certainty factor of -1 indicates a fact known to be false, and anything in between indicates a "maybe" of more or less certainty. MYCIN was one of the earliest AI programs that faced the issue of how to deal with uncertain data; it used a calculus of certainty factors to do this. The numbers associated with drugs in the second rule are probabilities, derived from hospital data, that the organism *Pseudomonas* will be sensitive to a drug.

MYCIN contains about five hundred such rules and can handle about one hundred different kinds of bacterial infections. In benchmark tests its performance compared very favorably with that of medical school faculty members and was better than that of medical students and residents at the Stanford Medical School (Yu et al. 1984). A typical session between a physician and MYCIN is shown in figure 4.2.

The MYCIN system performs a multiphase decision-making process:

1. Identify which organisms, if any, are causing the disease.
2. Determine which drugs are potentially useful.
3. Make drug therapy recommendations.

MYCIN works in a backward chaining style of reasoning to identify organisms. That is, it works backward from possible conclusions about the identity of the organism to the facts that would justify the conclusions. For instance, the rule base might contain rules of the following form:

If A then B.
If B then C.
If C then *E. coli*.

Given such rules, MYCIN would try to determine whether the unknown organism is *E. coli* by determining whether it satisfies condition C. If it didn't know this, it would try to infer it by reasoning back to see whether condition B is satisfied. And so on. At some point it might request additional information or clinical data from the user. Backward chaining focuses the program's reasoning on the rules and data relevant to reach a conclusion and thus is often called *goal-directed* reasoning. It enables MYCIN to avoid asking the user unnecessary questions.

Once it has established the likely identity of the organism, MYCIN retrieves lists of relevant drugs, considers contraindications, and rank orders the drugs according to their prospects for being successful. Finally, on the basis of patient data such as weight, age, and sex, it makes actual treatment recommendations.

MYCIN is a paradigmatic example of an expert system. Even though the term *expert system* should refer to any system performing at expert level, it frequently refers to systems built on a knowledge base of rules. Though the rule-based approach seems straightforward and enticingly easy to implement, a "knowledge engineer" can spend untold hours debriefing experts, developing a manageable vocabulary in which to write the rules, debugging the rules, and tuning the system. The first task requires

1) Patient's name: (first-last)
** **FRED BRAUN**
2) Sex: *(Questions 1-3 request*
** **M**   *background patient data.)*
3) Age:
** **55**
4) Are there any cultures for Fred Braun which may be related to
   the present illness, and from which organisms have been
   grown successfully in the microbiology laboratory?
** **Y**

--------CULTURE-1--------
5) From what site was the specimen for CULTURE-1 taken?
** **BLOD**
   = BLOOD   *(System corrects typing error.)*
6) Please give the date and time when CULTURE-1 was ob-
   tained.
   (mo/da/yr time)
** **JUN 20, 1977**
The first organism isolated from the blood culture of 20-JUN-77
(CULTURE-1) will be referred to as:

--------ORGANISM-1--------
7) Enter the laboratory-reported identity of ORGANISM-1:
** **UNKNOWN**   *(Typically identity is not yet known.)*
8) The stain (gram or Ziehl-Neelsen acid-fast) of ORGANISM-1:
** **NEG**   *(Preliminary lab results give some clues.)*
9) Is ORGANISM-1 rod or coccus (etc.):
** **ROD**
10) What is the form of the individual organism (e.g. lancet-
    shaped for cocci, fusiform for rods, etc.)?
** **FUSIFORM**

                    (. . . more questions follow in order to gather
                    sufficient information to infer the identity
                    and significance of the infecting organisms . . .)

23) What is the suspected portal of entry of the gramneg rod from
    the blood culture of 20-JUN-77 (ORGANISM-1) into this sterile
    site?
** **GI (6)**   *(User indicates the uncertainty of his response.)*
24) Is Fred Braun a burn patient?
** **N**
25) Is Fred Braun a compromised host (e.g. alcoholic, sickle-cell-
    disease, immunosuppressed)?
** **N**
26) Is Fred Braun febrile?
** **Y**

                    (. . . after about 50–60 questions, MYCIN prints
                    the diagnostic hypotheses on
                    which therapy will be based . . .)

Figure 4.2
A typical MYCIN consultation session. (From Buchanan and Shortliffe 1984.)

My therapy recommendations will be designed to treat for organisms that are either very likely or, although less likely, would have a significant effect on therapy selection if they were present. It is important to cover for the following probable infection(s) and associated organism(s):

INFECTION-1 is BACTEREMIA

<ITEM-1> E. COLI [ORGANISM-1]
<ITEM-2> KLEBSIELLA [ORGANISM-1]
<ITEM-3> ENTEROBACTER [ORGANISM-1]
<ITEM-4> KLEBSIELLA-PNEUMONIAE [ORGANISM-1]

(. . . questions follow to evaluate possible therapy choices, and finally MYCIN prints its therapy recommendations . . .)

[REC-1] My preferred therapy recommendation is as follows:
In order to cover for items <1 2 3 4>:
Give: GENTAMICIN   *(One drug covers 4 possible identities.)*
Dose: 119 mg (6.0 ml) q8h IV for 10 days [calculated on basis of 1.7 mg/kg]
Comments: Modify dose in renal failure.

Figure 4.2 (cont.)

knowing enough about the domain of the system to be able to talk with experts about technical matters and analyze their problem-solving behavior. The second often requires going beyond what is found in textbooks to include other concepts, typically of an informal nature or not clearly enunciated by the expert. The third requires experimenting with the rule set; it is rare indeed that the initial program contains all and only the necessary rules. And the fourth requires the ability to optimize system performance by clever ordering and structuring of the rule base. These tasks are often grouped under the rubric "knowledge acquisition bottleneck."

Nonetheless, the expert systems approach exemplified by MYCIN is very powerful. It is best suited to problems involving a narrow, well-delineated area of expertise that is too complex and dynamic to be modeled with simpler techniques like decision tables.

Legal Reasoning: The HYPO Program   Our third example AI system is a *case-based reasoning* system called *HYPO* (Ashley 1990; Ashley and Rissland 1988; Rissland, Valcarce, and Ashley 1984). Case-based reasoning (CBR) is a type of reasoning in which one tries to solve a new problem by using solutions from similar past problems. For instance, in developing a new plan or design, say, for a house, one adapts an already existing one: that is, on the basis of "specs" or desired features for a solution to the new problem, one retrieves and attempts to modify old solutions that are judged to be close enough to be amenable to being retailored to the new situation. There are many examples of such CBR-type problem solving in design fields like architecture and mechanical engineering. Even certain aspects of cooking, such as coming up with new recipes or menus, are examples of such design-oriented or planning-oriented CBR.

Another type of CBR is the sort of precedent-based reasoning used in legal reasoning: that is, presented with a new fact situation, one generates arguments pro and con an interpretation or treatment of it based on interpretations and outcomes made in similar, past cases. Precedent-based CBR is typically used in areas where there are competing interpretations of a given situation. It is used in areas as diverse as foreign policy, law, and everyday interactions with children and students. For instance, based on past precedents, a new regulation limiting what a federally funded artist may exhibit or publish may be interpreted as being an unconstitutional abridgment of an artist's freedom of speech. As another example, a teacher might decide to accept a student's late homework without loss of credit based on how past similar late-paper cases were handled. Anglo-American common law is a paradigmatic example of such reasoning since it is based on the doctrine of precedent that dictates that similar cases should be decided similarly. Of course, a critical question is, What counts as "similar"?

In both styles of case-based reasoning—which we can call *design-oriented* and *interpretation-oriented* CBR—key issues are representation and indexing of cases, assessing similarity between cases, and using relevant precedent cases to solve new problems. All CBR systems contain a knowledge base of cases, mechanisms to index and retrieve cases, and methods to assess similarity and relevance. In addition, design-oriented CBR systems contain methods to adapt cases and interpretation-oriented CBR systems contain methods to generate rationales or arguments for possible interpretations.

HYPO is a CBR system that operates in the area of law concerning the protection of trade secrets, such as knowledge used to produce and market new computer hardware. HYPO analyzes a new case (the "current fact situation" or "cfs") and, on the basis of known precedent cases and ways of analyzing them, formulates skeletons of arguments supporting interpretations (e.g., it was or was not an unlawful misappropriation) espoused by the opposing sides, the plaintiff and the defendant. HYPO's output includes both a case citation summary, giving a summary of relevant cases for each side, and a "3-ply" argument, in which side 1 first makes its best points by citing its best cases, then side 2 responds in a counterpoint by attacking side 1's analysis and offering its own best cases and an alternative analysis favorable to its point of view, and finally, side 1 has the opportunity to rebut side 2's analysis. At the heart of such precedent-based argumentation is assessment of case similarity and "on-pointness," construction of analogies with favorable precedents, and distinguishing away of unfavorable ones. See figure 4.3 for an example fact situation and 3-ply argument.

HYPO, like any CBR system, uses several sources of knowledge about cases. The first major category of knowledge in HYPO is its knowledge base of cases, the *Case-Knowledge-Base*. HYPO uses a set of hierarchical frames to represent the factual features and relations of its cases. The same representation is also used for the current fact situation. The frames have slots for information about various facts of cases, such as PLAINTIFF, DEFENDANT, TRADE-SECRET. Each of these in turn might be represented in frames. For example, several levels of subframes are used to represent facts about the TRADE-SECRET.

The second major category of knowledge in HYPO is knowledge of legal factors, which are called *dimensions*. Dimensions are used to index cases, to assess the strength of a case from a particular legal point of view, and to compare cases with respect to this viewpoint. Dimensions encode the knowledge that the presence of certain facts enables a case to be addressed from a certain point of view. For instance, two typical ways to approach a trade secrets case are (1) focus on the number of disclosures of the putative secret made by the plaintiff to others, and (2) focus on the relative expenditures of time and money made by the plaintiff and defendant. In addition to stating what information is necessary for a given dimension to apply, a dimension states how to assess the strength of a case along that dimension and to compare cases from this

⇒   Point For Defendant as Side 1:

Where: Plaintiff disclosed its product information to outsiders. Defendant should win a claim for Trade Secrets Misappropriation.

Cite: Midland-Ross Corp. v. Sunbeam Equipment Corp. 316 F. Supp. 171 (W.D. Pa., 1970).

⇐   Response for Plaintiff as Side 2:

Midland-Ross Corp. v. Sunbeam Equipment Corp. is distinguishable because: In Midland-Ross, plaintiff disclosed its product information to more outsiders than in Crown Industries

Counterexamples:

Data General Corp. v. Digital Computer Controls Inc. 357 A.2d 105 (Del. Ch. 1975), held for plaintiff even though in Data General plaintiff disclosed its product information to more outsiders than in Midland-Ross Corp. v. Sunbeam Equipment Corp.

⇒   Rebuttal for Defendant as Side 1:

Data General Corp. v. Digital Computer Controls Inc. is distinguishable because: In Crown Industries, Plaintiff disclosed its product information in negotiations with defendant. Not so in Data General. In Data General, plaintiff's disclosures to outsiders were restricted. Not so in Crown Industries.

Note:
Plaintiff's response would be strengthened if: Plaintiff's disclosures to outsiders were restricted. Cf. Data General Corp. v. Digital Computer Controls Inc. 357 A.2d 105 (Del. Ch. 1975)

Figure 4.3
The basic components of a typical 3-Ply Argument: a Point for Side 1 (in this case, the defendant), a Response for Side 2 (the plaintiff), a Rebuttal for Side 1, and a suggested hypothetical to strengthen the Response. (From Ashley 1990.)

point of view. For instance, according to the first approach, which in HYPO corresponds to the dimension called *voluntary-disclosures-made*, the more disclosures made by the complaining party (the plaintiff), the worse off the plaintiff is since the plaintiff is responsible for letting the cat out of the bag, so to speak. The second approach, represented in the dimension called *competitive-advantage-gained*, encodes the second way of looking at a misappropriation case, in which all things being equal, the greater the discrepancy in expended resources, the worse off the defendant is because large disparities in savings indicate that the defendant somehow gained an unfair competitive advantage. Each dimension has certain factual prerequisites. For instance, for *competitive-advantage-gained* to be applicable, HYPO must know facts such as that the plaintiff and the defendant manufacture competing products and the amount of time and money they expended in conjunction with their products. The latter facts are particularly important since they allow HYPO to compare cases on this dimension. Dimensions thus encode prerequisite facts to lines of argument or analysis, knowledge that certain prerequisites are key, and methods to compare cases along the dimensions. They are at the heart of HYPO's definitions of case similarity and relevance.

The overall processing of HYPO goes as follows. HYPO begins by analyzing a new problem case (the cfs), which is input directly into the frame representation used for cases. It analyzes the current fact situation to determine which dimensions are applicable, or nearly applicable (that is, they would be applicable if one more key fact were known). HYPO then retrieves from its Case-Knowledge-Base all cases that are considered relevant, where a case is deemed to be *relevant* if it shares at least one applicable, or nearly applicable, dimension with the current fact situation. This initial set of relevant cases is HYPO's first cut at gathering a set of relevant precedents to use in argument.

Next, HYPO determines which cases are more on-point, or more relevant, than others by imposing an ordering on the set of relevant cases. The most relevant cases are called *most on-point*. HYPO finds the most on-point cases by sorting the initial set of relevant cases according to an order that considers the overlap of the set of dimensions shared between the cfs and a relevant case. Most on-point cases are those cases that are maximal according to this ordering of relevant cases.

To be precise, case 1 is considered more on-point than case 2 if the set of dimensions case 1 shares with the fact situation contains the set case 2 shares with the fact situation. For example, suppose for simplicity that the set of applicable dimensions in the current fact situation is A, B, C, D; that A, B, C are applicable in case 1; and that B and C are applicable in case 2. In this instance case 1 will be more on-point than case 2. Note that if there were a case 3 with applicable dimensions B, C, D, it would be neither more nor less on-point than case 1: both share quite a number of legal aspects (i.e., dimensions) with the cfs, but neither one subsumes the analysis of the other. In this situation both case 1 and case 3 would be considered most on-point cases. Situations like this, in which neither of a pair of cases is "more" on-point than the other, arise because cases often address different aspects and comparing them is a bit like comparing apples and oranges. Note also that case 2 can be compared with both case 1 and case 3 (along the dimensions B and C) and that with respect to both, it is less on-point.

From the set of most on-point cases, HYPO next chooses the "best" cases for each side to use in its points and counterpoints in the 3-ply arguments. Since some most on-point cases might be good for one side and some for the opposing side, each side needs to focus on those most on-point cases that are best for it and at the same time be wary of those that are best for the other side since these will surely be used to make counterarguments. Thus, HYPO's next step is to further winnow down the set of relevant cases.

Best cases for a particular side (say, the plaintiff) are defined as those cases that in addition to being most on-point were won by the plaintiff and share at least one favorable dimension with the case at hand. Obviously, a case that held against you, even if most on-point, is not one that you would like to cite in arguing your case. Furthermore, it is not wise to rely on a case that is strong in ways that your case is not, for then your opponent may "distinguish away" this case by saying that the reason it was resolved as it was is that it had these other strong points that yours does not.

Having found the best cases for each side—the last in a series of steps to winnow down the set of cases initially retrieved from the Case-Knowledge-Base—HYPO is now in a position to play out various lines of argument about the current case. Figure 4.3 shows a 3-ply argument. HYPO also uses hypotheticals to point out how a particular case could be strengthened. For instance, in figure 4.3, HYPO suggests that "plaintiff's response would be strengthened if...." The study of hypotheticals is an interesting research area in itself (Rissland and Ashley 1986; Rissland 1989).

In summary, HYPO is an example of a precedent-based CBR program. It is an example of a program that proposes computationally well defined definitions for key CBR notions such as "similarity," "relevant," "most on-point," and "best case." With its knowledge of how to compare cases, it is able to perform various key steps, such as distinguishing and drawing analogies, used in legal reasoning.

4.2 Knowledge Representation

In this section we present a survey of the standard tools of symbolic knowledge representation; other approaches are covered in the section on connectionism and neural nets. Intuitively, a knowledge representation technique is a way of representing knowledge, that is, a way of encoding it for use by a computer program. A knowledge representation scheme is a system of formal conventions—sometimes called its *syntax*—together with a way to interpret what the conventions mean—sometimes called its *semantics*.

Any knowledge representation scheme has two parts: a knowledge base and an interpreter that manipulates it. Both aspects of knowledge representation—the knowledge base and the interpretive process—are necessary. Neither one alone represents much of anything more than, say, bat, ball, and players alone represent the game of baseball: one needs to know what to do with them (for instance, as described in the rules of the game).

A representation makes explicit certain ingredients and aspects of information and can greatly affect how easy it is for a program to perform different tasks. For instance, representing mathematics for a computer theorem prover requires both a knowledge base of true propositions and a mechanism that combines them to infer new true propositions. A representation that is good for computer theorem proving might not be good for modeling human mathematical skills.

We will see that there is no one right or universally correct representation for knowledge. The choice depends on various factors, for example, the needs of the system, the researcher's purposes for representing the knowledge, and the requirement of finding the representation that best mirrors the structure of the domain knowledge or makes explicit that aspect of the domain knowledge the researcher wants to emphasize. Moreover, we will see that each representation scheme has certain strengths and weaknesses and that each can be affected by certain well-known problems: the credit assignment problem, grainsize, the right primitives problem, and so forth. (For expository reasons we will consider these problems with respect to particular knowledge representation schemes; keep in mind, however, that each one applies to many, or even all, knowledge representation techniques.) In choosing a representation, then, the cognitive scientist will attempt to make the best match between desiderata and technique and will remain aware of the assumptions—some psychological, some computational, some philosophical—that go along with each choice.

Much of the AI work on knowledge representation provides examples of AI researchers grappling with fundamental problems of meaning and taking (even if implicitly) an epistemological stance that is somewhat "reductionist"; that is, they take the view that knowledge can be broken down until one eventually reaches a set of primitives that need not be broken down further. Although this view can be quibbled with philosophically, it is not a bad stance for the AI researcher, who must handle these questions pragmatically but in as principled a manner as possible.

Before we discuss particular methods, let us look at a list of critical questions to ask about any knowledge representation scheme.

Critical Questions for Knowledge Representation Schemes

Every representation scheme has its pros and cons; every scheme is good at capturing certain kinds of knowledge and not so good at capturing other kinds. Every scheme has its costs and benefits either to the program or to the person encoding the knowledge for the program or maintaining it. As an educated "consumer" of knowledge representation methods, a cognitive scientist should be able to evaluate the method with respect to the problem at hand and determine which scheme provides the best match of strengths to needs.

The following questions are useful in evaluating knowledge representation schemes:

1. *How perspicuous is the representation?* Does it permit a concise and transparent encoding of the knowledge? Or does it require the knowledge to be forced into its representational conventions in an uncomfortable way?

2. *How efficient is the representation?* Is simple knowledge encoded simply? Can knowledge that is used in more than one way or place be separated out or must it be repeated?

3. *What is the scope and grainsize of the knowledge that can be represented?* That is, what portion of the world can be represented and in what detail?

4. *What is the basic vocabulary of "representational primitives"?* What primitives are provided by the representation, and what concepts can be expressed in those primitives?

5. *How easy is it to modify the knowledge?* Is it possible to change just a few pieces of information, or does changing just a few pieces require changing a great many more, as well? That is, how modular is the representation?

6. *What kind of acquisition is possible or not possible?* How is new knowledge related to old knowledge? How are possible conflicts between old and new handled? Will the representation support generalization or specialization?

7. *What kind of retrieval is possible?* Is it possible to find knowledge via associations or hierarchical access? How are chunks of related knowledge retrieved?

8. *What kind of reasoning is possible?* Is it possible to make logical deductions? Is it possible to do some sort of induction? Is it possible to continue even in the face of missing or uncertain knowledge?

9. *What is the division of labor between the knowledge base and the interpretive program?* Must everything be encoded ahead of time, or can the interpreter fill in the gaps or generate new knowledge when it is needed? What knowledge is explicit? Implicit?

10. *How can the representation itself be modified or extended?* Can new primitives be created and used? Can the representational conventions be modified? What are the implications of such changes for the interpreter?

This is a very long list of questions, and many are interrelated. They can be paired according to the issues they address:

1 and 2: the ease of encoding,
3 and 4: expressive adequacy,
5 and 6: acquisitional adequacy,
7 and 8: inferential adequacy, and
9 and 10: the scheme itself and its maintenance.

It is probably too much to ask that every question be answered before choosing and using a representation scheme, but considering such a list—even if not in complete detail—is one of the best ways to make sure the scheme chosen matches the requirements of the project. Grappling with these questions is also a way to become familiar with the knowledge domain; they provide an entry point into the epistemological analysis the system designer must do.

In the next section we survey a handful of the best-known representation schemes. As you are reading, you might wish to consider how each representation fares in light of the preceding questions.

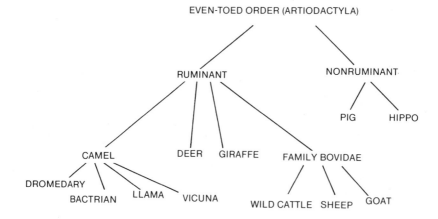

(a)

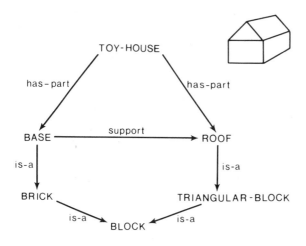

(b)

Figure 4.4
Examples of networks. (a) A concept hierarchy. The links are all *is-a* links. (b) A semantic network expressing some of the structure of a toy house. (c) A network showing some of the linkages between a particular proposition and general conceptual knowledge about human beings and flowers.

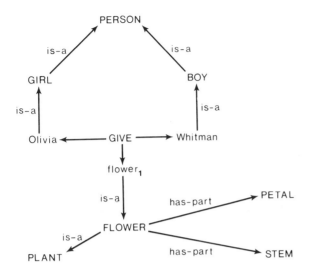

(c)

Figure 4.4 (cont.)

Survey of Standard Knowledge Representation Techniques

Semantic Nets   As we saw in chapters 2 and 3, a *semantic network*, or simply *net*, is a set of nodes and connecting links that represent propositional information. Knowledge resides in the structure of the net and in the processes that operate on it. Semantic networks were actually first developed by AI researchers (Quillian 1968) working on language understanding and have continued to be widely used and discussed (Brachman 1983, 1985).

Perhaps the simplest type of net—and the most frequently used in AI—is an *is-a* or *a-kind-of* (AKO) hierarchy, where the links express the *is-a* or *a-kind-of* relation between nodes. For example, part of the ruminant subfamily of mammals can be represented by the network fragment depicted in part (*a*) of figure 4.4. Such hierarchies have been used to great advantage by programs that operate in knowledge domains where the hierarchical nature of the knowledge is important. For instance, the AM program uses an *is-a* hierarchy to represent certain types of mathematical functions. In such networks, one is usually careful to distinguish between *is-a* in the sense of set inclusion, as in the statement "prime numbers are a kind of number" and *is-a* in the sense of one item being a member of a particular set, as in the statement "2 is a prime number." The semantics of these two different types of links—one between sets or classes of objects and the other between an individual object and class—are closely related yet different enough to require slightly different treatment.

Another type of net can be used to show how an object can be decomposed into other objects. Typical links in this type of network are *is-a-part-of* or *has-part*. This sort of network was used by Winston's (1970) concept-learning program, described later in this section. The network in part (*b*) of figure 4.4 contains the net for a house made of children's blocks. The *has-property* link is another type of frequently used link; it is used to associate a property with a node.

Of course, semantic nets can also be used to represent aspects of natural language, such as of the sentence *Olivia gave Whitman a red rose*. We could embed this bit of net into the larger scheme of our knowledge about the world and arrive at a network like the one shown in part (c) of figure 4.4. Note that we have used a "give" link in addition to the more standard links.

Such examples raise the *grainsize* and *right primitives* problems concerning the expressive adequacy of a representation. They are not unique to semantic nets but are relevant to any representation scheme. They are either troublesome or interesting issues, depending on one's point of view as either programmer or philosopher. For instance, just how many links are important in capturing the meaning of such a simple sentence as *Olivia gave Whitman a red rose*? Must we also "explode" the flower node into its constituent parts and each of these further still until we get down to the elements in the periodic table of chemistry? Won't this lead to a hopeless tangle? What about different senses of the word *gave*? Olivia gave Whitman a cold, an idea, a kiss, a punch in the nose?

Though one could obviously refine the nets given in figure 4.4 so that these particular problems are patched over, similar ones will crop up in the revised nets as well. There are no "right" answers to the problems touched on here: what primitives to use in a representation, what level of detail to use, and how to represent situations that change over time. Such problems are epistemological. That is, they raise questions about the nature of knowledge. The psychologist takes an empirical approach, asking how the problems are typically resolved by the human mind. AI workers often take a pragmatic approach and stop unearthing more questions and the knowledge needed to deal with them when they think they have enough to allow the program to accomplish its purpose, whether it be answering questions about stories or solving algebra word problems.

The is-a type of semantic net is particularly good for tasks involving movement of information between individuals and classes. Particularly important is the *inheritance* of information from class to subclass and from class to individual, such as the knowledge that dromedaries possess the attributes associated with ruminants, and ruminants those associated with mammals; hence, if we endow the scheme's interpreter (the process that manipulates the net) with transitivity, dromedaries also inherit properties of mammals, such as that they nurse their young.

This is very useful when we need to reason about dromedaries but do not know much about them. However, what we know about ruminants or mammals might be enough to answer questions like "Do dromedaries chew their cud?" or "Do dromedaries nurse their young?" Of course, many questions (for instance, "Do dromedaries have two humps?") would require specific knowledge of dromedaries.

As a pragmatic approach, we could try to encode information as high up in the hierarchy as possible (for instance, encode the fact of "having two eyes" at the mammal level) and let it be inherited downward (for instance, to the dromedary level). This of course places certain requirements on the interpreter and implies certain costs for using knowledge implicitly embedded in the representation.

The opposite approach would be to encode the information explicitly (for instance, to encode "having two eyes" on every node for which it is true). This removes some of the burden from the interpreter but exacts costs in terms of the neatness, efficiency, and ultimate perspicuity of the representation.

Other questions can be asked about inheritance as well. For instance, should it be restricted? Should there be a way, for example, to block the inheritance of "having two eyes" onto an individual animal that because of a mishap has only one? (See Brachman 1985 for an interesting discussion of such problems.) A good rule of thumb in this approach is to inherit values downward and assume them to be true unless told otherwise.

The opposite of inheritance may be said to be *induction:* moving from the characteristics of individuals to those of classes. This seems to be a much harder problem, but one that has central connections to psychology and concept learning. For instance, if all the ruminants one has encountered have an even number of toes, should one infer that this is true of *all* ruminants (true, barring accidents or genetic mutations) or more radically of all mammals (false)? How far up a hierarchy should specific facts be pushed, and how far down should general ones be inherited? One approach that will emerge in our discussion of the learning system LEX is to keep pushing up until one encounters a reason to stop.

Another was used by Winston in an early AI attack on the problem of inductive learning, which we will call *ARCH-LEARNER* (Winston 1970). It uses semantic nets. The program learns certain concepts, like that of an "arch" built of children's blocks, by being shown examples and nonexamples of the concept. The nonexamples, called *near misses*, are of a very special kind: they fail to be positive examples in exactly one respect (hence their name). A concept is learned through successive refinement of an initial model of the concept. In a sense the program is building a model or theory of what "archness" is. The whole process is driven by the exemplars (as compared with knowledge about buildings or physics), which is not so different from the way humans learn in many cases. Both the concept and the presented examples (i.e., positive examples and near misses) are represented as semantic nets with arcs like *is-a, part-of*, and *supports*.

For instance, suppose the program's current representation of an arch specifies that an arch has three subparts—a top, a left side, and a right side—and that each is-a kind of rectangular block, or brick. This representation captures the kind of arch shown in part (*a*) of figure 4.5. Now suppose the teacher shows the program the structure depicted in part (*b*) of figure 4.5, with the comment that this is not an arch. Since the only difference between what the program knows so far and this new nonexample is the touching of the base blocks, the program infers that this must be a difference that makes a difference; that is, it learns that the two support blocks of a true arch must not touch. This is reflected in the semantic net representation by the addition of a *must-not-touch* link between the two base blocks.

By processing further examples and nonexamples presented by a teacher, the program refines the arch concept (that is, the semantic net representing the arch concept). For instance, suppose the teacher next shows the program an arch whose top is a triangular block, such as the one shown in part (*c*) of figure 4.5, and says that this too is an example of an arch. This will cause the program to generalize by changing an is-a link for the top to point to a more general kind of block in its known hierarchy of block types, which includes such wedges. This example teaches the program that the concept of arch is more general than it had supposed. If another near miss is shown where the top is not supported by the two side blocks, as in part (*d*) of figure 4.5, the program learns that the support relationship between the top and the sides is necessary. This causes the *supports* link to be changed to a *must-support* link. The resulting concept of arch is shown in figure 4.6.

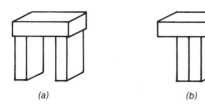

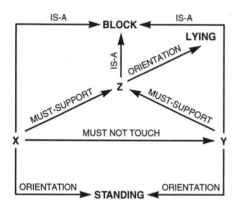

Figure 4.5
Arches and non-arches. (*a*) An arch. (*b*) A near miss: support columns cannot touch. (*c*) An arch: the lintel does not have to be a brick. (*d*) A near miss: the columns have to support the lintel. (Adapted from Winston 1970.)

Figure 4.6
The final concept of arch, following the training examples of figure 4.5. (Adapted from Winston 1970.)

In this way, ARCH-LEARNER evolves a model—in semantic network form—of what is involved in the concept "arch." The success of this approach depends heavily on the quality and order of the examples presented to the program by its teacher.

The decision of how the program should modify arcs in its semantic nets, if at all, is made by comparing the current representation of the concept with a representation of the presented example. Such a comparison is possible because both concept and presented example or nonexample are represented in semantic nets using the same kinds of arcs and nodes. This "single representation trick" greatly simplifies the comparison.

Further, since a near miss can fail to be an example in only one way, the blame for the failure can be assigned and the concept updated accordingly. If there were multiple differences, it would be hard to tell which difference made a difference; this is a version of what is known in the literature on learning programs as the *credit assignment* problem. The credit assignment problem was recognized very early in research on game playing, as a result of trying to ascertain just what move in a particular game led to a player's ultimate win or loss. For instance, which move was responsible for the successful or catastrophic checkmate: the original pushing of a pawn (unlikely) or the moves immediately preceding the checkmate (more likely)? The problem is how to judge.

Frames   It is frequently very natural to manipulate several pieces of information as if they were one unit. For instance, in certain contexts the whole cluster of network nodes and arcs representing the concept of an arch might be manipulated as a whole. Furthermore, there are often prototypical clusterings of information (such as constituent parts and their properties) that one would like to bundle together computationally. When combined with some ideas on data structures from computer science, these notions of prototype and *chunking*, which as we saw in chapter 2 have long been recognized in the psychological literature, lead to the idea of a frame (Minsky 1975).

A *frame* is a collection of slots and slot *fillers* that describe a stereotypical item. A frame has slots to capture different aspects of what is being represented. The filler that goes into a slot can be an actual value, a default value, an attached procedure, or even another frame (that is, the name of or a pointer to another frame). Unless otherwise identified, slot fillers in our examples are actual values.

For instance, the frame to represent a typical chair might look like this:

```
CHAIR
    SPECIALIZATION-OF: FURNITURE
    NUMBER-OF-LEGS:
        DEFAULT: 4
        IF-NEEDED: use procedure COUNT 'EM
    NUMBER-OF-ARMS: 0, 1, or 2
    SEAT:
    BACK:
        DEFAULT: same as SEAT
    STYLE:
    GOOD-FOR: sitting
```

The frame to represent a typical desk chair might look like this:

```
DESK-CHAIR
    SPECIALIZATION-OF: CHAIR
    NUMBER-OF-LEGS:
    NUMBER-OF-ARMS:
        DEFAULT: 2
    SEAT: cushioned
    BACK: cushioned
    STYLE: high-tech
    GOOD-FOR: sitting at a desk
```

Notice that the CHAIR frame has a default value of 4 for the NUMBER-OF-LEGS slot. This represents the knowledge that we usually expect chairs to have four legs; it is not always the case—think of a three-legged milking stool—but it is very often so. In general, a *default* value is a value that we assume to be true unless we are told otherwise. For instance, in discussing the semantic net for mammals, we treated the value 2 as the default value for the number of eyes; in a specific case this might be wrong, but in general it is a very good assumption. Assuming a default value is also appropriate for the number of wheels (4) on a car. There are exceptions—a certain kind of British car has three wheels—but in the preponderance of cases we can safely assume the default value and proceed with our task. Default values are useful because they encode certain expectations about the world, as do frames themselves, and they allow processing to proceed even in the face of missing data. However, if an incorrect assumption is very costly, we might not rely on the use of a default value, like 4 for the number of legs on a chair; instead, if we have it, we might use a procedure attached to the frame, like COUNT 'EM, to get an accurate value. The use of default values and attached procedures distinguishes a frame from an ordinary data structure, or index card. A slot can also be left unfilled (the BACK slot), list alternatives (the NUMBER-OF-ARMS slot), or point to yet another frame (the SPECIALIZATION-OF slot).

Frames can stand in a hierarchical relation to one another. DESK-CHAIR is a specialization of, a kind of, CHAIR. The SPECIALIZATION slot allows one frame to point "up" to another frame; generalization and other types of pointers are also possible. Having such pointers in frame slots allows the frames themselves to be arranged into networks. (Note that for simplicity we suppress the distinction between "subset of" and "member of," using the term "specialization of" to refer to both.) Networks of frames are frequently arranged in an is-a hierarchy, just like semantic networks. Networks of frames have been used to represent knowledge in complex domains like mathematics and law in the AM and HYPO programs.

In frame-based systems filling in slot values is a major activity. Using an inherited value (that is, the value from the same slot of another frame, typically one higher up in the hierarchy) is an easy way to obtain a value. For instance, the filler for the NUMBER-OF-LEGS slot of the DESK-CHAIR frame could be inherited from the same slot (actually the default value) of the CHAIR frame. When values from frames higher up are missing (as in the BACK slot of the CHAIR frame) or are not reliable enough, attached procedures can be used to determine them.

Frames are particularly good at representing "chunked" knowledge such as a person's understanding of complex concepts, like those from mathematics, or a whole section of a semantic net, like that representing the concept of an arch, although designing the right frame representation—just like designing the right link and node types for semantic nets—can be far from simple. Once designed, however, frames allow for expectation-driven processing. That is, because they represent the stereotypical situation, frames allow us to look for the expected and, when we note an exception, to record this difference and act on it. For instance, if we examine chairs in light of the CHAIR frame, which has a default value of 4 for NUMBER-OF-LEGS, and if we note that a particular chair, like a stool, has only three legs, we can (1) distinguish it from the run-of-the-mill type of chair and (2) treat it differently (for instance, in reasoning about how stable it is to stand on).

Frames can provide prescriptive knowledge that can help a program or person to understand a domain better by using the slots as generators of tasks to do—such as questions to answer. This was the approach taken independently by two researchers, Lenat and Rissland. As we have seen, Lenat's goal in developing the program AM was to model the creative discovery of mathematical concepts. Rissland's goal was to describe mathematical understanding of rich mathematical domains like linear algebra. Although these researchers' goals were different, their representations were remarkably similar. Both used similar frames in their representations for mathematical knowledge. Lenat included more procedural knowledge and a powerful interpreter that knew how to spawn new concepts; Rissland included more structural refinement of the knowledge that emphasized the different types of mathematical knowledge and their connectivity.

In brief, Rissland (1978) developed three types of frames and three semantic nets for CONCEPTS, RESULTS, and EXAMPLES. The three types of frames had similar slots (such as NAME, WORTH, EPISTEMOLOGICAL-CLASS, IN-SPACE-POINTERS), and each type could be organized in a net reflecting a different type of linkage. For instance, the linkage important among results (for example, theorems) was logical deduction, and the linkage important among examples was generation. The three semantic nets of frames, called *spaces*, were *Concepts-space*, *Results-space*, and *Examples-space*. These spaces were connected through interframe linkages. A typical frame for an example is shown in part (*a*) of figure 4.7. The use and representation of examples by Rissland was a precursor to case-based reasoning.

A typical frame in Lenat's AM scheme is shown in part (*b*) of figure 4.7. Unlike Rissland's scheme, AM had only one network of frames. In this representation, knowledge about examples was "linked to" the concept exemplified. There were no explicit links between exemplars. This was quite adequate for Lenat's purpose of studying the discovery of set and number theory concepts in the setting of the natural numbers. It would have been inadequate for Rissland's purpose because the connectivity between examples and other items of knowledge is an important ingredient of a mathematician's understanding. Also, in domains where examples have more structure than they do in the domain of the natural numbers, more knowledge about examples and their relationships would be needed (for instance, to accomplish the task of generating extreme cases). Thus, these two schemes demonstrate how differing purposes can lead to similar but different representations of the same general subject matter.

Scripts   As we saw in chapter 2, some stereotypical knowledge is episodic or sequential in nature and is well represented by scripts. A *script* is an elaborate causal chain about a stereotypical event. It can be thought of as a kind of frame where the slots represent ingredient events that are typically ordered in a particular sequence. For instance, as any parent will attest, there is a typical script for attending a preschool child's birthday party, which goes something like this:

> Go to party house.
> Give present to birthday child.
> Play games.
> Sing songs.
> Have snacks.
> Watch birthday cake being brought in.
> Watch birthday child blow out candles.
> Sing "Happy Birthday."
> Eat cake.
> Watch birthday child open presents.
> Play some more.
> Get cranky.
> Go home.

NAME: Cantor set

CLASS: Reference, Counterexample

RATING: Very important

STATEMENT:

SETTING: The Real numbers
CAPTION: The Cantor set is an example of a perfect, nowhere dense set
that has measure zero. It shows that uncountabale sets can
have measure zero.

DEMONSTRATION:

AUTHOR: Standard
MAIN-IDEA: Delete "middle-thirds"
CONSTRUCTION:

0. Start with the unit interval [0, 1];
1. From [0, 1], delete the middle third (1/3, 2/3);
2. From the two remaining pieces, [0, 1/3] & [2/3, 1], delete their middle thirds, (1/9, 2/9) & (7/9, 8/9);
3. From the four remaining pieces, delete the middle thirds;
N. At Nth step, delete from each of the 2^{N-1} pieces its middle third.

The sum of the length of the pieces removed is 1; what remains is the Cantor set

PICTURE:

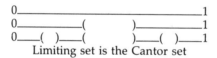

Limiting set is the Cantor set

REMARKS: Cantor set is good for making things happen almost everywhere

LIFTINGS: Construction of general Cantor sets

WITHIN-SPACE POINTERS:

BACK: Unit interval
FORWARD: Cantor function, general Cantor sets, 2-dimensional Cantor set

INTER-SPACE POINTERS:

CONCEPTS: Countable, measure zero, closed, perfect, geometric series
RESULTS: Perfect sets are uncountable; countable sets have measure 0

BIBLIOGRAPHIC REFERENCES: [*Names of texts containing further information*]

(*a*)

Figure 4.7
Frames for mathematical concepts. (*a*) A frame that emphasizes the structure of mathematical knowledge. The frame is from a network of example frames and has links to other example frames. It also has links to two other networks for concept-frames and results-frames. (From Rissland 1978.) (*b*) AM's frame for the concept "prime," oriented toward the generation of conjectures and new concepts. The frame is part of a single network and is tied to other concepts by generalization and specialization links. (From Davis and Lenat 1982.)

NAME: Prime numbers

DEFINITIONS:

   ORIGIN: Number-of-divisors-of $(x) = 2$

   FORMAL LOGIC: For all z, if z divides x, then either $z = 1$ or $z = x$

   ITERATIVE: For $x > 1$: For i from 2 to the square root of x, i does not
           divide x

EXAMPLES: 2, 3, 5, 7, 11, 13, 17

   BOUNDARY: 2, 3

   BOUNDARY-FAILURES: 0, 1

   FAILURES: 12

GENERALIZATIONS: Numbers; numbers with an even number of di-
                visors; numbers with a prime number of divisors

SPECIALIZATIONS: Odd primes; pairs of prime numbers whose differ-
                ence is 2

CONJECTURES: Extremes of number-of-divisors-of; all integers can be
              uniquely factored into a set of prime divisors

INTUITIONS: A metaphor to the effect that primes are the building blocks
             of all numbers

ANALOGIES: Maximally divisible numbers are converse extremes of num-
             ber-of-divisors-of; factor a nonsimple group into simple
             groups

INTEREST: Conjectures tying primes to times; to divisors-of; to related
           operations

WORTH: 800

(b)

Figure 4.7 (cont.)

Scripts have been used in natural language tasks such as the understanding of short stories (Schank and Abelson 1977; Lehnert et al. 1983). Understanding in this context means that a program can answer questions about what it has read. For instance, consider the following story:

> Whitman went to Olivia's fourth birthday party. After she blew out the candles and everyone sang, he gave her a new truck.

Now one could ask, "Why did Whitman give Olivia a truck?" We would answer, of course, "For a birthday present." We would also have no trouble naming at least one song sung at Olivia's party or answering questions about the candles. We would have no trouble answering such questions because we can understand this little story in light of a script that is very familiar to us. We know the sequence of events for such birthday parties and have no trouble filling in missing details or providing reasons not explicitly mentioned.

To understand the story and answer such questions requires not only specific knowledge about children's birthday parties but also commonsense knowledge about the world, such as that the truck in question is a toy and not a Toyota for a four-year-old's party. (Note: the answer might be different for adults.) The need for enormous amounts of such knowledge is related to the problem of *commonsense knowledge and reasoning:* that is, reasoning about things from everyday life, which we, "of course," all know. One aspect of this problem is that commonsense knowledge is vast; therefore, to represent all we might ever need is a tremendously difficult and pervasive problem, even if the individual bits of knowledge are not very complicated or deep. Another aspect of the problem concerns the commonsense physics of everyday life (metallic objects, like pennies, make a rattling sound when shaken in certain kinds of containers, like piggy banks; when a glass is knocked over, the contents will spill; and so on). This is a long-standing problem in AI (Minsky 1963) and has been attacked from the entire spectrum of approaches to AI ranging from McCarthy's use of logical formalisms (McCarthy 1980) to Minsky's use of frames (Minsky 1975). There are several ongoing efforts in AI to grapple with such problems. For instance, Lenat and coworkers are seeking to build an encyclopedic repository of everyday commonsense knowledge in the CYC project (Guha and Lenat 1990).

Scripts can point to other scripts and contain subscripts, just as frames can. Our birthday party script probably should include or point to a subscript for buying the birthday present; this in turn might point to a script about acquiring the money needed to buy it. Also, as pointed out in connection with semantic nets, this process of breaking down the constituents in the representation—here, the subacts in the scripts—can continue until we reach a fine-grained level and spell out the details of such actions as the "physical transfer" of objects. In their attack on this problem Schank and his coworkers developed a small set of a dozen or so representational primitives that were adequate for understanding everyday episodes. For instance, they distinguished between the primitive PTRANS, representing the physical transfer of an object between individuals, and the primitive ATRANS, representing an abstract transfer of possession or ownership. So, for example, ATRANS would be used in representing the second element of the birthday party script (give the present to birthday child). A simple handing over of an object as in "Hand the present to the birthday child" would use PTRANS.

Rule-Based Representations   In chapters 2 and 3 we introduced the concept of *production rules.* These *if-then,* or *situation-action,* pairs encode the knowledge that if a certain situation obtains, then a certain action should be taken. In AI this type of representation has been particularly useful in domains that require making deductions by stringing together if-then statements. Such *rule-based* representations have been used in many expert systems where expert knowledge is often of a rulelike nature, or at least can be gainfully represented that way. The production rule approach is particularly useful in tasks requiring categorization (Clancey 1984), as in the medical diagnosis program MYCIN.

Other well-known successes using this type of knowledge representation scheme include programs to deduce the chemical structure of molecules from their mass spectrograms and chemical formulas (DENDRAL) (Lindsay et al. 1980), to configure computer hardware (R1/XCON) (McDermott 1982), to interpret oil well drilling data (DIPMETER-ADVISOR) (Davis et al. 1981), and to analyze pulmonary function tests (PUFF) (Harmon and King 1985). Their use in real-world applications has become legion.

A production system has three parts:

1. A rule base (the collection of if-then rules)
2. A context
3. An interpreter

The rules represent the knowledge. The context represents the current state of the system's conclusions, that is, the facts known so far. The interpreter knows how to apply the rules to the context. The system works by looking at the context, seeing which rules apply, selecting one rule to apply, drawing that rule's conclusion, writing it into the context, and repeating the cycle. This can be summarized by saying that a production system has a basic three-part cycle:

1. Matching
2. Conflict resolution
3. Action

As we mentioned earlier, production systems can work either forward or backward. In a forward-chaining system, matching is done between data and preconditions of rules; in backward chaining, matching is done between goals/subgoals and consequents of rules. Thus, in the matching phase of a forward-chaining system, the interpreter must be able to tell whether the left-hand side of a rule—the *antecedent* or *if* part—is satisfied by the facts in the context. In the conflict resolution phase, if the context satisfies more than one rule, the interpreter selects one of them to apply. In the action phase the interpreter adds the selected rule's conclusion—its *consequent* or *then* part—to the context.

To see how a forward-chaining production rule system might work, consider the task of identifying an animal. (Note that this particular problem could be solved simply with a decision tree and does not really require the power of a production system; nevertheless, it is illustrative.) We need some rules, an interpreter, and some facts about the class of animals we wish to identify. Suppose that the knowledge base consists of the following rules:

1. If the animal chews its cud, then it is a ruminant.
2. If the animal is a ruminant and has humps, then it is a camel.
3. If a camel has one hump, then it is a dromedary.
4. If a camel has two humps, then it is a bactrian.
5. If an animal has one or two humps, then it has humps.

And suppose that the interpreter works as follows:

1. Find all rules whose left-hand side obtains and label them "applicable."
2. If more than one rule is applicable, then deactivate (remove the "applicable" tag from) any rule whose action would add a duplicate fact to the context.
3. Execute the lowest-numbered applicable rule. If none, quit.
4. Reset applicability of all rules. Return to step 1.

Conflict resolution is handled in step 3. Step 2 is needed to keep the system from spinning its wheels by drawing the same conclusion over and over again.

Now suppose we are told that the animal we wish to identify kicks, chews its cud, and has two humps. These facts are placed in the context, which we indicate in square brackets:

[kicks, chews-cud, humps = 2]

Now we begin our identification. In cycle 1, step 1, the applicable rules are 1 and 5. Neither rule would add a duplicate fact to the context, so neither is eliminated through deactivation in step 2. Since we take the lowest-numbered rule in step 3, rule 1 is used and its conclusion is written into the context:

[kicks, chews-cud, humps = 2, ruminant]

In cycle 2 the applicable rules are 1 and 5. Since rule 1 would lead to a redundant addition to the context, rule 5 is used and its conclusion is written into the context:

[kicks, chews-cud, humps = 2, ruminant, humps]

In cycle 3 the applicable rules are 1, 2, and 5. By the redundancy rule, rule 2 is selected and its conclusion is written into the context:

[kicks, chews-cud, humps = 2, ruminant, humps, camel]

In cycle 4 the applicable rules are 1, 2, 4, and 5. Rule 4 is selected and its conclusion is written into the context:

[kicks, chews-cud, humps = 2, ruminant, humps, camel, bactrian]

In cycle 5 no new rules are made applicable. That is, the system has invoked every rule it could and made every conclusion it could. Thus, the system's final conclusions are the facts now in its context, in particular, that the unknown beast is a bactrian camel. In this example we have used rules in a *forward-chaining* manner; that is, we started with data and reasoned "forward" toward conclusions. This is in contrast to the backward-chaining approach used in MYCIN. Forward chaining approaches are often called *data-driven* and backward-chaining approaches, *goal-driven*. The latter work best when the program has a plausible set of possible conclusions; the former, when the program has much data but no hunches about the conclusions. We could work the camel example in a backward-chaining manner using the same rules but making appropriate modifications to the workings of the interpreter. For example, we could attempt to determine whether the unidentified animal is a ruminant by determining whether it is a cud chewer. Of course, it is possible to combine both styles of reasoning in a more sophisticated system.

It is interesting that the research on human problem solving, reviewed in chapter 3, suggests that the productions of human experts are highly data-driven, leading to a forward-chaining style of reasoning. This may be because relevant productions can be selected by a highly efficient parallel activation process. In humans, backward chaining is more typical of the general problem-solving strategy used by novices and by experts when confronted with a problem that requires particularly novel use of expert knowledge.

To use the production rule approach, the researcher must resolve several problems. Obviously, the rules must be expressed, which typically means that someone must first extract the content of the rules from an expert and settle on a vocabulary for expressing the rules. Next comes the problem of specifying how the interpreter is to work. This largely involves deciding how to resolve conflicts. Some obvious strategies are

1. Use the lowest-numbered rule (as we have just done).
2. Use the rule with the highest current priority.
3. Use the most specific rule.
4. Use the rule that refers to the fact most recently added to the context.
5. Use an arbitrary rule.

Each of these approaches carries with it certain assumptions, some of which might be significant in terms of the particular system being developed. For instance, approach 1 assumes that rules are numbered according to usefulness, importance, or some other measure of goodness; approach 2 requires some way of defining, setting, and resetting priorities.

Perhaps more interesting are the grainsize and right primitives problems. For rule-based representations, these problems involve not only selecting a vocabulary that is meaningful but also specifying how to tell if an object possesses a quality or is an instance of a concept. Rules are ultimately built up by conjoining components called *predicates*, or *relations*, that answer "Yes" or "No" about a given quality. (We will discuss predicates further when we consider logic-based representations.) For instance, in an actual encoding of the rules for the camel problem, rule 1 would involve a predicate for CHEWS-CUD in the antecedent and a RUMINANT in the consequent. To use a predicate like RUMINANT, the system ultimately needs a way of answering "Yes" or "No" to the question "Is this animal a ruminant?" Of course, the easiest way is for the user to tell the system the answer directly. Another way is for the system to infer the answer by backward chaining or by applying some test procedure; for instance, rule 1 tells the system that if the animal chews its cud, then it is a ruminant. Of course, the problem with the backward-chaining approach is what to do when the rules run out. This occurs when the system designer doesn't know how to break concepts down any further. For instance, there is no rule in our example to enable the system to determine if the CHEWS-CUD predicate applies. If the user cannot answer this question, the system is stuck. Another problem in some domains is that certain properties or concepts do not have crisp, black-and-white boundaries. Some are a matter of degree (baldness), and some simply do not admit tight definitions (chair). Such concepts arise in everyday situations involving what philosophers call "natural kind" categories (e.g., chairs). Most legal concepts are of this type, even such familiar ones as "income" or "contract." In the law, as in everyday life, difficulties in reasoning with such concepts are handled by use of past cases that addressed the concept and then reasoning analogically. These problems arose earlier in our discussion of human concepts and reasoning in sections 3.1 and 3.3.

Several researchers are experimenting with hybrid approaches using rules and cases in a variety of domains and in a variety of computational architectures. In such approaches, for instance, cases can be used to aid rule-based reasoning. For instance, when rule-based reasoning reaches an impasse, past determinations (cases) about open-textured concepts can be used to help resolve their interpretation in a new situation.

Two recent AI and law systems that reason in statutory legal domains—that is, legal domains based on statutes, which are the rules passed by legislative bodies—combine reasoning with rules and reasoning with cases in interesting ways. For instance, one system called GREBE (Generator of Exemplar-Based Explanations) (Branting 1991) uses past exemplars and nonexemplars to help determine whether the facts in a new situation should be classified as a positive or negative instance of legal concepts necessary for applying legal rules (from an area of workers' compensation law). GREBE reasons analogically with these past exemplars by mapping over their explanations to the new case. GREBE's notions of analogy and the use of exemplars draw heavily on work modeling analogy as a mapping between representation structures, such as semantic nets (Falkenhainer, Forbus, and Gentner 1989), as well as on traditional AI tools of knowledge representation and search.

Another mixed paradigm system called CABARET (Rissland and Skalak 1991) brings together elements of the three systems—AM, MYCIN, and HYPO—introduced earlier, in an opportunistic processing style to generate analyses (for a subsection, the so-called home office deduction, of federal income tax law). CABARET combines classic rule-based reasoning (using forward and backward chaining) with the type of case-based reasoning used in HYPO in a computational architecture based on an agenda, the type of control scheme used in AM. In CABARET, the reasoning is more opportunistic than in GREBE in that difficulties or observations made from either type of reasoning can serendipitously set up tasks to perform with the other type of reasoning. For instance, in addition to the use of cases to aid in reasoning with open-textured concepts needed in rule-based reasoning, CABARET can take observations resulting from case-based reasoning, such as the existence of a preponderance of cases supporting one point of view, to set up tasks for rule-based reasoning, like the verification of the view suggested by the cases.

A mixed paradigm system from a nonlegal application is ANAPRON (Golding and Rosenbloom 1991), which uses cases and rules on the task of proper-noun pronunciation. ANAPRON uses cases to represent exceptions to general rules about how to pronounce names; if the exceptional cases are compelling enough, ANAPRON will use the pronunciation suggested by the case rather than the one indicated by the rule. In experiments with ANAPRON, it was shown that the use of both cases and rules greatly improved the performance based on cases or rules alone and that the increase in performance was monotonic on both aspects; that is, adding more rules or more cases led to improved performance. In addition, when ANAPRON used its complete rule set (approximately 650 rules) and case base (5,000 cases), its performance was as good as that of human experts.

It is interesting to note that in addition to rule and case hybrids using symbolic AI techniques there are also symbolic-subsymbolic hybrids addressing some of the same problems (such as the indexing of cases) as the symbolic hybrids we have just mentioned. One such system combining symbolic and connectionist techniques is the SCALIR system (Rose and Belew 1991). It uses a connectionist network—based on the backpropagation algorithm we discussed in chapter 2—to retrieve relevant cases and text needed for other reasoning tasks. SCALIR also operates in a statutory legal domain (copyright law).

Another recent hybrid that draws on both symbolic and statistical approaches is Stanfill and Waltz's (1986) MBRTALK system. Called a "memory-based reasoning" system by its developers, it uses a large number of cases (approximately 4,500) and a highly parallel approach to indexing them. It is implemented on the "Connection Machine," which embodies a highly distributed, parallel architecture involving thousands of processors.

It is likely that in the future there will be many more hybrid systems: hybrids of symbolic approaches as well as symbolic and connectionist ones. In such mixed paradigm systems, controlling the reasoning will present interesting problems. One promising approach for organizing such systems is the blackboard architecture, which we discuss in chapter 5. The CABARET system is actually an early example of this approach since an agenda can be considered a special case of a blackboard architecture.

Logic-Based Representations   Many AI applications make use of the formal reasoning tools of mathematical logic. The most widely used representation is *first-order predicate calculus* (FOPC), which specifies formal rules for reasoning about propositions that concern sets of objects. For example, FOPC can formally express the kinds of inferences discussed in section 3.3, such as

Premises: All rabbits like carrots
              Peter is a rabbit

Conclusion: Peter likes carrots

As we noted in section 3.3, in order to make this inference, a deduction system must have both the inference rule *modus ponens* and a rule (called *for-all elimination* or *universal specialization*) to connect the general proposition about all rabbits with the proposition about a particular rabbit.

FOPC was developed in the late nineteenth and early twentieth centuries by Gottlob Frege and jointly by Bertrand Russell and Alfred North Whitehead. They were particularly interested in developing a logical foundation for mathematics; they also recognized and began to develop the notion that formal logic could represent nonmathematical information and reasoning processes.

The use of formal logic in AI provides an interesting contrast with human reasoning. In chapter 3 we saw that people tend to reason with concepts and heuristic rules that efficiently yield useful conclusions most of the time but may yield logically incorrect results or fail to yield a correct result that is actually logically implied by the data at hand. In addition, people tend to think of concepts in terms of prototypical instances or "family resemblance" rather than in terms of strict logical definitions using necessary and sufficient conditions. This straightforward logical approach is often called the "classical" approach; in its pure form it is mostly discredited as a cognitive model (Smith and Medin 1981).

On the other hand, formal logical systems such as FOPC were explicitly developed with the goals of logical soundness and completeness in mind. Therefore, some researchers believe that if formal logical systems could be efficiently implemented on computers, they might outstrip human intelligence by being error-free and by coming up with correct results that humans might fail to obtain.

Logicians work with assertions like "Fido is a dog" or "A is a block and A is on my table" or "My table has four legs." In FOPC such statements could be written as follows:

DOG(Fido)
BLOCK(A) AND ON(A, My-Table)
EQUALS (4 NUMBER-OF-LEGS(My-Table))

DOG, BLOCK, ON, and EQUALS are examples of predicates. As we saw in chapter 2, when a predicate is applied to its arguments, it yields a truth-value. A predicate is a function that can take on values *true* or *false*.

These examples concern individual objects Fido, A, and My-Table. To represent statements about classes of individuals in our universe of discourse—either about all of them or about some of them—we must introduce into our notation what are called *universal* and *existential quantifiers*. For instance, to represent a statement about all dogs ("All dogs bark"), we must use a variable, x, and the universal quantifier (For all ...), which allows the variable to range over the set of all dogs. We could write this as follows,

For all $x \in$ Dogs, BARK(x)

where ∈ is short for "belongs to" or "in" and "Dogs" denotes the set of all dogs. Alternatively, we could use the implication arrow (⇒) and let the variable x range over all individuals in our realm of discourse (not just dogs):

For all x, DOG(x) ⇒ BARK(x)

To represent the statement "Some dogs bark," we use the existential quantifier (There exists …) and phrase the statement as "There exist some dogs that bark":

There exists x ∈ Dogs, BARK(x)
or
There exists x, DOG(x) AND BARK(x)

To encode the assertion that "Everybody loves somebody sometime," we would use both quantifiers and a three-place predicate (a predicate function of three variables) LOVES(x, y, t) to represent that the condition of love holds between the first variable and the second variable at the time of the third variable:

(For all x ∈ Persons)(There exists y ∈ Persons)(There exists t ∈ Time)
LOVES(x, y, t)

In addition to predicates FOPC can also make use of functions. Functions can take on values other than true or false. Examples of functions are COLOR, NAME, FATHER, NUMBER-OF. This allows us to represent statements like "There are blocks of two different colors" or "George is his own grandpa":

(There exists x ∈ Blocks)(There exists y ∈ Blocks)
(NOT (EQUALS (COLOR(x), COLOR(y))))
EQUALS (George, FATHER(FATHER(George)))

Note that whether such statements are actually true or not is a totally different concern.

FOPC is called "first-order" because it only allows quantification over individuals in the domain of discourse and does not allow quantification over such things as predicates or sets of individuals as in the assertion "All predicates are two-valued." A higher-order calculus would be necessary to encode the last statement. However, for most purposes in AI, FOPC has all the expressive power needed.

If-then statements are a particularly useful kind of assertion involving the use of implication (symbolized ⇒). We have already seen examples of such statements in the discussion of rule-based representation. To express them in the formalism of predicate calculus, we would pay particular attention to the quantification and the predicates involved:

1. (For all x) [CHEWS-CUD(x) ⇒ RUMINANT(x)]
2. (For all x) [(RUMINANT(x) AND HUMPS(x)) ⇒ CAMEL(x)]
3. (For all x) [(CAMEL(x) AND EQUALS(NUM-HUMPS(x), 1)) ⇒ DROMEDARY(x)]
4. (For all x) [(CAMEL(x) AND EQUALS(NUM-HUMPS(x), 2)) ⇒ BACTRIAN(x)]
5. (For all x) [(EQUALS(NUM-HUMPS(x), 2) OR EQUALS (NUM-HUMPS(x), 1)) ⇒ HUMPS(x)]

We have now introduced the vocabulary of FOPC. It includes *names*, which denote a specific element of the domain of discourse (e.g., Fido); *variables*, which range over elements (e.g., *x*); *predicates*, which take on the values true and false (e.g., BARK); *functions* (e.g., COLOR); the *existential* (There exists) and *universal* (For all) *quantifiers*, which apply only to variables; and *connectives* (e.g., AND, OR, NOT, IMPLIES). In fact, one can confine oneself to AND and NOT or OR and NOT as the connectives to use in FOPC since $A \Rightarrow B$ is logically equivalent to [(NOT *A*) OR *B*].

Formal syntactic rules must also be specified for creating complex expressions, such as the examples just discussed. Expressions in FOPC are often called *well-formed formulas* (WFFs). We will not give the rules for forming WFFs here, but WFFs are built up by putting together individual WFFs into more complex WFFs with the use of the connectives.

Perhaps the most important aspect of formal logic is that there are well-understood rules for deriving new truths from other known truths. Modus ponens is an example of a rule specifying how to make valid inferences. Such rules allow the deduction of new assertions from a knowledge base of existing assertions; moreover, if the assertions in the knowledge base are true, then so are the derived statements. This is the basis of theorem proving, whether by machine or by person. Thus, one of the most powerful uses of logic in AI is to use WFFs to represent assertions about a domain and a theorem prover to deduce new facts, which will be certain to be true.

The inference rule modus ponens is one example of a rule for deriving valid assertions from other assertions. Another is *universal specialization* (US), which states that if an assertion is true about all individuals, it is true about a particular individual:

Rule US: Given an individual *I* and the assertion (For all *x*)P(*x*), infer P(*I*).

Both rules were introduced informally in section 3.3. They apply in the case of the mortality of Socrates:

Premises:	1. (For all *x*) [HUMAN(*x*) $\Rightarrow$ MORTAL(*x*)]
	2. HUMAN(Socrates)
Apply US to 1:	3. HUMAN(Socrates) $\Rightarrow$ MORTAL(Socrates)
Apply modus ponens to 3 and 2:	4. MORTAL(Socrates)

As this example illustrates, logical deduction involves considerable detail; deductions must be made explicitly and precisely.

Formal reasoning is a potentially powerful tool, and a formal proof procedure, called the *resolution method* (Robinson 1965), has been developed that runs efficiently on digital computers. Resolution involves rewriting if-then statements in terms of equivalent statements using AND, OR, and NOT and then combining them in a special way. Resolution is most successful when the set of statements and facts is not too large.

Two examples of applications of logic and theorem provers have been question-answering systems and planning systems. For instance, if we know that a pig is a kind of even-toed animal that is not a ruminant,

EVEN-TOED(pig) AND NOT RUMINANT(pig)

we could answer questions like "Is it true that every even-toed animal is a ruminant?" by trying to prove

(For all x) [EVEN-TOED(x) $\Rightarrow$ RUMINANT(x)]

and returning "pig" as an explicit counterexample.

A classic planning application is STRIPS (Fikes and Nilsson 1971), which treats the problem of moving a robot from an initial state to a goal state by proving a theorem about the existence of the goal state. For instance, if the robot is at point A, boxes are located at points B, C, and D, and the problem is to gather the boxes "at" some other common point, this goal would be represented as a theorem to prove:

(There exists x) [AT(Box1, x) AND AT(Box2, x) AND AT(Box3, x)]

Some of the strengths and weaknesses of formal logic have been known since the 1930s, when the first *metamathematical* theorems were proved. These theorems concerned the general properties of formal logical representations. FOPC, for example, can be shown to be *sound* and in certain domains *complete*. The soundness theorem demonstrates that any assertion derived by the rules of inference from other true assertions will also be true. The completeness theorem establishes that there is a procedure that systematically constructs proofs for and lists all valid formulas. Thus, the theorem demonstrates that there actually is a proof for any true statement. Although these theorems apply only to straightforward set-theoretic domains, they are impressive in their scope, and nothing like them exists for formal systems that use networks, frames, or productions to do reasoning. On the other hand, the *undecidability* and *incompleteness* theorems establish profound limitations of formal logical systems. Church's undecidability theorem states that there can be no procedure for deciding in a finite number of steps whether a formula has a proof. Thus, if the procedure of the completeness theorem has not listed a particular formula after some number of steps, it may be because the formula is false or it may be because the formula will show up later in the list. The practical effect of undecidability is that no proof procedure can avoid wasting time trying to prove falsehoods or giving up too soon trying to prove statements that are actually true. Gödel's incompleteness theorem states that when FOPC is enriched enough to contain elementary arithmetic, the completeness theorem fails, and there are true statements about the domain of discourse that are not provable with any fixed, formal proof procedure.

The implications of the undecidability and incompleteness results for AI have been discussed for many years (for an introduction, see Hofstadter 1979). Most researchers now agree that the results do not preclude the possibility of artificially intelligent machines. However, it can be argued that humans and computers are limited by the results in the same ways. Any information-processing system, biological or electronic, that is restricted to a fixed formal deduction system will be limited by undecidability and incompleteness. To the extent that human beings have means to overcome these limitations, it is conceivable that the same means could be implemented on machines. Such means might include heuristic reasoning and enrichment of the knowledge base through interaction with an environment.

The lofty plane of metamathematics has not been the only source of debate about the use of logical representations. It has proven to be difficult to extend FOPC from mathematical domains, where facts are universal and eternal, to real-world domains, where facts change with time and situational context. Resolution theorem provers have also suffered from performance problems. They tend to get bogged down in the plethora of intermediate details that are generated in logical proofs. It has proven difficult to develop heuristics that identify plausible lines of proof or focus on the assertions that are crucial to proving a theorem. Such difficulties have led to what some have called the "neat-scruffy" debate: the view that knowledge is neat and clean and can be circumscribed and manipulated logically versus the view that knowledge and reasoning are intrinsically messy and heuristic and thus logical methods are bound to fail. Some researchers continue to work on extending FOPC to handle nonmathematical knowledge (we will see one approach in chapter 10; for another approach, see McCarthy 1980). Their goal is to preserve the strengths that come from well-defined concepts and reasoning techniques that can be shown to be logically sound. Other researchers adopt other representations and processes that have less well known properties but that ease some of the problems with logical representations.

Consider the legal domain. At first glance the law looks neat and rulelike. For example, we might think, "If there's a contract and one party has breached it, then the other can recover damages." But then the question becomes, "What's a contract?" We could try to solve this question in turn with a rule: "If there's consideration and a mutual bargain, then there's a contract." Now, of course, we must decide what constitutes consideration. In the law there really is no end to such backward chaining. So in fact we have bumped into a particularly vexing form of the grainsize and right primitives problem: in the legal context there is no ultimately satisfying grainsize or set of primitives. Furthermore, the difficulty with legal concepts is that they are *open-textured*, as opposed to mathematical concepts, which are *close-textured*. In calculus a function is either continuous or not, according to some precise definition; in law there are no watertight definitions. No matter what representation scheme we use in the legal domain—semantic nets, frames, production systems, or logic—we will of necessity have to grapple with such problems.

One approach is to assume that to a first approximation such a domain is neat (for instance, has well-defined concepts or reasoning processes). Another is to modify an existing representation scheme or reasoning mechanism to deal with the scruffy problems. AI workers take both approaches. For example, in the legal domain researchers are trying to use traditional representation schemes as well as supplementing them with new modes of reasoning. Gardner (1987) uses a traditional form of network supplemented by the heuristic use of examples. Rissland and Ashley's HYPO (Ashley 1990) uses traditional frames supplemented with case-based reasoning. Rissland and Skalak (1991) integrate case-based reasoning with traditional rule-based techniques. For a general discussion of recent progress in the area of AI and legal reasoning, see Rissland 1990.

Suggested Readings

Artificial Intelligence (Winston 1992), *Introduction to Artificial Intelligence* (Charniak and McDermott 1985), *Logical Foundations of Artificial Intelligence* (Genesereth and Nilsson 1987), and *Artificial Intelligence and the Design of Expert Systems* (Luger and Stubblefield 1989) are textbooks in AI. The second of these books includes a brief introduction to the LISP programming language. The four volumes of *The Handbook of Artificial Intelligence* (Barr and Feigenbaum 1981, 1982; Cohen and Feigenbaum 1982; Barr, Cohen, and Feigenbaum 1989) survey the field of AI at an intermediate level. Various collections such as *Readings in Knowledge Representation* (Brachman and Levesque 1985) and *Readings in Artificial Intelligence* (Webber and Nilsson 1981) reprint many classic research papers. One of the oldest collections—now a true classic—is *Computers and Thought* (Feigenbaum and Feldman 1963); another is *The Psychology of Computer Vision* (Winston 1975). Very interesting and thought-provoking books by some of the founders of AI include *The Society of Mind* (Minsky 1986) and *Unified Theories of Cognition* (Newell 1990).

References

Ashley, K. D. (1990). *Modeling legal argument: Reasoning with cases and hypotheticals.* Cambridge, Mass.: MIT Press.

Ashley, K. D., and E. L. Rissland (1988). A case-based approach to modelling legal expertise. *IEEE Expert.* 3 (3), 70–77.

Barr, A., P. C. Cohen, and E. A. Feigenbaum, eds. (1989). *The handbook of artificial intelligence.* Vol. 4. Reading, Mass.: Addison-Wesley.

Barr, A., and E. A. Feigenbaum, eds. (1981). *The handbook of artificial intelligence.* Vol 1. Los Altos, Calif.: Morgan Kaufmann.

Barr, A., and E. A. Feigenbaum, eds. (1982). *The handbook of artificial intelligence.* Vol. 2. Los Altos, Calif.: Morgan Kaufmann.

Brachman, R. J. (1983). What IS-A is and isn't: An analysis of taxonomic links in semantic networks. *IEEE Computer* 16 (10), 30–36.

Brachman, R. J. (1985). I lied about the trees. *AI Magazine* 4 (3), 80–93.

Brachman, R. J., and H. J. Levesque, eds. (1985). *Readings in knowledge representation.* Los Altos, Calif.: Morgan Kaufmann.

Branting, L. K. (1991). Building explanations from rules and structured cases. *International Journal of Man-Machine Studies* 34 (6), 797–838.

Buchanan, B. G., and E. H. Shortliffe (1984). *Rule based expert systems: The MYCIN experiments of the Stanford Heuristic Programming Project.* Reading, Mass.: Addison-Wesley.

Charniak, E., and D. McDermott (1985). *Introduction to artificial intelligence.* Reading Mass.: Addison-Wesley.

Clancey, W. J. (1984). Classification problem solving. In *Proceedings of the American Association for Artificial Intelligence.* Austin, Tex.

Cohen, P. R., and E. A. Feigenbaum, eds. (1982). *The handbook of artificial intelligence.* Vol. 3. Los Altos, Calif.: Morgan Kaufmann.

Davis, R., H. Austin, I. Carlbom, B. Frawley, P. Pruchnik, R. Sneiderman, and A. Gilreath (1981). The dipmeter advisor: Interpretation of geological signals. In *Seventh International Joint Conference on Artificial Intelligence.* Vancouver, B.C., Canada.

Davis, R., and D. B. Lenat (1982). *Knowledge-based systems in artificial intelligence.* New York: McGraw-Hill.

Falkenhainer, B., K. D. Forbus, and D. Gentner (1989). The Structure-mapping engine: algorithm and examples. *Artificial Intelligence* 41, 1–63.

Feigenbaum, E. A., and J. Feldman, eds. (1963). Computers and thought. New York: McGraw-Hill.

Fikes, R. E., and N. J. Nilsson (1971). STRIPS: A new approach to the application of theorem proving to problem solving. *Artificial Intelligence* 3, 251–288.

Gardner, A. v. d. L. (1987). *An artificial intelligence approach to legal reasoning.* Cambridge, Mass.: MIT Press.

Genesereth, M. R., and N. J. Nilsson (1987). *Logical foundations of artificial intelligence.* Los Altos, Calif.: Morgan Kaufmann.

Golding, A. R., and P. S. Rosenbloom (1991). Improving rule-based systems through case-based reasoning. In *Proceedings of the Ninth National Conference on Artificial Intelligence.* Anaheim, Calif.

Guha, R. V., and D. B. Lenat (1990). Cyc: A midterm report. *AI Magazine* 11 (3), 32–59.

Harmon, P., and D. King (1985). *Expert systems.* New York: Wiley.

Hofstadter, D. R. (1979). *Gödel, Escher, Bach: An eternal golden braid.* New York: Basic Books.

Lehnert, W., M. Dyer, P. Johnson, C. Yang, and S. Harley (1983). BORIS: An experiment in in-depth understanding of narratives. *Artificial Intelligence* 20, 15–62.

Lenat, D. B. (1977). Automated theory formation in mathematics. In *Proceedings of the Fifth International Joint Conference on Artificial Intelligence.* Cambridge, Mass.

Lenat, D. B., and J. S. Brown (1983). Why AM and Eurisko appear to work. In *Proceedings of the American Association for Artificial Intelligence*. Washington, D.C.

Lindsay, R., B. G. Buchanan, E. A. Feigenbaum, and J. Lederberg (1980). *DENDRAL*. New York: McGraw-Hill.

Luger, G. F., and W. A. Stubblefield (1989). *Artificial intelligence and the design of expert systems*. Redwood City, Calif: Benjamin/Cummings.

McCarthy, J. (1980). Circumscription: A form of non-monotonic reasoning. *Artificial Intelligence* 13, 27–39.

McDermott, J. (1982). R1: A rule-based configurer of computer systems. *Artificial Intelligence* 19, 39–88.

Minsky, M. L. (1963). Steps toward artificial intelligence. In Feigenbaum and Feldman 1963.

Minsky, M. L., ed. (1968). *Semantic information processing*. Cambridge, Mass.: MIT Press.

Minsky, M. L. (1975). A framework for representing knowledge. In Winston 1975.

Minsky, M. L. (1986). *The society of mind*. New York: Simon and Schuster.

Newell, A. (1990). *Unified theories of cognition*. Cambridge, Mass.: Harvard University Press.

Polya, G. (1957). *How to solve it*. New York: Doubleday Anchor Books.

Quillian, M. R. (1968). *Semantic memory*. In Minsky 1968.

Rissland, E. L. (1978). Understanding understanding mathematics. *Cognitive Science* 2, 361–383.

Rissland, E. L. (1989). Dimension-based analysis of Supreme Court hypotheticals. In *Proceedings of the Second International Conference on AI and Law*. Vancouver, B.C., Canada.

Rissland, E. L. (1990). Artificial intelligence and law: Stepping stones to a model of legal reasoning. *Yale Law Journal* 99 (8), 1957–1982.

Rissland, E. L., and K. D. Ashley (1986). Hypotheticals as a heuristic device. In *Proceedings of the American Association for Artificial Intelligence*. Philadelphia, Penn.

Rissland, E. L., and D. B. Skalak (1991). CABARET: Statutory interpretation in a hybrid architecture. *International Journal of Man-Machine Studies* 34, 839–887.

Rissland, E. L., E. M. Valcarce, and K. D. Ashley (1984). Explaining and arguing with examples. In *Proceedings of the American Association for Artificial Intelligence*. Austin, Tex.

Ritchie, G. D., and F. K. Hanna (1984). AM: A case-study in AI methodology. *Artificial Intelligence* 23, 249–268.

Robinson, I. A. (1965). A machine-oriented logic based on the resolution principle. *Journal of the ACM* 12, 23–41.

Rose, D. E., and R. K. Belew (1991). A connectionist and symbolic hybrid for improving legal research. *International Journal of Man-Machine Studies* 35, 1–35.

Schank, R. C., and R. P. Abelson (1977). *Scripts, plans, goals and understanding: An inquiry into human knowledge structures*. Hillsdale, N.J.: Erlbaum.

Shortliffe, E. H. (1976). *Computer-based medical consultations: MYCIN*. New York: American Elsevier.

Smith, E. E., and D. L. Medin (1981). *Categories and concepts*. Cambridge, Mass.: Harvard University Press.

Stanfill, C., and D. Waltz (1986). Toward memory-based reasoning. *Communications of the ACM* 29, 1213–1228.

Webber, B. L., and N. J. Nilsson, eds. (1981). *Readings in artificial intelligence*. Los Altos, Calif.: Morgan Kaufmann.

Winston, P. H. (1975). Learning structural descriptions from examples. In Winston 1975.

Winston, P. H., eds. (1975). *The psychology of computer vision*. New York: McGraw-Hill.

Winston, P. H. (1992). *Artificial intelligence*. 3rd ed. Reading, Mass.: Addison-Wesley.

Yu, V. L., L. M. Fagan, S. W. Bennet, W. J. Clancey, A. C. Scott., J. F. Hannigan, R. L. Blum, B. G. Buchanan, and S. N. Cohen (1984). An evaluation of MYCIN's advice. In Buchanan and Shortliffe 1984. Revised version of Antimicrobial selection by a computer: A blinded evaluation by infectious disease experts. *Journal of the American Medical Association* 242 (12), 1279–1282 (1979).

Chapter 5
Artificial Intelligence: Search, Control, and Learning

5.1 Search and Control

Artificial intelligence (AI) programs and analyses pose what can be called the *problem of what to do next*. For problems that can be viewed as an exploration of alternatives—as in looking ahead through game positions to see which move to make—the programs must select which alternative to consider next (in other words, how to explore the space of alternatives). This is the issue of *search*. In problems where the task has been broken down into subtasks, it must be decided how to coordinate the performance of the subtasks: when to do which and how to decide when to do which. This is the issue of *control* and the closely related issues of how to organize and structure the program. Search and control are two aspects of the problem of what to do next, and control can in fact be viewed as search writ large. Questions of search and control cannot be avoided, and how an AI program designer chooses to resolve them is related to other choices, like knowledge representation, that have certain implications for control style.

In this section we briefly describe some of the fundamental types of search techniques and control schemes. Although search is an important component of human problem solving, our approach in this section is not limited to modeling or describing search in human cognition. Human search strategies are very strongly constrained by the physical implementation of cognition in the brain, primarily by limitations on working-memory capacity and on the speed of serial operations. In AI we can approach search as a general issue in the design of intelligent systems, exploring the formal properties of a wide range of techniques with the knowledge that many of them can be implemented efficiently enough on computers to be useful.

Introduction to Search
Search techniques can be divided into two major types: *blind* search and *heuristic* search. Blind search techniques use only the structure of the space of alternatives in selecting the next alternative to consider; any "legal" possibility is as worthy of consideration as another. Heuristic search techniques, on the other hand, add measures to select the most "promising" or "plausible" alternative (or in other words, to ignore the least promising ones). This approach requires developing measures to gauge promise and plausibility.

The problem of getting from one place to another in a strange city can be viewed as a search problem. In blind search the traveler could only make use of the structure of the search space—the layout of the city—and could ask no questions about which route is shortest or quickest. In heuristic search the traveler would be better informed and would be able to use information about which streets are slow because of traffic

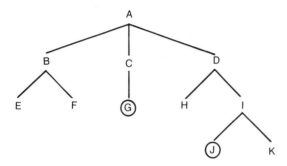

Figure 5.1
An example of a tree. The goal nodes are circled.

congestion, which streets curve and meander and are not the shortest routes, and so on. When there is a real cost involved in a search—for instance, the traveler is on foot and carrying a heavy suitcase—the advantages of informed, heuristic search over "dumb," blind search are apparent. Heuristic does have disadvantages, however. The information used to inform the search must be acquired, at some cost, and it must be accurate, to avoid errors.

To employ AI search techniques, the space of alternatives must be structured into a *graph* or a *tree*. Semantic nets are one type of graph. We will deal here only with trees, since they are simpler. In a tree—as opposed to a graph—a given node can be reached by only one path.

A tree in an AI program is a collection of *nodes* and *arcs* arranged in a manner reminiscent of the structure of a tree in nature: it has a *root* node, emanating from which are *branches*, which in turn divide into more branches. The number of branches springing from a node—its *branching factor*—is a measure of the number of alternatives. The depth or number of *levels* is another important descriptor for a tree. In the tree in figure 5.1 node A is the root node. It has three offspring or *successor* nodes: B, C, and D. This tree is not at all deep: it has only three levels (counting the level below the root node as "one," as is usually done). It is also not bushy, the greatest number of branches springing from a node being three.

Familiar examples of trees are one's family tree, the classification system for the plant and animal kingdoms, and the hierarchical chain of command in an organization where no one answers to more than one boss. Family trees can be drawn in at least two ways: (1) the root node represents the person making the tree, two branches from that node represent the person's parents, two branches from each of those nodes represent the person's grandparents, and so forth; (2) the root node represents some ancestor, and the branches from the root node represent that person's offspring. The first approach to drawing family trees leads to a uniformly structured *binary tree*: each node has exactly two branches emanating from it.

Such trees can have a large number of nodes. For instance, the number of nodes in the first type of family tree doubles with each generation. Trees arising in AI applications, such as game playing, can be so large that one must use clever ways to explore them. The point was nicely made by the mathematician Claude Shannon, who estimated the number of possible board states in chess to be 10^{120}, a number so large that even at the rate of one billion calculations per second, the history of the universe would not provide enough time to examine all the alternatives.

In the study of search the tree of alternatives represents three typical kinds of situations:

1. States: Each node represents a "snapshot" of a state of the problem.
2. Problems or goals: Each node represents an alternative or ingredient subproblem or subgoal.
3. Game state: Each node represents the state of the game after a player's legal move.

In the first type of tree, the search is called *state space* search; in the second, *problem reduction*; and in the third, *game playing*.

We can use the classic problem known as the Tower of Hanoi to illustrate the different approaches. A simplified version of the problem can be posed as follows:

> Given three graduated discs (large, medium, and small) and three pegs (A, B, and C), where the three discs are arranged on peg A so that the largest is on the bottom and the smallest is on the top: Move the discs to peg C so that they end up in the same order (largest on the bottom, smallest on the top). Only one disc may be moved at a time, and a larger disc may not be put on top of a smaller one.

Some of the states for the three-disc version of the problem are shown in figure 5.2. Note that the figure depicts both the series of states leading to the specified solution (tower stacked on peg C) and those leading to an analogous situation (tower stacked on peg B). Moreover, it includes a certain amount of redundancy, since several states are depicted more than once (the initial state, for example, appears again in level 2); this is to avoid drawing a graph (which would allow more than one way to arrive at a given state) instead of a tree.

The Tower of Hanoi problem can also be represented using a problem-reduction approach (see figure 5.3). In this approach the root node represents the original problem of moving the 3-tower on peg A to peg C. This could be broken down into three subproblems: (1) move the 2-tower (the small and medium discs) from peg A to peg B; (2) move the big disc from peg A to peg C; and (3) move the 2-tower from peg B to peg C. This solution to the three-disc version of the problem suggests a (recursive) solution to versions of the problems using N discs: (1) move the $N - 1$ tower out of the way to peg B; (2) move the biggest disc from peg A to peg C; (3) move the $N - 1$ tower onto peg C. Note that the first and third subproblems are also problems to solve; the second step is a "primitive" action and requires no further reduction.

Perhaps a more typical example of a problem easily handled with a problem-reduction approach is

> Get from your dorm to your parents' home.

This problem can be reduced to several subproblems: (1) get from your dorm to the bus station; (2) get from the bus station to the airport; (3) get by plane from that airport to the airport in your hometown; and (4) get from the airport in your hometown to your parents' home. Some of these subproblems might require further reduction: perhaps you'll need a cab to get to the bus station. Some can be solved in more than one way: to get from your hometown airport to your parents' home, you can either get a

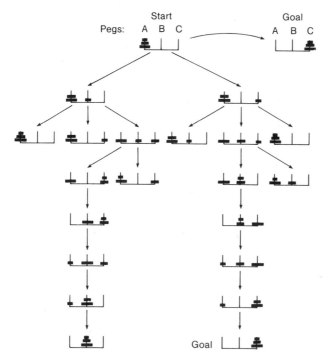

Figure 5.2
Part of the search space for the three-disc Tower of Hanoi puzzle. Only some of the states in the search space are illustrated here, including a complete search path to the goal state, in which all three discs are on peg C.

cab or have your parents pick you up. The idea in working with problem-reduction trees is to break the original problem down into smaller, and presumably easier, subproblems, and these subproblems into subsubproblems, until a level is reached that can be handled by "primitive" operations that the system can perform without further problem solving. In the travel example all of the four subproblems that are immediate offspring of the original problem must be solved in order to solve it, an example of an AND breakdown, but the fourth subproblem has two alternative solutions, "get a cab" or "have your parents pick you up," an example of an OR breakdown. The main point about the AND-OR distinction in the problem-reduction approach is that if a solution satisfies one OR node, there is no need to explore its siblings; and if one branch under an AND node fails to be satisfied, there is likewise no need to explore further.

A typical game tree problem occurs in playing tic-tac-toe. Supposing that your opponent has marked the center square, find your best, if possible winning, move (where alternate levels in the tree represent alternate players' options). Part of the tree for tic-tac-toe is shown in figure 5.4.

In this chapter we will treat search only in the context where the nodes represent states. Search in problem-reduction trees is much the same, with the addition of techniques to handle the AND-OR distinction. We will not explore the specialized techniques required by game tree search.

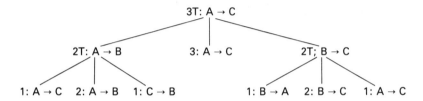

(a)

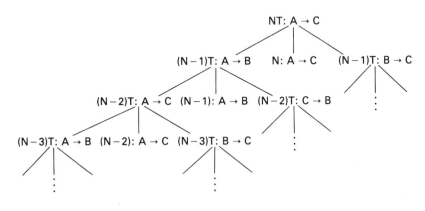

(b)

Figure 5.3
The problem-reduction approach to the Tower of Hanoi puzzle. A problem with any number of discs can be solved by successively breaking it up into subproblems that involve smaller numbers of discs. Each node in the search tree represents a subproblem. The smallest disc is numbered 1 and the largest disc, N. A subtower that contains the M smallest discs is called the M-tower, or MT. Thus, the notation 2T: $A \rightarrow B$ means "Move the subtower containing the two smallest discs from peg A to peg B," and the notation 2: $A \rightarrow B$ means "Move disc 2 from peg A to peg B." (a) A problem-reduction tree for the three-disc puzzle. The goal of moving the 3-tower is broken down into subgoals that involve moving the 2-tower and moving disc 3, which can be done directly. The goals of moving the 2-tower can be broken down into subgoals that involve moving disc 1 and disc 2 (note that the 1-tower is equivalent to disc 1). (b) A problem involving N discs can be decomposed in the same manner.

The important thing to remember about search techniques—like knowledge representations—is that each has its advantages and disadvantages. Choosing the most appropriate one depends on the kind of trees to be searched. Are they bushy? Are they deep? Where are the goal nodes?

In any search problem the programmer usually wants to use a method that is guaranteed to find a solution (if it exists). If at all possible, the programmer also wants the method to find a "good" or "optimal" solution and to do so efficiently. A typical way to measure efficiency is by counting the number of nodes examined in the search; the smaller the number the more efficient the search. The entire set of alternatives (nodes) is called the *search space*, and that part actually examined (presumably containing far fewer nodes) is called the *search tree*. Searching can be viewed as constructing or unmasking the search tree as the search proceeds.

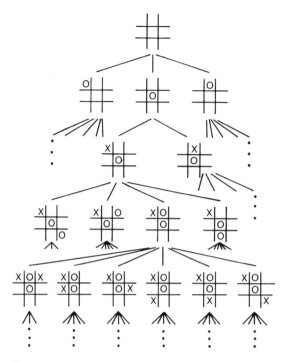

Figure 5.4
A small part of the game tree for tic-tac-toe. Player O moves first, and the possible moves generate the first level of the tree. The possible responses of player X generate the second level of the tree, and so on. Only a few of the possible positions are shown. Note that if two positions can be superimposed by rotating the paper and/or viewing the game in a mirror, they can be treated as equivalent. Thus, O's nine possible opening moves can be reduced to three categories that are strategically distinct.

Blind Search Techniques

There are many standard *blind search* techniques. We will briefly describe four of the most widely known: breadth-first, depth-first, uniform cost, and hill-climbing search. For a detailed treatment, see Nilsson 1971.

A search program always starts from some initial or *start* node and searches for a *goal* node or state. Though there is only one start node, there may be more than one goal node. In game-playing search, for instance, given an initial position (such as the opening board configuration), there may be several winning (goal) positions. In the example tree in figure 5.1 the root node is the start node, and there are two goal nodes G and J (circled) at the lowest level.

Breadth-First and Depth-First Search   *Breadth-first search* expands and examines nodes in order of their proximity to the start node. It examines all nodes at a given level or depth before considering those at the next. In other words, it considers every node n arcs or levels down from the start node before considering any node $n + 1$ arcs or levels down, so that (for example) level 1 is completely considered before any attention is given to level 2.

To use an everyday example, a breadth-first approach to a library research project would involve finding a survey article with a good reference list and proceeding to consider every work on that list (before considering any of the references those works

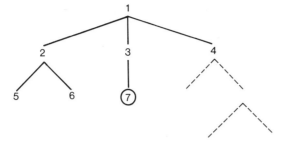

Figure 5.5
Breadth-first search, of the tree in figure 5.1. The names of the nodes are replaced with numbers that denote the order in which the nodes are searched. The dashed branches of the tree are not explored because the search terminates when a goal node is reached.

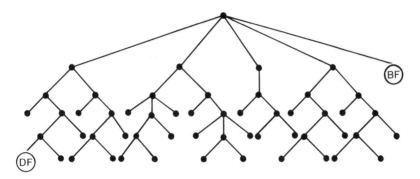

Figure 5.6
Easy and difficult searches. Using a breadth-first search algorithm, the node labeled BF is reached early in the search, and the node labeled DF is reached much later. Using a depth-first search algorithm, the opposite is the case: node DF is reached early, and BF much later. Thus, the usefulness of a search algorithm can depend on the location of the goal nodes in the search space.

point to); this gives a "broad" look at the subject. Breadth-first behavior allows the searcher to proceed cautiously. For instance, given six alternative financial investments, a breadth-first approach forces the investor to consider all of them before considering the alternatives opened up by any one. Figure 5.5 illustrates how the tree given in figure 5.1 would be searched using a breadth-first search technique. Notice that the search proceeds level by level.

Breadth-first search is careful and conservative. It is guaranteed to find the shortest path to a solution node. However, if the goal nodes are buried deep in the tree, it is wasteful. In the library research task, for instance, breadth-first search requires considering all of the first-level references—no matter how interesting or dull— before considering any of the second-level references—no matter how potentially relevant they may seem. Examples of good and not-so-good search paths for breadth-first search are shown in figure 5.6. The optimal kind of tree for breadth-first search is one in which the goal nodes are located in the uppermost levels; the worst is one in which they are buried very deep.

Depth-first search explores all of one branch before considering a sibling branch. That is, it expands nodes descending from those most recently considered, and only when it reaches a node with no offspring does it consider alternatives (siblings). Sometimes depth-first search is called a leftmost (or rightmost) *mouse scan* because it follows the principle "Explore the leftmost (rightmost) branch every time there is a choice; when a dead end is reached, back up to the last choice and take the next leftmost (rightmost) branch."

Carrying out the library research task in a depth-first manner would entail picking a work from the reference list of the original article, then picking one from the reference list of that work, and so on. In the investment example, instead of considering all initial alternatives, the investor would consider one of them in depth by following through on its implications and the implications of those implications. In other words, a depth-first searcher is going deep along one particular line of thought (branch of the tree) before considering any other.

Given the tree of figure 5.1, depth-first search would consider nodes in the order shown in figure 5.7. Depth-first search proceeds branch by branch. Note that it considers the rightmost node of level 1 only until after it has considered all the nodes— deep and shallow—on the branches to the left. Thus, the worst kind of tree for (leftmost) depth-first search would have goal nodes on a branch far to the right. Examples of good and not-so-good search paths for depth-first search are shown in figure 5.6.

Depth-first search is aggressive but potentially dangerous. The danger comes from descending a branch, in which the goal nodes are very deep or not present, and never returning, or at least not returning quickly. Because of this possibility, search program designers often use a slight variation called *depth-first-with-bound* that keeps the search from going deeper than a specified level before backing up. It is exactly the same as pure depth-first search except that an additional test for depth is inserted.

It is easy to specify rigorously the algorithms for breadth-first and depth-first search. To do this requires defining certain terms. A node is said to be *open* if it is a candidate for immediate further consideration but has not been expanded yet. *Expanding* a node means finding all its successor nodes. A node is *closed* if it has been examined, expanded, and put aside. A node is *unknown* if it has not been dealt with in any way. We will always assume that we have at our disposal the available operators necessary for expansion. Given this terminology, one procedure for breadth-first search is as follows:

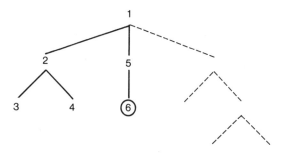

Figure 5.7
Depth-first search of the tree in figure 5.1. The names of the nodes are replaced with numbers that denote the order in which the nodes are searched. The dashed branches of the tree are not explored because the search terminates when a goal node is reached.

1. Put the start node S on the OPEN list. If S is a goal node, the search ends successfully.
2. If the OPEN list is empty (that is, there are no more alternatives to consider), no solution exists and the search ends unsuccessfully.
3. Remove the first node from the OPEN list; call it N. Put N on the CLOSED list.
4. Test N. If N is a goal node, the search ends successfully; otherwise, continue.
5. Expand N. If N has no successors, go to step 2.
6. Put all successors of N at the end of the OPEN list and cycle back to step 2.

This specification of breadth-first search can easily be modified to specify depth-first search. All that is needed is to modify step 6 so that the successors of N are placed at the beginning of the OPEN list instead of the end. In breadth-first search OPEN is what computer scientists call a *queue*: the first entry in is the first entry out. In depth-first search OPEN is a *stack*: the last entry in is the first entry out.

Search with a Cost Function   Breadth-first and depth-first search are very simple (and useful) search techniques that depend only on the structure of the tree being searched. In these algorithms no numerical measures are used to choose between nodes. Any successor is considered as good as any other successor in the sense that any order in which the expansion procedure produces them is acceptable. In many problems, though, such as the library research and financial investment tasks, intuition suggests that all successors are not equally good, and some method is needed for ordering or choosing among the successors. Uniform cost and hill-climbing search are two of the most common blind search techniques that rely on measures for choosing nodes.

Uniform cost search is used when there is a cost associated with the arcs. The idea is to find the cheapest path to a goal node and always to explore the alternative with the cheapest cost path examined so far. When all arcs are rated equally costly, say, of cost 1, uniform cost search is exactly the same as breadth-first search. Figure 5.8 illustrates the uniform cost search of a tree that has a cost associated with each arc. Table 5.1 displays the actions and results of each step in the search.

The algorithm is similar to the breadth-first and depth-first algorithms, but instead of choosing the first node on the OPEN list as the next node, the algorithm chooses the node with the lowest cost. If multiple nodes are tied for the lowest cost, a goal node is chosen if there is one, or else the choice is made randomly.

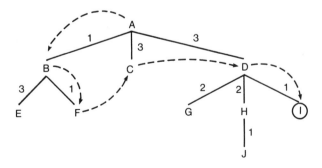

Figure 5.8
Uniform cost search. Each arc in the tree has a cost, which is shown as a number. The goal node is circled. The dashed arrows illustrate the order of the uniform cost search.

Table 5.1
The uniform cost algorithm. For the tree shown in figure 5.8 the algorithm opens and closes nodes in the order shown. The changes in the open and closed lists resulting from each node expansion are also shown. The algorithm proceeds through the tree by selecting the lowest-cost node on the open list. In the final step node I and node E have the same cost. However, I is selected because it is a goal node.

Actions	List of open nodes	Costs of open nodes	List of closed nodes
Open A	A	0	
Close A	B	1	
Open B, C, D	C	3	
	D	3	
Close B	C	3	A
Open E, F	D	3	B
	E	4	
	F	2	
Close F	C	3	A
	D	3	B
	E	4	F
Close C	D	3	A
	E	4	B
			F
			C
Close D	E	4	A
Open G, H, I	G	5	B
	H	5	F
	I	4	C
			D
Select I as goal			

The last blind search technique we consider is *hill-climbing search*, which was used most heavily in some early AI research. Unlike uniform cost search, which selects from all the unexplored alternatives whose cost has been calculated so far, hill-climbing search chooses which alternative to explore by selecting the best alternative from only the immediate successors of the node last visited.

The suggestive name of this method comes from the fact that if we imagine the space of alternatives as a landscape with knolls and hills whose height corresponds to some measure of goodness, we are trying to find the highest peak. At each step of the climb we ask which next step gains the most height.

Hill-climbing search requires making choices about which points (nodes) to sample from a landscape with vastly many points. Other considerations are how big an incremental step to take and whether, and how often, to adjust step size. Such questions are easy to appreciate if we think about the physical task of climbing a mountain.

Perhaps more important, continuing with the mountain-climbing metaphor, it is easy to imagine situations that would cause hill-climbing search to fail. For instance, hill-climbing search could direct the exploration up a secondary peak or a foothill, which it would never leave; such trapping by secondary maxima means that hill-climbing search is not guaranteed to find a global optimum. Another problem is posed by mesas and plains; the hill-climbing process can get stuck exploring uninteresting territory and pass right by a maximum. Researchers have developed various techniques to cope with false maxima and other shortcomings of hill-climbing search; for instance, occasionally the program can take a step in a random direction.

The algorithm for hill-climbing search is somewhat similar to that of uniform cost search. In particular, instead of the "global" cost function used in uniform cost search, hill-climbing search uses a "local" gradient function to measure the change in altitude in going from a node to its successors.

Heuristic Search Techniques

Any problem with many alternatives at each step presents a combinatorial explosion of possibilities to consider (recall the estimate of 10^{120} for the number of possible moves in chess). Since it is utterly impossible to explore all of these alternatives, the question becomes how to control the exploration. The blind search methods do bias the exploration one way or another but ultimately lead to exploring the whole search space if there are no goal nodes. At the very least, they trigger exploration of more alternatives than are desirable. The idea behind heuristic search is to use information about the domain, the search space, and especially the nature of the goal nodes to limit the exploration to only the most promising alternatives. The crux of the issue is determining how to assess promise.

Heuristic information can be used to decide which node to expand next. This can be done, for instance, by estimating the "distance" of the current node from a desired goal node, that is, by guessing about the unexplored intervening portion of the search space. Doing this, of course, requires having a way to calculate such an estimate.

There are several algorithms for heuristic search. Perhaps the best known of these— and the only one we will consider here—is the A^* *algorithm*, which builds directly on the idea of uniform cost search.

In addition to the cost functions used in uniform cost search, the A^* algorithm requires some *evaluation* functions. In particular, it requires a function, called h for its heuristic nature, to measure the cost that would be incurred in going from a node to a goal node. Since this function is usually not known with complete accuracy, an approximation, called h^*, is used. For the A^* algorithm to find an optimal solution of minimal cost, h^* must underestimate the true h; such an h^* is called *admissible*. (That is, formally, it is necessary that $h^*(x) < h(x)$ for each node x.)

The A^* algorithm chooses which node to explore by selecting the one for which the distance from the start plus the estimated distance to the goal is the least. (Recall that uniform search ignores any estimates of cost to reach a goal.)

Written out formally, the A^* algorithm looks very similar to the basic outline of the blind search techniques, especially uniform cost. Again, most of the action centers on how nodes are selected from the OPEN list. And, of course, the extra cost functions complicate matters somewhat.

To write down the A^* algorithm, we need more notation. Keep in mind that we are simply manipulating cost functions—both the actual cost incurred so far from the start node and a heuristic estimate of the cost that might be incurred in reaching a goal node. More specifically, the function f^* calculates cost by adding together the exact cost, g, of the path from the start node S to a node N and the estimate of the cost, h^*, of the path remaining to be traveled from N to a goal node. Again, for this algorithm to work properly, the heuristic function h^* must underestimate the actual cost h. To recap:

$$c(i, j) = \text{cost of arc from node } i \text{ to node } j$$
$$g(N) = c(S, N), \text{ where } S \text{ is the start node and } N \text{ is any other node}$$
$$h^*(N) = \text{estimate of actual cost } h(N) \text{ to reach a goal node from } N$$
$$f^*(N) = g(N) + h^*(N)$$

The procedure for the A^* algorithm is as follows:

1. Put the start node S on the OPEN list. Calculate $f^*(S) = 0 + h^*(S)$. (Note that $g(S) = 0$.)
2. If the OPEN list is empty, no solution exists and the search ends unsuccessfully.
3. Select from the OPEN list the node that minimizes the function f^*. If several nodes qualify, select a goal node, if there is one; otherwise, select one randomly. Call it N. Put N on the CLOSED list.
4. If N is a goal node, the search ends successfully; otherwise, continue.
5. Expand N. If N has no successors, go to step 2.
6. For all successors j of N, calculate $f^*(j)$:
$$f^*(j) = [g(N) + c(N, j)] + h^*(j).$$
Put all successors (tagged with their value of f^*) on the OPEN list. Go to step 2.

Figure 5.9 illustrates the A^* algorithm by applying it to the three-disc Tower of Hanoi problem. The insight that the solution involves moving the 2-tower to peg B and moving disc 3 to peg C is captured by the following method of calculating h^*:

$h^* = $ 4 + sum of the points from list below

−2 if the 2-tower is alone on peg B (a subgoal has been reached)

−2 if disc 3 is on peg C (a subgoal has been reached)

−1 if disc 2 is alone on peg B (part of a subgoal has been reached)

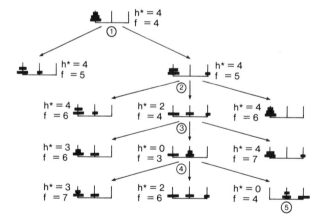

Figure 5.9

The A^* algorithm applied to the three-disc Tower of Hanoi problem. The calculation of h^* is explained in the text. The cost of a single arc is assumed to be 1, making f for a node equal to the sum of h^* and the number of arcs from the start to the node. The circled numbers denote the order in which nodes are closed by the A^* algorithm. The algorithm is assumed to have randomly chosen to close the second node, since the node has the same estimated cost as the unclosed node to its left. The algorithm begins to break down if the fifth node is expanded because of defects in h^* discussed in the text.

− 1 if disc 3 is alone on peg A (disc 3 can now be moved)

+ 1 if disc 2 is at the bottom of peg C (contrary to the subgoals)

+ 1 if disc 3 is on peg B (contrary to the subgoals)

The search in figure 5.9 has reached the state with the 2-tower on peg B and disc 3 on peg C. The h^* function begins to fail at this point because it does not reflect the subgoal of moving the 2-tower from peg B to peg C. It is an interesting exercise to continue the search in figure 5.9, observing the breakdown of h^*. Try to fix up h^* so that it works correctly, reaching the goal efficiently and never overestimating the number of moves to solution. Could the resulting h^* be generalized to any N-tower problem?

Program Architecture and Control

In dealing with the issue of control, we are dealing with questions about how information is to flow among the program's submodules, how these submodules interact, and how the submodules themselves are to be designed. For instance, in considering how processes are to communicate, access, and share information, we must ask, Is every process to have access to every bit of information? Or do some processes have more priority than others? Or is there a prescribed flow of information among the processes? These are questions of communication and coordination. Such issues are intimately bound to the internal architecture of the system and its submodules.

In this section we briefly discuss five control schemes. In addition to illustrating our discussion with systems, such as AM, MYCIN, and HYPO, which we have already introduced, we briefly discuss two additional programs, the classic GPS and HEAR-SAY-II programs.

The three-phase control cycle—matching, conflict resolution, and action—used in rule-based (expert) systems was introduced in chapter 4. It can be either backward or forward chaining. The MYCIN system exemplifies the overall control structure of a *backward chaining*—or *goal-directed*—production system. In backward chaining the system is trying to establish goals and subgoals—that is, the consequents or *then* parts of *if-then* rules—by working backward to establish the needed intermediate conclusions and facts—that is, the rule antecedents or the *if* parts of relevant rules. In such a system, the question of what to do next—that is, which rule antecedents to try to establish—is governed by the rules and conflict resolution scheme. The system looks for rules whose consequents match the antecedents present in the context, and the rule actually applied depends on the system's conflict resolution scheme (e.g., rule importance, inverse recency of rule firing). The search carried out in such a backward-chaining goal-directed system can often be described in terms of a breadth-first or depth-first search of an AND-OR goal tree since unwinding the *if* sides of rules amounts to solving subgoals, structured by the logical relations present in the rules (see figure 5.10).

The depth-first approach to backward chaining is sufficiently useful across a variety of AI tasks that it has been used as the basis of the programming language PROLOG. Because PROLOG program statements are essentially statements in a restricted class of well-formed formulas (so-called *Horn clauses*) of propositional logic, it is called a *logic-programming* language. (Of course, the same label could be applied to many rule-based systems.)

RULES	AND-OR GOAL TREE

If A and B then E. coli

If R or S then A

If C and D then B

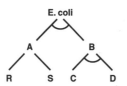

Figure 5.10
A simple example of how if-then rules can define a goal tree. To satisfy an AND-goal, both the subgoals (linked by a curved tie) must be satisfied. To satisfy an OR-goal, at least one of the subgoals must be satisfied.

When certainty factors are used to rate the reliability of intermediate conclusions—as is the case in MYCIN—the search carried out by the system is kind of heuristic best-first search since the most certain lines of reasoning are pursued before, and perhaps to the exclusion of, other lines of reasoning. The control scheme of backward chaining with certainty factors used in MYCIN is the basis of many commercially available expert systems shells. The control regime in MYCIN was motivated by analyses of the heuristic goal-directed way medical experts perform diagnosis, which is a kind of classification task. In general, the goal-directed approach is useful in classification tasks where there are a few possible classes, or hypotheses.

Many production systems use a *forward-chaining* or *data-driven* regime. (Recall from chapter 4 our example classifying types of camels.) Here the rules can be viewed as little processes that "watch" the context and add their conclusions to the context when they are allowed to "fire." In forward chaining, the system is in effect repeatedly applying the inference rule modus ponens. In chapters 2 and 3 we saw that there is considerable evidence for this kind of data-driven control in skilled human performance.

AM exemplifies a second type of control scheme, which is built around an *agenda*, an ordered list of tasks to do. Every time a new task is added to the agenda, it is placed according to the ordering. Typical orderings are based on priority, recency, importance, and interestingness. AM uses an agenda scheme based on interestingness, which engenders a "most-interesting-first" kind of search. Obviously, the control scheme of production systems can be viewed as a specialized kind of agenda: the ranking of the rules used by the conflict resolution scheme specifies an agenda. In this way, the interestingness ratings in AM serve a purpose analogous to that of certainty factors in MYCIN: they focus attention on the best—most interesting, most certain—tasks to do. In AM the actual generation of possible tasks to perform, like proposing a new concept (see the discussion in chapter 4), is dictated by procedures attached to various frames in AM's store of general and mathematical knowledge.

This brings us to our third type of control structure, found in frame-based systems like AM and HYPO: *procedural attachment*. In this scheme procedures are invoked when the frame, or slot, to which they are attached is manipulated by the system. For instance, in the CHAIR frame example of chapter 4, if the system needs to have a value for the NUMBER-OF-LEGS slot, it can run the procedure COUNT 'EM. As another example, a frame representing the concept of a right triangle could have an attached procedure for testing whether the legs of the triangle satisfy the Pythagorean theorem.

It could be invoked via inheritance when considering the frame for a specific triangle, say, a 3-4-5 triangle, farther down the is-a hierarchy. Through procedural attachment the frame under consideration prompts new processing related to it, and by traversing linkages, such as is-a links, between frames, the system can fan out in its activation of procedures.

A more complex kind of control is provided by the fourth type of control scheme: the *blackboard system* (Hayes-Roth 1985). In spirit, blackboard architectures are similar to the types of control we saw with rule-based systems. A *blackboard* is a central repository of information that all the processes, called *knowledge sources* (*KSs*), can monitor much as brokers might monitor a real blackboard in a brokerage office. Based on expertise, each KS is assigned to watch for a particular kind of event or information. For instance, there could be a commodities KS (broker) that watches the blackboard and "shouts"—makes its conclusions known to other KSs—when it sees a trade in a commodity about which it is knowledgeable.

Blackboard systems can be considered a generalization of production systems, in which KSs take the place of rules. The major difference is that in a blackboard scheme the KSs can be quite complex, and the blackboard can be partitioned into "levels" or subregions to which only some KSs pay attention. A rule set can also be partitioned by adding preconditions to rules to specify context, but the blackboard scheme seems a much cleaner way to divide up the problem-solving responsibilities among the KSs. In addition, there can be KSs whose only task is to control the scheduling of other KSs, for instance, by considering the cost of invoking a KS, the benefit of using any conclusion the KS might reach, and the likelihood that the KS might be successful. Such "scheduling" KSs serve a role analogous to that of interestingness ratings in AM and certainty factors in MYCIN: they help focus the processing (said another way: they help prune down the space of possible or pending tasks). Although it is highly flexible, the communication among KSs can be quite complex. There is some controversy about whether the blackboard scheme is a good model of human cognition. The philosopher Daniel Dennett explores this hypothesis in his book *Consciousness Explained* (Dennett 1991).

The blackboard approach was first used in the *HEARSAY-II* speech-understanding program (Erman et al. 1980). In the HEARSAY-II system a continuous stream of speech data is given to the program, which has KSs at many levels of speech information, ranging from KSs that know only how to process low-level segments of speech like phonemes, to those that know how to process syllables and words, to those that know how to process high-level structures like linguistically valid phrases. A noteworthy feature of this architecture is that data and small chunks of information *flow up* to be handled by KSs with more global concerns, and results from the higher-level KSs *flow down* to constrain the processing of the lower-level KSs.

For example, the lower-level processes might not have enough information to choose between the hypotheses of identifying a word as *taxes*, *taxis*, or *Texas*, on the basis of phonemic data; these choices would flow up. Meanwhile, a top-level knowledge source might have hypotheses that the phrase being processed is *no new _____*"; this information would flow down. Based on linguistic constraints, and others, the system would narrow its hypotheses to *No new taxes* or *No new taxis*; further information would be needed to select between these two interpretations. Speech understanding can be quite complicated; for instance, word boundaries are often hard to pin down. Consider what it would take to handle the situation where there were more high-level choices, such as *no nude* _____, as well as more choices for the third word in the phrase, such as *access* or *axes*. The HEARSAY-II architecture creates a control style involving both *top-down* (or goal-driven) processing and *bottom-up* (or data-driven) processing. Such a blackboard architecture where information is available for several or all processes to view and opportunistically act on is the antithesis of the standard programming style of using explicit procedure calls.

A fifth type of control scheme is *means-ends analysis* (introduced in chapter 3), in which the system uses a simple, uniform control loop: at any step of its problem solving, the system chooses what to do next on the basis of the perceived difference between its current state and the goal state. In other words, what matters in this approach is the difference between "where you are" and "where you want to get to." What to do in response to the measured difference is encoded in a difference operator table, which indexes relevant procedures, or operators, based on differences. (Once again, relevance does not guarantee success.) For instance, solving the problem of how to get from your dorm to your parents' home might require the following difference operator table:

If the distance is greater than 500 miles, take a plane.
If the distance is between 10 and 500 miles, go by car.
If the distance is between 2 and 10 miles, go by bus or by bicycle.
If the distance is less than 2 miles, walk.

This control scheme was first introduced in the landmark program *GPS* (General Problem Solver) of Newell and Simon (1972). The GPS style of architecture creates a processing style of decomposing problems into subproblems and is indeed a very general approach to problem solving. Means-ends analysis is a very simple style of control when compared to blackboards.

Means-ends analysis turned out to be less successful than hoped because of its lack of domain-specific knowledge. It is a universal "weak" method, having a wide range of applicability but not the power of control schemes that can make more efficient use of domain-specific knowledge. These conclusions closely parallel the results of psychological research on GPS. As we saw, human problem solvers use a GPS-like control scheme when they lack expert knowledge of a problem domain.

5.2 Learning

Learning, by which we mean any process whereby a person or a machine increases its knowledge or improves its skill, is a topic that combines all of the other themes we have been discussing: representation, search, and control. A wide variety of activities in people and programs are subsumed under the topic of learning. These range from simple rote learning to learning from examples to learning how to learn.

Learning is one of the most difficult issues known to researchers in AI and cognitive science. This is so for two reasons. First, learning subsumes some of the most difficult problems from the other areas of AI: representation, search, and control. One cannot design a learning system without addressing issues in these areas, even if only in the minimal sense of selecting an "off the shelf" method.

Second, it is fairly easy to achieve some initial successes with a learning system but exceedingly difficult to sustain the learning. The immediately learned first results are often a direct result of good choices concerning representation, search, and control.

This phenomenon can lead to the criticism that the results were "built in" or implicitly already known to the system. Though no one would seriously advocate a program starting with absolutely no knowledge, what counts as too much or just enough is debatable. In fact, this debate is fundamentally unresolvable in general since one person's (or machine's) learned result can be another's basic fact.

Learning is an important area of research for several reasons. First, as is true with much AI research, understanding a machine's performance of a given task (here, learning) enhances understanding of both machine and human performance of the task. Second, providing computers with the ability to learn greatly enhances their capabilities and thus their usefulness. Third, it is not feasible for humans to be responsible for all the improvement in computer programs; the programs must take some responsibility for themselves. The human resources are simply not available to hand-tool every system; this is especially so given the proliferation of expert systems in real-world applications.

Historical Overview

Machine learning has long been a topic of interest. In the 1940s researchers focused on self-organizing systems, stimuli, and feedback. Their hope was that somehow out of an unknowing system possessing some general capabilities would arise knowledge; in this, however, they were disappointed.

In the early 1960s there was a transition to using certain AI ideas about memory, search, and retrieval for learning. Selfridge's *PANDEMONIUM* program was one of the earliest efforts; it combined the older technique of adaptive control with newer ideas on learning to tackle the pattern-recognition problem of identifying letters (Selfridge 1959). This program improved its performance by tuning numerical parameters. It introduced the new idea of an independent knowledge source, called a *demon*, that "shouts" when it sees something of interest about which it knows something (for instance, A-ness or W-ness). The demon is really a forerunner of the knowledge sources used in blackboard systems.

A program that we will call *CHECKER-PLAYER*, achieved championship level checker-playing performance and represents another early landmark in research on machine learning (Samuel 1959). It could learn in two ways: (1) by acquiring knowledge through rote memorization about specific board positions and moves ("book moves"), and (2) by improving the evaluation function used to evaluate board positions in its search of the game tree. Better evaluation functions improved system performance because the system could more accurately evaluate board positions (in essence enabling the system to look down deeper into the game tree). CHECKER-PLAYER's approach to learning emphasized search, rote memorization, and adaptive tuning of evaluation functions (the quest for good evaluation functions can be viewed as a search through the space of all such functions).

In the 1970s Winston developed the *ARCH-LEARNER* (discussed in section 4.2 in conjunction with semantic nets). This program was based not on heavy search or numerical tuning but on representation and use of domain knowledge; it heralded the start of a new era in machine learning. This shift in emphasis to representation issues was also apparent in the field of AI as a whole. ARCH-LEARNER was instrumental in providing impetus for work in machine learning to focus on issues of concept acquisition and representation, particularly of a symbolic as opposed to a numerical nature.

Since the late 1970s the emphasis in machine learning has been on knowledge-intensive learning and the study of learning algorithms. This new era in learning research began with the work of Lenat on the program *AM* and Mitchell on the program *LEX*. As we have seen, AM is a program that performs concept discovery in mathematics. Among the key elements of learning, AM emphasizes knowledge acquisition more than improvement in task performance. It never gets better at discovering (and is not supposed to); in fact, its ability to discover interesting new concepts flattens out after its initial rush of successes. (Lenat tried to address this problem in his *EURISKO* program, whose task was to discover the kind of heuristics that made AM successful (Lenat 1983).) LEX is a program that learns how to improve its ability to solve problems in integral calculus by actually trying to solve problems. Both programs combine powerful search and control schemes with a rich, well-represented base of domain knowledge. LEX also uses a very explicit learning algorithm, which we will examine shortly.

Since the mid-1980s, there has been an explosion of interest in machine learning. Though we cannot treat them all in detail, several recent machine learning approaches deserve mention. Some of them constitute approaches to the problem of concept learning, which was introduced in section 3.1.

ID3 (Quinlan 1983, 1986) is an inductive algorithm for learning decision trees from examples. The input to ID3 is a set of examples, each labeled as a positive or negative example of a single concept. More recent programs, like *C4.5* (Quinlan 1992), can learn the decision trees for several concept classes at the same time. In these systems each example is represented as a vector of attribute-value pairs. The values can be symbolic, Boolean, or numeric. The output is a decision tree, which represents a decision procedure for determining how to classify an example.

Since the examples are labeled with respect to concept class and status as positive or negative example, the algorithm is called a *supervised* learning algorithm (since this information is tantamount to having a teacher, for instance, as in the case of ARCH-LEARNER).

In a decision tree each node specifies either a class name or a specific test that partitions the space of instances at that node into the possible outcomes of the test. Each subset of the partition corresponds to a subclassification problem, which is, in turn, solved by a subtree. For instance, a decision tree for deciding whether an example is a fire truck might contain a Boolean test, like Is-the-color-red?, which results in two branches, one for NO and one for YES, to subdecision trees for carrying out the classification in the subcases of red and nonred instances. The question of which attributes to test first—that is, which to place nearer the root of the decision tree—is answered by considering an information-theoretic utility measure of the test; the idea is to ask the most "useful" or discriminating questions first, where utility of the question is measured by how well the test partitions the instances into classes. ID3 is a very useful, efficient, and well-understood algorithm. The original ID3 algorithm could handle only one concept class into which to classify instances and did not handle numeric-valued attributes all that well; newer versions of the algorithm do both. In addition, the decision trees can be generated incrementally in the newer ID5 and ID5R systems (Utgoff 1989).

COBWEB (Fisher 1987) is another inductive learning algorithm. COBWEB incrementally creates a concept hierarchy by performing clustering of input examples. As in ID3, the input is an object described by a vector of attribute-value pairs. Each attribute has a symbolic name and can take symbolic, Boolean, or numeric values. As with ID3, subsequent refinements handle numeric attributes better than the original algorithm. The output is a "classification tree," which is essentially a concept hierarchy; that is, each node in the tree describes a concept description, which specifies for each attribute the probability that the attribute can take a specific value.

Unlike ID3, COBWEB is an *unsupervised* learning algorithm (since there is no teacher to say what concepts are to be learned or which examples are to be considered positive or negative examples of them). COBWEB thus actually performs two closely related tasks: categorization and classification. COBWEB develops categories and then a means to classify instances into them. By comparison, ID3 only did classification since it was given the categories to begin with.

For example, having decided that it should form a category that we would call *mammal*, COBWEB might then describe this class by the probability with which the attributes like *Body-cover, Live-birth, Number-of-chromosomes* take various values. (*Body-cover* would be a symbolic attribute taking values like hair, fur, no-hair, and so on; *Live-birth* would be a Boolean attribute taking as its value either true or false; and *Number-of-chromosomes* would be a numeric attribute taking a positive integer.)

COBWEB uses a heuristic measure, called *category utility*, to decide the utility of forming a concept class. This measure was originally developed as a means for predicting so-called basic level categories in human classification hierarchies (as discussed in the work of Rosch and others, for example, Rosch and Mervis 1975). During the course of creating the concept hierarchy, COBWEB can create and eliminate categories, for instance, by splitting or merging subclasses. The decision of which classes to include in the tree, and where, is based on the category utility of each of the choices.

Other systems that inductively build similar concept classification trees are *UNIMEM* (Lebowitz 1987) and *CYRUS* (Kolodner 1984). Kolodner's CYRUS grew out of the work of Schank and his colleagues on dynamic memory. CYRUS creates a memory of specific instances and inductive generalizations of subsets of them (called EMOPS for "episodic memory organization packets") that are all arranged in a decision tree. Considered as a case-based system—CYRUS, like HYPO, was one of the originals—its cases include generalized patterns as well as specific instances (HYPO, by comparison, includes only specific instances). Indexing is done by working down the decision tree, which structures the case memory (unlike HYPO, whose case base is unstructured).

In summary, both ID3 and COBWEB are inductive learning systems that do not require a deep model of the domain in which they are learning, although, of course, having a "good" set of features to represent the input—that is, to describe instances— can require artful knowledge engineering. (The *right primitives* problem, discussed in chapter 4, and the *new term* problem, discussed later in this chapter, are issues here as well.) Both algorithms require the use of a conceptual or an information-theoretic utility measure. One (ID3) is supervised, and the other (COBWEB) is not.

By contrast, the next approach to machine learning, *explanation-based generalization* (EBG), and the slightly more general technique called *explanation-based learning* (EBL) use an easily understood approach—generalizing a proof—and no utility measures (Mitchell, Keller, Kedar-Cabelli 1986). However, EBG requires much stronger domain knowledge.

EBG is a deductive, supervised approach to learning that uses domain knowledge to constrain the search for a concept description. An EBG system learns by explaining a particular instance in terms of a proof and then generalizing that explanation (proof) to serve as the concept description. There have been a great many systems that use an EBG approach.

The input to an EBG system is a goal concept, a domain theory, a positive example of the concept, and an "operationality" criterion. The operationality criterion specifies what counts as an acceptable description of a concept (e.g., that the concept be described in terms of perceptually observable characteristics). Using the domain theory, EBG constructs an operationally acceptable description of the concept by reasoning about the positive example. Specifically, using the domain theory, EBG first constructs an explanation—that is, a proof—of why the example is a positive example of the goal concept. EBG next examines this proof to determine a set of sufficient conditions under which the explanation holds (the attributes of the positive example *actually used* in the proof provide a set of sufficient conditions for membership in the concept class). EBG then attempts to generalize these sufficient conditions to provide both a general description of the concept and a proof justifying the generalization; the generalization must also satisfy the operationality criterion.

The major strength of EBG is that it is always clear why an object has a particular classification since there is a proof and there are no mysterious inductive leaps or manipulations of utility measures. On the other hand, EBG places onerous demands indeed on the domain theory. One usually needs the domain theory to be correct, complete, and consistent: a domain theory is said to be *correct* if it does not "explain" any negative examples of the concept, *complete* if it "explains" all positive examples, and *consistent* if it is both correct and complete. (In terms of Venn diagrams, the set comprising the concept—made up of positive instances of the concept—is exactly the set explained by the domain theory. If the set of instances explained by the domain theory is smaller than the concept's, the domain theory is not complete; if it is larger, it is not correct.) One could argue that if one's domain theory is so good—complete and correct—then most of the work has been already accomplished. In recent years research has been done on loosening these constraints on the domain theory.

Of course, the idea of creating a general description by looking at the proof of one (very good, prototypical) example is cognitively appealing; we make such "greedy" generalizations all the time. In psychology, forming a generalization by examining one instance goes by the name of *metonymy*. It is well known that people form general conclusions by aggressive generalizations (sometimes incorrect) from a very few examples. Note that a "bad" example or inappropriate generalization can completely corrupt the validity of the generalization. However, EBG, by requiring the use of proof, tempers the generalizations.

EBG can be compared with human problem solving in domains like mathematics or physics. In mathematics one of the best heuristic methods for creating a proof of a general conjecture is to prove it in a special case and then argue either that this proof can be generalized (no part makes use of anything specific to the special case) or that any general case can be reduced to the special case (in a "without loss of generality" argument). For instance, in analytic geometry one might examine how to prove some statement about circles in general by trying to prove it about a special circle, like the circle of radius 1 with center at the origin, and then generalize the proof or show how the general case can be reduced to the special one, for instance, by translation or scaling (both of which can be accomplished by a change of variables). Even though in high school geometry, for instance, one is always cautioned about relying on a special case to prove a general proposition, the EBG approach—prove the special case and then generalize the proof—is very powerful and perfectly correct when properly used.

Note that we have already encountered the idea of using the justification of a single precedent example to help explain concept membership in the GREBE program discussed in chapter 4 in conjunction with mixed paradigm systems. In GREBE an explanation of why a specific precedent case was considered a positive or negative example of a legal concept is reused in a new problem case. In GREBE, as opposed to EBG, however, there is no generalization but rather an analogical mapping of the old justification structure—particularly the sufficient conditions—onto a new example.

Another learning system, which is derived in part from the phenomena of skill acquisition and problem solving discussed in chapters 2 and 3, is *SOAR* (Newell 1990). SOAR, a general problem-solving architecture with a production-rule memory, uses *chunking*, or knowledge compilation, (discussed in chapter 2) to acquire rules from past problem-solving experience (Laird, Rosenbloom, and Newell 1986).

The input to SOAR is a specification of a problem as a state space search problem: a problem space, operators, an initial state, and a goal state. The output is a sequence of states connecting the initial and goal states. The key aspect of SOAR as a learning system is that it updates its rule-based memory by saving problem-solving chunks so that it can solve similar problems more quickly in the future.

SOAR works by repeatedly executing the following problem-solving cycle until a goal state (and thus a solution) is found or until it is unable to continue. SOAR's problem cycle is similar to the fundamental *match-resolve conflicts-act* cycle of rule-based systems. First, SOAR fires all eligible production rules, in parallel; this so-called elaboration phase adds information to what is known about objects and creates preferences for acquiring more information about some aspect of an object. Next, SOAR decides what information acquisition task from the first step is the most preferred. If no one task is preferred over others or there is a conflict between tasks or no tasks were suggested, then SOAR has reached a so-called impasse in this second, decision phase since in essence it does not know what to do next. SOAR responds to an impasse by creating a subgoal to resolve the impasse and recursively calling on its problem-solving methods. When an impasse is resolved, SOAR attempts to gather information that will prevent similar impasses in the future. This third, chunking phase is accomplished by (1) collecting conditions of a chunk, that is, those portions of working memory that existed when the impasse occurred and were used in resolving the impasse, and the chunk's actions, that is, those steps resolving the impasse; (2) generalizing the chunk by converting certain specific information, like named working-memory elements, to variables; and (3) optimizing the chunk (which is a piece of program code). Thus, SOAR caches generalizations of solutions to past problems so that they can be used in the future.

There are some interesting comparisons to be made between EBG and SOAR. For instance, SOAR's chunks are analogous to the operationalized sufficient conditions (the generalization) based on the special example in EBG. Both supply an instance from which sufficient conditions for a result may be harvested, generalized, and reused in the future. Of course, the generalizations made in EBG are based on deductive mechanisms and those in SOAR are based on subgoaling, an approach not usually thought of as deductive (although, strictly speaking, backward chaining through a rule set is a deductive approach).

From a psychological viewpoint, SOAR's approach of resolving an impasse in the course of problem solving is ubiquitous. Also, even though EBG was not intended to be a cognitive model and SOAR was—in fact, Newell (1990) calls it an example of a unified theory of cognition—EBG does have a certain amount of cognitive verisimilitude since it captures a feature of learning from problem solving.

There are now an abundance of projects experimenting with the SOAR architecture. It has been successfully applied in a variety of domains, ranging from the acquisition of typing skill to the solution of syllogisms. One criticism of SOAR is that there is no notion of how to evaluate the utility of a chunk or delete marginally useful ones. Thus, as SOAR solves more problems, it accumulates more chunks and may become slower because deciding which chunk to apply can take more time than solving the impasse. This problem of determining utilities has been addressed in subsequent research. It can also be thought of as the problem of indexing and relevance assessment well known to workers in case-based reasoning. Note that SOAR cannot really carry out CBR-style reasoning since it "throws away" its cases and only keeps their generalizations. Thus, although SOAR can capture a cognitively interesting style of reasoning it misses out on pure example- or case-based reasoning.

Connectionist learning, introduced in chapter 2, has received considerable attention in AI. Of particular note is the backpropagation (BACKPROP) algorithm. As discussed in chapter 2, it is a weight-training algorithm for connectionist networks. In essence, it is a supervised inductive learning algorithm that learns from examples since its input is a set of training examples, represented as vectors of numeric values plus the example's classification, and its output is a decision process—that is, a (revised) configuration of the network's weights—to classify instances as positive or negative examples of concepts.

A strong point of the algorithm is that it does not require much knowledge engineering to use it. It can be considered a universal "weak" method since it does not make extensive use of domain knowledge: it can be applied to any network. In essence, BACKPROP is an algorithm for dealing with the credit assignment problem. BACKPROP looks back over its computations and distributes credit and blame in a particular way to those nodes in the network that "deserve" it.

The input and output representations used in a network are critical to the success of BACKPROP. The algorithm is most likely to develop a useful representation in the hidden units if the network starts out with reasonably good initial representations. The representation discovered by BACKPROP also depends on the number of hidden units. If there are too few, the network may not have the capacity to compute the desired function, and it will arrive at inadequate generalizations. If there are too many, the network may store the training examples directly, as a kind of lookup table, and be unable to generalize to new examples. As pointed out in section 3.2, BACKPROP is also sensitive to the content of the training set and to the manner in which it is presented. A final problem with the connectionist approach to learning is that the nature of the learned representation is very difficult for a human to decipher. As we saw in chapter 2, for example, a significant amount of research was required to discover how the trained hidden units in NETtalk represented the mapping from text to phonetic representation.

Today the field of machine learning—both symbolic and connectionist—is extremely active. Much of the work investigates different algorithms and control structures for learning and relies on already understood search and representation techniques.

General Issues in Learning

In discussing a learning system, several clusters of questions are relevant.

1. *What is the computational architecture of the learning system?* Which component actually does the learning? Who or what component critiques the performance so that the learning component can improve it? What knowledge does the system possess?

2. *What is the role and source of examples?* How are examples, or "training instances," used to drive the learning system? Who provides them: an external or an internal teacher? What properties do or should they have? What kinds are there? How are they organized? How are they generated? How is their order of presentation determined?

3. *What types of learning is the system capable of?* Does the system learn by "rote" memorization or by being told exactly what to do? Can it fill in missing details by using deduction, induction, or analogy? Can it handle unreliable data? Can it take advice? Does it learn incrementally from one example or problem experience at a time, or does it proceed from an entire set taken all at once?

4. *What is the influence of the initial knowledge?* What conceptual and representational primitives does the system start with? At what level and in what detail is the knowledge represented? How is the domain knowledge structured? Is there a domain hierarchy? Is there a case base of past experiences? Is there an inherent bias in the knowledge representation scheme and can it be shifted when appropriate?

5. *What learning algorithms are used and what actually is learned?* How does the learning system generalize or specialize, do induction, reason analogically, or otherwise modify or improve itself? Does it learn new solutions, new classifications, new categories, new ways to organize and index its knowledge? Does it learn from its past mistakes so that it doesn't make the same blunder twice?

Even this handful of questions raises an abundance of interesting learning issues. In addition, there is the issue always present with AI systems of how to judge the success of the effort: how do we know if a system has successfully learned? As usual, various approaches are possible. We will discuss the five points in turn, digressing briefly between points 3 and 4 to look at the LEX system.

Issue 1: The Architecture of Learning Systems

A learning system can be viewed as having several "conceptual" components:

1. The knowledge base
2. The performance element, which performs in the task domain
3. The critic, which evaluates and critiques the performance element
4. The learning element, which knows how to change, and presumably improve, the system, particularly the performance element and the knowledge base
5. The hypothesis or problem generator, which poses the next task for the system to work on
6. The environment or world from which the system receives its new information, particularly examples

For instance, in a hypothetical system for learning a mathematical skill like solving high school algebra problems, the *knowledge base* might contain relevant mathematical knowledge about classifications of equations (e.g., linear, quadratic), general concepts (e.g., solution, root, factor), methods (e.g., plugging in integer values, moving the unknown to the left-hand side, eliminating square roots, using the quadratic formula), past problems and solutions (e.g., $x^2 = 1$ has two roots $+1$ and -1), and past dead ends or mistakes (e.g., "plugging in" whole numbers in $x^2 = 2$ or $x^2 = -1$). The *performance element* would know how to actually solve equations; this includes, of course, knowing how to access and apply knowledge (say, a particular formula) from the knowledge base or adapt an old solution to solve a new problem. The critic would review the performance of the performance element and isolate good and bad steps in the solution, where steps leading to a successful solution might be judged good and steps leading to dead ends bad. The *learning element* would know how to change the system in response to this review, for instance, by adding new concepts or refining old ones (such as "pairs of roots," "double roots") or by annotating a method with respect to its appropriate applications (including when not to use a method). The *problem generator*—often, a human teacher—would then pose a new problem or select a new example from the system's *environment*, and the cycle would repeat itself. The LEX system uses a decomposition similar to this. In fact, certain researchers see a decomposition into these six components as a useful generic framework to describe all learning systems (Buchanan et al. 1978).

From this description of a learning system, we can see how information flows back and forth between the system's environment and its knowledge base. From presented examples, the system learns new knowledge; in the reverse direction, on the basis of its knowledge, the system selects or generates new hypotheses and problems from its environment. Since the environment often consists primarily of examples or cases and the knowledge base usually consists of rules or results, such a system fits what is known as a *two-space* model of learning (Simon and Lea 1974) with an *Examples-space* and a *Rules-* or *Results-space*. If a third space is set aside for concepts, as suggested by Rissland (1978) and Sridharan (1985), the system is known as a *three-space* model. With either model the important point is that much of the learning activity occurs in the interactions between the various kinds of knowledge found in the different spaces.

In the multispace model the learning cycle consists of the system making mappings between spaces. For instance, the performance element, critic, and learning element cause the system to use information extracted from the examples to increase its knowledge of results (as through generalization or specialization of a rule); the teaching aspect of the system, embodied in the hypothesis or problem generator, allows the system to go back to its environment for more examples and problems. For the most part, learning research has concentrated on mappings from examples to concepts and results. However, when AM proposed new concepts and conjectures to be investigated with examples, it was mapping information in the reverse direction. LEX deliberately attempts to build the complete cycle into its architecture.

Each component of a learning system raises many issues. With regard to the knowledge base, we have already considered many relevant issues in discussing representation: expressiveness of the representation, modifiability, extendibility, ease of inference, and so forth. With regard to the performance element, several issues arise that overlap with control: complexity of the task and its implementation; flow and availability of information among the components; transparency; self-awareness; and modifiability of the components. With regard to the environment and the learning element, several issues arise that are unique to learning systems, such as the role and source of examples.

Issue 2: The Role of Examples

If you think of yourself as the learning system, then the importance of the quality and source of the examples—that is, problems or experiences—is obvious. This is even more true when you are working on your own, for then you are your own teacher. Thus, an important question concerns the source of examples: do they come from an external "teacher," or are they generated by the learning system itself? In either case thinking up good examples requires expertise. The goodness of the examples is tied to how well they match the needs of the learning system. Thus, either the system or its teacher must know something of what it is trying to teach or, at least, have general goals and ideas about what is good for learning. Three important factors concerning the use of examples by learning systems are the quality, source, and epistemology of the examples.

The Quality of Examples   The fundamental question concerning the quality of examples is, Are the examples easy to interpret? This question deals primarily with the quality of the system's learning experiences. A central issue is whether there is a close match (or a significant difference) between the representation of the example and the representation of the system's knowledge. Typically, this boils down to asking whether the spaces of examples, concepts, and results employ the same representation vocabulary (descriptive predicates, features, and so on). If so, the learning system has minimal work to do in interpreting the example. For instance, in ARCH-LEARNER the examples were very straightforward, since there was a total match between the representation of the environment (that is, positive examples and near misses) and the representation of the knowledge base (for instance, the emerging concept of "arch"). Using a common representation to eliminate translation problems has been dubbed the *single representation trick*. It is employed because translating between representation schemes can be difficult, even for human beings.

Even if the environment and the knowledge base use the same representation scheme, the difference in generality between them can influence how straightforward the examples are. There can be a small difference, such as that between variables and constants, where all the system needs is to plug in the values or manipulate the variables' ranges of values. Or there can be a great difference, such as that between viewing $3x + 2$ as an instantiation of the form $ax + b$ and viewing it as an instance of a more abstract idea like a "linear transformation." The greater the difference, the harder the job of interpreting the example.

Another aspect of the perspicuity of examples is whether they are correctly classified and free of extraneous details. For instance, are positive and negative exemplars correctly classified as such? It is obviously much easier for a system to learn if it does not have to worry about the quality of its examples. Consider what would happen to ARCH-LEARNER if the near misses were incorrectly classified.

The Source of the Examples   The fundamental question concerning the source of examples is, Where does the responsibility for the intelligent selection of examples lie? Does an external teacher decide what examples the system will consider? Or does the system itself do this? Since it is possible to isolate heuristics for picking examples, such as "Use the next most general case" or "Examine extreme cases," guidelines for intelligently selecting examples can be embedded in the system, with the result that the system is self-teaching to some degree. This was the approach used in AM.

Since learning is sometimes susceptible to the order in which examples are presented, part of intelligently selecting examples is determining their order of presentation. This is of concern especially in situations involving incremental learning. For instance, think of ARCH-LEARNER learning with a different order of presentation. If one "false step" can bring the whole learning effort to its knees, then the learning is not very robust.

In addition to ascertaining which properties the examples should have, there is the problem of actually finding or generating them. The teacher or some component of the system itself must have the expertise to do this. It is true that in some domains (such as elementary mathematics) the examples are easy to generate; for instance, to generate another example of an integer, just add 1. In other domains (such as law and medicine) it is not so easy. If the examples are easily generated, a learning system can get by (as AM does) with very minimal example generation capabilities and still rely heavily on examples in learning. If this is not the case, the generation of examples becomes a challenging subproblem in itself (Rissland 1981).

The Epistemology of the Examples   The fundamental question concerning the epistemology of examples is, What kinds of examples are there and how are they organized? For instance, examples can be categorized with respect to the observation that different ones serve different purposes in learning and are appropriate at different stages. The following types have been identified (Rissland 1978):

1. Start-up examples, which require minimal prior knowledge and are good initial cases to try
2. Reference examples, which are standard textbook cases, good at any stage
3. Counterexamples, which limit overgeneralizations or falsify incorrect ideas
4. Anomalies, which do not fit in with current knowledge but require further analysis
5. Model examples, which are templatelike paradigmatic examples

In addition, the Examples-space has structure. It is no more an unorganized heap of knowledge than the Rules-space is. The issue is to determine what relations among the examples should be used in representing the space. For instance, should the examples be organized into a semantic net: often (as in mathematics and law) one example is built from others, in which case the Examples-space can take on a network structure using a relation that may be called *constructional derivation* (Rissland 1978). Another approach might be to organize the examples together with some partial generalizations into a decision tree (as in CYRUS (Kolodner 1984)).

Up until a few years ago few researchers concentrated on the Examples-space aspect of learning. However, with the advent of interest in case-based systems, there is now a growing sense that much can be learned by examining this topic.

Issue 3: Types of Learning
There are several ways of describing the type of learning a system does. For instance, types of learning can be classified according to the following criteria:

1. The type of learning algorithm
2. The underlying knowledge representation scheme
3. The domain of application
4. The degree of match between the examples and the system's knowledge
5. The presence or absence of a teacher
6. Whether the examples are presented incrementally or all at once

We have already considered several examples of the possible types of learning algorithm: the concept development method used in ARCH-LEARNER, the inductive approaches used in ID3 and COBWEB, and the deductive approach used in EBG, or the connectionist approach used in BACKPROP. We will consider another, the candidate elimination algorithm, when we discuss the program LEX.

With regard to the knowledge representation scheme and domain of application, there is obviously a wide range of possibilities, although basing classification on these factors does not necessarily shed that much light on learning issues themselves.

How well the presented examples match the system's knowledge leads to categorizing types of learning in the following way:

1. Learning by rote memorization: The system does nothing other than memorize what it is told in exactly the form in which the information is presented (an example is storing board positions in CHECKER-PLAYER).

2. Learning from examples: The system (such as LEX or ARCH-LEARNER) tries to generalize on its experience with the example.

3. Learning by analogy: The system is given an analogous task and asked to "map" over the solution (examples are case-based systems like HYPO and GREBE).

4. Learning by being given directions: The system is told the answer in a high-level way but must instantiate and fill in the details (very few systems really do this; most are planning systems).

The presence or absence of a teacher leads to two categories: *supervised* learning, where the system has a teacher, and *unsupervised* learning, where the system is on its own. Of the systems we have studied, ARCH-LEARNER is highly supervised ("highly" because the choice and ordering of examples and near misses is critical). ID3 is supervised. LEX, when it includes its problem generator, is unsupervised. COB-WEB is unsupervised. AM is mostly unsupervised ("mostly" because the user can influence the system through interactions with it—for instance, by giving an AM-discovered concept a name and thereby indirectly boosting its interestingness).

LEX: A Case Study in Learning
In this section we examine an example system, Mitchell's LEX, in terms of the sixfold conceptual breakdown of learning systems. The domain of LEX (Learn by Experimentation) is the calculus. It learns to integrate symbolic mathematical expressions (Mitchell 1983; Mitchell, Utgoff, and Banerji 1983). LEX is related to a much earlier program called SAINT (Symbolic Automatic INTegrator) (Slagle 1961). SAINT used heuristic rules to do integration problems. LEX's task is to *learn* such heuristics—in other words, to learn the kind of knowledge that was built into SAINT to make it a powerful problem solver.

LEX acquires and modifies heuristics by iteratively cycling through the processes of (1) generating a practice problem, (2) using the current state of its available heuristics and other knowledge to try to solve this problem, (3) analyzing and criticizing the steps in attempting to obtain a solution, and (4) refining the heuristics.

The Architecture of LEX   The LEX program contains four modules: Problem Solver, Critic, Generalizer, and Problem Generator. LEX's knowledge base consists primarily of two sorts of domain-specific knowledge: a collection of if-then rules representing integration techniques, and a hierarchy of classes of mathematical functions and objects. Its environment consists of integration problems with integrands that are instances of the mathematical functions and expressions it knows about.

The functions of the four modules are as follows:

1. Problem Solver (LEX's performance element) tries to solve the problem at hand (implemented as a problem-reduction kind of search for a solution node, that is, one with no integrand symbol) with its available store of operators, including the current status of its heuristics.

2. Critic analyzes the trace of a successful solution to glean positive and negative instances. A positive instance is a problem state on a path that led to a successful solution; a negative instance is a problem state on a path that led away from the solution.

3. Generalizer (LEX's learning element) rewrites its knowledge of heuristics on the basis of what the Critic tells it: it narrows the most general statement of the heuristic on the basis of negative instances and generalizes from the most specific on the basis of positive instances.

4. Problem Generator poses new problems to solve that will help to further refine knowledge of the heuristics.

The flow of control among these modules is shown in figure 5.11. The corpus of rules represents the operations done in integral calculus. These include heuristic "algorithm-like" (to use Slagle's term) transformations as well as "book knowledge" procedures such as common antiderivatives and standard transformations. For example:

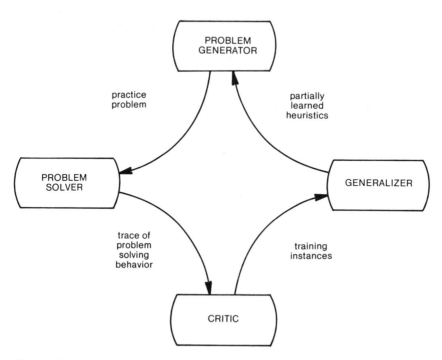

Figure 5.11
The architecture of the LEX system. (Redrawn with permission from Mitchell, Utgoff, and Banerji 1983.)

OP1: $\int r \cdot f(x)\,dx \Rightarrow r \cdot \int f(x)\,dx$

OP2: Integration by parts
$\int u\,dv \Rightarrow uv - \int v\,du$

OP3: $1 \cdot f(x) \Rightarrow f(x)$

OP4: $\int f_1(x) + f_2(x) \Rightarrow \int f_1(x)\,dx + \int f_2(x)\,dx$

OP5: $\int \sin(x)\,dx \Rightarrow -\cos(x) + C$

OP6: $\int \cos(x)\,dx \Rightarrow \sin(x) + C$

The hierarchy shown in figure 5.12 lays out LEX's second major source of knowledge: relationships between major classes of functions.

LEX's Task   LEX improves its performance of integration by discovering what classes in its concept hierarchy a rule should be restricted to for best results. For instance, in the case of OP2, integration by parts (IBP), LEX is to learn how to "bind" the *u* and the *dv*. As students of calculus soon learn, there is some art in choosing the *u* and the *dv*. LEX tries to acquire and express that expertise.

For instance, suppose LEX is trying to learn IBP—that is, to refine OP2 to narrower classes for *u* and *dv*. Suppose the first problem LEX tries is this:

$$\int 3x \sin(x)\,dx$$

At the completion of one cycle IBP has been refined and is narrowed to a range of possibilities from most specific to most general:

Most specific: Apply IBP with $u = 3x$ and $dv = \sin(x)\,dx$
Most general: Original form of OP2

That is, the "right" time to use IBP is certainly not just in the case of the most specific example the system has worked and probably not in every case (which is what the

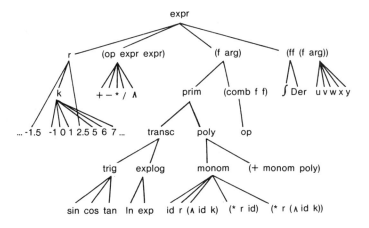

Figure 5.12
The conceptual hierarchy of the LEX system. The hierarchy is based directly on the syntax of symbolic expressions in mathematics. For example, an expression can be composed of an algebraic operator $(+, -, *, /, \wedge)$ followed by two expressions. The hierarchy also captures major classes of functions. For example, *sin*, *cos*, and *tan* are grouped together as trigonometric functions, which are in turn part of the class of transcendental functions. (Redrawn with permission from Mitchell, Utgoff, and Banerji 1983.)

original form of OP2 implies). The appropriate kinds of problems for IBP lie some-where in between. Possibilities between these two extremes include

Apply IBP to $\int 3x\,\text{trig}(x)\,dx$ with $u = 3x$ and $dv = \text{trig}(x)\,dx$
Apply IBP to $\int \text{poly}(x)\sin(x)\,dx$ with $u = \text{poly}(x)$ and $dv = \sin(x)\,dx$
Apply IBP to $\int kx\,\text{trig}(x)\,dx$ with $u = kx$ and $dv = \text{trig}(x)\,dx$ (k is an integer)

By incrementally narrowing this range of possibilities, LEX eventually learns the condi-tions that govern the application of IBP.

The narrowing of the range of possibilities is done by the learning element, the Generalizer. It uses an algorithm called the Candidate Elimination Algorithm (CEA). Basically, the idea is to generalize from positive examples and to specialize from negative examples and thus eliminate candidates from the space of hypothesized ranges for the heuristic. Positive examples hint that a heuristic might apply to a wider range of cases, and negative examples suggest that there is a class of cases to which the heuristic does not apply. The class hierarchy provides the way to generalize and specialize; for instance, if a technique applies to both *cos(x)* and *sin(x)*, then LEX says it applies to their common generalization, *trig* (the class consisting of all types of trigono-metric functions). It does not leap to the most general conclusion that it is true for all types of functions; instead, it makes a conservative, *least* generalization. Similarly, if a technique fails for *expln* (the class including both exponential and logarithmic func-tions), LEX does not assume it fails for everything subsumed under the *expln* class but remains optimistic and says it might work for one of the next most specific subclasses, *exp* (exponential functions) or *ln* (logarithmic functions).

An example of one cycle of LEX starting with the problem $\int 3x\cos(x)\,dx$ results in the flow of information summarized in figure 5.13. We discuss the CEA in more detail in the next section.

Critique of LEX   LEX does quite well but still can make mistakes. The following are three criticisms of LEX:

1. It is not always true that because a technique applies to both *cos* and *sin*, it is true for all trigonometric functions like *tan*.
2. Because LEX does not have concepts like "even integer" and "odd integer," it cannot learn some of the usual tricks involving integrals of powers of *sin* and *cos* (which involve one trick for odd powers and another for even powers).
3. LEX fails to notice some things that are obvious to mathematicians like group-ing in

$$\int (\sin x)^2\,dx + f(x)\,dx + (\cos x)^2\,dx$$

to take advantage of a well-known identity and arrive at

$$x + \int f(x)\,dx.$$

Criticisms 1 and 2 are about the shortcomings of LEX's initial vocabulary—a right primitives problem complaint—and its inherent "bias" (for instance, given LEX's con-cept hierarchy, it tends to make certain kinds of generalization, such as generalizing from *sin* and *cos* to *trig*). To this one could respond that every initial knowledge base is likely to be deficient or biased in some way, and one must start somewhere. In fact, researchers have begun to address the question of how to shift such bias (Utgoff 1983, 1986). A more general issue is that learning can and should happen on several fronts:

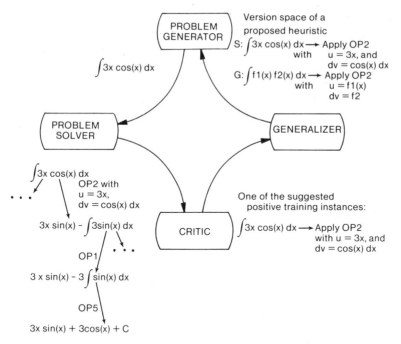

Figure 5.13
An example of the flow through LEX's learning cycle. The Problem Generator delivers a practice problem
to the Problem Solver. The Problem Solver solves the problem by applying a series of operators. The
Critic selects an aspect of the solution that might be used to build a new heuristic. The Generalizer
constructs a version space for the heuristic, which is bounded by a most specific version, S, and a most
general version, G. The version space is narrowed by cycling through further, related practice problems.
In this example solutions to further problems would reveal whether S could be generalized to expressions
of the form $\int kx \operatorname{trig}(x)\,dx$. (Redrawn with permission from Mitchell, Utgoff, and Banerji 1983.)

the system should learn not just the rulelike aspects but the concepts as well. For that
matter, it would be desirable for other elements such as the Problem Generator to learn
also (the Problem Generator should get better at posing problems). This discussion
leads to the next level: learning how to learn. The successors to LEX, a successor to
SAINT, can be considered steps in that direction.

Criticism 3 is of a type that has been called the *superhuman human fallacy*: if a system
can't do all the big (and little) subtle (and obvious) things an expert can do, it isn't very
good. Since one can always say this, it isn't very helpful. More useful is specifying the
range of expert performance the learning system should try to achieve. This goes back
to the issue of how to evaluate a learning system, a topic we will not pursue here, but
currently a central concern of researchers in machine learning, and AI, in general.

Criticism 1 also points to something that might be considered a weakness of the
CEA. In effect, the CEA generalizes a statement to a parent node whenever it is true
for two offspring nodes. A more conservative approach to generalization would require a change in the algorithm.

In spite of such criticisms, LEX is an exceedingly interesting and powerful paradigmatic example of a learning system. It is based on important principles and is
carefully implemented.

Issue 4: A Priori Knowledge
It is obvious that what the system knows initially greatly affects what it can represent
and learn. We have already dealt with an aspect of this in discussing representational
issues, particularly the right primitives problem.

Of particular concern from the learning point of view is the question of what
concepts or types of improvement are accessible to a system. For instance, LEX cannot
learn certain integration tricks because it does not have the concepts of "odd" and
"even" integer. To be able to acquire the new tricks, LEX would have to revise its
representation knowledge by acquiring these new terms. This is an example of what
learning theorists call the *new term* problem, an ever present problem in learning
research. One way to attack it is to focus on shifting the bias of the system.

Utgoff has contributed to research on this aspect of learning. He defines bias as all
the factors "that influence hypothesis selection"—that is, any concepts or criteria such
as the following that cause the system to act the way it does (Utgoff 1986):

1. The concept description language in which the hypotheses are described
2. The space of hypotheses that the program can consider
3. The procedures that define the order in which hypotheses are to be considered
4. The acceptance criteria that define whether a search procedure may stop with
   a given hypothesis or should continue searching for a better choice

Given that any system has some bias, the interesting question then becomes, How
can we give the system a different bias, in particular, one that might improve its
learning abilities? This is really an aspect of the problem of learning how to learn. For
instance, if the bias is too strong, the system is too highly focused and has too small a
space of hypotheses to search—a space that may not even contain the right hypothesis. If the bias is too weak, the system is permitted to consider a large—perhaps far
too large—number of hypotheses. A correct bias is one that allows the concept learner
to select the target concept; an incorrect one does not.

Utgoff's particular interest is in shifting LEX-like systems from an overly strong to
a weaker bias. He does this in a three-step process: (1) recommending (via heuristics)
new concept descriptions (for instance, odd integer, even integer) to be added to the
concept description language; (2) translating these recommended concept descriptions
into the representation formalism used by the system; and (3) melding in these
concepts so that the structure of the program's hypothesis space is maintained (for
instance, odd-integer and even-integer is-a integer). The recommendation phase is accomplished by closely examining the trace of the performance element for steps where
key operations—like dividing by 2—were performed and seeing if this operation was
common among some of the solutions—like those requiring an even-numbered expo-
nent in steps involving integration of powers of sin and cos. This sort of learning is
also being explored in EBG.

Issue 5: Algorithms for Learning
Various algorithms are available for the learning element to use. For instance, in
learning new rules by generalizing, a system could adopt the following strategies:

1. Change constants to variables
2. Drop conditions
3. Add options

4. Extend the range of quantification
5. Climb an is-a hierarchy

For instance, ARCH-LEARNER employs the fifth technique when it modifies the requirement that a part "be a wedge" to the requirement that it "be a block" (since a wedge is a-kind-of block).

Conversely, in learning new rules by specializing, a system could adopt these strategies:

1. Restrict the range of variables
2. Add conditions
3. Drop options
4. Restrict the range of quantification
5. Descend an is-a hierarchy

The CEA used in LEX has elements of both specialization and generalization. It relies on the presence of a hierarchy specifying the generalization/specialization possibilities in the domain.

The CEA is easily described using the idea of *version spaces* (Mitchell 1982). Version spaces are simply a mechanism to represent the range of possibilities spanned between the most specific and most general cases known. Since the concept hierarchy implicitly specifies how to generalize or specialize, only the most specific instances and the most general instances need be stored. All the intermediate cases are implicitly represented and can be generated by generalizing (or specializing) to higher (or lower) classes in the hierarchy.

The meat of the algorithm is what is done to the set of most specific instances, called S, and the set of most general instances, called G, in response to a positive or negative instance, called E:

If the example E is positive, generalize S as little as possible:
1. Remove from G any rules not covering E, and
2. Update S to contain all maximally specific common generalizations of E and S.

If the example E is negative, specialize G as little as possible:
1. Remove from S all rules that cover E, and
2. Update G to contain all maximally general common specializations of E and G.

The key is to take the least common generalization and the greatest common specialization. (This is exactly analogous to taking the least maximum and the greatest minimum of two numbers: for instance, 16, 3, and 1,056 are maximums for 2 and 3, but 3 is the smallest maximum; 2, -5, and -107 are all minimums for 2 and 3, but 2 is the greatest minimum.)

Analysis of a Learning Episode in Legal History
Examples of CEA-like refinement of rules and concepts are to be found in the legal domain. A famous example is the development of the doctrine concerning the liability of a manufacturer to a third party injured by a defective product. For instance, if you buy a defective car, a wheel falls off, and you are hurt, the manufacturer of the car must compensate you for your injury even though you bought the car from an intermediate vendor (say, a car dealership) and not directly from the manufacturer.

Originally there was no relationship of liability between manufacturers and third parties because the law required *privity* of contract, that is, an immediate seller-purchaser relationship between manufacturer and injured party. This situation, as we know from daily experience in a consumer-oriented society, has changed.

The change in the legal rule—which might be stated as "no privity, no liability"—begins with the case *Thomas and Wife v. Winchester*, decided in the New York Court of Appeals in 1852. In this case Mr. Thomas had a prescription for dandelion extract for his ailing wife filled by his local druggist. The druggist filled the prescription from a jar labeled as dandelion; the jar came from Winchester, a drug manufacturer. Unfortunately, the jar actually contained belladonna, a substance that looks somewhat similar but causes very different effects. Mrs. Thomas got very ill, suffered "derangement of the mind," and eventually recovered. Mr. and Mrs. Thomas sued Winchester.

The Thomases won. The court justified making an exception to the privity of contract rule because mislabeled poisons, like belladonna, were so "imminently dangerous" that they deserved an exception. Belladonna was to be considered "inherently" dangerous, like a loaded gun in the hands of a child unaware of danger. Thus, after this initial case an exception to the privity rule was created; in time the exception would grow to swallow up the rule itself.

The *Thomas and Wife v. Winchester* case marks the end of the first stage of what the legal scholar Edward Levi (1949) views as a three-stage process. In the first stage a concept is created. In the second it is initially refined to cover specific positive cases and exclude negative ones and is then expanded, almost too far. In the third it is redefined. It is interesting to compare Levi's analysis of legal evolution with the growth of knowledge in other domains like astronomy (Kuhn 1962) or mathematics (Lakatos 1976).

For the next fifty years or so the New York Court of Appeals handed down decisions (see table 5.2) that allowed exceptions to the privity rule for items considered "imminently dangerous" in and of themselves, like belladonna and loaded guns. It did not extend the exception to include a more general class of items that became dangerous when defective (for instance, items like carriages and steam boilers). During this period the court was both (1) defining the category of "imminently dangerous" items by including or excluding examples on a case-by-case basis (that is, if the court allowed recovery for third-person injury from an item under the rubric of the "imminently dangerous" exception, it was in the class; if the court didn't, it wasn't) and (2) refusing to extend the exception's coverage to a more general class of items. Thus, by the turn of the century (and the end of Levi's stage two) the exception covered a range of cases from the most specifically to the most generally "imminently dangerous." The situation is summarized in figure 5.14.

Table 5.2
Summary of "inherently dangerous" cases

Case	Date	Item	Finding
Thomas v. Winchester	1852	Belladonna	Liable
Loop v. Litchfield	1870	Balance wheel	Not liable
Losee v. Clute	1873	Steam boiler	Not liable
Devlin v. Smith	1882	Painter's scaffold	Liable
Torgesun v. Schultz	1908	Bottle of aerated water	Liable
Statler v. Ray Mfg. Co.	1909	Coffe urn	Liable

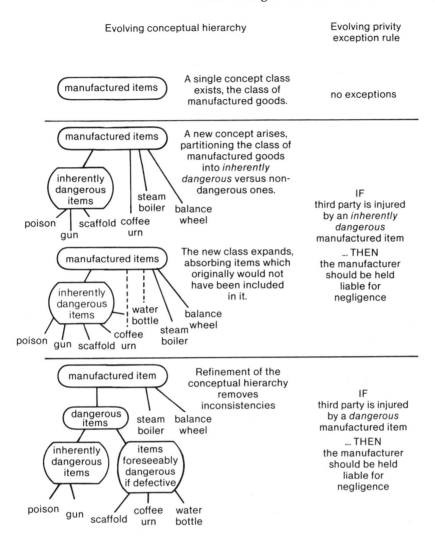

Figure 5.14
The evolution of a legal doctrine

However, through its decisions in this middle period (1852–1915) the court was also pushing the boundaries of the "imminently dangerous" class to include some items like coffee urns and hairwash that do become dangerous when defective. Nevertheless, at this point the court believed the "rule" of the exception could be summed up as follows:

> One who manufactures articles inherently dangerous, e.g., poisons, dynamite, gunpowder, torpedoes, bottles of water under pressure, is liable in tort to third parties.... On the other hand, one who manufactures articles dangerous only if defectively made, or installed, e.g., tables, chairs, pictures or mirrors hung on the walls, carriages, automobiles, and so on is not liable to third parties for injuries caused by them, except in cases of willful injury or fraud.
> *Cadillac Motor Car Co. v. Johnson* (1915)

Thus, the court held to its previously drawn line not to extend the exception up the hierarchy. On the other hand, the class of articles deemed "imminently dangerous" seemed to be expanding more and more to include many items that seemed more naturally to belong to the more general class of "dangerous if defective."

The pressure to break through the hierarchical barrier and extend the exception finally became too much in 1916. In that year the court decided the case *MacPherson v. Buick*. In this case MacPherson, a third party, was allowed to recover for injury caused by a defective Buick, an item dangerous only if defective. Thus, a new specific positive case gave the rule its final push.

The opinion stated:

> We hold, then, that the principle of *Thomas v. Winchester* is not limited to poisons, explosives, and things of like nature, to things which in their normal operation are implements of destruction. If the nature of a thing is such that it is reasonably certain to place life and limb in peril when negligently made, it is then a thing of danger. Its nature gives warning of the consequences to be expected. If to the element of danger there is added knowledge that the thing will be used by persons other than the purchaser, and used without new tests, then, irrespective of contract, the manufacturer of this thing of danger is under a duty to make it carefully. That is as far as we are required to go for the decision of this case.

Thus, at the conclusion of the third stage of evolution of this legal doctrine, the principle of the exception to the privity rule has been extended and now covers a range from a most specific class of items like belladonna and loaded guns to a most general class of items considered "dangerous if defective." The swollen extension of the "imminently dangerous" concept, which occurred during the second stage, has stopped and even been contracted. As the result of these three stages, the exceptions have swallowed up the rule of privity of contract so that a manufacturer can now be assumed to be liable (in tort) to third parties.

In summary, this historical example from the legal domain has illustrated how the conceptual frameworks provided by AI can be applied. In particular, it shows how the law can be seen to function as a system that refines concepts and rules on the basis of positive and negative examples. We have emphasized its rule-refinement aspects and discussed how it can be viewed as an example of CEA-like learning. (You might find it interesting to reexamine the concept refinement in view of another learning algorithm such as the one used by ARCH-LEARNER and to note the strengths and weaknesses of this analytical approach, for instance, with respect to the handling of near misses.)

For background material on this episode of legal history, see Berman and Greiner 1980 or Levi 1949. An article by the legal scholar Max Radin gives a very CEA-like description of this legal episode (Radin 1933).

Suggested Readings

Artificial intelligence (Winston 1984) and *Introduction to Artificial intelligence* (Charniak and McDermott 1985) are textbooks in AI. The second of these books includes a brief introduction to the LISP programming language. The four volumes of *The Handbook of Artificial Intelligence* (Barr and Feigenbaum 1981, 1982; Cohen, and Feigenbaum 1982; Barr, Cohen and Feigenbaum 1989) survey the field of AI at an intermediate level. The series entitled *Machine Learning: An Artificial Intelligence Approach* (Michalski, Carbonell, and Mitchell 1983, 1986) present collections of papers concerning recent research on learning; the journal *Machine Learning* is the primary source for articles on state-of-the-art techniques in machine learning.

References

Barr, A., P. C. Cohen, and E. A. Feigenbaum, eds. (1989). *The handbook of artificial intelligence.* Vol. 4. Reading, Mass.: Addison-Wesley.

Barr, A., and E. A. Feigenbaum, eds. (1981). *The handbook of artificial intelligence.* Vol. 1. Los Altos, Calif.: Morgan Kaufmann.

Barr, A., and E. A. Feigenbaum, eds. (1982). *The handbook of artificial intelligence.* Vol. 2. Los Altos, Calif.: Morgan Kaufmann.

Berman, H. J., and W. R. Greiner (1980). *The nature and functions of law.* 4th ed. New York: Foundation Press.

Buchanan, B. G., T. M. Mitchell, R. G. Smith, and C. R. Johnson, Jr. (1978). Models of learning systems. In J. Belzer, A. G. Holzman, and A. Kent, eds., *Encyclopedia of computer science and technology.* Vol. 11. New York: Marcel Dekker.

Charniak, E., and D. McDermott (1985). *Introduction to artificial intelligence.* Reading, Mass.: Addison-Wesley.

Cohen, P. R., and E. A. Feigenbaum, eds. (1982). *The handbook of artificial intelligence.* Vol. 3. Los Altos, Calif.: Morgan Kaufmann.

Dennett, D. C. (1991). *Consciousness explained.* Boston, Mass.: Little Brown.

Erman, L. D., F. Hayes-Roth, V. R. Lesser, and D. R. Reddy (1980). The HEARSAY-II speech-understanding system: Integrating knowledge to resolve uncertainty. *Computing Surveys* 12, 213–253.

Fisher, D. H. (1987). Knowledge acquisition via incremental conceptual clustering. *Machine Learning* 2, 139–172.

Hayes-Roth, B. (1985). A blackboard architecture for control. *Artificial Intelligence* 26, 251–321.

Kolodner, J. L. (1984). *Retrieval and Organizational Strategies in Conceptual Memory: A Computer Model.* Hillsdale, N.J.: Erlbaum.

Kuhn, T. S. (1962). *The structure of scientific revolutions.* Chicago: University of Chicago Press.

Laird, J. E., P. S. Rosenbloom, and A. Newell (1986). Chunking in SOAR: The anatomy of a general learning mechanism. *Machine Learning* 1, 47–80.

Lakatos, I. (1976). *Proofs and refutations.* Cambridge: Cambridge University Press.

Lebowitz, M. (1987). Experiments with incremental concept formation: UNIMEM. *Machine Learning* 2, 103–138.

Lenat, D. B. (1983). EURISKO: A program that learns new heuristics and domain concepts: The nature of heuristics III: Program design and results. *Artificial Intelligence* 21, 61–98.

Levi, E. H. (1949). *An introduction to legal reasoning.* Chicago: University of Chicago Press.

Michalski, R. S., J. Carbonell, and T. M. Mitchell, eds. (1983). *Machine learning: An artificial intelligence approach.* Vol 1. Palo Alto, Calif: Tioga.

Michalski, R. S., J. Carbonell, and T. M. Mitchell, eds. (1986). *Machine learning: An artificial intelligence approach.* Vol 2. Palo Alto, Calif.: Tioga.

Mitchell, T. M. (1982). Generalization as search. *Artificial Intelligence* 18, 203–226.

Mitchell, T. M. (1983). Learning and problem solving. In *Proceedings of the Eighth International Joint Conference on Artificial Intelligence.* Karlsruhe, Germany.

Mitchell, T. M., R. Keller, and S. Kedar-Cabelli (1986). Explanation-based generalization: A unifying view. *Machine Learning* 1, 47–80.

Mitchell, T. M., P. E. Utgoff, and R. Banerji (1983). Learning by experimentation: Acquiring and refining problem-solving heuristics. In Michalski, Carbonell, and Mitchell 1983.

Newell, A. (1990). *Unified theories of cognition.* Cambridge, Mass.: Harvard University Press.

Newell, A., and H. A. Simon (1972). *Human problem solving.* Englewood Cliffs, N.J.: Prentice-Hall.

Nilsson, N. J. (1971). *Problem-solving methods in artificial intelligence.* New York: McGraw-Hill.

Quinlin, J. R. (1983). Learning efficient classification procedures and their application to chess end games. In Michalski, Carbonell, and Mitchell 1983.

Quinlin, J. R (1986). Induction of decision trees. *Machine Learning* 1, 81–106.

Quinlin, J. R. (1992). *C4.5 programming for machine learning.* San Mateo, Calif.: Morgan Kaufmann.

Radin, M. (1933). Case law and stare decisis: Concerning Präjudizienrecht in Amerika. *Columbia Law Review* 33, February, 119–212.

Rissland, E. L. (1978). Understanding understanding mathematics. *Cognitive Science* 2, 361–383.

Rissland, E. L. (1981). Constrained example generation. Technical report 81-24, Department of Computer and Information Science, University of Massachusetts at Amherst.

Rosch, E., and C. B. Mervis (1975). Family resemblances: Studies in the internal structure of categories. *Cognitive Psychology* 7, 573–605.

Samuel, A. L. (1959). Some studies in machine learning using the game of checkers. *IBM Journal of Research and Development* 3, 210–229. Reprinted in E. A. Feigenbaum and J. Feldman, eds. (1963). *Computers and thought.* New York: McGraw-Hill.

Selfridge, O. G. (1959). PANDEMONIUM: A paradigm for learning. In *Proceedings of the Symposium on Mechanization of Thought Processes.* National Physics Laboratory. London.

Simon, H. A., and G. Lea (1974). Problem solving and rule induction: A unified view. In L. Gregg, ed. *Knowledge and cognition.* Hillsdale, N.J.: Erlbaum.

Slagle, J. (1961). A computer program for solving problems in freshman calculus (SAINT). Doctoral dissertation, MIT, Cambridge, Mass. Reprinted in E. A. Feigenbaum and J. Feldman, eds. (1963). *Computers and thought.* New York: McGraw-Hill.

Sridharan, N. S. (1985). Evolving systems of knowledge. *AI Magazine* 4, 108–121.

Utgoff, P. E. (1983). Adjusting bias in concept learning. In *Proceedings of the Eighth International Joint Conference on Artificial Intelligence.* Karlsruhe, Germany.

Utgoff, P. E. (1986). Shift of bias for inductive concept learning. In Michalski, Carbonell, and Mitchell 1986.

Utgoff, P. E. (1989). Incremental induction of decision trees. *Machine Learning* 4, 161–186.

Winston, P. H. (1984). *Artificial intelligence.* 2nd ed. Reading, Mass.: Addison-Wesley.

Chapter 6

Linguistics: The Representation of Language

Linguistics is the branch of cognitive science that is concerned with human language. Its goal is to understand how linguistic knowledge is represented in the mind, how it is acquired, how it is perceived and used, and how it relates to other components of cognition.

A language is a system that uses some physical signal (a sound, a gesture, a mark on paper) to express meaning. As we have seen, information-processing systems are devices that represent information in symbolic form. They are computational in the sense that these symbolic representations can be manipulated and transformed to create new representations. There is, of course, a broader sense in which language is not only a special cognitive system but also a highly complex form of behavior that impinges on personality, emotional state, personal interaction, cultural development, and social structure. Just the same, we will argue that it is possible to study language as a distinct cognitive system, abstracting away from questions of communication, aesthetics, persuasiveness, and other applied or functional concerns. Moreover, we suppose that our narrowed investigation of language will be a necessary preliminary to understanding how linguistic knowledge interacts with these other aspects of human life.

For now, then, we will restrict our attention to the goal of understanding the nature of *grammars*—formal theories of linguistic knowledge itself, independent of other aspects of cognition, socialization, or behavior. A grammar must be able to characterize what we know about the physical signals on one end of the linguistic equation, as well as what we know about meaning on the other end. In addition, it must provide an account of how the two are connected.

Languages may be described by systems of rules and principles that constitute scientific hypotheses about the nature of the linguistic knowledge possessed by native speakers. These rules and principles purport to account for the pattern of the language—the range of possible moves in the language game that are consistent with a set of linguistic conventions. It is crucial to understand that grammars are intended to *describe*, not to *prescribe*, linguistic systems. That is, *descriptive linguistics* attempts to detail the underlying knowledge that is reflected when someone speaks or understands language. Unlike the *prescriptive linguistics* associated with traditional grammarians, a cognitive linguistic theory is not concerned with legislating social norms or rendering aesthetic judgments about language usage.

Some English speakers say *hoagie*, others, *submarine*, and still others, *grinder* for a particular kind of sandwich. These differences distinguish different *dialects* of English. Similarly, some English speakers pronounce the *r* in *poor*, but for others this word sounds more or less the same as *paw*. These alternative pronunciations, too, indicate different regional (or social) dialects. Indeed, even the structure of sentences can vary across dialect groups. For example, many speakers of Parisian French say *Je sais pas* instead of the standard *Je ne sais pas* (in English, "I don't know"). In a western Massachusetts dialect, "So don't I" can be used interchangeably with "I do too" to indicate agreement, as in "I really want to go swimming.... So don't I!"

These variations in vocabulary, pronunciation, structure, and meaning can be described by providing slightly different accounts of the linguistic knowledge possessed by speakers of distinct dialect groups. This characterization carries over to speakers who systematically dangle prepositions (for example, those who say *I know which chair you are sitting on* instead of *I know on which chair you are sitting*) or split infinitives (producing, for example *She wanted to completely disassociate herself from them*). To a descriptive linguist, these are not considered errors to be corrected, but rather facts to be described as part of a theory of knowledge.

Within this field of variation is a range of common linguistic patterns that constitutes what is informally called the English language (better understood as a cluster of closely related, variant dialects). Furthermore, certain patterns are systematically excluded. Consider the sentences in examples (1) through (4), which represent different orderings of certain English words:

(1)   The dog irritated Mary.

(2)   Mary irritated the dog.

(3)   *Dog the Mary irritated.

(4)   *Irritated the Mary dog.

Only (1) and (2) are well-formed orderings in English; we will characterize them as *grammatical* sentences; (3) and (4), marked with an asterisk, are *ungrammatical* strings of words. Any speaker of any language has acquired the ability to systematically distinguish grammatical from ungrammatical utterances. In the case at hand, only certain patterns of words constitute English sentences, and English speakers have the ability to identify and use them when speaking or understanding the language. English speakers also have a grasp of principles of pronunciation, word structure, and meaning that constitutes their knowledge of English.

The use of language feels like second nature to us once we have acquired the relevant body of linguistic knowledge. But we must not lose sight of the complexity and variety of the patterns that must be learned. The speaker of any language recognizes a vast array of structures: simple declarative affirmative sentences like (1) and (2), questions such as *Did the dog irritate Mary?*; negations such as *The dog did not irritate Mary*; sentences with parts emphasized, as in *It was the dog that irritated Mary*; sentences with parts that are truncated, as in *I would like to leave on Friday, and Mary on Saturday*; and so forth. Moreover, speakers of different languages learn different patterns. Compare the English question in (5) with the German equivalent in (6):

(5)   Did John see the man?

(6)   Sah Johann den Mann?
       saw John   the man

In Sinhala, a language of Sri Lanka, the order of elements differs from the basic English order, even in simple declarative affirmative sentences:

(7)   The woman eats rice.

(8)   Noona   bat kanəwa.
       woman-the rice eats

(The symbol [ə] represents the sound that also occurs in English at the end of a word like *sofa*.)

Having articulated the perspective of descriptive linguistics, we must consider more closely the nature of a speaker's knowledge of a language. Initially, it is not obvious in which terms linguistic regularities are best captured. Perhaps a standard representation in terms of a database (see chapter 3) or a simple list of options might seem appropriate. There is, however, reason to believe that grammars are best represented in terms of *generative rules*—explicit algorithms that characterize the structures of a particular language.

To pursue this point, notice that many of the sentences we use (such as those you are now reading) have never before been produced in your experience. Not only the content, but also the specific sentence structure may be novel. Yet the task of understanding these sentences seems to present no untoward problems of linguistic interpretation: we can effortlessly identify such sentences as grammatical and derive their meaning. Consequently, our linguistic knowledge must go beyond finite lists of words or sentences. To account for a fluent speaker's creative ability to recognize and use novel patterns, we assume that speakers know rules and principles that define a sense of that patterning. A grammar of a language, then, can be thought of as a set of such rules and principles.

The body of knowledge that is characterized by a grammar is sometimes referred to as *linguistic competence*. Just as the rules of chess define the range of possible moves and legal positions, but do not otherwise direct the course of the game, the rules of a competence grammar define the class of possible linguistic structures, but do not completely determine actual language behavior. There is, for instance, no upper bound on the number of sentences that are grammatical in any known natural language. The grammar of every human language contains mechanisms with which a finite set of rules can characterize an infinitely large set of possible expressions. *I despise the dog* is a sentence of English; so is *I despise the dog and Melba doesn't like the cat*; so is *I despise the dog, Melba doesn't like the cat, and Sue could live without the iguana*; and so on, without limit. There is no reason in principle to rule out grammatical sentences of any particular length so long as they fit the pattern of English conjunctions. Of course, at a certain point some sentences may become too long or complex for speakers to use or understand. Even simpler grammatical sentences may be subject to errors in perception or production. We have all had the experience of initially failing to understand a normal sentence, or of producing a strange and unintended utterance. These are matters of linguistic *performance*. By contrast, a theory of competence is not intended to provide an account of what we actually say at a given place and time, or of the nature of the psychological and neural mechanisms that implement linguistic knowledge in actual behavior. In chapters 7 and 11 we will see how linguists collaborate with other cognitive scientists in addressing some of these other important issues.

Competence grammars are highly complex. Articulating the grammar of even a single language is an imposing and challenging intellectual task. This is because the rules of a language are generally not consciously known by speakers of that language, and they have never been completely codified by previous grammarians. Let us consider two cases in point. All native speakers of English know that the plural of *dog* is *dogs*, and that the plural of *cat* is *cats*. When English speakers produce these plurals, they instinctively sound the plural marker (spelled *-s*) as a "z" sound in the first case and as an "s" sound in the second. There is, it turns out, a rule for constructing plurals in English that generates a different representation for the plural ending depending on the phonetic properties of the final sound of the word, as we will see in detail below.

As a second example of common linguistic knowledge, consider the behavior of the word *that*. *That* plays several distinct roles in English sentences. For one thing, *that* can appear prenominally (before nouns) in noun phrases like *that turkey*. It can function as a pronoun, as in *Don't touch that*. Let us focus our attention on its third role as a *complementizer*, a word that introduces *subordinate clauses* (sentences within sentences).

In the following example we see something of the behavior of this *that*. The subordinate clauses are italicized:

(9)   a. Irving believed *that pigs can fly*.
      b. *That sugar is sweet* is obvious to everyone.
      c. The pain *that I feel* is unpleasant.
      d. The dog *that bit me* is missing now.

In (9a) *that* is optional—the sentence is grammatical even if the complementizer is not present. By contrast, (9b) is an instance of a construction in which the complementizer cannot be omitted. The pair of sentences (9c) and (9d) presents yet another puzzle. Both examples involve the same type of construction (the *relative clause*), yet the complementizer is required in (9d) and optional in (9c).

The rules and principles that govern the distribution of *that* appear to have little to do with the meaning of the utterances in question. In fact, it is not immediately clear what the privileges of occurrence for *that* are, although all competent speakers of English "know" its principles of distribution. In the case of the relative clauses, the necessity or optionality of the complementizer seems instead to depend on whether the "head" of the clause (*the pain* in (9c) and *the dog* in (9d)) is functioning as the subject or the object of the verb in the relative clause. But this does not appear to explain the distribution of *that* in the first two examples.

These kinds of subtleties in the distribution of a word like *that* are tacitly grasped by any speaker of English, yet they are features about which school-taught grammar never speaks, and it is exceedingly unlikely that parents have ever instructed their children regarding the rule. How then do we come to have such knowledge? In what form is such knowledge represented in the mind? Questions of this order, posed at a fine-grained level of detail, are paradigmatic examples of problems in cognitive science.

We will return to discuss some of these problems below, but for now we wish to emphasize that although speakers apparently know how to determine the correct form of English plurals and the distribution of *that*, they cannot articulate the principles that inform these judgments. Furthermore, virtually all the important features of linguistic knowledge have this character: linguistic competence is unconscious or *tacit* knowledge that speakers possess, but cannot articulate and are unaware of.

Just the same, much of grammar is learned apparently effortlessly by all normal human children substantially before the age of five. Children acquire language with virtually no direct instruction, with little or no systematic presentation of relevant data, and with the added load of many other developmental tasks. Indeed, there is considerable reason to believe (see chapter 9) that the data that are available to children for grammar construction *underdetermine* the goal—children are not provided with enough evidence in their linguistic environment to directly account for what they come to know.

This state of affairs constitutes a problem of major proportions for cognitive science, at large. How is it that the young organism can acquire a body of knowledge that, in important regards, is learned without benefit of direct instruction, and in support of which there is insufficient information in its environment? Many contemporary linguists, following Chomsky (1965, 1975, 1980, 1986, 1988), hold that general learning mechanisms or properties of information processing at large cannot account for the acquisition and form of grammars. Rather, the problem of grammar acquisition seems best explained by positing powerful special principles that are present in the language learner by virtue of its biological constitution—ultimately, properties of the human genome that are innate in the organism.

It is important to understand that this does not amount to the claim that any particular grammar, or rule of grammar, is inborn. What is thought to be innate is a set of properties that guide and constrain the organism as it develops linguistic knowledge, and that determine the form of particular linguistic rule systems. Furthermore, the grammars of all natural languages are thought to exhibit certain commonalties that cannot plausibly be accounted for in terms of other kinds of nonlinguistic constraints on learning. This conclusion is motivated by the following observations: (1) all dialects of all natural languages pose the same sort of challenge to the learner—the grammar of every language is similarly underdetermined by linguistic experience, but still efficiently acquired; and (2) any child has the capacity to acquire any natural language (given the proper circumstance) regardless of genetic heritage. Consequently, whatever the biological specialization for language learning turns out to be, it must be capable of playing a role in the acquisition of any human language.

These conclusions are supported by the identification of linguistic *universals* (properties common to all languages) that do not appear to have analogs in other cognitive domains (see below). Moreover, there is mounting evidence (some of which is presented in chapter 7) that the human brain is specially structured and organized to support language. Finally, there is a substantial body of biological research that suggests that genetic predispositions can play a major role in learning and behavior in other organisms (see, for example, Alcock 1989; Marler and Sherman 1985). The natural communication systems of many species exhibit complex interactions between genetic structure, development, and learning of the general sort that are apparent in human language.

We now begin a closer investigation of two of the major components of the theory of linguistic competence. We look first at *phonology*, the study of sound systems; then we turn to *syntax*, the study of the sentence structures that provide a bridge between sound and meaning. We defer our exploration of *semantics*, the study of meaning, until chapter 10, since meaning is most fruitfully investigated jointly by linguists, philosophers, and other cognitive scientists.

6.2 Phonology

The Goals of Phonology

The phonological component of a grammar comprises the rules that determine how linguistic representations are pronounced. Although a language can consist of an infinitely large set of sentences, each language has (at a given time) a finite *lexicon*, a dictionary of the language's primitive sound-meaning pairs (*morphemes*). A morpheme may be word sized, like *elephant*, or smaller, like the plural morpheme *-s*; the word *elephants*, then, consists of two morphemes. Words and morphemes, of course, can be combined (under the constraints of syntactic and other rule systems) to form sentences.

A very simple and straightforward account of phonological knowledge (let us call it T_1) might have the following character:

> The phonological component of a grammar consists of a list of the words of that language, with the pronunciation of each word given as a faithful acoustic image coupled with direct instructions to the vocal tract about how to produce that image, and instructions to the perceptual system about how to recognize it.

T_1 assumes no rules; there is only a kind of database, a dictionary of direct representation of sounds. Consider a word like *cat*. On T_1, there will be a dictionary entry something like [kæt], in which we use a special *phonetic representation*. We can think of each symbol as a set of instructions regarding the phonetic characteristics, or *features*, of a particular sound segment. (See tables 6.1 and 6.2 for information about phonetic symbols and features for English.)

Now, to return to an earlier problem, what of the plural form *cats*, consisting of the basic morpheme *cat* and the plural morpheme *-s*? On T_1, we will simply have a second entry, [kæts], containing the phonetic information appropriate to this new word. In the same way, the dictionary will contain two entries for the singular and plural of the word *dog*: [dag] in the singular, [dagz] in the plural. You will observe, however, that the final segment in *dogs*, representing the plural, is not identical to the final segment in the plural *cats*: in the former the plural is [s], in the latter, [z]. That is, in the case of *cats*, we make a friction sound (a *fricative*) with the front of the tongue, without vibrating the vocal cords; in the case of *dogs*, we make a similar fricative but with the vocal cords vibrating. Moreover, in a pair like *glass/glasses*, the plural ending has yet another pronunciation, [əz].

If it were simply the case that the plural pronunciations of words like *cat*, *dog*, and *glass* were arbitrary and unpredictable (like the sound shapes of the basic words themselves), this situation would not be especially troublesome. After all, the word that refers to cats might just as well have been *blorb*, had the history of English proceeded differently. Perhaps, then, the pronunciation of the plural for each given word is equally arbitrary and is simply a fact that must be specified in the lexicon for each relevant word.

It is a simple matter to show that this is not so. If it were, we should expect to find some word with a sound shape like *cat*—perhaps *bat*—with a plural ending pronounced as [z] or [əz]. We might also expect to find a word like *dog*—*cog*, for example—with a plural other than [z]. But every speaker of English knows, unerringly, that this is not so. *[bætz] or *[kagəz] simply could not be the pronunciation of the plural of any word of English.

Table 6.1
Phonetic symbols

Symbol	Description	Examples
	Consonants	
p	voiceless (vl.) bilabial stop	pit, spit, tip
b	voiced (vd.) bilabial stop	bit, rabbit, bib
t	vl. alveolar stop	top attack, gnat
d	vd. alveolar stop	dig, adopt, tad
k	vl. velar stop	cat, akin, tack
g	vd. velar stop	got, again, lag
m	bilabial nasal	man, amen, rum
n	alveolar nasal	nut, nanny, sin
ŋ	velar nasal	singer, ring
f	vl. labiodental fricative	fat, laugh, huff
v	vd. labiodental fricative	vat, liver, shiv
θ	vl. interdental fricative	thick, ether, both
ð	vd. interdental fricative	this, either, lathe
s	vl. alveolar fricative	sit, asset, Liszt, this
z	vd. alveolar fricative	zit, lazy, fizz, is
š	vl. alveopalatal fricative	ship, nation, ash
ž	vd. alveopalatal fricative	leisure, beige
č	vl. alveopalatal affricate	chip, itchy, rich
ǰ	vd. alveopalatal affricate	judge, edgy, ridge
w	vd. labiovelar glide	why, wick, away, row
y	vd. palatal glide	yes, boy, beyond
l	vd. lateral liquid	lip, allot, call
r	vd. central liquid	rip, arrears, car
h	vl. glottal fricative	hat, heap, ahead
	Vowels	
i	high front tense unrounded	beet, heap, believe
I	high front lax unrounded	bit, ship
e	mid front tense unrounded	bait, hay, eight
ε	mid front lax unrounded	bet, met
æ	low front lax unrounded	bat, rat, at, attach
u	high back tense rounded	boot, through, lose
U	high back lax rounded	put, look
o	mid back tense rounded	boat, blow, road
ɔ	mid back lax rounded	bore, bought
ʌ	mid back lax unrounded	but, begun
a	low back lax unrounded	pot, mock, car
ə	mid central lax unrounded	sofa, about, photograph

Table 6.2
Feature definitions

Feature	Definition
Consonant	Sound made with a constriction in the vocal tract
Vowel	Syllabic sound made with open vocal tract
Voiced	Vocal cords are vibrating
Voiceless	Vocal cords are not vibrating
Stop	Airstream is completely blocked
Nasal	Airstream passes through nasal cavity
Fricative	Airstream is partially obstructed, friction noise
Affricate	Stop sound with a fricative release
Liquid	Consonant without significant obstruction
Glide	Vowel-like but nonsyllabic sound
Bilabial	Articulated at both lips
Labiodental	Articulated with teeth and lower lip
Interdental	Articulated between the teeth
Alveolar	Articulated behind the teeth at alveolus
Alveopalatal	Articulated between alveolus and hard palate
Velar	Articulated at soft palate
Labiovelar	Articulated at lips and soft palate simultaneously
Lateral	Articulated with sides of the tongue
Central	Articulated with tongue in center of oral cavity
Glottal	Articulated at the glottis, or voice-box
Front	Tongue is at front of oral cavity
Back	Tongue is is at rear of oral cavity
High	Tongue is raised
Mid	Tongue is neither raised nor lowered
Low	Tongue is lowered
Tense	Tongue root is tensed
Lax	Tongue root is relaxed
Round	Lips are rounded
Unround	Lips are spread

In fact, careful observation will demonstrate that the distribution of the three plural pronunciations is entirely predictable: it depends in a strictly systematic fashion on the phonological shape of the word that is pluralized. If *cat* had been *blorb*, its plural would have been pronounced with a [z]. Had it been *blorch*, its plural would have been *blorches*, with [əz]. Every speaker of English knows this to be true even though the words *blorb* and *blorch* are not listed in their mental lexicons. We are therefore led to the conclusion that English speakers know a *phonological rule* that determines the pro unciation of plurals and that is independent of any list of words in actual use.

These facts suggest that the theory T_1 is inadequate as an account of our knowledge of linguistic sound structure: morphemes can have alternate pronunciations whose occurrence is predictable, and T_1 fails to have this kind of predictive power. A similar state of affairs exists as words and morphemes combine into sentences, which may on occasion be pronounced in *more* than one way. Consider the sentence that is written *Do you want to?* This sentence consists of four words whose phonetic representations, in isolation, are roughly [du], [yu], [want], and [tu]. It is possible to pronounce this sentence simply by concatenating these representations: [du yu want tu] is a grammatical English utterance. Nevertheless, it is somewhat unusual—the kind of pronunciation that might be used only in an exceptionally formal, deliberate, and self-consciously careful speech style. There are, in fact, a variety of more likely pronunciations that would be appropriate in less formal, but otherwise grammatical usage. Several of these are given in (10):

(10)   a. [də yə wan tu]
       b. [də yə wan tə]
       c. [də yə wanə]
       d. [dyə wanə]
       e. [jəwanə]

The utterances in (10) are given roughly in order of increasing informality and casualness of style. In (10a) the unstressed vowels of the first two words have been "reduced" to the very brief central vowel [ə]. In (10b) all the vowels but that of the stressed main verb have been so reduced, and the [t] of the main verb *want* has been eliminated. In (10c) the [t] of the final *to* has been deleted as well, and in (10d) the vowel of the first word, the auxiliary *do*, has been treated likewise. Finally, in (10e) the [d] that remains of *do*, and the [y] of [yə] from *you*, have been fused into a [j], a "soft *g*." Say the sentence *Do you want to?* to yourself several times, out loud and rapidly, and you will assure yourself that all of these utterances are indeed real pronunciations, including (10e), where virtually no part of the utterance can be simply decomposed into the original dictionary pronunciations of its component words.

It should be apparent that an account of English must involve some rather elaborate computational relationships between very disparate structures, if we are to model the knowledge that all of the pronunciations in (10) are related. It might be suggested, however, that the variant pronunciations in (10) are not solely a matter of linguistic knowledge. It might be the case that increasing informality and rapidity of speech causes the physiological mechanisms of production to lose their precision of control. Thus, we might look for an explanation for these facts in the domain of motor control rather than in phonology. But there is evidence that such an explanation is unsatisfactory in this and many similar cases. Consider the process that converts [want tu] to [wanə]. The same kind of effect can be seen in the case of the phrase *going to*, which is typically realized phonetically in rapid speech as [gʌnə], sometimes written *gonna*. Consider the sentences in (11):

(11)   a. I'm going to leave.   [aym goiŋ tu liv]
       b. I'm gonna leave.   [aym gʌnə liv]

If the pronunciation in (11b) were a matter of motor control, we would have a right to expect a sentence like *I'm going to New York* to behave identically under rapid speech conditions. That is, we should expect to find casual pronunciations like **I'm gonna New York*. But this appears not to be a possible pronunciation. The process in question seems to depend on more than the physiological state of the vocal tract under rapid production conditions. Among other things, it appears to depend on the syntactic structure of the utterance. The reduced *to* in *I'm gonna leave* is part of an infinitive verb; in the ungrammatical **I'm gonna New York* the reduced *to* is a part of speech that linguists call a preposition. Clearly the process of contraction that produces forms like *wanna* and *gonna* cannot have a motoric explanation if it depends crucially on syntactic information of this sort. Finally, lest the reader think that the facts can somehow be explained by an appeal to other phonetic differences between the utterances in question, consider the pair of sentences *I'm going to split* (under the colloquial meaning of "leave") and the phonetically identical *I'm going to Split* (where "Split" is the name of a city in the former Yugoslavia). The contracted form [aym gʌnə split] can only mean that you are intending to leave, not that you intend to go to the Balkans. Since these sentences differ only in syntactic structure, we are left with no alternative but to conclude that these phonetic facts are to be explained by appealing to (rules within) a theory of grammar.

The Nature of Phonetic Representations
Before we proceed to develop a more adequate theory of phonological knowledge, let us pause briefly to discuss the nature of representations in phonology.

A phonological theory must have a notation for displaying the phonetic shape of utterances. We have already made use of such a system when we represented the word *cat* as [kæt]. These *phonetic representations* are, in some respects, close to being pictures of actual pronunciations. But, as we will see shortly, they are not in any sense "reproductions" of actual utterances.

Let us look in more detail at a representation like [kæt]. Note that we always use square brackets to indicate that we are dealing with a phonetic representation rather than a written form in conventional spelling. It is essential to understand that [kæt] is not an unanalyzable whole. It consists (at least) of a chain of discrete symbols that each represents *one and only one* particular sound segment. Furthermore, the sound that is represented by each symbol—[k], [æ], [t]—is itself a cluster of many interrelated physical events. [k] represents a sound in which the airstream from the lungs is completely obstructed in the oral cavity by the back of the tongue against the *velum*, or soft palate. This produces a *velar stop* consonant. At the same time, we note that the vocal cords (part of the larynx in the neck) are not vibrating since [k] is a *voiceless* stop. By contrast, [æ] represents a vowel sound that is made with no vocal tract obstruction, and with the vocal cords set in vibrating motion; it is a *voiced* sound. Moreover, the airstream is shaped by the tongue, which is lowered, fronted, and relaxed: [æ] is a *low front lax* vowel. As for [t], it is also a voiceless stop consonant, like [k], but in this case the airstream is completely blocked by the closure of the tongue tip against the ridged area just behind the teeth, the alveolus: [t] is a *voiceless alveolar stop*. (Had we set the vocal cords to vibrating, a [d] would have resulted—a *voiced alveolar stop*. The voiced counterpart of a [k] is a [g], a *voiced velar stop*.) It should be clear that phonetic representations like [kæt] are, in a sense, shorthand accounts of a much richer and more complex picture of an actual physical event.

We know a great deal about the anatomical, physiological, and acoustic properties of linguistic sounds, and such information can be essential to an adequate understanding of phonological phenomena. Electromyographic analysis enables us to specify the states of the dozens of muscles that are activated in the production of any speech event. X-ray methods allow us to visually observe the anatomic states of the vocal tract in motion, and sound spectrography provides a detailed picture of the physical, acoustic properties of speech signals. With these and other methods we are capable of constructing highly refined phonetic records that are multidimensional accounts of observable, physical phonetic events. Nevertheless, there is an important virtue in the relative shorthand of the phonetic representation. Different speakers actually produce speech sounds that are physically distinct, and sometimes dramatically so. Imagine a four-year-old girl, and a forty-year-old man with a chronic hoarse voice, pronouncing the word [kæt]. Sex, age, health, emotional state, even rate of speech will result in very different phonetic pictures. If we compared two forty-year-old males with hoarse voices, we would find remarkably different phonetic descriptions of what is arguably the same word, since their vocal tracts are likely to be quite different in shape. In fact, even were we to compare successive pronunciations of the same word by the same speaker, we would likely find significant physical differences from one pronunciation to the next.

What is of interest to the phonologist, as a cognitive scientist, is the fact that speakers of the same language can recognize that it is the *same word* that is intended in each case by each speaker. Factors like age, sex, emotional state, bad colds, and alcohol may conspire to make actual performances physically distinct, but there must be some level of phonetic description at which all possible distinct tokens of the same word are represented in essentially the same fashion. Put another way, factors like colds and age are not relevant to the particular system of knowledge—the grammar—that determines whether an utterance is part of the language, and what part it is. Our linguistic capacity (the competence grammar, and its implementing mechanisms) manages to normalize the great variability in speech performance by establishing representations that contain only linguistically significant information.

Phonemic Representation
We must now ask ourselves a fundamental question: What *does* constitute a linguistically significant property of pronunciation? In other words, what kinds of knowledge ought to be accounted for in a cognitive theory of phonology?

Some such aspects of pronunciation suggest themselves quite readily. Consider, for example, the difference between the [s] and [z] sounds in a pair of words like *sap* and *zap*. Native speakers of English know instantly, without introspection, that these are different words. The physical difference between [s] and [z] appears to be the only factor that distinguishes the two words. Both sounds are fricatives made by creating a partial obstruction between the tongue and the alveolar ridge. The difference between the two is strictly a matter of vocal cord vibration: [s] is voiceless, [z] is voiced. This physical difference is neither random nor controlled by extralinguistic factors like age or drunkenness. Speakers of English know that the difference between these sounds can be exploited to represent a difference between words in the lexicon. We will refer to this distinguishing property of sounds as *phonemic*, and to sounds like [s] and [z] as distinct *phonemes*.

In general, the most straightforward way of determining whether two sounds should be represented as distinct phonemes is to apply the *minimal pair test*. This test can be conceived in various ways. One way to apply the test involves substituting a phonetically different sound, say, [z], for the initial segment [s] of a word like *sap*. If we pronounce [sæp] with an initial [z], it simply becomes [zæp]. The latter is, of course, a perfectly good pronunciation in English just as [sæp] is, but it is the pronunciation of a different word.

A second way of applying a minimal pair test involves comparing two phonetic representations that differ from one another in one and only one segment. If the two forms in question are distinct words (that is, distinct in meaning), then the two segments under comparison are to be represented as distinct phonemes. We can see this (again) for [s] and [z] by applying the minimal pair test to the words *loose* [lus] and *lose* [luz]. These forms differ only in their final segment and are distinct in meaning; hence, the phonetic difference constitutes a systematic phonemic contrast.

There is, furthermore, no way to *predict* that the final segment of a word like *loose* will be [s], or that the final segment of *lose* is [z]. The occurrence of one or another phoneme is an arbitrary fact about each word. There is nothing inherent in the grammar of English that makes [z] the "correct" final segment of *lose* except for the simple fact that it is so. This is another crucial property of phonemes.

A central task of phonological theory is to characterize the nature of representations in the mental lexicon keeping separate entities in the lexicon distinct from one another. It follows that phonemic distinctions must be a crucial part of such lexical representations. The theory, then, must capture the notion of the phoneme in some explicit fashion. If, contrary to fact, all linguistically significant phonetic properties of words were also signals of a systematic phonemic distinction, there would be a simple solution: phonological theory could largely consist of a closed set of symbols (like table 6.1), each representing a single phoneme. We would, in addition, need a set of rules that govern the order and combination of phonemes (phonologists call these *phonotactic* rules) that tell us, for example, that [s] and [z] may not occur contiguously. Under such a theory, forms like [sæp] and [zæp] would constitute legal words, and indeed they occur in the English lexicon. The theory would also predict, correctly, that a form like [pæz] should be a possible word of English, whereas *[pæsz] is not.

However, although a theory of this sort has merit, our first assumption—that all linguistically significant sounds are phonemic in nature—cannot be maintained. As a case in point, consider the pronunciation of an English word like *pat*. We may for the moment represent this form phonetically as [pæt]. ([p], which we have not yet discussed explicitly, is a voiceless stop like [t] and [k]. Its stop closure is *bilabial*; that is, it is made with both lips sealed together.)

If you moisten the back of your hand and pronounce the word normally, while holding your lips close to your moistened hand, you will notice that a distinct puff of air accompanies the [p] at the onset of the word. We will refer to this puffed *p* as *aspirated*. Now do the same for the word *spat*. You will observe that there is no comparable aspiration accompanying the [p] in this word. We find instead an *unaspirated* voiceless bilabial stop. You can observe the same effect somewhat more dramatically by lighting a match and holding it in front of your lips during the pronunciation of each word. Aspirated [p] will cause the match to go out, whereas unaspirated [p] will not.

The physical difference between these two events may not be apparent to every reader; it is not perceptually salient to most speakers of English, and English speakers may be quite firm in their conviction that the two kinds of *p* are, in some quite potent sense, the same. But the physical difference is clear, as the two sound spectrograms in figure 6.1 demonstrate.

Here, then, are two phonetically distinct events. Are they phonemically distinct? Recall that substituting [z] for [s] in the initial segment of *sap* yielded a pronounceable, yet different, word of English. Suppose we try to transpose aspirated *p* (we will represent this as [pʰ]) with unaspirated [p] in a selection of English words. By contrast, we do *not* create new and different words of English. What results are bizarre, deviant pronunciations that cannot be English words. *[pæt] without aspiration sounds uncomfortably close to the English word [bæt], *bat*, where [b] is a voiced bilabial stop—but not close enough to sound like a real English word. *[spʰæt] sounds overstrenuously articulated, noisy, and wrong.

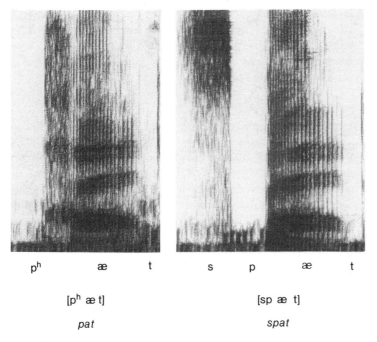

Figure 6.1

Sound spectrograms of utterances of *spat* and *spat*. Time is represented on the horizontal axis of each spectrogram, and frequency (pitch) is represented on the vertical axis. The degree of darkness at a particular point indicates the amount of energy present at that time and frequency. Note that the portion of the spectrogram corresponding to the /pæ/ is different for *pat* and *spat* owing to the presence of aspiration in *pat* and its absence in *spat*.

Both pronunciations are, of course, physically possible. Indeed, there are many languages where it is possible for initial [p] (and other sounds as well) to occur aspirated as well as unaspirated—the feature of aspiration is used phonemically in such languages. A good example is Assamese, a language of northeastern India. Consider the contrasting forms in (12):

(12) a. [pat]   'leaf'
      b. [pʰat]   'split'
      c. [bat]   'road'
      d. [bʰat]   'boiled rice'

In Assamese there is a phonemic contrast not only between the ordinary unaspirated voiceless [p] and the voiceless aspirated [pʰ], but also between these and the voiced unaspirated and aspirated pair [b] and [bʰ]. All of these sounds can occur relatively freely in various positions within words.

As a consequence of these observations, we are led to the conclusion that the occurrence of aspirated versus unaspirated voiceless bilabial stops in English is rule governed. We will refer to the pattern of occurrence that these sounds exhibit as *complementary distribution*. This kind of distribution, governed by rule, stands in opposition to the *contrastive distribution* that is exhibited by sounds that are phonemically distinct, and whose distribution cannot be predicted by rule. The simple theory T_1 that we suggested earlier is thus inadequate. There are indeed sound distinctions that must be represented phonetically but cannot be characterized as distinct phonemes. In the following section we will develop a richer theory of sound structure that accounts both for phonemic contrast and for the kind of systematic phonetic variation that is exemplified in the case of aspiration in English.

A Theory of Phonemes and Their Variants

We have identified two goals that a phonological theory must meet: (1) to characterize the set of distinctive contrasting sounds (phonemes) in the language, and (2) to characterize the distribution of sounds that are not distinctive. Simply increasing the vocabulary of phonetic symbols (to include aspirated stops, for instance) does not accomplish these goals. As we have noted, the relationship between aspirated and unaspirated voiceless bilabial stops seems to be regular and predictable. It is arguably part of the speaker's active rule-governed knowledge of the language, and not simply a general description of the distribution of elements in the lexicon. Suppose an English speaker has reason to coin a new word, for instance, a form represented in conventional spelling as *paff*. It is a safe bet that any English speaker will pronounce this hypothetical word with an initial aspirated stop, as [pʰæf]. But such a word could not have been included in any lexicon of previously learned words of English, or even in a complete lexicon of all the words of English.

Consider also the evidence provided by speech errors. A speaker intends to produce a word like *flap* [flæp]. Inadvertently, the production system slips, and the speaker emits [pʰlæp], anticipating, as it were, the final [p]. Final [p] is not normally aspirated in English, nor is initial [f]. But when speakers commit this kind of error, the anticipatory [p] will be aspirated.

These kinds of evidence confirm our assertion that English speakers represent their knowledge about aspiration in a form that is *independent* of the phonetic form of actual words. We will formally represent this knowledge by means of the concept of the phonological rule. A first approximation to the particular rule that governs English aspiration is given below:

(13) *English Aspiration* (version 1)
All instances of word-initial voiceless bilabial stops are aspirated.

This rule makes no special reference to any particular form in the English lexicon. In this general form, it will hold for all lexical items, as well as for possible forms that have not yet been entered into the lexicon. Moreover, if we assume that the rule of Aspiration is part of the actual process of producing utterances (as well as a description of phonological knowledge, in the competence sense), we can explain why mistakenly produced utterances also exhibit aspiration.

In the case of a phonemic contrast, say, between [p] and [b], speakers report effortlessly that these are different sounds. But they cling just as steadfastly to the belief that [p] and [pʰ], which are in fact related by a phonological rule, are the "same" sound. We want our theory to account for these perceptions in a straightforward, plausible fashion. It seems unlikely, for example, that speakers search their lexicon for minimal pairs when asked if two sounds are the same or different. Nor is it likely that our perception of sameness is established on the basis of some metric of phonetic similarity, for [p] and [pʰ] are no more or less different from one another than [p] is from [b]. Both pairs differ by exactly one feature (aspiration in the first case, voicing in the

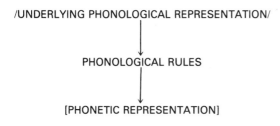

Figure 6.2
The structure of phonological knowledge

second), yet only the [p]/[b] pair presents a phonemic contrast that is perceived as different.

These considerations have led phonologists to the conclusion that phonological knowledge cannot be characterized adequately by a theory that provides only phonetic representations. We will claim that there is a second level of representation at work, a level of mental representation that is more distant from the actual physical phonetic events than is phonetic representation itself. We refer to this as the *underlying phonological representation* (*UPR*). The overall picture of the grammar that is implied by these assumptions is given in figure 6.2.

By hypothesis, sounds that are in complementary distribution share a single common phoneme in UPR. (We enclose such entities in slash marks—for example, /p/—to distinguish them from elements of phonetic representation.) The lexicon, where all (and only) phonemic properties are marked, consists of forms in UPR; phonological rules then apply to such forms to convert them into phonetic representations. Thus, the rule of Aspiration can now be understood to apply to lexical entries that contain a phonemic /p/ that is not marked for aspiration. Just in case this /p/ is in the initial position of a word, it is converted by rule into [pʰ]. In any other position /p/ will be realized phonetically, with no change, as [p]. These two phonetic variants, [p] and [pʰ], are referred to as *allophones* of the phoneme /p/, related to that phoneme by rule. In such a model our commonsense conviction of the apparent identity between physically distinct sounds like [p] and [pʰ] can now be understood as a real identity—not at the physical level, not in phonetic description, but at a deeper level of mental representation.

To illustrate these ideas, let us consider more concretely the *derivations* (formal mappings between levels of representation) of some actual words—say, *pat*, *spat*, *sap*, and *zap*. The UPRs of these words, the form in which they are entered in the lexicon, will be /pæt/, /spæt/, /sæp/, and /zæp/. (How might you determine why /s/, /z/, and /æ/ are presumed to be distinct underlying phonemes of English?) It now remains to apply relevant phonological rules (*P-rules*) to these UPRs. Thus far we have seen only one rule in English, Aspiration. The relevant derivations for the above forms are given in (14):

(14) Underlying
representation   /pæt/   /spæt/   /sæp/   /zæp/

P-rules
  Aspiration   pʰ   not applicable

Phonetic
representation   [pʰæt]   [spæt]   [sæp]   [zæp]

Rules and Features

We will now examine the nature of phonological rules in more detail. Consider again the phenomenon of aspiration in English. In our first formulation of the Aspiration rule, we limited our attention to the phoneme /p/. The fact is that other sounds, for example, /t/, behave identically to /p/ with respect to aspiration. The minimal pair test will assure us that /p/ and /t/ are indeed contrasting phonemes: witness the lexical contrast between *pick* and *tick*, *spill* and *still*. In word-initial position we find only aspirated [tʰ]; in other positions, plain [t]. We must therefore modify the Aspiration rule so that it applies to /t/ as well as /p/:

(15)   *English Aspiration* (version 2)
        Word-initial /p/ and /t/ are aspirated.

Phonologists are concerned not only with making correct observations, but also with explaining them, and, as in any science, seek explanations that lead to clearer and deeper understandings. In this spirit, *why*, one might ask, are /p/ and /t/ both aspirated under the same conditions? It is possible, of course, that they are only accidentally and randomly grouped together with respect to aspiration. Had the historical development of English been different, perhaps /n/ and /p/ rather than /p/ and /t/ might have behaved alike.

However, the fact is that the grouping of /p/ and /t/ is a very common phenomenon in the grammars of the world's languages; the grouping of /n/ and /p/ is rare indeed. We want to be able to find a nonarbitrary way of characterizing this asymmetry, and we can readily find one when we consider the phonetic features that characterize the sounds in question. The phonetic segments [p] and [t] share a number of articulatory characteristics by virtue of both being voiceless stops: they are both made with a simple, complete closure of the vocal tract, within the oral cavity, with nonvibrating vocal cords. If we assume that these features are not only descriptions of physical phonetic states, but also abstract properties of the phonemes that underlie them in mental representation, we can recast the rule of Aspiration in a form that captures the unity of /p/ and /t/ in a principled manner:

(16)   *English Aspiration* (version 3)
        Voiceless stop sounds are aspirated in word-initial position.

Comparing the first two versions of the Aspiration rule with the third, we note a crucial difference. The first two are formulated in terms of particular phonemes, treated as unanalyzable wholes. But the most recent version of the rule is formulated in terms of particular properties, or phonological features, of groups of phonemes. There is nothing about the first two versions of the rule that would preclude any other arbitrary segment from being involved in the process. Thus, we might expect the second version of the rule to eventually come to apply to /p/, /t/, and /n/. As we noted, such groupings do not (commonly) arise. But the third version of Aspiration makes a specific and testable claim: *any* voiceless stop in English will be aspirated in the appropriate environment. Thus far we have discussed only two such stops, /p/ and /t/. But if there are other voiceless stop phonemes in the language, the new Aspiration rule predicts that they will behave identically with /p/ and /t/. In fact, there is another: /k/, the velar voiceless stop. Its phonemic status can be determined simply enough by the minimal pair test: compare *pill*, *till*, and *kill*. The aspiration of /k/ in initial position, as predicted, is evident in forms like *kill* (but appropriately missing in *skill*).

Phonological theory has far greater explanatory and predictive value, then, if we regard phonemes not as atomic wholes, but as sets of component phonological features. The features serve two purposes: first, they provide a *description*, at the level of phonetic representation, that is appropriately close to the physiological and acoustic nature of speech events; second, they allow a proper *classification* of phonemes at the level of underlying phonological representation. Cognitive representations in the phonological domain are thus highly abstract in certain ways, but closely linked to the physical nature of the organism and the world in other respects. Furthermore, there is good reason to believe that phonological features are not idiosyncratically defined for each particular language. Instead we believe that a uniform set of features is made available within universal grammar, as a fixed property of the architecture of the language acquisition system. We will see some evidence for this view shortly.

Morphophonemic Alternation: The Case of English Plurals
Earlier in this chapter we saw that the plural ending in English can take three phonetically distinct forms: [s], [z], and [əz]. A number of interesting problems remain to be considered in this regard.

First, in the theory we have developed above, each of these plural forms would seem to require distinct phonemic representations. We might expect the underlying form of [s] to be /s/, and of [z] to be /z/. But [əz] poses something of a problem. /z/ is certainly a phoneme, but it is not at all apparent that there is a /ə/ phoneme. The minimal pair test will fail to find a single case where two words differ uniquely in that one contains a /ə/ contrasting with some other vowel (at least in monosyllabic words where the vowel is stressed). What then can the underlying phonological representation of [əz] be?

The second problem is that even if we could account for the underlying nature of [ə], we would be left with three distinct underlying representations for what is transparently the same morpheme of English, the meaning-bearing element that represents plurality. Surely the theory of phonological knowledge of English ought to be able to capture this fundamental identity of [s], [z], and [əz] in a unitary fashion. But the theory of phonemes we have developed seems to force three separate lexical representations on us when we ought to have only one.

Let us step back for a moment and recall that the distribution of the three forms is, in fact, predictable. In the current theory this kind of predictability is represented in the form of P(honological)-rules. What would such rules be like in the case of the English plural? Consider the actual distribution; table 6.3 outlines the circumstances in which we find each type of ending. On examining the first column, we discover that the final segment of each noun stem—the basic, nonplural form—is voiceless. Similarly, all of the nouns that take the [z] ending have voiced final segments. The third column renders things a little less clear. Some of the words end in a voiceless segment (for example, the [č] of *latch*), and some end in a voiced segment (for example, the [ǰ] of *judge*). However, careful observation leads to a revealing discovery: all of the words in the third column end in consonants that are acoustically noisy, and each has two distinct noise sources. The [s] and [z] endings, for instance, involve friction noise between the tongue and roof of the mouth, and also noise produced by the airstream as it passes the teeth. We can capture this acoustic similarity by characterizing the final segments in the stems of the third column by the phonological feature *strident*.

Table 6.3
Distribution of the three versions of the English plural morpheme

[s]	[z]	[əz]
ship/ships	hub/hubs	glass/glasses
gnat/gnats	dud/duds	gaze/gazes
tick/ticks	bag/bags	lash/lashes
laugh/laughs	cur/curs	garage/garages
depth/depths	shill/shills	latch/latches
	ram/rams	rouge/rouges
	shin/shins	judge/judges
	hoe/hoes	
	shiv/shivs	
	lathe/lathes	

There appear, then, to be three generalizations at work here: (1) if a noun ends in a strident sound, it takes the [əz] ending; (2) if it ends in a (nonstrident) voiced sound, it takes the [z] ending; and (3) if it ends in a (nonstrident) voiceless sound, it takes these [s] ending. We might take these statements to be rules that govern the assignment of three lexical plural morphemes. But such an analysis misses the thrust of the problems posed earlier, namely, that [ə] has no direct phonemic counterpart, and that the three phonetic forms in question represent the single concept of the plural in English, in spite of the apparent phonemic differences among them. We ought then to consider revising our theory in order to capture the unity of the plural phenomenon.

In fact, this is a simple matter to accomplish. Let us claim that there is indeed only a single lexical representation of the plural morpheme assuming, by hypothesis, that it is /z/. The process of forming a plural in English consists of affixing the plural /z/ to a noun stem in underlying phonological representation. Consider the nouns *gnat*, *bag*, and *glass*. These have the lexical phonemic forms /næt/, /bæg/, and /glæs/, respectively. After affixing the plural /z/, we have the composite underlying representations in (17):

(17)   /næt + z/
         /bæg + z/
         /glæs + z/

In order to account for the [z] that occurs in forms with final voiceless segments, like *bags*, we need do nothing at all, and /bæg + z/ will surface phonetically as [bægz] with no additional steps. In order to account for the [s] that occurs in forms like *gnats*, we posit a rule of the form in (18):

(18)   *Devoicing*
         When a morpheme /z/ is preceded by a final unvoiced segment,
         devoice the /z/; that is, convert it to [s].

The Devoicing rule will not apply to /bæg + z/ because the final /g/ of the stem is voiced. But the rule will apply to a form like /næt + z/, because the final /t/ of the stem is voiceless; hence, the /z/ plural affix is converted by Devoicing to [s], yielding [næts].

It remains to account for the plural of words like *glass*. Recall that the underlying representation of the plural is /glæs + z/. [ə] must eventually appear between the /s/ of the stem and the plural affix. Since this vowel is not present in underlying representation under this account (and has no special phonemic counterpart in any case), we must postulate a rule to accomplish its *insertion* into the representation:

(19) [ə]-*Insertion*
When a /z/ morpheme is affixed to a stem with a final strident segment, insert [ə] between the stem-final segment and the affix.

The rule of [ə]-Insertion will apply appropriately to /glæs + z/. Observe that the rules in question must apply in a particular order. If Devoicing were to apply first, /glæs + z/ would surface incorrectly as *[glæsəs], since /z/, preceded by a voiceless /s/, would trigger Devoicing. The ordering relation [ə]-Insertion/Devoicing, in addition to the rules themselves, must therefore be a part of the phonological grammar of English.

The generality of this analysis becomes clear when we observe that the insertion/devoicing phenomenon is not simply a description of noun plural formation in English. In fact, we find the same distribution of [s], [z], and [əz] when we examine the third-person singular ending of English verbs—*walks* [waks], *nags* [nægs], *hitches* [hičəz]. The possessive ending behaves in the same fashion—*Mark's* [marks], *Bob's* [babz], *George's* [ǰorǰəz]. In each case we hypothesize that the underlying representation is /z/—phonologically identical to the plural, but differing in meaning and syntactic function—and the rules of [ə]-Insertion and Devoicing apply.

An examination of this broader domain also provides direct evidence that the underlying form is indeed /z/, and not /s/ or /əz/ or something else. Notice that a decision to treat the underlying form of the plural as /s/, as its conventional spelling might suggest, would change the logic of the derivation considerably. In particular, were we to make this assumption, the Devoicing rule we have posited would need to be replaced by a corresponding Voicing rule—one that changed the plural marker /s/ into [z] in the environment of a word-final voiced consonant. However, by considering the phenomenon of "*is*-contraction" in English, where we find variation between phrases like *Bob is (here)*, and *Bob's (here)*, we find independent evidence that English contains a *Devoicing* rule, in turn motivating our original assumption treating the plural marker as underlying /z/. The underlying representation of *Bob is (here)* is /bab Iz/ and must surface as [babz]. The contraction process consists of deleting the /I/ of *is* and affixing it to the preceding noun. Once this contraction is accomplished, an environment arises where [ə]-Insertion and Devoicing can apply—on the assumption that those rules operate over /z/, in this case, the second segment of *is* ([iz]). Indeed, we find just the same outputs that we saw in the case of the plural, the third person, and the possessive: *Mark is here* surfaces, after contraction, as [marks hir]; *George is here*, as [ǰorǰəz hir]; and *Bob's here*, unchanged by rule, as [babz hir]. The hypothesis that the underlying form of the English plural is /z/ turns out to have exactly the right predictive value when it comes to understanding the completely unrelated phenomenon of contraction. Thus, we have supporting evidence for our apparently arbitrary decision to assume (in spite of orthographic appearance, where relevant forms are always written "s") that the plural is underlyingly /z/.

Hierarchical Representations
On the view that has been developed thus far, phonological representations are linear-segmental and two-dimensional: that is, a representation contains a row of phonemes, each of which consists of a column of features. The familiar roman alphabet roughly represents a linear string of phonemes. Each written symbol or combination of symbols

corresponds (ideally) to one phoneme. Not all writing systems are like this, however: many of them use symbols that do not correspond to single phonemes, but to groupings of phonemes that are generally called *syllables*. We have seen ample evidence that phonemes themselves are not merely artifacts of our writing systems, but fundamental elements of phonological representation. We will now consider some evidence that the same is true of the syllable.

Consider, again, the case of aspiration. You will recall that we have claimed that voiceless stops are aspirated in word-initial position in English—for example, [pʰIt]. But this is not the whole story. In a word like *appear*, the medial /p/ is also aspirated, as is the /t/ in *attack* and the /k/ in *akin*. However, the rule we adduced earlier does not account for these facts, since the relevant voiceless stops are not word-initial.

We can nevertheless provide a perspicuous general account of aspiration, if we assume that phonological representations are organized not only into segmental chains, but also into higher-order syllable structures. The syllable is a notion that is intuitively easy to grasp: it is a grouping of segments that seem to us to cohere together. Thus, even if *paka* is not a word of English, virtually any speaker will be able to break it down into syllables—*syllabify* it—as *pa-ka*. Indeed, it is a fairly safe prediction that speakers of every language will make the same syllable break. Even in more complex cases, when native speakers may be less sure of where the syllable breaks are, they are quite uniformly able to say how many syllables there are in a word.

Researchers have long sought a measurable definition of the syllable, hoping to find that the intuitive notion corresponded to a physical event like a breathing pulse, or a unit of muscular effort. Such efforts have failed. The syllable appears instead to be best interpreted as a unit of cognitive organization. It is helpful (and, as it turns out, theoretically significant; see below) to regard a phonological representation as consisting in part of a sequence, or *skeleton*, of C and V elements. Syllables can then basically be defined in terms of the organization of C and V elements in the skeleton.

Every syllable must normally contain a vowel (V) *nucleus*, the core of syllabic organization (with the occasional exception being cases like English *button* in which a sonorous consonant—in this case, /n/—serves as the peak of the syllable). Indeed, it appears that the ability of speakers to count syllables, even when they cannot say how they are broken up, is a function of counting the vowel nuclei. Vowels are the most perceptually salient elements of the syllable—largely accounting for its overall duration, and carrying the syllable's pitch or tonality.

It is quite possible to identify some elementary general principles of syllabification. One such principle appears to be that successive sequences of C and V are organized with the C element as the beginning, or *onset*, of the syllable. A string like *pataka* will always be syllabified as *pa-ta-ka*, not as *pat-ak-a*. The principle that guarantees this is the *Maximal Onset Principle*. The principle says that—all things being equal (but see below)—consonants are organized into the onset of a following syllable rather than the end of a preceding one. So, to consider an actual example, a word like *attract*, [ətrækt] with the skeleton CVCCVC, should be syllabified as CV-CCVC—[ə-trækt] rather than [ət-rækt]. Languages do, however, differ in the complexity they allow in onsets. Whereas some languages permit only simple CV syllables, others permit more complex syllable onsets. In English, for example, the onset may contain as many as three consonants: for instance, the word *spree*, whose skeleton contains the single CCCV syllable /spri/.

The syllabic nucleus itself may be complex, as in the case of English *diphthongs* like /oi/ in *boy*, where two nonidentical segments are each associated with a distinct

Figure 6.3
Syllabic nucleus of /oi/

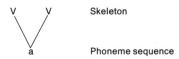

Figure 6.4
/a/ attached to two Vs in the skeleton

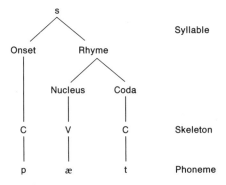

Figure 6.5
Hierarchical syllable structure for the one-syllable word *pat*

V-slot (figure 6.3). In cases where vowel sequences are identical—in languages such as Sinhala, where the word *maasə* 'month' contrasts with *masə* 'meat'—it has been convincingly argued that a skeletal nucleus of the form VV is associated with a single phoneme. The length of the vowel is a consequence of having two elements in the skeleton, rather than two distinct vowel phoneme segments in a linear string (figure 6.4). English also permits complex syllable *offsets*, or *codas*, which follow the vocalic nucleus: for example, *brisk*, whose skeleton is the single CCVCC monosyllable /brIsk/.

There is good reason to think that the nucleus and coda are themselves grouped together in a hierarchical fashion, into a *rhyme* constituent. The term is due in part to the fact that it is this constituent that "rhymes" in conventional poetry—*sit, pit, bit*—whereas the onset does not participate in this kind of normal rhyme scheme. The rhyme also plays a crucial role in the determination of stress patterns in many languages (including English). Rhymes that are complex, which contain a nucleus plus a coda, or a "branching" nucleus—a diphthong or long vowel—tend to be the most prominent, or stressed, syllable in words.

The overall hierarchical picture of the syllable that emerges is illustrated in figure 6.5 for the one-syllable word *pat*. The rhyme constituent is obligatory: every syllable in every language must contain at least a V nucleus. Consonantal onsets and codas

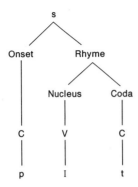

Figure 6.6
Syllabification for *pit*

are optional in some languages: English allows both, either, or neither: *beat* [bit], *bee* [bi] , *eat* [it] , *oh* [o].

We noted above that there are some apparent counterexamples to the Maximal Onset Principle. An English word like *constrain* has the skeletal structure CVCCCCVC. The Maximal Onset Principle might appear to mandate that this word be syllabified as CV-CCCCVC—*co-nstrain*. Of course, no English speaker would report such a syllabification. Indeed, we want to rule out the possibility of a monosyllabic English word beginning with a sequence like */nstr/—even though such initial sequences are possible in other languages. (Russian, for example, has onsets like /mst/ in the name *Mstislav*.) Therefore, we must specify, for each language, the set of consonant sequences that can serve as onsets. The Maximal Onset Principle is overridden when such language-specific constraints would be violated.

Although there is a great deal more to say about the organization of syllable structure that is beyond the scope of this discussion (more discussion regarding the evidence for syllables will be found in chapters 9 and 11), for present purposes it suffices to assume two things about phonological representation. First, phonological representations are hierarchical in the sense discussed above, and second, the Maximal Onset Principle (at least in part) defines the relationship between syllabified segments. We can now return to the problem of characterizing the English Aspiration rule. We have seen that voiceless stops are aspirated in word-initial position, and also in words like *appear*. Our initial formulation of the rule does not account for these latter cases. But an obvious generalization emerges when we think in terms of syllable structure.

All word-initial segments are, by definition, in the onset of the first syllable. Thus, *pit* is syllabified as in figure 6.6. Under the Maximal Onset Principle, a word like *appear* will have the syllabic structure illustrated in figure 6.7. If we make the plausible assumption that syllable structures are part of the underlying representation of words, then their properties should be "visible" to phonological rules that operate over them. It becomes a simple matter to reformulate the Aspiration rule in a way that generalizes to the necessary cases:

(20) *English Aspiration* (syllabic version)
Aspirate all syllable-initial voiceless stops.

(There are, however, some medial voiceless stops that do not aspirate. For example, the medial /p/ in *happy* is not aspirated. A careful examination of the range of cases will

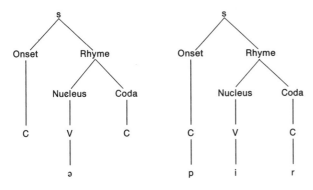

Figure 6.7
Syllabification for *appear*

show that aspiration occurs only when a voiceless stop is in the onset of a stressed syllable. Kahn (1976) has argued that the onsets of unstressed syllables in English are actually *ambisyllabic*. That is, they also serve as codas of the preceding syllable. Selkirk (1980) argues that consonants in the onset of unstressed syllables are resyllabified by a special rule of English, which changes basic syllable structure (as defined by the Maximal Onset Principle)—reassigning the consonant to the coda of the preceding syllable. Hence, such consonants would not be subject to the Aspiration rule (20).)

English aspiration is a generalization that cannot be captured in a purely linear representational framework without great descriptive complication. (As an exercise, the reader may wish to try to formulate the Aspiration rule to cover the full range of cases without making use of notions like the syllable.) Indeed, the last decade and a half of research has led to the conclusion that many other phonological phenomena are also best understood in a nonlinear "three-dimensional" framework. In an early development of this view, Goldsmith (1976) showed that tone languages, whose words may be distinguished solely by differences in pitch, are best described in an *autosegmental* framework, one in which the features of pitch are represented as discrete elements on a separate tier of representation (like syllables), rather than as inherent features of segments within a linear string. An example of an analysis that is illuminated by this perspective can be found by examining some data from the African language Etung. In this language one-syllable words (for example, (21a)) can be associated with high pitch (H), low pitch (L), rising pitch (R), or falling pitch (F). But in words of more than one syllable (21b–c)), only simple high and low pitch are normally exhibited:

(21) a. | H | L | F | R |
|---|---|---|---|
| kpa 'first' | kpe 'even' | na 'it is' | no 'how' |

    b. | H H | L L | H L | L H |
|---|---|---|---|
| nse 'father' | egu 'evening' | oda 'platform' | ekat 'leg' |

    c. | H H H | L L L | H L L | L H H |
|---|---|---|---|
| ekue 'forest' | eyuri 'dress' | akpuga 'money' | bisone 'spoon' |

If tones are to be characterized by phonological features that inhere in individual segments (say, vowels), we must posit four such features: high, low, rising, and falling. But a puzzle presents itself: why can the putative tone features rising and falling only occur on vowels in words of one syllable?

Figure 6.8
Two representations of "tone melodies" in Etung

Figure 6.9
Tones exhaustively linked to vowels in Etung

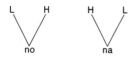

Figure 6.10
Representations of contour tones

An autosegmental analysis can provide an insightful account of these facts. Tone languages such as Etung have lexical representations that consist of (at least) a phoneme tier and an independent tonal tier. The tone "autosegments" H and L—representing high and low pitch—can occur on the tonal tier. But, as with phonemes, only certain sequences of tones are permitted. Suppose that for Etung, only H, L, LH, and HL "tone melodies" are allowed. In a two-syllable word with an HL or LH melody, each tone will be associated with one vowel according to a *well-formedness constraint* requiring that every tone must be associated with a vowel, and every vowel with a tone. The representations in figure 6.8 obtain. When the number of syllable nuclei exceeds the number of tones on the tone tier, the well-formedness condition requires that the tone(s) exhaustively link to all vowels (or syllable nuclei; in Etung, nasals may serve as syllable nuclei along with vowels, at least in word-initial position) (see figure 6.9).

In the one-syllable cases the picture is simple when a single H or L melody occurs—the word exhibits high or low tone by straightforward association. But when an LH or HL melody occurs, the story is more interesting. The well-formedness condition requires that all tones be linked to vowels. In one-syllable words *both* tones must be linked to the single vowel. This gives rise to *contour* tones, represented in figure 6.10.

The phonetic interpretation of these representations is quite straightforward—a low-high sequence is heard as a rise; a high-low, as a fall. There are no rises or falls in the multisyllabic words above simply because such forms have enough vowels to link with each tonal autosegment without forming a contour. This is a formally simpler account of this phenomenon than is possible in a linear-segmental model; no separate rising or falling features—with skewed distributions—are needed to describe these contoured tones.

The decision to treat tone as an autosegment (in tone languages) also receives support from other quarters. For example, Goldsmith (1976) has demonstrated that

Figure 6.11
Metrical structure for *persist*

Figure 6.12
Metrical structure for *perfect*

tonal autosegments can be inserted or deleted independently of the segments or syllables with which they will be associated phonetically, as part of morphophonemic processes. And, indeed, the segmental material to which a tone is linked can be altered or even deleted without affecting its associated tone. Furthermore, lexical representations in tone languages can have "floating" tonal autosegments—morphemes that are not associated with any particular phoneme at all, but have a purely intonational affect. This independence of tones and segmental phonemes (see Goldsmith 1990 for details) provides compelling support for the notion that phonological representation must be richer than the conventional picture of a linear string of segments.

Liberman and Prince (1976), Selkirk (1984), Prince (1983), Hayes (1980, 1982), and others have also developed related frameworks to account for metrical structure—patterns of stress, rhythm, and intonation. On these views, the perceptual salience of certain parts of words and phrases can be captured by representing the individual syllable structures of a multisyllabic word in a hierarchical representation that is independent of the linear string of phonemes.

In such a metrical theory, a stressed syllable is represented as *strong* (S) relative to a *weak* (W) syllable with which it is paired. On this view, stress is inherently not a phonetic property of a syllable that can be represented by a feature—it is a matter of *relative prominence* that is always defined with respect to some other element in a nonlinear representation. A two-syllable word like *persist* [prsIst], with stress on the second syllable, is assumed to have the metrical structure given in figure 6.11. By contrast, an adjective like *perfect* [prfIkt] has the metrical structure in figure 6.12. Note that the verb *to perfect* has the same stress pattern as *to persist*, which is also a verb. In general, English verbs tend to have final stress, even when their associated nouns have stress on the first syllable.

Metrical "trees" like those above can also be used to represent stress in structures more complex than single words. Thus, noun phrases generally exhibit the overall metrical pattern W-S, that is, with main stress on the first syllable of the rightmost element. This is the stress pattern typical of phrasal structures (figure 6.13). The main prominence (in isolation) of the first syllable of *pretty* is reduced because the second element, *flower*, has an overall greater prominence in the phrase. As a result, the first syllable of *flower* is the most prominent (most stressed) element in the whole phrase. Compound nouns like *blackboard*, consisting of the adjective *black* and the noun *board*, and having a special lexical meaning (a surface to write on with chalk), follow a distinct metrical pattern, with stress on the *leftmost* element (figure 6.14).

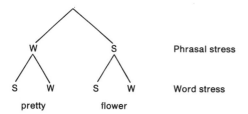

Figure 6.13
Stress pattern for the phrase *pretty flower*

Figure 6.14
Metrical structure for the compound *blackboard*

Figure 6.15
Grid representations for *perfect* and *persist*

The interaction of word stress, phrasal stress, and compound stress gives rise to highly intricate patterns of prominence and intonation. These phenomena are quite complex and provide data for a very rich research program. Some linguists, notably Prince (1983) and Selkirk (1984), have developed a somewhat distinct approach in which stress is represented with a grid of associated *beats*, or rhythmical elements, rather than hierarchical tree structures (figure 6.15). Although this grid allows us to express somewhat different relationships than the metrical tree we considered above, like the tree structures, the grid can be viewed as a distinct autosegmental tier. Like tones, the elements of this tier can act independently of information at other levels of representation.

In ongoing research, linguists compare these and other representational systems in an attempt to discover the nature of the cognitive system that mediates the metrical properties of language. In general, all of these nonlinear approaches have tended to shift some of the burden of phonological description from the processlike rules and rule orderings we discussed above, to properties of richer hierarchical representations themselves. Moreover, many of these properties—such as the organization of syllables into onset and rhyme constituents, or the possible locations of stress—are held to be consequences of human cognitive architecture (the species-general linguistic capacity, or *universal grammar*) rather than peculiarities that must be stated in the grammars of particular languages.

6.3 Syntax

Some Preliminaries

Languages are cognitive systems that enable human beings to express an infinite range of meanings in a physical, (typically) acoustic form. However, having investigated a theory of phonological representation, we are still far from an understanding of how linguistic sounds are paired with semantic interpretations. Indeed, one of the central mysteries of natural language can be couched in this way: how is it that the movement of air molecules, and attendant changes in pressure, can ultimately be treated by human beings as meaningful?

Obviously, meanings must be correlated with morphemes and words, but there must also be a procedure for assigning meaning to phrases, sentences, and larger discourses. Current linguistic theory maintains that there is a highly articulated sub-component of grammars—the *syntax*—that mediates the pairing of sound and meaning. As in the case of phonological theory (or, indeed, any currently developing theory), there are a number of alternative approaches to the study of syntax. However, to permit us to examine syntax in some depth, we will concentrate on the theory of generative grammar currently being developed by Chomsky and others known as Government and Binding (GB). (For references to and summaries of other approaches, see Sells 1985 and Wasow 1989.)

There are several motivations for positing a level of syntactic representation. Consider a sentence like *Herb and Rae went to the beach* in which there appears to be an intuitive boundary between the subject of the sentence, *Herb and Rae*, and the predicate, *went to the beach*. The syntactic structure of the sentence can be informally sketched as follows:

(22)   [[Herb and Rae][went to the beach]]

Sometimes we have clear intuitions (introspective beliefs and judgments) about this kind of structural categorization. Asking a native speaker to "divide a sentence into its two main parts" will fairly reliably give the structure in (22). There is also considerable experimental evidence within psycholinguistics to support the view that the mental representations of sentences involve higher-order structure of this sort. Fodor, Bever, and Garrett (1975) provide a good overview of these results. Levelt (1970), for instance, showed that when subjects are asked to judge the "relative relatedness" of adjacent words in a sentence, responses showing a high degree of relatedness cluster around syntactic boundaries like those indicated in (22). In experiments using more complex sentences, Fodor and Bever (1965) inserted brief clicks into sentences and asked subjects to locate the noise. Subjects' performance was best when the click coincided with a syntactic boundary.

In certain cases, however, our intuitions about syntactic structure are not always clear and may be subject to disagreement among speakers. Moreover, we ought not investigate the properties of a language simply by asking speakers to tell us about its structures. Although people often believe that they have insight into such matters, it does not make for good science to rely on the layperson's hunches about language any more than it would to employ such an approach in the study of an organ like the brain, or the mechanisms of visual perception.

Consequently, cases in which experimental evidence is unavailable, or in which we may not yet know where to look for experimental confirmation, will require other ways of establishing the structure that we associate with sentences. Fortunately, there are tests that can be applied that provide linguistic evidence for assigned structure. Among these tools are *constituency tests*. In this regard, consider the following *ambiguous* sentence, a case in which a single string of words can be assigned more than one semantic interpretation.

(23)   The people talked over the noise.

This sentence might be interpreted to mean that the people spoke so as to overcome an interfering sound. In this case a plausible syntactic analysis of the sentence might be as in (24):

(24)   [The people][talked [[over][the noise]]]

Here, the verb is *talked*, and the rest of the predicate consists of a prepositional phrase *over the noise* (which in turn consists of the preposition *over* and its object *the noise*).

Alternatively, the sentence might be interpreted to mean that the people discussed the noise. Under this interpretation, a reasonable constituent analysis might look like this:

(25)   [The people [[talked over][the noise]]]

This analysis of (23) treats the verb as complex, consisting of the simple verb *talked* and the particle *over*. But if this grouping is correct and the string *talked over* forms a constituent (a structural unit), we should be able to substitute another verb for it—for instance, *discussed*—and still have a sentence that preserves the same relationships between structure and meaning. In the case of (24), however, we cannot make such a substitution. Instead, we can substitute a phrase like *in spite of the interruptions* for *over the noise*, consistent with the claim that the latter constitutes a structural unit in (24) (though not in (25)). We refer to this as the *substitution test*. In the case at hand this test reveals that a single sentence can correspond to two quite different propositions, each of which has a distinct syntactic (and logical) structure, hence, a different cognitive representation.

Additional confirmation for the conclusion that (23) can be associated with two different syntactic representations comes from considering the following example:

(26)   The people talked the noise over.

Notice that unlike (23), (26) can only mean that the people discussed the noise, and not that they overcame it. But why does the second meaning disappear? Our explanation is that when (23) is structured as in (25), it can be *transformed* into an alternative representation in which the particle *over* appears at the end of the predicate. Other complex verbs such as *call up* and *egg on* also allow displacement of the particle:

(27)   a.   The committee [called up] the candidate.   ↔   The committee called the candidate up.
        b.   The fans [egged on] their opponents.   ↔   The fans egged their opponents on.

Prepositional phrases, however, do not allow a repositioning of the preposition at the end of the phrase:

(28) a. The man stood quietly [behind the tree]. ↔ *The man stood
          quietly the tree behind.
      b. The duck worried about the football. ↔ *The duck worried the
          football about.

So, when (23) has the meaning and the structure of (25), *over* counts as a particle and can be dislocated to the end of the predicate. This explains why (26) can carry the meaning of (23) that is supported by (25). In contrast, when (23) has the meaning and the structure of (24), *over* counts as a preposition. Since prepositions cannot dislocate (see (28)), *over* cannot dislocate in this analysis. Thus, on its representation in (25), (23) can be turned into (26), but not on its representation in (24). This provides a strong argument for taking meaning to be assigned on the basis of syntactic structure, and not directly to words and sentences themselves. By applying constituency tests such as the substitution test and by examining distributional patterns in a language, linguists can determine the nature of the syntactic structure.

We argued earlier that the inherent creativity of language, and the ability of the human information-processing system to acquire and process it, cannot be explained if we view the language ability simply as a mental list of sentences. Such a list of sentences would need to be infinitely long, a fact at odds with the assumption that all of our cognitive capabilities must be representable within finite-sized systems (our brains). Our most recent considerations add a second reason to resist a conception of the language faculty as a list of sentences—the interpretation of sentences requires the assignment of a particular syntactic structure. We have suggested that a more promising conception of linguistic knowledge is that speakers know the patterns of their language, and that those patterns can be represented as a set of rules and principles that define the infinitely large class of permissible sentences.

The Goals of a Grammar
What would an appropriate set of such rules and principles look like for a language like English? To approach this question, consider first the simpler case of an abstract formal language that consists exclusively of sentencelike strings containing any number of instances of the symbol "B" followed by a single occurrence of the symbol "A." A grammar for this language contains the initial symbol "A," and a rule that dictates that the symbol "A" can *dominate* (consist of) the string of symbols "B A":

(29) A → B A

The application of such a rule yields the string "B A"; the symbol "A" dominates the two symbols "B A," as the rule specifies (figure 6.16). Notice, however, that this rule can apply *recursively*—it may reapply to its own output. If we reapply the rule once, the lower occurrence of "A" will dominate the string "B A." If we reapply it twice, we get the result shown in figure 6.17. There is, in fact, no limit to the number of times the rule may be applied in a derivation.

Figure 6.16
Tree representation of a derivation employing the rule A → B A

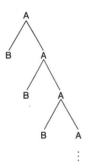

Figure 6.17
An example of a recursive derivation

Suppose we consider each occurrence of a symbol that does not dominate any other symbol a terminal element. The sequence of terminal elements constitutes a well-formed string, or sentence of the language. In the case of figure 6.17, the sentence we have generated is "B B B A." Since there is no upward bound on the number of times that this rule can be recursively applied, there is an infinite number of sentences in this formal language. Accounts in current linguistic theory hold that the syntax of natural languages can be characterized by a grammar that employs recursion in this sense to provide for the essential creativity of linguistic systems.

Note that all the sentences generated by our simple grammar will be of the form "$B^n A$"—some number n of "B"s followed by exactly one "A." Any other string is ungrammatical—it is not a part of the language, and the grammar will not be able to generate (assign a structure to) it. The syntactician undertakes to determine just which finite set of rules is adequate to the task of defining the syntactic patterns of a particular language. The primary goal of syntactic theory from the perspective of the cognitive scientist is to model the system of knowledge that determines which utterances constitute the language, and to contribute to an explanation of how that knowledge is acquired and used.

As we have pointed out, the criterion of grammaticality is not to be found in grammar books, but in the judgments of speakers. We test claims about syntactic structure and the adequacy of a particular hypothesis against data in the form of intuitions of native speakers. All speakers of English will, without hesitation, report that the string *girl the the hippopotamus without a is not a sentence of English. Neither is *girl the kissed boy the, even though we can make more sense of this string. Furthermore, we can produce and understand a sentence like Melvin ate a bulldozer that he believed was trying to turn him into a watermelon and determine that it is grammatical, in spite of the fact that it expresses a bizarre claim. Indeed, Chomsky (1957) observed that a sentence like Colorless green ideas sleep furiously is grammatical (that is, fits the pattern of English) even though it is nonsensical.

Syntacticians do not ordinarily rely on the production of speakers' actual utterances in gathering their data. For one thing, speakers may not necessarily produce the types of sentences that we wish to investigate even though they are within their grammatical competence. For another, actual utterances may involve errors in performance: shifts of attention, limits on memory, drunkenness, and so forth, can produce outputs that are not actually consistent with the grammar (and whose inconsistency has a different kind of explanation).

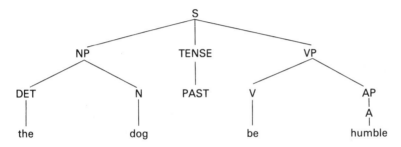

Figure 6.18
Phrase marker for the sentence *The dog was humble*

As a result, we must provide a laboratory-like environment in which we artificially induce the kind of linguistic behavior that we want to examine. Syntacticians typically proceed by asking questions of native speakers; "Is '...' a grammatical sentence?" is normally all that is needed once a subject has a rough-and-ready understanding of what is meant by grammaticality. By and large we can develop a substantial and highly consistent body of data in this fashion. We typically need not resort to more formal experimental procedures, although in unclear cases we may well want to do so. In part, this consistency is achieved by investigating constructions that are shared by many speakers of a given dialect or language.

The Theory of Grammar: Phrase Structure
We have already seen evidence that the syntactic properties of sentences cannot be described solely in terms of linear sequences of words. But linear order is an important part of a characterization of grammaticality for many (though not all) languages. In English *new books* is a well-formed phrase, whereas **books new* is not. By contrast, in Sinhala *pot alut*—literally 'books new'—is grammatical, but **alut pot* is not. Syntactic theory must therefore characterize a level of representation that allows us to capture the notion of syntactic constituency, permits a characterization of the linear order of elements within and between units, and admits of (at least some) variation among dialects and languages. One form that such representations can take is the *phrase structure tree*, or *phrase marker*.

Phrase markers are upside-down treelike structures in which the nodes are labeled by syntactic category. For a sentence like *The dog was humble*, the phrase marker will have roughly the form shown in figure 6.18. Some of the symbols appearing in the phrase markers that we will discuss are listed in table 6.4.

Although you are no doubt familiar with terms like *noun*, it may not be so clear what a *Noun Phrase* (NP) is. Although the subject or object of a sentence sometimes is a single noun (for example, a proper noun like *Seymour*), other sentences contain subjects or objects consisting of a sequence of words. For example, in figure 6.18 we find the subject NP *the dog*. The sentence would have been equally grammatical with a subject as complex as *the only other book that I have ever read that I can remember the title of*, or *every other armadillo in the town*. Furthermore, these same sequences of words can also appear in object position, for example, after the verb *liked* in the string *I liked . . .* We can categorize all sequences of words (phrases) that can appear in subject (or object) position by assigning them to the category NP, noting that phrases that occupy this slot contain at least one noun.

Table 6.4
Symbols used in phrase markers

Symbol	Name	Examples
S	Sentence	A girl walked the dog.
NP	Noun Phrase	the dog, a girl
DET	Determiner	the, a, some
N	Noun	dog, girl
TENSE	Tense Marker	PAST, PRESENT
VP	Verb Phrase	walk the dog
V	Verb	walk, kiss
AP	Adjective Phrase	very smart, tall and thin
A	Adjective	interesting

Next we will address the TENSE node. We have made an unintuitive assumption in figure 6.18: the tense marker appears in the tree in front of the verb rather than following it (as we might expect by observing that ordinary past tense verbs like *walked* exhibit a past tense marker, *-ed*, suffixed after the verb stem). There are some important reasons for this decision, which we will survey later in the discussion. We should also note that English phrase markers contain only two possible tenses, PAST and PRESENT. Other languages have more complex tense systems, but English is restricted to past and present tense forms of the verb. Reference to future time is accomplished by means of a "helping" or auxiliary verb, for example, *will*, which precedes the verb stem.

In our analysis, the verb's tense is determined by selecting either PAST or PRESENT as the node under TENSE. Notice that the verb itself is inserted in the phrase marker in its basic unaffixed form. By convention, the TENSE node specifies the tense of the verb immediately to its right, and the tense of the verb is determined by the value of the tense marker chosen in the tree. The tree for the sentence *The dog is humble* differs from figure 6.18 only in that the node under TENSE is PRESENT rather than PAST.

The explanation of the need for the Verb Phrase (VP) and Adjective Phrase (AP) categories is parallel to the explanation for the category NP. In each case we find that although some sentences exhibit simple adjectives and verbs, others contain complex phrases. For example, instead of the simple adjective *humble* in figure 6.18, we might have had the complex AP *more humble than the lowliest snail*, or *very, very humble*. Similarly, *died*, *chased the cat*, and *gave his owner a hard time* are all VPs that might have substituted for *was humble* in the example phrase marker.

Two final, brief comments. The Determiner (DET) category comprises a class of words including *some*, *every*, and *a*, in addition to *the*. These introduce and specify common nouns. The S node, at the top of the tree, can be thought of in two ways: as the symbol for Sentence, and also as the Start symbol that begins each phrase marker.

Not every arrangement of nodes into a phrase marker corresponds to an English sentence. For example, in English the subject NP typically precedes the VP predicate. Therefore, reversing the first NP and the VP in figure 6.18 results in the ungrammatical string *was humble the dog. A competent speaker of English must know a set of rules and principles that distinguish possible from impossible phrase markers. Although some of these restrictions will be particular to a given language, others may follow from general properties of language. However, it is not always clear at the outset whether any given syntactic property is to be attributed to a language-specific rule or a general linguistic principle. Consequently, we will begin by assuming that every feature of the language under investigation must be spelled out by a rule, and later suggest ways in which some of these rules might be replaced by general principles.

The rules that describe constituency relations and linear order are called *phrase structure rules*. Here are the rules we need to construct the phrase marker in figure 6.18:

(30)   S→ NP TENSE VP
       NP → DET N
       TENSE → {PRES, PAST}
       VP → V AP
       AP → A

The rules shown in (30) tell us that a sentence (S) consists of an NP, a TENSE node, and a VP, in that order. This rule encodes the basic order of English subjects and predicates. The second rule specifies that an NP dominates a determiner followed by a noun. The TENSE rule provides the two tense alternatives in English. Exclusive choices are listed within braces, set off by commas. The next rule dictates that a VP includes a Verb followed by an Adjective Phrase, and the final rule indicates that an Adjective Phrase dominates an Adjective. Although each of these rules requires considerable amendments to be complete and accurate, this small grammar is sufficient to generate the phrase marker in figure 6.19, which is the same as that in figure 6.18, without its lexical items.

In order to associate the bottom nodes of the tree with actual lexical material (words), we must apply the process of *lexical insertion*. To accomplish this, we require a list of vocabulary words called the *lexicon*, which specifies a syntactic category for each entry as well as information about its phonological form and semantic interpretation. In the case of verbs, a *subcategorization frame* is also specified to indicate which syntactic categories may cooccur with each particular verb (its *complement structure*). Notice, for instance, that *be* can appear with an NP as well as an AP:

(31)   Dogs are [$_{NP}$ a responsibility]$_{NP}$

(32)   Dogs are [$_{AP}$ quite bothersome]$_{AP}$

Verbs like *perspire* and *elapse* differ from *be* in that they cannot cooccur with NPs at all:

(33)   A carpenter perspired.

(34)   *A carpenter perspired sweat.

(35)   The time remaining in Rover's life elapsed.

(36)   *The time remaining in Rover's life elapsed two hours.

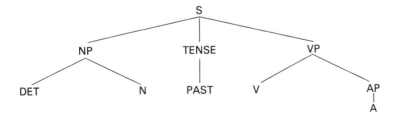

Figure 6.19
Phrase marker for the sentence in figure 6.18 before lexical insertion

By substituting *expelled* for *perspired*, and *exceeded* for *elapsed*, we reverse the pattern of grammaticality judgments in (33) through (36). Each verb, then, must be associated with a range of appropriate complements. Sample partial lexical entries for some of the vocabulary under consideration might look like this:

(37)   be, /bi/, V, _____{NP, AP}
       perspire, /prspair/, V, _____∅
       elapse, /ilæps/, V, _____∅
       expel, /ɛkspɛl/, V, _____NP
       exceed, /ɛksid/, V, _____NP
       time, /taim/, N
       the, /ðʌ/, DET

On the basis of such lexical information, we can select the appropriate words and insert them into trees.

Transformations

In addition to the phrase structure and lexical components of the grammar, collectively known as the *base*, there is a second type of syntactic rule that has played an important role in linguistic theory, the *transformation*. Unlike phrase structure rules, this class of rules does not characterize phrase structure trees. Rather, transformations rearrange phrase markers in certain ways. The rule discussed above that optionally moves a particle to the end of a VP (particle movement) is an example of a transformational rule.

Another type of phenomenon that has yielded to transformational analysis is so-called *wh-question formation*. Wh-questions are sentences that ask "Who? Where? Why? What?" and so forth, in contrast to yes/no questions, which merely require an affirmative or negative answer. Examples of English *wh*-questions are given in (38) and (39):

(38)   Who spilled it?

(39)   What is the problem?

Wh-question words in other languages may not, of course, begin with the letters *wh-* (even in English, *how* questions are of the *wh*-question type), but such questions typically involve a query correlated with some major constituent of the sentence, such as the subject or object NP. In English the question word takes the place of some such constituent and usually appears at the beginning of the sentence.

In (38), because we are questioning the subject, it is not possible to detect any shift in position. But in (39), where we are questioning a noun phrase at the end of the VP, the question word appears in sentence-initial position. Linguists have analyzed these types of questions by assuming that the question word is initially generated in a normal *argument position* (as subject or object), but is consequently moved to sentence-initial position by a transformation. The structure for (39) that is generated by the phrase structure rules is shown in figure 6.20.

Notice that we are assuming that *what* is a noun, and that it is generated by the phrase structure rules for NPs. The transformation of *Wh-Movement* then applies to rearrange the phrase marker in figure 6.20, moving *what* to the front of the S. Another transformation, *Inversion*, will also apply to reverse the order of the verb and subject. Figure 6.21 shows an informal representation of these two movements.

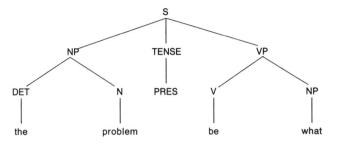

Figure 6.20
Phrase marker generated by phrase structure rules for the sentence (39), *What is the problem?*

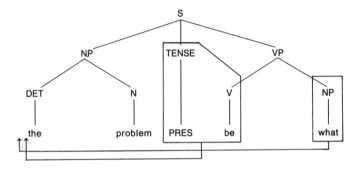

Figure 6.21
Informal representation of transformations applying to the phrase marker in figure 6.20 in the derivation of (39), *What is the problem?*

Perhaps it is not clear why we could not simply generate the word *what* in sentence-initial position in the initial phrase marker rather than appealing to a transformation to move it to the front of the sentence. The reason is that there is a *dependency* between the fronted question word and its initial argument position that would not be accounted for by this more direct analysis. The dependency may be stated as follows: whenever there is a question word at the front of a sentence, there is also a corresponding *gap*—a missing constituent—inside the sentence. Thus, in (38) there is a missing subject; in (39), a missing object. Sentences in which these positions are filled, and a question word occurs as well, are ungrammatical:

(40) *Who *John* spilled it?

(41) *What is the problem *the book*?

In the framework we are developing, if we were to directly generate question words in initial position, we would not be able to correlate sentence-initial *wh*-words with the corresponding gaps in argument position. We can, however, explain the facts in the transformational account. On this analysis, the only way to produce a question word at the beginning of a sentence is for that question word to have been moved there from its normal position, where it was initially placed by the phrase structure rules. Thus, it is an automatic consequence of the transformational movement that a gap is left behind.

The transformational account also predicts that question formation should be possible in subordinate clauses. (42) and (43) present some relevant examples:

(42)   I know who Bill insulted.

(43)   John knows Mary knew what Nancy considered.

In the case of (42), before *Wh*-Movement, the question word *who* was in object position in the subordinate clause. It is moved to the front of the subordinate clause to form (42), as (44) informally indicates:

(44)   I know <u>who</u> Bill insulted ＿＿＿
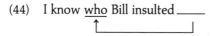

In (43), *what* started out as the subject of the lowest subordinate clause:

(45)   John knows Mary knew <u>what</u> Nancy considered ＿＿＿
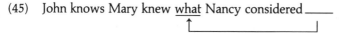

Furthermore, the *what* can move two clauses up, as in (46):

(46)   John knows <u>what</u> Mary knew ＿＿＿ Nancy considered ＿＿＿
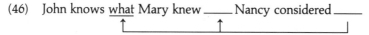

Finally, it is possible in both of these cases to move the questioned word all the way to the front of the main clause. Further rules apply, in this case, to insert a form of the auxiliary verb *do*, but (47) and (48) gives the basic idea of how this works:

(47)   <u>Who</u> do I know Bill insulted ＿＿＿

(48)   <u>What</u> does John know ＿＿＿ Mary knew ＿＿＿ Nancy considered ＿＿＿
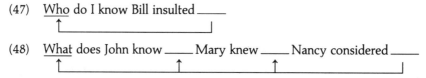

The full range of these constructions can be accounted for if we assume that the *Wh*-Movement transformation moves a question word to the front of an S. This type of formulation allows the rule to move the *wh*-word to either of two positions in constructions like those above, which contain more than a single S node.

Question formation, then, involves a *movement transformation*: the derivation involves *moving* a constituent to a new position in the phrase marker. We will now briefly discuss another type of transformation: a *deletion* rule.

(49)   Moe added salt, and Curly did too.

(50)   Max preferred the mackerel, and Bill the brill.

(51)   Herman owned some dogs, and Mary owned some too.

In each of these sentences there is a phrase that is "understood" but not overtly present. In (49), for instance, what Curly is understood to have done is to have *added salt*. Similarly, Bill is understood to have *preferred the brill*, and what Mary owned was *dogs*. These sentences are derived by deletion transformations from the structures that underlie the following sentences:

(52)   Moe added salt, and Curly added salt too.

(53)   Max preferred the mackerel, and Bill preferred the brill.

(54)   Herman owned some dogs, and Mary owned some dogs too.

The rule that converts the tree corresponding to (52) into the one corresponding to (49) deletes a VP, in this case *added salt*. There is an interesting special condition that must be met in order for this rule to apply: there must be a copy of a VP that is the potential deletion target elsewhere in the sentence, or the larger discourse. For example, it would not be possible to apply the VP-Deletion rule to the structure underlying (55) in order to derive (49):

(55)   Moe added salt, and Curly added pepper too.

Another way of putting the point is that this type of deletion transformation can only remove material that is redundant, and therefore *recoverable* from the sentence that results after the rule applies. In the case of (49) and (52), this recoverability condition is met.

The examples in (50) and (53) involve a rule that deletes verbs, sometimes known as *Gapping*. In the case of (51) and (54) a rule of *Identical Noun Deletion* is at work. For both of these rules, the conditions on recoverability of deletion obtain. Notice that the principle of recoverability of deletion has a very powerful practical motivation—it must be possible for a hearer to determine exactly what constituent meaning is missing in order to interpret elliptical sentences. Since the preservation of meaning is what is involved, this may well be a case where general properties of human information processing are at work, interacting with the form and functioning of linguistic rules.

A Case Study

We will now examine more closely a special problem in the syntactic analysis of English, *case marking*, and consider its relevance for universal grammar. Case marking is a device for varying the form of a word, typically to provide an indication of the role that it plays in a sentence. For example, in (56) the third person pronoun appears in a different form depending on whether it is the subject or the object of *accused* (*he* is in the *nominative* case, *him*, in the *accusative* case):

(56)   After John saw Irv leave the victim's room, he accused him of the murder.

In general, English appears to have relatively little case marking, especially in comparison to a language like Finnish, which has more than a dozen distinct case types. Furthermore, English speakers draw systematic case distinctions only in the pronoun system (and to indicate possession with the *genitive* marker, *'s*). By contrast, Japanese, which provides case markings for subject and object—*ga* and *o*, respectively—attaches them quite generally to subjects and objects:

(57)   Jon-ga   hon-o   yonda.
       John (subj) book (obj) read
       'John read the book.'

However, although it may appear that English employs very little case marking, we will show that case relations actually play a highly significant role in English syntax, a role that may in part be determined by properties of universal grammar.

We begin this analysis by advancing an abstract hypothesis: all nouns in English *bear* case, but it is only in the pronoun system that case is *marked* by an overt phonological form. Is such a claim plausible? Are there other circumstances in English grammar where a significant morpheme or syntactic category may not have a

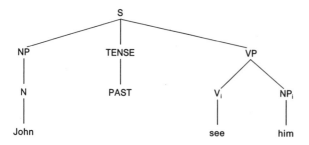

Figure 6.22
Phrase marker enriched with indices

phonetic realization? Although most English nouns are pluralized by adding the suffix /z/, there are exceptions such as *deer*, which are superficially invariant in the singular and plural. That is, *The deer grazed peacefully* is ambiguously about either one deer or more than one deer. Notice that it will not do to suggest that *deer* is neither singular nor plural—that it does not bear plurality—because in the cases like (58) in which the verb inflects for number, *deer* must be plural since *were* is the third person plural form of the verb, which can only appear with plural subjects:

(58) The deer were grazing peaceably.

The logic of the situation with regard to English case is similar. We know that pronouns must be assigned case because they display it phonetically; we must look for additional evidence if we wish to claim that other forms (nouns in general) also are assigned case—evidence from which we can deduce the presence of case even where it is not overtly marked.

We begin by formalizing the claim that all nouns in English are *case-assigned* by adopting the *Case Filter* (from Chomsky 1986):

(59) *Case Filter*
Every NP must bear a case.

According to (59), there can be no grammatical phrase markers in which NPs do not have a case. Typically, the noun in subject position of any grammatical sentence will receive nominative case marking, and the object, accusative case marking.

We further hypothesize that case marking is *assigned*. For example, we will treat the transitive verb as assigning accusative case to its object. On this view, the verb "deposits" a case property on the object NP, by analogy to the way electrons are transferred from electron donors to electron recipients in chemical models. We can indicate this formally by annotating a verb that has assigned a case and the NP to which it has assigned it with the same index, as in figure 6.22. In this case *see* and its object are coindexed with the index *i*. Since an NP that is coindexed to a verb has been assigned the accusative case by that verb, the third person object pronoun appears in the accusative case (*him*). If the object of *see* had been other than a pronoun, case assignment (and coindexing) would proceed in the same manner. For example, if *Bill* had been the direct object, the phrase marker in figure 6.23 would result. That is, we can generalize case assignment so that verbs case-assign their objects regardless of whether the assigned case shows itself in the form of an overt morphological marking.

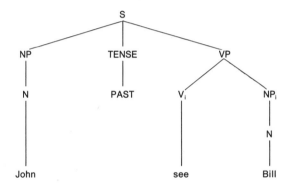

Figure 6.23
Indexed phrase marker for *John saw Bill*

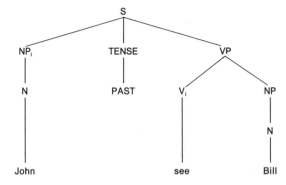

Figure 6.24
Illegal indexed phrase marker for *John saw Bill*

In a moment we will turn to evidence in favor of this assumption, but first we examine the case assignment mechanism we have introduced a bit more closely.

How does case assignment succeed in linking a transitive verb to its object and transferring case? Suppose we start off with the simplest assumption, namely, that a verb can case-mark any NP. If this were so, we would expect the phrase marker in figure 6.24, in which *see* case-marks the subject *John*, as an alternative to the one in figure 6.23. Since case is not overtly displayed on proper nouns, it might not seem problematical that the subject in figure 6.24, *John*, is coindexed with *see*. However, in situations where subject position is filled by a pronoun, it is clear that accusative case cannot be assigned to subject position:

(60)   *Her saw Bill.

(61)   She saw Bill.

We must therefore rule out the possibility of transitive verbs freely case-assigning any NP. We can eliminate this option by specifying a *domain* in which case assignment must take place. We will say that case assigners (in this case, verbs) can assign case only to NPs that are in their *governing domain*. This domain is defined as follows:

GOVERNS

Figure 6.25
Graphic representation of the notion "governing domain"

(62)   A node α is in the governing domain of a node β if the first branching
node that dominates β also dominates α (where a branching node is one
that dominates at least two other nodes).

The simplest circumstance that satisfies this definition is illustrated in figure 6.25.
In this case α governs β (and vice versa) because the first branching node that dominates α, namely, X, also dominates β. Below we will see other phrase structure configurations that fit the definition of government. For now, though, let us formalize the
principle of case assignment as follows:

(63)   *Case Assignment under Government*
A case assigner can assign case only to an NP within the governing
domain of the case assigner.

We must now account for how case is assigned to subject position. Recall that the
Case Filter requires *every* NP to be assigned case. Furthermore, the facts of English (as
evidenced by the form of subject pronouns) demand that it be nominative case that is
assigned. First, we must identify a case assigner that can assign case to subject NPs.
Our hypothesis is that it is the TENSE node that plays this role, assigning nominative
case to NPs in subject position. Notice that TENSE is an appropriate choice in that
it governs the subject NP, providing some motivation for our earlier decision to place
TENSE before rather than after the verb.

Now consider the phrase marker of the sentence *He saw him*, incorporating the two
chains of indices that are required by the assumption that the nodes V and TENSE each
separately coindex NPs within their governing domains (see figure 6.26). Here TENSE
has case-assigned the subject NP, and V has case-assigned the object NP. Since TENSE
assigns nominative case, the subject receives that case; since V assigns accusative case,
the object is so marked.

We have limited our comments so far to the details of simple sentences in formalizing the account of English case assignment we want to defend. The sentences are
simple in two senses. For one thing, they do not involve any florid constructions. But
in a more technical sense they are simple because each contains a single *clause*, a
constituent with the basic properties of a sentence. English, as well as other natural
languages, also allows constructions that can involve one or more *subordinate* clauses
in addition to the *main* clause. Some examples of such constructions are given in (64)
through (68), with the subordinate clauses italicized:

(64)   The position *you are defending* is preposterous.

(65)   *After sizing up the situation*, John died.

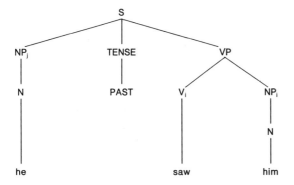

Figure 6.26
Indexed phrase marker for the sentence *He saw him*

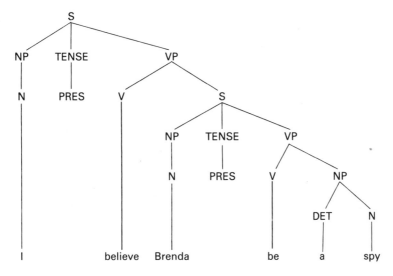

Figure 6.27
Phrase marker for the sentence (66), *I believe Brenda is a spy*

(66) I believe *Brenda is a spy*.

(67) *That beans are magical* became obvious.

(68) I suspect *that you feared that I knew Verna sneezed*.

Although the syntax of these constructions is complex (and fascinating), we will restrict our attention to points that bear on the analysis of abstract case, case assignment, and government. Several of these considerations provide interesting arguments in support of this analysis of case. Observe that (69), which is almost synonymous with (66), differs somewhat in its syntactic structure:

(69) I believe *Brenda to be a spy*.

First of all, the verb *to be* appears in a *tenseless* (or *infinitival*) form in (69), whereas the same verb occurs in (66) in its present tense form, *is*. The phrase markers for (66) and

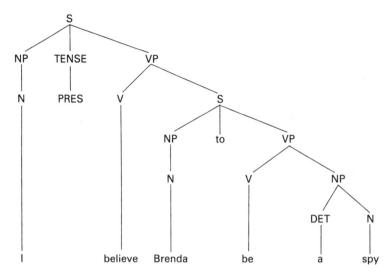

Figure 6.28
Phrase marker for the sentence (69), *I believe Brenda to be a spy*

(69) are roughly as given in figures 6.27 and 6.28; case indexing is suppressed for clarity. Another important detail to notice is that in figure 6.28 there is no TENSE marker of the usual sort in the lower S, just the infinitive marker *to*. This accounts for the fact that *be* appears in its untensed *uninflected* form. Given our previous assumptions about case assignment, we can now account for a very interesting further differ-ence between the structures in figures 6.27 and 6.28 that is not immediately apparent. In the following set of data we have substituted pronouns for *Brenda* where it occurs in the earlier examples:

(70)   I believe she is a spy.

(71)   *I believe her is a spy.

(72)   *I believe she to be a spy.

(73)   I believe her to be a spy.

These data show that the subject position of the tensed subordinate clause is assigned nominative case—just like the subject position in simple sentences; we see this in (70). But the subject position of tenseless subordinate clauses is assigned accusative case, as, for example, in (73). We can explain these phenomena in the following way. We have claimed that it is TENSE that is responsible for assigning nominative case to subject NPs. The coindexing operations for the phrase marker in figure 6.27 and for sentence (70) will proceed uneventfully, and nominative case will be assigned to each subject position (in both the main and subordinate clauses); accusative case will be assigned to the object NP in the lower subordinate clause in figure 6.29 (assuming that *believe* does not assign case into tensed subordinate clauses).

Consider, by contrast, the phrase marker in figure 6.30, which underlies the sentence (73). Since there is no TENSE node in the subordinate clause to assign nominative case to the subject of that clause, the theory predicts that nominative case will not appear

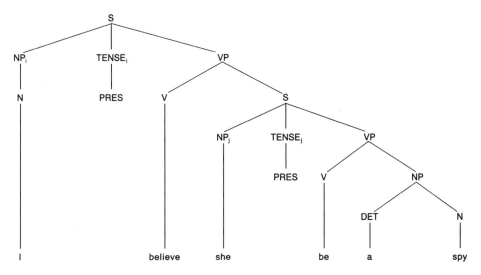

Figure 6.29
Phrase marker for the sentence (70), *I believe she is a spy*, after coindexing

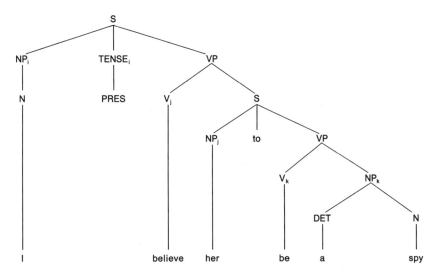

Figure 6.30
Phrase marker for the sentence (73), *I believe her to be a spy*, after coindexing

in this position. This, of course, leaves us with the question of what does assign case to *her* in (62). One standard assumption is that *believe* can be recruited to assign case to the subject position of tenseless subordinate clauses, perhaps because (unlike in the case of (61)) it is the closest potential case assigner that governs the embedded subject position. Since *believe* is a verb, we expect accusative case to be assigned, as desired.

Given the constellation of assumptions that we have developed, we can account for what appears, at first blush, to be a very curious correlation between tense and case. More evidence for this connection is to be found in contrasts like the following:

(74)   Mary $\begin{Bmatrix} \text{took} \\ \text{considers} \end{Bmatrix}$ him to be a fool.

(75)   Mary $\begin{Bmatrix} \text{made} \\ \text{considers} \end{Bmatrix}$ him a believer.

(76)   Mary $\begin{Bmatrix} \text{concluded} \\ \text{determined} \end{Bmatrix}$ that he was a spy.

Concentrating on the case form of the subject of the subordinate clause, we note that the contrast between (74) and (76) is expected: subjects of tenseless clauses are accusative, and subjects of tensed clauses are nominative. The interesting case is (75). Here the subordinate clause (if, indeed, it is a clause) apparently contains neither a tense marker nor the infinitival *to*. The case form of the third person pronoun is accusative (compare: *I consider he a spy*), patterning with (74) rather than (76), in this regard.

Again, this is the expected result, given our framework of assumptions. Since the embedded material in (75) does not include TENSE, there is no case assigner available capable of assigning nominative case. Rather, the higher verb must case-assign the pronoun, resulting in accusative case marking.

This pattern can also be observed in sentences containing complements to the verb *see*:

(77)   John saw her leave.

Here again, the complement to the verb, *her leave*, is untensed (compare *Her leave* with *She left*). Consequently, case assignment of *her* cannot come from within the subordinate clause and must be assigned by the higher verb, *saw*. Notice, incidentally, that this account of case assignment directly explains why strings like *Him/He a believer* and *Her/She leave* cannot appear as main clauses in standard English: in both of these examples there would be no available case assigner. This guarantees that these strings can only appear as complements to verbs that are capable of assigning case to subordinate structures (for example, (75) and (77)).

One final piece of evidence in favor of our theory of abstract case assignment speaks more directly to the claim that all NPs are case-assigned (even if they do not reveal any overt case marking). We have claimed that verbs assign accusative case to their direct objects. We might be more specific by restricting this principle to *transitive* verbs—verbs that take a direct object. *Intransitive* verbs (those that do not appear with direct objects) obviously cannot assign accusative case. Suppose, then, that we stipulate that intransitive verbs do not assign case, as a basic property of all intransitive verbs. We can extend this generalization to include passive verbs. That is, just as

simple intransitive verbs cannot cooccur with lexical objects (for example, *John perspired sweat*), neither can passive verb phrases (for example, *John was arrested the police*).
Put another way, passive verb phrases are intransitive, suggesting that they, too, fail
to assign case.

Against this background, let us reconsider the following contrasts:

(78) a. John believed $\left\{ \begin{array}{c} \text{she} \\ \text{Brenda} \\ \text{*her} \end{array} \right\}$ was a spy.

     b. John believed $\left\{ \begin{array}{c} \text{*she} \\ \text{Brenda} \\ \text{her} \end{array} \right\}$ to be a spy.

(79) a. It was believed $\left\{ \begin{array}{c} \text{she} \\ \text{Brenda} \\ \text{*her} \end{array} \right\}$ was a spy.

     b. *It was believed $\left\{ \begin{array}{c} \text{she} \\ \text{Brenda} \\ \text{her} \end{array} \right\}$ to be a spy.

The pattern in (78) is usual. In (78a) the tense marker in the lower clause will assign
nominative case to the lower subject, explaining why *Brenda* or *she* can appear in the
embedded subject position. *Her* is ungrammatical since it would require accusative case
assignment. In contrast, in (78b), in the absence of a tense marker in the lower clause,
believed assigns accusative case to the embedded subject, accounting for the grammaticality of *Brenda* and *her*, but not *she*. (79a) also follows the expected generalizations.
The case of the subject of the subordinate clause must be nominative, as assigned by
the tense marker in the lower clause. Thus, just as in (78a), either *Brenda* or *she*, but not
her, is suitable as the subject in the subordinate clause. Notice that in each of these
three cases, either the nominative form (*she*) or the accusative form (*her*) is possible, and
so is the non-case-marked name *Brenda*. On our analysis, the choice of pronoun shifts
with the choice of case assigner (either TENSE, for nominative, or the main clause verb,
for accusative). The proper name can receive either nominative or accusative case and
therefore is generally compatible. However, this generalization appears not to obtain
in (79b).

The puzzle is, Why are *none* of the possibilities for the embedded subject grammatical in (79b)? Let us consider each option in turn. First, since the subordinate clause is
infinitival, there is no tense marker available to assign nominative case to embedded
subject position, explaining the impossibility of *she* in subject position. In fact, case
cannot be assigned from within the subordinate clause, since there are no governing
case assigners in the clause. In this regard, the subordinate clause patterns with (78b).
Of course, in such a circumstance, it fell to the higher verb *believed* to assign (accusative) case to the lower subject. In (79b), however, the main clause contains the passive
verb phrase *was believed*, which, because it is intransitive, is incapable of assigning
accusative case to the lower subject. This explains why the third candidate, *her* (the
accusative form), is ungrammatical in (79b).

We have ruled out the nominative form of the pronoun in (79b) because there is no nominative case assignment, and the accusative form because there is no accusative case assignment. But why can't Brenda, the overtly non-case-marked proper name, appear as the embedded subject of (79b)? The explanation depends on the crucial difference between case *marking* and case *assignment* to which we are committed. Even though *Brenda* is not overtly marked for case, it must, on our account, be assigned either nominative or accusative case. But in (79b) there is no case assigner available to assign case to the subject of the subordinate clause. Consequently, if *Brenda* were to appear in this position, it would go without being assigned case, violating the Case Filter and rendering the sentence ungrammatical.

Although we have barely scratched the surface of even one tiny corner of English syntax, we are already able to glimpse the deductive richness and explanatory depth that one hopes for in the scientific investigation of a language. Moreover, the study of aspects of grammar such as case theory has come to occupy a prominent position in current syntactic research because it has turned out that they figure importantly in our understanding of the grammars of many disparate languages. The most ambitious claim we might pursue is that the abstract principles that we uncover are *universal*— that they apply to *every* natural language. We turn next to this, perhaps the most important area of ongoing research in linguistic theory.

6.4 Universals

According to much of current linguistic theory, certain linguistic properties (for example, the Case Filter and the Maximal Onset Principle; see below) are principles that are reflected by every natural language. Consequently, although certain properties hold for each individual language, they are not best understood as having been coincidentally written into the grammar of each language. Instead, linguists, following the pioneering work of Chomsky (1965) and Ross (1967), have located such principles in universal grammar (UG). UG is not a grammar in the usual, generative sense of the term. Rather, UG comprises the features that are instantiated in the grammars of all natural languages. Principles of UG are perfectly general, and the rule systems of individual languages will only need to state the idiosyncratic properties of the languages they generate.

The principles of UG have also been claimed both to play a central role in the acquisition of language by children and to constitute species-specific, domain-specific, innate properties of mind. The role of the principles of UG in language acquisition is discussed in some depth in chapter 9. For now, it will suffice to emphasize that these principles are taken to limit the range of hypotheses that children will normally consider during the course of acquisition. Let us examine how this way of conceptualizing the process of language acquisition proceeds.

When a child is faced with the task of deciphering the pattern revealed by some subset of sentences of a language, there will be a number of systems of rules that are consistent with the available data (for instance, the sentences the child is exposed to), although ultimately divergent in the languages they generate. The child's learning problem can be seen as that of figuring out which of these possibilities to reject. The principles of UG are thought to aid in this task by delimiting the live options—only those grammars that are consistent with UG will be available to the child as candidates for capturing the pattern of the language. Without this restriction on hypothesis formation, the child's task seems daunting, and, some linguists have contended, impossible. Research and debate concerning the role of UG in language learning are at the center of the ongoing work in linguistics and cognitive science.

The claim that the principles of UG are species specific turns on the proposition that only humans have language ability. Of course, different species certainly have effective communication systems, and some may even possess systems that are languagelike in significant regards. Yet most cognitive scientists have come to the conclusion that whatever such abilities amount to, they appear to be distinct from the human capacity (see, for example, Premack 1986). In turn, linguists have reasoned that although the principles of UG may well be (part of) what enables humans to learn language, the absence of these properties and the learning advantages they afford may explain why other organisms cannot acquire human languages.

The principles of UG have also been asserted to be domain specific—to govern the shapes of grammars and thereby direct the course of language acquisition, but to have no direct impact on other cognitive capacities or in other learning domains. This position typically forms a part of the *modularity thesis* that ascribes different cognitive abilities to separate faculties of mind (see Fodor 1983; Piatelli-Palmerini 1980; Garfield 1987). On this view, since language is a distinct cognitive capacity, the principles of its theories should not be expected to characterize other capacities. This entails that the principles of UG, in particular, are specific to language, and also that the way children learn language may be importantly unrelated to the way they learn anything else.

Finally, the principles of UG have been claimed to be innate (see Chomsky 1965, 1980). As such, they are taken to be a part of the organism's biological endowment, ultimately to be identified in terms of human genetics. The argument, roughly put, is that such principles are not simply inducible from the primary data available to children—yet learners cannot form adequate hypotheses about their own languages without such principles. They must, perforce, be innate. If notions like the Case Filter are indeed a part of the biological system that guides the formation of grammars, it should not be surprising to find that abstract case plays a crucial and widespread role in English even though there is little overt evidence for case marking. We should also find evidence that these kinds of principles are at work even in languages that exhibit no overt manifestation of case whatsoever. Such results would be impressive indeed, and much of current linguistic research is directed toward uncovering this kind of evidence. Although there are alternative accounts of the relationship between grammars and cognition (see Gazdar et al. 1985), and several rival accounts of the details of syntactic theory (see Sells 1985; Wasow 1989), much current linguistic research is directed at working out the details of case theory and other subtheories of generative models of linguistic knowledge.

The task of elucidating the properties of universal grammar would be relatively straightforward if all languages uniformly embodied a fixed and unvarying set of principles. But matters are not so simple. The details of case assignment vary from language to language. Syllable structure can vary significantly, and there is no single stress system that follows inexorably from principles of metrical structure. Facts such as these threaten to vitiate the important claims that have been made about UG. Indeed, if part of the empirical appeal of UG was that its claims are testable against the data of any natural language, the failure to account for the data of even one language is deeply problematic.

In an attempt to solve these problems, generative linguists remain committed to the view that the grammars of particular languages reflect a set of core properties captured by the principles of UG, but hold that these basics are subject to a (limited) degree of variation as well—*parameters* that mark the range of possible human languages. Before we turn to some examples of the principles-and-parameters view of things, an analogy may be useful.

Consider the great variety that seems to exist in handwoven rugs. On entering a rug store, we may be struck by the great wealth of different designs: colors, patterns, and sizes all vary according to the country of origin, the maker, and so forth. Yet when we examine the rugs more closely, it is possible to discern some interesting, though much less obvious, similarities. Two rugs that appear when viewed from the usual distance to be constructed from utterly different weaving patterns turn out, when viewed at close range, to be built up from identical knots—which happen to be oriented differently and made from wool of different thicknesses. As these two simple parameters vary, highly similar rugs (at a certain level of examination) take on strikingly distinct superficial appearances. The universal linguistic properties that we have considered may well have this character—admitting of small variations on relatively abstract parameters that, from afar, create the appearance of great diversity.

A Phonological Example

According to the theory we have been describing, many of the identifying details of the world's languages can be viewed as small variations on universal themes. Consider, again, the matter of syllable structure. At the heart of the syllabification process is a set of fundamental—and invariant—principles. Many phonologists maintain that universal grammar requires all languages (as a consequence of the Maximal Onset Principle, among others) to have at least some syllables of the form [CV ...], with an onset. No language is known to violate this principle. Nevertheless, it is subject to parameterization: some languages, like Klamath, a Native American language of Oregon, require *every* syllable to be of this form. Others, like English, permit *some* onsetless syllables. Similarly, all languages exhibit syllables with vowels at their nucleus. But the appearance of two vowels or of consonants in nuclear position is parameterized: some languages exhibit long vowels, diphthongs, or sonorants as nuclear consonants. Others forbid them and admit only single vowels in the nucleus. Finally, the "coda parameter" regulates the appearance of consonants in syllable-final position. No fixed principle determines whether a language must have syllables beginning and ending with consonents (*closed syllables*): they are "optional," subject to what we may describe as a simple "yes/no" parameter. Set to "yes," the parameter permits syllables like [... VC]; English is an example. Set to "no," the parameter prohibits them, Hawaiian and Italian being cases in point. But if a language chooses the "yes" option, a core principle of universal grammar still requires that it *must also* allow open syllables without a final consonant. Thus, the range of syllable structures that is available to languages is quite broad—but still set within rather stringent limits.

Some Syntactic Principles and Parameters

The application of the theory of principles and parameters to problems in syntactic analysis has been one of the most important programs of research in contemporary linguistic theory. Following Chomsky (1986), linguists have decomposed syntactic theory into a number of subtheories, each one of which contains parameterized principles that define its core properties. These subtheories include case theory, *binding theory*, *bounding theory*, *theta theory*, and *X-bar theory*. We have already considered problems in case theory, which is responsible for establishing the principles of case assignment. The central principle in case theory is the Case Filter—the (universal) principle that requires that NPs must be assigned case. In fact, the principle may be more general, for in some languages (for example, Russian and German) it has been proposed that certain adjectival phrases are marked for case. Thus, the principle may take the form "all *XPs* must receive case," with the value of *X* being set somewhat differently for different languages. If this is correct, we would expect languages all to involve case, but to assign it and mark it in somewhat different ways.

Binding theory concerns itself with the *anaphoric* properties of pronouns, reflexives, and lexical NPs. These principles capture the structural circumstances under which certain expressions (for example, pronouns) can depend on an antecedent for their interpretation. For example, *John* and *he* can be naturally construed to be the same person in (80), but not in (81):

(80)   John thinks [that Scruffy likes him]

(81)   Scruffy thinks [that John likes him]

One part of binding theory constrains the interpretation of personal pronouns like *him*, as follows:

(82)   *Binding theory*
       A pronoun must be free in its local *X*.

Pronouns that are *free* are interpreted independently of potential antecedents. For English, *X* works out roughly to *clause*. What this amounts to is that English personal pronouns cannot depend for their interpretation on antecedents that are locally contained in the same clause as they are. Thus, *him* can refer to the same person as *John* in (80) because *John* is the subject of the higher clause, whereas *him* is the object of the lower clause. In (81) both *John* and *him* are contained in the same clause, and so *him* must be interpreted as being free from *John*; that is, *him* and *John* cannot refer to the same person.

Other languages also limit the interpretations of pronouns, but in ways that may be somewhat different from the pattern in English. In particular, languages can differ in the setting for the parameter *X* in binding theory, producing contrasting distributions. In Icelandic, for example, the personal pronoun *hann* 'him' appears, at first, to follow the English pattern in subordinate clauses:

(83)   Jón segir að [Maria elskar hann]
       Jón says that Maria loves him

The interpretation of (83) is parallel to that of the English translation; *Jón* and *hann* can refer to the same person. In tenseless subordinate clauses, however, the patterns diverge:

(84)   Jón skipaði mér að [raka   hann]
       Jón ordered me to shave him

Whereas in the English translation *him* can refer to Jón, *hann* cannot refer to Jón in the Icelandic sentence. This is because in Icelandic the value of the parameter *X* in the binding theory clause that applies to pronouns is set differently from the value for

English. The value for Icelandic is "tensed clause," meaning that potential antecedents must not be members of the smallest *tensed* clause containing a corresponding personal pronoun. In (83) *hann* is in a separate tensed clause from *Jón*. In (84), however, although these two terms are in separate clauses, the smallest tensed clause containing *Jón* also contains *hann*.

Once again we have profitably compared and contrasted two different linguistic systems within the principles-and-parameters framework of UG. Similar inquiries have also been undertaken into the other subdomains of linguistics. Bounding theory, for example, concerns itself with how distant a moved element can be from its corresponding gap. In some languages a moved element must appear within the same clause as does the gap, whereas other languages permit greater distance between the two. *Subjacency* is the hypothesized universal principle that establishes these restrictions on movement:

(85) *Subjacency*
      A moved element may not cross X.

where X, as in the previous example, is a parameter that can be set in a small number of ways (for example, a clause boundary or two clause boundaries), specific to each language. See if you can figure out what the value for X is in the case of English.

Theta theory is the part of linguistic theory that explores the assignment of *thematic roles* to arguments. Thematic roles determine the action structure of the sentence by distinguishing who is doing what, to whom. For example, if we understand *John* as the *agent* in (86), then he is taken to be the initiator of the action:

(86) John rolled down the hill.

It is possible, however, to construe *John* as receiving an action (as a *patient*), as well, although this interpretation is easier to assign in (87):

(87) The rock rolled down the hill.

Theta theory is interested in the principles that mediate the assignment of these roles, and like the other subdomains of the grammar, it contains principles that are thought to be universal. The central principle of theta theory is the *Theta Criterion*, which requires that every argument position must be assigned exactly one thematic role. In the case of (86), for example, this principle entails that if John may be a either the agent or a patient, then he cannot be taken to be both simultaneously, or neither at all. This criterion and the related theory are currently objects of considerable attention by linguists who are exploring the application of these principles (along with any parameterization) across the languages of the world.

Finally, the subdomain of universal grammar that characterizes the phrase structure of each natural language can also be looked at from the perspective of its principles and parameters. Earlier we noted that although it is possible to write out a phrase structure grammar for each language that generates the initial phrase markers of that language, there are cross-linguistic generalizations in this aspect of grammar that suggest an alternative approach. Indeed, some time ago linguists noticed that there are regularities in word order and constituent structure both within and across languages that deserve to be captured by the principles of UG. X-bar theory, which is the universal principle at the heart of this component of the grammar, is an attempt to distill universal principles of phrase structure and constituency. To the extent that

X-bar theory succeeds, the phrase structure rules for each language can be simplified and will only need to record the features of phrase markers that are idiosyncratic in a particular language. Proposed principles include the claim that in all languages a phrase of the form XP must contain an occurrence of X, which is called the *head* of the phrase. That is, NPs must contain nouns as heads, VPs must contain verbs as heads, and so on.

The ordering of subconstituents within a constituent is one locus of variation across languages. In some languages adjectives follow the noun (for example, Hebrew), in some they precede it (for example, English), and in some both alternatives are possible (for example, French). Nevertheless, there are certain subregularities that generally obtain. For example, languages like Japanese, which is verb-final, also tend to be postpositional (objects of prepositions follow prepositions), contain relative clauses that precede the noun they modify, and have adjectives that precede the noun. These are languages in which the *Head Parameter*—the parameter that establishes in which periphery (left or right) of a constituent phase its head will be located—is set to the value "heads right." In Hebrew, in contrast, where the verb is VP-initial, there are prepositional phrases, relative clauses follow the nouns they modify, and adjectives follow the noun, the setting is "heads left." Although languages sometimes tolerate some exceptions to these ordering generalizations (for example, English—try to set the Head Parameter and note any exceptions!), the Head Parameter generally makes accurate predictions about connected aspects of word order across languages. In this regard, it is an important component of the theory of Universal Grammar.

Challenges to the Theory
Chomsky's system of UG has been extremely influential in guiding the development of research projects in many areas of cognitive science. Yet, like any important idea, the position we have sketched has been seriously criticized, frequently amended, and in some cases jettisoned in favor of alternative frameworks. We close our discussion of UG by briefly noting some of the interesting areas of continuing research on UG, with special attention to the more general psychological and biological claims that have been made for UG.

The hypothesized innate universal grammar is often compared (by Chomsky and others) to a bodily organ—albeit a "mental organ"—that is organized in brain and other neural tissue. Although the details of the biological basis of the linguistic capacity are by no means well understood (see chapter 7), it is often claimed that UG represents a modular, highly specialized capacity—and it is sometimes suggested that it has a specialized genetic basis. That is, the notion of linguistic innateness has been taken to mean that there must have been highly specific natural selection in the course of human evolution for the details of UG. This view is sometimes further popularized to suggest that there are specific genes for language. But there is little evidence to support this notion. In fact, few organ systems or behaviors are the products of single genes. There is certainly little basis in contemporary molecular biology to support the notion that specific informational states, like the Case Filter or abstract principles of syllabification, could be somehow directly encoded in human chromosomes. The challenge, then, is to reconcile Chomsky's claims about the biological basis of language with what is known about genetic mechanisms and evolutionary principles.

There is also room for doubt about the claims of species specificity that have been made for the language organ. It has been discovered, for example, that mammals other than humans exhibit *categorical perception* (Kuhl and Miller 1975), the tendency to perceive what are in fact distinct points along a continuum as falling into discrete clumps of data. Humans have been claimed to rely innately on categorical perception to distinguish voiced from voiceless sounds. That is, despite considerable actual acoustic variation, we hear sounds only as voiced or voiceless, with no apparent middle categories of perception. Although it is clear how categorical perception is useful in speech perception, Kuhl and Miller's evidence that nonhumans exhibit this phenomenon is surprising. Although categorical perception may not technically qualify as one of the principles of UG (in that it is more a perceptual property than a narrowly linguistic one), findings such as these fuel the hopes of those who maintain that there must be substantial overlap between the cognitive properties of humans and nonhumans.

Finally, there are also hesitations concerning the claim that the properties of universal grammar are strictly modular—that is, that they pertain only to linguistic representation and acquisition and the like, and do not follow from more general architectural or other characteristics of cognition. It is difficult, of course, to attribute broader (or analogous) functions to highly abstract properties like the Case Filter, and the implausibility of this attribution has been taken by some researchers to be strong evidence for modularity. But much more will need to be known about cognition before we can determine with any confidence whether some of the innate mechanisms that subserve language turn out to have a broader organismic significance.

Again, motivation to pursue this inquiry comes from the phenomenon of categorical perception, which has also been demonstrated in certain nonlinguistic domains, for example, between certain musical sounds related on an acoustic continuum, such as the plucking and bowing of a violin string (Cutting and Rosner 1974). These results suggest that some capacities that support language learning may not be specifically "linguistic," but are instead part of more general cognitive capacities. Can this reduction be accomplished for the principles of UG? Certainly the universals we have sketched, for instance, the Case Filter, do not obviously admit of this kind of account, though further research may indeed show that they do follow from more general aspects of cognitive architecture. Indeed, researchers like Lieberman (1985) have argued that all linguistic universals are ultimately a function of general biological mechanisms, a view shared, in certain respects, with Piagetian psychologists. But many generative linguists remain skeptical that the elimination of UG in favor of general biological and cognitive properties is possible, and any strong conclusions seem premature.

Summary and Reprise

Adult learners of new languages struggle (much like linguists) to acquire some understanding of their language. The struggle will go on for some time, and it typically ends in an imperfect (if hard-won) mastery. Very young children learning their first language (or languages) face the same general task, complicated by the limited experiential resources of infancy and an apparent lack of any linguistic context in which to embed new knowledge. Despite these limitations, children enjoy an ease of language learning that adults envy.

The child's course of learning is not instantaneous, or free from errors and missteps. But there does appear to be a highly systematic pattern to the range of false steps that children take. Moreover, there appear to be types of errors that children learning any language simply do not make. For instance, children learning questions typically go through several stages of development, some of which involve utterance types that differ in interesting ways from the adult system. But certain differences do not emerge. For instance, children never seem to misjudge the appropriate position of question words on the basis of evidence like *I know what John ate*; they do not hypothesize a rule to the effect that question words in English are to be placed in the middle of sentences. In the same vein, children never seem to hypothesize, on the basis of frequent exposure to words with closed syllables, that *all* English words involve such syllables (by contrast, many children for a considerable time produce only open syllables). There is no a priori reason why children do not entertain these alternative hypotheses, yet they fail to do so even in the face of data that are consistent with them. It is intriguing to conclude that they do not do so because they *cannot*, that UG enforces a general constraint on the form of rules that precludes them from deducing constructs like "the middle of a sentence." Such constraints vastly simplify the learning task by restricting the range of possible hypotheses. By setting such limits on the kinds of knowledge representation that the organism can learn—whether by highly specific neural constraints, or as a consequence of more general constraints on development—evolution has facilitated the acquisition of the extraordinarily powerful, flexible, and creative systems we call language.

Suggested Readings

A broader introduction to linguistic theory and the study of language in general can be found in *An Introduction to Human Language* (Gee 1993). Several of Noam Chomsky's works also provide an accessible perspective on theoretical issues and on the intellectual context of recent work; see in particular *Rules and Representations* (1980) and *Language and Problems of Knowledge: The Managua Lectures* (1988). *The Language Lottery* (Lightfoot 1982) and *How to Set Parameters* (Lightfoot 1991) provide a perspective on the biological nature of language, language acquisition, language change, and universal grammar. *Generative Phonology: Description and Theory* (Kenstowicz and Kisseberth 1979) and *Autosegmental and Metrical Phonology* (Goldsmith 1990) provide an introduction to generative phonology. The *Problem Book in Phonology* (Halle and Clements 1982) provides a series of phonological problems drawn from the languages of the world. *A Course in Phonetics* (Ladefoged 1982) contains background information on articulatory and acoustic phonetics. For work in contemporary syntactic theory, see *Introduction to Government and Binding* (Haegeman 1991) and *Introduction to the Theory of Grammar* (Van Riemsdijk and Williams 1986). Finally, for a comparison of various competing contemporary approaches to syntactic theory, see *Lectures on Contemporary Syntactic Theories* (Sells 1985) and "Grammatical Theory" (Wasow 1989).

References

Alcock, J. (1989). *Animal behavior: An evolutionary approach*. Sunderland, Mass.: Sinauer Associates.

Chomsky, N. (1957). *Syntactic structures*. The Hague: Mouton.

Chomsky, N. (1965). *Aspects of the theory of syntax*. Cambridge, Mass.: MIT Press.

Chomsky, N. (1975). *Reflections on language*. New York: Pantheon.

Chomsky, N. (1980). *Rules and representations*. New York: Columbia University Press.

Chomsky, N. (1986). *Knowledge of language: Its nature, origin, and use*. New York: Praeger.

Chomsky, N. (1988). *Language and problems of knowledge: The Managua lectures*. Cambridge, Mass.: MIT Press.

Cutting, J. E., and B. S. Rosner (1974). Categories and boundaries in speech and music. *Perception and Psychophysics* 16, 564–570.

Fodor, J. A. (1983). *Modularity of mind.* Cambridge, Mass.: MIT Press.

Fodor, J. A., and T. G. Bever (1965). The psycholinguistic reality of linguistic segments. *Journal of Verbal Learning and Verbal Behavior* 4, 414–420.

Fodor, J. A., T. G. Bever, and M. F. Garrett (1975). *The psychology of language.* New York: McGraw-Hill.

Garfield, J. (1987). *Modularity in knowledge representation and natural-language understanding.* Cambridge, Mass.: MIT Press.

Gazdar, G., E. Klein, G. Pullum, and I. Sag (1985). *Generalized phrase structure grammar.* Cambridge, Mass.: Harvard University Press.

Gee, J. P. (1993). *An introduction to human language.* Englewood Cliffs, N.J.: Prentice-Hall.

Goldsmith, J. (1976). An overview of autosegmental phonology. *Linguistic Analysis* 2, 23–68.

Goldsmith, J. (1990). *Autosegmental and metrical phonology.* Oxford, U.K., and Cambridge, Mass.: Blackwell.

Halle, M., and G. N. Clements (1982). *Problem book in phonology: A workbook for introductory courses in linguistics and modern phonology.* Cambridge, Mass.: MIT Press.

Hayes, B. (1980). A metrical theory of stress rules. Doctoral dissertation, MIT, Cambridge, Mass.

Hayes, B. (1982). Extrametricality and English stress. *Linguistic Inquiry* 13, 227–276.

Kahn, D. (1976). Syllable-based generalizations in English phonology. Doctoral dissertation, MIT, Cambrige, Mass.

Kenstowicz, M., and C. Kisseberth (1979). *Generative phonology: Description and theory.* New York: Academic Press.

Kuhl, P., and J. Miller (1975). Speech perception by the chinchilla: Voiced-voiceless distinction in alveolar plosive consonants. *Science* 190, 69–72.

Ladefoged, P. (1982). *A course in phonetics.* 2nd ed. New York: Harcourt Brace Jovanovich.

Levelt, W. J. M. (1970). A scaling approach to the study of syntactic relations. In F. B. Flores d'Arcais and W. J. M. Levelt, eds., *Advances in psycholinguistics.* New York: American Elsevier.

Liberman, M., and A. Prince (1976). On stress and linguistic rhythm. *Linguistic Inquiry* 8, 249–336.

Lieberman, P. (1985). *The biology and evolution of language.* Cambridge Mass.: Harvard University Press.

Lightfoot, D. (1982). *The language lottery.* Cambridge, Mass.: MIT Press.

Lightfoot, D. (1991). *How to set parameters.* Cambridge, Mass.: MIT Press.

Marler, P., and V. Sherman. (1985). Innate differences in singing behaviour of sparrows reared in isolation from adult conspecific song. *Animal Behaviour* 33, 57–71.

Piatelli-Palmarini, M. (1980). *Language and learning.* Cambridge, Mass.: Harvard University Press.

Premack, D. (1986). *Gavagai!* Cambridge, Mass.: MIT Press.

Prince, A. (1983). Relating to the grid. *Linguistic Inquiry* 14, 19–100.

Riemsdijk, H. van, and E. Williams (1986). *Introduction to the theory of grammar.* Cambridge, Mass.: MIT Press.

Ross, J. R. (1967). Constraints on variables in syntax. Doctoral dissertation, MIT, Cambridge, Mass.

Selkirk, E. (1980). The role of prosodic categories in English word stress. *Linguistic Inquiry* 11, 563–605.

Selkirk, E. (1984). *Phonology and syntax: The relation between sound and structure.* Cambridge, Mass.: MIT Press.

Sells, P. (1985). *Lectures on contemporary syntactic theories.* Palo Alto, Calif.: Center for the Study of Language and Information.

Wasow, T. (1989). Grammatical theory. In M. I. Posner, ed., *Foundations of cognitive science.* Cambridge, Mass.: MIT Press.

Chapter 7

Neuroscience: Brain and Cognition

7.1 Introduction to the Study of the Nervous System

In the previous chapters we have taken a computational approach to cognition, analyzing information processes as computations over abstractly defined representations. Although human and animal cognition is physically realized in the nervous system, the computational level of analysis has allowed us to study cognition without paying much attention to its physical implementation. In this chapter we introduce *neuroscience*, the field that encompasses the levels of analysis that are required for the study of physical processes and structures in the nervous system. There are several reasons to extend our study of cognition to include its biological underpinnings.

First, the question of how nervous systems achieve the kinds of complex information processing that we have been studying is intrinsically fascinating. Questions about how to complete the chain of scientific understanding from mind to brain, from thought to neuron to molecule and perhaps on to subatomic particle, are among the most interesting in science.

Second, research on the nervous system can help test some of the theories that have been developed in cognitive psychology and linguistics. We saw in chapter 2, for example, how the discovery that visual areas of the brain are differentially active during imagery is an important piece of evidence for the existence of a spatially organized buffer for visual imagery.

Third, as we saw in our study of connectionism, the potential importance of neuroscience to cognitive science goes beyond the likelihood that neuroscience is a source of evidence for autonomously developed computational theories. The information processes that a system is capable of carrying out efficiently are strongly constrained by its computational architecture. The capabilities of an architecture arise directly out of its physical structure. Thus, knowledge about fundamental principles of structure and process in the nervous system should be able to contribute to the initial construction of a theory of cognitive architecture. Ideally, a theory of the architecture would be the joint product of findings at the computational and biological levels of analysis. Connectionist researchers have reached for this ideal by trying to build principles of neural computation into their conceptions of cognitive architecture. There is considerable controversy about whether the principles that have been suggested are the right ones and even whether the whole enterprise is premature, given our primitive understanding of neural computation, but the vision cannot be faulted. In order to convey a sense of what is known in neuroscience and how it relates to analysis at the cognitive level, this chapter covers quite a bit of territory. Some of what is presented falls into the area that has come to be called *cognitive neuroscience*, the active intersection between the two fields. Other material is currently rather remote from the central concerns of cognitive science, but could become more important as research advances. The cognitive scientist should be conversant with neuroscience, ready to establish new connections when they become possible.

A fourth reason for linking the study of cognitive science and neuroscience is that the understanding of the relationship between the physical structure of the nervous system and its information-processing capacities has many potential practical applications. Increased understanding of the biological substrates of cognition will contribute to the development of better physical and behavioral treatments for damage to the nervous system caused by accident or disease. More generally, such knowledge will aid in the design of learning environments that are tuned to the physically determined strengths of human information processing and will suggest new ways in which computer systems can be used to compensate for its weaknesses. Researchers have also begun to envision new types of computers with highly parallel hardware that exploits some of the design principles of the nervous system (Hecht-Nielsen 1990).

7.2 Organization of the Central Nervous System

Introduction: Levels of Description

The nervous system has been studied at many different levels. Neurobiology gives a very different picture of what the brain is doing than psycholinguistics or neuropsychology. As Sejnowski and Churchland (1989) have pointed out, these divisions of study are somewhat arbitrary and serve the convenience of scientists and the techniques that are used in their research. They describe seven different levels (see figure 7.1), organized along a spatial scale. At the top of the scale are neural systems organized around general functional characteristics, such as the speech articulation system. At the bottom of the scale are neurotransmitters, the chemicals that carry signals between neurons, the cells in the brain that process information. At present our

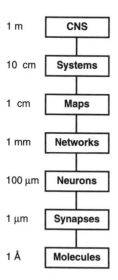

Figure 7.1
Scale of size and unit of function in the nervous system

knowledge of neural processes at the molecular or synaptic level is much more detailed than at the neural network and map levels. Future research is likely to restructure these descriptive levels as we learn more about the brain's own states of internal representation.

Basic Neuroanatomy

The human nervous system is divided into central and peripheral systems. The *central nervous system* is made up of the brain and spinal cord and can be thought of as the control center for interpreting sensory input and directing our thoughts and actions. The *peripheral nervous system* functions to carry information from the body and the outside world to the central system and back. For understanding cognitive functions, we are most interested in a review of the central nervous system (CNS).

Neuroanatomy refers to the general structural organization of the brain and spinal cord, including its major physical and functional divisions. Neuroanatomy is difficult to learn because new brain structures developed on top of older ones during the course of evolution, producing a highly complicated organ with many regions tightly packed together and extremely complex interconnected pathways among them. Figure 7.2 illustrates the major regions of the CNS and some of its principal structures. The lowest functional division is the spinal cord, which connects the brain to the body's organs and muscles. The middle division is the *brain stem*, which is made up of the diencephalon (between brain), the midbrain or mesencephalon, and the hindbrain or rhombencephalon. The highest division is the *forebrain*, which includes the cerebral cortex, basal ganglia, olfactory bulbs, and limbic system. There are complementary left and right structures at every division in the brain, with the exception of the pineal body.

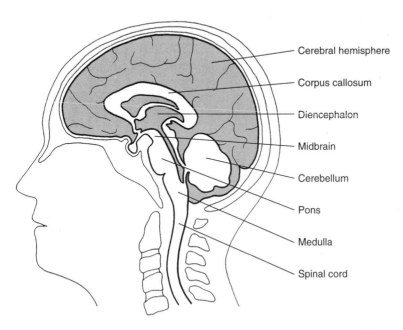

Figure 7.2
A midsagittal diagram of the principal structures of the brain. (From Kandel 1991a.)

The diencephalon consists of three thalamic (inner chamber) structures and the pituitary gland. The epithalamus is made up of the pineal body and other cell groups, or nuclei, called the habenula. The hypothalamus is composed of over twenty small nuclei. They are involved in nearly all aspects of behavior, including regulatory functions of sleep, appetite, reproductive cycles, and body temperature. These functions are affected through the release of chemicals called hormones into the blood stream that are then transported to other tissues in the body and brain. The *thalamus*, made up of a cluster of smaller nuclei, is located dorsally (on top) and anterior (in front of) to the rest of the midbrain. The thalamus functions as part of the sensory relay system that receives input from all sensory organs except the nose and relays these signals to the cortex. For example, the *lateral geniculate nucleus* (LGN) receives input from the eyes, and the *medial geniculate nucleus* (MGN) receives auditory projections.

The midbrain is organized into two sections that are physically divided by the cerebral aqueduct. This narrow cavity is part of the ventricle system in the brain, which is filled with cerebrospinal fluid, cushioning the brain from shock and possibly playing a role in filtering metabolic wastes. The area lying above the aqueduct is called the tectum and primarily consists of the superior and inferior colliculi, nuclei that receive projections from visual and auditory organs, respectively. Below the aqueduct is the tegmentum, made up of sensory and motor fibers passing between the forebrain and the peripheral nervous system, and a number of motor nuclei, such as the substantia nigra (which when damaged produces the symptoms of Parkinson's disease).

The hindbrain is made up of the pons, medulla oblongata, and cerebellum. In the pons are a variety of sensory and motor nuclei that govern vestibular (balance and postural orientation) and motor functions. The medulla oblongata consists primarily of fiber tracts that pass information between the spinal cord and the cortex. In addition, it contains a complex mixture of fibers, called the reticular formation, that travel up and down the brain stem from the diencephalon through the hindbrain.

Overlying the brain stem is the *cerebellum*. Its cellular organization is remarkably uniform throughout, as compared, for example, to the cortex, which has regionally organized characteristics. The cerebellum has connections to structures throughout the rest of the brain. Although it was once thought to be specialized primarily for sensory-motor coordination, recent research suggests roles in learning (McCormick and Thompson 1984) and possibly other higher cognitive functions (Courchesne et al. 1988).

The forebrain is divided into four regions: the cerebral cortex, the limbic system, olfactory bulbs, and basal ganglia. Sometimes the thalamus is placed with the forebrain group. The limbic (border) system is made up of several structures. The major nuclei include the hippocampus (seahorse), amygdala, septum (partition), mammillary bodies, fornix, and cingulate (girdle) gyrus, which together surround and sheathe the brain stem. These structures form connections with parts of the hypothalamus, thalamus, and cortex through the cingulate gyrus. Because of their interconnections with the olfactory bulbs they were once called the rhinencephalon and thought to analyze olfactory information. More recently the hippocampus has received intense study for its role in the formation of memory (Squire 1987) and in spatial orientation (O'Keefe and Nadel 1978).

The basal ganglia are formed from several large nuclei that surround the thalamus and lie in the medial (middle) region below the cortex. These structures, including the putamen (shell), the globus pallidus, and the caudate, have extensive connections with

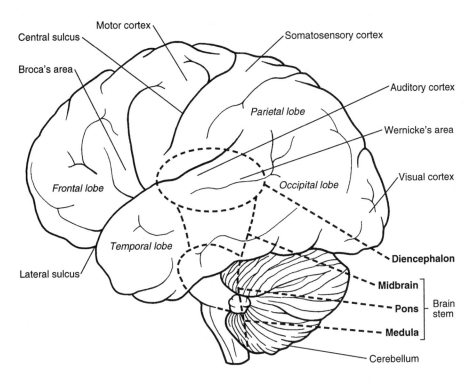

Figure 7.3
The main parts of the central nervous system and cerebral cortex. (From Kandel 1991a.)

the cortex and thalamus as well as portions of the midbrain, such as the red nucleus and substantia nigra. They play a significant role in the initiation and control of movement.

Cerebral Cortex   Approximately 1.5–3 mm thick, the *cerebral cortex* consists of four to six layers of cells that are spread out over a large surface area of 100,000–200,000 mm^2 (Cherniak 1990). As the cortex increased in size during the course of evolution, folds and wrinkles appeared, presumably to allow more cortical tissue to fit into the skull without expanding the size of the cranium. This folding process produced characteristic ridges (called gyri or lobules) and clefts (called fissures or sulci if shallow).

These ridges and clefts are not identical in any two individuals, but they are relatively uniform and can be divided into four major regions (see figure 7.3). The *occipital lobes* are located in the posterior (back) part of the cortex. They serve as the primary sensory system for vision. The *temporal lobe*, located lateral (to the side) and ventral (below) to the prominent lateral or *Sylvian fissure*, serves at least three functions: primary and secondary processing of auditory information, long-term storage of sensory information (such as the identity of visual objects) (Mishkin and Appenzeller 1987), and processing of emotional qualities associated with sensation. The *parietal lobe* is strategically located posterior to the *central sulcus* and anterior to the occipital lobe. Its multiple connections with occipital, frontal, and temporal lobes suggest a functional role in the cross-modal integration of sensory information. Recent research also has suggested a functional role in locating visual objects and directing visual attention

(Andersen, Siegel, and Essick 1987). The *postcentral gyrus* of the parietal lobe contains the *somatosensory cortex*, which is the primary sensory area for afferent (incoming) signals from the surface of the body, such as touch and pain.

The *frontal lobe* is composed of the cortical tissue that is anterior to the central sulcus. The frontal lobe has a complex array of connections with other cortical regions and with subcortical structures. Until the 1930s the frontal lobes were most often described as the seat of human intelligence, including functions such as foresight, self-awareness, and ethical judgments. Today theories of frontal lobe function are more complicated and include components of motor control (both fine-motor control and complex limb movements that involve tactile or visual guidance), speech production (associated with Broca's area), and higher mental functions, such as planning or structuring activities around a goal. The *precentral gyrus* of the frontal lobe contains the *primary motor cortex*, which sends efferent (outgoing) signals to the spinal motor systems, producing muscle movement.

Comparative Neuroanatomy
The anatomy of the human brain is similar to that of the rat or monkey. Although early neuroanatomists hoped to find types of neural cells that were unique to humans, this has proved not to be the case. However, the human brain is different in other ways. When the size of the human brain is compared with the brain size of other animals, taking body weight into account, humans have the largest brains of all mammals—six times as large as a cat's brain and almost three times as large as a chimpanzee's (dolphins rank a close second to humans) (Stephen, Bauchot, and Andy 1970). Humans fare even better when the relative size of the cortex is used for comparison.

Compared with other primates, humans are born with a brain that is small relative to its adult size. Macaque monkeys are born with brains that are 60 percent of their adult weight. The proportions for chimpanzees and humans are 46 percent and 25 percent, respectively. These relationships appear to be due to the rate of brain growth that occurs after birth. During fetal development the brain grows at the same rate in macaque, chimpanzee, and human. At birth the rates of brain growth slow down markedly for macaque and chimpanzee, but human brains continue to grow at the rapid fetal rate for about two more years. Apparently, the increase in the size of the human brain was achieved evolutionarily by prolonging development after birth.

The significance of the facts about brain size is in some dispute. Differences in size could be the result of more cells, more cell processes (such as the size of dendritic branches or the number of axonal connections between neurons), or increased cell density. Using one method to estimate the density of cortical cells, Changeux (1985) reported that cell density and the relative frequency of different types of cells for a given cortical region are fairly constant across a number of species from mouse to human. He suggested that the human advantage is in the sheer number of cells, estimating humans to have from three to four times the number of cortical cells as other primates. Using other methods, Passingham (1982) calculated that with larger brain volume, human cortical cells are spaced farther apart than the cells in the brains of other primates. He suggested that in certain cortical areas the human brain has more connections per cell rather than more cells. The increased volume is not found in primary sensory regions of the cortex, such as the occipital lobe or parts of the temporal lobe, suggesting that the main evolutionary pressure on brain development in humans was to enlarge cortical areas involved in the cross-modal integration of information, such as the parietal and frontal cortex.

The functional organization of the human brain also may be different from that of the brains of other mammals. For example, Passingham (1982) has suggested that because certain behavioral functions appear to be localized in one cortical hemisphere, such as language in the left hemisphere, humans may have a brain that can process information more efficiently. We will return to this topic later in the chapter.

Cellular Systems

Neurons   The cells of the brain are generally divided into two categories: the nerve cells or *neurons* and others called *glial* cells. Neurons are intensively studied because of their unique computational properties. Although their biological processes are much like those of other cells, neurons have the special ability to receive and transmit information to other neurons, muscles, and glands, sometimes over great distances. Most neurons send signals to many other neurons and also receive signals from many other neurons.

Glial cells, which are much more numerous than neurons, are not well understood, but they are known to serve several functions. They are involved in the removal of unnecessary or excess substances. Glial cells often absorb excess neurotransmitter chemicals at synapses (a process described below) and have been observed to multiply and remove cellular debris at sites of brain damage. In vertebrates (animals with spinal cords) glial cells provide two special functions. They establish the blood-brain barrier to filter the blood supply to the brain and also form myelin on the axons of some neurons (both functions are described below in more detail).

The brain is the most metabolically active organ in the body, accounting for 15 to 20 percent of the body's oxygen utilization but only 2 percent of total body weight. Neurons are always active and require a constant supply of energy in the form of blood glucose to remain alive. As a neuron's level of activity increases, its need for energy rises as well and glucose is taken up more rapidly. Special imaging techniques, such as *positron emission tomography* (PET), have been developed to provide pictures of the brain by labeling glucose with a radioactive isotope. The labeled glucose is intravenously injected and differentially absorbed by those regions of the brain that are metabolically most active during the time period when the isotope is still active. Once the isotope has been absorbed into the cells, it remains there, and the subject's brain can be imaged without harmful effects. PET scans are one of the few procedures available that can provide functional brain images in humans. This technique is particularly useful for localizing behavioral functions to specific brain locations. It requires finding a task that involves areas of the brain differentially and keeping a subject at the task for two minutes without distraction or interruption while the image is being recorded.

If the supply of oxygenated blood to the brain is interrupted, through a heart attack or stroke, for example, the loss of oxygen disrupts cell metabolism and neurons begin to die within minutes. Because the genetic material in the soma of adult neurons cannot initiate the process for cell duplication (unlike glial cells), neurons cannot reproduce to replace lost cells. Thus, any brain damage in adults is permanent. Neurons are vulnerable in other ways as well. Their functioning can be disrupted by toxic substances from the environment or even by naturally occurring chemicals in the bloodstream such as amino acids. For protection, a blood-brain barrier has evolved that acts to selectively filter the brain's blood supply. Glial cells, which have fatty membranes, tightly sheathe most of the blood vessels in the brain. Small molecules, such as oxygen, can easily pass through this membrane tissue, but larger ones, such as glucose, require special transport mechanisms to get across the barrier. For a drug to directly affect brain function, its molecular structure must be small enough to fit through the glial membrane or be soluble in the fatty tissue and so transportable across the membrane. In a few locations in the brain the blood vessels are not wrapped in glial tissue, which allows these brain regions to monitor the composition of the blood for substances such as hormones.

Although neurons vary considerably in shape and size (see figure 7.4), they generally have three major parts: the *cell body* or *soma*, the *dendrites* (Greek for tree), and the *axon*. The soma, whose diameter is usually smaller than 50 micrometers (one-millionth of a meter), contains the cell's nucleus and many other small structures (called organelles) that carry out processes necessary for the cell's health. Radiating out from the cell body are the dendrites and the axon. Each type of neuron has many dendritic fibers, which form a characteristic shape that distinguishes it from other types. For example, the dendrites of the Purkinje cells in the cerebellum have a complex coral

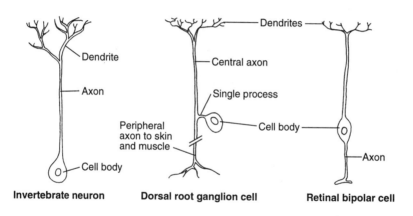

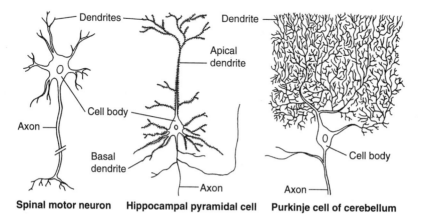

Figure 7.4
Examples of different types of neurons. (From Kandel 1991b.)

shape, whereas the pyramidal cells in the cortex have dendrites that branch less frequently and extend farther (figure 7.4). The dendritic tree of a single neuron receives input from as many as several thousand other neurons through synaptic contacts (which are described below). Input is also received on the soma. In some types of neurons the contact points along the dendrites bulge up, producing little knobs called spines, which change in shape and size with experience, serving to expand the surface area of contact.

Each neuron has only one axon, which has been estimated to make up to 4,000 contacts with the dendrites and somas of as many as 1,000 other neurons (Cherniak 1990; Shepherd 1990b). The axon is connected to the cell body or a large dendrite at a junction called the *axon hillock*. Axons are constructed like fine cylindrical tubes that taper as the tube extends from the soma. At the end of the axon, many small collateral branches extend to make contact with other neurons. As these branches end, the tissue expands into a small bulb known as the *axon terminal*. Some axons are quite short and extend less than a millimeter, whereas others axons, such as those that carry information to or from the spinal cord, can be several feet long.

Neurons are electrically charged, somewhat like a battery, carrying a negative charge inside relative to the outside of their cell membrane. In a resting state the voltage difference or potential between the inside and outside of a neuron is about -70 millivolts. This charge is due to an unequal distribution of charged particles, called ions, between the inside and outside of the cell. Positively charged ions, such as sodium (Na^+), are found in higher concentrations outside the cell, whereas negatively charged ions, such as cell proteins (P^{2-}), are more concentrated inside the cell. Other ions, such as potassium (K^+), calcium (Ca^{2+}), and chloride (Cl^-), are also unequally distributed. This distribution is maintained by the cell membrane, which contains tiny channels, specialized for transporting each type of ion. In its resting state the membrane is semipermeable to K^+, allowing these ions to move relatively easily between the inside and outside of the cell through the potassium channel. However, at rest the membrane is impermeable to Na^+. Cell proteins are too large to pass through the ion channels and remain in the soma. The combined distribution of these ions produces a negatively charged cell.

The cell's charge would eventually run down, were not it for a mechanism in the membrane, called the *sodium-potassium pump*, which pumps potassium back into the cell and sodium out. The cell's negative potential is maintained primarily by keeping Na^+ ions outside of the cell, as potassium channels allow K^+ to leak back into the cell. Ion channels also are activated by changes in the potential of the cell.

Local and Action Potentials   Within neurons information is conducted in two different ways. Long-distance transmission occurs via *action potentials*, which travel along the surface of the axon from the soma to the axon terminals. To assimilate incoming information in the dendrites and soma, neurons use *local potentials*. Sometimes local potentials also function to transmit information over very short distances (less than a micrometer) between two adjacent neurons. Action potentials produce a large, all-or-none signal that is brief (1–10 milliseconds) and travels unattenuated and at a rapid rate (as high as 100 meters per second). Local potentials are small and graded, and propagate passively, rapidly degrading as electrical resistance is encountered.

Changes in local potentials of dendrites and the soma are produced by synaptic contact with other neurons (a process described below). These synapses either electrically excite or inhibit the receiving neuron. The charge of the soma can be depolarized (say, from −70 millivolts to −60 millivolts) if the sum of the local potentials synaptically generated by other neurons is large enough. The more excitatory synapses that occur at the same time, the larger the local potential.

Action potentials begin at the axon hillock. The hillock is very sensitive to changes in the membrane potential of the cell. When the potential in the hillock is depolarized to a critical threshold, the ion channels, which are sensitive to voltage changes, open briefly (about half a millisecond) to allow Na^+ to rush into the cell. Because the concentration of Na^+ outside the cell is much higher than inside, Na^+ is driven inside the cell by processes that tend to equalize the concentrations (diffusion, due to the concentration gradient, and electrostatic pressure, due to the charge gradient). This influx of positive ions rapidly depolarizes the cell further, achieving a positive 50-millivolt charge, at which point the sodium channels close (see figure 7.5).

Meanwhile the potassium channels are also opened to allow K^+ to flow out of the cell through the diffusion process. Because potassium channels open more slowly and the concentration gradient for sodium is more out of balance, the Na^+ influx dominates

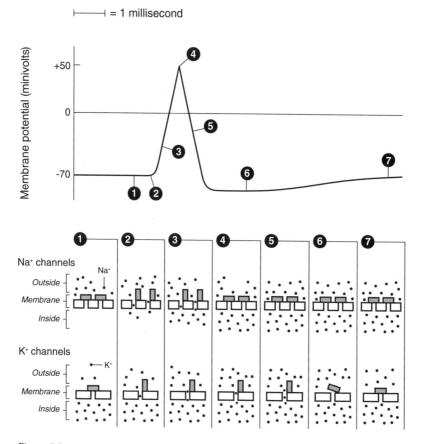

Figure 7.5
Schematic diagram of changes that occur in a neuron's membrane potential during an action potential. Refer to the text for an explanation. (From Thompson 1994.)

the initial changes in the cell's membrane potential. However, after the sodium channels close, the potassium channels remain open. The cell is then negatively repolarized as K^+ continues to leave the cell and as Na^+ is actively transported out of the cell by the sodium-potassium pump. When the cell begins to reach its resting potential, the potassium channels close. However, this process takes a few milliseconds, during which the membrane is actually hyperpolarized (at, say, -75 millivolts) until the sodium-potassium pump and the leaking of Na^+ to the outside of the cell can return the membrane potential to its resting level.

When the hillock begins to depolarize, the adjacent region of axon membrane becomes depolarized as well by the influx of Na^+. These positive ions make the inside of the cell less negatively charged. This reduction in membrane potential is sufficient to trigger adjacent sodium channels, causing them to open and thus moving the action potential farther down the axon membrane. When the sodium channels are open, this region of the membrane cannot be electrically stimulated to produce another action potential until the channels close and the membrane begins to repolarize. This portion of the action potential is called the *refractory period*. Because of the refractory period, the action potential is propagated in only one direction, away from the soma, advancing along that part of the axon membrane which is electrically at rest. Each step in this process is illustrated in figure 7.5.

To speed up the rate at which action potentials are conducted, some axons are sheathed with *Schwann cells*, a type of glial cell. Schwann cells produce a fatty substance called *myelin* that wraps around the axon in multiple layers. Myelin is an electrical insulator that isolates the axon membrane from the extracellular fluid and thus from changes in electrical potential caused by the movement of ions across the membrane. If the myelin sheath were continuous along the axon, the action potential could not propagate. However, every millimeter or so there are small gaps in the myelin, called *nodes of Ranvier*. The electrical current associated with the influx of Na^+ at one node is directly and very rapidly conducted to the next node, causing a depolarization at that node. In this way the action potential jumps from one node to the next. In unmyelinated axons, where the action potential must be propagated continuously along the membrane, conduction speed is rarely more than a few meters per second, but myelination can increase the speed to up to 100 meters per second.

Human infants are born with minimal myelination, mainly in primary sensory and motor areas, but myelination continues throughout childhood, past the age of fifteen. The myelination process has a profound effect on the development of cognitive and motor functions. For example, infants begin to walk at about the time that the peripheral motor neurons that control leg muscles complete myelination. Some researchers have speculated that myelination in associative and frontal cortex may play an important functional role in the development of language and other higher cognitive functions (Huttenlocher 1979). Multiple sclerosis (MS) is a degenerative disease in which patches of myelin and sometimes axons in the motor and sensory tracts are destroyed.

In addition to conducting action potentials, axons provide a conduit for the transportation of chemical substances between the soma and the axon terminal. Certain chemicals, called *neurotransmitters*, used in the synaptic transmission at the axon terminal (described below) are manufactured in the soma and then go through anterograde (forward) transport to the axon terminal, where they are stored in synaptic vesicles. These chemicals also undergo retrograde (backward) transport from the terminal to the soma so they can be reused. A slow (one millimeter per day) anterograde transport system carries material important for cell growth and regeneration. A faster (10–20 millimeters per day) system carries the transmitter material. Some neurotransmitters (such as acetylcholine, which is involved in synaptic transmission in the peripheral nervous system to active muscle tissue) are manufactured at the axon terminal.

The firing rate of a neuron can range from a few action potentials per second to several hundred depending upon the amount of excitatory or inhibitory input. Changes in the firing rate represent a basic computational property of the nervous system. When a neuron changes its firing rate in response to a particular stimulus characteristic, the neuron is probably involved in the computational analysis of that attribute.

Synapses *Synapses* are the basic building blocks for neural computation. A synapse is a site at which electrical or chemical transmission occurs between neurons. The changes that occur in the firing rates of neurons are controlled by the synaptic activity. Most synaptic transmission in the mammalian brain is chemical. The sending (or presynaptic) cell releases a neurotransmitter, which binds to the membrane surface of the receiving (or postsynaptic) cell, causing a change in its local potential. Some transmissions are *excitatory* and depolarize the postsynaptic cell, driving it toward its firing threshold and thus making it more likely that an action potential will be generated. Other transmissions are *inhibitory* and hyperpolarize a cell, driving the membrane potential below its resting level, reducing the likelihood that an action potential will be produced.

The process of chemical transmission between neurons is called *exocytosis* (out of the cell). Exocytosis takes less than a millisecond. A neurotransmitter is contained in tiny vesicles in the presynaptic terminal. Each vesicle contains about 10,000 molecules of the transmitter chemical. When an action potential reaches the axon terminal, the change in voltage triggers the opening of calcium ion (Ca^{2+}) channels. These ions diffuse into the cell, further depolarizing the terminal and causing the vesicles of neurotransmitter to fuse with the terminal membrane and open to the outside of the cell, releasing the transmitter chemical into a very small space roughly 20 nanometers wide (called the *synaptic cleft*) between the pre- and postsynaptic membranes. The vesicles are thought to be reformed out of the terminal membrane.

The Fast Synaptic System   Once released into the synaptic cleft, the neurotransmitter diffuses across the space and attaches to molecular receptors on the postsynaptic membrane (see figure 7.6). These receptors are large protein molecules embedded in the cell membrane with one surface area sticking out. This surface has a region with a precise shape that matches the configuration of the transmitter molecule so that the transmitter can attach itself to this region like a key fitting a lock. In some receptors the attachment of the transmitter alters the receptor's molecular structure so that a channel is opened to the outside of the cell, allowing certain types of ions to diffuse into or out of the postsynaptic cell. Whereas the ion channels involved in the transmission of the action potential are electrically gated—that is, they open or close to changes in the voltage of the cell—these postsynaptic receptors are chemically gated, so that ion channels open and close in the presence of certain neurotransmitter chemicals.

Whether the postsynaptic cell is excited or inhibited depends upon the flow of ions. Excitation causes what is called an *excitatory postsynaptic potential* (EPSP). An EPSP is a depolarization of the cell membrane, driving the membrane potential in a positive direction toward its firing threshold (see the area marked 3 in figure 7.5). An inhibitory

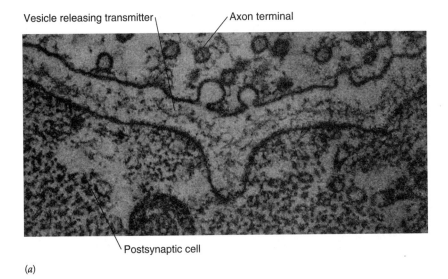

Vesicle releasing transmitter   Axon terminal

Postsynaptic cell

(a)

Synaptic vesicles

Synaptic cleft

Presynaptic membrane

Transmitter molecules

Postsynaptic membrane

(b)

Figure 7.6
(a) shows an electron microscope photograph of a synapse. (b) is a schematic diagram of this process, showing a synaptic vesicle fusing with the presynaptic membrane to release neurotransmitter into the synaptic cleft. (From Steven 1979.)

synaptic transmission produces an *inhibitory postsynaptic potential* (IPSP) and has the opposite effect of hyperpolarizing the cell, driving its potential below its normal resting level. Acetylcholine, a neurotransmitter that occurs in synapses between motor neurons and muscle cells in the peripheral nervous system, is excitatory because Na^+ channels open at the receptor site and allow positively charged ions to flow into the cell and depolarize it. On the other hand, gamma-aminobutyric acid (GABA) is an inhibitory neurotransmitter because its receptors open Cl^- ion channels, allowing ions to flow into the cell and causing hyperpolarization via their negative charge. In general, the action of the neurotransmitter depends upon the receptor molecules. The same neurotransmitter can be excitatory at some synapses and inhibitory at others; for example, acetylcholine inhibits heart muscle fibers.

Neurotransmitter chemicals are rapidly inactivated so that the timing of the signal is precisely controlled; otherwise, postsynaptic neurons would continue to respond until the brain went out of control (something like an epileptic seizure). Inactivation occurs in several different ways. The neurotransmitter chemical can simply diffuse from the synaptic junction into intercellular space, enzymes in the synaptic cleft can bind to the neurotransmitter and inactivate it, or the transmitter chemicals can be recycled back into the presynaptic terminal and reused, a process called *pinocytosis*.

Second Messenger Systems   Other neurotransmitters, such as dopamine and norepinephrine, operate by different and more elaborate mechanisms than chemically gated ion channels. These neurotransmitters affect the concentrations of certain chemical substances in the postsynaptic cells, which in turn cause a chain of chemical events that eventually act on the ion channels directly. This type of postsynaptic effect is termed a second messenger system.

Second messenger systems are extremely complicated and involve a sequence of many chemical events, each of which has multiple effects on other chemical processes in the postsynaptic cell (see figure 7.7). For example, many neurotransmitters use cyclic adenosine monophosphate (cAMP) as a secondary chemical messenger. The precursor to cAMP is adenosine triphosphate (ATP), which is a source of energy that is formed by the metabolism of blood glucose. When the transmitter binds to the postsynaptic receptor, it activates an enzyme, adenylate cyclase, which catalyzes the conversion of ATP into cAMP. In turn, cAMP can act on other biochemical machinery, such as protein kinase (an enzyme that alters the permeability of ion channels), the sodium-potassium pump, the genetic activity of the cell nucleus, and so on. Thus, information from the neurotransmitter, or the first messenger, is multiplied and amplified as the message is passed from one chemical reaction to another. The net result is that a weak signal from the transmitter receptor can produce large and long-lasting effects on the postsynaptic potential. This system is relatively slow. Whereas the chemically gated transmission takes less than a millisecond, second messenger systems require several milliseconds, and some chemical responses can take up to several minutes to be completed.

Some neurotransmitters function in both the fast synaptic and the second messenger systems. For example, in the peripheral nervous system acetylcholine receptors use the fast synaptic system mediated by sodium ion channels; however, in the brain and spinal cord acetylcholine's effects are produced through a second messenger system. Dopamine also uses at least three different types of receptors. The first dopamine receptor (D1) activates a second messenger system, whereas D2 activates chemically gated ion channels.

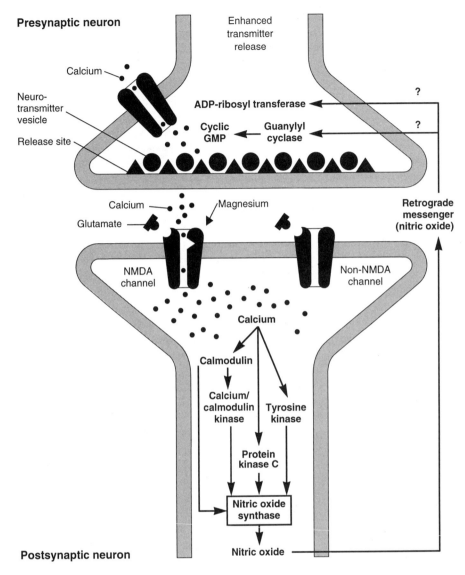

Figure 7.7
Mode of long-term potentiation. Refer to the text for an explanation. (From Kandel and Hawkins 1993.)

Synaptic Modulatory Mechanisms   Synaptic effects are modulated by many different mechanisms, which control the size and the duration of the EPSP or IPSP. At least two different mechanisms are known. First, Kandel and his colleagues (Hawkins et al. 1983) reported that the strength of a synaptic connection could be modulated by the activity of a third neuron, which was active at the same time as the presynaptic neuron. This modulatory effect was first found in the study of the classically conditioned gill-withdrawal reflex in a sea snail (aplysia), but it has not yet been seen in the mammalian nervous system. In the aplysia the modulatory neuron stimulates the presynaptic neuron through a serotonin receptor, which leads to activity in the presynaptic neuron that increases the influx of Ca^{2+}. This increased level of calcium ions, in turn, results in more neurotransmitter being released, producing a larger EPSP or IPSP.

Second, Hebb (1949) proposed that coincidental activity in pre- and postsynaptic neurons strengthens the synaptic connection between them. In a classic Hebbian synapse changes are produced in both the pre- and postsynaptic cells, making the connection between them more efficient, whereas in the modulatory synapse increases in synaptic strength are primarily the result of changes that occur in the presynaptic neuron. The mammalian hippocampus has been the site of much recent research on Hebbian synapses (Lynch and Baudry 1984). When a hippocampal pathway is rapidly stimulated for a short period, producing action potentials, synaptic strengths can increase for days or even weeks (Bliss and Lomo 1973). This change has been called *long-term potentiation* (LTP). The associative type of LTP requires the conjunction of two inputs and seems to involve a genuinely Hebbian synapse (Wigstrom and Gustafsson 1985). The release of the neurotransmitter glutamate (the most common in the hippocampus) initiates the postsynaptic changes. Glutamate depolarizes the postsynaptic cell by binding to a type of receptor called non-NMDA (N-methyl D-aspartate). This depolarization, in conjunction with the presence of appropriate neurotransmitters, opens a channel in another type of receptor called NMDA, which is usually blocked, allowing Ca^{2+} to enter the postsynaptic cell. The calcium ions trigger a chain of second messenger events that induce LTP. The long-term maintenance of LTP, however, appears to require presynaptic changes that increase the release of neurotransmitter, perhaps in a chemical feedback message sent by the postsynaptic cell. Several researchers now think that nitric oxide may be that messenger (Kandel and Hawkins 1993).

Neurochemical Systems

The brain contains many different chemical substances that influence synaptic communication between neurons—at least forty by most recent accounts. Why there are so many different neurochemicals is the subject of much speculation and intense study. One suggestion is that a variety of chemicals have been adapted to serve a multitude of functions during evolutionary development, each one acquired at a different time and place (Iversen 1979).

Neurochemicals have been most recently categorized as *neurotransmitters* or *neuromodulators*. Neurotransmitters are released in synapses to conduct information locally between two neurons, whereas neuromodulators are released in the cerebral spinal fluid or the bloodstream and thus affect a large population of neurons. Several different criteria have been used for defining a neurotransmitter: (1) the chemical is synthesized in the presynaptic neuron; (2) it is released from the synaptic terminal; (3) it produces an EPSP or IPSP; and (4) it is removed from the synaptic cleft or deactivated (Feldman and Quenzer 1984). At present only nine neurochemicals have received widespread acceptance as neurotransmitters (Pinel 1990). Neurotransmitters were once thought to have specific anatomical pathways of their own in the brain. Neurons were identified by the neurotransmitter they released, and imaging techniques were employed to produce neuroanatomical maps of the different neurotransmitter systems. However, new evidence demonstrates that some neurons secrete more than one neurotransmitter or have receptors that respond to different types of neuromodulators and neurotransmitters (Snyder 1986). Furthermore, assigning functional specificity to the neurochemical pathways remains elusive. In addition to their overlapping anatomical locations, neurotransmitters differ in their modes of action. Some neurotransmitters modulate the effects of another transmitter on a postsynaptic cell. Some have their effects through postsynaptic chemical receptors, and others act to modulate voltage-sensitive channels in presynaptic terminals. Still others modify second messenger systems in postsynaptic cells. We are just beginning to understand the full range of neurotransmitter function.

Neuromodulators act more globally, yet appear to have behavioral effects that are highly specific. They can be found in the central nervous system as well as in other areas of the body, such as the gastrointestinal tract (e.g., substance P, enkephalins, somatostatin). Very small amounts of some neuromodulators have been shown to produce profound behavioral effects. For example, an injection of a nanogram (one billionth of a gram) of the peptide angiotensin II can produce intense and prolonged drinking behavior in animals that were not thirsty. Some neuroscientists have interpreted these data to suggest that neuromodulators are specialized for triggering brain activity associated with particular behavioral functions, such as regulating emotional states or the balance of body fluids.

Neurochemicals that exist naturally in the body are called *endogenous* and are distinguished from *exogenous* substances, such as drugs, which can produce profound psychological and neurophysiological effects. Some drugs are so potent that neuroscientists began searching for endogenous substances with the hypothesis that if drugs are so strong, there must be endogenous substances in the brain that have similar neurophysiological properties. Hughes and Kosterlitz (Hughes et al. 1975) discovered two endogenous neurochemicals that acted like morphine, a narcotic drug that is highly addictive and a powerful analgesic for pain. They called these substances enkephalins. Snyder and his colleagues (Snyder 1980) injected radioactively labeled morphine into a laboratory animal and then studied where the isotope would be found in the animal's central nervous system, photographing slices of the brain using film that was sensitive to the presence of the isotope. They discovered that certain regions of the brain and spinal cord contain cells with chemical receptors that have a specific affinity for opiates (so named for the opium poppy from which morphine is derived). Hughes and Kosterlitz showed that enkephalins bound to the opiate receptors just like morphine.

Psychoactive and Neuroleptic Drugs   Many other *psychoactive* drugs may produce their effects by mimicking, enhancing, or disrupting the effects of endogenous neurochemicals. For example, several hallucinogens have molecular structures that resemble those of neurotransmitters. LSD is structurally similar to serotonin, and mescaline resembles norepinephrine and dopamine. Caffeine inhibits the enzyme that degrades cAMP in the second messenger system of postsynaptic cells. Cocaine blocks the reuptake of norepinephrine, with the result that more neurotransmitter remains in the synaptic cleft to stimulate receptors. This information does not explain why caffeine acts as a mild psychological stimulant, why LSD distorts sensory perceptions, or why cocaine produces a euphoric effect. However, understanding the behavioral effects of these drugs must certainly include a clear picture of their neuropharmacological properties.

Neuroleptic drugs, so called for their clinical effect on brain function, have received intensive scrutiny in an effort to better understand the biological basis for the mental disorders they treat. Many of these drugs were prescribed over the years because they were clinically effective, but no one knew why they worked. Neuroscientists have been studying how they affect brain function in the hope of finding evidence about the biological bases of mental disorders.

The best example of this approach has been the study of schizophrenia, a mental disorder widely treated with a class of drugs called phenothiazines. Research now indicates that phenothiazines block the receptor sites for the neurotransmitter dopamine, specifically, the third type of dopamine receptor (D3), thus forming the basis for the dopaminergic hypothesis for schizophrenia: if phenothiazines improve schizophrenic symptoms and also block dopamine receptors, perhaps the symptoms are a product of too much dopaminergic activity in the central nervous system (Snyder 1976). Of course, the story is not necessarily simple. One or more of a number of presynaptic and postsynaptic processes could be involved in schizophrenia. Because of the complicated nature of the synaptic process, it is difficult to pin down exactly what the problem is. Additionally, psychological factors, such as stress, might alter neurochemical functions, further complicating the picture. Still, results from this line of research are promising. Other disorders, including depression, mania, obsessive-compulsive disorders, Alzheimer's disease, and Parkinson's disease, have also been the subject of extensive neurochemical study. The potential to alleviate many of the debilitating effects of brain disease by neurochemical means still holds great promise for the future.

Neural Development

How the brain grows from a single cell to a complex structure of billions of neurons largely remains a mystery. During gestation the brain grows at an average rate of several hundred thousand neurons per minute. Animal research has revealed much about the sequence of developmental events, but most of the finer details about what controls and directs the events remain to be discovered. By roughly three weeks after conception, the dorsal surface of the developing embryo contains a small patch of cells that will eventually form the entire human nervous system. Over the next week this plate of approximately 125,000 cells forms a groove that folds over on itself and then fuses to become a tube. This tube eventually becomes the spinal canal and ventricles. Once the neural tube is formed, cells rapidly proliferate, and after forty days of gestation the tube has developed three bulges that eventually become the forebrain, midbrain, and hindbrain (see figure 7.8).

Cells undergo a fixed sequence of events during development: *proliferation, migration,* and *aggregation.* The timing of these processes is critical and varies for different species and for different parts of the nervous system. First, cells divide along the inner wall of the neural tube in a region called the ventricular zone. Each neuron passes through a number of divisions (mitosis), eventually losing the capacity for further division. Neurons stop dividing when they begin migration. Proliferation continues in some parts of the nervous system until a gestational age of about twenty-eight weeks for humans.

Once mitosis is over, cells begin a migration away from the ventricular zone toward the outside wall of the neural tube, forming progressively thicker layers of cells. Generally, larger neurons with long axonal projections begin migration before smaller neurons. Migrating cells move along glial cells, which set up long fibers that act like scaffolds extending from the ventricular zone to the outside wall of the neural tube. Neurons follow these glial processes at a slow rate, on the average of a tenth of a millimeter per day. Cells that eventually occupy the same cortical location always begin migration together.

When neurons reach their definitive "addresses," they aggregate with other neurons to form cortical layers or nuclei. Cells of the same kind tend to group together and

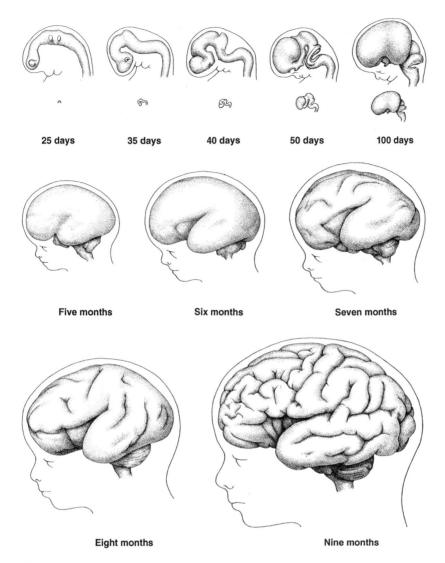

| 25 days | 35 days | 40 days | 50 days | 100 days |

| Five months | Six months | Seven months |

| Eight months | Nine months |

Figure 7.8
Human brain development from 25 days gestation until birth. Figures are enlarged for ages 25 to 100 days (approximate size displayed below). (From Cowan 1979.)

align themselves in a preferred orientation; for example, in the cortex pyramidal neurons are oriented with their dendrites spread out toward the surface of the brain and their axons projecting below. This aggregation process is now thought to be mediated by certain molecules on the surface of the neuron (Rutishauser et al. 1988).

Cell migration errors are not unusual. Through staining and microscopic study, aggregates of neurons can be found in the wrong cortical layer, an abnormality called an *ectopia*. Another migration error called *dysplasia* occurs when a pocket of neural tissue is missing cells (see figure 7.9). In one animal study about 3 percent of the neurons out of the population examined migrated to the wrong location (Cowan 1979).

Several human developmental disorders are associated with cell migration errors. Probably the most carefully studied example is developmental dyslexia, a fairly

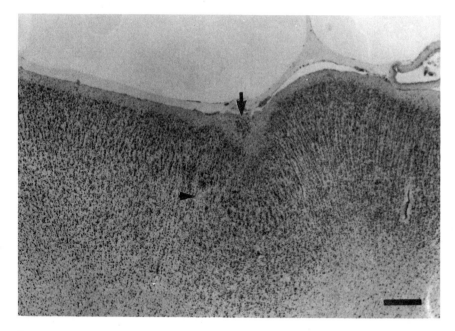

Figure 7.9
An example of an ectopia (arrow) and a dysplasia (arrowhead). Bar in lower right corner equals 500 μ.
(From Galaburda et al. 1985.)

frequent condition (2–5 percent of the population) in which children with normal intelligence and educational opportunity have difficulty learning to read. The research of Galaburda, Rosen, and Sherman (1989) has documented several cases where large numbers of ectopias and dysplasias have been found in the brains of dyslexic patients, which were studied after the patients' deaths. It has not yet been determined whether cell migration errors are present in all cases of dyslexia or whether such errors actually cause reading problems.

This example suggests the possibility that some developmental disorders may be the product of disruptive events that occurred during critical phases of neural development. Because different parts of the brain are at different stages of development during gestation, the timing of a disruption is critical and controls where the abnormality will appear in the brain and the severity of the abnormality. What could cause such disruptions is the subject of considerable speculation; environmental factors, such as viruses, and genetic defects have both been suggested.

Once migration and aggregation are completed, cells undergo a process of differentiation in which axons grow, synaptic connections are formed, and circuits are pruned down to functional pathways. The early stages of the differentiation process are under genetic control. Studies of neural development in simpler invertebrate nervous systems have shown that for each member of a species, growing neurons follow specific paths and form precise connections with other neurons (Bastiani et al. 1985). Three different hypotheses have been proposed to explain how this takes place: (1) that chemical signals are transmitted between the pre- and postsynaptic cells to guide the growing axon (Sperry 1963); (2) that the chemical or physical signal is laid down in a pathway for the axon to follow (Singer, Nordlander, and Egar 1979); (3) that the relative position of the cell bodies in an aggregate of growing neurons influences the direction of axon growth so that the synaptic terminals of the axons end up in the same relative position as their cell bodies (Easter et al. 1985).

Following the growth of axons, the number of synapses and the density of synaptic contacts are significantly reduced. Synaptic reduction is commonly assumed to be caused by competition between neurons for functional connections, although the mechanisms underlying these changes are unknown. One hypothesis suggests that some cells die because they fail to receive a necessary nutrient provided by a successful synaptic contact (Cowan 1979). Studies from different species have suggested that from 15 to 85 percent of the initial neuronal population may die during the period of synaptic consolidation. However, humans may not lose neurons to the same degree as other species. Recent studies of human brains have shown a decrease in synaptic contacts without the accompanying cell death (Huttenlocher 1990).

Cell differentiation continues for a long time in humans. Studies of the primary visual cortex have suggested that the density of synaptic connections rapidly increases from about the second month of postnatal life, reaching adult values around the age of five months, and then overproducing for the next three to five months. Connections are then gradually eliminated over the next nine years, reaching adult values by the age of ten (Leuba and Garey 1987). Other parts of the cortex may show a different time course; for example, neuronal density in the frontal lobe does not reach adult values until around seven years of age, and synaptic consolidation may continue through late adolescence (Huttenlocher 1990).

Developmental Plasticity   Development in a vertebrate nervous system is marked by progressive phases of overgrowth and subsequent regressive phases in which excess neurons and neural connections are eliminated. Prenatal progressive events include cell proliferation, migration, and aggregation among similar cell types, as described above. Postnatally, cell processes continue to proliferate, producing an abundance of synaptic contacts. Children's synaptic concentrations remain nearly double adult values in some cortical regions until puberty (Huttenlocher 1990). Regressive events begin prenatally with the death of excess neurons, which continues until about the age of two. The pruning of excess synapses and axon collaterals begins postnatally and continues throughout childhood and adolescence (Changeux and Konishi 1987; Cowan et al. 1984; Purves 1988; Rakic 1979).

Developmental changes in cerebral functioning can be studied more directly with PET imaging techniques that measure the rate of cerebral glucose metabolism. The developmental course of the PET data is consistent with neurobiological and microscopic evidence. Cortical metabolic values of newborn babies are 30 percent lower than those of adults, then increase to exceed adult values by the age of two to three years, presumably reflecting the increased metabolic activity necessary to support the many additional synaptic contacts. These PET values remain high until the age of about ten, then gradually decline until they reach adult levels around the age of sixteen to eighteen (Chugani and Phelps 1990).

Regressive events are thought to be the result of competitive interactions between neurons or their processes for some required resource (e.g., a nutritional factor that is necessary for the health of the cell, or electrical stimulation) that is in limited supply (Purves 1988). When a neuron or its processes are deprived of this resource, the size of the axonal and dendritic arbors is reduced, processes are withdrawn from the region of competition, or the cell degenerates (Changeux and Danchin 1976; Rakic 1986). Through a process of competitive elimination, selective rather than random connections are lost, producing functionally segregated cortical areas. For example, Rakic (1986) has shown that ocular dominance columns in the LGN, which are groups of cells that selectively respond to one eye or the other, are primarily formed by the pruning of axon collaterals from the inappropriate eye.

Early in development there are critical time periods for the establishment of certain behavioral functions. The neural substrates of these behavioral functions develop only if the nervous system receives certain environmental inputs during the critical period. Environmental deprivation can produce profound and permanent impairments, and environmental variation can produce variation in neural development. Critical periods have been demonstrated for a wide variety of behaviors, and in some cases the associated developments in the nervous system have been identified. In the visual system closing one eye during the first few months of life results in more neurons in layer IV of the primary visual cortex being devoted to sensory input from the open eye. The number of layer IV neurons that still can respond to input from the closed eye is correspondingly reduced by 80 percent, thus producing permanent visual damage in that eye (Hubel and Wiesel 1977).

Experiments with white-crowned sparrows and other songbirds have demonstrated that these birds have an innate capacity to develop a basic song pattern specific to their species, but only during the first few months of life (Konishi 1985; Nottebohm 1970). Although the neural correlates have not been identified, an analogous development occurs in human speech. At the age of eight months infants are able to hear the difference between two speech sounds from a foreign language that they have never heard before and that their caretakers cannot distinguish; however, by twelve months of age they lose this ability and can discriminate only speech contrasts from their native language (Werker et al. 1981).

Critical periods for behavioral development correspond to periods during which neural differentiation is occurring in those parts of cortex involved in the behavior. The increase in synaptic density appears to provide a degree of plasticity or flexibility for the formation of behavioral functions. So, for example, because synaptic density continues to remain high in the visual system up to the age of four years, the visual condition known as strabismus (in which the visual axis of one eye tends to deviate from the correct line of sight) can be treated during this period by occluding the sight of the good eye and forcing the use of the squinting eye (Assaf 1982). Presumably a functional plasticity associated with the use of the frontal cortex would persist longer, since synaptic reduction does not begin in this region until about the age of seven.

The plasticity gained from synaptic overproduction also appears to provide the brain some reserve capacity to recover from damage. Many studies have shown age to be a very important factor in successful recovery. In young children, for example, language impairments produced by brain injury are brief, and normal functioning is usually restored when the injury occurs before the age of five, although the severity and location of the injury can impede recovery (Aram, Ekelman, and Gillespie 1990; Kolb and Whishaw 1990).

Since the damaged tissue cannot regenerate itself, linguistic function must have been assimilated into other parts of cortex. The most striking evidence for this conclusion comes from case studies of hemidecorticate patients, who had one cortical hemisphere removed a few weeks after birth because of a rare disease that left only one hemisphere normal and healthy. Since language functions are localized to the left hemisphere in most people, follow-up studies were remarkable in that many linguistic functions were normal in the patients who had their left hemisphere removed (Dennis and Whitaker 1976). A similar recovery would not occur from a hemispherectomy in adulthood. Although the right hemisphere was not able to process some linguistic tasks well (for example, distinguishing the difference between "the man's lost wallet" and "the lost man's wallet"), patients performed normally on most of the tasks given, including all of the academic tests.

7.3 Neural Representation

The study of the biological properties of the synapse and neuron is an important enterprise, but it cannot by itself tell us how the nervous system represents and transforms meaningful information. To understand how representations and computations are encoded neurally, we must study the properties of interconnected networks of neurons as well. For the cognitive scientist, the study of neural representation and computation is the most exciting, and challenging, frontier of neuroscience.

Structural Principles

Higher cognitive abilities, such as memory consolidation or visual perception, are often associated with large anatomical regions such as the hippocampus or occipital lobe. These regions can be broken down into smaller and smaller structural components, ranging from somewhat smaller anatomically identifiable cortical regions to neural circuits to particular types of neurons or synapses. A full understanding of how the brain achieves some cognitive ability requires understanding the computational functions contributed by each level of structure. For example, the hippocampus can be divided structurally into the dentate gyrus, CA3, and CA1 regions, and different aspects of memory function can be ascribed to these substructures. Rolls (1990) has hypothesized that CA3 serves as an autoassociation system to retrieve the memory of specific autobiographical episodes. Enough is known about the neuroanatomy of CA3 and the response properties of the different types of neurons contained in it that Rolls was able to develop a network model that exhibits some of the required computational properties and is faithful to certain aspects of the neuronal data. Our understanding of the neural implementation of various functions is typically incomplete and still unfolding. Nevertheless, several organizational principles in the nervous system have been well demonstrated. We will touch on a few here; for a more complete discussion, consult some of the readings listed at the end of the chapter.

Experimental Techniques   Charting the structural and functional components of the brain has not been easy. Research has relied heavily on three procedures. The first technique involves destroying selected neurons and then studying what other parts of the brain show degeneration as a result of the damage. By tracing the path of degeneration, neuroanatomists hope to discover functional pathways between brain regions. The problem with lesion procedures has been the inability to localize damage to specific cells. Fibers from other cells that may just be passing through the target region also may be destroyed, resulting in their degeneration as well. The recent discovery of acids that selectively destroy neurons with somas in a specific region and not fibers of passage has revived interest in this procedure.

The second technique, which was mentioned earlier in this chapter, involves the introduction of dyes that are taken up by the neural tissue to highlight particular cells or selected parts of them. In the last twenty years new staining procedures have advanced rapidly. One procedure, called *autoradiographic tracing*, uses the anterograde transport system in neurons to determine where a cell's axon terminates. Amino acids are labeled with tritium and injected into the targeted brain site. These acids are taken up by neurons, converted to proteins, and transported down their axons to the synaptic terminal. Sometimes the labeled chemicals are transported to the postsynaptic cells. This transportation takes a few days, after which the animal is killed, and the brain tissue is sliced and prepared in a way that highlights the tritium-stained cells in a photograph. Another procedure uses retrograde tracing to map from synaptic connections back up to the cells from which the axons originate. The most common technique uses horseradish peroxidase (HRP), an enzyme found in horseradish and other plants, which is taken up by the synaptic terminals and transported back up the axon to the cell body. Double labeling, using both techniques, provides a much more precise description of neural pathways than has been possible with older staining or lesion procedures. New techniques for labeling neurotransmitters also have been invented to identify precisely the neurochemical pathways of the brain. Most recently, optical dyes, sensitive to electrical changes or fluctuations in ion concentrations, have been developed that are taken up by synaptically active cells, providing the potential to identify functional neural pathways operating under relatively normal conditions (Grinvald et al. 1986).

A third technique involves recording the electrical activity of single cells. Extracellular recordings are made with microelectrodes, very sharp needles that can be inserted into the brain to monitor the changes in electrical potential of a single neuron. Intracellular recordings are made by micropipettes, very tiny glass tubes that can be inserted into the cell body of a neuron. Although intracellular recordings can only be made for a few minutes, microelectrodes can record for long periods. Using these techniques, neuroscientists have been able to measure the responses of individual neurons to external sensory stimuli. Individual neurons have been shown to increase (or decrease) their firing rates in response to specific features of sensory input, such as the angle of orientation of a visual line display, its direction of movement, or its color (Hubel 1988). However, many neurons that are several synapses beyond primary sensory input do not respond to any simple stimulus characteristic but may be part of an assembly of cells that performs a particular computational function necessary for perception, movement, or thought. Many such neurons receive inputs from multiple sources, suggesting a coordination or integration role. Functions studied at these higher levels include the recognition of complex stimuli, such as faces (Perrett, Mistlin, and Chitty 1987) or the coordination of motor movements for reaching and locomotion (Georgopoulos and Grillner 1989). For a further discussion of these issues, see the section below on computational maps.

Functional Pathways   Many different pathways have been discovered in the CNS that carry sensory and motor information. One of the first discoveries was made in 1822 by François Magendie. He reported that the dorsal root of the spinal cord carried sensory information from the peripheral to the central nervous system, but that the ventral root transported motor output to the muscles. This discovery established the principle that different parts of the CNS could be specialized for different functions and that functional pathways could exist to carry specific information.

We know most about the sensory input and motor output systems. Our bodies have five exteroceptive sensory systems, which perceive stimuli from outside the body: vision, touch, hearing, olfaction (smell), and taste. All five sensory systems appear to be organized in a similar fashion. In the classical model, sensory systems are hypothesized to be organized hierarchically, with each major receptor organ passing sensory information along a pathway to the thalamus, which then relays the input to the cortex. Each sensory system has a special part of the thalamus devoted to processing its input. For example, visual information from the retina of the eye is carried to the LGN of the thalamus. The cortex also has primary sensory regions, devoted to sensory input (see figure 7.3). Information is passed from the primary cortex to secondary sensory regions and then to the association cortex, where information from different sensory modalities is integrated. In the simplest model a single stream of information follows a sequential progression, moving from receptors to higher brain regions, gradually being transformed from raw sensory data into perceptual representations. Each level of the system analyzes the information available at that stage and then passes its analysis on to the next level (see figure 7.10).

A hierarchical model of this kind was once proposed for the visual system (Hubel and Wiesel 1977). The model accounts for considerable neurophysiological data. First, there are light-sensitive receptor cells in the retina that signal the intensity of the light at a particular point in the incoming image. The retina's output neurons (called ganglion cells), however, respond to intensity *changes* in small regions of the image. This shift from signaling intensity at a point to signaling local contrast can be seen as the

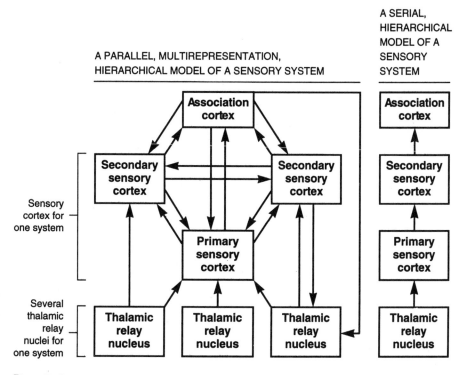

Figure 7.10
Two different models of sensory processing. (Adapted from Pinel 1990.)

first step in a process of object recognition. The regions of local contrast in the image can be seen as early information about the edges or contours of objects. The contrast signals are relayed through the LGN, and the next step in the hierarchy is accomplished by cells in the primary visual cortex (called *simple cells*) that detect contrast boundaries at specific angular orientations in small regions of the image. These *edge* and *line detectors* can be seen as organizing the local, unoriented contrast information coming from the retina into small, oriented segments of the boundaries of objects in the image. Further steps in the process would be associated with other cells in the visual cortex that respond to the presence of an oriented boundary over a larger region of the image (*complex cells*) or that respond to corners or terminated lines (*hypercomplex cells*). Eventually the construction process was hypothesized to reach cells in the medial-temporal region that are specialized to respond to complex shapes, such as a hand or face (Desimone and Gross 1979) or perhaps even specifically to the face of one's grandmother (Barlow 1972).

Although the early evidence on the response properties of neurons in the visual system was consistent with this classical model of a single hierarchical visual pathway, recent evidence has suggested that the system is organized into a number of parallel pathways (see figure 7.10). Information about shape, color, motion, and binocular disparity appears to be processed in distinct parallel channels (Hubel 1988). The parallelism is already present in the ganglion cells. In the primate retina there are two types of ganglion cells, which can be distinguished by the sizes of their cell bodies, the shapes of their dendritic trees, and their response properties. Although the small cells (P-cells) and large cells (M-cells) are intermixed in the retina, their axons project to distinct layers of the LGN. The P-cells project to the *parvocellular* layers and the M-cells to the *magnocellular* layers of the LGN. The separation between the two pathways is maintained, and they are further subdivided, as visual analysis develops in the visual areas of the cortex (Livingstone and Hubel 1987). Computation in the visual system is still thought to be hierarchical in the sense that later stages of the system deliver more reliable and meaningful information about the visual world in comparison with earlier stages, whose outputs code local properties of the visual image that are often not reliably correlated with properties of the visual world (see chapter 12). For example, early stages of the color pathway cannot represent the surface color of an object independently of the color of illuminating light, whereas later stages of the pathway can.

Not much is known about how increasingly meaningful information is developed in the parallel channels of the primate visual system or about how the information is integrated to produce visually guided behavior and object recognition. However, detailed studies of the neural substrates of two perceptually driven behaviors, the sound localization response of the barn owl and the jamming avoidance response of the electric fish (Konishi 1991), have shown that it is possible to analyze a sensory pathway in detail. In both cases the sensory analysis is carried out in two separate parallel channels, which eventually converge on the neurons that code for the critical property.

The analysis of the barn owl begins with the observation that when the owl hears a sound, it turns its head in the direction of the sound source. This head orientation is accurate in both the horizontal (azimuth) and vertical (elevation) directions. Thus, if the source of a sound is 30 degrees to the left and 15 degrees above the axis of the current head orientation, the owl will turn its head upward and to the left the appropriate amounts. By playing experimentally controlled sounds through earphones, researchers were able to show that the horizontal and vertical components of the orientation response are controlled by two different aspects of the sound. Horizontal localization is based on interaural time differences. Because the owl's ears are separated horizontally in space, a sound in the environment is delivered to the two ears in slightly different ways. Consider a 100-hertz (cycles per second) sound that originates to the left of the owl. The sound will reach the left ear slightly before it reaches the right ear. Another difference arises from the fact that the sound oscillates sinusoidally with time. The sine wave for a 100-hertz tone reaches its peak energy value 100 times per second. Each energy peak will reach the left ear slightly before it reaches the right ear. The sine waves at the two ears are said to be *out of phase* with each other. Complex sounds are mixtures of many frequency (or pitch) components. The experiments showed that the owl uses the phase differences at all audible frequencies rather than the initial difference in onset time for horizontal localization.

Because the owl's right ear is angled slightly upward and the left ear is angled downward, differences in the properties of a sound as it arrives at the two ears can also be used to determine the sound's elevation. The behavioral experiments showed that intensity (or *amplitude*) differences between the two ears were used in this case. A sound that is above the owl is slightly louder in the right ear than in the left and vice versa. As a result of the behavioral studies researchers knew that the auditory system must extract a combination of interaural time and amplitude differences from the incoming sound. This combination specifies the horizontal and vertical values of the sound and hence its direction in space. A code for the combination must be passed on to the visual and motor systems, since the owl turns its head toward sounds in its environment and tries to visually locate the source of the sound.

Konishi and his colleagues (Konishi 1991) were able to locate *space-specific* neurons in the exterior nucleus of the inferior colliculus, a midbrain structure that is part of the auditory system. Single-cell recordings showed that each space-specific neuron fired when a sound occurred in a particular spatial direction. Using experimentally controlled sounds delivered through earphones, the researchers were able to show that the neurons were in fact selective for combinations of interaural time and amplitude differences. The space-specific neurons appear to be the output neurons for the sound localization computation. They directly encode the information that triggers sound localization behavior. Anatomically, they are at the top of the owl's auditory pathway, and their axons project to the optic tectum, a midbrain structure involved in vision containing neurons that respond to both auditory and visual inputs. Electrical stimulation of these auditory-visual neurons causes quick head movements of the kind that are also induced by sound.

The neural circuitry leading up to the space-specific neurons is sketched in figure 7.11. The initial transduction of sound is accomplished by receptor cells in the *cochlea*, a structure in the inner ear. Receptor cells fire in response to particular frequencies. Their rate of firing is correlated with the intensity of the incoming sound, and they tend to fire in phase with the incoming sound. Thus, frequency, amplitude, and phase information are all available at the receptor level. Further amplitude and phase processing, however, occurs in two separate, parallel pathways. The output of each cochlea projects to both a magnocellular nucleus and an angular nucleus. Magnocellular nucleus neurons tend to fire in phase with a particular frequency component of the sound in the source ear. Their responses are *phase-locked* with the incoming stimulus.

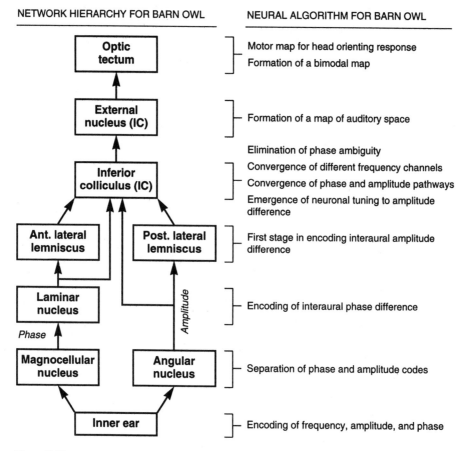

NETWORK HIERARCHY FOR BARN OWL

NEURAL ALGORITHM FOR BARN OWL

Optic tectum — Motor map for head orienting response
Formation of a bimodal map

External nucleus (IC) — Formation of a map of auditory space

Inferior colliculus (IC) —
Elimination of phase ambiguity
Convergence of different frequency channels
Convergence of phase and amplitude pathways
Emergence of neuronal tuning to amplitude difference

Ant. lateral lemniscus

Post. lateral lemniscus — First stage in encoding interaural amplitude difference

Laminar nucleus — Encoding of interaural phase difference

Phase

Amplitude

Magnocellular nucleus

Angular nucleus — Separation of phase and amplitude codes

Inner ear — Encoding of frequency, amplitude, and phase

Figure 7.11
An anatomical and functional mapping of the auditory system of the barn owl. (From Konishi 1991.)

These neurons are not sensitive to variations in amplitude, however. In contrast, angular nucleus neurons fire more rapidly in response to higher amplitudes but are not sensitive to phase.

At the next stage in the phase-processing pathway, the phase-locked signals from the two ears are combined in the laminar nuclei. Laminar neurons respond to particular interaural phase *differences* at particular frequencies. At further stations shown in figure 7.11 the phase signals are transformed into an unambiguous code for interaural time differences by removing frequency dependence and some ambiguities in the phase signals. Interaural differences in amplitude are first encoded at a nucleus in the posterior lateral lemniscal nuclei and are rendered unambiguous by the processing at further stages. The two pathways converge in the inferior colliculus with neuronal selectivity for specific spatial directions finally emerging in the exterior nucleus of the inferior colliculus.

Sound localization in the barn owl provides a relatively simple, concrete illustration of the simultaneous parallel and hierarchical organization of sensory pathways. Although this pathway extends from a sensory organ to various nuclei in the brain stem rather than from thalamus to cortex, the architectures depicted in figures 7.10 and 7.11 are similar. The hierarchical nature of the sound localization pathway is very clear. Computationally, the representations at higher levels in the pathway represent behaviorally relevant information more explicitly and unambiguously than the representations at lower levels. Neurons at the top of the hierarchy encode the behaviorally relevant property of spatial direction. Neurons somewhat lower in the hierarchy encode two independent dimensions of spatial direction. Neurons that are still lower in the hierarchy encode stimulus properties that are useful inputs to the computation of the two dimensions, and so on. Anatomically, it is possible to trace the forward-feeding connections among cell populations that are responsible for the levels of representation. In some cases the detailed circuitry of the connections helps explain how a higher-level representation is computed from a lower-level one. For example, the axonal projections from the magnocellular nuclei to the laminar nuclei appear to be organized as delay lines, which allow phase-locked signals that originate at different times at the two ears to arrive simultaneously at laminar neurons.

Sound localization in the barn owl also illustrates other principles of neural coding. One principle is that of *place-coding*. Nervous systems often dedicate specific neurons to the representation of a given type of information. The location of a neuron at a particular place in the neural circuitry and its interconnection with other neurons determine its computational role. A simple example is provided by the fact that cells in the occipital cortex are devoted to vision, whereas cells in the postcentral gyrus are devoted to sensations from the body surface. At a finer grain neurons in a particular region of the visual cortex correspond to a particular region of the retina, and neurons in a particular region of the somatosensory cortex correspond to a particular region of the body surface. In the barn owl we see more subtle examples of this principle. Groups of neurons are dedicated to the representation of more abstract properties, such as monaural phase, monaural amplitude, interaural time differences, interaural amplitude differences, and direction in auditory space. The significance of place-coding is brought out further in the sections below on cortical columns and maps.

In addition to its place in a neural network, a neuron's computational role hinges on details of its moment-to-moment behavior. In the angular nucleus of the barn owl, for example, the amplitude of a sound at a particular frequency is encoded by the rate at which frequency-selective neurons fire. In the magnocellular nucleus, however, phase is encoded by timing action potentials to correspond to the phase of the stimulus. To see that the rate and timing of impulses represent two distinct coding strategies, recall that two neurons could be firing at the same rate but still be out of phase with each other. Rate and phase of firing are well-established bases for neural codes. Other time-varying properties of neuronal activation, such as the probability of firing during a brief interval, may be added to this short list. However, a point made about connectionist models in chapter 2 can be reiterated in a somewhat different form here. It is not thought that the timing of a train of neural impulses can encode arbitrarily complex information in the manner of a text being transmitted over a telegraph line via Morse code.

The study of sound localization in the barn owl is instructive as an example of a research program in computational neuroscience that has advanced to the point where evidence from a cognitive-level analysis of a behavior has converged with evidence from neurophysiology and neuroanatomy to favor a rather detailed model. This is the kind of convergence that we can look forward to in the study of the cognitive capacities of humans and other primates, but for the most part it is a goal rather than a reality. In judging the current state of cognitive neuroscience, it is a good model to keep in mind. However, the specifics of the example should not be overgeneralized. The single-neuron encoding and the parallel-hierarchical organization of the computation may or may not characterize other capacities in other organisms.

Columnar Organization   The primary cortex of all five sensory systems contains vertical columns of cells that tend to respond to the same kinds of sensory input. Each column receives input from the same general area in the peripheral sensory organ, thus encoding the location of sensory input. In the visual system this means that adjacent columns of cells in the occipital lobe correspond to overlapping parts of the visual field. Microcolumns also have been discovered inside the larger place-columns (Hubel 1988). These substructures organize information into left- and right-eye input as well as columns that show a preference for contrast boundaries of particular orientations (see figure 12.10).

Topographic Maps   Because spatial relationships between cortical columns correspond to the spatial organization found between adjacent neurons in the sensory organs, primary sensory cortical areas provide detailed representations of sensory input patterns, which are called *topographic maps*. Such maps have been found in the visual, somatosensory, and auditory cortices, but gustatory and olfactory maps have not yet been discovered (however, see Skarda and Freeman 1987 for a discussion of olfactory representation). Each map displays systematic variation for a particular stimulus attribute. In the visual and somatosensory systems, the mappings correspond to the two-dimensional topography of the retina (retinotopic) and body surface (somatotopic), respectively. The primary auditory cortex is mapped tonotopically, with the anterior portion responding to high-frequency tones and posterior regions responding to progressively lower frequencies.

These cortical maps maintain a correspondence with peripheral sensory neurons, so that higher concentrations of sensory cells in one region will produce a central map with more space devoted to that region. Consequently, cortical maps of the hands and face, which have many more sensory neurons than the feet, can appear quite distorted in relation to the size of the body part (see figure 7.12).

Multiple cortical maps appear to exist for each sensory modality in their respective cortical regions. Many retinotopic maps, for example, have been discovered on the cortex of nonhuman primates; the macaque monkey has roughly twenty different visual maps, which are interconnected by over eighty pathways. These maps represent different stimulus attributes, such as the orientation of contrast borders or the direction of movement of visual objects (Swindale, Cynader, and Matsubara 1990). Maps also may perform different computations on the same attribute, or facilitate the speed with which certain computations are performed (Dudai 1989). As researchers learn to tune their experiments to the proper attributes, many more maps probably will be discovered.

Substantial experimental evidence suggests that cortical maps can change with experience and even vary between individuals (Merzenich 1987; Pons, Garraghty, and Mishkin 1988). Merzenich and his colleagues have demonstrated these changes in a most striking way. Through the use of multiple microelectrodes they recorded from different regions in the somatosensory cortex of an owl monkey while stimulating the surface of the monkey's hand and digits. In this way they were able to map the

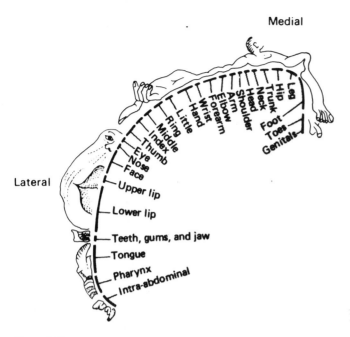

Figure 7.12
Illustration of the primary somatosensory regions corresponding to different parts of the body (From Kandel and Schwartz 1985.)

monkey's hand and digits onto the somatosensory cortex (see figure 7.13). The monkey then received an hour and a half of daily training in which it rotated a disk with its second, third, and occasionally fourth digits in order to receive a food reward. After twenty weeks of training, the researchers remapped the cortex and discovered that the cortical representation of the used digits had markedly expanded. These results suggest a plasticity or ability of the cortex to adapt to experience that previously had not been thought possible.

Cortical maps also vary among individuals. Thirty-five years ago Woolsey (1960) proposed a theory that the auditory cortex was tonotopically organized, with high-frequency tones more anterior than low-frequency tones. Early attempts to test Woolsey's theory suggested he was wrong. When researchers recorded from neurons in a specific region of auditory cortex, they found that cells in different animals responded to a wide range of frequencies rather than to the same frequency, as Woolsey had suggested. When experimental procedures improved, allowing more cells to be recorded from one animal, researchers discovered that different cells from the same region responded to similar frequencies in an individual animal, thus supporting the tonotopic theory (Merzenich, Knight, and Roth 1974). They also found that the part of the auditory cortex that responded to a given frequency varied from one animal to another.

The lesson from this research is clear. Topographical mapping is an important organizing principle that is consistently followed in all sensory modalities studied so far. However, the spatial organization of cortical maps changes with experience, and individual differences are likely to be considerable.

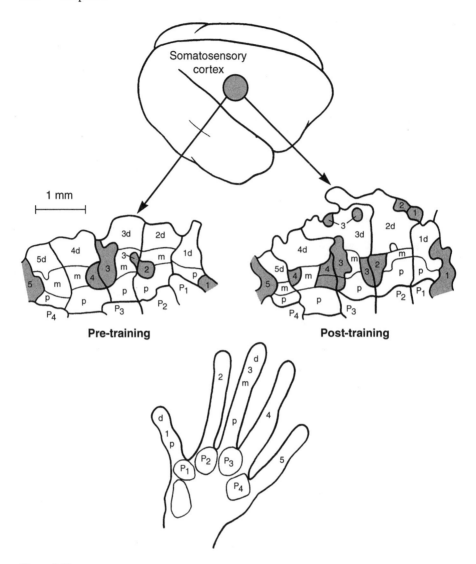

Figure 7.13
A topographical map of the somatosensory cortex of an adult owl monkey's hand. The hand surface of a normal monkey is coded in the bottom figure. Each digit is numbered (thumb = 1); d = distal, m = middle, p = proximal parts of the digits; P1–P4 = the palmar pads at the base of the digits. The surface of the hand is represented in a cortical map in the somatosensory cortex, illustrated in the middle figures. On the left is the cortical map before training. Each cortical area has neurons that respond to touch in the corresponding region of the hand. The gray areas are the dorsal surface of each digit. The right figure shows the same cortical region of the same animal after training. Over twenty weeks, monkeys were trained for one and one-half hours each day to use the distal parts of digits 2 and 3. Notice the increased size of the cortical areas that responded to tactile stimulation in digits 2 and 3. (Adapted from Jenkins and Merzenich 1987.)

Computational Maps   The cortex also contains *computational maps* that do not correspond to the topography of sensory neurons. These maps represent more abstract information that figures in cognition or behavior. We saw above, for example, that the barn owl's inferior colliculus (a subcortical structure) contains neurons that code for particular spatial directions. The neurons are arranged in an orderly map, in which neighboring neurons respond to neighboring directions and in which changes in azimuth and elevation are defined along roughly perpendicular axes (Konishi 1986). For echolocation the mustached bat emits a complex spectrum of sounds and then listens to the echoes that return from targets (biosonar). Suga's research (1990) has revealed a central auditory system that not only encodes the frequency, amplitude, and time delay of the echoes but also contains computational maps for target velocity and range.

Maps can also encode combinations of two or more types of information. Topographical information can combine with computed information, within or across sensory modalities (Dudai 1989). In the barn owl we saw that the axons of the space-specific neurons in the inferior colliculus project to the optic tectum, which contains a visual-auditory map of space that responds to both auditory and visual input and that triggers head movements. Swindale and his colleagues (1990) provide an interesting description of how visual orientation and direction maps interact to maintain continuity and completeness in our cortical representations of visual scenes.

Distributed versus Single-cell Representations

We saw in chapter 2 that an issue of single-unit versus distributed coding arises in connectionist modeling. Connectionist models, of course, are typically not specified in any detail at the neural level of analysis. For example, in a network with single-unit coding, each unit might be implemented at the neural level by many neurons in a distributed manner. Nevertheless, we can imagine taking single-unit coding all the way down to the neural level, using single neurons to encode features, concepts, propositions, or schemas. In this case the standard apocryphal example of the grandmother unit would be a single neuron that fired if and only if you were thinking of your grandmother—the so-called grandmother cell. Just as in a connectionist net, such a cell would have to be connected to many other cells, involved in processing visual input, kinship concepts, and so on; nevertheless, activity in this cell would be a necessary and sufficient condition for grandmother cognition.

It is sometimes thought that single-cell coding is unreliable and therefore would be selected against during evolution. Imagine losing your concept of your grandmother when the single cell that encodes her dies randomly as you struggle through the last mile of a marathon. Evolution could guard against this possibility, however, by providing multiple copies of each coding unit. Thus, there might be ten copies of your grandmother cell and a miniscule probability that more than one or two of them would die off in a lifetime, barring a major brain injury or disease. In such a brain, there would be single-unit coding that is resistant to damage.

A theory of single-cell representation is initially attractive conceptually because it is easy to understand how items of information are represented and easy to understand the functional role of the individual neuron in cognition. The theory is also initially attractive methodologically. Since we know how to record the activity of single neurons, we can immediately start looking in experimental animals for neurons whose activity is uniquely correlated with, say, the recognition of some particular object. This strategy is not so easily implemented, however. For example, to show that a cell is a grandmother cell, we would at least have to show that it fires vigorously to grandmother and not to anything else. But, confronted with a neuron that is fairly well removed from the sensory-motor periphery, we might have to test thousands of objects to find one that it prefers, and if we hit upon a preferred object, we might have to test thousands more to show that the cell does *not* fire to each of those. Further, if we found that the cell responded to some degree to other objects (though not as strongly as to grandmother), we simply would not be able to conclude that the cell does not play a role in the representation of nongrandmothers. So, there is no simple empirical method to test for single-cell representations. We cannot easily confirm or disconfirm the existence of such representations by just wandering through the cortex and testing the response properties of individual neurons. We need a more complete theory of neural representation that makes testable predictions about the anatomy of and the course of processing in entire neural pathways or networks.

Distributed neural encoding is somewhat harder to imagine, but, as we saw in chapter 2, the initial conceptual hurdles are cleared by connectionist models that successfully employ distributed codes in networks of neuronlike units. To repeat, there is no assumption in these models that individual units correspond to single cells at the neural level of analysis, but the models demonstrate that distributed coding is a viable possibility in the brain. Cognition of the proverbial grandmother might now be represented by a distinctive pattern of activity over a population of neurons, all of which are also involved in encoding other concepts. Following the lead of connectionist networks in which knowledge of each piece of information is encoded in the pattern of weights across *all* of the units in the net, we can imagine an extreme case in which knowledge of grandmother (and all other concepts) is encoded in synaptic patterns across all of the trillion or so cells in the cerebral cortex. Currently, this possibility is not being actively pursued by researchers, because, as we have seen, there is abundant evidence that the brain is highly organized structurally. It is unlikely, for example, that the visual recognition of your grandmother involves patterns of activation across the entire primary motor cortex. It is more likely that distributed codes are restricted to functional regions of the brain, such as the cortical maps just discussed.

Like single-cell representations, distributed codes cannot be found through simple fishing expeditions in the brain. Even with the best techniques for simultaneously recording from more than one neuron, for example, it might be difficult to record from enough of the neurons involved in a distributed code to figure out how the code works. If a particular distributed representation depends on only a fraction of the cells in some cortical region, it might also be difficult to find many of those cells. Worse, the fact that a certain profile of activity occurs in a number of cells under some conditions and not in others does not by itself demonstrate that distributed coding is involved. After all, in a network with single-unit coding all of the cells will have some level of activity all of the time, and the profile of activity in some group of cells might well be similar under similar circumstances. For example, activity in the cell that encodes grandmother cognition might well be accompanied by strong activity in the cells that encode gray-hair cognition and twinkling-eye cognition, weak activity in the cell that encodes beard cognition, and middling activity in the cell that encodes a particular nose shape that sort of matches grandmother's. As in the case of single-unit coding, what is required is a detailed theory and data about anatomical structure and patterns of activity at more than one level in a pathway.

Both local and distributed coding are known to occur in nervous systems. In the barn owl, for example, individual space-specific neurons at the top of the auditory pathway code for particular directions. At lower levels in the hierarchy, however, the coding of spatial direction is distributed between the amplitude and phase pathways. At the inner ear the information about the direction of the auditory stimulus is distributed across virtually all of the receptors in the two ears. Generally, distributed coding is a necessity toward the periphery of sensory systems for at least two reasons. First, cognitively or behaviorally significant information in the stimulus has to be extracted from a multiplicity of often ambiguous cues in the input. For example, single units for sound direction could not exist in or near the inner ear of the barn owl because information from the two ears has to be compared to establish direction. Or, just as obviously, there could not be grandmother detectors on the retina, because when grandmother is in view the information about her is distributed across a fairly large area of the retinal image and therefore across many receptor cells. To recognize grandmother, the outputs of these cells must be combined, and the relevant information coming from them (e.g., hair color) must be separated from the irrelevant (e.g., level of illumination). Second, it is often physically impossible to use single units to encode information that is meaningful and locally available at the periphery. The wavelength of the light at a particular spot on the retinal image is a case in point. Hundreds or thousands of units, each selective for a particular wavelength, could not be packed into each point on the retina. Instead, sensitivity to variations in wavelength is accomplished by just three types of receptors.

The retinal cones are an example of *coarse coding* in the nervous system. Each type of cone responds across a broad region of the visible spectrum. The medium wavelength ("green") cones, for example, have a peak sensitivity around 530 nanometers, but their sensitivity falls off rather gradually around this peak. Because of their broad tuning, the green cones do not represent any particular wavelength. Further, their output is a joint function of their sensitivity and the intensity of the incoming light. Their response to an intense light at, say, 500 nanometers can be stronger than their response to a dim light at 530 nanometers. The result of this trade-off between wavelength and intensity is that a single type of receptor cannot encode wavelength (and therefore color) information at all. However, the combination of the responses of the three broadly tuned cone types (each with a different peak sensitivity) does encode wavelength information. This combination constitutes a distributed code, which can be represented as a vector of three numbers or a point in a three-dimensional space. Even though none of the cone types has the ability to encode wavelength information by itself, the combination gives us the ability to perceive many thousands of colors. Generally, the profile of responses from a population of coarsely tuned units can specify a value with great precision.

The ability of neural systems to develop codes that are more precise than the resolving power of the individual input neurons is known as *hyperacuity*. In addition to color vision, the visual system exhibits a number of other hyperacuities. For example, people can make spatial discriminations involving distances that are smaller than the distance between adjacent receptor cells on the retina. Bats can discriminate distances as small as 1.0 to 1.5 centimeters using the time delays between the return of their echoes (Suga 1990). The discrimination requires a sensitivity to time differences in the range of 0.06 to 0.09 milliseconds, but the sensitivity of individual auditory neurons is only 0.13 milliseconds. A fertile hypothesis is that distributed coarse codes are a general strategy for achieving hyperacuities (Baldi and Heiligenberg 1988). The research of Georgopoulos and his colleagues (1986) illustrates one approach to pursuing this hypothesis. They recorded the activity of cells in the motor cortex after training monkeys to reach for different spatial locations. Most of the cells showed a response preference for a particular direction of movement, but they were broadly tuned to a range of directions. The response curves of different cells also overlapped considerably. It was impossible to predict the actual direction of movement from the activity of any single neuron. However, the average response of the entire cell population predicted the exact direction of arm movement. Similar results have been obtained for other motor (Schor, Miller, and Tomko 1984) and visual (Steinmetz et al. 1987) behavior.

In the case of arm movement (as well as some other motor behaviors) the response of a cell population represents its overall average response. It is possible that at a higher level of representation the average is represented by finely tuned direction-specific neurons. In other cases, taking the average response over the population would destroy the information it encodes. For example, averaging the responses of the three retinal cone types would produce a single broadly tuned response curve similar to that of each of the individual cones, with no capacity to encode wavelength information. In these cases any higher-order grandmother units would have to capture properties of the profile of responses over the population. Alternatively, vectors of activation can be mapped directly onto other vectors with no intervening local code.

The hypothesis that distributed coding is employed very widely by the nervous system currently guides a great deal of work in computational neuroscience (Churchland and Sejnowski 1992). The hypothesis is supported by the known cases of distributed coding and by the finding that neurons in sensory and motor cortical areas tend to be broadly tuned. It is also supported by the necessity that even where local coding holds at the top of a processing hierarchy, there must be distributed coding at lower levels. Where there is a grandmother cell, there must be distributed information about grandmother below the level of that cell. The hypothesis is also fueled by the theoretical arguments for distributed coding that have emerged from connectionist research (Hinton, McClelland, and Rumelhart 1986, and chapter 2). With distributed coding, similar objects or concepts have similar codes, sharing many elements or having similar values on many features. The system can respond to a novel input vector by exploiting its correlations with familiar vectors. It can map incomplete or noisy inputs to decent outputs. The high-dimensional spaces created by distributed representations contain plenty of room for encoding vast numbers of objects or concepts and their variants, produced by different points of view or different interpretations. Adjustable weights allow distributed systems to learn complex mappings from experience. Such systems continue to respond reasonably even when their connections and weights have sustained significant damage. These properties, which seem to be properties of nervous systems, are a natural consequence of distributed coding, and it is often argued that it is not clear how to achieve them in systems that rely extensively on local coding. The strongest form of the theoretical argument is that distributed codes should be maintained throughout a system, mapping vectors onto vectors, without passing through stages of local coding. Much of the evidence is consistent with this view, but it is consistent as well with a view that gives a strong role to local coding at higher levels of representation, which also has its theoretical proponents (Trehub 1991). The general debate about strategies of neural coding and computation can only be settled by detailed models and empirical evidence.

Innate or Learned Representations

Philosophers and scientists have proposed conflicting views on exactly how representations are formed in a developing nervous system. In general terms the empiricist position argues that neural representations are a reflection of environmental stimulation. Neural circuits are programmed as if the brain were a blank slate to be written on by experience. The opposing nativist position hypothesizes that representations are innate and biologically "hardwired." Neural circuits are already in place to subserve specialized functions, and the "right" kind of sensory input triggers the activation of such prewired circuits.

Neurodevelopmental and genetic considerations suggest that both positions have merit. The major neural pathways and structures are very similar in all mammals, suggesting a high degree of genetic hardwiring to guide the design. Members of the same species produce nearly identical neural circuits during the early stages of neural development. However, Changeux (1985) has pointed out that genes are not likely to be responsible for the diversity and specificity of all synaptic connections. Studies of the eye in a simple organism such as the water flea reveal that the number of sensory neurons and the number of ganglion cells with which they make contact are the same for insects that are cloned and thus genetically identical; but the number of synapses between these cells and the shape of their axonal branches vary from one clone to another (Macagno, Lopresti, and Levinthal 1973). When we consider the more complicated nervous system of mammals, the variability is only likely to increase.

Considerable research has documented environmental influences on brain development. Animal experiments have shown that enriched environments increase the size of the cortex, the density of glial cells, and the density and number of synaptic connections (Diamond 1984). Research with the visual system also has shown that sensory deprivation early in life can lead to severe abnormalities in visual cortical cells and produce blindness, but deprivation later in life does not produce ill effects (Kratz, Spear, and Smith 1976).

Acknowledging the influences of both genes and the environment, several neuroscientists have suggested the theory that learning proceeds from a "selective, Darwinistic mechanism" (Changeux 1985; Dudai 1989; Edelman 1987). The key idea is that the brain spontaneously produces what Changeux has called *prerepresentations*, which correspond to the transient but discrete electrochemical activity of an assembly of neurons. These autonomous patterns of activity are endogenous; that is, they exist apart from any sensory input. Inputs from sensory receptors and the cortical maps they project to create a *primary percept*. Percepts interact with prerepresentations of the brain to produce resonant states in which the prerepresentation is stabilized and a memory or *mental image* is formed. For resonance to occur, a certain degree of "match-up" has to exist between the percept and the prerepresentation; too much dissonance will interfere with learning. Resonance is produced when neurons fire in phase with one another, creating a temporally coupled volley of activity (Von der Malsburg and Willshaw 1981). This resonant pattern reinforces itself through a strengthening of synaptic connections between neurons in the assembly, thus "storing" the memory.

Mental representations are not the direct product of sensory input, nor are they hardwired into functional circuits by the genome. Rather, stable neural states are selected from among a variety of spontaneously generated neural activation patterns through an interaction with sensory input. The idea is that prerepresentations are genetically inherited, but only those endogenous activation patterns that prove to be functionally useful through experience are stabilized to form the mental structures of the mind. This stabilization process occurs during the critical period of neural development when some neural connections are stabilized into functioning circuits and other synaptic contacts regress. Presumably neural architecture can be influenced by evolution in the same way as other physical traits. Those prerepresentations that provide the right kind of raw material to form mental representations give the animal a selective advantage.

Although these ideas are likely to remain speculative for some time, they nevertheless have directed considerable interest to the level of cell assemblies. In the study of complex representations, most neuroscientists now recognize the need to monitor the activity of large assemblies of neurons, not just record the activity of single cells. Techniques to provide such functional mapping do not yet exist, although several new experimental procedures, such as optical dyes (Grinvald et al. 1986) or mapping brain activity using multiple electrodes (Abeles and Gerstein 1988), hold promise.

7.4 Neuropsychology

Theoretical and Methodological Considerations

The study of the neural substrates of higher cognitive functions, such as memory, language, or consciousness, is often referred to as *neuropsychology*. Traditionally, neuropsychologists have studied how cognitive functions are physically implemented by studying people or animals with damaged brains. Performance by a person with damage to a known area in the brain can be compared with performance by people with intact brains or damage to other areas. The differences in performance can be used to generate or test theories about the roles played by various areas of the brain in cognitive functioning. In recent years this line of research has been vigorously pursued as part of the framework of cognitive science for several reasons. First, neurological patients sometimes exhibit strikingly selective cognitive deficits, which suggest that some of the detailed representations and processes that have been hypothesized at the cognitive level of analysis are implemented in localized areas of the brain. Second, recent methodological advances in cognitive psychology have made possible much more detailed assessments of the cognitive impairments of neurological patients. Third, contemporary cognitive scientific theories have generated a host of new neuropsychological theories. The flowering of neuropsychological research within cognitive science has also been accelerated by the development of new methods for observing the working brain. Localized patterns of activity during cognition can now be observed in the intact or damaged brain using methods such as magnetic resonance imaging (MRI), positron emission tomography (PET), or the recording of event-related potentials (ERP). Although their spatial and temporal resolution is limited, these methods allow researchers to observe directly some of what must be inferred in the traditional method of correlating cognitive performance with the locations of brain lesions.

Traditional and much of contemporary neuropsychology is a top-down enterprise, in which theories from the cognitive level of analysis are brought to bear on neuropsychological data. Advances in our knowledge of neural circuitry and the growth of connectionist and neural network models are beginning to bring bottom-up considerations to the field, however. Neuropsychology researchers must now pay attention to relevant data about neural circuits, and they must consider network models in addition to more classical cognitive models, which are often couched at a higher level of analysis and employ highly structured representations and rules. Currently, there is lively debate within neuropsychology over the relative weight to be given to traditional cognitive models and their supporting data versus network models and neurobiological data. Many traditional cognitive models, of course, were not designed with any general theory of neural computation in mind, and the gross anatomical data about brain lesions traditionally associated with neuropsychology say little about the organization of neural circuits. Theorists who are oriented toward the reduction of cognitive models to neural models (Churchland 1986; Sejnowski 1986) tend to argue that all neuropsychological theories should be based at least in part on well-supported characteristics of neural computation and, where possible, microstructural neuroscientific data.

The detailed study of *acquired dyslexia* (the loss of reading skills through brain damage) represents one of the more successful examples of the top-down approach to neuropsychological research (Coltheart, Patterson, and Marshall 1987; Patterson, Marshall, and Coltheart 1985). Researchers have systematically analyzed the patterns of reading errors produced by dyslexic patients to gain insight into how the reading system is structured. The overall structure of a theoretical model resulting from this line of research can typically be represented as a flowchart, such as the one in figure 7.14. Each box in the chart represents a computational module, or component, that takes one or more representations as input and maps that input onto an output representation. The label in a box describes the output representation that is computed by that module. The arrows in the chart represent the flow of information among the modules. Figure 7.14 represents a model, proposed by Marshall and his colleagues (Marshall and Newcombe 1981), which contains two parallel information-processing routes for the reading of individual words. One route is based on sight vocabulary and is known as the *lexical* or *direct* route. The other route, called the *phonological* route, relies on regularities in the correspondence between spelling and sound and on the morphological and phonological structure of spoken language. This route can "sound out" a word in the absence of a direct processing route.

In the current model word recognition begins with an analysis of visual features to provide information for identifying letters or whole words. In the phonological route letters are grouped or parsed together into syllabic units, which are then coverted to the proper phonemes. This conversion process is based on rules or regularities acquired from spelling experience (Venezky 1970). The phonological outputs of the conversion process are then passed to a further process that blends them back together to produce the whole word. The early stages of development of the phonological route are evident when young readers sound out words. In the lexical route words also are parsed in the early stages to identify the base root of a word (e.g., *antiabortion* becomes *anti/abort/ion*). Then lexical memory is accessed to recall the meaning and proper pronunciation of the base and any prefixes and suffixes. The word parts are then resynthesized for proper pronunciation. The two routes are hypothesized to operate in

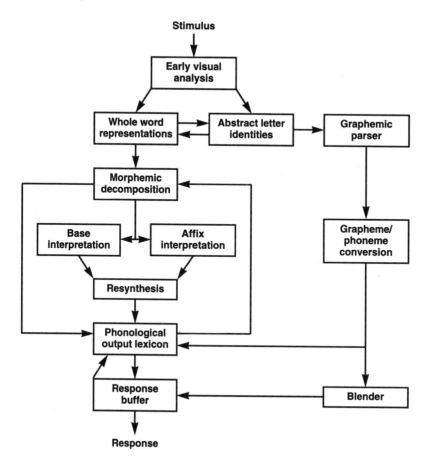

Figure 7.14
Symbolic model of reading

parallel so that whichever subsystem completes the word identification process first will control how the word is pronounced.

This model has had considerable success in accounting for the variable reading performance of acquired dyslexic patients. For example, patients with a condition called *phonological dyslexia* have difficulty pronouncing unfamiliar words, even simple nonwords such as *troat*, but otherwise may have no trouble reading. In this case the phonological route is thought to have been damaged, leaving intact the lexical route and its access to a previously learned reading vocabulary. The opposite problem is thought to exist for a condition called *surface dyslexia*. In this case the patient cannot access lexical information and so must sound out every word by reading through the phonological route. Because the phonological route follows spelling rules in deriving a pronunciation, surface dyslexics frequently mispronounce words with unique pronunciations, such as "yacht," or words that have some irregularity, such as *come* or *have* (the rule says that *e* at the end of the word should make the vowel long). Surface dyslexics also have trouble understanding what they read because access to lexical memory is impaired.

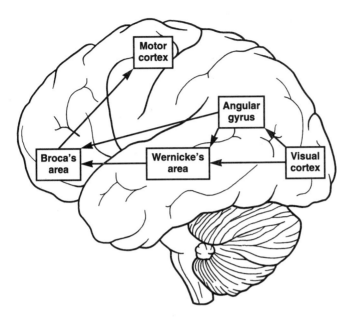

Figure 7.15
The Wernicke-Geschwind model of reading as represented in different cortical regions

Models of this kind have been mapped onto the brain (see figure 7.15) by correlating the location of brain damage and patterns of reading impairment with the processing components of the models (Benson and Geschwind 1982). Visual input is processed along two parallel pathways from occipital to parietal, temporal, and then frontal regions. In the phonological route visual information is converted to an auditory code as the word form passes through language regions in the left hemisphere. This conversion has been determined to take place in a region of the parietal lobe called the angular gyrus, since patients who suffer damage to this region lose the ability to sound out words. The lexical route is presumed to circumvent the angular gyrus and to access semantic information directly from the temporal lobe, based on the visual word form. Motor programs for controlling speech output are hypothesized to be located in a part of the frontal cortex known as Broca's area (see the discussion of language below).

Regardless of the research strategy that is followed, neuropsychology is an extraordinarily difficult enterprise. The neuropsychologist faces three sorts of methodological problems.

The first problem is shared with all cognitive scientists. Like any cognitive scientist, the neuropsychologist typically has a computational theory of the cognitive process under study. Whether this theory is a traditional symbolic theory or a more microstructural connectionist theory, it can be wrong. The proposed representations, components, or computational processes might be incorrect.

The second problem is shared with all cognitive scientists who are interested in the brain. In addition to a computational theory of some cognitive process, the neuropsychologist must have a theory of how the computational model is realized in the brain. The computational theory does not dictate the physical-realization theory.

Given the current state of our knowledge, there is almost always more than one possibility for mapping the computational theory onto the brain. A simple mapping that associates parts of the computational model with discrete parts of the brain would be incorrect, for example, if one computational component were implemented in several anatomically distinct areas of the brain rather than in one brain "center."

The cognitive neuroscientist is thus juggling two theories, each of which can fail in various ways, making it difficult to interpret data and to assign credit or blame when the data suggest a revision of the theories. Many researchers hope that this double difficulty of cognitive neuroscience will be converted into an advantage as knowledge advances. Computational and neural models, supported by behavioral and neurobiological data, should ultimately become mutually constraining. Research at one level of analysis should strongly suggest or rule out possibilities at other levels. Arguments over the merits of cognitively versus neurally inspired models aside, the prospect of converging evidence from different levels of analysis suggests that all levels should be pursued simultaneously and as cooperatively as possible in what Churchland (1986) calls a coevolutionary research strategy. For some higher cognitive processes the current problem is that not enough reliable knowledge is available at lower levels of analysis to strongly constrain the higher levels, hampering the dynamic of coevolutionary research.

The third problem for neuropsychology is specific to working with subjects who have suffered brain injury or have other kinds of neurological abnormalities. The attempt to understand the workings of an extraordinarily complex system by observing its behavior when parts of it have been capriciously damaged is obviously fraught with difficulties. To begin with, the neuropsychologist faces the additional burden of developing a theory of how the computational model of normal cognition performs when it is "lesioned" and of mapping these cognitive lesions onto physical lesions. The general empirical strategy in neuropsychology has been to show that damage to a specific brain area selectively impairs some aspect of performance and spares other aspects (which in turn may be impaired by damage to another brain area). When brain injuries *dissociate* various aspects of normal cognitive performance from each other, it becomes possible to map the injured brain areas onto the components of cognitive models that are responsible for the aspects of performance that are impaired or spared. Even in cases where the dissociation is complete, however, the mappings proposed are not logically necessary (Shallice 1988). For example, Churchland and Sejnowski (1992) argue that "lesioned" connectionist networks can exhibit dissociated performance even though they do not consist of discrete modules that are interconnected by pathways that carry different representations. One way this can happen is that, as the weights on hidden units are adjusted during learning, units can come to specialize on one or another aspect of the structure of a domain (e.g., vowels vs. consonants). If units with similar specializations are physically clustered, they could be selectively lesioned, causing a selective performance impairment.

The problems with interpreting neuropsychological data are further complicated by other factors. Naturally occurring brain damage (typically caused by stroke, trauma to the head, or infection) does not respect computational categories, and it is usually quite diffuse, involving several major areas. Localized lesions are rare. When patients with similar cognitive performance are grouped together for purposes of study, the groups are never homogeneous. The subjects usually have a variety of lesions of different sizes and in somewhat different locations. Even in a fairly homogeneous group, there might still be considerable individual differences in the organization of cortical maps (see the earlier discussion of topographical maps). Imaging techniques used to identify brain injury also have limitations. Computerized tomography (CT), the most frequently used brain scan, cannot image a lesion smaller than 1 to 2 centimeters and does a poor job in identifying subcortical damage. Another factor to consider is the cause of the damage. Grouping patients with different types of injury is problematic. Head trauma almost always produces diffuse damage; tumors can produce electrical abnormalities; and brain function can be affected by related medical conditions, such as cynotic heart disease, which can slow down metabolic activity by depleting oxygen supply. Many patients with brain damage also take psychotropic drugs, such as the seizure preventive Tegretol, yet the effects of these drugs on cognitive functions are not well understood. Finally, the patient's age at the time of the injury and his/her time for recovery (the interval between when the injury occurred and when testing took place) can be important factors in performance. Taken together, these concerns constitute a formidable challenge to the neuropsychologist. No study of a group of brain-damaged patients ever controls for all the factors because too many patients would be eliminated from the group.

One approach to this problem has been to avoid studies that involve groups of patients and instead to make detailed case studies of individuals with brain damage. Case-history studies have attempted either to provide a comprehensive assessment of an individual's cognitive functions (the approach pioneered in the former Soviet Union by Luria) or to analyze in detail a specific cognitive function (the British approach recently championed in this country by Caramazza). There are strong opinions on both sides about the relative merits of group or case studies in neuropsychology (Caramazza and McCloskey 1988).

As research progresses, the challenges of neuropsychology should be met by a combination of improved techniques, such as the use of high-resolution brain scans and the expanding database of carefully studied subjects, and convergent data from other sources. One area where the value of converging evidence can be seen is color vision and cognition. Certain aspects of color vision performance, such as color matching, discrimination, and naming, have been very well characterized in laboratory studies. The underlying neurophysiology up to the primary visual cortex is also well understood, and it fits together very well with the perceptual data. Although the basic character of the perceptual data has been known for over one hundred years, the fit with the physiological results came with a fertile period of coevolution that began with the development of modern neurophysiological methods, such as the techniques for recording the responses of single neurons. Given that we have a good handle on some of the phenomena of color perception and cognition and that we know a good deal about how color is initially represented in the cortex, we have a good chance of being able to put neuropsychological observations about color to good theoretical use. Davidoff (1991), for example, integrates a wide range of neurophysiological and perceptual-cognitive data with findings concerning various impairments involving color, such as the selective, total loss of color vision caused by cortical injury (acquired achromatopsia) or the selective loss of the ability to name colors when other aspects of color perception and cognition are intact (color anomia). As converging sources of evidence accumulate in other areas of research, neuropsychological data will make a clearer contribution to the overall scientific picture in those areas as well.

Memory

Memory is a good illustration of the study of a cognitive faculty for which neither the cognitive nor the neurobiological theory and data are as detailed or secure as they are for color vision. The contemporary neuropsychological study of human memory began with the study of HM, a patient who underwent a radical surgical procedure to control his constant epileptic seizures. Medications had proved ineffective, and so the parts of HM's brain that were producing the seizure activity were removed (Scoville and Milner 1957). To everyone's surprise, when HM recovered from surgery, he was profoundly amnesic and could not remember events that occurred after the surgery. HM had no trouble recalling events from his childhood or utilizing information that he had learned prior to the surgery. His short-term memory skills were normal. Therefore, the surgery affected his ability to store or retrieve new long-term memories. HM has a disorder called *anterograde amnesia*, the inability to recall events that occur after the onset of the amnesia. (*Retrograde amnesia* refers to the loss of memory for events that occurred prior to the amnesia.) For HM the amnesia is so profound that he cannot remember what he was doing even a few minutes ago. He is forever stuck in the present, or as he himself described it, "Every day is alone in itself, whatever enjoyment I've had, and whatever sorrow I've had.... It's like waking from a dream. I just don't remember" (Milner, Corkin, and Teuber 1968, 216).

The case of HM redirected attention to the study of storage and retrieval processes as well as different aspects of long-term memory. As we discussed in chapter 3, HM and other amnesic patients like him have difficulty with semantic and episodic memory. Semantic memory refers to memory for facts, such as the meaning of a word or the birth date of a grandson, and episodic memory refers to recall of specific autobiographical events, such as a boat trip last Fourth of July or yesterday's breakfast (Squire 1987). In our sketch of the cognitive architecture we classified both of these kinds of memory as declarative, the kind of memory that can be learned in just one trial or experience, and can be voluntarily and consciously accessed, usually through more than one sensory modality. We contrasted declarative memory with procedural memories, which are built up over repeated exposures, are manifested by changes in performance rather than by conscious recollection, and are modality specific. Figure 7.16 presents a classification scheme for types of memory.

As we pointed out in chapter 3, studies suggest that the procedural memory system is intact for amnesic patients. Milner (1965) was the first to demonstrate that HM could

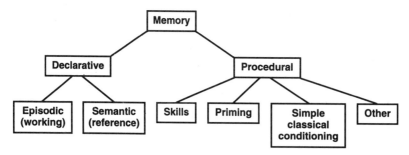

Figure 7.16
Model of memory systems. (From Squire 1987.)

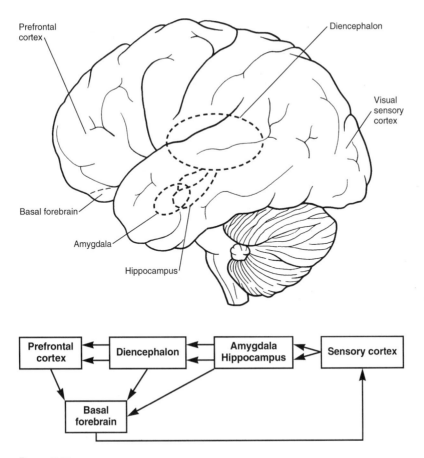

Figure 7.17
The flowchart and anatomical locations of a model for visual memory functions

Broca's aphasia patients are characterized by slow and effortful speech in which each word can require several seconds to produce and speech sounds are slurred or re-arranged. For example, Gardner (1974) reports this conversation with a Broca's aphasia patient:

I asked Mr. Ford about his work before he entered the hospital.
"I'm a sig ... no ... man ... uh, well, ... again."
"Let me help you," I interjected. "You were a signal ..."
"A sign-nal man ... right," Ford completed my phrase triumphantly.
... "I see. Could you tell me, Mr. Ford, what you've been doing in the hospital?"
"Yes, sure. Me go, er, uh, P. T. nine o'cot, speech ... two times ... read ... wr ... ripe, er, rike, er, write ... practice ... get-ting better."
"And have you been going home on weekends?"
"Why, yes ... Thursday, er, er, er, no, er, Friday ... Bar-ba-ra ... wife ... and, oh, car ... drive ... purnpike ... you know ... rest and ... tee-vee." (Gardner 1974, 60–61)

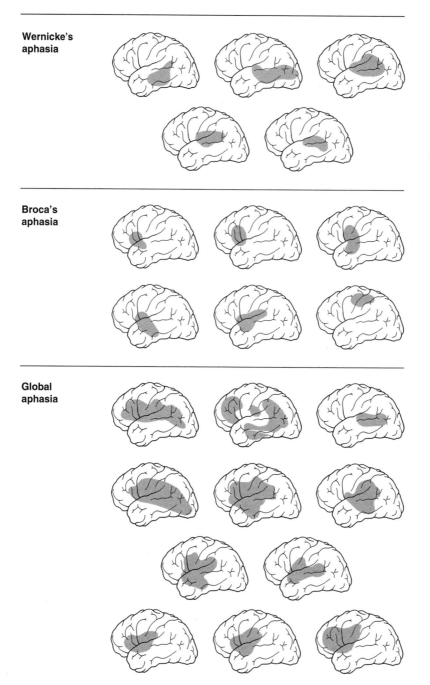

Figure 7.18
Figures showing the site of brain damage (dark areas) for different individuals. Top group suffered from Wernicke's aphasia, middle group from Broca's aphasia, and bottom group from Global aphasia. (From Kolb and Whishaw 1990.)

About ten years after Broca's report, Wernicke described a second language center located in the temporal lobe. Whereas patients with Broca's aphasia talk in a slow, deliberate manner, using simple grammatical structures, those with Wernicke's aphasia have poor speech comprehension, and although speech is fluent, they often confuse the sounds of words and mix up syllables to create neologisms (new words) or scramble phrases together to produce word salad. Again, another example from Gardner's book:

> "What brings you to the hospital?", I asked the 72-year-old retired butcher four weeks after his admission to the hospital.
> "Boy, I'm sweating, I'm nervous, you know, once in a while I get caught up, I can't mention the tarripoi, a month ago, quite a little, I've done a lot well, I impose a lot, while, one the other hand, you know what I mean, I have to run around, look it over, trebbin and all that sort of stuff." (Gardner 1974, 68)

In addition, the writing skills of Wernicke's aphasics are usually impaired.

Since Wernicke's time, neurologists and neuropsychologists have continued a functionalist approach to the study of neurolinguistics. The method involves a careful examination of the linguistic skills of brain-damaged patients to correlate their speech impairments with the site of their brain trauma. Goodglass and Kaplan (1972) have produced a classification system that is commonly used to analyze linguistic functions. This system includes two types of comprehension disorders, visual and auditory, and eight types of expressive disorders, which cover areas such as articulation, grammar, fluency, and writing. Most aphasic patients have impairment in many of these categories, involving both expressive and receptive functions. Although many neuropsychologists who study aphasia hope and expect that someday each of these functions will be localized to discrete anatomical locations, so far this goal has not been reached. One reason may be the extent of most patients' brain damage. Aphasia is commonly caused by strokes. The middle cerebral artery, a blood vessel in the brain that nourishes these language regions, is particularly susceptible to arteriosclerosis, a disease in which blood vessels thicken and are weakened with age. When a blood vessel is occluded or bursts, large portions of brain tissue die, typically producing a lesion that is not localized to a specific functional area.

Other explanations for the difficulty in localizing such functions may be either that the brain does not organize linguistic processes by Goodglass and Kaplan's categories (Marshall 1986) or that such functions are more broadly distributed and not localized. In practice only about 60 percent of aphasic patients exhibit patterns of linguistic impairment that fit into the current classification schemes.

Linguistic aphasiology research has adopted an information-processing approach to provide a much more detailed description of linguistic function (Caplan 1987). Using theoretical concepts derived from linguistics and cognitive psychology, aphasiologists have studied the impaired linguistic performance of aphasic patients to map their deficits into subcomponents of a language-processing system. Many interesting refinements of linguistic theory have resulted from this work. For example, several studies have examined the role syntactic structures play in sentence comprehension. Consider these three sentences:

(1)   The girl is chasing the big dog.

(2)   The dog the girl is chasing is big.

(3)   The dog the girl is chasing is barking.

Although sentences (1) and (2) convey the same meaning, the order of the nouns is reversed in sentence (2), requiring the reader to use syntactic information to assign the proper thematic roles to the dog and the girl to determine who is doing the chasing. Syntactic information also is useful in sentence (3), although lexical-pragmatic information can be used to determine thematic roles since girls do not bark. When sentences like these are given to Broca's aphasia patients, they have a very difficult time comprehending sentence (2) but not (1) or (3), suggesting the presence of several different systems involved in language comprehension (Caramazza and Zurif 1976). However, Broca's aphasics are not completely impaired in their grammatical judgments. Linebarger, Schwartz, and Saffran (1983) reported that Broca's aphasics who were severely impaired in their syntactic comprehension were still able to make reasonably good judgments about whether sentences were grammatically correct. This finding suggests that grammatical systems must be broken down further into parsing operations that determine constituency and a separate stage in which the sentence structure created by the parser is interpreted.

The issue of localizing linguistic functions to particular brain regions is problematic. Although considerable evidence suggests the principle of gross localization of major linguistic functions, more elementary stages of linguistic processing appear to be distributed and to vary between individuals. Some of the most problematic evidence comes from studies conducted by Ojemann and his colleagues (Ojemann 1983), who attempted to map speech zones during neurosurgery. Ojemann used a weak electrical current to stimulate selected surface areas of the cortex while patients were engaged in verbal tasks. During the procedure patients remained awake and alert because there are no pain sensors on the surface of the brain. If their performance was disrupted, then the site of the electrode indicated a speech zone. Their results supported the general concept of Broca's and Wernicke's language zones; however, stimulation in both regions had quite similar effects, disrupting both expressive and receptive functions. In addition, the boundaries varied considerably from one individual to another, and many other regions outside of these zones also affected linguistic functions. Furthermore, many different tasks, such as phoneme perception (distinguishing *ba* from *da*) or copying orofacial movements (such as sticking the tongue out), could be disrupted from the same site.

Other brain structures besides the cortex have often been overlooked when discussing language functions. In 1866 Hughlings-Jackson (1932) was the first to suggest that subcortical structures are important to normal language function. Recent studies have demonstrated language disorders in patients with thalamic lesions (Ojemann 1975) and in Parkinson's patients who have basal ganglia damage (Lieberman, Friedman, and Feldman 1990). Together these data suggest that the language system is extremely complex, involving many cortical and subcortical structures.

Left Brain/Right Brain—Cerebral Dominance
A curious feature of the brain's organization is that the symmetrical halves of the brain respond to sensory input from the opposite or contralateral side of the body. The somatosensory system is almost completely crossed so that the right half of the brain controls the left side of the body and vice versa. The visual system is slightly more complicated (see figure 7.19), with the nasal (near the nose) portions of the visual field crossing while the peripheral visual fields remain ipsilateral (same sided). Thus, if the eyes are focused straight ahead, the left visual field is mapped onto the right visual

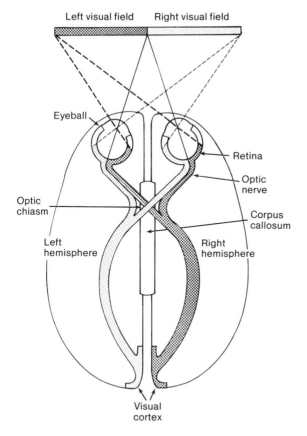

Left visual field   Right visual field

Eyeball

Retina

Optic
nerve

Optic
chiasm

Corpus
callosum

Left
hemisphere

Right
hemisphere

Visual
cortex

Figure 7.19
Central visual pathways. Light from the left visual field projects to the left eye's nasal and right eye's temporal parts of the retina. These regions send optic fibers to the right cortical hemisphere. Similarly, light from the right visual field projects to the left cortical hemisphere.

cortex and vice versa. The auditory system also is contralaterally organized, although ipsilateral projections exist as well.

Another unusual feature is that one cerebral hemisphere is usually dominant for particular behavioral functions. For example, the vast majority of people show a right-handed preference, suggesting left hemisphere cerebral dominance for manual motor functions. Many other cognitive functions, such as language, are also lateralized to the left hemisphere, although some, such as visual-spatial abilities, show a right hemisphere preference (Bryden 1982). Why higher cognitive functions, such as language, should lateralize to a dominant hemisphere has been the subject of intense speculation and recent biological investigation (Geschwind and Galaburda 1984). One hypothesis suggests that the two hemispheres are not as physically symmetrical as once thought and that important anatomical and cellular differences may be at the heart of certain functional differences. For example, Geschwind and Levitsky (1968) have shown that a region known as the *planum temporale*, located in the temporal lobe near the primary auditory corex (see figure 7.20), is larger in the left hemisphere for about 80 percent of the brains examined, suggesting a possible role in the left hemisphere's dominance for linguistic functions.

Split-Brain Studies Since the 1940s *commissurotomy* has been used as a last resort treatment for some patients with intractable seizures. This is a rare neurosurgical procedure in which the fibers of the corpus callosum that connect the two cerebral hemispheres of the brain are cut. The surgery is thought to prevent the spreading of epileptic discharge from one hemisphere to the other, thus helping to control seizure activity. Two groups of patients who have had commissurotomies have been carefully studied, revealing important differences in the way the two hemispheres function. The California group consists of about two dozen patients who underwent complete commissurotomies in the 1960s. They were extensively examined by Sperry and his colleagues (Gazzaniga 1970; Sperry 1968). During the 1970s a second group of patients underwent partial commissurotomies at Dartmouth Medical School and were studied by Gazzaniga and his colleagues (Gazzaniga and LeDoux 1978).

Study procedures took advantage of the fact that sensory systems are contralaterally organized for the two hemispheres. If visual information was only briefly displayed to the left visual field (so as to avoid eye movements that would shift the field of vision), or if objects were handled only by the left hand, the sensory information would be conducted only to the right hemisphere. With the corpus callosum severed, information from one hemisphere could not be transferred cortically to the other hemisphere, providing the opportunity to directly examine the cognitive processing capabilities of each hemisphere.

In general, split-brain studies confirmed that the control of speech is localized to the left hemisphere (LH) for most people. For most subjects the LH was able to respond verbally to questions or other visual displays, whereas the right hemisphere (RH) was unable to do so. Gazzaniga (1983) reported that only three out of twenty-eight patients from the Dartmouth group showed any evidence of RH linguistic function, and in all three cases evidence suggested the RH may have assumed a role in language because of LH damage early in life. According to Gazzaniga, only two patients in the California group showed evidence of RH language function, although Zaidel disagreed and claimed that as many as six patients had RH language (Zaidel 1983). Part of the disagreement may be due to differences in how linguistic responses are defined. None of the patients from the California group were able to write or speak with the RH. However, several were able to complete some linguistic comprehension tasks with the RH, such as matching simple, concrete nouns spoken out loud with pictures selected by the left hand or following oral commands to make a fist or raise the left arm. Zaidel also devised a contact lens that would block one part of the visual field so that patients could visually examine objects for a longer period of time and still ensure that the information was selectively processed only by one hemisphere. Using this lens, Zaidel extensively studied two patients and reported a surprising degree of linguistic comprehension in the RH, roughly equivalent to a ten-year-old level, although comprehension of complex sentences, such as "Before touching the red circle, pick up the green square," was still compromised. More recently Gordon (1980) reported that if the LH was occupied doing a task, the RH could respond to a verbal command, suggesting that the LH may dominate and inhibit the RH from functioning linguistically (Smith 1966).

The split-brain studies also supported the notion of the RH as specialized for visual-spatial functions, although this conclusion is based on only a small selection of RH responses. For most of the split-brain patients, the RH rarely responded at all (Churchland 1986). When there were responses, the RH was superior to the LH on such tasks as drawing figures, analyzing part-whole relationships for geometric shapes, and manipulating spatial relationships.

Remarkably, none of these hemispheric disconnection effects are seen in patients who were born without a callosum. In very rare cases the callosum fails to form during fetal development, a condition known as callosal agenesis. The few studies conducted with these patients have shown both hemispheres able to process verbal and spatial tasks (Ettlinger et al. 1972; Saul and Sperry 1968). Although most split-brain patients cannot respond verbally to pictures shown to the RH, even though their left hand can select the correct objects, callosal agenesis patients have no such difficulty. The nervous systems of the callosal agenesis patients may have compensated during development for the lack of a corpus callosum, recruiting subcortical connections to communicate between hemispheres.

Hand Preference   About 90 percent of people prefer to use their right hand when they write, eat, or need to use one hand to perform other skilled activities. Because some people are comfortable using more than one hand for different unimanual tasks, researchers now treat hand preference as a continuous variable, with some people strongly lateralized to one side and others more nearly ambidextrous. To measure an individual's hand preference, questionnaires have been constructed to sample hand use on a variety of tasks. Such tests produce scores that represent an average performance, called a laterality quotient. When Oldfield (1971) surveyed 1,000 undergraduates at the University of Edinburgh, he found that students who preferred to use their right hand did so quite consistently, whereas those who preferred the left hand tended to be more ambidextrous. This finding suggested that right-handedness is the norm, and those who are not right-handed vary to differing degrees from that normal condition.

Several neurobiological explanations of handedness have been proposed, but none has received widespread acceptance. Recent studies have demonstrated several anatomical asymmetries associated with hand preference (Kolb and Whishaw 1990). On measures of cerebral blood flow, and relative sizes of left-right cortical regions, such as the width of frontal or occipital lobes, up to 60 percent of the right-handers generally show strong lateralization, whereas left-handers show the opposite asymmetry or no differences. The functional significance of these facts, however, is hard to explain. Behavioral studies of left- and right-handers suggest that left-handers have more bilateral representation of function (Springer and Deutsch 1989). For example, a procedure known as the Wada test is often used with patients who are about to undergo neurosurgery to determine which half of the cortex controls speech production. In the Wada procedure one hemisphere is temporarily anesthetized by an injection of sodium amobarbital into the carotid artery that provides the blood supply to that hemisphere. Studies of hundreds of patients have shown that 96 percent of right-handers have speech lateralized to the left hemisphere and 4 percent to the right. However, only 70 percent of left-handers have speech lateralized to the left hemisphere; of the others, 15 percent have speech lateralized to the right and 15 percent have bilateral speech representation (Rasmussen and Milner 1977). One might then conclude that the structural asymmetries are behind these functional differences, but a careful examination of individuals suggests that is not case. At present no one has produced a convincing explanation to account for the significance of the structural differences.

A new hypothesis was proposed by Geschwind and Galaburda (1987), suggesting a hormonal theory to account for the association among left-handedness, immune disorders, and learning disabilities. In one study, 500 strongly lateralized left-handers were compared to 900 strongly lateralized right-handers by questionnaire. Compared to right-handers, results showed that left-handers had about two and a half times the incidence of migraine headaches, thyroid conditions, and immune disorders particularly involving the gastrointestinal tract, such as celiac disease, Crohn's disease, or ulcerative colitis. Left-handers also had ten times the rate of developmental disorders, including dyslexia, stuttering, language disorders, hyperactivity, autism, and Tourette's syndrome. A second study with another 1,400 subjects replicated these results. Noticing that these disorders occur more frequently in men and that the male hormone, testosterone, is known to affect the developing nervous system in nonhuman species, Geschwind and Galaburda proposed that exposure to higher concentrations of testosterone slows the growth of the left hemisphere and affects the immune system during fetal development, producing immune malfunctions and disrupting cortical organization to affect handedness and cognitive development.

For example, microscopic studies of the brains of a small sample of dyslexics have shown a cortical symmetry between the left and right regions of the planum temporale (see figure 7.20), an area thought to be involved in language processing, whereas in normal readers this region is larger in the left hemisphere 76 to 84 percent of the time (Galaburda, Rosen, and Sherman 1989). In dyslexics the planum also has high concentrations of ectopias and dysplasias, abnormalities produced by the neural migration errors described above. Geschwind and Galaburda's hormone hypothesis suggests that the dyslexic left hemisphere is smaller and contains structural abnormalities because of exposure to high concentrations of testosterone during fetal development.

A single mechanism that could account for so many different neural conditions is appealing; however, two recent pieces of evidence have weakened this hypothesis. First, studies of neural development in animals have shown that cortical asymmetry

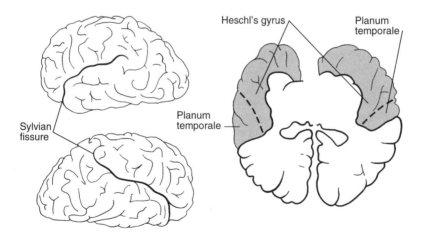

Figure 7.20
Differences in the anatomy of the two hemispheres can be found in the temporal lobe. As seen in the left figure, the Sylvian fissure rises more steeply in the right hemisphere. This difference is related to the size of the planum temporale, which is located along the surface of the Sylvian fissure (exposed in the right figure). The planum is larger in the left hemisphere. (From Kolb and Whishaw, 1990.)

develops as a result of synaptic reduction and cell death in the smaller hemisphere (Sherman, Rosen, and Galaburda 1989), suggesting that the hypothesis that testosterone inhibits left hemisphere development to produce abnormally symmetrical hemispheres is probably wrong. Apparently the normal hemispheric asymmetry is produced by neural reduction in the right hemisphere rather than greater cell proliferation in the left, and so symmetry is the result of more cells and synaptic connections remaining intact in the right hemisphere. It remains to be seen whether these results also hold true for humans, since neural cell death during human development may not be as extensive as animal studies would suggest (Huttenlocher 1990). Second, the higher incidence of some developmental disorders in males has recently been questioned. For example, several researchers (DeFries 1990; Finucci and Childs 1981) have suggested that boys are overrepresented in the dyslexic population because of sampling bias. If gender differences in some of these disorders turn out to be culturally defined and not biologically based, then the testosterone hypothesis would have to be modified or abandoned.

7.5 Computational Neuroscience

Computational neuroscience is a new term used for the study of the biological implementation of information processes. This research approach is an attempt to relate psychological models of behavior to neurobiological functions. Constructing computer models, which can mathematically define and simulate the computational components of neural systems, is an important part of this approach and a necessary adjunct to neurobiological experimentation. Sejnowski, Koch, and Churchland (1988) cite three reasons. First, a computer model can capture complex interactions among neural components, making the analysis of complex, nonlinear brain functions more accessible. Second, model simulations can provide novel explanations for complex behaviors. Simulations often suggest new experiments that could then test the model's predictions. Third, computer models can provide a vehicle for conducting simulated experiments that cannot be performed in vivo.

At a recent symposium on computational neuroscience (Schwartz 1990), many questions were raised about the enterprise: Can research on simple invertebrate nervous systems be generalized to more complex mammalian brains? Can the neural basis of cognition best be understood by a study of the logical functions of the brain, or must computational models also be designed with the neural "hardware" in mind? What spatial and temporal scales should be used in computational models—should modeling work focus at the synaptic-neuronal level, or should cell assemblies and cortical mapping schemes be studied? All points of view are represented in the neuroscientific community, and it is premature to predict which efforts will be most successful. However, some general guiding principles have emerged. First, known neurobiological principles are the standard against which model simulations must measure their success. Otherwise, neuroscientists are engineering designs of their own, as computer scientists would design an intelligent machine, not discovering how the brain functions; computational neuroscience is the study of "natural" intelligence, not artificial intelligence. Second, models can be realistic and incorporate as much biological detail as possible or can be simplified, providing a conceptual framework for study of algorithmic solutions. Both approaches have merit.

Connectionist Models

At present classical symbolic models cannot be reduced to neurobiological terms. We saw in chapters 2 and 3 that many connectionist models also have been developed to account for cognitive phenomena without any detailed assumptions about the underlying neural architecture. Smolensky (1988) and others have argued that connectionist models concern a subsymbolic, or microstructural, level of analysis that is lower than that of classical symbolic models but still above and in many respects autonomous from the physiological level of analysis. Nevertheless, connectionists have deliberately attempted to incorporate what is sometimes called *brain-style processing* into their models. Connectionist models are sometimes called *artificial neural networks*, suggesting that the processing units are analogous to neurons or cell assemblies in the brain. Connectionist models have in fact been rapidly assimilated into the neuroscience community (Gluck and Rumelhart 1990; Grossberg 1988; Hanson and Olson 1990; Nadel et al. 1989; Schwartz 1990).

Some neuroscientists (Crick, 1989; Shepherd, 1990a) have argued that current connectionist designs make many unrealistic assumptions, and they have encouraged network modelers to develop systems that incorporate more features of real neural architecture. On the one hand, some connectionist models have characteristics for which there is no neuroscientific evidence. The backpropagation learning algorithm, for example, requires that each forward path through a network be paired with a backward path along which error signals can be sent. In the model it is easy to imagine sending the error signals back along the very lines that carry activation forward through the net, but nerve fibers are not bidirectional, and there is currently no evidence for the precisely matched forward and backward paths that the model requires (Crick 1989; Zipser and Rumelhart 1990). On the other hand, there is ample evidence for the computational relevance of many features of real neural networks that are often not incorporated into model networks. For example, real neurons generate streams of action potentials, which have both a frequency and a phase, whereas the units in many network models generate simple numerical values, which lack phase information. Real neural networks contain multiple neurotransmitters and many distinct morphological types of neurons. Most artificial networks do not incorporate these distinctions. The net input to a unit in a typical connectionist model is a weighted sum of its inputs. In real neural networks there is evidence for microcircuits within dendritic trees that compute complex, nonlinear functions rather than simple summations. This finding supports an approach that takes the synapse, rather than the neuron, to be the basic unit of neural computation (Shepherd 1990a). Currently, network models vary widely in neural realism. The connectionist models discussed in this book fall at the abstract end of the spectrum.

In spite of attempts to make them more neurobiologically realistic, models always fail to incorporate some relevant details of actual neural networks and rest on some assumptions that are not fully supported by evidence. Limitations on neural realism are partly a matter of the need for better empirical information and partly a matter of the difficulties of simulating models on computers. A more important factor, however, is the belief that in some cases a simple model will yield greater scientific insight than a more complex one because it shows clearly how some features of the brain contribute to a particular function. In the quest to understand the brain at the physiological level of analysis, the key issue concerning any particular type of model is whether it succeeds in giving us insights into neural computation.

Abstract connectionist models are in fact yielding insights into brain function. Zipser (1990), for example, trained a connectionist network to compute the correct spatial direction of an object using the pattern of activation on the retina and the position of the eyes as inputs. Visual systems must compute this function because an object at a particular position in space casts an image onto different parts of the retina depending on the direction of gaze. The true direction of the object must be recovered by combining information about retinal position with information about eye position. The backpropagation algorithm was used to train a network consisting of input units that encoded retinal and eye position, a layer of hidden units, and output units that encoded true spatial direction. The input representations were designed on the basis of evidence about the actual inputs to the visual cortex. Following training, the response characteristics of the hidden units in the model closely resembled the electrophysiological behavior of parietal neurons recorded in macaque monkeys. These neurons were suspected of being involved in computing visual location (Zipser and Andersen 1988). This result demonstrated that the position computation can be acquired through experience, and it showed how neurons with particular response properties might arise during learning. Issues concerning the biological plausibility of backpropagation are less important than they might initially appear in this research because any learning algorithm that minimizes error in weight space (see chapter 2) will yield the same result. Although the model is extremely simple and unrealistic in some respects, its very simplicity makes for a stronger scientific result. Zipser was able to determine exactly which characteristics of the model produced hidden units with the desired response characteristics. Several other researchers have reported successes using similar approaches (Anastasio and Robinson 1989; Lehky and Sejnowski 1988).

A potentially powerful feature of this research is the use of learning algorithms to develop hypotheses about internal neural representations. Experimental techniques for recording and interpreting the patterns of activation among large sets of neurons are only just beginning to be developed and are still a long way from providing detailed information about representational states. It is difficult, therefore, to construct a representational theory directly from neurobiological data. If data is available on input and output representations, however, a model with hidden units can be simulated, and the representations developed by the hidden units can be studied to develop hypotheses about what to look for in the brain.

The vision of cooperative interaction among levels of research may be coming closer to realization. Empirical results in neurobiology can guide the construction of network models, and the results of model simulations can be used to guide further research on the brain.

Suggested Readings

The Brain (Thompson 1994) provides a very readable introduction to neuroscience. There are many good sources of information about basic neuroanatomy and neurophysiology: *Fundamental Neuroanatomy* (Nauta and Feirtag 1986) and *Synaptic Organization of the Brain* (Shepherd 1990b) are among the best. In *The Computational Brain* Churchland and Sejnowski (1992) provide a connectionist approach to computational neuroscience that includes detailed discussions of many neuroscientific details. *The Man Who Mistook His Wife for a Hat and Other Clinical Tales* (Sacks 1985) is a delightful introduction to clinical neuropsychology. *Fundamentals of Human Neuropsychology*

(Kolb and Whishaw 1990) is an excellent reference source. For a readable introduction to connectionist modeling, see *Connectionism and the Mind* (Bechtel and Abrahamsen 1991); for a more advanced review, see *Parallel Distributed Processing*, Vols. 1 and 2 (Rumelhart and McClelland 1986; McClelland and Rumelhart 1986).

References

Abeles, M., and G. L. Gerstein (1988). Detecting spatiotemporal firing patterns among simultaneously recorded single neurons. *Journal of Neurophysiology* 60, 909–924.

Amaral, D. G. (1987). Memory: The anatomical organization of candidate brain regions. In F. Plum, ed., *Handbook of physiology: Higher functions of the nervous system*. Bethesda, Md.: American Physiological Society.

Anastasio, T. J., and D. A. Robinson (1989). Distributed parallel processing in the vestibulo-oculomotor system. *Neural Computation* 1, 230–241.

Andersen, R. A., R. M. Siegel, and G. K. Essick (1987). Neurons of area 7 activated by both visual stimuli and oculomotor behavior. *Experimental Brain Research* 67, 316–322.

Aram, D. M., B. L. Ekelman, and L. L. Gillespie (1990). Reading and lateralized brain lesions in children. In K. von Euler, I. Lumberg, and G. Lennerstrand, eds., *Brain and Reading*. Hampshire, England: Macmillan.

Assaf, A. A. (1982). The sensitive period: Transfer of fixation after occlusion for strabismic amblyopia. *British Journal of Ophthalmology* 66, 64–70.

Baldi, P., and W. Heiligenberg (1988). How sensory maps could enhance resolution through ordered arrangements of broadly tuned receivers. *Biological Cybernetics* 59, 313–318.

Barlow, H. B. (1972). Single units and sensation: A neuron doctrine for perceptual psychology? *Perception* 1, 371–394.

Bastiani, M. J., C. Q. Doe, S. L. Helfand, and C. S. Goodman (1985). Neuronal specificity and growth cone guidance in grasshopper and drosophila embryos. *Trends in Neuroscience* 8, 257–266.

Bechtel, W., and A. Abrahamsen (1991). *Connectionism and the mind*. Cambridge, Mass.: Blackwell.

Benson, D. F., and N. Geschwind (1982). The alexias. In H. S. Kirshner and F. R. Freemon, eds., *The neurology of aphasia*. Lisse, Holland: Swets and Zeitlinger.

Bliss, T. V. P., and T. Lomo (1973). Long-lasting potentiation of synaptic transmission in the dentate area of the anaesthetized rabbit following stimulation of the perforant path. *Journal of Physiology* 232, 331–356.

Bryden, M. P. (1982). *Laterality: Functional asymmetry in the intact brain*. New York: Academic Press.

Caplan, D. (1987). *Neurolinguistics and linguistic aphasiology: An introduction*. New York: Cambridge University Press.

Caramazza, A., and M. McCloskey (1988). The case for single-patient studies. *Cognitive Neuropsychology* 5, 517–528.

Caramazza, A., and E. B. Zurif (1976). Dissociation of algorithmic and heuristic processes in language comprehension: Evidence from aphasia. *Brain and Language* 3, 572–582.

Changeux, J., and A. Danchin (1976). Selective stabilization of developing synapses as a mechanism for the specialization of neural network. *Nature* 264, 705–712.

Changeux, J., and M. Konishi (1987). *The neural and molecular bases of learning*. New York: Wiley.

Changeux, J.-P. (1985). *Neuronal man: The biology of mind* (Laurence Garey, trans.). New York: Oxford University Press.

Cherniak, C. (1990). The bounded brain: Toward quantitative neuroanatomy. *Journal of Cognitive Neuroscience* 2, 58–68.

Chugani, H. T., and M. E. Phelps (1990). Imaging human brain development with positron emission tomography. *Journal of Nuclear Medicine* 32, 23–26.

Churchland, P. S. (1986). *Neurophilosophy*. Cambridge, Mass.: MIT Press.

Churchland, P. S., and T. J. Sejnowski (1992). *The computational brain*. Cambridge, Mass.: MIT Press.

Coltheart, M., K. E. Patterson, and J. C. Marshall (1987). *Deep dyslexia*. 2nd ed. London: Routledge and Kegan Paul.

Courchesne, E., R. Yeung-Courchesne, G. A. Press, J. R. Hesselink, and T. L. Jernigan (1988). Hypoplasia of cerebellar vermal lobules VI and VII in autism. *New England Journal of Medicine* 318, 1349–1354.

Cowan, W. M. (1979). The development of the brain. In D. Flanagan, ed., *The brain*. New York: W. H. Freeman.

Cowan, W. M., J. W. Fawcett, D. D. O'Leary, and B. B. Stanfield (1984). Regressive events in neurogenesis. *Science* 225, 1258–1265.

Crick, F. H. C. (1989). The recent excitement about neural networks. *Nature* 337, 129–132.

Davidoff, J. (1991). *Cognition through color*. Cambridge, Mass.: MIT Press.

DeFries, J. C. (1990). Genetic etiology of reading disability: Evidence from a twin study. Paper presented at the meeting of the National Dyslexia Research Foundation, Rancho Mirage, Calif.

Dennis, M., and H. A. Whitaker (1976). Language acquisition following hemidecortication: Linguistic superiority of the left over the right hemisphere. *Brain and Language* 3, 404–433.

Desimone, R., and C. G. Gross (1979). Visual areas in the temporal cortex of the macaque. *Brain Research* 178, 363–380.

Diamond, M. C. (1984). Age, sex, and environmental influences. In N. Geschwind and A. M. Galaburda, eds., *Cerebral dominance*. Cambridge, Mass.: Harvard University Press.

Dudai, Y. (1989). *The neurobiology of memory*. New York: Oxford University Press.

Easter, S. S., D. Purves, P. Rakic, and N. C. Spitzer (1985). The changing view of neural specificity. *Science* 230, 507–511.

Edelman, G. M. (1987). *Neural Darwinism: The theory of neuronal group selection*. New York: Basic Books.

Ettlinger, G., C. Blakemore, A. D. Milner, and D. Wilson (1972). Agenesis of the corpus callosum. *Brain* 95, 327–346.

Feldman, R. S., and L. F. Quenzer (1984). *Fundamentals of neuropsychopharmacology*. Sunderland, Mass.: Sinauer.

Finucci, J. M., and B. Childs (1981). Are there really more dyslexic boys than girls? In A. Ansara, N. Geschwind, A. Galaburda, M. Albert, and N. Gartrell, eds., *Sex differences in dyslexia*. Towson, M. D.: Orton Dyslexia Society.

Galaburda, A. M., G. D. Rosen, and G. F. Sherman (1989). The neural origin of developmental dyslexia: Implications for medicine, neurology, and cognition. In A. M. Galaburda, ed., *From reading to neurons*. Cambridge, Mass.: MIT Press.

Galaburda, A. M., G. F. Sherman, G. D. Rosen, F. Aboitiz, and N. Geschwind (1985). Development dyslexia: Four consecutive patients with cortical anomalies. *Annals of Neurology* 18, 222–233.

Gardner, H. (1974). *The shattered mind*. New York: Vintage Books.

Gazzaniga, M. S. (1970). *The bisected brain*. New York: Appleton-Century-Crofts.

Gazzaniga, M. S. (1983). Right hemisphere language following brain bisection: A 20 year perspective. *American Psychologist* 38, 525–537.

Gazzaniga, M. S., and J. E. LeDoux (1978). *The integrated mind*. New York: Plenum Press.

Georgopoulos, A. P., and S. Grillner (1989). Visuomotor coordination in reaching and locomotion. *Science* 245, 1209–1210.

Georgopoulos, A. P., A. B. Schwartz, and R. E. Kettner (1986). Neuronal population coding of movement direction. *Science* 233, 1416–1419.

Geschwind, N., and A. M. Galaburda (1984). *Cerebral dominance: The biological foundations*. Cambridge, MA: Harvard University Press.

Geschwind, N., and N. Galaburda (1987). *Cerebral lateralization: Biological mechanisms, associations and pathology*. Cambridge, Mass.: MIT Press.

Geschwind, N., and W. Levitsky (1968). Left-right asymmetry in temporal speech region. *Science* 161, 186–187.

Gluck, M. A., and D. E. Rumelhart (1990). Neuroscience and connectionist theory. In *Developments in connectionist theory*. Hillsdale, N.J.: Lawrence Erlbaum.

Goodglass, H., and E. Kaplan (1972). *The assessment of aphasia and related disorders*. Philadelphia: Lea and Febiger.

Gordon, H. W. (1980). Right hemisphere comprehension of verbs in patients with complete forebrain commissurotomy: Use of the dichotic method and manual performance. *Brain and Language* 11, 76–86.

Graf, P., L. R. Squire, and G. Mandler (1984). The information that amnesic patients do not forget. *Journal of Experimental Psychology: Learning, Memory, and Cognition* 10, 164–178.

Grinvald, A., E. Lieke, R. D. Frostig, C. D. Gilbert, and T. N. Wiesel (1986). Functional architecture of cortex revealed by optical imaging of intrinsic signals. *Nature* 324, 361–364.

Grossberg, S., ed. (1988). *Neural networks and natural intelligence*. Cambridge, Mass.: MIT Press.

Hanson, S. J., and C. R. Olson (1990). Connectionist modeling and brain function. In J. L. Elman, ed., *Neural network modeling and connectionism*. Cambridge, Mass.: MIT Press.

Hawkins, R. D., T. W. Abrams, T. J. Carew, and E. R. Kandel (1983). A cellular mechanism of classical conditioning in Aplysia: Activity-dependent amplification of presynaptic facilitation. *Science* 219, 400–405.

Hebb, D. O. (1949). *The organization of behavior.* New York: Wiley.

Hecht-Nielsen, R. (1990). *Neurocomputing.* Reading, Mass.: Addison-Wesley.

Hinton, G. E., J. L. McClelland, and D. E. Rumelhart (1986). Distributed representations. In Rumelhart and McClelland 1986.

Hubel, D. H. (1988). *Eye, vision, and brain.* New York: Freeman.

Hubel, D. H., and T. N. Wiesel (1977). Functional architecture of macaque visual cortex. *Proceedings of the Royal Society of London. Series* B 198, 1–59.

Hughes, J., T. W. Smith, H. W. Kosterlitz, L. A. Fothergill, B. A. Morgan, and H. R. Morris (1975). Identification of two related pentapeptides from the brain with potent opiate agonist activity. *Nature* 258, 577–581.

Hughlings-Jackson, J. (1932). Notes on the physiology and pathology of learning. In J. Taylor, ed., *Selected Writings of John Hughlings-Jackson.* London: Hodder.

Huttenlocher, P. R. (1979). Synaptic density in human frontal cortex: Developmental changes and effects of aging. *Brain Research* 163, 195–205.

Huttenlocher, P. R. (1990). Morphometric study of human cerebral cortex development. *Neuropsychologia* 28, 517–527.

Iversen, L. L. (1979). The chemistry of the brain. In D. Flanagan, ed., *The brain.* New York: W. H. Freeman.

Jenkins, W. M., and M. M. Merzenich (1987). Reorganization of neocortical representations after brain injury: A neurophysiological model of the bases of recovery from stroke. In F. J. Seil, E. Herbert, and B. M. Carlson, eds., *Progress in brain research.* New York: Elsevier.

Kandel, E. R. (1991a). Brain and behavior. In E. R. Kandel, J. H. Schwartz, and T. M. Jessell, eds., *Principles of neural science.* 3rd ed. Englewood Cliffs, N.J.: Prentice-Hall.

Kandel, E. R. (1991b). Nerve cells and behavior. In E. R. Kandel, J. H. Schwartz, and T. M. Jessell, eds., *Principles of neural science.* 3rd ed. Englewood Cliffs, N.J.: Prentice-Hall.

Kandel, E. R., and Hawkins, R. D. (1993). The biological basis of learning and individuality. In J. Piel, ed., *Mind and brain.* New York: W. H. Freeman.

Kolb, B., and Whishaw, I. Q. (1990). *Fundamentals of human neuropsychology.* New York: W. H. Freeman.

Konishi, M. (1985). Birdsong: from behavior to neuron. *Annual Review of Neuroscience* 8, 125–170.

Konishi, M. (1986). Centrally synthesized maps of sensory space. *Trends in Neuroscience* 9, 163–168.

Konishi, M. (1991). Deciphering the brain's codes. *Neural Computation* 3 (1), 1–18.

Kratz, K. E., P. D. Spear, and D. C. Smith (1976). Postcritical-period reversal of effects of monocular deprivation of striate cells in the cat. *Journal of Neurophysiology* 39, 501–511.

Lehky, S. R., and T. J. Sejnowski (1988). Network model of shape-from-shading: Neural function arises from both receptive and projective fields. *Nature* 333, 452–454.

Leuba, G., and L. J. Garey (1987). Evolution of neuronal numerical density in the developing and aging human visual cortex. *Human Neurobiology* 70, 11–18.

Lieberman, P., J. Friedman, and L. S. Feldman (1990). Syntax comprehension deficits in Parkinson's disease. *Journal of Nervous and Mental Disorders* 178, 360–365.

Linebarger, M. C., M. F. Schwartz, and E. M. Saffran (1983). Sensitivity to grammatical structure in so-called agrammatic aphasics. *Cognition* 13, 361–392.

Livingstone, M. S., and D. H. Hubel (1987). Psychophysical evidence for separate channels for the perception of form, color, movement, and depth. *Journal of Neuroscience* 7, 3416–3458.

Lynch, G., and M. Baudry (1984). The biochemistry of memory: A new specific hypothesis. *Science* 224, 1057–1063.

Macagno, E. R., U. Lopresti, and C. Levinthal (1973). Structural development of neuronal connections in isogenic organisms: Variations and similarities in the optic system of Daphnia magna. *Proceedings of the National Academy of Sciences* 70, 57–61.

Marshall, J. C. (1986). The description and interpretation of aphasic language disorder. *Neuropsychologia* 24, 5–24.

Marshall, J. C., and F. Newcombe (1981). Lexical access: A perspective from pathology. *Cognition* 10, 209–214.

McClelland, J. L., D. E. Rumelhart, and the PDP Research Group (1986). *Parallel distributed processing: Explorations in the microstructure of cognition.* Vol. 2: *Psychological and biological models.* Cambridge, Mass.: MIT Press.

McCormick, D. A., and R. F. Thompson (1984). Cerebellum: Essential involvement in the classically conditioned eyelid response. *Science* 223, 296–299.

Merzenich, M. M. (1987). Dynamic neocortical processes and the origins of higher brain functions. In J. P. Changeux and M. Konishi, eds., *The neuronal and molecular bases of learning*. New York: Wiley.

Merzenich, M. M., P. L. Knight, and G. L. Roth (1974). Representation of cochlea within primary auditory cortex in the cat. *Journal of Endocrinology* 61, 231–249.

Milner, B. (1965). Memory disturbance after bilateral hippocampal lesions. In P. M. Milner and S. E. Glickman, eds., *Cognitive processes and the brain*. Princeton, N.J.: Van Nostrand.

Milner, B., S. Corkin, and H.-L. Teuber (1968). Further analysis of the hippocampal amnesic syndrome: 14-year follow up study of HM *Neuropsychologia* 6, 215–234.

Mishkin, M., and T. Appenzeller (1987). The anatomy of memory. *Scientific American* 256 (6), 80–89.

Nadel, L., L. A. Cooper, P. Culicover, and R. M. Harnish (1989). *Neural connections, mental computation*. Cambridge, Mass.: MIT Press.

Nauta, W. J. H., and M. Feirtag (1986). *Fundamental neuroanatomy*. New York: Freeman.

Nottebohm, F. (1970). Ontogeny of bird song. *Science* 167, 950–956.

O'Keefe, J., and L. Nadel (1978). *The hippocampus as a cognitive map*. New York: Clarendon Press.

Ojemann, G. A. (1975). The thalamus and language. *Brain and Language* 2, 1–20.

Ojemann, G. A. (1983). Brain organization for language from the perspective of electrical stimulation mapping. *Behavioral and Brain Sciences* 6, 189–230.

Oldfield, R. C. (1971). The assessment and analysis of handedness: The Edinburgh Inventory. *Neuropsychologia* 9, 97–114.

Passingham, R. E. (1982). *The human primate*. San Francisco: W. H. Freeman.

Patterson, K. E., J. C. Marshall, and M. Coltheart (1985). *Surface dyslexia*. London: Erlbaum.

Perrett, D. I., A. J. Mistlin, and A. J. Chitty (1987). Visual neurons responsive to faces. *Trends in Neuroscience* 10, 358–364.

Pinel, J. P. J. (1990). *Biopsychology*. Boston: Allyn and Bacon.

Pons, T. P., P. E. Garraghty, and M. Mishkin (1988). Lesion-induced plasticity in the second somatosensory cortex of adult macaques. *Proceedings of the National Academy of Sciences* 85, 5279–5281.

Purves, D. (1988). *A trophic theory of neuronal organization*. Cambridge, Mass.: Harvard University Press.

Rakic, P. (1979). Genetic and epigenetic determinants of local neuronal circuits in the mammalian central nervous system. In F. O. Schmitt and F. G. Worden, eds., *The neurosciences: Fourth study program*. Cambridge, Mass.: MIT Press.

Rakic, P. (1986). Mechanisms of ocular dominance segregation in the lateral geniculate nucleus: Competitive elimination hypothesis. *Trends in Neuroscience* 9, 11–15.

Rasmussen, T., and B. Milner (1977). The role of early left brain injury in determining lateralization of cerebral speech functions. *Annals of the New York Academy of Sciences* 299, 355–369.

Rolls, E. T. (1990). Spatial memory, episodic memory and neuronal network functions in the hippocampus. In L. R. Squire and E. Lindenlaub, eds., *The biology of memory*. New York: Schattauer Verlag.

Rumelhart, D. E., J. L. McClelland, and the PDP Research Group (1986). *Parallel distributed processing: Explorations in the microstructures of cognition*. Vol. 1: *Foundations*. Cambridge, Mass.: MIT Press.

Rutishauser, U., A. Acheson, A. K. Hall, D. M. Mann, and J. Sunshine (1988). The neural cell adhesion molecule (NCAM) as a regulator of cell-cell interactions. *Science* 240, 53–57.

Sacks, O. (1985). *The man who mistook his wife for a hat and other clinical tales*. New York: Summit Books.

Saul, R., and R. Sperry (1968). Absence of commissurotomy symptoms with agenesis of the corpus callosum. *Neurology* 18, 307.

Schor, R. H., A. D. Miller, and D. L. Tomko (1984). Response to head tilt in cat central vestibular neurons: I. Direction of maximum sensitivity. *Journal of Neurophysiology* 51, 136–146.

Schwartz, E. L., ed. (1990). *Computational neuroscience*. Cambridge, Mass.: MIT Press.

Scoville, W. B., and B. Milner (1957). Loss of recent memory after bilateral hippocampal lesions. *Journal of Neurology, Neurosurgery, and Psychiatry* 20, 11–21.

Sejnowski, T. J. (1986). Open questions about computation in cerebral cortex. In McClelland and Rumelhart 1986.

Sejnowski, T. J., and P. S. Churchland (1989). Brain and cognition. In M. I. Posner, ed., *Foundations of cognitive science*. Cambridge, Mass.: MIT Press.

Sejnowski, T. J., C. Koch, and P. S. Churchland (1988). Computational neuroscience. *Science* 241, 1299–1306.

Shallice, T. (1988). *From neuropsychology to mental structure*. Cambridge: Cambridge University Press.

Shepherd, G. M., ed. (1990a). The significance of real neuron architectures for neural network simulations. In Schwartz 1990.

Shepherd, G. M., ed. (1990b). *The synaptic organization of the brain*. 3rd ed. New York: Oxford.

Sherman, G. F., Rosen, G. D., and A. M. Galaburda (1989). Animal models of developmental dyslexia: Brain lateralization and cortical pathology. In A. M. Galaburda, ed., *From reading to neurons*. Cambridge, Mass.: MIT Press.

Singer, M., R. H. Nordlander, and M. Egar (1979). Axonal guidance during embryogenesis and regeneration in the spinal cord of the newt: The blueprint hypothesis of neuronal pathway patterning. *Journal of Comparative Neurology* 185, 1–22.

Skarda, C. A., and W. J. Freeman (1987). How brains make chaos in order to make sense of the world. *Behavioral and Brain Sciences* 10, 161–195.

Smith, A. (1966). Speech and other functions after left (dominant) hemispherectomy. *Journal of Neurology, Neurosurgery, and Psychiatry* 29, 467–471.

Smolensky, P. (1988). On the proper treatment of connectionism. *Behavioral and Brain Sciences* 11, 1–74.

Snyder, S. H. (1976). The dopamine hypothesis of schizophrenia: Focus on the dopamine receptor. *Journal of American Psychiatry* 133, 197–202.

Snyder, S. H. (1980). Brain peptides as neurotransmitters. *Science* 209, 976–983.

Snyder, S. H. (1986). *Drugs and the brain*. New York: W. H. Freeman.

Sperry, R. W. (1963). Chemoaffinity in the orderly growth of nerve fiber patterns and connections. *Proceedings of the National Academy of Sciences* 50, 703–710.

Sperry, R. W. (1968). Hemisphere deconnection and unity in conscious awareness. *American Psychologist* 23, 723–733.

Springer, S. P., and G. Deutsch (1989). *Left brain, right brain*. New York: W. H. Freeman.

Squire, L. R. (1987). *Memory and brain*. New York: Oxford University Press.

Steinmetz, M. A., B. C. Motter, C. J. Duffy, and V. B. Mountcastle (1987). Functional properties of parietal visual neurons: Radial organization of directionalities within the visual field. *Journal of Neuroscience* 7, 177–191.

Stephen, H., R. Bauchot, and O. J. Andy (1970). Data on the size of the brain and of various parts in insectivores and primates. In C. R. Noback and W. Montagna, eds., *The primate brain*. New York: Appleton-Century-Crofts.

Stevens, C. F. (1979). The neuron. In D. Flanagan, ed., *The brain*. San Francisco: W. H. Freeman.

Suga, N. (1990). Computation of velocity and range in the bat auditory system for echo location. In Schwartz 1990.

Swindale, N. V., M. S. Cynader, and J. Matsubara (1990). Cortical cartography: A two-dimensional view. In Schwartz 1990.

Thompson, R. (1994). *The brain*. New York: W. H. Freeman.

Trehub, A. (1991). *The cognitive brain*. Cambridge, Mass.: MIT Press.

Venezky, R. L. (1970). *The structure of English orthography*. The Hague: Mouton.

Von der Malsburg, C., and D. Willshaw (1981). Cooperativity and brain organization. *Trends in Neuroscience* 4, 80–83.

Weiskrantz, L., and E. K. Warrington (1979). Conditioning in amnesic patients. *Neuropsychologia* 17, 187–194.

Werker, J. F., J. H. V. Gilbert, K. Humphrey, and R. C. Tees (1981). Developmental aspects of cross-language speech perception. *Child Development* 2, 349–355.

Wigstrom, H., and B. Gustafsson (1985). On long-lasting potentiation in the hippocampus: A proposed mechanism for its dependence on coincident pre- and postsynaptic activity. *Acta Physiology Scandinavia* 123, 519–522.

Woolsey, C. N. (1960). Organization of cortical auditory system: A review and a synthesis. In G. L. Rasmussen and W. F. Windle, eds., *Neural mechanisms of the auditory and vestibular systems*. Springfield, Ill.: Charles C. Thomas.

Zaidel, L. (1983). A response to Gazzaniga: Language in the right hemisphere, convergent perspectives. *American Psychologist* 38, 342–346.

Zipser, D. (1990). Modeling cortical computation with backpropagation. In M. A. Gluck and D. A. Rumelhart, eds., *Neuroscience and connectionist theory*. Hillsdale, N.J.: Lawrence Erlbaum.

Zipser, D., and R. A. Andersen (1988). A back propagation programmed network that simulates response properties of a subset of posterior parietal neurons. *Nature* 331, 679–684.

Zipser, D., and D. A. Rumelhart (1990). The neurobiological significance of the new learning models. In Schwartz 1990.

Zola-Morgan, S., and L. R. Squire (1985). Amnesia in monkeys following lesions of the mediodorsal nucleus of the thalamus. *Annals of Neurology* 17, 558–564.

Chapter 8

Philosophy: Foundations of Cognitive Science

8.1 Philosophy in Cognitive Science

All sciences used to be branches of philosophy. A science is born when it breaks off from philosophy and begins to be pursued by specialists. Physics, biology, and chemistry are all sciences that were born in this way a rather long time ago, but all began as branches of philosophy. Cognitive science, and the disciplines it comprises—psychology, linguistics, neuroscience, and computer science (omitting, for the moment, philosophy itself)—are young sciences, each having emerged from philosophy within the last hundred years or so. Psychology was born as an independent science in the last few decades of the nineteenth century. Neuroscience had its beginnings around the same time, though its real development into a promising theoretical enterprise is much more recent. Linguistics as we know it today began to emerge in the 1920s and is still very much in the process of becoming independent, with certain of its problems, particularly those having to do with logic and semantics, still falling as much in the domain of philosophy as in its own. Computer science has existed only since about 1950 (though its roots are primarily in mathematics).

Historical Background

Cognitive science, the fusion of these disciplines, is younger still, only several decades old. So it, even more than its component disciplines, is thoroughly entwined with its philosophical roots. These roots are to be found in the seventeenth century, when philosophers began to find new ways of addressing problems about the nature of thought and the mind. Debates began about the relation between mind and body, the relation between language and thought, the relation between thoughts or perceptions and the objects thought about or perceived, whether ideas are innate or acquired, and the nature of the embodiment of mind. Amid this intellectual ferment, two figures stand out as grandfathers of the cognitive approach: René Descartes and Thomas Hobbes.

Descartes argued that all of our knowledge of the external world is mediated by *representations*—mental objects that somehow stand for things outside. Thought, he contended, always involves the manipulation, through inference or other mental processes, of these representations. This is not as obvious as it might seem at first. After all, it could be (and many have argued that it is the case) that our knowledge of the world consists merely of our being able to do certain things and that it in no way involves manipulating internal symbols (whether they are made of immaterial soul-stuff as Descartes thought, or of gray matter, or of silicon). One natural way to think about these representations is that adopted by many of Descartes's contemporaries—as mental images of what they represent. Another, more plausible, and ultimately more influential way is as sentences (or as remarks of some kind) in an internal language of thought, or perhaps in the native language of the speaker. What makes the contention that thought is representational so interesting are the implications Descartes saw in this position, implications that have helped to shape not only all subsequent philosophical thought about the mind but current cognitive science as well.

The first implication Descartes noticed was that these representations have no necessary connection to the things they represent. Of course, fortunately for us (and, Descartes thought, only through the good graces of the deity), they tend to bear some consistent relation to the things they represent and hence are fairly well able to serve their function of guiding our activity in the real world. But, Descartes suggested, even if there were no external world at all, we could have the same representations that we do now (just as, though there are in fact no unicorns, there are pictures of unicorns, and just as, though we have pictures and reported sightings of yetis, we don't know whether these yeti representations correspond to actual yetis). Of course, we would be mistaken in thinking that they represented reality, but they would be the same mental states. They would feel the same, would interact with each other in the same way, and would guide behavior in the same way. (Of course, who is to say that we are not in that state right now?) Because of the skeptical worry that this position sometimes raises, let us for now call Descartes's insight *representational skepticism*.

The second interesting implication of Descartes's view is that one can study the mind without paying any attention at all to the reality it purports to represent and think about. After all, on this view, since what we are studying is just the nature and interrelations of symbols and processes going on inside a mind, and since those symbols and processes would be what they are even if nothing but that mind existed, why bother paying attention to anything but those symbols and processes themselves? The suggestion is not that nothing other than the mind in fact exists—a view called *solipsism*—but rather that if we study the mind as if solipsism were true, we can say everything scientifically interesting that we would ever want to say about it. For this reason, the view is called *methodological solipsism*. (For more discussion of methodological solipsism, see Putnam 1975b or Fodor 1981, chap. 3.)

The third interesting inference that Descartes drew from his *representational theory of mind* is that mind and body are two completely different kinds of thing. This view, for which Descartes is perhaps best known, is usually called *Cartesian dualism*. Most often dualism is interpreted as the belief in a ghostly soul-stuff permeating our bodies in some mysterious (nonspatial) way and running them for us. This is probably roughly how Descartes thought of it. But we can think of Cartesian dualism in a slightly more sophisticated light: mental things, like beliefs, images, and thoughts, are what they are because of what they represent. This, after all, is the central insight of the representational theory of the mind. Now, they represent what they represent because of how they behave in the mind (after all, we just saw that it can't be because of any relation they bear to the external world). The point is that very different kinds of things (brain states, states of computers, ink marks on paper, sounds) could all represent the same thing. For instance, consider the situation depicted in figure 8.1.

The figure shows John, John's name (*John*), the image of John in Bill's head, Bill's thought about John, the sounds Bill makes when he calls John, Bill's picture of John (in whatever style Bill is working in these days), and a magnetic record of 'John' in a computer. Except for John, each of these things is a representation of John. But these representations have nothing whatever in common physically. What makes them

Figure 8.1
John and some representations of John

about John must therefore be, a modern-day Cartesian can reason, something non-physical. Hence, what makes a representation the representation that it is, this line of reasoning continues, is some nonphysical fact about it. Mental objects, considered as mental, are therefore nonphysical kinds of things. This is not to say that representations are not also physical things. After all, the image in Bill's head, the painting, the name tag, the sounds, and the computer record are all physical, but the kind of thing they all are—a representation of John—is a nonphysical kind of thing.

These three central tenets of the representational theory of mind—representational skepticism, methodological solipsism, and Cartesian dualism—have been extremely influential in the history of thought about the mind. All three tenets are represented to some degree in contemporary cognitive science. They are Descartes's legacy.

Hobbes introduced one twist on Descartes's view that is interesting for our purposes. (Do not be misled—Hobbes and Descartes had very different views of the mind and differed from one another radically on many points, but this particular one of Hobbes's insights can usefully be grafted onto the Cartesian theory we have just outlined to yield an intriguing picture.) Hobbes suggested that "all reasoning is but reckoning." By this he meant that thought can be understood as a kind of calculation, perhaps often unconscious, using formal operations on symbols stored in the mind. With Hobbes's dictum in mind, we can see the completion of Descartes's model of mind as a prototype for contemporary cognitive science. Not only are our mental states and processes to be conceived of as forming a sort of autonomous representational system; in fact, they are all to be thought of as in some sense *mathematical* (or at least *linguistic*—but at any rate, in some sense *formal*) objects, at least at some level of description, and the operations our minds perform on them when we think are to be conceived of as *computations*. Again, note that this elaboration is neither obvious nor in any sense necessarily true. It could well be (as many current connectionists maintain) that although we represent the world, our representations are not in any appropriate sense distinct formal objects themselves. These fruits of seventeenth-century philosophy contain the seeds of contemporary cognitive science.

Over the next three hundred years the Cartesian approach to the philosophy of mind went in and out of fashion and was refined and blended with other approaches. At the end of the nineteenth century philosophy gave birth to psychology. That first psychology, sometimes called *introspectionism*, was very Cartesian in its orientation, but it soon gave way to *behaviorism*, a decidedly anti-Cartesian school of psychology. Then, in the early 1950s, a remarkable development occurred. Behaviorism began to give way to *cognitive psychology*, a brand of psychology that takes seriously the computational version of the representational theory of mind. (Though the reasons for this development in psychology are many and complex, one can say with some justice—as we will see shortly—that the reasons for the demise of behaviorism and the rise of cognitive psychology had to do with the difficulties behaviorists had in extending their rather simple models of habit formation and learning to theories of complex behavior, reasoning, memory, problem solving, language acquisition, and the like— exactly the things Descartes and Hobbes found most interesting. The patterns of failure suggested that theories of a very different kind—describing internal representational structures in detail (or perhaps brain processes)—would be necessary to account for this range of phenomena.) At the same time philosophy began to swing back in the Cartesian-Hobbesian direction, linguistics (in Chomsky's very Cartesian form) began to emerge as an exciting science, and computer science emerged as a full-fledged discipline. Motivated by that same Cartesian-Hobbesian vision of the mind as a calculating device operating on representations, computer scientists began the quest for artificial intelligence. Cognitive science was conceived.

The Role of Philosophy
Clearly, philosophy has played an important role in the history of cognitive science and in the history of the ideas it embodies. The philosopher also has a place in the ongoing practice of cognitive science. Philosophy is a foundational discipline. Not only does it do the spadework that makes the construction of other disciplines possible; it also pays constant attention to the foundations of those disciplines as they are practiced. Philosophers assist scientists in defining their enterprise and in clarifying what they are studying, what their methods ought to be, and what relations hold between the entities studied by the various disciplines. This function is particularly important in a new, interdisciplinary enterprise like cognitive science, in which the entities being studied—abstract mental and computational processes—are often difficult to pin down and in which practitioners of different disciplines are working on related problems in rather different ways. The philosopher helps these collaborators to formulate their problems and models and to think more clearly about the nature and structure of the objects and processes under discussion. Philosophers have worried about these questions about the mind and language for a few millennia, and, if nothing else, they know where it is easy to get muddled. We can distinguish three areas of philosophical contribution: defining the enterprise and getting a synoptic view of it (*philosophy of science*); concerning itself with the nature of the abstract structures being studied by cognitive science, and their relation to more concrete things (*metaphysics*); and thinking about the interrelations between representations, and how the mind organizes and uses them to generate knowledge (*epistemology*).

In the following sections of this chapter we will apply all of these philosophical contributions: we will attempt to gain a synoptic view of the enterprise of cognitive science, consider ontological questions that it raises, discuss knowledge (how it is represented in the mind and how, if at all, it could be represented in a machine), and explore the current state of the field.

8.2 The Enterprise of Cognitive Science

Behaviorism

The first fifty years of this century saw the study of the mind dominated by a school of psychological thought known as *behaviorism*, led by I. P. Pavlov, John Watson, Edward Chace Tolman, Clark Hull, and B. F. Skinner. Behaviorism arose as a reaction against introspectionism. The introspectionists studied the contents and structure of consciousness by having carefully trained subjects introspect, that is, "look inside" their minds and report what they observed, under carefully controlled conditions and while performing particular cognitive tasks. Introspectionist psychology failed largely because of the fallibility of introspection, which was, after all, its principal instrument. But the features of introspectionist psychology most directly responsible for its collapse were the tremendous disagreements over fundamental data between different laboratories and the lack of any unified, testable theory to explain these data.

The behaviorists argued that the problem lay in the subjectivity of the introspectionist method. They contrasted this method, whose data could be directly observed only by the subject and could not be independently verified, with the methods of the physical and biological sciences, where data are always public and therefore independently observable, or objective. Some behaviorist critics went so far as to suggest that the very phenomena the introspectionists claimed to be studying—the mind, consciousness, attention, and cognitive processes, among others—could not even be shown to exist and were therefore not proper objects of scientific inquiry at all. The behaviorists proposed to replace introspectionism with an objective science of behavior modeled on the more successful physical sciences.

Behaviorism was not confined to psychology. Philosophers such as Gilbert Ryle, Ludwig Wittgenstein, Rudolph Carnap, Otto Neurath, and Moritz Schlick argued that if they were to be at all useful to a science of psychology, such *mentalistic* terms as *thought, belief, mind,* and *consciousness* had to be redefined in terms of, or replaced with, more objective terms that referred only to publicly observable movements of the organism or to events in its environment.

The behaviorists attempted to discover *scientific laws*, that is, universal generalizations that would describe, predict, and explain the relations between the *stimuli* organisms encountered in their environment and the *responses*, or movements, they produced in the presence of those stimuli. The principal area investigated by the behaviorists was learning. Laws were sought, for instance, that would predict the rate at which rats would press bars when they received food rewards on a variable rather than a fixed schedule.

As an approach to explaining simple sorts of behavior, particularly of cognitively simple animals in carefully restricted situations, behaviorism was rather successful. But when the behaviorists attempted to understand more complex behavior, they encountered difficulties. It became apparent that there simply are no good ways to describe very complex behavior such as speech that allow the formulation of explanatory laws. For example, try to develop a generalization that enables you to predict under what circumstances someone will use an adverb, just as a physicist can predict the orbit of a planet. Moreover, much behavior (again, linguistic behavior provides an excellent example) does not seem to be under the direct, lawlike control either of stimuli in the environment or of past reinforcement or punishment histories. Rather, it seems to be generated by complex cognitive structures, including those responsible for the thought being expressed and such structures as the grammars studied by linguists.

Behaviorism claimed that all mentalistic terms can be redefined in terms of observable, physically describable behavior. But consider any mentalistic term—say, "thinking that the queen of England is the richest woman in the world." A behavioral definition of that term might run like this: " 'Thinking that the queen of England is the richest woman in the world' = $_{df}$ (abbreviation for "is by definition") *being disposed to say things like 'The queen of England is the richest woman in the world'; being disposed to answer the question 'Who is the richest woman in the world?' with 'The queen of England, of course'; and so on.*" (Definitions like this, with many variations, have been suggested by defenders of various versions of behaviorism.)

But such definitions cannot work, for several reasons. First, the *and so on* at the end of the definition is not just an abbreviation for a lot of dispositions that we are just too lazy to specify. The number of dispositions necessary to fill out such a definition is boundless, and even if endless definitions make sense, they are certainly of little use to a scientific discipline.

Second, many things that do not have the requisite beliefs nonetheless have the named dispositions—for example, the tape recorder with the tape loop that endlessly plays "The queen of England is the richest woman in the world."

Third, there is the case of things that do have the belief in question but lack any of the supposedly defining behavioral dispositions. Suppose you are being tortured by the Renganese secret police, who want to know who the richest woman in the world is so that they can kidnap her, hold her for ransom, and solve their national debt problems. You know the answer. But do you have the disposition to answer their questions correctly? Certainly not! (And assuming you did crack under torture, for a die-hard behaviorist, your answer could be of no use to your captors. Although their interpreter might come to say things like "The queen of England is the richest woman in the world," the Renganese secret police speak only Renganese. So they would only come to say things like "Hoya pata Englaterri nyool chen mikya"—which is a different thing to say and hence bespeaks a different belief, on the standard behaviorist account.)

Fourth, a behaviorist might try to rescue the account by saying that the dispositions are dispositions to say things only when a speaker *wants* to evidence the belief, or when the speaker *believes* that no harm will result, or some such thing, and that not only English words count, but so do any translations of them, that is, any words that *mean the same thing*. But both of these attempts, though perhaps the only hope for saving the theory, lead down the garden path to circularity. The goal of behaviorism was to define mentalistic terms using only behavioral terms, but this strategy for rescuing failed definitions relies upon using mentalistic terms themselves to define other mentalistic terms. Thus, behaviorism appears to succumb not only to empirical difficulties, but to conceptual confusion as well.

The failure of behaviorism provided one motivation for adopting the cognitive approach. Behaviorism's difficulties made it clear that in order to really understand complex cognitive capacities, it is necessary to look inside the organism—to pay attention not only to the stimuli impinging upon the organism and its responses to them (though these are certainly important) but also to the internal processes that mediate between perception and action. But what was lacking until recently, when computer science developed, was a suitable model for the internal processing that could support such behavior.

The Computer and Cognitive Science

The necessary model for internal processing was supplied by the digital computer. Computer science showed cognitive scientists that it was possible to explain the intelligent behavior of a complex system without presupposing the intelligence of its components by employing the idea of an information-processing system and the computational model of explanation. This model also demonstrated the possibility of analyzing meaning in terms of *functionally interpreted* states of physical systems (what Newell and Simon (1976) have called the idea of a *physical symbol system* introduced in chapter 2). Finally, all of this suggested a model of the relation between mind and body that is respectably *physicalistic*, in that it does not posit a dualism of substance, but that avoids the pitfalls of behaviorism and does not involve reducing the mental to the physical. Let us first see how the digital computer gives r se to each of these ideas, and then turn to their realization in the enterprise of cognitive science.

For many years, especially in the heyday of behaviorism, it was thought that there were only two ways to explain intelligent behavior: physicalistically or mentalistically. Mentalistic explanations operated by reference to the "internal workings of the mind" or, as Ryle (1949) called it, the "ghost in the machine." Such explanations were looked upon with disfavor because it was argued (by Ryle, among others) that any mentalistic explanation could only "explain" intelligence by appealing to structures or processes that were themselves intelligent.

As an example, consider a hypothetical debate between yourself, as a cognitive scientist, and a philosopher of Ryle's school. You want to explain your ability to come up with examples in a discussion of philosophy of mind by appealing to internal processes. "Well," the philosopher might say, "come up with some plausible candidate processes (not necessarily all of the details)." You might reply, "There is a process that selects important features of the topic under discussion, and a 'librarian process' that checks my memory store of philosophical examples for examples that have some of those features, and a 'pattern matcher' that finds the closest one to what I need, and an 'augmenter' that fixes up the details just right."

With only this much in hand, the philosopher can argue, "These internal processes are all well and good, but each must be applied intelligently. If the 'feature selector' is to do any good, it must select the right features; if the 'librarian' is to do its job well it must select the best examples; and so forth. And all of these tasks require intelligence. Therefore, your explanation of your ability requires us to explain the intelligence of your subsystems, and we are back where we started, only with more problems. So much for ghosts in machines."

The advent of digital computers has provided a model of explanation that suggests a reply to this argument (which we may call *Ryle's regress*). Imagine how we explain the ability of a computer to do the things it does. We posit subprocesses to explain the actions of processes, sub-subprocesses to explain the actions of subprocesses, and so on, until we reach the level of elementary information processes. Although the action of the whole program may appear to require brilliance (especially if it reliably generates good philosophical examples), the processes into which it decomposes at the first level (the "main" subroutines) require only moderate brightness. As we go down through the *levels of decomposition* in the explanation, the spark of intelligence required for the processes at each level gradually dims, until we reach the machine language instructions, which are easy to implement mechanically. The ghost is exorcized by gradually reducing it to simple formal operations as we elaborate the explanation.

From the idea of an information-processing system it is but a short step to the idea of a physical symbol system. We will make both of these concepts much more precise later, but for now note that what a computer does is process *symbols*. Symbols always have a dual nature. On the one hand, they are physical things (like the ink on this page, or the electrical impulses and magnetic records in the computer); on the other hand, they stand for things other than themselves. The computer processes these symbols according to rules, and the meanings of the symbols are tied up with these rules. But the computer does not need to "know" the meanings of the symbols. It performs its operations on symbols by means of procedures that depend only upon their physical characteristics. The trick, of course, is to get the physical and meaningful (or semantic) characteristics of the symbols, the rules, and the machine employing them to match up in the right way. This is the essence of an information-processing system: that it encodes information about the world, operates on that information in some way that can be characterized as meaningful, and is structured as a set of functionally organized, interacting parts. The digital computer is a perfect example of these ideas, and it has provided dramatic evidence that intelligent performance can be the product of a physical symbol system.

The final item in our catalogue of ideas given to cognitive science by the digital computer is an account of the relation between mind and body that is neither objectionably dualistic (as in a naive Cartesian theory of mind) nor objectionably reductionistic (as in a naive behaviorist theory of mind). The idea, known as *functionalism*, is that mental states, such as beliefs, and mental processes, such as considering or deciding, are nothing but physical states described functionally. The same physical state in differently organized systems might yield different mental states; the same mental state might be realized very differently in different physical systems.

This is the case with computers. When a small personal computer and the largest supercomputer perform the same computation, they have little in common from a physical standpoint, though functionally they may be identical. Similarly, a computer performing a particular computation using a particular machine language subroutine may in one program be deciding on a chess move (if that subroutine in that context is a "position evaluator"), and it may in another program be deciding whether to buy pork bellies (if in that context it is an "expected gain estimator"). The low-level computational states (and so, perhaps, the physical states) are the same, but the high-level functional interpretations they receive are radically different.

This fact about computers certainly suggests an intriguing question: Might the same be true with human minds? Our psychological states might not be reducible to our physical states, since different physical states might be correlated with the same psychological state, and vice versa. But this does not entail a dualism of substance. Each particular (or *token*) psychological state is some particular physical state (a view known as *token identity theory*), but no *type* of psychological state is a type of physical state, and vice versa. This means that there need be no mystery about what kind of thing any particular psychological state or process is—it is some particular physical state or process—but we need not be committed to the view that whenever that physical state or process occurs in a person, the same psychological state or process is occurring in that person, or vice versa.

These are the ways in which the digital computer facilitated the transition from behaviorism to cognitive science. Let us now turn to the questions the cognitive scientist asks of the philosopher of science. What is cognitive science's characteristic method of asking, attacking, and answering questions? How exactly does it conceive of the mind? We begin with the idea of an information-processing system.

Information-Processing Systems

What is an information-processing system? This question goes right to the heart of the structure of cognitive science, since more than anything else, the view of the mind as an information-processing system is what characterizes and unifies the field. We discussed the general concept of an information-processing system in chapters 1 and 2, and we will introduce other basic distinctions here in order to set the stage for the rest of our discussion.

The first distinction is between *digital* and *analog* representations. Although the digital computer is the dominant technology in present-day computing, there is another type of electronic computer, which is based on analog computation. A mundane example will illustrate the characteristics of these analog computers. Most people buy things using digital monetary systems that are restricted to fixed denominations: dollars and cents, pounds and shillings, and so on. But in some places people use analog money systems in which goods are exchanged for quantities of some material, say, gold or silver. Gold has a certain advantage over dollars and cents: the value of a piece of gold is directly proportional to its weight, an intrinsic physical characteristic. In digital money systems, such as the U.S. system, no such simple relationship holds between the values of coins and bills and any of their physical properties. That is, there is no function relating value to weight, size, or any other basic physical characteristic. Instead, for each type of bill and coin there is a rather arbitrary relation between some cluster of physical characteristics and a particular fixed value. A penny is identified by a set of physical characteristics, but there is no law of physics that will allow us to predict the characteristics of the nickel and dime from the characteristics of the penny. Further, this kind of arbitrary mapping requires that some coin represent the smallest value in the system.

A nice consequence of the direct physical relation used for gold is that it can be used to represent *continuous* monetary values, because weight varies continuously. Weight, and therefore gold, also has no minimum value (we are ignoring questions that arise at the atomic scale). Suppose you have some particularly worthless object, say, an outdated textbook, good for nothing but holding up table legs. Suppose you want to sell it to a neighbor with a rickety table for .7 cents. A transaction in dollars and cents is impossible, but gold meets your requirements. If gold is worth $200 an ounce, then .0000035 ounces of gold is exactly what your neighbor owes you for the book. The analog system appears to be more natural, precise, and flexible.

There is a problem, however. In any computational system we not only need representations; we also need to be able to process them. The apparent precision of the analog system depends on the accuracy of the device used to measure the relevant physical quantity. In order to measure the gold needed to purchase your book, your neighbor's scale would have to be accurate to the ten-millionth of an ounce. This problem is not restricted to attempts to weigh tiny amounts. It arises whenever we need precision that exceeds the capacity of the scale. If the scale is accurate to the hundreth of an ounce, then its range of error at $200 per ounce is $2. Under these conditions dollars and cents are more accurate (as long as the eyesight of the person handling the money is good enough to distinguish the coins).

Analog systems have advantages. They have a certain simplicity and directness because meaningful values are directly represented as physical quantities. Straightforward physical processes that operate on the physical qualities can therefore have an immediate interpretation. Continuous values can be represented. Also, certain computational problems that are solvable by analog computation lead to unmanageable combinatorial explosions when approached digitally. An example due to Dreyfus (1979) illustrates this point. Suppose you have a map of a complicated railway system linking all of the towns in a region, and you want to figure out the shortest route between two towns. You could write a digital computer program to solve the problem, but any program you wrote could be shown to consume rapidly increasing and finally impractical amounts of time as the number of cities served by the system increased. Instead, you could make a "string-net map" of the system, by tying pieces of string of lengths proportional to the rail links together in such a way that the pattern of links and towns matches the pattern of string pieces and knots. Then you could just grasp the two knots matching the two towns and pull. The taut string path would represent the shortest rail route.

Analog systems also have disadvantages. They always have a margin of error determined by the accuracy of their measuring devices. If values must be held over time, or passed along from process to process, the errors can accumulate rapidly and render the output useless. Because meaningful values and transformations are directly represented by simple continuous physical characteristics and processes, analog systems also tend to be inflexible special-purpose devices. A string-net map is not the right device to schedule trains and keep track of passenger reservations, for example. Thus, it is not clear how a complex and flexible symbol system could be implemented on a strictly analog computer.

The advantage of the digital system is that there is no margin of error. The quantities it represents are always precise. Even a worn penny and a torn dollar bill represent one dollar and one cent exactly. In digital computers symbols are also assigned to physical values in such a way that perturbations of physical qualities rarely cause error. Digital computation, however, often seems awkward and unnatural because of the indirect relationship between complex symbolic structures and physical operations.

Several factors determine what kind of system of representation is appropriate for any particular task. One important variable is the kind of equipment available. If you have good mints and poor scales, choose a digital monetary system; given good scales but poor mints, an analog system might work better. Another important variable is the nature of the task to be accomplished.

An information-processing system may represent and encode information in either a digital or an analog form. If it is to operate digitally, using such perfectly precise, error-free (and hence information-preserving) operations as arithmetic, linguistic, and logical operations, the information must be encoded digitally. If the system is to operate analogically, exploiting the speed and fine-grained nature of such analog processes as rotation, expansion, or continuous amplification, the representations it employs must be analogical.

Just which, if any, human information processes are digital, and which, if any, are analog, is a fascinating philosophical and psychological question. The controversy that most often raises this question concerns the reality of mental imagery. The dispute is generally couched in these terms: Are all mental representations linguistic in form, or are some pictorial, operated on by processes that can be characterized with terms such as "mental rotation" or "scanning with the 'mind's eye'"? Linguistic representations, of course, are digital. The units of representation are the set of phonemes, or the lexicon of the language, depending on the level of analysis one chooses. The operations on them are the operations of logic, arithmetic, and syntax. Mental images, however, are analog. The units of representation are "pictures" in "mental space," and their dimensions vary continuously. The operations on them are also described spatially, and are continuous. Whether humans use both types of representation in thinking or only one (and if so, which) is an open question in cognitive science. In chapter 2 we discussed the theory that an intrinsically geometric image representation and associated processes are built into human biology (in addition to the references cited there, a good philosophical source is Block 1980c). According to such theories, continuous quantities such as space, size, and angle of view are built into image representation and are transformed by built-in operations for scanning, zooming, rotating, and so on. Although analog imagery theories have been hotly disputed, some theorists believe that they point the way to the discovery of a number of special-purpose analog subsystems in the human mind.

Research on connectionist networks provides a new context for the contrast between analog and digital computation. As we saw in chapter 2, the connection weights, net inputs, and activation values in networks typically vary continuously. Vectors of activation values or weights can often be interpreted as points in multidimensional spaces. Values are computed numerically using continuous transformations, such as the logistic function. Such features suggest that connectionist networks can be thought of as analog computers. On the other hand, the inputs and outputs of connectionist networks often are not numerical analogs of physical quantities. The XOR network described in chapter 2, for example, learns to compute a digital function, although it employs an analog style of computation. Thus, the sense in which connectionism represents an alternative to digital computation is an open question. Later we will return to the issues posed by competing cognitive architectures.

Whether an information-processing system is digital or analog, it is *intentional*. "Intentionality" and its cognates are philosophers' terms for *aboutness*. The thought that the full moon is beautiful is intentional, because it is about, or contains, the full moon. The words in this book are also intentional: they have content; they are about cognitive science. Insofar as the information contained in and processed by an information-processing system is about anything—that is, insofar as it functions representationally—the states and processes of that system are intentional.

Just what it takes for a system or a state of a system to be intentional, and just what it is to represent one thing rather than another, are difficult matters. As noted in chapter 1, it seems at least necessary for there to be an *isomorphism* (sameness of structure) between the representational components of the system and the contents of those representations and processes. Ideally, there would be some structure-preserving mapping between the components of the system that do the representing and the things in the world (or out of it) that they represent. Thus, if all pointers are sporting dogs, and all sporting dogs are carnivorous, then for a person (or a computer database) to represent this set of relations, a structure such as figure 8.2 should be present. The information represented in semantic nets is carried by the structure of the nodes and links. The reason that this net can represent the information it does is that the relations

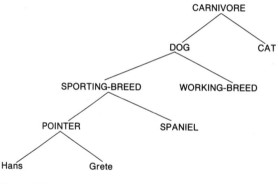

Figure 8.2
Dog hierarchy

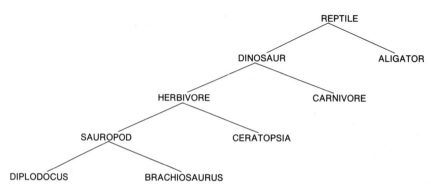

Figure 8.3
Dinosaur hierarchy

between the nodes in the net are isomorphic to the relations between the corresponding entities and classes of entities in the world.

But this relation of isomorphism is not sufficient to make the net *about* dogs and related matters. Consider the net shown in figure 8.3. This net is isomorphic to the one represented in figure 8.2. But even though they are each about something, they are not about the same things. What would capture this difference? One answer is that the ways in which these nets hook up with perception and action would differ. For instance, the "dog net" would be active when throwing sticks for Grete, and the "dinosaur net" would be active when strolling through the dinosaur exhibit of a museum. The point is that intentionality requires not only isomorphism but also some kind of *appropriate causal relation* (sometimes called *input-output relations*) to the world. Not only must the representational structures in the mind or machine be isomorphic to what they represent, but since, as our two examples show, any mental structure will be isomorphic to a host of different things (and vice versa), a representational structure, in order to represent some state of affairs, must typically be triggered by that state of affairs, or something like it, and must typically trigger behavior appropriate to that state of affairs, or something like it.

These two features of an information-processing system may not be sufficient for it to be intentional. Many philosophers argue that more is necessary as well (Searle

1980). But they seem clearly necessary, and they seem at least to be central features of the representational power of human and artificial information-processing systems. Reflection on the nonsufficiency of isomorphism for representation raises the possibility, however, that isomorphism might not even be necessary for intentionality. Some cognitive scientists reflect on the capacity of connectionist networks to employ distributed representations. They note that there is sometimes no obvious feature of these representations that is isomorphic to what is represented, and they would argue that intentionality requires only reliable causal relations of particular kinds between representational states and perception, action, and other representational states, and that no further isomorphism requirement must be attached.

One final characteristic of information-processing systems remains to be discussed: their *modularity on functional dimensions*. This is a point about what kinds of parts these systems decompose into. Compare three objects: an anvil, an automobile engine, and a story-understanding computer. In order to understand the "behavior" of the anvil under various stresses or weather conditions, we can simply decompose it into a set of adjacent regions and investigate their behavior. But suppose that we tried to explain how an automobile engine works by dividing it exhaustively into a set of adjacent one-inch·cubes and then explaining (1) the behavior of each cube and (2) their interactions. Imagine what some of these pieces would contain. One might include part of a piston, part of an intake valve, some empty space, and a bit of the wall of a cylinder. Another might include a piece of carburetor, a piece of air filter, and part of a wing nut. Many cubes would be largely empty. There would be no way to explain the operation of the engine taking this set of cubes as its fundamental parts.

It would be much better to decompose the engine into its "natural" modules: the fuel system, the electrical system, the ignition system, the exhaust system, and so forth, to explain the behavior of each of these systems (perhaps by decomposing them into their natural components), and then to characterize the interactions among these systems. The interesting thing about this strategy (the only one capable of providing an explanation) is that the components into which it divides the engine will in general be related not spatially but functionally. They subserve the same or related functions, and these functions are hierarchically arranged: the fuel system delivers fuel to the cylinders; the carburetor (a component of the fuel system) mixes the gasoline and air; the needle valve assembly controls the amount of gasoline admitted to the carburetor; and so forth. This kind of explanation of how something works is called a *systematic explanation* (Haugeland 1978).

This kind of functional organization is characteristic of information-processing systems as well. The only difference is that in information-processing systems, unlike automobile engines, the parts of the system, their functions, and the ways in which they are interconnected are characterized intentionally, that is, by reference to their representational properties. For instance, a chess-playing computer would decompose not into adjacent one-inch cubes, but into such things as a position decoder, a move generator, a look-ahead device, a tree-pruning routine, position-evaluation routines, and so forth. Each of these components is characterized functionally, rather than physically. Indeed—and this is an important feature of information-processing systems—there is a sense in which it does not matter what physical stuff the components are made of as long as they generate the right output for each input. Moreover, each function, and hence each device, is characterized intentionally. This, then, is the essence of an information-processing system: a system of representations and representation manipulators that decomposes functionally, and whose functions and components are characterized intentionally. Cognitive science is the attempt to understand the mind as just such a system.

Later in this chapter we will turn to some of the specific philosophical problems that arise from thinking of the mind as an information-processing system (henceforth IPS). Much of the philosophy of cognitive science is taken up with those problems. But first we consider the general structural features of IPSs more carefully to see what it means to think about thinking from an IPS point of view.

The Structure of Cognitive Science

Once we adopt an IPS view of the mind, we think of cognitive processes (deciding, planning movement, retrieving a memory), cognitive states (believing that cognitive science is fun, desiring a cold drink), constructing a visual percept in response to light impinging on our retinas, or solving a difficult puzzle like Rubik's cube as manifestations of a complex set of computational operations on neurally encoded symbols, carried out by a complex IPS, of whose operations we are largely unaware. Those symbols represent not only the things about which we are consciously thinking but also a host of items used internally to the system, of whose very existence we are unaware, such as texture gradients or stack heights.

On this model, our cognitive states—our beliefs, desires, moods, hopes, and fears— are states of this IPS. Exactly what this means is a matter of some dispute (see section 8.3). But the rough idea is that just as a computer's moving its pawn to king's four is, when carefully examined, just an informational characterization of a particular physical state of that computer (voltage high on such and such a line, and so forth), your moving a pawn to king's four is just a way of informationally characterizing your physical state, including perhaps the movement of your arm, as well as the current pattern of neural firings. Cognitive psychology attempts to elucidate the nature of the information processes that mediate between our neural wetware on the one hand, and our beliefs and other conscious states on the other.

This approach invites speculation concerning the medium in which all of these information processes are represented and carried out. The physical symbol system hypothesis, developed in chapters 1 and 2, identifies information processing with symbol manipulation, which involves structured representations and structure-sensitive operations. Fodor (1975, 1987) has extended this view to argue that there is an internal language of thought, innately specified, by means of which all humans represent the world to themselves. Other researchers, inspired by connectionist modeling, argue that human information processing might not involve, properly speaking, computations over symbols at all, despite the fact that it can *mimic* such processing (Churchland 1989; Smolensky 1988). Given its centrality to thought about the nature of mental representation and mental processes, this debate over the internal medium of thought—whether there is one, and if so what it is—has become increasingly salient in the foundations of cognitive science.

Understanding the IPS model of the mind makes it clear just why AI plays such a central role in cognitive science. After all, in the absence of such a model, it would be strange to lump neuroscience, psychology, linguistics, and the philosophy of mind, all seemingly about humans, with AI, a branch of computer science, seemingly about machines. But if the mind is understood as an IPS, as an abstractly characterized formal structure for manipulating representations, then it would seem that it (or portions of it) can in principle be implemented on a digital computer. Consequently, by studying particular programs running on machines, AI can be seen as a domain for experimenting with cognitive models of the mind in order to divine the structure of human programs. This enterprise would be incoherent in the absence of the IPS model of the mind but is perfectly natural within that model.

Given the IPS viewpoint, the cognitive science discipline that might not seem to fit (if one adopts a classical, as opposed to a connectionist, model of thought) is neuroscience. Although at times we have said that in a sense it doesn't matter what hardware (or wetware) a program runs on, from the IPS viewpoint there is a sense in which it can make a good deal of difference. A chess-playing program on a supercomputer might also run on a personal computer or on a set of filing cards manipulated by thousands of clerks. It might generate identical output for identical input and decompose identically in each of these implementations. But it will run at very different speeds on these devices, taking months to generate each move when implemented by clerks and cards, minutes on a personal computer, and milliseconds on a supercomputer. It might be still faster on a dedicated chess machine, a computer designed solely to play chess. Understanding just how, in detail, the program is implemented by these various systems, and what accounts for their performance characteristics, would be an interesting task. This is one motivation for cognitive neuroscience—to find out how our "software" is implemented on our wetware, and how this implementation affects our cognitive performance. Furthermore, the design of a machine determines that certain programs will be more efficient than others on that machine. As an example, consider a machine with a fast adder and a slow multiplier (and suppose that these functions were represented directly on bits of hardware). Then it might turn out that for certain problems, it would be faster to compute a product by means of a series of addition operations than by a single multiplication operation. Given data about how fast an unknown program ran on such a machine, and a knowledge of its hardware, we might be able to get some important clues about the structure of the program. Similarly, if neuroscientists can tell us interesting things about the strengths and limitations of our nervous systems, from an information-processing standpoint, this, together with performance data, might yield valuable clues about the architecture of the programs we "run." Finally, of course, if neuroscience can provide a radically different model of a computing device (for example, a connectionist model), we might be led to rethink the very model of computation that undergirds the computational model of mind. Some cognitive scientists (for instance, P. M. Churchland 1984, 1989; P. S. Churchland 1986) urge just such a neuroscience-based approach to the study of mind. Remembering that there are currently many viable approaches both to cognitive science and to the philosophy of mind, some computational and some not, it is now time to investigate the philosophical problems raised by conceiving of the mind as an information-processing device of some sort, and by conceiving of a research program in this way.

8.3 Ontological Issues

Ontology

The *ontology* of mind is the study of the nature of psychological states and processes and their relation to physical states and processes. We will consider four central ontological problems raised by cognitive science. These are by no means the only interesting ontological problems posed by the field, but they are among the most far-reaching and intriguing. First, we will consider what has become cognitive science's version of the mind-body problem: the problem of specifying the kind of relation that holds between psychological and physical events in representational information-processing systems such as human beings and artificially intelligent computers. Second, we will consider how to interpret information-processing theories of human intelligence. Are psychological processes really carried out by the brain in some kind of biological analog of LISP code, or are the programs written by psychologists and computer scientists engaged in cognitive simulation merely useful calculational devices for predicting our behavior? Third, we will ask specific questions about the nature of certain kinds of contentful psychological states such as beliefs, desires, hopes, and fears. Fourth, we will ask what kind of account cognitive science should offer us of the felt quality of our inner experience.

Functionalism

It is useful to begin a discussion of the relation of psychological to computational to physical states with a discussion of *Turing machines*. A Turing machine is a simple kind of computing machine. It is usually described as comprising a *tape* (of any length), divided into discrete cells, upon each of which a single character is written (usually a 0 or a 1); a *read/write mechanism* capable of reading the character on a given cell of the tape, writing a new character, and moving one cell in either direction; a *finite list of internal "states"* the machine can be in; and a *machine table* prescribing for each possible machine state, and each character that the machine might scan while in that state, what character it should write on the tape, which direction it should move after writing that character, and what state it should shift into. These components of the Turing machine are depicted schematically in figure 8.4. In this figure the model Turing machine is in state 2, scanning a 1, and so will print (that is, in this case, leave alone) a 1, move left one cell, and go into (that is, remain in) state 2.

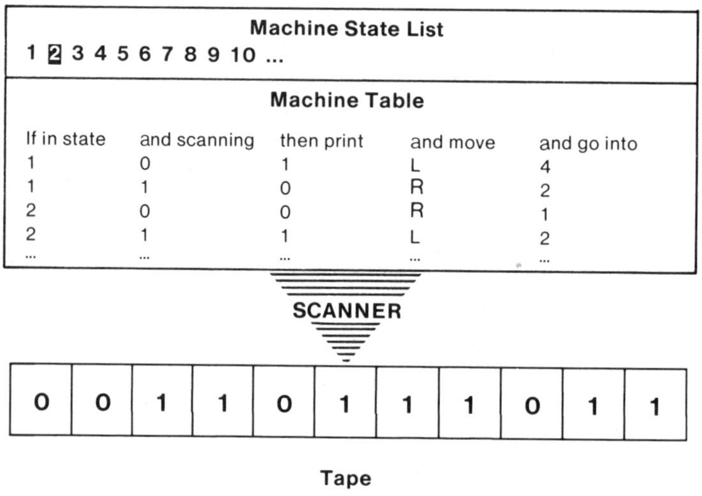

Machine State List
1 2 3 4 5 6 7 8 9 10 ...

Machine Table

If in state	and scanning	then print	and move	and go into
1	0	1	L	4
1	1	0	R	2
2	0	0	R	1
2	1	1	L	2
...	...	...	...	...

SCANNER

0	0	1	1	0	1	1	1	0	1	1

Tape

Figure 8.4
Diagrammatic representation of a Turing machine

Despite its simplicity, in terms of the tasks it can accomplish, the Turing machine is the most powerful computational device possible. It is almost certainly true that any computational process that can be performed can be performed by a Turing machine, and it is certainly true that any computation that can be performed by a digital computer can be performed by a Turing machine. In fact, because of the existence of a so-called *universal Turing machine*, a machine that takes a coded version of other Turing machines as inputs, and then emulates their behavior, it is further true that this one machine, the universal machine, itself possesses all of the computational power that any computing machine can possess.

How are Turing machines relevant to an account of the relation between the mind's information-processing states and the brain's biological states? The Turing machine has given cognitive science a persuasive model of what this relation might be and of what the nature of mental states might be. The generic term for the theories inspired by this model, which are embodied to some extent or other by cognitive science, is *functionalism*. In the following three sections we will distinguish several different varieties of functionalism and ask which, if any, constitute plausible theories of the nature of mind. The varieties of functionalism we will consider are *machine functionalism, psychofunctionalism*, and what we will call *generic functionalism*.

Machine Functionalism   The simplest Turing machine model of the relation of psychological to biological states is that adopted by *machine functionalism*. The machine functionalist notes that the Turing machine is both a physical system and an abstract computing device. Whenever it is in a particular physical state, it is also in a particular machine state, and it is performing some particular calculation (say, adding two numbers or emulating some other Turing machine). And there is no great mystery, no "mind-body problem," about how the physical machine manages to be at the same time a computing machine—that is, about how its machine or computational states are related to its physical states. If someone were to ask how this merely physical machine could possibly be performing the "mental operation" of adding, we would simply point out that each machine state of the system just is a physical state of the system under a computational description.

Machine functionalism asserts that the same might be true of human beings. After all, a Turing machine can represent any information-processing system humans instantiate. They, like us, are finite (though unbounded) physical systems. Hence, if we are physically instantiated information-processing systems, as cognitive science would have it, then we are functionally equivalent to some Turing machine. Since for a Turing machine to be in a particular machine state (its analog of a psychological state) is for it to be in a particular functionally interpreted physical state, it is overwhelmingly plausible to assert that for us, to be in a particular psychological state is to be in a particular functionally interpreted physical state (presumably a biological state of the central nervous system). After all, this line of reasoning continues, a Turing machine can be realized in any kind of physical medium, including both metal and neural matter. It would seem that in the case of humans, then, neural states are to be thought of first as machine states and then as psychological states. On this view, the task of cognitive science is to uncover the machine table that characterizes the machines that human beings instantiate. (For the classic exposition of this view, see Putnam 1960.)

Machine functionalism captures the idea that what is essential to the psychological nature of a mental process or state is not its particular physical realization (though this may be important for various theoretical and practical reasons) but its computational role in the information-processing system. Hence, it provides an account of how people, intelligent Martians, and suitably programmed digital computers could have the same psychological states and processes, simply by virtue of instantiating, albeit in vastly different physical media, the same Turing machine table.

Psychofunctionalism   Even this liberal view of the link between the physical and the psychological nature of information-processing states may be too restrictive, however. One essential component of a Turing machine is its fixed finite list of machine states. But even though the number of machine states for any Turing machine is finite, the number of possible computations that a machine can perform is, in general, infinite. Consider the following example. Suppose that we have a Turing machine capable only of performing addition. Call it A. Even though A may have a very simple machine table, involving only a few states, if we choose to characterize A, not by reference to its machine states, but by reference to what we might call instead its *computational states*, we will see that A is in fact capable of being in an infinite number of states. For A might be adding 2 and 3, or it might be adding 666,666 and 994. It might be "carrying 2," or it might be "writing the answer." Although each of these computational states is equivalent to some sequence of machine states and tape sequences, none is identifiable with any single state, and by virtue of the unboundedness of the set of possible sequences of machine states, there are infinitely many possible computational states of A.

The view that human psychological states are to humans as a Turing machine's computational states are to the Turing machine is known as *psychofunctionalism*. Two general types of reasons motivate psychofunctionalism as opposed to machine functionalism. The first concerns the apparent unboundedness of the class of human psychological states we would like our theories to cope with; the second concerns the criteria we would adduce for ascribing psychological states to humans or machines. Let us consider these in turn.

Suppose that human beings are Turing machines. Then human beings have finitely many possible machine states. How many beliefs could you, as one human being, possibly have? Not at one time, of course, or even actually in one lifetime; but how large is the list of possible beliefs that you are capable of holding, by virtue of your psychological makeup? Could you, for instance, believe that 2 is the successor of 1, that 3 is the successor of 2, and so on, for all natural numbers? If you think that for any belief of this form, you could form that belief and hold it, then you think that you could hold infinitely many possible beliefs. And we haven't even gotten past the most elementary arithmetic! Nor have we touched on desires, hopes, fears, and the multitude of subconscious processes necessary to a complete psychology. Considerations such as these motivate the view that the number of possible psychological states that a complete cognitive science must account for vastly outstrips the number of machine states possible for any Turing machine (though any Turing machine of even small complexity is capable of infinitely many computational states). Of course, this does not imply that the brain might be capable of assuming infinitely many physical states. Quite the contrary. The point is that just as a much richer description of a finite Turing machine results from talking about its computational states than from talking about its machine states (in the sense that there are many more of the former than the latter), so a much richer (and hence possibly psychologically more fertile) description of human brains would result from talking about their computational states than from talking about their machine states.

Even if by some chance there are only finitely many psychological states in which humans are capable of being, there would be reasons to prefer the psychofunctional account of psychological states. Suppose we have two Turing machines, T^1 and T^2. Both are adding machines, and both are made of the same material. But suppose that their machine tables and sets of machine states are different. Whereas T^1 adds by successively incrementing the first addend by 1 the number of times specified by the second addend, T^2 adds by incrementing the second addend by 1 the number of times specified by the first addend. Moreover, they accomplish their tasks using a different set of machine states. Now, it seems fair to say that when these two machines are adding a pair of numbers, they are, in an important sense, doing the same thing. If we count them as "believing" anything about the sums they compute, then they "agree" in all of their "beliefs," even though they share no machine states. Hence, it seems that the computational level of description is, for some purposes, at least, a useful one for the description of Turing machines. Is this true for people?

Here the case seems, if anything, clearer. For even if it seems far-fetched to attribute beliefs to machines, or odd to think that the computational level would be a particularly interesting level of description for them, it is certainly true that among the psychologically interesting facts about people are the things we believe, fear, doubt, and so on. And even if we are, underneath our surface psychology, Turing machines, many different Turing machines could realize these surface states. Further, it seems that our criteria for attributing these states to ourselves and each other have nothing whatever to do with our views about the machine tables underlying our cognitive processes, but instead have something to do with the relations that these states have to other such states, to the inputs we receive from our environments, and to the behavior we produce in response to them. For instance, if you are disposed to say, "Goats are wonderful," to argue vigorously with those who doubt the virtues of goats, to act in an admiring and friendly way toward goats, to infer from the fact that goats are nearby that something wonderful is nearby, and so on, then others will feel pretty comfortable in ascribing to you the belief that goats are wonderful. And this belief, though it may be supported by some set of your machine states, tape states, and so forth, need not be identified with any particular machine state. Moreover, it certainly need not be the case that there is some machine state that is such that anyone who shares your belief is in that state. Psychofunctionalists argue that psychological states bear a relation to those holding them that is analogous to the relation that computational states bear to their Turing machines, and this has seemed a much more liberal, and indeed more plausible, way to apply the Turing machine metaphor to the task of understanding the nature of mental states.

Generic Functionalism   As liberal as psychofunctionalism appears in its account of the psychophysical relation, it is possible to develop an account that is still less restrictive, yet still recognizably functionalist. In order to understand this *generic functionalism*, it is necessary to step back from the Turing machine metaphor and to consider what it is that makes an account functionalist in the first place. Both machine functionalism and psychofunctionalism develop the general idea of functionalism using the Turing machine as the leading idea. But that is really not an essential feature of the functionalist approach. The kernel of the approach is really in the insight that psychological terms such as *belief, desire, pain, memory,* and *perception* need not be understood as some kind of shorthand either for neurophysiological descriptions or for behavioral descriptions.

The claim that these psychological terms stand for neurophysiological descriptions (a view called *central state identity theory,* or *CSIT*) implies that when someone says that John remembers eating vanilla ice cream and that Bill does, too, then that person is claiming that by virtue of sharing a particular memory, John and Bill share a particular brain state. It would, of course, be an unfortunate consequence of this view that only beings who are neurophysiologically like human beings can have psychological states, thereby ruling out in a single a priori stroke the possibility of intelligent (or even sentient) Martians or computers. In some cases it rules out the possibility of two people sharing any states as well. Suppose, for example, that John lost the left half of his brain in an auto accident at an early age, and Bill lost the right half of his in the same accident; fortunately, however, both were young enough that they have completely recovered with no loss of function, so that despite their apparently similar attitude toward vanilla ice cream, they in fact share no psychological properties.

Thinking that our psychological vocabulary is a set of shorthands for behavioral descriptions is, of course, behaviorism. On this view, to ascribe to both Mary and Sue the desire for a pet unicorn would be to assert that they share a set of behavioral dispositions, including the tendency to chase and attempt to capture any passing unicorns, to say things like "I wish I had a pet unicorn," to search the "Pet Store" section of the Yellow Pages tirelessly for a store carrying unicorns, and so forth. Suppose, though, that Mary is so painfully unassertive that she never openly expresses what she wants, and moreover that she has never heard of the Yellow Pages; and suppose that Sue is a brash and cosmopolitan individual who makes all her wishes known. On the behaviorist account, Mary and Sue could not possibly share this desire (or probably any other, for that matter). Clearly, the behavioral account is inadequate.

The Scylla of CSIT has this much in its favor: it lets Mary and Sue share a desire, despite their personality differences, and gives a fairly straightforward answer to any question about the nature of the psychophysical relation. Unfortunately, it delivers the wrong answer on John and Bill, and it rules out intelligent Martians and computers altogether. The Charybdis of behaviorism has this in its favor: it lets Bill and John share an attitude, despite their different neurophysiological makeup, by virtue of being disposed to say and do the same relevant things. But it fails where Mary and Sue are concerned (and elsewhere, as we have seen).

Functionalism navigates the narrow strait by giving each side its due. The functionalist agrees with the behaviorist that the connections between psychological states and the organism's input and output are central to that state's nature, and that psychological states are independent of particular physical realizations in particular organisms or machines. But the functionalist also agrees with the identity theorist that it is important to look at the inside of the organism, and the interrelations of internal states, in assigning psychological predicates to physical correlates. The functionalist differs from both in suggesting that the right way to understand the mind-body relation is via what is called the *token-identity* theory, that is, that particular (or *token*) psychological events are to be identified with token physical events. Both the behaviorist and the identity theorist subscribe to the stronger *type-identity* theory, which holds that each kind (or *type*) of psychological event is to be identified with a type of physical (for the identity theorist) or behavioral (for the behaviorist) event. And it is the greater flexibility of the token-identity position that provides the compass that guides the passage.

We have digressed at this length because it is important to get a picture of the general position staked out by functionalism in order to see that although the models of machine functionalism and psychofunctionalism inspired by Turing machines might be strong versions of this view, they are not the only possible versions. Generic functionalists can deny that particular psychological states are to be identified with particular computational or machine states of some Turing machine used to model the mind, while allowing that token psychological states are to be identified with token physical states under one or another scheme for identification, without being committed to the particular scheme. Generic functionalists will agree with their brand-name cousins that whatever this scheme is, it must pay attention to the functional role that the psychological state in question plays in the system being studied—that is, to its relations to inputs, outputs, and other internal states. In short, generic functionalists accept all of the general tenets of functionalism while withholding commitment to any particular version of the mapping from the psychological to the physical. This has the advantage of "looking before leaping" in the absence of concrete evidence for the stronger claims of the brand-name versions and therefore appeals to those of a conservative temperament; but it has the disadvantage of not suggesting a particular research program or line of investigation for determining just how to map psychological states onto physical states and therefore is unappealing to those who want a bold conjecture to test.

Whether generic functionalism is compatible with radical connectionism is a matter of some debate. In a network with hidden units and distributed representations, a psychological state, say, believing that the queen of England is the richest woman in the world, would be stored somehow in the network's set of connection weights. Different learning histories that included the acquisition of this belief would produce different weights. In fact, it is quite possible that two learning histories would produce different values for every single weight in the network. Nevertheless, it is conceivable that some functional property of the weight vector might be discovered that is a necessary and sufficient condition for the possession of the belief. For example, the property might concern the propensity of the network to produce certain pattern of activation over its hidden units when the belief is relevant to the current situation. It is possible, then, that one could be a generic functionalist and a connectionist at the same time (though neither of the stronger versions of functionalism we have considered would be available to a connectionist). On the other hand, either we might fail to discover any such property, or we might find that all the properties that seem to be correlated with the belief are too distributed and temporally unstable to qualify as the belief itself. Generic functionalism would seem to required a belief to be a stable, internal, computationally discrete property, capable of playing a causal role in cognition (Ramsey, Stich, and Garon 1991). Finally, a property of the weights that we wish to identify with the belief might sustain that interpretation only in the context of appropriate input-output relations and by itself deserve no special interpretation at all (to anticipate the considerations in favor of naturalism to be discussed below). Such results might lead to the conclusion that functionalism of any type and connectionism are incompatible and represent genuine alternative to each other. Another alternative, introduced in chapter 2, is to argue that any plausible connectionist model of cognition will turn out to be an implementation of a classical model (Fodor and Pylyshyn 1988). This debate may be with us for some time.

Interpreting the Theories   We have, then, a sketch of the ways in which one can think of the relation between the mind and body if one adopts the computational view of mind embodied by cognitive science. But there are different ways to adopt scientific theories. On the one hand, one could adopt a cognitive theory as literally true and assert that the processes and structures it posits are actually "in the head" (a *realistic* interpretation). On the other hand, one could just suppose that the theories make true predictions about such things as behavior, reaction times, error patterns, and so forth, but not assert that the structures they posit actually reflect psychological reality (an *instrumentalist* interpretation). Before we explore these positions in any detail, let us digress somewhat. Suppose that we, as cognitive scientists, are confronted with a chess-playing computer, playing tolerably good chess. Our task is to offer a theory explaining how the machine works, a theory that will enable us not only to understand its play but also to predict as well as possible what its next move will be in particular situations.

Briefly, considering distinctions drawn earlier, there are three general strategies we could adopt (described in more detail in Dennett 1971). We could describe transistor by transistor, wire by wire, and pixel by pixel, how the current flows through the machine, how it is affected by the depressing of keys, and how it results in the change in luminosity of various regions of the video display (the *hardware strategy*). Or we could abandon that electro-Herculean task in favor of describing line by line, sub-routine by subroutine, the program the machine runs in order to play chess, explaining how it encodes board positions, how it represents the values of various parameters, what mathematical operations are performed on these parameters, and so forth (the *program strategy*). Or, dismayed by that prospect as well (quite a daunting one even for a professional programmer), we might offer a theory something like this: "The machine evaluates the current position, looking for threats to pieces, possible forks, and discovered checks. It takes care of those first. Then it looks ahead about two moves, evaluating each possible position according to the balance of material and threats to pieces. It especially worries about losing its major pieces. And one more thing: It knows lots of openings, but only about five moves of each" (the *mentalistic strategy*).

What are the relative advantages and disadvantages of these strategies? First, if (and that's a big "if") the hardware strategy could be made to work, it would give an accuracy of predictive power unmatched by either of the other strategies. The hardware strategy could even predict (something the other strategies could not even do in principle) when smoke would come out of the back of the machine. The problem, of course, is that such an explanation is impossible in practice; moreover, although it tells how this machine really works in one sense, it fails utterly to tell how the machine plays chess. To see this, let us consider another machine, running exactly the same program, but made out of wooden gears instead of silicon chips. Any explanation of how one machine plays chess should be an explanation of how the other plays as well, since they run exactly the same program. But the hardware explanation of our silicon-based computer will be irrelevant to—and certainly false of—its wooden cousin; hence, whatever it does explain, it does not explain our machine's chess-playing ability per se.

The program strategy avoids this problem since it would assign the same explanation to the two physically dissimilar but computationally equivalent computers. Moreover, the explanation would be easier to come up with. These are this strategy's principal advantages. On the other hand, it has a few disadvantages of its own. First, though it is infinitely easier to come up with a program explanation of the abilities of such a system than it is to come up with the corresponding hardware explanation, it is still very difficult, and the explanation might be so complicated that it would provide no real insight into the ability at all. Second, there is much that the program explanation will be unable to handle, such as machine malfunctions that are perfectly amenable to a hardware explanation but are simply outside the scope of the program strategy. Third, the program approach encounters a problem analogous to the problem of rigidity that the hardware approach encounters, though it emerges at a slightly higher level. Consider two machines, alike in hardware, that run programs that implement the same general chess-playing strategies but are written in different programming languages, using different types of underlying subroutines, data structures, and control. Ideally, the explanation of how they play chess should be the same for both. But that would require a "higher," more abstract level of description than the program strategy.

That more abstract level, of course, is what we have called the mentalistic strategy. Here, instead of talking about transistors or cogs, subroutines or addresses, we talk about plans, goals, desires, beliefs, knowledge, and so forth. The disadvantages of this strategy compared with the first two are plain: its predictions will be far less exact, and its explanations in particular cases that much more suspect. It will be completely unable to handle both hardware malfunction and software "bugs." But its advantages are impressive as well. A reasonable amount of close observation will yield reasonably good theories at this level, and the theories will be relatively easy to test and to implement for prediction. Most of all, explanations at this mentalistic level will generalize to all machines using the same kinds of strategies.

Let us focus on the program and mentalistic explanatory strategies, since these are the explanatory strategies most characteristic of cognitive science. A cognitive scientist interested in how people play chess would be primarily interested in understanding what kinds of strategies they employ, or, if the scientist was operating at a more fundamental level, what kind of "program" they are running. Now, the relevant question is this: When interpreting a theory expressed at one of these levels, do we interpret claims that particular programs are being executed, or that particular goals and intentions are being acted on, as possibly literally true, and the processes they posit as in some sense real (a realistic interpretation)? Or do we interpret these theories only as useful predictive instruments, with no claim to real truth, but only to usefulness in prediction and explanation, perhaps pending the development of an explanation of the relevant phenomena in terms of processes with a better claim to reality, perhaps a hardware theory (an instrumentalistic interpretation)?

Both positions can be defended. On the one hand, the advantages of the mentalistic strategy argue in favor of a realistic interpretation of cognitive theories. These theories capture important functional commonalities between human beings, perhaps between human beings and intelligent computers. If there are features that humans share with other physically distinct information-processing systems that explain important aspects of the functioning of both, this argues that such features ought to be treated as real properties of persons qua intelligent organisms. According to this line of reasoning, theories that explain our behavior by virtue of these processes ought to have every claim to truth.

On the other hand, the instrumentalist would counter, one could treat all of the arguments in favor of adopting the mentalistic strategy, or indeed the program strategy, as supporting the usefulness of these perspectives for predicting the behavior of complex systems but still assert that they say nothing whatever about the truth of program or mentalistic theories or about the reality of the processes the explanations posit. Indeed, the instrumentalist might continue, the fact that, as we ascend the hierarchy of abstraction from the hardware to the mentalistic approach, we lose considerable accuracy and scope of predictive power is strong evidence that what we are doing is trading truth for convenience, accepting a good instrument for human purposes instead of a clumsy, though literally accurate, one. Therefore, the instrumentalist concludes, when we develop program and mentalistic theories of the mind, or of artificially intelligent systems, what we are doing is developing increasingly sophisticated instruments whose accuracy can only be vouchsafed by realistically interpreted theories at the hardware level.

Though some have adopted this instrumentalistic attitude, most cognitive scientists and philosophers of cognitive science accept some version of a realistic interpretation of the theories of cognitive science. They grant that neural matter and silicon are real and that they are the substrata of the higher-level phenomena that cognitive science is interested in explaining and describing in its cognitive theories. But, they argue, all of this does not impugn the reality of the higher-level phenomena supported by hard- or wetware. Those phenomena, too, are real, for they can be shared by objects of radically different hardware constitution and are therefore in some very important sense independent of hardware phenomena. Cognitive scientists' theories study these structures and are true by virtue of making true claims about these abstract structures and processes.

Even though the instrumentalist-realist dispute is very much open in cognitive science (Dennett 1978, 1982; Stich 1983), in what follows we will assume a realistic interpretation of cognitive theories and hence that whatever psychological or computational information processes or states cognitive science requires actually exist, if cognitive science is to be viable.

We have done a good deal of ontological spadework: we have developed the outlines of the functionalist view of the mind that underlies the cognitive science approach, and we have seen what it would be to pursue cognitive science with a realistic interpretation of its theories. We are now in a position to examine particular kinds of psychological phenomena—to ask just how cognitive science should understand them and how they fit into a functionalist philosophy of mind, and what constraints a coherent philosophical account of these phenomena might place on the shape of cognitive theory.

We will take two broad classes of psychological states as examples for the remainder of this ontological investigation. First, we will examine the psychological states that philosophers call *propositional attitudes*. These are states such as belief, desire, hope, and fear that seem to have as their contents *propositions*, or assertions about the world. When, for instance, you *believe that snow is white*, the clause *that snow is white* is a proposition and appears to be the content of your belief. Belief is but one attitude you might take toward that proposition. You might also *doubt, fear*, or *hope* it. Propositional attitudes are interesting to cognitive science because they are *relational*. They seem to involve a certain relation of the individual to the world, or at least to a proposition about the world. Second, we will examine *qualia*, or the felt character of psychological states, such as *what chocolate tastes like* or *what red looks like*. These states are interesting to cognitive science for the opposite reason: they seem to be *nonrelational*. Examining the ontological problems posed by these two classes of phenomena should give us a good feel for the range of ontological issues raised by a realistic, functionalistic theory of mind and hence for the information-processing approach to the study of mind generally. We begin with the propositional attitudes.

Propositional Attitudes
Cognitive science is concerned with propositional attitudes because cognitive science sees its task as explaining the cognitive processes and states of people and other intelligent information-processing systems. Human beings (and perhaps some other intelligent information-processing systems) at least appear to have propositional attitudes. Cognitive science hence owes us, if not an explanation of these states, then at least an explanation of why we appear to have them. And even if the propositional attitudes of which we are immediately aware, such as belief, desire, and the rest, were explained away, instead of merely explained, the problem they pose would remain. Part and parcel of the idea of an information-processing system is the idea that the states of such a system, physical though they may be, are interpretable as having content, even if they are only representing something as mundane as arithmetic operations. On this account, then, even a calculator might be representing the fact that $3 + 4 = 7$, and we would still have to explain just what it is about the machine that constitutes its states' having the content that they do.

Nevertheless, it is not at all clear just what, if anything, cognitive science ought to be expected to tell us about propositional attitudes. For one thing, it is not yet clear whether propositional attitudes are the kinds of things that will appear in a recognizable form in a complete psychology (in the way that gold does both in commonsense talk and in chemistry) or whether they are merely creatures of the commonsense world that have no place in mature science (as the class of precious metals per se has no place in chemistry). Nor is it clear what the boundaries of the domain of cognitive science will be. For all we know now, a cognitive theory may eventually be developed that is adequate to explain a wide range of phenomena, but belief may fall naturally into the domain of a noncognitive portion of psychology. So positions on the place of propositional attitudes in cognitive science vary widely: some hold that cognitive science must provide a complete information-processing account of what belief is and of how it is related to such things as memory and behavior; some that certain aspects of belief will be amenable to cognitive explanation but that others might require a more sociological treatment; some that belief itself is a commonsense notion that will have to be replaced with a more refined concept for the purposes of science; and some that belief is at bottom an incoherent notion that has no place in an accurate description, cognitive or otherwise, of the psychological world. In the discussion that follows we will consider a range of possible approaches to providing cognitive explanations of the nature and role of the propositional attitudes, recognizing that these approaches do not exhaust the possibilities and that it is not obvious to what extent belief is a proper subject of cognitive theory. Such philosophical theorizing about the propositional attitudes may, however, contribute significantly to characterizing the limits and nature of the enterprise of cognitive science by delimiting the nature and range of phenomena to which it is suited and by sketching the form that a theory would have to take in order to accommodate at least these states and processes.

Propositional attitudes (henceforth simply "beliefs") are problematic for a number of reasons. For our purposes, the central problem is that they look like the kinds of things that should be identified and grouped according to their content, but real scientific and commonsense difficulties stand in the way of doing that.

An example will begin to spell out these difficulties. Suppose that Kilroy is the world's leading cognitive scientist, a renowned goatherd, and Sam's next-door neighbor. Betty knows nothing of Kilroy's glorious caprine successes but has long admired his work in cognitive science. Sam, on the other hand, though blissfully ignorant of Kilroy's career in cognitive science, is in awe of his champion goats. Now, suppose that as Sam and Betty are enjoying a beer at the local dive, in strolls Kilroy. Betty comes to believe *that the world's greatest cognitive scientist has entered the bar*. Sam, on the other hand, comes to believe *that the world's greatest goatherd has entered the bar*. They are, of course, both right, and what makes each right is that each correctly believes *that Kilroy has entered the bar*. The very same fact makes both of their beliefs true. Both of their beliefs are about Kilroy. In fact, a mind-reading bartender would truthfully report that both believe *that Kilroy has entered the bar*. And there's the problem. On the one hand, if the content of their belief is what matters, they do seem to believe the same thing. On the other hand, if the functional role that belief plays in their internal information-processing system is what matters, they do not believe the same thing, since although Betty's belief is connected with other beliefs about cognitive science, Sam's is connected with other beliefs about goats. Hence, they have different relations to other beliefs, inputs, outputs, and so forth, with the result that on any functionalist account they are different beliefs. Therefore, if cognitive science is to realize the dream of a functionalist account of the mind as an information-processing system, and if it is to account for beliefs in this scheme—to treat beliefs, not as classified by their content, but as classified by their functional role in the internal economy of the information-processing system—the question then is, How can cognitive science do this, while at the same time doing justice to the obvious fact that beliefs are beliefs just because they are about things?

The approach to belief that attempts to identify beliefs with particular internal information-processing states is called *individualism*. Two general types of individualism can be distinguished in recent work on the problem of belief: *methodological solipsism* (Fodor 1980; Putnam 1975a; Stich 1983) and *naturalistic individualism*.

Methodological Solipsism   Solipsism as a metaphysical thesis is the position that nothing exists outside of the mind of the solipsist. It is hence a very lonely doctrine, and not one frequently defended anymore. Understood methodologically, rather than metaphysically, however, solipsism is more plausible and has more adherents (most of whom recognize each other's existence). The idea is this: we can study mental states and processes without paying any attention at all to the external world they ostensibly represent, and indeed without even assuming that it exists. Rather than explicitly denying the existence of an external world, which would be both absurd and beside the point, we can, the methodological solipsist asserts, ignore the external world for the purposes of cognitive science, in particular, for the purposes of characterizing and attributing beliefs to subjects. The way to do this, the methodological solipsist continues, is to restrict our cognitive science to discussing formal (that is, computationally characterized) operations on formal (that is, characterized only by reference to their shape) tokens, or states of the organism or computer, and explicitly refusing to discuss any possible interpretation or meaning those states or processes might have for the system in its environment.

Methodological solipsism is motivated by the observations that an information-processing system has no access to the world except through its beliefs and that its processing certainly cannot be sensitive to the interpretations assigned to its internal states. If it is operating on a symbol—say, the English word *you*—the processor will do whatever it does to it regardless of who happens to be in front of it—in fact, regardless of whether anybody happens to be in front of it. Information-processing systems process information by manipulating what are to them meaningless symbols, according to physically determined rules. What makes what they do information processing is that we can later interpret those symbols, states, and processes as meaningful, in light of what we know about the organism's interaction with its environment.

In developing the view motivated by these intuitions, we begin by characterizing the states and processes of our information-processing system purely formally, as a set of uninterpreted formal symbols manipulated by the system according to a set of uninterpreted formal rules, like a complex game or a highly systematic, but possibly meaningless, computer program written in a very abstract computer language. This forms the core of our cognitive theory of the information-processing system in question. Each state of that system, each belief, doubt, perception, intention, and memory, will eventually be identified with one of these as yet uninterpreted states. Then we interpret. We try to assign meanings to the smallest symbols and processes of the system in such a way that the entire system, under this translation scheme, turns out to be functioning sensibly, having mostly true beliefs, making mostly good inferences, and interacting plausibly with its environment. When we succeed in this interpretive task, we are done.

The feature of this approach that deserves emphasis is this: when Betty believes that the world's greatest cognitive scientist has just entered the bar, what is happening as far as cognitive science is concerned is that Betty has processed (in the way that is interpreted as belief in a good cognitive theory of Betty's processor) a formal string of mental symbols (ultimately neurally represented) that are interpreted (in the light of the total behavior of Betty's information-processing system) as a representation of the fact *that the world's greatest cognitive scientist has just entered the bar*. The same can be said for Sam when he believes *that the world's greatest goatherd has just entered the bar*. Neither of them has a representation that is in any essential way connected with Kilroy. Their respective internal cognitive states would presumably be shared by two quite different people, who upon seeing Bill Clinton enter the bar, and having bizarre beliefs about him, believe that the world's greatest cognitive scientist, and the world's greatest goatherd, have entered the bar. On this account, the representations have only to do with the concepts involved, and they mean what they do regardless of what they refer to in the world, if anything. So Kilroy himself plays no part in the cognitive story about Sam's and Betty's beliefs. He does, however, happen to explain the truth of both of their beliefs, by virtue of his happening to satisfy both descriptions that are the best interpretations of the descriptive terms in Sam's and Betty's respective belief-symbols. Thus, methodological solipsism is able to explain how cognitive science could account for the representational character of cognitive states while referring only to internal information processes in characterizing the nature of those states.

A further argument for methodological solipsism is due to Stich (1983), who calls it the argument from the *autonomy principle*. The autonomy principle states that the proper matter for cognitive explanation includes only those states and processes that are realized entirely within the physical bounds of the organism. For example, someone's *being to the west of the World Trade Center* (ignoring the fact that this is not even plausibly a cognitive property) would be ruled out by the autonomy principle as the kind of property with which cognitive science should concern itself. Stich uses what he calls the *replacement argument* to defend the autonomy principle:

> Suppose that someone were to succeed in building an exact physical replica of me—a living human body whose current internal physical states at a given moment were identical to mine at that moment. And suppose further that while fast asleep I am kidnapped and replaced by the replica. It would appear that if the crime were properly concealed, no one (apart from the kidnappers and myself) would be the wiser. For the replica, being an exact physical copy, would behave just as I would in all circumstances. Even the replica himself would not suspect that he was an imposter. But now, the argument continues, since psychology is the science which aspires to explain behavior, any states or processes or properties which are not shared by Stich and his identically behaving replica must surely be irrelevant to psychology. (Stich 1983, 165–166)

This argument needs some refinement to handle certain properties, such as those determined by social relations, but these need not concern us now. The point of the example should be clear. Stich's replica's psychology must be the same as his, and so it must be that the only physical properties that make a difference to Stich's psychology are properties of his body. If that is true, then there is no need for a cognitive theory to pay attention to anything outside Stich's body, and that is what methodological solipsism comes to—that for the purposes of cognitive science, an organism's information-processing states can be characterized without reference to their meaning or their connection with the external world.

This view of mental states as essentially uninterpreted information-processing states that can be identified and explained by cognitive science without reference to their content, but that derive content as a result of our interpreting them in light of the way they and the organism or machine to whom they belong are embedded in the world, has gained much favor within cognitive science, particularly among linguists, computer scientists, and philosophers. But some (for example, Pylyshyn 1980; Bach 1982; McGinn 1982, 1990) are uneasy and suggest that more attention needs to be paid to the meaning of internal states than methodological solipsism permits. They agree with the methodological solipsist that beliefs are internal information-processing states of the individual but deny that they can be identified and explained without looking beyond the individual. The methodology they propose is hence a kind of *naturalism*, by virtue of paying attention to the organism's situation in and relation to nature, but is *individualistic*, in that it continues to view the states themselves as located firmly within the bounds of the individual. We will now examine considerations that lead some to adopt naturalistic individualism.

Naturalistic Individualism   Pylyshyn (1980) has noted that certain kinds of explanation might be difficult, if not impossible, to provide in a methodologically solipsistic cognitive science. Suppose, for instance, that we ask the solipsist to explain Mary's behavior:

It simply will not do as an explanation of, say, why Mary came running out of a certain smoke-filled building, to say that there was a certain sequence of expressions computed in her mind according to certain expression-transforming rules. However true that might be, it fails on a number of counts to provide an explanation of Mary's behavior. It does not show how or why this behavior is related to very similar behavior she would exhibit as a result of receiving a phone call in which she heard the utterance "this building is on fire!", or as a consequence of hearing the fire alarm, or smelling smoke, or in fact following any event interpretable as generally entailing that the building was on fire. The only way to ... capture the important underlying generalisation ... is to ... [interpret] the expressions in the theory as goals and beliefs....

Of course the computational [methodologically solipsistic] model only contains uninterpreted formal symbols.... The question is whether the cognitive theory which that model instantiates can refrain from giving them an intentional [meaningful] interpretation. In the above example, leaving them as uninterpreted formal symbols simply begs the question of why these particular expressions should arise under what would surely seem (in the absence of interpretation) like a very strange collection of diverse circumstances, as well as the question of why these symbols should lead to building evacuation as opposed to something else.... What is common to all of these situations is that a common interpretation of the events occurs.... But what in the theory corresponds to this common interpretation? Surely one cannot answer by pointing to some formal symbols. *The right answer has to be something like the claim that the symbols represent the belief that the building is on fire....* (Pylyshyn 1980, 161; emphasis added)

The point of Pylyshyn's argument is fairly straightforward. A good cognitive explanation of behavior that is motivated by beliefs ought to explain how those beliefs are related to the behavior and to the circumstances that give rise to them. If the beliefs are characterized by the theory as uninterpreted symbols, and if believing is characterized as an uninterpreted process in the believer, then the theory cannot explain their connection either to behavior or to stimulation—or for that matter, to other beliefs. In any real explanation, this objection goes, the content of the belief plays a role. The symbols in Mary's head cause her behavior *because* they represent the fact that there is fire, and any symbols that did not represent that fact would by themselves not explain her behavior. The conclusion that a naturalistic individualist draws is that in a cognitive theory internal information-processing states must be identified by their content, and in order for this to happen, one must of course examine their connections not only to other cognitive states and processes but also to the organism's environment.

This argument charges methodological solipsism with being a useless research strategy. Another line of argument in favor of naturalistic individualism denies the very coherence of the solipsistic strategy. Methodological solipsism insists that information-processing states and processes are to be taken by cognitive theory as uninterpreted formal states and processes and that they are to be identified without paying attention to any relations between the organism and the environment. Now (the naturalist points out) we all agree, as cognitive scientists, that information-processing states are not to be identified physically, for then we could not generalize about information-processing systems realized in physically different substrata, such as human beings and artificially intelligent but perhaps functionally equivalent computers.

The challenge is then posed to the methodological solipsist: given something you have reason to believe is an information-processing system and whose behavior you wish to explain as a cognitive scientist, your task is to decide which of its physical states and processes are going to count as functional or computational states and processes. And of course you cannot, for the reasons we have just discussed, simply stare at the neurons and figure it out. Well, the naturalist continues, I can think of only one way to do it: watch the organism interact with the environment, see how the neural stuff acts when confronted with particular types of stimulation—when the organism performs certain kinds of actions, and solves certain kinds of problems—and interpret the states accordingly. And that, it will be agreed, is a very naturalistic strategy. (But see Fodor 1987 for a determined, though controversial, argument for the compatibility of such a naturalistic research program with a solipsistic psychology, and Garfield 1991 for a reply.)

The point is that simply to make the initial move from the physical level of description to the functional or computational level, as we must in order to do cognitive science at all, is to interpret the system, and the only way to get the data that justify a particular interpretation is to pay attention to naturalistic phenomena. On this account, then, methodological solipsists are wrong in two ways: first, they are wrong in thinking that there is such a thing as an uninterpreted formal description of a physical system, and second, they are wrong in thinking that solipsistic data alone could justify even a minimal interpretation of the states of a physical system as information-processing states.

We have seen powerful arguments for both versions of individualistic interpretations of the propositional attitudes. Which position, if either, is in fact correct is still a hotly debated issue concerning the foundations of cognitive science. But before leaving the subject of the propositional attitudes altogether, we will take a brief look at nonindividualistic accounts of belief. Such accounts are offered by Burge (1979, 1982), McGinn (1990), and Garfield (1988, 1990, 1991), and considered by Stich (1983).

Nonindividualistic Conceptions   Nonindividualists take naturalism one step further. They agree that in order to specify the nature of any belief, it is necessary to talk about its content, and that it is impossible to talk about the content of any belief without paying attention to the world outside, including such things as the causes of the belief, the things the belief is about, and the meanings of the words the speaker uses in formulating the belief. Nonindividualists draw a further moral from this need to pay attention to naturalistic data. They infer that belief itself may be a naturalistic phenomenon, that is, that it may be essentially a relation between an organism or machine and the world, rather than a state of the individual organism or machine itself.

An analogy will help to clarify and motivate this point. Individualists treat beliefs as something like internal sentences. The methodological solipsist differs from the naturalistic individualist only in that the former thinks that we can tell what sentences are in someone's head just by looking inside, whereas the latter thinks that we need to look around at the world as well. But suppose that believing *that roses are red* is not so much like writing "Roses are red" in the "belief register" of a person's brain as it is like being related to what "Roses are red" means. The inscription "Roses are red" by itself is not a sentence about flowers. You can see this by imagining a swirl of gases in a far-off nebula, or billions of hydrogen atoms scattered across light-years of intergalactic space, that happen to have the same shape as an English inscription of "Roses are red." These things make no assertions about flowers. What makes an inscription a sentence expressing a thought about the world is instead its relation to a language and to a community of users of that language. A sentence's being a statement is hence a relational fact about that sentence, much as Harry's being a brother (where Harry is a person who has a brother) is a relational fact about Harry. It is not a fact about Harry per se, in isolation from his environment; rather, it is a fact about one relation between Harry and his environment, in particular between Harry and his family.

Note, for instance, that nobody could tell by just examining Harry—not even his doctor performing the most thorough physical—that he is a brother. Nor, says the anti-individualist, could anyone tell—even by means of the most thorough neural examination—what someone believes. This is just to say that believing *that roses are red* is a relational fact in the same way that an inscription's meaning is. To hold that belief involves a relation among a believer, the corresponding behavior, roses, redness, and a language. On this account, belief is more like brotherhood than like height. It is not a characteristic of the individual, but one of the relations that individual bears to the world.

Those cognitive scientists who adopt this view of belief take one of two attitudes toward the place of belief in cognitive science. Either they decide that belief is not the right kind of thing for cognitive science to study and that it should concern itself only with individualistic phenomena, or they decide that cognitive science must be broadened to encompass not only the nature of the internal information processing of organisms and machines but also their information-theoretic relations to their environments. Both of these approaches involve certain attractions; both are fraught with difficulty. On the one hand, banishing belief is motivated, if belief turns out to be relational, for the reasons suggested by the autonomy principle. But banishing belief seems to involve banishing a central psychological phenomenon from the domain of psychology, and it is not clear what would be left for cognitive science to study. Broadening the purview of cognitive science to encompass relational facts about information-processing systems seems attractive in that it offers the greatest promise of explaining a wide range of cognitive phenomena. On the other hand, there is much to be said for focusing on the already difficult, but somewhat circumscribed, domain of individual information-processing systems in isolation. It should also be noted that such a naturalistic view of belief provides a very natural way of accommodating connectionist models of cognition that defy functionalist or otherwise symbolic interpretation with a realistic view of the propositional attitudes. This may well be despite the fact that no distributed connectionist state of your brain by itself can be identified as the belief, say, that the queen of England is the richest woman in the world. But even if individualism is false, that would not impugn the reality of your belief that she is. For that belief may well comprise a complex set of relations you bear by virtue of that distributed state to external things, such as sentences of English and Elizabeth II, among others.

One final remark about the place of propositional attitudes in cognitive science before we turn to qualia. We have now seen good arguments not only for identifying propositional attitudes both solipsistically and naturalistically but also for construing them individualistically and nonindividualistically. Indeed, it appears that their very nature as states that connect the organism to the world gives them a Janus-like character. On the one hand, in order to figure in internal information processing, they seem to be necessarily individualistically construed; on the other hand, in order to have content, they seem to be necessarily relational. Without content they seem to lack explanatory power, and without autonomous internal existence they seem psychologically and computationally inert. Therefore, some have suggested, perhaps the right conclusion from these conflicting considerations is that the concepts of belief, and of propositional attitudes generally, are incoherent—in other words, that despite the folklore about human beings as believers, doubters, hopers, and fearers, we in fact are never in any of those states, simply because there is no such thing as a propositional attitude. On this view, to say that you believe that roses are red is as false as it is to say that you are Santa Claus or that you live in a round square house. Here the central task of cognitive science is to construct the notion of an information-processing system in a way that involves no states such as belief at all. This view is developed in various ways by Stich (1983), Ramsey, Stich, and Garon (1991), P. M. Churchland (1984), and P. S. Churchland (1986). Just how such a view would look, and just how it would account for our persistent belief in belief, is not at all clear. Nor is it clear that analogous problems about content will not be raised for the structures that supplant belief in such a theory. The place of propositional attitudes in the computational theory of mind is far from settled, but it is clear that given the central role that the notion of a contentful state plays in cognitive science, it will be important to resolve these problems.

Qualia

The difficulties raised by the propositional attitudes derive from their relational character. It is intriguing that the other class of states thought to raise special problems for cognitive science, the qualia, are thought to raise special problems precisely because they are not relational in character.

The word *quale* (plural *qualia*) is the philosopher's term for the "felt" or "experienced" character of mental states. For instance, although *tasting chocolate* is not a set of qualia, *what chocolate tastes like* (more precisely, *what it feels like to taste chocolate*) is a set of qualia. In order for chocolate tasting to take place, there must actually be some chocolate in rather close proximity to the taste buds of the taster. We could even imagine a mechanical chocolate taster tasting chocolate while experiencing nothing (having no qualia), perhaps only examining the chocolate for the FDA. On the other hand, we could imagine experiencing what it is like to taste chocolate (having chocolate qualia) in the absence of any chocolate, by means of hypnosis or drugs. So the qualia that normally accompany a particular functionally characterized state are at least conceptually separable from the state itself. Whether they are also in fact separable—that is, whether these states can in fact occur without their corresponding qualia, and whether qualia associated with a state can in fact appear without the corresponding state—is another question, one perhaps both philosophical and empirical.

Some psychological states have no intrinsic qualitative character. Believing that the earth revolves around the sun or doubting that the moon is made of green cheese has no particular qualitative character, though each may have a particular functional character. In general, propositional attitudes seem to have no typical qualitative character, but perceptual states, and perhaps emotions and moods, appear to be typically qualitative. Of course, many questions suggest themselves at this point. Are moods and emotions qualitative because they involve some kind of perceptual states, or do they have qualia all their own? Do all perceptual states have associated qualia, or are there some kinds that do not? But we will not ask these questions. Rather, we will ask how qualitative states differ from propositional attitudes, what possible problems they pose for cognitive science, and whether cognitive science needs to worry about them at all.

The central difference between qualitative states and propositional attitudes is that attitudes always seem to involve a relation between their subject (the believer, hoper, doubter, and so on) and the object of the attitude (the proposition believed, doubted, hoped to be true, and so on). The relation is not easy to characterize, but it seems nonetheless clear that when someone believes something, that person is related by the belief relation to *something*. The qualitative character of a perceptual state, on the other hand, seems to be a *monadic* property of that state, that is, a simple fact about that state of mind, not involving its relation to anything else. Examples of other monadic properties are *being red, weighing one hundred pounds*, and *being a dog*. These are properties that things have that do not involve their relations to other things, as opposed to properties like *being to the left of, being heavier than*, or *being the favorite animal of*, which essentially involve relations to other things. Some argue that the propositional attitudes are monadic properties of persons (Quine 1960; Sellars 1968) and others argue that they are not (Fodor 1978; Stich 1983), but discussion of this view would take us far from both cognitive science and our concern with qualia.

Why Qualia Are Problematic   In order to see the possible problems that qualia raise for cognitive science, we must focus on the functionalist theory of mind that we have seen to underlie cognitive science. What makes functionalism a plausible theory of mind is that it offers a good way to identify the psychological states of a natural or artificial system with its physical states: namely, in terms of the relations that they bear to each other, and to the input and output of the system. And these relations are all that matter. On the functionalist view, the intrinsic properties of the state, such as what kind of material the state is realized in, or how long it lasts, or how much noise the system makes getting into it, are irrelevant to its psychological descrption. All that is important here are the relations that the physical state to be described psychologically bears to other psychologically describable physical states of the system.

Those who have suggested that qualia pose special problems emphasize this essential role that the relational (as opposed to the intrinsic) properties of states play in functionalism. They contrast the plausibility of construing propositional attitudes in this way with what they suggest is the implausibility of construing the apparently nonrelational qualia in this way (Block 1978, 1980a; Block and Fodor 1972). A few of the examples often used to make this point will help:

> Imagine a body externally quite like a human body, say yours, but internally quite different. The neurons from the sensory organs are connected to a bank of lights in a hollow cavity in the head. A set of buttons connects to the motor-output neurons. Inside the cavity resides a group of little men. Each has a very simple task: to implement a "square" of a reasonably adequate machine table that describes you. On one wall is a bulletin board on which is posted a state card, i.e., a card that bears a symbol designating one of the states specified in the machine table. Here is what the little men do: Suppose the posted card has a 'G' on it. This alerts the little men who implement G squares— "G-men" they call themselves. Suppose the light representing input I_{17} goes on. One of the G-men has the following as his sole task: When the card reads 'G' and the I_{17} light goes on, he presses output button O_{191} and changes the state card to 'M'. This G-man is called upon to exercise his task only rarely. In spite of the

low level of intelligence required of each little man, the system as a whole manages to simulate you because the functional organization they have been trained to realize is yours. A Turing machine can be represented as a finite set of quadruples (or quintuples, if the output is divided into two parts)—current state, current input; next state, next output. Each little man has the task corresponding to a single quadruple. Through the efforts of the little men, the system realizes the same (reasonably adequate) machine table as you do and is thus functionally equivalent to you.

I shall describe a version of the homunculi-headed simulation, which is more clearly nomologically possible. How many homunculi are required? Perhaps a billion are enough; after all, there are only about a billion neurons in the brain.

Suppose we convert the government of China to functionalism, and we convince its officials that it would enormously enhance their international prestige to realize a human mind for an hour. We provide each of the billion people in China (I chose China because it has a billion inhabitants) with a specially designed two-way radio that connects them in the appropriate way to other persons and to the artificial body mentioned in the previous example. We replace the little men with a radio transmitter and receiver connected to the input and output neurons. Instead of a bulletin board, we arrange to have letters displayed on a series of satellites placed so that they can be seen from anywhere in China. Surely such a system is not physically impossible. It could be functionally equivalent to you for a short time, say an hour. (Block 1978, 278–279)

Now, it is argued, though it might be plausible that such a homunculi-headed body, whether its homunculi are internal, as in the first case, or external, as in the second, shares all of your propositional attitudes, including, naturally, the belief that it is not a homunculi-head, it would be *implausible* to think that such a creature would share your qualia. Suppose, for instance, that you are completing the last hundred meters of a marathon, and the Peoples' Republic of China (and its robotic input-output device) is in the process of functionally simulating you. It, like you, believes that it is finishing the race. Its robot, like you, is sprinting, or staggering, toward the finish line. Its cognitive processes, like yours, are, by hypothesis, slightly addled. Granting a functionalist account of belief, all of this seems perfectly plausible (give or take a bit of science fiction). But could the Peoples' Republic of China (or its inanimate, remote-controlled robot) feel the same pain (or elation) that you feel at the end of a grueling race? It might believe that it is in intense pain, but what would it be for one billion people and a robot, no one of whom is individually in pain (in any relevant sense), to collectively feel pain, as a result of the inputs to a robot to which they are only connected via walkie-talkies and satellites?

It is the bizarreness of this suggestion that leads many to suggest that qualia pose a special problem for cognitive science. The problem appears to be that (1) qualia are psychological phenomena and are essential to many psychological states (like being in pain, for instance, or seeing red)—hence that they are within the domain that cognitive science ought to cover—but that (2) unlike the propositional attitudes, which are amenable to the relational account offered by functionalism, the qualia of psychological states are monadic, intrinsic features of those states, and not functional attributes. This is demonstrated, the argument continues, by the fact that there can be functionally identical systems, one of whom has qualia (you) and one of whom does not (Peoples'

Republic of China + robot). This is often called the *absent qualia problem*. Hence, the argument concludes, qualia are not functionally characterizable. Hence, states with an essential functional character are not functional states. Hence, not all human psychological states are functional states. Hence, functionalism is not an adequate account of the mental. Hence, insofar as cognitive science is committed to functionalism (and we have seen that it may be rather deeply committed to it), cognitive science is in trouble.

There are two general strategies that a functionalist cognitive scientist could adopt in replying to this qualia-centered charge: deny that cognitive science ought to concern itself with qualia, or meet the argument head on and show that the purported counterexamples (the homunculi-heads) are not real counterexamples, either because they are impossible or because they in fact have qualia. We will consider each of these replies in turn.

Banishing Qualia   The task of cognitive science, when applied to human psychology, is to explain and characterize human psychological phenomena as cognitive. In particular, though all psychological states have some noncognitive properties (such as being realized on a digital computer or in a human brain), these noncognitive properties are not the business of cognitive science. Furthermore, by virtue of being functionalist, cognitive science has an account of what it is for a property to be cognitive: it is for that property to be a functional, information-processing state of the system in question. If functionalists could argue persuasively that qualia not only are not functional states (just what the absent qualia objector urges against them) but also are not really part of the domain of cognitive psychology at all, they would have a strong reply to the qualia objection—in effect, that claim (2) is right—qualia are not functionally characterizable or explicable—but claim (1)—that they are within the purview of cognitive science—is wrong, and hence functionalists should no more be worried about their inability to explain them than they are worried about their inability to explain the common cold.

The argument begins by noting that many psychological states are qualitative. But that no more guarantees that they are necessarily qualitative, when considered just as psychological states, than the fact that some psychological states are neurological guarantees that they are necessarily neurological when considered just as psychological states. Hence, some properties of any psychological state—in particular, physical properties—though they serve as underpinnings for psychologically important properties of that state, are themselves irrelevant to the psychological identity of the state. Furthermore, the very examples that both the functionalist and the absent qualia objector offer suggest that functionally identical states might differ qualitatively, in just the way that we have seen that they can differ physically. Now, functionalism independently provides a good theory of the nature of psychological states. Given this fact about the possible physical dissimilarity between cognitively identical states, these examples should suggest only that qualitative character is to a psychological state just as physical character is to it—a character that many, or perhaps even all, states have, but one that is accidental to their cognitive nature and hence not within the purview of cognitive psychology. On this account, the right way to think about psychological states is as functional states, which typically have qualitative character but whose qualitative character is not essential to their psychological nature. Explaining and characterizing this qualitative character is no business of cognitive science on this account, except insofar as we are concerned to explain the particular physical realization that a psychological state might have. Such an account might vary from system to system. Of course, one would have to add that explaining the belief that one is having qualia of a given type would fall within the purview of cognitive science on this account, since beliefs are functional states according to the theory we have been exploring. But on this view, beliefs about one's own qualia no more entail the need for an explanation of the qualia than beliefs about elephants call for a theory of elephants. To the extent that one is comfortable exiling qualia from the domain of psychology, this is an attractive position (Churchland and Churchland 1981).

Qualia Functionalized   If one wanted to keep qualia within the domain of cognitive science and therefore wanted to defend a functionalist account of qualia, one might argue something like this: The very examples that defenders of qualia employ against cognitive science are incoherent. These examples suppose that there are possibly two kinds of states, both of which are typically caused by the same sorts of things, and which typically cause the same sorts of beliefs that one is in a state of a particular qualitative character. For example, we are to imagine that on finishing the race described earlier, you are in state Q_1, which is caused by running a marathon and which causes one to believe that one is in pain, but the Chinese homunculi-headed robot is in state Q_2, which is also caused by running a marathon and which also causes one to believe that one is in pain. However, state Q_1 produces a true belief that one is having pain qualia, whereas state Q_2 produces a false belief of the same kind. Now, what could account for this difference?

There seem to be two possible ways to answer this question. One could simply say that there is no difference—that any state that has such and such causal properties by virtue of such and such functional relations is qualitative—hence, the homunculi-heads and their cousins the computers, intuitions to the contrary, have qualia. Or one could insist that there is some nonfunctional fact about genuinely qualitative states such as Q_1, not shared by such ersatz states as Q_2, that accounts for their being genuinely qualitative.

There is considerable reason to argue that the homunculi-heads do, appearances and intuitions to the contrary, have qualia. After all, what more could you say about a pain, or a sensation of red, other than that it is the very thing that is typically caused by (...) and gives rise to all the (very complex) set of beliefs, desires, and so on that (...) and dispositions to do (...). Obviously, "..." will become very complicated and will be no easy matter to spell out, but that is the task of cognitive science and is what makes it hard and interesting. And imagine trying to convince someone (something) that has just been injured (broken), and is sincerely telling you that it is in pain, and is acting as though it is in pain, that it is mistaken in thinking that it is in pain, because, though it has all of the right beliefs, desires, and behavior, and for all of the right reasons, it lacks qualia.

On the other hand, if defenders of qualia maintain that there is something nonfunctional about qualitative states that distinguishes them from their ersatz counterparts, they have the difficult task of telling us what that is. One reason that it is difficult is this. The distinguishing quality must be something that makes a difference in people's cognitive lives—that makes real qualitative states different from ersatz qualitative states (Davis 1982)—or else there is no difference between the two, and the argument is over. Presumably, this difference must involve the ability of genuine qualitative states to produce some effects on our beliefs, desires, and so on, that ersatz states cannot; otherwise, what would the difference come to? But if that is true, the functionalist can reply, then since our beliefs are functional, we can define genuine qualitative states functionally in terms of the beliefs they cause, and ersatz states functionally in terms of the different beliefs they cause. Hence, on this view, if there is a difference between real and ersatz qualitative states, it is a functional difference, and so qualia are functional. Therefore, the apparent examples of nonfunctional differences between real and ersatz qualia (the internal and external homunculi-heads) are not real examples, since it is impossible for a system to be functionally equivalent to but qualitatively different from us (Shoemaker 1981, 1982).

This reply exerts considerable pull unless one adopts the view (explicitly denied by the defender of functionalism in the last paragraph) that there is a difference (hard to capture though it may be) between real and ersatz qualitative states that does not show up in the interactions of these states with functionally characterized states but is instead an irreducible, introspectible, and monadic property of these states themselves. The defender of qualia can argue that just as many things (the sight of an elephant, drugs, fever) can produce in us the belief that we are seeing an elephant, so many things (pain, dreams, ersatz pain) can produce in us the belief that we are in pain. But it would not follow from the fact that ersatz and real pain bore the same relations to all functional states that they are, or feel, the same, just as it would not follow from the fact that some drug and the sight of an elephant both typically cause one to believe that one is seeing an elephant that the drug and the elephant are the same thing. And, the defender of qualia would conclude, as mental states, qualia are within the domain of cognitive science, for to feel pain is not, like being in a particular neural state, merely an accidental feature of a psychological state, it is that psychological state itself; hence, if cognitive science is to say anything about the mind, it must say something about qualia, and if functionalism is incapable of capturing qualia, something must change in cognitive science.

This debate is obviously complicated, and it remains one of the interesting areas for philosophical research in the ontology of cognitive science. It is, of course, possible (Searle 1980) that the problems about propositional attitudes that we have raised and the very different-looking problems about qualia are really two sides of the same underlying problem about the ability of functionalism and the computational paradigm to account for meaningful states generally. Those sympathetic with this outlook have suggested that the problem is to be located in the view, essential to the cognitive paradigm, that physical realization is inessential to psychological properties—that the mental can be abstracted from its physical substrate. Those who take a more biological view of the mental reject this assumption; they argue that the psychological is essentially biological and hence that the problems we have seen about propositional attitudes and qualia are simply problems that arise when one mistakenly treats intelligence and mentality as abstract, information-processing concepts. This is a dispute that goes to the heart of the ontological foundations of cognitive science. We have only touched the surface.

8.4 Epistemological Issues

We now turn to the epistemological issues relevant to cognitive science. *Epistemology* is the branch of philosophy concerned with the nature, structure, and origins of knowledge. Traditionally, the major issues in epistemology with which philosophers have concerned themselves have been the analysis of the concept of knowledge and the nature of the justification of belief. But cognitive science has forced a reconception of what epistemological issues demand attention, and currently issues about the structure and organization of the representation of knowledge are coming to center stage. We will first discuss the nature of what has come to be called the *knowledge representation problem*—the problem of just how to represent large bodies of knowledge in such a way that they can be mobilized to guide behavior and to understand and produce language. We will then examine a few of the special problems about how to understand the concept of knowledge in the context of cognitive science.

The Knowledge Representation Problem
Artificial intelligence (AI) is so central to cognitive science because it both embodies the computational model of cognition and serves as a test of the enterprise. If we could build intelligent information-processing systems on digital foundations, that would show that digital information-processing systems can be intelligent and would provide a powerful reason for believing that humans can be described in that way; should it prove impossible to build such systems, or should serious principled difficulties arise, that would constitute powerful evidence that cognitive science is headed in the wrong direction. Among the most powerful tests of an AI system is its ability to understand natural language.

Understanding natural language requires a vast array of knowledge, and it is important that the knowledge be arranged in such a way that at a moment's notice the system can draw upon just the right bit to help it understand the text it is reading or hearing. Haugeland (1979) drives this point home with a few apt examples:

(1)   I left my raincoat in the bathtub because *it* was still wet. (p. 621)

(2)   When Daddy came home, the boys stopped their cowboy game. *They put away their guns and ran out back to the car.* (p. 625)

(3)   When the police drove up, the boys called off their robbery attempt. *They put away their guns and ran out back to the car.* (p. 625)

Strictly speaking, the italicized texts are all ambiguous. The *it* in (1) could refer to the bathtub, but that is not the most likely interpretation. The second sentences in (2) and (3) are identical. But they mean very different things, and no speaker of English would pause for a moment over the ambiguity. For anyone with the right kind of common sense and linguistic ability, these texts are unambiguous in context. The question is, How do we (and how should an AI system) represent the knowledge that enables us to understand natural language in cases like this in such a way that we can mobilize it just when we need to in order to effortlessly disambiguate texts like these?

This is no trivial problem. Suppose that the way we understand (1) is by retrieving the fact *that putting a raincoat in a bathtub makes sense if the raincoat is wet, but not if the bathtub is.* This would be a pretty strange piece of knowledge to have floating around in our heads. Think of how many others like it we would need to have if this were really how we worked: *that grizzly bears don't like champagne, that there is no major league baseball on Uranus,* and so on ad infinitum. Probably, then, this is not the right account.

We have explored some of the strategies that the field of AI uses in order to try to solve this knowledge representation problem. Frames and scripts are one approach. But even frames, with all their flexibility and power, are not clearly adequate to tasks like those posed by this collection of mundane texts. As Haugeland (1979) points out, although both a bathtub and a raincoat frame would contain the information that the respective objects could get wet, neither would plausibly contain just the piece of information we need. It would also appear that production or other rule-based systems would have great difficulty with such texts. These systems are even less flexible than frame systems and more prone to being led down "garden paths" of misinterpretation. This kind of problem may be best viewed as akin to a pattern-matching problem. For instance, some researchers claim that recognizing letters, words, or familiar objects is something that is more easily accomplished by connectionist systems than by classical systems. Solving these problems may not require a great many (or even any) explicitly stored statements or rules, but instead a well-tuned network that reliably maps stimulus patterns into actions. It may be that by virtue of a well-tuned cognitive-neural connectionist network, human beings reliably and with no explicit reliance on propositional knowledge or inference rules simply map the "raincoat" situation onto the action of putting the raincoat into the bathtub, and that is all there is to it. Maybe much of our knowledge is like that. This, of course, would represent a dramatic reconceptualization of what and how we know.

The problem of how we in fact represent the myriad bits of information we obviously represent about the world in a way that allows us to find just what we want when we want it is still unsolved. It is a central problem of cognitive science.

Procedural, Declarative, and Tacit Knowledge
In discussing knowledge representation, we have been talking about knowledge almost exclusively as though it is "knowledge that . . ." or (to use the philosopher's term) *declarative knowledge*, that is, knowledge of the truth of declarative sentences (for example, "Putting a raincoat in a bathtub makes sense if the raincoat is wet, but not if the bathtub is"). But it is far from clear that all of our knowledge is of this form.

Traditional epistemology distinguishes between *knowing how* and *knowing that*. Though this distinction is not the same as the one psychologists draw between procedural and declarative knowledge, the two are closely related. Much of our knowledge-that is probably encoded declaratively, since much of it is mobilized in controlled processes. Similarly, the kinds of automated, production-style skills we have are typically demonstrated in situations where "know-how" is the most apt characterization of the knowledge in question. An example of a piece of procedural knowledge that is also know-how is *knowing how to ride a bicycle*. We might also know declaratively that a bicycle has two wheels and that we must balance in order to ride it. But it is a very different thing to know that we have to balance it and to know how to accomplish that feat, as any child with training wheels will testify. Not only can we have some knowledge-that without having the corresponding knowledge-how; we can also know how to do something without knowing that we do it in the way that we do. However, these distinctions do not coincide exactly. We may, for instance, know how to solve a tricky puzzle by virtue of representing declaratively a set of rules for its solution, and it may be correct to say that a baby knows that crying will lead to feeding, even if all that is represented is a production rule mediating a highly automated procedure that fires when the baby's stomach is empty. In what follows we will oversimplify somewhat and refer to knowledge-that as declarative knowledge and knowledge-how as procedural knowledge, examining only the cases where the distinction collapses.

Given that some knowledge appears to be declarative and some appears to be procedural, we can begin to ask some interesting questions. Is there some knowledge that is *necessarily* procedural or *necessarily* declarative? Is some knowledge more efficiently represented procedurally or declaratively? Is linguistic knowledge more accurately characterized procedurally or declaratively? Does it make any real difference how we choose to represent a particular item or kind of knowledge? Could all knowledge be represented one way or the other? Is knowing what the word *hammer* means more like knowing that it has six letters or like knowing how to use a hammer? Does the distinction between classical and connectionist models of the architecture of cognitive systems correspond to or crosscut the procedural/declarative or the how/that distinction?

In another version of the argument we have called Ryle's regress, Ryle (1949) argued that procedural knowledge is more fundamental than declarative knowledge—that is, that all declarative knowledge presupposes some procedural knowledge, but not vice versa. In particular, many tasks requiring intelligence, such as reading, problem solving, speaking one's native language, and carrying on a conversation, are guided by procedural rather than declarative knowledge. Ryle was concerned to argue against what he called "the intellectualist legend" according to which in order to do anything intelligently was to do it guided by some internally represented declarative knowledge about the task. Ryle argued that this view was committed to an infinite regress of such data structures. For if to do anything intelligently is to do it in a way guided by some declarative knowledge, then to use the relevant declarative representations for a particular intelligent task intelligently would require using declarative knowledge about which information to use, how to use it, and so forth, and to use that knowledge intelligently would require a further data structure, and so on ad infinitum. To use any information without consulting the relevant meta-information would be to use it unintelligently; hence, the entire operation would be guided unintelligently and therefore would be unintelligent. Hence, Ryle argued, any view of intelligent action that requires that action to be guided by declarative knowledge in order to be intelligent must be misguided.

Of course, the point of this argument is not that there is no declarative knowledge, or even that intelligent behavior is not often guided by declarative knowledge. Plainly, there is and it is. Rather, the point is that it cannot be declarative "all the way down." At some point (perhaps often, appearances to the contrary, at the very top) the regress of declarative representations must bottom out with at least the knowledge of how to use the relevant declarative representations. Since this knowledge cannot be declarative, on pain of the regress, all declarative knowledge presupposes at least the knowledge of how to access and use that knowledge, whereas procedural knowledge presupposes no declarative knowledge. Hence, the argument concludes, procedural knowledge is the most fundamental kind of knowledge.

Not surprisingly, given the role of declarative representations in contemporary approaches to cognitive science, not all cognitive scientists are persuaded by this argument. Fodor (1981) expresses one reply in this way:

> Someone may know how to X and not know how to answer such questions as "How does one X?" But the intellectualist [cognitive] account of X-ing says that, whenever you X, the little man in your head [control routine of the program you run] has access to and employs a manual on X-ing; and surely, whatever is

his is yours. So again, how are intellectualist theories to be squared with the distinction between knowing how and knowing that?

The problem can be put in the following way. Intellectualists want to argue that cases of X-ing involve employing rules the explication of which is tantamount to a specification of how to do X. However, they want to deny that anyone who employs such rules *ipso facto* knows the answer to the question "How does one X?"

What, then *are* we to say is the epistemic relation [way of representing] an agent necessarily bears to rules he regularly employs in the integration of behavior? There is a classical intellectualist suggestion: if an agent regularly employs rules in the integration of behavior, then if the agent is unable to report these rules, then it is necessarily true that the agent has *tacit* knowledge of them. (Fodor 1981, 73–74; reprint of Fodor 1968)

The regress, this line of argument suggests, is generated only if we worry in the wrong way about how the behavior is executed. If we insist, with Ryle, that for the behavior to be executed intelligently is one thing, requiring guidance by declaratively represented rules, and for it to be merely executed is another, requiring no such guidance by representations, then we will fall prey to the regress. But suppose instead that to execute the behavior requires that the system represent something like an internal manual (Fodor's term for a structure of declaratively represented information). Suppose further that the relevant declarative representation is *tacit* (hence unconscious or unavailable to introspection) and that the system is wired so as to access that information in order to execute the behavior. We can then treat the intelligence of behavior as a description of the quality of the information used by the system, or of the procedures that make use of it, and no regress arises.

This reply to the regress involves two key insights. The first is the insight that there can be declarative knowledge that is not conscious, that the organism is unable to articulate—that is, tacit knowledge. To attempt to argue that the knowledge that guides a particular performance is procedural simply on the grounds that the person or machine performing the procedure cannot explain how it does it is to ignore the possibility that much of our knowledge, whether procedural or declarative, is inaccessible to our introspection.

The second key insight behind this cognitive reply to Ryle's regress is that in order for behavior to be guided by an internal declarative representation, it does not follow that the system needs a further declarative representation to guide its access to the first representational structure. At some point, this reply points out, the operation *Get the information necessary for dialing the telephone* can be "wired into" the system, and an executive whose only job is to access the right information at the right times does not have to do much more than recognize those times. Hence, even for behavior to be guided intelligently (that is, by a good representational structure), all that is needed is that a rather dumb executive routine recognize that it is time to activate that particular structure. Then the knowledge contained in that structure can be used by dumb processes to guide intelligent behavior. And that is the way that large computer operating systems work.

This line of argument is certainly plausible, and it may ultimately be the correct reply to the regress argument. However, it is important to note that several key issues are swept under the rug in adopting this reply, issues that are central to the epistemology of cognitive science. First, if the bulk of the knowledge that guides intelligent behavior is to be represented explicitly, albeit tacitly, in internal "manuals" or some other kind of declarative data structure, with a relatively dumb executive acting as librarian for the system, it is necessary to specify what the content of these manuals will look like. It is well and good to focus on things like dialing telephones, tying shoes, stacking blocks, and other such simple, self-contained operations. But is there to be a manual for conducting a conversation about the weather, for doing literary criticism, or for selecting a movie? What gets put in what manual? This, of course, is a problem that goes beyond merely declarative data structures and can be raised as well for highly procedural knowledge representation systems, such as production systems. It is the problem of what knowledge to put where, of how to organize it for quick access, and of how to design an executive adequate for the access task.

Second, even if there were a way to partition the knowledge we represent into a tidy library of manuals for guiding behavior, it is by no means clear that the "dumb executive librarian" that would have the job of selecting the right manual at the right time would have such an easy job that it could be very dumb. It takes a certain amount of judgment to know whether it is appropriate to take the *Run for Your Life* manual off the shelf rather than, say, the *Fundamentals of Self-Defense* manual. Maybe both are part of the *How to Cope with Danger* manual. Once the books get *that* fat, however, the library loses much of its point, for vast amounts of procedural knowledge will be needed even to help find the right chapter.

Considerations such as these suggest that it is probably necessary when thinking about knowledge representation to think about employing a healthy mix of procedural and declarative strategies for representing necessary knowledge (not only the knowledge necessary for text understanding but also the knowledge necessary for guiding action) and that simply solving the problem of how to represent knowledge about some small portion of the world (or a "microworld") may leave untouched the larger and more fundamental problem of how to represent and organize the large amounts of information necessary to get around in a world that resists tidy compartmentalization. It is also important, these considerations suggest, to remember that to "know" something, whether it be knowledge-how or knowledge-that, is not necessarily to know consciously; it is only to somehow represent the relevant information in a way that makes it accessible for information processing.

Linguistic Knowledge

As an example of the usefulness of the concept of tacit knowledge in cognitive theorizing, let us consider the representation of specifically linguistic knowledge. Two epistemologically interesting claims are often made about linguistic, especially syntactic, knowledge: (1) that although we have no conscious access to them, and although we frequently violate them, we *know* (the as yet scientifically unknown) rules of the syntax of our native language and (2) that our knowledge of certain universal principles and parameters of syntax is innate.

These claims initially sound puzzling since, although the notion of tacit knowledge makes sense, we might think that the only grounds for asserting that a set of rules is represented tacitly in a system is that the system always obeys them. After all, we are by hypothesis denied the evidence of the system's reciting the rules to us. But we do not always obey the rules of our grammar. Given that any knowledge we have of these rules must be tacit, and that the only grounds for attributing tacit knowledge of a set of rules to a system is that it obeys them, and that we do not always obey the rules of our grammar, why can we nonetheless legitimately say that we tacitly know those rules?

The answer to this puzzle involves distinguishing, as in chapter 6, between our linguistic *competence* and our linguistic *performance*. Our linguistic performance is what we actually do. It depends on many factors that have nothing to do with our linguistic knowledge or with cognitive science: what we know, how tired we are, how much we've had to drink, what music we've been listening to, and so on. Our linguistic competence describes what we are able to do, under ideal conditions, simply by virtue of our knowledge of our language. A model of English competence is a model of the idealized speaker of English. The business of linguistic theory is to explain ideal behavior, linguistic competence, and not the countless deviations from competence occasioned by the slings and arrows of outrageous fortune. (The task of explaining such deviations is left to other branches of cognitive science, such as cognitive psychology, psycholinguistics, and, in extreme cases, neuroscience.) Now, if the task is to explain our linguistic competence, and if the best explanation of our linguistic competence involves suggesting that we follow a highly articulated set of rules, then it seems that we are forced to the conclusion that we somehow represent those rules in a way that enables us to guide our behavior. And that, given the fact that we are completely unable to say what those rules are, suggests that we tacitly know them. Now, of course, this is not to say whether these rules are represented declaratively or procedurally, classically or connectionistically (and whether, if the latter, in a way that actually lets us isolate the representation of particular rules at all), or at what level of analysis their representation is to be found. That is no concern of linguistics, or even of epistemology, but rather of empirical psycholinguistics. What turns out to be the most efficient form in which to represent linguistic knowledge will depend a great deal on other as yet undiscovered facts about the structure of the human information-processing system. But it does seem clear that the facts that we do not accurately follow our grammar and that we cannot articulate it in no way impugn the assertion that we tacitly know it.

This completes our brief survey of some of the major epistemological issues that confront a philosopher of cognitive science. There is clearly much scope for work to be done, but it should also be clear that philosophy has a substantial contribution to make, both to the process of coming to a synoptic understanding of the nature and commitments of cognitive science and to the assessment, reformulation, and revision of cognitive theory and research.

8.5 *The State of Cognitive Science*

We have surveyed the structure and ontology of cognitive science and some of the epistemological problems it poses. We have developed the idea of an information-processing system and explored the value of that idea as a framework for understanding the mind. It is an extremely fruitful idea. This is obvious from the pace and results of research in cognitive science. It is also remarkable evidence in favor of this approach to the study of the mind that it has sparked such a thorough and exciting convergence of ideas and research among psychology, philosophy, neuroscience, computer science, and linguistics. The view of the mind that emerges is both scientifically and philosophically compelling.

We have also seen that in cognitive science philosophy is not a mere "commentator" on the activities of the other disciplines. Philosophy functions as a team player, helping to define problems, criticize models, and suggest lines of inquiry.

But we have also encountered some outstanding philosophical problems confronting cognitive science. There is the matter of what brand of functionalism looks best as an account of the mind-body relation. Each version has certain advantages, but each is beset with deep philosophical difficulties as well. There is the problem of whether to adopt a realistic interpretation of cognitive theory, and of what the consequences would be. A sound account is needed of the nature both of the propositional attitudes and of qualia. Disquiet about the nature of these complementary classes of psychological states leads to deeper worries about the connection between mind and its physical substrate that penetrate to the very foundations of the cognitive approach. These are not mere conceptual playthings. They are ontological problems that must be soluble if the cognitive approach is coherent. This situation, of course, is not unique to cognitive science. All sciences pose philosophical problems, and the existence of difficulties does not necessarily indicate that those difficulties are insuperable.

The epistemological issues confronting cognitive science also raise a myriad of outstanding issues: the knowledge representation problem, which is both formidable and central to the enterprise; the procedural-declarative issue and the many problems of detail it raises; and fortunately other problems that philosophy has already helped to solve as well as to pose. Again, however, noticing difficulties is not tantamount to noticing certain failure, and nothing we have said about either ontological or epistemological issues could be interpreted at this stage as evidence of the imminent demise of cognitive science, only of much work, and much philosophical work at that, to be done.

Even if we had very good reason to believe that one or more of the problems raised in this chapter was indeed insoluble, and that because of its intractability the information-processing approach to understanding intelligence and human behavior was ultimately doomed, this would not be a reason to give up on cognitive science. After all, Newtonian physics ultimately turned out to be false, but had it not been pursued, relativistic physics could never have been born. Similar analogies can be found in all of the sciences. It is a fact of scientific progress that the advent of each new, more-close-to-true theory or approach is made possible only through the work of earlier scientists pursuing an ultimately false or ultimately unworkable approach. The point of science, including cognitive science, is always to pursue the best research program going, and to push it as far as it will go. It will either turn out to be correct, or, if not, it will almost certainly lead to the discovery of a better approach.

Suggested Readings

Brainstorms (Dennett 1978) offers a number of essays on topics in the philosophical foundations of cognitive science, focusing primarily on questions concerning intentionality and the interpretation of intentional psychological theories but discussing a number of other related topics as well. For more discussion of the relation of mind to brain and of the role of neuroscience in cognitive science, see *Matter and Consciousness* (P. M. Churchland 1984) or *A Neurocomputational Perspective: The Nature of Mind and the Structure of Science* (P. M. Churchland 1989). For a more detailed view of the relevant neuroscience in a philosophical context, see *Neurophilosophy* (P. S. Churchland 1986); for a more popular treatment, see *Minds, Brains, and Science* (Searle 1984).

Further discussions of philosophical problems raised by AI can be found in "Semantic Engines" (the introduction to Haugeland 1981) and *Artificial Intelligence* (Haugeland 1985), in *Gödel, Escher, Bach: An Eternal Golden Braid*, a wide-ranging, more popular, and often highly entertaining and intriguing treatment (Hofstadter 1979), and in two particularly skeptical treatments of AI, *What Computers Can't Do: A Critique of Artificial Reason* (Dreyfus 1979) and *Minds, Brains, and Science* (Searle 1984). Good discussions of the nature of psychological explanation and the structure of cognitive theory are to be found in *The Nature of Psychological Explanation* (Cummins 1983) and *The Science of the Mind* (Flanagan 1984), and an especially careful treatment of the role of computational models in psychological theory in *Computation and Cognition* (Pylyshyn 1984). For interesting challenges to the reality of such commonsense psychological states as propositional attitudes, see (from the perspective of neuroscience) *Matter and Consciousness* (P. M. Churchland 1984) and *Neurophilosophy* (P. S. Churchland 1986) and (from a more computational perspective) *From Folk Psychology to Cognitive Science: The Case against Belief* (Stich 1983). *Representations: Philosophical Essays on the Foundations of Cognitive Science* (Fodor 1981) and *The Modularity of Mind* (Fodor 1983) offer articulate expositions and defenses of the functionalist, computational model of mind, as does Computation and Cognition (Pylyshyn 1984). *Belief in Psychology: A Study in the Ontology of Mind* (Garfield 1988) offers a critical survey of a number of proposals regarding the attitudes and a defense of a naturalistic account of mind. *Mental Contents* (McGinn 1990) provides a detailed examination of the scope and limits of such a naturalism. For treatments of epistemological issues in cognitive science, see *Cognition and Epistemology* (Goldman 1986) and *Language, Thought, and Other Biological Categories* (Millikan 1985). *Simple Minds: Mental Representation from the Ground Up* (Lloyd 1989) offers a compelling integrated vision of the embodiment of mind in simple organisms and machines, as well as in humans, and a sensitive exploration of the tension between classical and connectionist models.

References

Bach, K. (1982). *De re* belief and methodological solipsism. In Woodfield 1982.

Block, N. (1978). Troubles with functionalism. In Savage 1978. Also in Block 1980b.

Block, N. (1980a). Are absent qualia impossible? *Philosophical Review* 89, 257–274.

Block, N. ed., (1980b). *Readings in philosophy of psychology*. Vol. 2. Cambridge, Mass.: Harvard University Press.

Block, N., ed. (1980c). *Imagery*. Cambridge, Mass.: MIT Press.

Block, N., and J. A. Fodor (1972). What psychological states are not. *Philosophical Review* 81, 159–181. Also in Fodor 1981.

Burge, T. (1979). Individualism and the mental. In French, Uehling, and Wettstein 1979.

Burge, T. (1982). Other bodies. In Woodfield 1982.

Churchland, P. M. (1984). *Matter and consciousness*. Cambridge, Mass.: MIT Press.

Churchland, P. M. (1989). *A neurocomputational perspective: The nature of mind and the structure of science*. Cambridge, Mass.: MIT Press.

Churchland, P. M., and P. S. Churchland (1981). Functionalism, qualia, and intentionality. *Philosophical Topics* 12, 121–145.

Churchland, P. S. (1986). *Neurophilosophy*. Cambridge, Mass.: MIT Press.

Cummins, R. (1983). *The nature of psychological explanation*. Cambridge, Mass.: MIT Press.

Davis, L. (1982). Functionalism and qualia. *Philosophical Studies* 41, 231–249.

Dennett, D. (1971). Intentional systems. *Journal of Philosophy* 63, 87–106. Also in Dennett 1978 and Haugeland 1981.

Dennett, D. (1978). *Brainstorms*. Cambridge, Mass.: MIT Press.

Dennett, D. (1982). Beyond belief. In Woodfield 1982.

Dreyfus, H. (1979). *What computers can't do: A critique of artificial reason.* 2nd ed. New York: Harper and Row.

Flanagan, O. J. (1984). *The science of the mind.* Cambridge, Mass.: MIT Press.

Fodor, J. A. (1968). The appeal to tacit knowledge in psychological explanation. *Journal of Philosophy* 65, 627–640. Also in Fodor 1981.

Fodor, J. A. (1975). *The language of thought.* Cambridge, Mass.: Harvard University Press.

Fodor, J. A. (1978). Propositional attitudes. *Monist* 61, 501–523. Also in Fodor 1981.

Fodor, J. A. (1980). Methodological solipsism considered as a research strategy in cognitive psychology. *Behavioral and Brain Sciences* 3, 63–73. Also in Fodor 1981 and Haugeland 1981.

Fodor, J. A. (1981). *Representations: Philosophical essays on the foundations of cognitive science.* Cambridge, Mass.: MIT Press.

Fodor, J. A. (1983). *The modularity of mind.* Cambridge, Mass.: MIT Press.

Fodor, J. A. (1987). *Psychosemantics: The problem of meaning in the philosophy of mind.* Cambridge, Mass.: MIT Press.

Fodor, J. A., and Z. Pylyshyn (1988). Connectionism and cognitive architecture: A critical analysis. *Cognition* 28, 3–71.

French, P. A., T. E. Uehling, and H. K. Wettstein, eds. (1979). *Midwest studies in philosophy.* Vol. 4: *Studies in metaphysics.* Minneapolis, Minn.: University of Minnesota Press.

Garfield, J. (1988). *Belief in psychology: A study in the ontology of mind.* Cambridge, Mass.: MIT Press.

Garfield, J. (1990). *Epoche* and *Sunyata:* Scepticism East and West. *Philosophy East and West* 40, 285–307.

Garfield, J. (1991). Review of Fodor, *Psychosemantics. Philosophy and Phenomenological Research* 52, 235–239.

Goldman, A. (1986). *Cognition and epistemology.* Cambridge, Mass.: Harvard University Press.

Gunderson, K., ed. (1975). *Language, mind, and knowledge.* Minneapolis, Minn.: University of Minnesota Press.

Haugeland, J. (1978). The nature and plausibility of cognitivism. *Behavioral and Brain Sciences* 2, 215–260. Also in Haugeland 1981.

Haugeland, J. (1979). Understanding natural language. *Journal of Philosophy* 76, 619–632.

Haugeland, J., ed. (1981). *Mind design: Philosophy, psychology, artificial intelligence.* Cambridge, Mass.: MIT Press.

Haugeland, J. (1985). *Artificial intelligence: The very idea.* Cambridge, Mass.: MIT Press.

Hofstadter, D. (1979). *Gödel, Escher, Bach: An eternal golden braid.* New York: Basic Books.

Lloyd, D. (1989). *Simple minds: Mental representation from the ground up.* Cambridge, Mass.: MIT Press.

McGinn, C. (1982). The structure of content. In Woodfield 1982.

McGinn, C. (1990). *Mental contents.* Oxford: Blackwell.

Millikan, R. G. (1985). *Language, thought, and other biological categories.* Cambridge, Mass.: MIT Press.

Newell, A., and H. A. Simon (1976). Computer science as empirical enquiry. *Communications of the Association for Computing Machinery* 19, 113–126. Also in Haugeland 1981.

Putnam, H. (1960). Minds and machines. In Putnam 1975b.

Putnam, H. (1975a). The meaning of 'meaning'. In Gunderson 1975. Also in Putnam 1975b.

Putnam, H. (1975b). *Mind, language, and reality: Philosophical papers.* Vol. 2. Cambridge: Cambridge University Press.

Pylyshyn, Z. (1980). Cognitive representation and the process-architecture distinction. *Behavioral and Brain Sciences* 3, 154–169.

Pylyshyn, Z. (1984). *Computation and cognition: Toward a foundation for cognitive science.* Cambridge, Mass.: MIT Press.

Quine, W. V. O. (1960). *Word and object.* Cambridge, Mass.: MIT Press.

Ramsey, W., S. Stich, and J. Garon (1991). Connectionism, eliminativism, and the future of folk psychology. In J. D. Greenwood, ed., *The future of folk psychology: Intentionality and cognitive science.* Cambridge: Cambridge University Press.

Ryle, G. (1949). *The concept of mind.* London: Hutchinson.

Savage, W., ed. (1978). *Perception and cognition: Issues in the foundations of psychology.* Minneapolis, Minn.: University of Minnesota Press.

Searle, J. (1980). "Minds, brains, and programs. *Behavioral and Brain Sciences* 3, 417–457. Also in Haugeland 1981.

Searle, J. (1984). *Minds, brains, and science.* Cambridge, Mass.: Harvard University Press.

Sellars, W. (1968). Some problems about belief. *Synthese* 19.

Shoemaker, S. (1975). Functionalism and qualia. *Philosophical Studies* 27, 291–315.

Shoemaker, S. (1981). Absent qualia are impossible: A reply to Block. *Philosophical Review* 90, 581–599.

Smolensky, P. (1988). On the proper treatment of connectionism. *Behavioral and Brain Sciences* 11, 1–74.

Stich, S. (1983). *From folk psychology to cognitive science: The case against belief.* Cambridge, Mass.: MIT Press.

Woodfield, A., ed. (1982). *Thought and object.* Oxford: Oxford University Press.

Chapter 9

Language Acquisition

All normal human children acquire at least one natural language in the process of their development. The successful completion of this task seems largely independent of race, religion, culture, general intelligence, or location. In fact, many would contend that the natural ability to acquire a language is the chief defining criterion for what it means to be human. Furthermore, it is easy to see why the process of language acquisition should draw such considerable attention from cognitive scientists. The information-processing system that develops in the child to subserve the language function can profitably be investigated from each point of view represented in the field. For example, linguists explore the representation of the knowledge that the child comes to represent, psychologists and researchers in artificial intelligence (AI) study the processes involved in the acquisition and deployment of linguistic knowledge, and philosophers investigate the implications of rival learning theories, for instance, with regard to the epistemological status of linguistic knowledge. Finally, although we will not explore such work here, neuroscientists provide insight into the nature of language acquisition by exploring the emerging neurological and brain mechanisms that underlie language development. For these reasons, among others, the study of language acquisition is at the confluence of the sovereign disciplines in cognitive science.

It may at first seem surprising that a process as omnipresent as language acquisition should be the focus of so much academic attention. Indeed, prior to studying this field, many casually assume that there is little difficulty in accounting for how children learn language—children are simply trained to speak by parents and others in their linguistic community. After all, since language is rule-governed, it is not unreasonable to assume that parents simply inculcate the appropriate rule systems in their children. On this view, children rather passively learn language because they are taught.

Very quickly, however, our confidence in this sort of analysis is shaken. Although linguistic knowledge is representable in the form of rule systems, the grammars that linguists write about are *hypotheses* about *unconscious* rules. We emphasize the hypothetical nature of these grammars to make the point that grammars, viewed from a research perspective, are scientific constructs. Therefore, it is presumptuous to assume that parents can fully articulate to their children linguistic rule systems that, in part, resist our best efforts at scientific inquiry. Furthermore, parents do not generally have access to the relevant rules of their language (recall, for instance, the analysis of phrase structure or pluralization in chapter 6). That is because our linguistic knowledge is unconscious. Although we may, from time to time, have cause to reflect on our language use, we simply do not have reliable access to the systematic body of knowledge that underlies our linguistic ability. Therefore, since parents cannot teach what they do not (know they) know, language acquisition must proceed somewhat differently than we might have thought.

The position that virtually all theorists have accepted is that parents generally teach children language only in a very indirect manner. Of course, parents contribute richly to the child's linguistic environment. They illustrate the language, in effect, modeling the end-state that the child is destined to attain. Still, it is up to the child to develop the ability to use language after the fashion of the linguistic community. The information-processing theory we are developing views the situation roughly as follows. The child is initially faced with a sea of linguistic data. From these data the child must abstract the pattern of the language being learned. If we concentrate on the parts of language examined in chapter 6 and agree that the best representation of the patterns of a language is a generative grammar of that language, then we can recast our position by identifying the child's task as that of deducing the grammar from the available linguistic data.

The child's situation is in certain regards quite similar to that in which linguists find themselves. Working from data that include utterances drawn from a language, linguists attempt to write grammars that define the well-formed syntactic, semantic, and phonological structures of that language. Children are also faced with specimens of a language, and their task, too, is to discover the operative rule systems. For this reason, the child has been metaphorically described as a "little linguist" (Valian, Winzemer, and Errlich 1981) to emphasize the fact that language learners must process the linguistic information that surrounds them and test hypotheses about the nature of their language against these data.

This active model of language acquisition stands in marked distinction to the passive model. It is active in the sense that the linguistic knowledge that the child must learn is not simply presented in the form of a grammar that can be internalized directly; instead, linguistic data are presented, and the grammar must be actively (but not consciously) deduced. As we have seen, the process of deducing a grammar from linguistic data is an imposing intellectual task when undertaken by adult scientists. In fact, if we compare the progress made in linguistic theory in the last thirty-five years to that made by any randomly selected language-learning child, we discover that in learning a native language, there is a sense in which the child accomplishes by puberty what linguists have not yet managed to do in several decades: extrapolate a complete grammar from linguistic data.

This circumstance raises a multitude of questions about the language-learning abilities of normal children. We must wonder what capacities children have by virtue of which they learn language with such facility. Our explanation for how children learn language will come from studying language, observing and experimenting with children, and designing theories of language acquisition that explain the growth of linguistic knowledge. After looking at a thumbnail sketch of the course of language development, we will turn to recent work in cognitive science that tries to explain the nature of language acquisition. We will conclude with a discussion of some of the philosophical implications of this work.

9.1 Milestones in Acquisition

Babbling
Most of our knowledge about the earliest stages of language development comes from observation and diary studies and some important experimental research. It is

useful to divide early acquisition into two stages: prelinguistic and linguistic. In the prelinguistic stages the child's language capacity matures without any clearly identifiable linguistic production. Still, at a very early age—in fact, before birth—children begin to develop in ways that bring them closer to language. The child's first vocalization is usually the birth cry, but well before this, even in utero, there is considerable growth of structure and function that will come to subserve language (for example, in the auditory system and the central nervous system). There is even some evidence that unborn fetuses are capable of remembering messages heard before birth (see Reich 1986). Very soon after birth, children can discriminate sounds on the basis of change in voicing, place of articulation, stress, and intonation.

Putting aside the biological changes facilitating language development that take place in the very early months of the child's life (Carmichael 1964) and the earliest cries and vocalizations, it is the babbling of young children at approximately six months of age that signals the onset of linguistic production. Emerging after the cooing and gurgling sounds that precede it, the babbling period features many sounds occurring in the languages of the world, although not always in the language the child is destined to learn. This stage seems prelinguistic by virtue of the fact that the sounds produced during the babbling phase appear not to be intended by the child to convey linguistic meaning. But since babbling is marked by a variety of sounds that *are* included in the child's target language, some researchers (for instance, Allport 1924) contend that babbling signals the beginning of the child's communicative linguistic ability. They point out, for example, that the sounds of the babbling stage provide the repertoire out of which children identify the phonemes of their language. However, McNeill (1970), citing work by Bever (1961), points out that the order in which sounds emerge during babbling is generally opposite to that in which sounds emerge in the child's first words. For example, back consonants and front vowels (e.g., [k], [g], and [i]) appear early in the babbling stage but quite late in subsequent phonological development. The linguist Otto Jespersen has noted, "The explanation lies probably in the difference between doing a thing in play or without a plan—when it is immaterial which movement (sound) is made—and doing the same thing of fixed intention when this sound and this sound only is required" (Jespersen 1925).

Unlike the cooing sounds that precede it, the sounds of the babbling period are typically organized into syllables. Initially these have C(onsonant) V(owel) structure, with CVC sequences emerging later (Goodluck 1991). Although the pitch contours of these early utterances often appear to imitate those of the target language, there is little reason to think that these signals exploit linguistic meaning in any systematic way. Finally, although there is evidence to suggest that children brought up in different linguistic communities babble somewhat distinctively, the differences are slight indeed. Apart from minor variations in intonation, the nature of children's babbling appears to be largely independent of their linguistic environment (see Reich 1986).

The First Words

The first indisputably linguistic stage of language acquisition seems to be the one-word stage. At this stage, which typically occurs within a few months of the child's first birthday, children produce their first words. Furthermore, most of the child's utterances are generally limited to no more than a single word. Table 9.1 gives a sample of typical one-word utterances. These first words are pronounced quite a bit differently by children than by adults. For example, Menyuk (1969) reports that the child responsible

Table 9.1
One-word utterances (Menyuk 1969)

Noun	Verb	Adjective	Preposition
light	go	nice	up
bottle	look	good	down
car	sit	pretty	on

for the early utterances in table 9.1 pronounced *bottle* as [batu], *car* as [ta], and *light* as [ai]. Several factors appear to contribute to the unusual pronunciations. Some sounds, such as [ð] (the "th" sound in *the*), appear to be outside young children's audible range prior to certain maturation of the nerve sheaths (Salus and Salus 1975). Sounds that are difficult for children to detect are obviously difficult for them to learn. Furthermore, some sounds appear to be articulatorily difficult for children. For example, it is quite common to find children who are quite linguistically advanced for whom the [r] sound seems all but impossible to pronounce. Sometimes sounds that present little difficulty in general can become difficult to produce in the environment of certain other sounds or in certain word positions. For example, children at the one-word stage frequently omit final consonant sounds, the pronunciation [ai] for *light* being a case in point. Final [l] sounds that constitute a syllable also provide an articulatory challenge, as witnessed in the pronunciation of *bottle* as [batu]. Notice that this example involves mispronouncing the final [l] sound as a [u] rather than omitting it completely. The pronunciation of [k] as [t] in *car* ([ta]) is another example of a substitution phenomenon.

Other very interesting classes of early phonological errors do not seem to be attributable either to auditory or to articulatory complexity. The simplest type involves sounds such as [æ], which, curiously, develops after many other vowels are in place. This is surprising in light of the fact that over three-quarters of young children's crying consists of the vowel [æ] (see Reich 1986), and, as Dale (1972) points out, [æ] occurs quite frequently in English in words such as *bad*, *cat*, and *hand*. Furthermore, these are words that children are likely to encounter, suggesting that the frequency of a sound in the child's linguistic environment may not be a good predictor of how readily that sound will be acquired.

The fact that children initially produce syllables with CV and later CVC structure also is at odds with the correlation we might expect to find between the form of *the primary linguistic data* (the totality of linguistic input available to the child) and the form of the child's verbal output. Early in the one-word stage, children who are exposed to a range of syllable types in English delete or substitute sounds in their own speech to conform to CV (and later CVC) skeletons (Goodluck 1991). Later, when they can articulate consonant clusters as the onsets of syllables, they still tend to simplify CCCV sequences (such as *straw* ([strɔ]) to either *traw* ([trɔ]) or *sraw* ([srɔ]) but, interestingly, not *staw* ([stɔ])) (Smith 1973). As Goodluck (1991) points out, this is a situation in which English-speaking children employ a consonant cluster sequence that does *not* appear in the language to which they are exposed ([sr]) while eschewing a cluster ([st]) that appears regularly (in CCV ... structures like *store*, *stop*, and so on). By investigating the principles of information processing that are at work in the course of language acquisition, researchers hope to explain these discrepancies between what the child hears and what the child says.

According to one theory of phonological development due to Jakobson (1968), "It is the frequency in the languages of the world, and not how frequent the phoneme is in the particular language the child hears, that is important" (Dale 1972, 212). Indeed, to return to our earlier examples, the [æ] sound is quite rare across the world's languages, and [sr] and [tr] clusters are more frequent than [str] or [st] clusters, just as this account would predict.

It is quite interesting to ask what feature of learning or cognition could account for this correlation between linguistic universals and the order of phonological development. Clearly, children are not aware of universal linguistic generalizations, and even if they were, it is not clear why this would facilitate the acquisition of the more widely distributed features of language. The explanation that we will advance below is that universally (or widely) distributed linguistic phenomena are readily learnable because of the nature of the human language-learning system. That is, the child's mind is naturally disposed to associate certain kinds of linguistic patterns with and identify certain kinds of features in a given range of primary linguistic data, and, therefore, these patterns and features are most widely distributed cross-linguistically. We will return to this point in a later section.

Another sort of phonological mistake that young children are prone to make that is probably not best explained articulatorily or auditorily involves certain systematic sound substitutions such as the following reported by de Villiers and de Villiers (1978) (see also Smith 1973 and Stampe 1972). One child they discuss pronounced the word *puzzle* as [p ∧ gl] and *puddle* as [p ∧ zl]. The explanation for why the child failed to pronounce the [z] in *puzzle* cannot be the unavailability of the sound in a phonetic repertoire, since the mispronunciation of the [d] in *puddle* shows that the [z] sound is available. Rather, the best explanation seems to require the assumption that children are learning complex representations and relations between sounds that linguists represent as phonological rules, and that they can entertain false hypotheses about the nature of these rules and representations, leading to mistaken pronunciations. Children seem to be learning a sound *system*, not merely an inventory of sounds.

Children at the one-word stage not only pronounce words differently than do the adults in their linguistic community but also mean different things by the words they use. For example, it is usual for children to innovatively coin some of their first words. Although some of these idiosyncratic forms are based on imperfect imitation, others are novel, and both types must, in effect, be learned by the child's parents to determine the child's meaning. When more conventional forms do emerge, many researchers have noted that children seem to express complex and sometimes unusual meanings by quite laconic utterances. It is as if they are producing one-word sentences that are intended to represent complete thoughts. This use of language, called *holophrastic speech*, indicates that children's conceptual development tends to outstrip their linguistic development at these early stages of acquisition. We must draw this conclusion cautiously, however, since judgments about what children mean at beginning developmental stages can be difficult to make with confidence.

In accessing these and other properties of the child's semantic system, we must consider the questions about the nature of meaning discussed in chapter 10. In particular, it is important to clarify just what sort of knowledge the child must master during the process of language acquisition. Frege's distinction between *sense* and *reference* is relevant; we can explore how children form and organize meanings and how they learn to refer.

In fact, initially, pairings of words with referents may not involve reference at all. Children's early uses of words may instead involve a looser type of association. At this stage, although children can sometimes successfully match words with an appropriate object, they may be able to do so only in the context of a ritual or game. For example, although children may be able to name an object in a picture book, they may fail to correctly label an actual occurrence of the same object. As children develop fully referential uses of words, they become able to name objects in the absence of prompting or a stereotypical context, to reason about objects that are referred to but absent, and later to retrieve requested objects by themselves from a remote location.

The concepts that children assign to words also pass through interesting stages of development. Clark (1973) and Anglin (1977) have shown that children's first meanings depart systematically in two rather opposite ways from those of the adult speech community. In certain cases children use words to refer to an inappropriately wide range of objects. For example, *car* might be used to refer to large objects that move or to any object providing transportation. In the opposite case children use words in an overly restrictive manner, referring to a sometimes drastically limited subset of the range of permissible referents. A child using *dog* only as the name of the family dog would be a case in point.

These *overextensions* and *underextensions* are quite frequent in the early speech of children but eventually decrease to the point where the child's lexicon is qualitatively similar to the adult's. Clark's account of semantic acquisition crucially involves the assumption that children learn word meanings by bundling together semantic features that collectively constitute the concept expressed by a term. In effect, this hypothesis about lexical development sees the child amassing a database whose primitives, semantic features, are associated as a group with a single node, in turn associated with a lexical item. If a child mistakenly associates too many or too few features with a given term, the resulting concept will be overly restrictive or overly general, respectively, leading to over- and underextension in reference. Although the details of this explanation are controversial (Carey 1978), the idea that children construct concepts out of some kind of conceptual primitives is less so. As in the case of phonological acquisition, then, there is evidence that children acquire abstract representations on their way to learning their language, even at the very earliest stages of acquisition.

Thus far in our investigation of the one-word stage we have concentrated on what children understand about the meaning and pronunciation of their first words. Before leaving this stage, however, we should briefly consider what is known about how children first identify *words* as the basic currency of language. The central question to ask in this regard is how children determine what the words of their language are. In particular, how are children able to individuate the words in the speech stream to which they are exposed?

Since typically there are no pauses between sounds in a word or between words in a phrase in normal articulation, children must generally rely on some cue other than intervening periods of silence to identify the parts of the speech stream. This requires parsing a continuous speech signal into constituents (for example, phonemes, morphemes, words, and phrases) that are not obviously physically demarcated.

Indeed, in certain cases children make mistakes in this task, for example, taking *I pledge allegiance* to be *I pledge a legions*. These sorts of errors sometimes persist and can even become part of the language. For example, the current form *an apron* derives historically from *a napron* (compare *a napkin*, which did not undergo this change). Generally, however, children are successful in identifying the correct units of analysis. In the absence of physical gaps between phonemes and words, then, how do children identify these basic elements of language?

In the case of phonemes evidence (due to Eimas et al. 1971) suggests that children are biologically specialized to identify phonemic sounds in speech. Very young children (on the order of two months of age) show sensitivity to voicing and other phonetic features that distinguish phonemes, suggesting that "language learners have relevant information *in advance* about the inventory of possible phonetic elements" (Gleitman et al. 1988, 154; emphasis added). In other words, phoneme detection seems to be an innate capacity of the language learner.

Evidence for this position comes from studies of the ability of very young children to detect features like voicing and aspiration, which are capable of distinguishing phonemes in many languages. For example, in English and many other languages vocal cord vibration occurring in a time frame from consonantal release to about 20–30 milliseconds after release is associated with the consonant, which is consequently perceived as voiced (for example, as [b] rather than [p]). There are, however, some languages (for instance, Thai and Spanish) that employ different time envelopes for voicing. So, just as English contains some relatively unusual linguistic properties (such as the vowel [æ] and the initial consonant cluster [str]), there are languages with unusual voice onset delays.

Furthermore, there may be a learning-theoretic consequence of the special voice onset time in Spanish. Studies of Spanish-speaking children suggest that up to the age of about six months, they continue to use the regular discrimination boundaries for voicing even though their target language employs different values (Lasky, Syrdal-Lasky, and Klein 1975). As Reich (1986) suggests, Spanish-learning children may be somewhat delayed in their ability to discriminate parts of the Spanish phonemic inventory. This provides indirect evidence that there is an innate phoneme detection capacity that is at least temporarily frustrated when the language to be learned exhibits idiosyncratic timing envelopes or other unusual features (see Goodluck 1991 for further discussion).

Although there is some support for the claim that phoneme detection normally exploits a biological capacity, in the case of identifying the words of a language we must pursue a different explanation. For although it may be possible for a child to be innately predisposed to identify the range of phonemes available in the languages of the world, it is implausible to believe that discovery procedures sufficient for the tens of thousands of vocabulary items in each language (past, present, and future!) could be part of human genetic endowment. How, then, does the child efficiently individuate words in the flow of language?

Gleitman et al. (1988) argue that word identification is initially bootstrapped by the child's attention to the feature of linguistic stress. That is, the parts of the speech stream that bear stress are salient for the child. This may explain why stressed syllables are the first to be pronounced (for example, *raff* for *giraffe*); why, when words have both stressed and unstressed forms (for example, *not/n't*), the former are learned first (Bellugi 1967); and why words that generally lack stress (for instance, function words in English) are omitted from early speech (but see below for another explanation). On this view, children at the one-word stage identify stressed syllables as their first "words," incorporating unstressed material at a later stage of development.

Thus, even though our first assumptions about language acquisition viewed children as simply acquiring sounds and meanings, our cursory investigation of the child's first words indicates that the strategies children use to extract linguistic patterns are quite sophisticated. Furthermore, even the linguistic knowledge acquired by the average one-year-old takes the form of a rich system of rules and representations that must be deduced from the child's experience with a linguistic community. Early linguistic development is marked by considerable progress, as well as by mistakes and mismatches between the child's and the adult's grammar. Indeed, it is often precisely the child's linguistic errors that provide the deepest insights into the nature of the acquisition process and the cognitive mechanisms of the child's emerging information-processing system.

The Emergence of Syntax

At the one-word stage of development we restricted our discussion to the semantic, phonetic, and phonological aspects of language development. As far as the child's early linguistic production is concerned, there is little evidence at this stage of mastery of the syntactic rule system. Most lexical items are uninflected, there do not appear to be distinct lexical categories, and answers to *wh*-questions are not reliably categorically correct (Radford 1990). As the child's utterances expand in length to two words, it begins to be possible to examine syntactic development, at least in a rudimentary fashion. Examples of two-word utterances might include *mommy sock, allgone sticky, more cookie,* and *fix shoe.* Just as in the one-word stage, the pronunciations and intended meanings of the spoken words may deviate from the adult model. For now, however, let us restrict our attention to syntactic structure.

A popular early hypothesis concerning the pattern of these two-word utterances (Braine 1963) contended that children organized vocabulary words into two lexical classes called *pivot* and *open.* It was claimed that children's two-word utterances were composed of either two open-class words or one open-class word and one pivot-class word, in either order. One-word utterances would be selected solely from the open class, with the result that pivot-pivot sequences and pivot singletons were supposed not to occur. The assignment of words to one class or the other would need to be discovered for each individual child by looking carefully at production data. If, for example, a child produced *ball* on one occasion and *hit* on another, each word would be assigned to the open class for the child in question, since only pivot words were argued to appear alone in one-word utterances. This theory would therefore predict that *ball hit* and *hit ball* should be possible utterances for this child. Conversely, any word used by the child that failed to appear alone in a single-word utterance would be assigned to the pivot class, and the theory would predict that no two such words would be strung together in a two-word utterance.

As researchers looked more closely at the utterances produced by children at the two-word stage, a number of counterexamples to the pivot-open hypothesis emerged. Nevertheless, even at this early stage of development the child seems to be following a grammar. The speech of twenty-eight-month-old Adam, a child studied by Roger Brown and his colleagues (Brown and Fraser 1963), was described by McNeill (1970) by the following three phrase structure rules:

$$(1) \quad S \rightarrow \begin{Bmatrix} (NP) & VP \\ NP & (VP) \end{Bmatrix}$$

$$(2) \quad NP \rightarrow \begin{Bmatrix} (DET) & N \\ N & N \end{Bmatrix}$$

(3) $VP \rightarrow (V) \, NP$

Sample utterances generated by this grammar include *doggie eat, that flower, Adam write,* and *put on.* As McNeill pointed out, it is unsurprising that the child's first grammar should be so simple. Nevertheless, despite the tiny number of rules, the concepts of optionality and order already seem to be in place, indicating that certain of the key principles of the developing linguistic system have emerged at this early stage of development.

As combinations of words emerge, the child begins to systematically establish relationships between them. The earliest such relations appear to include those of modifier-modified and agent-action. In the first case, taking *more cookie* as an example, the child must come to grasp that *more* specifies an amount of cookie and must not be interpreted as the subject of *cookie*, perhaps meaning that more stands for something that is a (kind of) cookie. The example *doggie eat* may well involve an interpretation in which the dog is the subject of *eat* and carries out the associated action. The point is that the order and juxtaposition of terms do not predict the nature of the semantic relationship between those terms in any simple manner, even in a language like English that is quite sensitive to word order in sentence construction. These semantic relations (sometimes called *thematic relations*) develop over time, apparently beginning at the two-word stage. Some researchers, such as Bloom (1970) and Bowerman (1973), have proposed that thematic relations constitute the first important structural relations that the child uses to construct multiword utterances, suggesting that the child's first grammar may be best described in thematic terms. Such a system might analyze sentences in terms of categories like agent and action instead of the syntactic categories Noun Phrase and Verb Phrase.

Against this, however, Radford (1990) argues that the increasing use of inflections and the growing ability to reply to *wh*-questions with answers in the proper syntactic category suggest that children have begun to understand parts of speech and to employ an essentially syntactic organization of the grammar, often before their second birthday. Radford also provides evidence that children at this stage organize sentences in terms of *hierarchical structure*, as, for example, in the case of rule (2), which analyzes a DET N sequence as a single constituent.

Another suggestion, made by Berwick and Weinberg (1983), is that children's early grammars are based on the assumption that each syntactic structure is correlated with exactly one thematic structure. Thus, at these early stages of development every NP-VP sequence would be interpreted by an agent-action relationship, and similarly for other syntactic sequences. However, there is some evidence that by the later portion of the two-word stage children are capable of associating a single syntactic structure with more than one thematic structure, and of associating a single thematic structure with more than one syntactic structure (Radford 1990). This suggests that by this stage children have developed abstract syntactic representations that they associate with thematic representations. In other words, children at the late two-word stage seem to have already developed an autonomous level of syntactic representation that mediates between sound and meaning, just as it does in adult grammars.

There are, of course, a number of ways in which the linguistic systems of children at this stage of development differ from the adult system. In addition to waging continued struggles with pronunciation and meaning, children deviate in quite interesting ways from the syntactic pattern of the adult speech community. Obviously, they produce much briefer sentences; moreover, most of their utterances are innovative in that they are not imitations of adult speech. Some of the examples of two-word utterances we have discussed—such as *allgone sticky*—clearly suggest that creative speech is already present. Why it should be that children pass through this stage of development remains poorly understood. It may turn out that extragrammatical factors such as limitations of memory or attention span account for restricted production. What is clear, however, is that children do indeed go through a procedure of grammar construction that is in evidence at the earliest stages of multiword utterances.

Beyond the Two-Word Stage
Although the one- and two-word stages of language development do not have precise beginnings and endings, they are plateaus reliably found in children's patterns of language acquisition. After the two-word stage, however, there do not seem to be easily identifiable stages corresponding in any simple way to the number of words per utterance. Moreover, soon after their second birthday, children learning inflected languages such as English begin to tackle the system of prefixes and suffixes that in part compose the morphology of their language, and this precipitates the need for a more fine-grained measure of linguistic development. The calculation of the *mean length of utterance* (MLU) in terms of the number of morphemes per utterance allows us to take the development of inflectional systems into consideration.

As the child's MLU shoots upward, the complexity of the grammar that generates each successive body of new data itself becomes more complicated both in the number and in the type of rules involved. Although Adam's grammar at twenty-eight months comprised only three phrase structure rules, at thirty-six months the same child's verbal output was analyzed by a grammar that Brown, Cazden, and Bellugi (1970) judged to include over a dozen phrase structure rules as well as several transformational rules, including a transformation for forming questions. The utterances produced by two- and three-year-olds are, again, often ill formed by adult standards. The following examples of the speech of two- to three-year-olds with MLU in the vicinity of five morphemes per utterance are typical (the utterances are taken from various sources):

(4)   Count a buttons.
      It fell in sand box.
      The monster's coming.
      Mommy try it.
      What that?
      No sit here.
      Where those dogs goed?
      Put truck window.

In contrast to the holophrastic speech of children at earlier developmental stages, the speech of children at this level of development has been described as *telegraphic speech*. The final example in (4) clearly illustrates what is meant by this label in that the child has omitted the small function words, in this case the determiner and the preposition, much as someone with an eye toward economy would phrase a telegram. Radford (1990) suggests that telegraphic speech generally arises because of the basic organization of children's early grammars, which fails to provide syntactic representation for functional categories.

The syntactic form of early questions is also quite intriguing. Both of the interrogatives in (4) reveal some difficulty with the process of auxiliary inversion, which places a verbal element (in these cases, *is* and *did*) to the left of subject position in *wh*-questions. In the case of *What that?* the verb *is* is omitted from the sentence, a typical feature of children's speech at this stage. The second question exhibits several departures from adult English. In addition to the previously noted omission of *did*, the tense of the sentence is displayed on the main verb as *goed*. As we will now see, the investigation of such illegal past-tense forms can reveal quite a bit about how the child organizes linguistic knowledge, even at this relatively early stage of development.

Irregularity and Linguistic Representation
It is quite common to find that children pass through a number of stages before they master correct irregular past-tense forms, such as the alternation between *go* and *went*. Kuczaj (1978) proposes that this developmental sequence begins with children occasionally using the *correct* past-tense forms of irregulars (for example, *went*), with the incorrect forms rarely in evidence. Next they begin to introduce forms such as *goed*, with some uses of the correct forms still persisting. In a third stage children add a second type of error that involves applying the regular past-tense rule to the irregular past-tense form (for example, *wented*), although again they continue to use the earlier forms (*went* and *goed*). Finally, the incorrect forms drop out of use, resulting in the reliable use of the correct irregular forms, although this process takes years to work to completion. In a careful study of the frequency of forms such as *goed*, Marcus et al. (1992) found that such forms are quite rare, with a median distribution of 2.5 percent in over 11,000 irregular past-tense utterances of the eighty-three children they studied. However, they were able to confirm that children's use of the incorrect forms continues at a constant rate for several years and that the introduction of these forms follows a period in which children use the correct forms (a phenomenon they call *U-shaped development*).

It is of considerable interest to establish why children take these backward steps during language acquisition. One explanation suggests that children at first simply imitate the correct past-tense form, *went*. At a later point, after they have acquired the general rule for past-tense formation, they creatively apply it to the base form *go*, even though they have never actually heard the form *goed* in their linguistic environment. At the next stage children appear to move closer to the idea that all past-tense forms should have overt past morphology (*-ed*), yielding a second class of incorrect forms. In time children must learn that the irregular past tense *went* is the only appropriate form, although many children resist this conclusion for some time.

In this case, then, the emergence of a linguistic rule actually leads the child away from identifying the correct linguistic forms. Of course, in regular cases this same rule constitutes a powerful learning device that allows the child to incorporate a large number of correct forms as a single class of phenomena rather than on a case-by-case basis. Finally, the persistence of incorrect forms over time provides intriguing evidence that reveals the extent to which the acquisition of linguistic knowledge is shaped by linguistic rule systems.

Although this emphasis on rule systems as explanations for cognitive phenomena is a hallmark of most classical approaches to cognitive science, in the connectionist paradigm it is assumed that the fundamental unit of processing and representation is an element that has more in common with a simple (if abstract) neuron. On this view, knowledge—whether information about the world, memory, or the representation of linguistic generalization—resides in a complex of connectivity that arises in the mind as the result of the interaction of myriad very simple processing units. In most connectionist theories, knowledge does not—indeed, cannot—take the form of abstract rules and higher-order structures that are typical of contemporary linguistic theories as well as of the accounts of language acquisition that draw inspiration from such theories. Notions like *transformational rule* or *phrase structure tree*, for example, can have no independent status in a connectionist model, since whatever knowledge they embody, like everything else in the mind, is ultimately built out of simple, relatively homogeneous processing units that are not uniquely dedicated to special tasks like the representation of linguistic knowledge. On the contrary, for the connectionist, there are no "executive or other overseer" units (Rumelhart and McClelland 1986a) that regulate cognitive systems.

Connectionist models have been developed in a number of domains of linguistic representation, though as yet there are few that are capable of handling the kinds of problems we have been discussing. However, one of the most interesting and controversial connectionist models is Rumelhart and McClelland's (1986b) account of the child's capacity to learn and use the English past-tense system, an analysis that bears on the discussion of irregular past tense forms that we have just developed.

To begin with, let us recall the analysis of past-tense forms provided by a symbolic linguistic theory of the kind described in chapter 6. We assume that the speaker has learned a set of phonological rules of essentially the following form:

(5) *Past-tense formation*
     If a verb stem ends in a voiced segment (for example, *hug*), add the past-tense ending /d/ to the end of the stem;

     If a verb stem ends in a voiceless segment (for example, *lick*), add /t/ to the end of the stem;

     Unless the verb stem ends in a coronal stop /t/ or /d/ (for example, *want* or *seed*), in which case, add /əd/ regardless of the voicing of the final segment.

In addition to these rules, about 150 verbs in English including *go, eat, hit, see,* and *leave* are unusual in that they undergo one of a set of special past-tense changes. These might involve an internal vowel change, as in *ring → rang* or *leave → left*, or, in the case of *go → went*, a completely irregular alternation. At the heart of our explanation of the developmental sequence for regular and irregular past-tense forms is the multilayered set of interrelated rules and representations crucially including (1) a lexicon of underlying representations, (2) a set of morphological principles for constructing complex words from basic underlying representations, (3) a set of phonological rules that determine the phonetic properties of those representations, and (4) a phonetic output consisting of direct instructions for pronouncing words.

In Rumelhart and McClelland's (1986b) model (henceforth RM), there are no phonological rules like those in (5), no morphological constructs such as *word* or *verb stem*, and no structural/positional notions such as *end of stem* or *word boundary*. The RM model's internal knowledge state is a connectionist network of weighted nodes that directly represents the probabilities that certain types of verbs will be associated with particular inflected (past-tense) phonetic forms. This is accomplished by *training* the model—providing it with sufficient examples of actual pairs of uninflected and past-tense forms. The only relevant mechanism in the model is a pattern associator with two layers of nodes, the first of which represents uninflected verbs as input, and the second of which produces inflected past-tense verbs as output.

On the whole, the RM model does a remarkable job of producing appropriate past-tense outputs without ever having been trained on or directly representing a rule. Furthermore, the model, if ultimately successful, would provide an account of linguistic knowledge in which the very notion of an explicit rule system was unnecessary. If connectionist models of this sort were able to accomplish this goal for the full range of linguistic generalizations that linguists can discern, much of the debate around the nature of linguistic representation might be resolved. In particular, there would be no grounds for assuming a special role for grammar, independent of other systems of knowledge; in effect, there would be no grammar. This is just as the (radical) connectionists would have it, since their view of cognition is that it is uniformly based on a nonmodular, homogeneous learning and representational system.

The RM model has been criticized on a number of counts, however. Pinker and Prince (1988) argue that the model fails in a number of crucial respects as an account of the English speaker's knowledge of the past-tense formation process. For one thing, when the model was asked to produce past-tense forms for verbs on which it had not been trained, it exhibited a high proportion of incorrect responses (33 percent). Recalling our earlier discussion of the *goed-went* alternation, we might ask how the connectionist model behaved in cases in which children produce incorrect past-tense forms for irregular verbs—precisely the cases of the overgeneralization of a rule to an exceptional irregular form that motivated us to provide a rule-based account of the phenomenon. Indeed, the RM model also overgeneralized in such cases. But, whereas in the course of maturation children ultimately acquire the correct, irregular adult forms, the model did not (see Marcus et al. 1992 for a discussion of further research on this topic).

Pinker and Prince (1988) also investigated the class of errors that the RM model made. Since children make certain errors on the way to acquiring adult linguistic competence, we would expect a successful model of language learning to fail part of the time, as well. However, Pinker and Prince argue that the RM model made mistakes of a sort that children do not make. For example, for the verb *sip*, it output **sept*, apparently following the alternation in *keep/kept*. It is noteworthy that the model was able to discern this particular (and rare) subregularity in English, but it generalized it inappropriately. The model also produced irregular-like forms that neither children nor adults ever exhibit—for instance, **membled* as the past tense of *mail*. Perhaps more significantly, for about 10 percent of the test verbs, the model could not reach a decision threshold—it did not output any past-tense form at all. Children who have begun to acquire the tense system do not appear to have this problem; they typically provide some morphophonemically altered form to denote past tense. This suggests that children have learned that past-tense verbs always have the underlying form V + PAST, where the morpheme PAST may be realized in a number of ways, but must be realized in some fashion. This abstract condition on verbal morphology appears to constrain children's performance. But no such constraint is built into the RM model; nor, apparently, does the model learn it.

Considerations such as these continue to fuel the debate between connectionist and classical symbolic models of cognition. Indeed, even in the specific case of irregular past-tense formation new observations about the course of acquisition and the possibility of providing a connectionist account of it continue to be registered (see Marcus et al. 1992). More generally, the connectionist paradigm will need to develop increasingly more convincing accounts of linguistic representation and language acquisition. If such accounts are forthcoming, the central insights of contemporary linguistic analysis and its account of the language acquisition device would need to be reconceived in their light.

Later Development

After the two-word stage children are involved in expanding their vocabularies, learning the range of constructions (negations, passives, and so forth) available in their language, honing their semantic and morphological systems, improving their pronunciations, and generally moving steadfastly closer to the conventions of the adult speech community. Some of these aspects of development require considerable time to fall into line with adult grammar. For example, the systematically correct use and interpretation of passive sentences can take until the early school years to emerge, and sentences that involve complicated rules of interpretation such as *The doll is easy to see* can tempt children into misinterpretations (in this case taking *doll* as the subject of *see*) at somewhat more advanced ages.

Despite these occasional bugbears, most of the linguistic system is mastered by the age of six or seven, certain matters of vocabulary, pronunciation, and stylistically complex constructions aside. Even this brief overview of linguistic development hints at the vast amount of information that must be acquired and consequently exposes the magnitude of the task that most all children quite easily accomplish in the first few years of their lives. This last comment sets the theme for the next section, which contains a more theoretical look at the process of language acquisition, by establishing our most central question: if language is so complex, and yet is acquired so rapidly and so well, what is it about language, and what is it about children, that accounts for this apparent paradox?

9.2 Theoretical Perspectives

The Poverty of the Stimulus

From the point of view of our theory of information processing, every child who develops the capacity to speak a natural language has internalized a system of representation that distinguishes the permissible structures in that language. On the hypothesis we are investigating, an interesting part of that system of representation can be characterized in the form of a grammar including a syntax, a semantics, and a phonology. Given our knowledge of the stages through which children pass on the way to acquiring this grammar, our knowledge of the linguistic environment in which the child learns, and the nature of the end-state—the grammar that is ultimately acquired—we can begin to ask how language acquisition proceeds.

Whatever the eventual explanation for language acquisition looks like, it must account for the relevant features of development. In addition to such properties as linguistic creativity and the interesting correlation between universal properties of languages and the order of acquisition, a number of other features of the task of language acquisition have received considerable attention from cognitive scientists. Three of these issues concern the *poverty of the stimulus* for language learning.

The stimulus in this case is the total input on which the child depends to determine the nature of the language being learned. This includes the utterances of parents, peers, and other people, the situations in which those utterances take place, the child's own utterances along with the correlated responses, and so forth. Many linguists and psychologists have contended that in the case of language acquisition, the stimulus situation is impoverished in the sense that there is not enough linguistic information in the environment to directly account for what the child learns. One of the points of such arguments is to deemphasize the importance of simple imitation of sounds, words, and sentences as a mechanism for language learning in favor of a view according to which the child abstracts linguistic rule systems on the basis of exposure to data from a speech community.

The first matter concerns the quantitative insufficiency of linguistic data. Consider the number of possible well-formed sentences in any natural language. Since natural languages feature linguistic devices such as coordination and subordination that involve recursive rules, the number of those sentences is infinite. Learning language therefore requires acquiring an infinite capacity, despite the fact that all children (and for that matter, all adults) are able to experience only a finite number of linguistic utterances during the course of acquisition. A simple model of language learning that posits imitation as the sole process of acquisition is consequently rendered implausible, since the child's linguistic environment is in principle too limited to make available for imitation all of the sentences that the child comes to have available as the language is acquired. Furthermore, even the sentences children produce in the one- and two-word stages on their way to acquiring an adult linguistic capacity are not limited to imitations. Thus, neither the magnitude nor the creativity of linguistic competence that children display very early on can be explained simply in terms of imitation of utterances from the linguistic environment.

The second argument for the poverty of the stimulus concerns not the quantity of linguistic experience, but its quality. Although informed estimates vary, the language that children hear is, to some extent, ungrammatical. In addition to the malformed utterances of other language-learning youngsters, children are exposed to the occasional linguistic mistakes of parents and other adults. Typically, these errors are not identified as such to the child attempting to acquire the language and must therefore count as an unvariegated part of the child's linguistic input. Nevertheless, children manage to acquire a grammar that does not in general incorporate these random mistakes. A related but even more complicated situation arises when children are raised bilingually. Since the utterances of one language are ungrammatical with respect to the other language, children must be able to keep the languages separate prior to knowing either language fully, even in cases in which there are no contextual clues to help. Indeed, although relatively little is known about bilingual acquisition, interlanguage confusion appears to be relatively rare. These natural abilities to distinguish relevant from irrelevant input do not seem to be easily accounted for in terms of properties of the linguistic environment.

The third argument for the poverty of the stimulus concerns the nature of linguistic knowledge and linguistic data. Children learning language are exposed to utterances of various lengths in associated contexts of use. They must ultimately determine which linguistic and nonlinguistic features of the input are important and which are only accidentally present. To complicate matters, these distinctive features can vary from language to language. Let us first consider a phonological example.

Children learning English must learn to disregard the pitch of a sound in determining their phonemic inventory, but to attend to voicing quality. Children learning Zulu must take pitch into consideration (since Zulu is a tone language), but not the random pitch differences between two different utterances of the same word or the equally irrelevant but more systematic differences in absolute pitch produced by men, women, and children. Children learning English also must disregard irrelevant inter- and intraspeaker variation. For example, the typical [b] sound made by an English-speaking mother and father will differ acoustically along a number of dimensions such as volume and duration that are not distinctive in the language, and these differences must be overlooked. Furthermore, the child's own utterances will differ acoustically from those of adults in dramatic ways. For instance, owing to the relative smallness of the child's vocal tract, the pitch of most utterances produced will be higher than those of parents and older siblings.

Parallel considerations apply in the domains of semantics and syntax. We have already discussed the tendency of young children to over- and undergeneralize word meanings. In part, these errors presumably arise from the child's mistaken assumptions about which aspects of a set of stimulus situations are formalized in a meaning. In the case of syntactic patterns, the child is constantly called upon to discriminate real generalizations from seductive pseudo-analogies. For example, in the sentence *The men expected to vote for themselves*, the antecedent for *themselves* is *the men*. When the same string of words appears as part of a longer sentence, for example, *I know which women the men expected to vote for themselves*, the antecedent of *themselves* switches to *the women* even though simple analogy might lead us to expect the same reference.

All this suggests that children cannot take the data they depend on for language acquisition at face value. As Chomsky (1980, 34) has put it, there is a "vast qualitative difference between the impoverished and unstructured environment, on the one hand, and the highly specific and intricate structures that uniformly develop, on the other." Although the raw data consist of sounds and contexts, children must somehow abstract rules and principles that refer to features of the environment that are linguistically important. These features may not always be particularly salient when judged by acoustic or perceptual criteria, and of course they vary from language to language. The correct linguistic generalizations will typically refer to distinctive features, case, tense, government, phrase structure, sets, quantifiers, and so forth, that are not directly given in the words and deeds the child observes. Furthermore, there will be a large number of tempting hypotheses that are consistent with the input data but are ultimately false; in this sense, the grammar is underdetermined by the data. An effective learning strategy must cope with these general restrictions on the nature of linguistic data.

The Linguistic Environment

Given the impoverished character of the natural linguistic environment, it is intriguing to ask how language acquisition manages to proceed as efficiently as it does. One possibility is that children might receive supplemental information that somehow simplifies the learning task. For example, parents might provide systematic reinforcement to children in the form of attention, praise, or services, increasing the probability that the child will produce grammatical utterances. Another possibility is that parents artificially simplify their children's linguistic environment by the repetition and special organization of utterances presented to them. *Motherese* is the name given to this simplified register used by parents (not just mothers!), which has been widely studied (see Snow and Ferguson 1977). Studies of English motherese have shown that it typically involves relatively short utterances with exaggerated intonation. The proportion of questions, declaratives, and imperatives differs from the norm, and it shifts significantly as the child develops.

Another factor that could work to simplify the acquisition task is feedback from parent to child that tells the child whether or not a given utterance is ungrammatical. *Positive feedback* provides some indication that the child has employed a grammatical utterance. It may take the form of repetition of the child's utterance, a smile, increased attention, or outright approval. *Negative feedback* corrects or otherwise distinguishes ungrammatical speech. Sometimes negative feedback can include a corrected version of the utterance the child had attempted.

Although it is clear that simplification of the linguistic environment, reinforcement, and feedback each play a role in easing the task of language acquisition, some research indicates that these factors are less important than is commonly assumed. In the case of reinforcement, parental reward seems to be correlated not with grammaticality but with appropriateness or veracity (see Brown and Hanlon 1970, Pinker 1989, and the references cited there for a recent discussion). Moreover, many researchers have noted that negative reinforcement is not generally available to the child (Baker 1979). Experimental research has also cast doubt on the effectiveness of at least some forms of negative feedback. Cazden (1965) examined the effect of systematically expanding the speech of twelve children between the ages of twenty-eight and thirty-six months. The expansion involved responding to the children's brief, telegraphic utterances with correct, fully fleshed out, adult versions of the sentences. For example, if a child uttered *Sam highchair*, the researcher might respond with *Sam is in the highchair*. Using a variety of measures including MLU, Cazden found that children in the expansion group experienced some acceleration in development when compared to a control group. However, a third group, which heard as many grammatical sentences as the expansion group that were merely conversationally related to the children's utterances, developed even more quickly. Cazden concluded that the amount of verbal interaction might be more important than its corrective character, although other conclusions are possible (for discussion, see Dale 1972).

As for simplification in the form of motherese, Newport, Gleitman, and Gleitman (1977) have argued that although certain aspects of syntactic development (such as the English auxiliary) do indeed correlate with the corresponding aspects of parental speech that are highlighted, other aspects of syntactic development (such as mastery of the syntax of subordinate clauses) seem independent of the facilitative effects of simplified registers. Here again, there is a connection between trends in acquisition and universal properties of languages:

> We have suggested in outline a position ... in which (1) the acquisition of universal aspects of language design proceeds in indifference to the details of varying linguistic environments, at least within the range of some gross syntactic simplifications (which would appear to occur necessarily in any world where

mothers wish to communicate with their children), and (2) individual differences in the linguistic environment, exemplified by the mother, exert their effects only on the acquisition of language-specific aspects of surface structure, and even then only through the listening biases of the child. (Newport, Gleitman, and Gleitman 1977, 145)

This bifurcation of language development into aspects that are language specific and those that are universally based corresponds to a distinction linguists make between the *core* and the *periphery* of a language. The core is the bulk of the language that instantiates universal principles within a restricted range of options. The periphery is the residual portion that is idiosyncratic. Apparently, the learning of these two different subsets of the language proceeds differently, parental shaping of linguistic development being most influential in the learning of the peripheral portion of the language. Furthermore, there is evidence that in some non-Western cultures, motherese may be limited, available at different stages in development, or nonexistent (Ochs and Schiefflin 1984).

In the face of such evidence suggesting that the child's linguistic environment, although different from the adult's in certain ways, nevertheless affords data that underdetermine the grammars being learned, many researchers have looked to the one other significant factor in the process of acquisition—the child—to attempt to explain how language is acquired.

In the case of biological organs (for example, the liver) it is common to expect the properties of the mature state to depend not only on the effects of day-to-day life but also on the nature of genetic information that guides the organ's development. It is common to search out a biological basis for the development of human physical systems, and although it has been less common to expect such a basis for the development of information-processing systems, Chomsky (1980) suggests that cognitive systems are equally likely to have a biological basis. Indeed, in the case of language Chomsky argues that because the grammar is typically underdetermined by the data, in order for language acquisition to proceed, the child's development must be guided by a set of linguistic principles that incline the child toward the correct grammar for the language being acquired. These principles, which are presumed to be innately specified in the same way that other genetic information is specified, supplement the linguistic data and the environmental cues to make the acquisition of language possible. We will now consider this position in more detail.

Innateness
In the process of deducing a grammar from linguistic data, the child is often faced with a situation in which there are a vast number of hypotheses from which to choose. Most of these involve a commitment to rules and principles that are incompatible with the adult grammar and would, in the long run, lead the child astray. If the child were to pursue each of these options in turn, the attainment of the adult grammar would be dramatically delayed. Furthermore, without the benefit of substantial amounts of systematic feedback to correct mistakes, it is not clear how the child could rebound from these errors and efficiently zero in on the correct grammar.

In fact, there is mounting evidence that the child is not left to test all the grammars that seem temporarily compatible with the linguistic data. The model of acquisition developed by Chomsky and his associates attributes to the child a learning strategy that restricts the range of grammars that must be evaluated at any given point in the process. The restriction involves a series of principles that describe the form that a grammar must take in order to be considered by the child. On this view, the child is instinctively directed away from hypotheses that, although compatible with a corpus of available data, incorporate rules and principles that do not systematically describe any humanly possible language. Furthermore, since these rules and principles of language acquisition presumably play the same learning-theoretic role regardless of the language being learned, they must be universal in nature. Viewed from a slightly different perspective, these learning principles constitute universal grammar—a specification of the grammatical properties that hold across all human languages.

Linguistic theory shoulders two separable, yet related, responsibilities in its role as a component of cognitive science (in addition to its direct goal of providing a description of each natural language): it is simultaneously a theory of the nature of human language and a theory of language learning. The plausibility of this theory of language depends in part on the success that linguistic theory enjoys in characterizing the principles of universal grammar. And to the extent that we are successful in fleshing out these universals, we can consider them as candidates for a hypothesis-restricting role in the acquisition process.

Cognitive scientists have determined a range of evidence that supports the rich (and still controversial) conception of universal grammar we are developing. One such consideration comes from the previously mentioned study of the child's primary linguistic data undertaken by Newport, Gleitman, and Gleitman (1977) in their investigation of the role of motherese in early acquisition. They found that motherese is most helpful in teaching aspects of language that are idiosyncratic, and least helpful in teaching aspects that are consistent with universal principles. On the account of language learning we have been discussing, we have stressed that the assist contributed by the hypothesized innate learning mechanism to the language acquisition task takes the form of universal grammatical principles. It follows, then, that this device will not facilitate or favor acquisition of nonuniversal aspects of languages. Nevertheless, such aspects need to be acquired. It is therefore understandable that in these cases the child would look to the resources of the linguistic environment—in this case, to the example being set by parents—to bootstrap the acquisition process. To acquire those features of language that are facilitated by universal principles, the child need not rely on environmental cues to the same extent. We can therefore explain the interesting correlation between universal aspects of grammar and dependence on motherese if we assume an innate basis for language acquisition.

Work such as this has motivated cognitive scientists to articulate rather specific models of universal grammar and to test them against linguistic and acquisition data. One current specification of universal grammar that is illuminating as an account of language and language learning is known as the *principles-and-parameters framework* (Chomsky 1986). On this approach, in addition to manifesting properties common to all languages (the principles), universal grammar is analyzed as comprising sets of severely limited alternative possibilities from which languages "choose" (the parameters). The introduction of this second aspect of universal grammar was prompted by the observation that although there are many regards in which languages may vary, often the variation itself is limited. By parameterizing universal grammar, we can account for uniformities that, although not universal, nevertheless suggest substantial generalizations about languages and, as we will see below, figure prominently in the theory of language acquisition.

To make the concept of a parameter clearer, let us consider a case in point. We noted in chapter 6 that languages differ in word order. Although the basic order for English is S(ubject) O(bject) V(erb), other languages use other basic orders, including SOV (Japanese) and VSO (Modern Irish). Nevertheless, if we look more closely at word order across languages, we find interesting commonalities within this sphere of differ- ence. For example, although it follows from the variation in word order that languages may differ in the order in which *heads* (verbs, nouns, adjectives, and prepositions) and their *complements* (for example, object NPs or modifiers) may occur with respect to each other, the two usual cases found across languages are head initial and head final. To capture this generalization, the *head parameter* is proposed as a parameter of universal grammar that admits of two settings: heads right or heads left. Each natural language can instantiate either one of the settings, and this determines the head-complement order throughout the language. In particular, this approach predicts that languages tend to adopt the same order across all phrasal categories: there are languages like English in which verbs, nouns, adjectives, adverbs, and prepositions tend to precede their objects and modifiers (for example, [[$_V$ *run*] quickly], [$_N$ [*books*] that I read], [[$_{Adj}$ *taller*] than Mary], [[$_{Adv}$ *rapidly*] as can be], and [[$_P$ *in*] the dirt]), and languages like Japanese in which the order is reversed.

Like the principles of universal grammar, parameters are construed as simultaneously explaining the nature of human language and playing a role in the acquisition of language. We turn next to some of the evidence bearing on this claim about the role of universal grammar in acquisition.

We begin by examining a proposed principle of universal grammar and consider its role in a theory of language acquisition, returning below to discuss how parameters fit into this model. Let us recall one of the linguistic descriptions discussed in chapter 6 concerning interrogative constructions. English *wh*-questions normally require locating the *wh*-word in a special position to the left of the subject (for example, *What did you touch?*). This position, called the *complementizer* position, is a typical landing site for *wh*-movement; there do not seem to be languages that locate question words in "counted" positions—for instance, in the middle of the sentence or after the third word—although we could easily imagine such possibilities. Suppose we consider this generalization about possible languages as a principle of universal grammar: move- ment must take place to structurally specified positions (not linearly specified posi- tions). This principle, known as *structure dependence*, will limit the range of possible rules for moving interrogative expressions in a way that will permit the English patterns but not the imaginable but unobserved linearly characterized possibilities (Chomsky 1975; Pinker 1989).

As an illustration of this analysis, suppose the data considered by a child learning English included several utterances like *Josephine knows exactly what John touched yester- day*, which involve a question construction in a subordinate clause. Since the *wh*-word is located to the left of the embedded subject position and not in its normal argument position after *touched*, this utterance displays *wh*-movement. How, then, will the child go about determining the constituent structure of this indirect question, and particu- larly the position of the *wh*-word? Numerous hypotheses about question formation are consistent with the information contained in this utterance, most notably, one that analyzes questions as being formed by moving the interrogative pronoun to the complementizer position at the front of each clause and one that assumes that *wh*- words can be moved to the middle of a sentence.

Whereas the first hypothesis is structure dependent, the second is clearly a linear hypothesis—one requiring that a sentence be analyzed in terms of a countable sequence of elements. Although coherent, succinct, and consistent with the data at hand, this account is ultimately incorrect as a general description of English *wh*-questions. Furthermore, on the present analysis, it is disqualified from consideration by the child because it is inconsistent with the universal principle of structure dependence. Consequently, we would not expect a child learning this construction to adopt the excluded linear hypothesis and to produce ungrammatical utterances (for example, *Do you know John what saw at the beach?*) that are based on it. The literature bears out the absence of these kinds of errors. Since only structural hypotheses (including the correct one) are available for the child to consider, this restriction of the hypothesis space saves the child wasted effort, limits the problem of recovering from incorrect rules, and cumulatively greases the wheels of the acquisition process.

In addition to considering the linguistic motivation for our general account of language acquisition, we can seek empirical support by examining relevant experimental studies of language learners. To pursue the claim that language learners enjoy a restriction of the hypothesis space imposed by the principle of structure dependence, Crain and Nakayama (1986) investigated how children learning "Yes"-"No" questions who were given data consistent with both a linear hypothesis and a structural hypothesis coped with these alternatives.

Presenting young children with declaratives like *The man is tall* and asking them to form the corresponding "Yes"-"No" question, Crain and Nakayama examined whether children would seize on a linear solution to question formation (for example, move the third word to the front of the sentence) or a structural solution (for example, invert the main clause auxiliary with the subject NP). Subjects consistently chose a structural analysis, as the present theory would predict. This sort of evidence contributes to the view that language learners are naturally disposed to construct hypotheses consistent with structure dependence, a principle of universal grammar.

Notice that the theory of language development we are discussing does not suggest that the actual rules of the target language are included in the child's learning mechanism. Clearly, children are not born with the full-blown grammars of all of the world's languages at their disposal, but only with an efficient strategy for learning these grammars.

The main conclusion we wish to draw is that children seem to operate with a plan for language learning that effectively leads them toward certain kinds of hypotheses and away from others. Inasmuch as this sort of preference is not based on any obvious general learning strategy, we infer that the human mind is predisposed to go about the task of language learning only along certain special paths. However, other researchers continue to ask whether these paths are indeed uniquely designed to support the complex task of language acquisition. Some are pursuing theories of acquisition that rely on general learning strategies that account for learning irrespective of cognitive domain (Anderson 1983). Such an approach might, in this case, seek support for the claim that all serial behavior issues from structure-dependent rules, subsuming the case of question acquisition under general properties of the acquisition system. In contrast, Chomsky (1975) has suggested that structure dependence, as well as other principles of universal grammar, are features of an acquisition device specific to language learning, supporting the so-called *modular* view of the architecture of the mind (Fodor 1983, Garfield 1987).

In addition to providing an account of the process of language acquisition in princi-ple and in practice, a theory of innateness based on the principles and parameters of universal grammar provides an explanation for previously noted correlations observed by Jakobson (1968) between the order in which various features of language are acquired and the distribution of those features across the world's languages. Two instances of this correlation that we have already discussed concern the relatively late acquisition of the vowel [æ] and the interesting acquisition sequence for syllable struc-ture in English.

As noted in chapter 6, the vowel [æ] is rare in the sound systems of the world's languages. Although [æ] presumably occurs quite frequently in the English-learning child's linguistic environment and is not demonstrably difficult to hear or articulate, it is nonetheless learned quite late. The vowel sounds [i], [u], and [a], on the other hand, are found in the phonological inventories of every language in the world, and they emerge prior to [æ] in the standard developmental pattern for English. We can explain these correlations if we assume that the principles of universal grammar somehow specify the universality of [i], [u], and [a] and thereby facilitate the acquisition of these sounds for the child. Since [æ] has no claim to being universal, its acquisition would not be facilitated in this way, accounting for the developmental lag.

Turning to the case of syllable structure, recall that CV is the syllable type most widely distributed across the world's languages and that consonant clusters—frequent in English—are relatively rare cross-linguistically (compared to singleton consonants); recall also the *st* clusters are rarer cross-linguistically than *sr* clusters, although *st* clusters are permitted in English and *sr* clusters are not. The early syllables produced by English-learning children tend to be of the universally more frequent CV type; later CVC syllables emerge, eventually giving way to syllables with consonant clusters. In the earliest clusters they produce, English-speaking children tend to include *sr* se-quences (more common cross-linguistically but prohibited in English) and omit *st* sequences (rare cross-linguistically but allowed in English). In both cases the child's developmental sequence tracks the frequency of distribution of syllable types across languages rather than the frequency of distribution in English.

As in the case of the acquisition of [æ], we must establish some connection between how broadly distributed a linguistic feature is across languages and how readily learn-able it is. In the case of syllable structure, the universality of CV syllables is presumably marked in the learning mechanism, thereby facilitating the acquisition of this syllable type. To account for the emergence of *sr* clusters (but not *st* clusters), we posit the *sonority hierarchy* as a universal principle of language learning. This hierarchy entails that each consonant in a cluster must be more sonorous than the consonant that precedes it (where the sonority of a sound is its relative loudness compared to other sounds with equal stress, length, and pitch). Since stops (for example, [p], [t], and [k]) are less sonorous than fricatives (for example, [s], [v], and [∂]), which in turn are less sonorous than [r] and [l], the usual cluster sequences *tr* and *sr* are expected, but *st* is not. By assuming that the sonority hierarchy is simultaneously part of linguistic theory and a property of the language acquisition device, we can account for the observed devel-opmental sequence and for the correlation between stages of development and the pattern of the distribution of linguistic features across languages. As before, to con-struct this type of explanation requires the assumption that learning principles and patterns as task specific and abstract as the sonority hierarchy are properties of a child's language-learning strategy.

A Parameter-Setting Model of Language Acquisition

In each of the examples of learning we have discussed, what was at stake was a universal principle that, marked exceptions aside, holds for all languages. Before concluding this section, we consider how the parameterized features of universal grammar fit into the picture of language learning we are developing. In parameter-guided learning an aspect of choice arises that complicates the relationship between the learning mechanism and the primary linguistic data. Whereas in the case of principle-driven language learning the child's primary burden is to determine which principle(s) are relevant to the analysis of a given data set, in the case of parameter-driven learning the child must determine which setting of which multivalued parameter is relevant.

To return by way of example to the head parameter discussed above, a child trying to learn head direction not only needs to determine that this parameter is applicable but also must calculate which setting of the parameter, heads left or heads right, is the correct choice for the language being learned. This determination in turn presupposes a successful analysis of phrases into heads and complements, rendering the acquisition of head direction a fairly involved process.

Much interesting research has recently been devoted to investigating just how children choose the correct setting of learning parameters in cases such as these. Among the various accounts of this mechanism is work by Hyams (1987) and by Wexler and Manzini (1987), which explores the idea that children come to the task of language acquisition with a default setting of at least some parameters. Hyams investigates the *pro-drop parameter*, which determines for a given language whether sentences normally require subjects. In pro-drop languages like Italian and Hebrew there are grammatical sentences that lack overt subjects, whereas the parallel cases in a non–pro-drop language like English require a subject. For example, *I speak* translates into Italian as either *Io parlo* or *Parlo; Io*, the first person pronoun, is optional.

Hyams (1987) discusses data suggesting that both Italian- and English-learning children initially take their language to be a pro-drop language. That is, even though English learners are not generally exposed to subjectless sentences (whereas Italian learners are), all learners pass through a stage in which they treat their target language as a pro-drop language. For the Italian learners, this is the right choice of parameter settings, but the English learners need to reset the pro-drop parameter in order to correctly (re)analyze their language. Hyams presents evidence that this resetting takes place when English learners discover other properties of English that are incompatible with their initial assumption that English is a pro-drop language.

Since the primary linguistic data available to English learners do not support the (incorrect) initial parameter setting, Hyams's analysis suggests that the assumption that a language is a pro-drop language is the default setting of the pro-drop parameter. In cases in which the default setting fits the language being learned, learning is facilitated, but a nonmatching default will temporarily lead the learner astray.

The Subset Principle

On the subject of default settings, researchers (for example, Wexler and Manzini 1987 and Berwick 1985) have proposed that there is an overarching learning principle that determines the order in which the settings of certain parameters will be established. The *Subset Principle* requires that children move successively from the most conservative parameter setting through progressively less conservative ones until they reach the setting that is correct for their target language. For the parameters to which this principle applies, the alternative parameter settings give rise to a hierarchy of languages $L_1, L_2, L_3 \ldots L_n$ where L_1 is a subset of L_2, L_2 is a subset of L_3, and, in general, L_{n-1} is a subset of L_n.

As an example, Wexler and Manzini (1987) discuss a parameterized approach to the binding theory (see chapter 6). According to the binding theory, all reflexives must be bound by antecedents, and antecedents are prohibited from being too far away from the reflexives that they bind: in *John likes himself*, *himself* and *John* are anaphorically linked, but in **John thinks Mary likes himself* they cannot be linked.

Although the binding theory requires reflexives to be bound within a certain domain, languages differ slightly in what counts as the appropriate binding domain. Wexler and Manzini suggest that the definition of binding domain should be parameterized, with each of the five (or so) possibilities found in the languages of the world constituting a different parameter setting. In the Icelandic sentence *Jón skipaði Haraldi að raka sig* 'Jon ordered Harald to shave himself', for example, *sig* and *Jón* can be anaphorically linked, but *John* and *himself* cannot be linked in the corresponding English sentence. This is because the characterization of binding domain in English prohibits a subject NP from intervening between antecedent and reflexive, but in Icelandic it does not. On the basis of these and other examples, Wexler and Manzini argue that English is more conservative than Icelandic when it comes to reflexive binding—any pattern that is grammatical in English will be acceptable in Icelandic, but not vice versa. If we limit our attention to reflexive binding, then, the grammatical possibilities in English are a subset of the those in Icelandic, an instance of the subset relations diagrammed in figure 9.1.

In such a situation the Subset Principle predicts that language learners will begin with the most conservative assumption about the domain of reflexive binding—in this example, choosing the English setting of the parameter. Of course, if the children are learning English, their initial parameter setting will be correct; but if they are learning Icelandic, they will need to reset the binding theory parameter to the less conservative setting required by that language. Prior to this resetting, the Icelandic-learning child's grammar will undergenerate the target language since only those patterns consistent

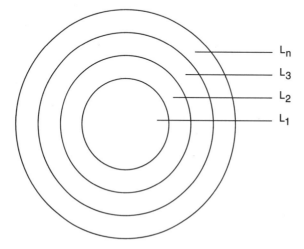

Figure 9.1
Languages in a subset relation

with the English setting of the parameter will be derivable. Consequently, the child will eventually confront grammatical Icelandic sentences that do not square with the initial grammar, and this will trigger the resetting of the binding theory parameter.

More experimental work is needed before we can be sure of the extent to which the Subset Principle guides language acquisition. From a theoretical perspective, however, one of the virtues of an approach to language acquisition in which learning moves through progressively less conservative grammars is that the learner is dependent only on the presence of positive linguistic data to motivate the resetting of parameters. Although the Subset Principle is still controversial (see Valian 1990), the work that is based on it contributes to one of the most exciting areas of current research in cognitive science, which seeks to illuminate language learning from a linguistic and an experimental point of view.

Philosophical Perspectives
The theory of language acquisition we have been discussing involves positing an innate component of the language-learning mechanism. In making the claim that a child has a predisposition toward considering certain kinds of grammars given certain ranges of linguistic data, we commit ourselves to a position that has been taken to support a version of philosophical rationalism (Chomsky 1968). (*Rationalism* is a view on which certain knowledge is known prior to experience.) On the innatist account of acquisition, universal grammar, to the extent that it characterizes the child's genetically specified language-learning device, qualifies as a kind of innately specified information that we may consider as evidence for rationalism. What is at issue is how broadly we construe knowledge.

Linguistic knowledge is generally unconscious, and that is surely true where principles and parameters of universal grammar are concerned. Some philosophers and linguists have made a distinction between *knowing how* and *knowing that* to try to clarify the status of unconscious linguistic knowledge (see chapter 8). In knowing that something is the case, we typically have conscious propositional knowledge about a given state of affairs. In contrast, we may know how to do something without being conscious of the procedure involved in our ability. Knowing that it is raining and knowing how to ride a bicycle are respective examples of these two rather different types of knowledge.

The knowledge of a grammar by virtue of which a speaker uses a native language also roughly qualifies as a specimen of knowledge of the second sort (Chomsky 1975). Thus, we analyze knowing how to speak English as an ability that can be explained by characterizing the grammatical knowledge that underlies the linguistic competence of a native speaker of English. That this linguistic knowledge is unconscious is not surprising, since in this regard it is no different from many instances of knowledge-how.

It is not on the basis of language-specific grammatical knowledge that we make a case for rationalism, however. Since children must learn the grammar of a language on the basis of exposure to primary linguistic data, we do not assume that grammars are innate. Thus, although we can agree that knowledge of grammar is an instance of knowledge-how, this has little direct bearing on the argument for rationalism. Rather, it is universal grammar that is the candidate for innate knowledge.

Consider the principle of structure dependence, as a specific example of a principle of universal grammar. Supposing it to be innate, in what sense can we say that a language-learning child *knows* this principle? Clearly, we cannot argue that principles of universal grammar are known in the propositional sense of knowledge (knowledge-that), since such principles are clearly not tokens of conscious awareness. It is also not clear that principles of universal grammar are instances of knowledge-how, at least in the sense that knowledge of a grammar is. All things being equal, if a person who knows a grammar and has the ability to use language can translate that competence into performance. The connection between principles of universal grammar and linguistic performance, however, is more indirect. Chomsky (1975, 23), adapting work by Kenny (1973), suggests that principles of universal grammar constitute a *second-order capacity*: an "innate capacity of [an organism] to construct cognitive structures" (grammars) that in turn constitute the knowledge-how underlying linguistic performance. On this view, the innately specified principles of universal grammar are learning principles and may be thought of as constituting knowledge of how to learn a grammar.

In recognizing principles of universal grammar as instances of knowledge, then, we must be willing to recognize a new level of knowledge represented at a fundamental level of the human information-processing system responsible for guiding language development. This account of mental capacity, which views the acquisition of cognitive structures as the outcome of the interaction of (in this case, linguistic) data and principles of learning (that is, universal grammar), offers a very rich and highly structured conception of the mind and its development. It is a very exciting and equally controversial outcome of recent work on language acquisition.

Learnability and Parsing
When a linguist proposes a grammar for a range of linguistic data, its success is measured according to several levels or criteria of adequacy. In order to be at all interesting, the proposed grammar must of course accurately account for the data at hand. It should also make predictions about additional linguistic data that will be borne out as increasingly larger amounts of data are considered. Above and beyond the success of hypothesized grammars for individual languages, linguists are interested in developing a theory of universal grammar that will do double duty. On the one hand, universal grammar specifies those linguistic properties and parameters that uniquely characterize the world's languages. On the other hand, universal grammar constitutes a hypothesis concerning the innately specified component of the child's language-learning mechanism.

Although linguists hope that evidence drawn from the study of linguistic universals and evidence drawn from the study of language development will converge in this way, there is no guarantee that they will. In particular, it is possible that a given principle will accurately characterize a linguistic universal but will fail to play an important role in the acquisition process.

Let us assume, for the sake of an example, that it turns out that the phonemic inventory of every language contained an even number of phonemes. Suppose this is proposed as a linguistic universal. It is unclear how such a principle could function as a learning principle, since it does not effectively restrict the hypothesis space that the child must search in any learning situation.

Thus, not all conceivable universal properties of languages will play a role in our theory of language learning (or *learnability*, as it has come to be called). In general, we will need to examine the consequences of incorporating a given principle into the theory and test these predictions against the actual course of acquisition (the earlier discussion of the principle of structure dependence being a case in point).

In certain cases, however, it becomes possible to reject a candidate principle on formal grounds without the need to test its predictions in this detailed manner. This is because not all hypothesized systems of universal grammar are feasible. *Feasibility* is a criterion of adequacy for universal grammar requiring that it not only characterize linguistic universals but also provide an account of language development that is consistent with the principles of a theory of acquisition (Wexler and Culicover 1980). Among other things, this will require that the proposed learning theory characterize human languages in a restrictive enough manner to account for learning on the basis of actual linguistic data in finite time.

Several factors are involved in this requirement. First, not all classes of languages are learnable in finite time. To the extent that a set of languages contains members that overlap so that the linguistic data do not distinguish them, it becomes difficult to decide which language is being learned. Wexler and Culicover (1980) describe a set of formal languages that overlap to such a degree that it is in principle impossible to select a unique grammar on the basis of any finite amount of linguistic data. A universal characterization of language must, of course, avoid this situation to attain feasibility.

Second, a successful learning theory must account for language acquisition on the basis of the type of linguistic data to which the child is actually exposed. For instance, given what is known about motherese and the child's linguistic environment in general, an account of learning must not rely too heavily on overly complex sentences involving multiple layers of embedded subordinate clauses, since these types of sentences are not in general available to the child; nor can it rely on too much long-term memory for previous linguistic data. It must also avoid relying on negative feedback, since this is neither frequently nor systematically available to the child (Baker 1979; Wexler and Culicover 1980; Pinker 1984).

It is possible to evaluate linguistic theories formally to see whether they are capable of accounting for language learning in finite time on the basis of reasonable conditions of acquisition. In fact, Wexler and Culicover (1980) discuss a version of linguistic theory derived from work by Chomsky (1965) that fails as a feasible theory of learnability. They suggest modifications of the theory, which, they go on to prove, can in principle account for language learning. We will not go into the technical details of the proofs; what is interesting about Wexler and Culicover's learnability conditions from the standpoint of this discussion is that many of them have proven to be of independent value to linguists in characterizing universal grammar (Culicover and Wexler 1977; Baker and McCarthy 1981). This sort of convergence contributes extra motivation for a system of universal grammar cum learnability theory.

A third aspect of the study of language that has yielded principles that partly converge with those of learnability theory and universal grammar is *parsability*. Just as languages must fall under certain principles in order to be learned in finite time, so they must have certain formal properties in order to be finitely parsable, as natural languages clearly are. Furthermore, natural languages are not only finitely parsable, but quite rapidly parsable, and the model of parsing should account for this property.

Marcus (1980) has developed a computationally implemented parsing system that addresses these concerns for English with a two-pronged approach that includes principles of parsing and a grammar of the language. His system accepts typed input and assigns syntactic structures of the general sort discussed in chapter 6. Berwick (1985) uses this system as the basis for a computationally implemented learning system that acquires new rules needed to parse a growing corpus of English sentences over time. The system begins with a fixed number of grammatical principles and can develop seventy to one hundred rules on the basis of exposure to several hundred sentences. In addition to acquiring new linguistic knowledge, the system puts that knowledge to use in the task of on-line parsing.

Berwick draws the intriguing conclusion that the requirements of the computation theory necessary to establish this learning system can be made quite compatible with those of a feasible learnability theory. Indeed, among the conditions that Berwick imposes on his learning model are the restrictions on long-term memory, complex data, and negative feedback that form an important part of Wexler and Culicover's account of learnability. In short, the demands of a theory of parsing seem to be compatible with the complementary theories of learnability and universal grammar, with important, ongoing work in artificial intelligence, psychology, and linguistics offering the promise of a most interesting unified theory.

Suggested Readings

For an introduction to the field of language acquisition, see *Language Acquisition: A Linguistic Introduction* (Goodluck 1991), *Language Development* (Reich 1986), and *First Language Acquisition: Method, Description and Explanation* (Ingram 1989). *Syntactic Theory and the Acquisition of English Syntax* (Radford 1990) explores the acquisition of early syntax from the perspective of contemporary syntactic theory. *Parameter Setting* (Roeper and Williams 1987) and *Language Processing and Language Acquisition* (Frazier and de Villiers 1990) are two anthologies that present a selection of work on language acquisition and theories of language and language processing. Philosophical discussions of innateness are covered in another anthology, *Innate Ideas* (Stich 1975).

References

Allport, F. (1924). *Social psychology*. Cambridge, Mass.: Houghton Mifflin.

Anderson, J. R. (1983). *The architecture of cognition*. Cambridge, Mass.: Harvard University Press.

Anglin, J. (1977). *Word, object, and conceptual development*. New York: W. W. Norton.

Baker, C. L. (1979). Syntactic theory and the projection problem. *Linguistic Inquiry* 10, 533–581.

Baker, C. L., and J. McCarthy (1981). *The logical problem of language acquisition*. Cambridge, Mass.: MIT Press.

Bellugi, U. (1967). *The acquisition of negation*. Unpublished doctoral disertation, Harvard University.

Berwick, R. (1985). *The acquisition of syntactic knowledge*. Cambridge, Mass.: MIT Press.

Berwick, R., and A. Weinberg (1983). *The grammatical basis of linguistic performance*. Cambridge, Mass.: MIT Press.

Bever, T. (1961). Pre-linguistic behavior. Ms., Harvard University, Cambridge, Mass.

Bloom, L. (1970). *Language development: Form and function in emerging grammars*. Cambridge, Mass.: MIT Press.

Bowerman, M. (1973). *Structural relationships in children's utterances: Syntactic or semantic?* In T. E. Moore, ed., *Cognitive development and the acquisition of language*. New York: Academic Press.

Braine, M. (1963). On learning the grammatical order of words. *Psychological Review* 70, 323–348.

Brown, R., C. Cazden, and U. Bellugi (1970). The child's grammar from I to III. In R. Brown, *Psycholinguistics*. New York: Free Press.

Brown, R., and C. Fraser (1963). The acquisition of syntax. In C. Cofer and B. Musgrave, eds., *Verbal behavior and learning: Problems and processes*. New York: McGraw-Hill.

Brown, R., and C. Hanlon (1970). Derivational complexity and the order of acquisition in child speech. In R. Brown, *Psycholinguistics*. New York: Free Press.

Carey, S. (1978). The child as a word learner. In M. Halle, J. Bresnan, and G. Miller, eds., *Linguistic theory and psychological reality*. Cambridge, Mass.: MIT Press.

Carmichael, L. (1964). The early growth of language capacity in the individual. In E. Lenneberg, ed., *New directions in the study of language*. Cambridge, Mass.: MIT Press.

Cazden, C. (1965). Environmental assistance to the child's acquisition of grammar. Doctoral dissertation, Harvard University, Cambridge, Mass.

Chomsky, N. (1965). *Aspects of the theory of syntax*. Cambridge, Mass.: MIT Press.

Chomsky, N. (1968). *Cartesian linguistics*. New York: Harper and Row.

Chomsky, N. (1975). *Reflections on language*. New York: Pantheon.

Chomsky, N. (1980). *Rules and representations*. New York: Columbia University Press.

Chomsky, N. (1986). *Knowledge of language: Its nature, origin, and use*. New York: Praeger.

Clark, E. (1973). What's in a word? On the child's acquisition of semantics in his first language. In T. E. Moore, ed., *Cognitive development and the acquisition of language*. New York: Academic Press.

Culicover, P., and K. Wexler (1977). Some syntactic implications of a theory of language learnability. In P. Culicover, T. Wasow, and A. Akmajian, eds., *Formal syntax*. New York: Academic Press.

Crain, S. and M. Nakayama (1986). Structure dependence in children's language. Language 63, 522–543.

Dale, P. (1972). *Language development*. Hinsdale, Ill.: Dryden Press.

de Villiers, J., and P. de Villiers (1978). *Language acquisition*. Cambridge, Mass.: Harvard University Press.

de Villiers, J., and P. de Villiers (1979). *Early language*. Cambridge, Mass.: Harvard University Press.

Eimas, P. D., E. R. Siqueland, P. Juscyzk, and J. Vigorito (1971). Speech perception in infants. *Science* 171, 303–306.

Fodor, J. A. (1983). *The modularity of mind*. Cambridge, Mass.: MIT Press.

Frazier, L., and J. de Villiers, eds. (1990). *Language processing and language acquisition*. Dordrecht: Kluwer.

Garfield, J. (1987). *Modularity in representation and natural language understanding*. Cambridge, Mass.: MIT Press.

Gleitman, L. R., H. Gleitman, B. Landau, and E. Wanner (1988). Where learning begins: Initial representations for language learning. In F. J. Newmeyer, ed., *Linguistics: The Cambridge survey*. Vol. 3: *Language: Psychological and biological aspects*. Cambridge: Cambridge University Press.

Goodluck, H. (1991). *Language acquisition: A linguistic introduction*. Cambridge, Mass.: Blackwell.

Hyams, N. (1987). The theory of parameters and syntactic development. In Roeper and Williams 1987.

Ingram, D. (1989). *First language acquisition: Method, description and explanation*. Cambridge: Cambridge University Press.

Jakobson, R. (1968). *Child language, aphasia, and phonological universals*. The Hague: Mouton.

Jespersen, O. (1925). *Language*. New York: Henry Holt.

Kenny, A. (1973). The origin of soul. In A. Kenny, H. Longuet-Higgins, J. Lucas, and C. Waddington, eds., *The development of mind: The Gifford lectures 1972–73*. Edinburgh: University of Edinburgh Press.

Kuczaj, S. A. (1978). Children's judgements of grammatical and ungrammatical past tense verbs. *Child Development* 49, 319–326.

Lasky, R. E., A. Syrdal-Lasky, and R. E. Klein (1975). VOT discrimination by four- to six-and-a half-month-old infants from Spanish environments. *Journal of Experimental Child Psychology* 20, 215–225.

McNeill, D. (1970). *The acquisition of language*. New York: Harper and Row.

Marcus, G. F., S. Pinker, M. Ullman, M. Hollander, J. Rosen, and F. Xu (1992). Overregularization in language acquisition. *Monographs of the Society for Research in Child Development* 57 (6).

Marcus, M. (1980). *A theory of syntactic recognition for natural language*. Cambridge, Mass.: MIT Press.

Menyuk, P. (1969). *Sentences children use*. Cambridge, Mass.: MIT Press.

Newport, E., H. Gleitman, and L. Gleitman (1977). Mother, I'd rather do it myself: Some effects and non-effects of maternal speech style. In Snow and Ferguson 1977.

Ochs, E., and B. Schiefflin (1984). Language acquisition and socialization: Three developmental stories and their implications. In R. Shweder and R. LeVine, eds., *Culture theory*. Cambridge: Cambridge University Press.

Pinker, S. (1984). *Language learnability and language development*. Cambridge, Mass.: MIT Press.

Pinker, S. (1989). Language acquisition. In M. Posner, ed., *Foundations of cognitive science*. Cambridge, Mass.: MIT Press.

Pinker, S., and A. Prince (1988). On language and connectionism: Analysis of a parallel distributed model of language acquisition. *Cognition* 28, 73–193.

Radford, A. (1990). *Syntactic theory and the acquisition of English syntax.* Cambridge, Mass.: Blackwell.

Reich, P. A. (1986). *Language development.* Englewood Cliffs, N.J.: Prentice-Hall.

Roeper, T., and E. Williams, eds. (1987). *Parameter setting.* Dordrecht: Reidel.

Rumelhart, D. E., and J. L. McClelland (1986a). PDP models and general issues in cognitive science. In D. E. Rumelhart, J. L. McClelland and the PDP Research Group, *Parallel distributed processing: Explorations in the microstructure of cognition.* Vol. 1. *Foundations.* Cambridge, Mass.: MIT Press.

Rumelhart, D. E., and J. L. McClelland (1986b). On learning the past tenses of English verbs. In J. L. McClelland, D. E. Rumelhart, and the PDP Research Group, *Parallel distributed processing: Explorations in the microstructure of cognition.* Vol. 2: *Psychological and biological models.* Cambridge, Mass.: MIT Press.

Salus, P., and M. Salus (1975). Development neurophysiology and phonological acquisition order. *Language* 50, 151–160.

Smith, N. V. (1973). *The acquisition of phonology: A case study.* Cambridge: Cambridge University Press.

Snow, C., and C. Ferguson, eds. (1977). *Talking to children: Language input and acquisition. (Papers from a conference sponsored by the Committee on Sociolinguistics of the Social Science Research Council.)* Cambridge: Cambridge University Press.

Stampe, D. (1972). What I did on my summer vacation. Doctoral dissertation, University of Chicago, Chicago, Ill.

Stich, S., ed. (1975). *Innate ideas.* Berkeley and Los Angeles: University of California Press.

Valian, V. (1990). Logical and psychological constraints on the acquisition of syntax. In Frazier and de Villiers 1990.

Valian, V., J. Winzemer, and A. Errich (1981). A "little linguist" model of syntax learning. In S. Tavakolian, ed., *Language acquisition and linguistic theory.* Cambridge, Mass.: MIT Press.

Wanner, E., and L. Gleitman (1982). *Language acquisition: The state of the art.* Cambridge: Cambridge University Press.

Wexler, K., and P. Culicover (1980). *Formal principles of language acquisition.* Cambridge, Mass.: MIT Press.

Wexler, K., and R. Manzini (1987). Parameters and learnability in binding theory. In Roeper and Williams 1987.

Chapter 10
Semantics

Language relates sound to meaning via syntactic structure. We turn now to what is considered by many to be the most captivating aspect of this relation, the study of meaning, called *semantics*. Semantics is a highly interdisciplinary area of inquiry. Researchers from all areas of cognitive science have contributed to our knowledge of meaning, with the fields of philosophy, linguistics, psychology, and artificial intelligence (AI) claiming the study of meaning as a core area of interest.

There are a variety of reasons why the study of meaning has been so popular, and particularly so in the last century. From the point of view of linguistic theory, the system of meaning that we all master in becoming native speakers of a language must be studied if we are to lay claim to understanding human language ability. Speakers have the competence to evaluate argument structure, identify contradictions and ambiguities, provide paraphrases, and use metaphorical and idiomatic constructions. These abilities, among others, constitute a domain of inquiry for the linguistic semanticist.

Philosophers have studied meaning for other reasons. One philosophical tradition of the twentieth century, the analytic tradition, urged that studying the linguistic form of philosophical puzzles—that is, the language in which the puzzles are couched—would illuminate their solutions. For example, philosophers such as Russell and Moore contended that the analysis of the meaning of sentences that make ethical or existential assertions can reveal considerable insight into ethics and ontology. Philosophers who study logic have also often found an interest in natural language. Although some logicians have felt that natural languages are too vague and ambiguous to yield to logical analysis, others have attempted to modify and extend their techniques with much success. One final attraction that the study of meaning has held for philosophers stems from the status of meanings themselves and related issues. Meanings have been variously analyzed as mental concepts, behaviors, ideas, and objects, among other things. The study of meaning also raises questions about consciousness, ontology, identity, intentions, and the mind that provide a severe test for most philosophical theories.

AI and psychology also count meaning as an important concern. Psychologists have studied meaning as it is involved in concept formation, affect, reasoning, and memory. They have also traditionally been interested in various topics in semantics at the intersection of linguistics and psychology (so-called psycholinguistics), including the acquisition of meaning by children, the analysis of ambiguity, and the process of interpretation. One topic in psycholinguistics that we take up below is the psychological plausibility of the semantic theory we will develop. Since our semantic rule system will turn out to be parallel in status to our syntactic rule systems in the sense that both are part of a theory of linguistic competence, similar philosophical questions arise about the psychological claims we are entitled to make for our account.

Research in AI has explored meaning with both direct and indirect goals in mind. In order to build an expert system, it is necessary to confront an array of problems concerning the representation of semantic information. Such systems must be able to interpret the meaning of their input, represent meaningful information in memory, draw inferences, and respond in a language that the user can comprehend. All these tasks involve aspects of meaning. More directly, many researchers in AI have felt that computational models of knowledge representation shed a new and different light on the nature of meaning. We will consider this point of view briefly at the end of the chapter.

10.2 Meaning and Entailment

Our study of semantics proceeds with two different but complementary purposes in mind. From a viewpoint that currently is shared by many linguists and philosophers, we will study the meanings of linguistic expressions. In this regard, we might begin by assigning a meaning to each terminal node in a surface structure phrase structure tree for a given sentence. These meanings would then be combined to determine the meaning of the whole sentence. Evidence that an analysis of sentence meaning must compose such meanings out of the meanings of subconstituents of the sentence comes from the consideration that there are an infinite number of meaningful sentences in any natural language that are readily understandable by native speakers. By assuming that speakers construct the meanings of larger expressions out of the meanings of their parts, we can explain this natural ability in a manner quite parallel to that by which we accounted for the ability of native speakers to spontaneously muster intuitions of grammaticality for novel utterances and for a theoretical infinity of sentences.

Following in a second, more narrowly philosophical tradition, we will consider the nature of entailment and argument structure. For some, this interest springs from a more general interest in the nature of rationality. For example, our native ability to reason tells us that it is legitimate to conclude (1c) if (1a) and (1b), the *premises* of the argument, are true,

(1) a. Johnny is a whale.
     b. All whales are mammals.
        Therefore
     c. Johnny is a mammal.

but that the conclusion in (2c) does not follow from (2a) and (2b):

(2) a. Johnny is a mammal.
     b. All whales are mammals.
        Therefore
     c. Johnny is a whale.

Logicians have traditionally investigated the logical structure of arguments to determine how to distinguish valid arguments (those arguments whose conclusions must be true if their premises are true, or, in other words, whose conclusions are *entailed* by their premises) from invalid arguments (those arguments the truth of whose conclusions is not entailed by the truth of their premises, or, in other words, the truth of whose premises is *compatible with* the falsity of their conclusions). Although our primary interest in this chapter will be in constructing an account of meaning, we will also discuss argument validity from two different points of view. Finally, after a discussion of such matters, we conclude the chapter by considering ways in which research in semantics makes contact with work on language processing in psychology and AI.

10.3 Reference

In our attempt to analyze the meaning of sentences we immediately face several central questions, including the most basic concern of all: What is meaning? This extremely vexed matter has received various answers throughout the years. Meanings have been variously treated as concepts, entities in a Platonic heaven, objects, and behaviors. Some philosophers have come to the conclusion that it may not even make sense to talk about meanings per se (Austin 1962). As a starting point, we might agree that language is, at its core, a symbolic system. This is to say that languages consist of forms of expression that *stand for* (or *refer to*) things. This is perhaps most plausible in the case of names: it is natural to say that the name *Churchill* refers to Churchill and that this exhausts its meaning. We will attempt to extend this insight to other parts of the language as well and claim, at least for now, that (for example) *snow* refers to snow. We might, then, provisionally accept the claim that to know the meaning of a word involves knowing what it can properly be used to refer to.

As we will see, this simple assumption is probably not correct as stated, but it will carry us quite a way in our study of meaning. Combining this principle with the idea that meanings of sentences are determined out of the meanings of subconstituents of sentences, we will embark on a program that specifies what the basic meaningful expressions in a language stand for and how to calculate the interpretations of sentences on the basis of these reference relations. Implicit in these notions is another leading idea: to know the meaning of a sentence is to know the conditions under which it is true (its *truth-conditions*), or, alternatively, to know what makes it true or how the world would have to be for it to be true. The combination of these ideas, called *compositionality* and *truth-conditional semantics*, is at the heart of much of semantic research in cognitive science. Both ideas were first developed systematically by the German philosopher and mathematician Gottlob Frege.

Let us begin our investigation of truth-conditional semantics by considering the following sentence:

(3)   Churchill smoked.

What are the references (or *semantic values*) of the constituent expressions? In the case of the subject, Churchill, the semantic value is the prime minister of Great Britain during World War II. We write this as follows.

(4)   ⟦Churchill⟧ = Winston Churchill

reading the "⟦...⟧" notation as *the semantic value of* ... and taking the expression on the right-hand side of the "=" to denote the man. What, then, does *smoked* have as its semantic value? Putting aside the matter of the tense (or time frame) of the verb, we can analyze the semantic value of intransitive verbs as sets of individuals; in this case,

(5)   ⟦smoked⟧ = {individuals who smoked}

The "{...}" notation is the standard notation from set theory for a set—roughly, a collection of things. Sets can be expressed either by a criterion for membership, as in (5), or by listing their members. So, we could have said:

(6)   ⟦smoked⟧ = {Groucho Marx, George Burns, Churchill ...}

Given that ⟦Churchill⟧ is Winston Churchill and ⟦smoked⟧ is the set of those who smoked, it remains to calculate the semantic value of the sentence as a whole. Now we can bring together the ideas of compositionality and truth-conditionality. The semantic value of the subject of this sentence is an individual, and the semantic value of the predicate is a set; what we need is a way of composing these semantic values to get a semantic value of the sentence. The natural composing operation is that of set membership, symbolized in set theory as "∈", since it is an operation that applies to individuals and sets. What is more, the result of applying this operation is *True* if and only if (*iff*) the individual belongs to the set, and *False* iff the individual does not. This gives us a systematic way to calculate the truth-conditions of such a sentence: it is true iff the individual denoted by the subject of the sentence is a member of the set denoted by the predicate. We can also see what the semantic values of sentences will be. Since they will be the result of composing the semantic values of their constituents, and these results are always either True or False, the semantic value of a sentence will be its truth-value. Let us now work these ideas out in more detail.

The truth-value of a sentence such as (3) can be computed by applying the rule given informally in (7) and more formally in (8):

(7)   A sentence S is true if the semantic value of the subject NP is an element of the semantic value of the predicate VP.

(8)   If a sentence S has the structure $\alpha\beta$, where α is an NP and β is a VP containing an intransitive verb, then ⟦S⟧ = True iff ⟦α⟧ ∈ ⟦β⟧.

In the case of (3) this amounts to asking whether

(9)   Churchill ∈ {individuals who smoked}

which, of course, he is.

Quantification: First-Order Quantifiers
The insight we are developing is that the semantic value of a sentence is calculated out of the semantic values of its parts and that the sentence as a whole has a truth-value as its semantic value. However, when we consider other examples, we encounter complications. For instance, it is not entirely clear what individual it might be that the subject NP *nothing* refers to in (10):

(10)   Nothing eats.

The apparent problem is that there is no individual for *nothing* to refer to. If we take a word's meaning to be its referent, and reference to be a relation between words and things in the world, then it would appear that the subject of this sentence is meaningless, which of course it is not.

One solution to this problem, which allows us to assign this sentence a semantic value, involves importing the first-order predicate calculus introduced briefly in chapter 4. (10) can be translated into a representation in this logic as follows:

(11)   (For all things x,) [It is not the case that x eats]

In the vocabulary of our logic, (11) is more formally rendered as (12a) or equivalently as (12b):

(12)   a. $(\forall x)[\sim x\ \text{eats}]$
        b. $\sim(\exists x)[x\ \text{eats}]$

"$(\forall x)$" is read "for all x...," "$(\exists x)$" is read "there exists an x such that ...," and "$\sim$" stands for "it is not the case that...." Notice that this sort of analysis does not really answer the question of what the word *nothing* refers to. Instead, *nothing* is translated into a new vocabulary that essentially treats it as "all things do not" or "there does not exist a thing that does." This of course only pushes the problem of interpreting (10) back a level, for now we need a rule of interpretation for the expressions in (11) and (12). The method of interpretation for such examples involves considering in turn each thing in the world and checking whether each such thing is in the set of eaters. If none are, then (12) (and (11)) are true—and therefore, so is (10), since we are taking the former to represent the meaning of the latter.

The symbol "$(\forall x)$" stands for the universal quantifier. Notice that it would appear in the logical translation (13b) of (13a) as well as in (12a).

(13)   a. Everything eats
        b. $(\forall x)[x\ \text{eats}]$

The existential quantifier "$(\exists x)$" can also appear in the position before the brackets in (13), as follows:

(14) $(\exists x)[x\ \text{eats}]$

The rule of interpretation for (14) will have us check for at least one individual in the world who is in the set of eaters. "$\exists x$," then, is a first-order predicate calculus representation for at least *one* (or, roughly, *something*). (The particular choice of the symbol "x" as a variable in these last examples is arbitrary, although conventional. Thus, substituting, say, "y" for "x" in (14) does not affect the interpretation of the formula.)

Let us step back for a moment to survey the method we have employed in our semantic analysis. In determining first under what conditions a sentence is true and then whether the sentence is in fact true, we are (1) translating the sentence into a symbolic notation (for now, the language of the first-order predicate calculus), (2) using the apparatus of set membership and an (informal) interpretation of the quantifiers, determining the truth-conditions of the resulting logical formula, and (3) determining whether those conditions in fact obtain in the world (or our model of it). We turn to this indirect interpretive approach in order to establish a systematic way of calculating semantic values.

An important feature of the analysis we have chosen is that it determines the semantic functions of two different members of a single syntactic category in different ways. So, where *nothing* in (10) and *Churchill* in (3) (which are both NPs) might appear to play the same semantic role, our analysis reveals that on closer inspection, they are interpreted by very different procedures. We will return to this point below.

Our approach to quantifiers like *all* and *some* runs into difficulties when we consider other kinds of quantifiers. Consider, for example, the following translation for *A dog barks* in which "&" stands for *and*:

(15)   (∃y) [y is a dog & y barks]

Since the rule of interpretation for "&" requires that each part of the conjunction be true in order for the whole sentence to be true, the rule for interpreting existentially quantified statements will ask us to determine whether there is at least one individual in the world who is in two sets: the set of dogs and the set of barkers.

So far, so good, but this sort of analysis cannot be readily extended to the seemingly parallel (16):

(16)   Most dogs bark.

Suppose, for example, that we invent a new quantifier symbol, "Δ," whose interpretation requires testing the individuals in the world to determine whether or not enough of them (say, more than half) are in the set of dogs and the set of barkers, in effect rendering (16) as (17) in the first-order predicate calculus with Δ:

(17)   (Δx)[x is a dog & x barks]

This cannot be a representation of (16), since (17) requires that most things be dogs (and barkers), whereas (16) seems only to require that most things that are dogs be barkers. In point of fact, (16) seems true, but (17) does not. (For further discussion, see Barwise and Cooper 1981.)

For these and several other reasons, many cognitive scientists no longer regard the simple version of the first-order predicate calculus that we have presented as the optimum representation for quantifierlike expressions in natural languages. A number of alternatives are currently being studied. Both Montague (1973) and Barwise and Cooper (1981) have developed methods of analysis that, although different in interesting ways, share a common insight that introduces an alternative to the analysis of quantification above.

To reconsider the case in (10), *Nothing eats*, suppose we attempt to assign a semantic value directly to *nothing*. We have already noted that there does not seem to be any relevant individual to which *nothing* might refer, but that does not rule out certain less obvious alternatives. Suppose, for example, that we analyze *nothing* as referring to a set of sets, which for ease of description we will call a *family* of sets. Which sets will be in this family of sets? Let us say that a set with no members, or what is called the *empty* set, is the only member of this family of sets. On this model, *something* will have as its semantic value a family of sets each of whose members has at least one member, and *everything* will have as its semantic value the family of sets whose only member contains everything in the universe of discourse as a member. If we adopt this analysis, it becomes possible to provide a rule that computes the semantic value of a sentence like (10) out of the semantic values of its parts as follows:

(18)   ⟦Nothing eats⟧ = True iff ⟦eats⟧ ∈ ⟦nothing⟧

Since ⟦eats⟧ is a set (namely, {things that eat}), it makes sense to ask whether it is a member of the family of sets that *nothing* refers to. The only member of that family of sets is the empty set, and so the sentence comes out false because the set of eaters is not empty (hence, not in the family of sets in question). But consider the sentence *Something eats*. Here the family of sets to which *something* refers contains as members those sets that contain at least one individual. Since the set of eaters contains many members, it will be a member of ⟦something⟧. Thus, if we inquire whether

(19) $[\![\text{eats}]\!] \in [\![\text{something}]\!]$

the answer is yes, and the sentence is true. By the same sort of reasoning, you should be able to determine the truth-value of $[\![\text{Everything eats}]\!]$.

This system of interpretation can also be extended to handle sentences involving other quantificational NPs, including determiners such as *a dog* in *A dog barks* (discussed earlier), and even the sentence involving *most* in (16). For example, in order to receive a treatment parallel to that received by *nothing* and *something*, *most dogs* will have to refer to a family of sets. (We leave aside the more technical question of what *most* itself refers to and how that semantic value is composed with that of *dogs* to generate the semantic value of the resulting NP. For discussion, see Barwise and Cooper 1981.) Which sets will that family comprise? It should be the family of sets each of which includes most dogs. *Most dogs bark* will then be true iff (20a) is true, which in turn is true iff (20b) is true:

(20)   a. $[\![\text{barks}]\!] \in [\![\text{Most dogs}]\!]$
        b. $\{\text{barkers}\} \in \{\text{all sets that contain most dogs}\}$

(20b) asks whether the set of barkers is one of those sets that has the property of containing most dogs. Now, of course, many sets contain most dogs. For example, the set of things that have fur contains most dogs, since dogs overwhelmingly have fur. Here we are interested in whether the set of barkers is to be found among the sets containing most dogs. Since few dogs do not bark, it is, and therefore (16) is true.

This approach to quantification in English involves treating the subject NP as a complicated set of sets and calculating whether or not the semantic value of the predicate is in that set. This seems "backward" compared to the manner in which we computed the semantic value of sentences such as (3) (*Churchill smoked*), in which we tested the semantic value of the subject of the sentence for inclusion in the semantic value of the predicate. That is, in light of the interpretation we have just offered of quantified NPs, we are committed to an asymmetrical analysis of sentences depending upon whether or not they contain names. Compare (21a) and (21b) with (21c):

(21)   a. $[\![\text{Something died}]\!] = \text{True iff } [\![\text{died}]\!] \in [\![\text{something}]\!]$
        b. $[\![\text{The dog died}]\!] = \text{True iff } [\![\text{died}]\!] \in [\![\text{the dog}]\!]$
        c. $[\![\text{Churchill died}]\!] = \text{True iff } [\![\text{Churchill}]\!] \in [\![\text{died}]\!]$

A New Theory of Names and Quantifiers
Montague (1973) has pointed out that it is possible to provide a uniform interpretation for names, descriptions, and quantified noun phrases. In order to achieve this parallelism between quantified and nonquantified sentences, we must revise our view of what names refer to. Earlier we suggested that a sentence ascribing a property to a named individual is true iff that individual is in the set of things having that property. Unfortunately, given our analysis of quantifiers, sentences with names in subject position receive a semantic analysis completely different from, and opposite to, that given to quantified sentences.

One solution to this problem is to assign families of sets as interpretations to names as well, taking names to be abbreviations for the bundle of properties possessed by the named individual. Thus, to *Churchill* we assign the family of sets each of which contains Churchill as a member. This is made explicit in the treatment of proper names proposed by Montague (1973). Using this approach, we interpret (3) as follows:

(22) $[\![\text{Churchill smoked}]\!] = \text{True iff } [\![\text{smoked}]\!] \in [\![\text{Churchill}]\!]$

Since the set of smokers contains Churchill, that set will be one of the members of the family of sets to which *Churchill* refers. Therefore, the set of those who smoked will be a member of the semantic value of Churchill, and the sentence is true.

To be sure, this analysis of proper names is controversial. In its favor is the fact that it allows us to treat all subject expressions uniformly. On the other hand, it does some violence to the intuition (developed in Kripke 1980) that the semantic function of a name is just to pick out its bearer. Intuitively, we think that *Churchill*, for instance, does nothing more than refer to Churchill. But the approach we have discussed has it referring to a family of sets. Regardless of the final verdict, we have seen that semantic analysis, like syntactic and phonological analysis, proceeds by hypothesis and justification and may not always conform to our first intuitions. In these regards, semantics has much in common with other areas of scientific inquiry, with the first-order predicate calculus and the analyses of Montague and of Barwise and Cooper constituting competing theories of quantification and naming. Although the latter approach has great potential, for ease of exposition we will concentrate on first-order predicate calculus as we continue our analysis. It has the advantage of being better known and somewhat less abstract, while still being a good illustration of a systematic analysis of logical form.

Domain of Discourse, Tense, and Indexicality
As is the case with any hypothesis, when we look more closely at the interpretations of a wide range of sentences, we discover additional data that our theory must confront. In fact, several interesting problems that we have suppressed have already cropped up. Thus, before extending our analysis to accommodate new facts, we note a few qualifications. First of all, when an NP such as *everything* is used in typical speech, there is normally an implicit narrowing of what is called the *domain of discourse*. That is, the universe over which we quantify (in other words, the stock of individuals about which we are talking) is limited, often by an implied criterion of relevance. Thus, a person who says *Everything is fattening* while in a restaurant is presumably talking about the food on the menu and not about everything in the universe. Even quantificational NPs such as *every man* fall under this generalization: in using such an expression, we typically make a comment about all the relevant men (whoever they may be in a given circumstance). If this intuition informs the analysis of quantification sketched above, we will limit our consideration to relevant individuals in the domain of discourse when we construct the sets and families of sets that figure in the calculation of semantic values.

Next, we need to consider tenses. *Churchill smoked* is true on its interpretation as a simple past-tense assertion when uttered at times after he acquired the habit. It was not true at his birth or at any time prior to that event. More generally, many sentences of natural languages can only be evaluated for truth or falsity relative to a moment of utterance and with respect to a time frame. The time frame is typically given by the tense marker in simple sentences. In simple cases such as the one under consideration past tense requires that the sentence *Churchill smoked* must have been true at some moment prior to the time of utterance. Present tense is more complicated. If you say *Birds eat*, you do not necessarily mean that they are doing so at present. It is more likely that you mean that they habitually eat or that they eat as a matter of course. It is possible to use present tense to refer to the present moment (as, for example, in reports of sporting events: "And Jones slides into third under the tag!"), but this is fairly uncommon.

These are some of the concerns with tense that a more thoroughgoing treatment of English semantics would need to analyze. Recently linguists and philosophers have developed richly detailed analyses of tense systems that address these and related facts within frameworks closely related to the one we have been examining (see Dowty 1982; Partee 1973), and temporal logics remain an active field of investigation.

A related phenomenon that also requires somewhat more elaboration of our semantic system is *indexicality*. Terms in natural languages like *I*, *you*, *now*, and *here* are said to be indexical, because they refer to different entities at different times and when used by different speakers in different situations. *Now* refers to the present moment now but to a different one when used at different times. *Here* is anywhere the speaker who uses it happens to be. The account of the interpretation of such expressions and of sentences that contain them requires a specification of how to fix the reference of these expressions depending upon these situational variables.

Ambiguity and Scope
Let us now test our theory against some new data. Consider, first, a class of ambiguities that involve quantification. Each of the following sentences has two different interpretations:

(23) a. Blik is not available in all areas.
      b. Somebody voted for every candidate.

Sentence (23a) can be used both to assert that the product is available only in some areas and to assert that it is available in none. Sentence (23b) means either that someone voted as many times as it took to cast a vote for each candidate or that no candidate failed to receive a vote (with the votes coming from possibly different voters). Part of the interest in these examples lies in the fact that their ambiguity does not appear to derive from ambiguities in word meaning. For instance, the ambiguity of (24) can be traced to the two different meaning of *record*; there is no *structural ambiguity* in the sentence:

(24) Mary broke the record. (disc or Guinness)

There does not seem to be a parallel explanation for (23a) and (23b). In these examples each component of each sentence has a single interpretation, yet each sentence has two interpretations. We conclude that there must be two different ways of combining the interpretations of the parts to produce the interpretations of the entire sentences. In the case of (23a), for example, the crucial issue is the point in the interpretation at which we factor the semantic value of the negation into the sentence. In other words, (23a) can be construed as asserting either (25) or (26):

(25) It is not the case that [Blik is available in all areas]

(26) For all areas, it is not the case that [Blik is available in them]

Sentence (25), which claims that there are at least some areas in which Blik is not available, would be represented in the first-order predicate calculus as (27a), where x ranges over areas, which is equivalent to (27b):

(27) a. $\sim (\forall x)$ [Blik is available in x]
      b. $(\exists x)$ [$\sim$ Blik is available in x]

By contrast, sentence (26) asserts that Blik is not available anywhere, which would be symbolized as (28a) or (28b):

(28) a. $(\forall x) \sim$ [Blik is available in x]
      b. $\sim (\exists x)$ [Blik is available in x]

In such cases we say that there are two ways of assigning *scope* to the negation operator and the quantifier. In (27a) negation has wide scope over the universal quantifier, because it occurs outside of the quantifier; in (28a) the universal quantifier has wide scope, because it occurs outside of the reach of the negation. In specifying the truth-conditions of quantified sentences, our semantic theory will assign different truth-conditions to these two readings, as a result of composing the interpretation of the sentence by assigning different relative scopes to negation and quantification. Consequently, (27a) will be true iff Blik's availability is not universal, and (28a) will be true just in case Blik is nowhere to be found. The important point here is that the first-order predicate calculus can both explain this ambiguity and assign the correct semantic interpretation to each of the readings by providing two permissible but mutually incompatible ways of translating this English sentence into the logic and of assigning truth-conditions to it.

A similar scope contest, this time between two quantifiers, is at work in (23b). (23b) can be represented either as (29)

(29) $(\exists x)(\forall y)$ [x voted for y]

(that is, some particular individual x is such that that individual voted for each and every candidate y), or as (30)

(30) $(\forall y)(\exists x)$ [x voted for y]

(that is, for every candidate y, there is at least one voter x such that x voted for y). Again, these two interpretations in our logic, one of which assigns the universal quantifier wide scope over the existential quantifier and one of which assigns scope in the reverse order, will have different truth-conditions, by virtue of interpreting the quantifiers in different orders and with different relative scopes when computing the truth-conditions of the sentence as a whole. This ambiguity thus receives an explanation parallel to that of (23a).

We have seen that a fairly rigorous account can be given of how the meaning of a sentence can be constructed from the meanings of its parts. So far we have been operating under the assumptions that the meaning of a linguistic item is its referent and that the reference of a sentence is its truth-value. In the following section we will see why this is in fact too simplistic a view of the nature of linguistic meaning and how our semantics must be enriched, and complicated somewhat, in order to account for more of the complexity of natural language.

10.4 Sense

In addition to the ideas of compositionality and of truth-value as sentence reference, Frege introduced the distinction between the *sense* and the *reference* of a linguistic item.

For the remainder of this discussion we will be exploring views in the tradition of Frege. Although this is not the only approach to semantic analysis practiced within cognitive science, it is important and representative. We will develop it at some length to give something of the flavor shared by many alternative theories.

When Frege introduced the sense-reference distinction, his purpose was to challenge a popular theory that analyzed meaning as reference. The account of semantic interpretation we have discussed so far is also essentially a referential theory in that it generally takes the semantic value of an expression to be its reference. Thus, Frege's arguments are quite relevant to our position, and they will incline us to add a new component to our semantic theory.

We have seen that the reference of a term is the thing in the world that a term (such as a name or a description) picks out, like Churchill for *Churchill* or {all red things} for *red*. The idea of sense is more abstract. Briefly, the aspect of the meaning of a word, by virtue of which we understand it and by virtue of which it succeeds in picking out its referent, is its sense. For a sentence, the sense is the way it describes the world, which, if accurate, makes it true, and which, if inaccurate, makes it false. Sense is therefore the feature of a linguistic expression that determines its reference, and it is what the mind grasps when it understands an expression.

To see this more clearly, we may consider the following pairs of examples:

(31) a. Churchill
      b. The prime minister of England during World War II

(32) a. ____ has a heart
      b. ____ has a kidney

(33) a. Clinton is Clinton.
      b. Clinton is the first Democratic U.S. president since Jimmy Carter.

(34) a. Carmen is a bat.
      b. Carmen is a winged mammal.

The members of each of these pairs are identical in reference but appear to differ in meaning. Consequently, our theory of meaning must be able to distinguish the interpretation of each member of the pair from the other. Unfortunately, as long as we assign their reference as their meaning, we will be unable to do so. Therefore, following Frege, we note that each of these examples has a different sense and thus a different way of picking out its referent. Although each expression in (31) picks out Churchill, (31a) does so by naming him, whereas (31b) is a description, whose meaning is in turn constructed from the meanings of its parts. Although it happens to be true of Churchill, there is a strong sense in which it need not have been. It could have been, for instance, that Chamberlain retained that office. Notice that adopting this style of semantic analysis gives up the claim that meaning equals reference and adopts the position that expressions that are coreferential may express different senses and therefore have different meanings.

Similarly, although (32a) and (32b) refer to the same set, they too have different meanings. That intuitively rather obvious fact can be demonstrated semantically. Since (32a) and (32b) are complex expressions, their semantic values should be composed from the semantic values of their parts. The only difference between (32a) and (32b) is that where (32a) contains *heart*, (32b) contains *kidney*. The mode of composition of the meaning of these phrases hence should be the same. However, the meanings of *heart* and *kidney* are different, since *heart* refers to the set of hearts and *kidney* to the set of kidneys. Thus, we would expect that the meanings of the descriptions would differ, despite the coincidence of their identical reference.

A related point brings into focus the sorts of problems that examples such as these pose for the analysis of meaning as reference. Suppose for the sake of argument that meaning is reference, and keep in mind that we are assuming that phrase and sentence meaning is compositional and that the reference of a sentence is its truth-value. Since on this account (32a) and (32b) have the same meaning, then so should (35a) and (35b), since they differ only in the same respects that (32a) and (32b) do:

(35)   a. The fact that John *has a heart* explains the circulation of his blood.
       b. The fact that John *has a kidney* explains the circulation of his blood.

But (35a) is true, whereas (35b) is false. Hence, these sentences differ in reference, though the two phrases in italics do not. We therefore need some account of meaning that will do justice to the difference in truth-value of sentences like (35a) and (35b) despite the identity of reference of pairs of phrases like (32a) and (32b), and the key should be assigning different meanings to (32a) and (32b) and hence dropping our assumption that reference is meaning.

Sentences (33a) and (33b) make this point in a slightly different way. (33a) is a logical, or a necessary, truth. It is logically impossible for it to be false, for everything is what it is. However, (33b), though true, is true not by virtue of logic but by virtue of the facts of history. It could have been otherwise, for instance, if Dukakis had won or if Clinton had decided not to run for office. This difference in logical status ought to be reflected in a difference in meaning of the two sentences, despite their agreement in truth-value and despite the fact that the description in (33b) picks out exactly the same individual as the name it replaces in (33a). In particular, the semantic theory should be able to explain why (33a) is a *necessary* truth, whereas (33b) is only a happenstance, or *contingent*, truth.

Sentences (34a) and (34b) are both true. But Fred, who can always recognize a bat when he sees one and who knows Carmen well, believes that bats are birds. Therefore, (36a) is true, whereas (36b) is false:

(36)   a. Fred believes that Carmen is a bat.
       b. Fred believes that Carmen is a winged mammal.

Ideally, a semantic theory could explain how this is possible despite the identical reference of *bat* and *winged mammal*, and of (34a) and (34b) (which are both true sentences), and despite the fact that (36a) and (36b) are alike in all respects except for the substitution of expressions that do not differ in reference. The key to the solution of all these puzzles lies in the introduction of sense as the meaning of linguistic expressions.

Possible Worlds
Let us consider first what the notion of sense should capture. The sense of a sentence should be, not its truth-value, but *what makes the sentence true or false*; the sense of a predicate expression should be, not the set to which it refers, but *what makes the predicate expression refer to that set*; and senses should be what we understand when we understand an expression. Informally, then, the sense of a sentence—what it ex-

presses—is what the world would be like if it were true, and a sentence is true if the world is in fact like that. Similarly, the sense of a predicate expression is the property that a thing would have to have in order to be in the set picked out by that predicate, and a set is the reference of a predicate if it is the set of individuals with the requisite property. To make these ideas clearer and more formal, we introduce a device that has been important to the development of natural language semantics in the Fregean tradition in the last few decades, the concept of a *possible world* (Montague 1973; Dowty, Wall, and Peters 1981). A possible world is nothing more than a way the world could have been, consistent with logic. So, another way of saying "Bush could have been reelected" would be "There is a possible world in which Bush had been reelected"; or, more fancifully, another way of saying "It is possible that lizards speak French" would be "There is a possible world in which lizards speak French." The logical device of possible worlds provides a tidy account of sense and its connection with reference that will in turn afford an explanation of both the similarities and the differences between such pairs of sentences as those in (31) through (36).

Let us develop our previous rough-and-ready notions of sense more carefully using possible worlds. We will say that the sense of a sentence, which we will call a *proposition* (to use the term in a new, technical manner), is just that set of worlds in which the sentence is true. It may seem strange at first to identify the meaning of a sentence with a set of possible worlds. But consider what this really means: when someone asserts a sentence, such as "Grass is green," for that sentence to be true is for this world (the *actual world*) to be in the set of worlds in which grass is green. If the person had said, "Grass is purple," we would have understood that sentence and known it to be false, because the actual world is not in the set of purple-grass worlds. The important thing to understand is that, although this sentence is false, we know what it would be for that sentence to be true—namely, for one of the possible worlds with purple grass to be the actual one.

Propositions, Necessity, and Propositional Attitudes
In this section we will first explore how the notion of possible worlds works for predicate expressions and then turn to the problem of combining the senses of subject and predicate expressions to come up with the propositions.

Recall that the sense of a predicate expression is a property, a usage that accords fairly well with our ordinary language use of the word. Note that when we understand a word like *red*, it would be odd to say that what we grasp is the set cf red things ({all red things})—the reference of *red*. Rather, what we grasp is *what it is to be red*. Using the language of possible worlds, we can say that what we understand is what it takes to qualify for membership in the set of red things in any possible world. Thus, when we understand *red*, if we were to go to another world (using our imagination), we would be able to identify the set of red things in that world. The property associated with a predicate, then, is the set comprising the set of things in the reference of that predicate expression in each possible world. The mechanism of possible worlds allows us to treat senses, which are conceptlike in nature, as sets of referents—sets of worlds (propositions), sets of sets (properties), and so forth. So, the property of redness includes, in this world, the set of all red things; in another world, the set of all red things in that world; and so on.

On this account, when we understand the meaning of an expression, we grasp not its reference but its sense. The sense of an expression, together with the way the world is, determines its reference. Thus, a proposition and the facts together determine a truth-value (for example, *Grass is green* and the greenness of actual grass determine True, whereas *Grass is purple* and the greenness of actual grass determine False). A property and the way the world is determine a set, which is the kind of thing that is the referent of a predicate expression (for example, the property of being red and the facts about what things are red determine {all red things}).

Next, let us consider the senses of names. The semantic function of a name is to pick out an individual. *Bush*, for instance, picks out Bush. Since we want to be able to say things like "It was possible for Bush to defeat Clinton" or "John believes that Bush won reelection," and we are attempting to describe the meanings of these sentences in terms of possible worlds, *Bush* must refer to Bush in each of these worlds. We will assume, then, that names designate the same individual in all possible worlds; the sense of a name is therefore the set consisting of its bearer, in each world. In discussing reference, we noted the elegant uniformity that can be achieved in the semantics of NP expressions, including names, by treating their semantic values as families of sets. It might appear that by treating names as designating their bearers in each possible world, we are in danger of losing this uniformity. But the danger is only apparent. For we can, on this approach, treat the semantic values of names as the families, not of sets to which their bearers belong, but of properties that they have, thus achieving exactly the same effect. We will see more of how this works shortly (see Dowty, Wall, and Peters 1981).

Let us consider how the enriched semantic theory handles the problematic pairs of sentences in (31) through (36), repeated here:

(31) a. Churchill
      b. the prime minister of England during World War II

(32) a. _____ has a heart
      b. _____ has a kidney

(33) a. Clinton is Clinton.
      b. Clinton is the first Democratic U.S. president since Jimmy Carter.

(34) a. Carmen is a bat.
      b. Carmen is a winged mammal.

(35) a. The fact that John has a heart explains the circulation of his blood.
      b. The fact that John has a kidney explains the circulation of his blood.

(36) a. Fred believes that Carmen is a bat.
      b. Fred believes that Carmen is a winged mammal.

Churchill in (31) refers to Churchill, as does *the prime minister of England during World War II*, but the semantic value of *Churchill* will pick out Churchill in every possible world, whereas the semantic value of *the prime minister of England during World War II* will pick out, in each world, whoever happens to hold that office. In the actual world these senses determine the same reference. But our intuition that this fact is merely happenstance is nicely accounted for by the possible-worlds semantics. Although in the actual world, being the prime minister was one of Churchill's properties, it is not so in all possible worlds. In other words, it is possible that Churchill was not prime minister during World War II. We thus explain both the sameness of reference of these expressions (Churchill) and their difference in sense (Churchill's properties, or Churchill in all worlds versus whoever, in any world, is prime minister of England during World War II in that world).

With respect to (32), we note that although in the actual world {things with a heart} = {things with a kidney}, this does not mean that these sets are the same in all worlds. The fact that we can describe a possible world where there are heartless but kidneyed creatures, or vice versa, tells us that the senses of these two expressions differ—that although their senses pick out the same set in the actual world, they pick out different sets in other worlds. It is hence no surprise that (35a) and (35b) express different propositions, by virtue of being composed of constituents with different senses, or that one of them expresses a proposition that is true in this world, whereas the other expresses a proposition that is false in this world.

Both occurrences of *Clinton* in (33a) pick out Clinton in every world. It would follow, then, that (33a) expresses a proposition true in all possible worlds—in other words, a logically necessary proposition. But whereas *Clinton* picks out Clinton in all worlds, *the first Democratic U.S. president since Jimmy Carter* picks out different individuals in many of the different worlds we might imagine. And of course, there are plenty of worlds where its sense picks out an individual distinct from Clinton, worlds in which (33b) is false. In some worlds, then, the family of Clinton's properties includes the property of being the first Democratic U.S. president since Jimmy Carter, whereas in others it does not; but in each world Clinton's property set is self-identical. We can therefore understand why these two sentences express different propositions—both true, but one true necessarily, and one merely contingently.

Finally, we return to the sentences in (34) and (36). The sentences in (36) attribute beliefs to Fred. As noted in chapter 8, philosophers have termed states such as beliefs *propositional attitudes*. We are now in a position to see just why it is so fruitful from the standpoints of both philosophy and linguistics to see these states as connecting persons to *propositions*, as opposed, say, to connecting them to the things referred to by the sentences they believe (truth-values, on the current analysis) or to the things referred to by the constituents of those sentences (objects and sets). We know that the sense of *Carmen* picks out Carmen (or, more exactly, the corresponding family of sets) in every world and that the senses of *bat* and *winged mammal* pick out sets of things in each world. Now, in this world those are the same sets, and if what Fred believed was related in some simple way just to the reference of either (34a), (34b), or of any of their constituents, it would be impossible for (36a) and (36b) to differ in truth-value. But suppose that Fred believes the *sense* of (34a) and disbelieves the *sense* of (34b). There are certainly plenty of worlds in which {bats} does not equal {winged mammals}. Fred believes that the actual world is one of those and that Carmen, although a member of {bats}, is not a member of {winged mammals}. So long as belief is the kind of thing that relates believers to propositions, rather than to the referents of the sentences that express them or to the referents of their constituents, we have no trouble, given the difference in sense between (34a) and (34b), in distinguishing (36a) from (36b).

Because it explains such a wide range of semantic phenomena, the notion of sense has gained great favor in semantics. This analysis allows us to retain our intuition that the semantics of complex expressions is compositional (that is, that complex meanings are built up systematically from the meanings of constituent parts) and the intuition that to understand a sentence is roughly to know under what circumstances it is true. This approach also has the virtue of providing the same types of interpretations for constituents of sentences that are syntactically similar, thus confirming an intuition that syntactic theory and semantic theory go hand in hand in the account of how we map from structure to meaning. Despite these many virtues, however, this approach to semantic theory does encounter certain problems, and alternative approaches that address some of these issues have been proposed.

10.5 Problems in Possible-Worlds Semantics

The first two of the three problems we will consider are closely related. They both arise from the fact that propositions are identified with the sets of worlds in which the sentences that express them are true. For instance, *A dog died* expresses the proposition that is the set of worlds in each of which at least one dog died; to believe that a dog died is to believe that the actual world is one of those; for it to be possible that a dog died is for there to be at least one world in which a dog died, and so on.

The first problem is the *problem of the equivalence of necessary truths*. Consider the following sentences:

(37) a. Churchill is Churchill.
      b. John believes that Churchill is Churchill.

(38) a. $2 + 2 = 4$.
      b. John believes that $2 + 2 = 4$.

(39) a. There are infinitely many prime numbers.
      b. John believes that there are infinitely many prime numbers.

Each of the sentences (37a), (38a), and (39a) expresses a necessary truth. That is, each of these sentences is true in every possible world. But, given the account we have developed of propositions, this means that they all express the same proposition and hence mean the same thing. But this seems wrong. (37a) is about Churchill, (38a) is an elementary truth of arithmetic, and (39a) is a theorem that requires some mathematical sophistication to prove. Moreover, if our semantics is really compositional, then since the (a) sentences of (37) through (39) mean the same thing, and since the only difference between the (b) sentences of (37) through (39) is that the content of John's belief is specified in each by the respective (a) sentence, it would seem that the (b) sentences should mean the same thing and therefore should have the same truth-value in all possible worlds. Clearly, they do not: John might have no problem with (37a) and (38a), for instance, but not know enough mathematics to even understand (39a), much less believe it, with the result that (39b) would be false. It seems that our semantic theory makes a false prediction here—namely, that all necessary truths express the same proposition, if we are to understand propositions as the meanings of sentences.

What seems to be wrong is that our way of classifying propositions is too coarse. That is, finer distinctions must be drawn between different propositions than those determined by noting the worlds in which each is true. Ideally, semantic theory should assign different interpretations to the (a) sentences of (37) through (39) and yet explain why they are all true in just the same possible worlds, in the way that our theory explains why (31) through (34) have different senses yet have the same reference in the actual world. An analysis that would meet this demand is the goal of much ongoing research in semantics (Barwise and Perry 1983, Cresswell 1985).

The second problem, the *problem of logical omniscience*, is very closely related to the first. Consider a Sherlock Holmes story, in which both Holmes and Watson know all of the clues in the case. Holmes performs his "elementary" deduction and now also knows who did it. Watson is still in the dark, however, and will remain so until Holmes patiently leads him through the train of complex but logically valid reasoning from the evidence to the conclusion. This all seems at least possible. The problem is that on the semantic analysis we have been considering, Watson's state of believing all the premises of Holmes's reasoning but of not yet believing the conclusion is an impossible state to be in. For consider: what makes Holmes's reasoning valid is that in all possible worlds where all of the premises are true (that is, where the evidence is as he says it is) the conclusion of his reasoning is true (the butler did it). But if Watson believes all the premises, and if what he believes by virtue of believing them is a proposition (that is, a set of worlds), and if the butler did it in all those worlds, then it would seem that Watson would believe the proposition that the butler did it. This is just the problem of the equivalence of all necessarily true propositions in different clothing. Our model is not fine grained enough to distinguish propositions from what they entail and hence does not allow for the existence of less-than-perfect deducers. The work of Cresswell (1985), Barwise and Perry (1983), and Kamp (1984), among others, has been directed toward the problem of developing model-theoretic treatments that preserve the advantages of the Frege-Montague approach but do not have these untoward consequences.

A third difficulty that this approach has encountered from the standpoint of cognitive science concerns the *psychological plausibility of semantic theory*. The semantic theory we have been developing has assigned very abstract sets, including even sets of possible worlds, as the meanings of linguistic expressions. Being abstract, sometimes downright unreal, and (most important) infinitely large representations, such set-theoretic entities cannot literally be represented in peoples' (finite) brains or even in machines. But as cognitive scientists, we are interested in an explanation of how actual information processing occurs, and we would like to know, in the case of language understanding, just how humans manage to understand linguistic expressions. The problem appears to be that as we have sketched compositional model-theoretic semantics, although it is (outstanding difficulties aside) an elegant compositional theory assigning meanings to linguistic expressions, it is not a finite representation. Consequently, it does not seem to be able to say much about human semantic processing, nor has any evidence in its favor derived from experimental results measuring human semantic performance been presented.

A plausible resolution (suggested in Partee 1979) is to point out that although model-theoretic semantics does not directly specify psychological or computational mechanisms that may be at work in natural language understanding, and although the semantic structures it posits are not literally in speakers' heads, it provides a useful abstract characterization of the psychologically and computationally relevant structures that mediate and explain language understanding. Consider, for clarification, a related problem with mathematical models. Multiplication can be described as a function mapping pairs of numbers into their products. However, no finite computation device (person or machine) can directly represent this infinite function, although our actual mental processes must be functionally parallel to the infinite function, at least over a wide range of cases. Similarly, the semanticist might say, although we do not believe that sets of possible worlds or families of properties are literally in speakers' heads, we are showing that whatever representations are in the heads of language understanders, by virtue of which they understand language, must be abstractly describable by these kinds of structures and that whatever kinds of psychological or computational processes operate on these representations must generally preserve this kind of structure. On this view, semantics provides a constraint on empirical theories —telling the experimentalist what kinds of theories would count as language-understanding mechanisms—and provides a guide to empirical research by suggesting models to investigate.

When viewed in this way, semantic research is seen as an indispensable tool in the effort to understand human linguistic information processing and in the effort to design machine understanding systems. It provides the initial abstract characterization of the goals to be achieved, constrains the range of models that can be proposed, and suggests processes that might work. When elaborated more completely, it may even describe essential features of the data structure involved in understanding language. In the next section we will consider briefly the ways in which semantics is infused into the cognitive psychology of language processing and into AI research in natural language processing, and the ways in which these fields contribute to research in linguistics and philosophy.

10.6 Cognitive and Computational Models of Semantic Processing

Let us begin by clarifying the distinction between *proof-theoretic* and *model-theoretic* analyses of argument validity. Recall our earlier discussion of argument structure centering on examples (1a–c) and (2a–c). In the logical tradition there are two ways of distinguishing arguments. A proof-theoretic approach would translate the premises of these arguments into a logical representation such as the first-order predicate calculus. By appealing to axioms (certain logical assumptions) and rules of deduction, we can prove that certain sentences follow from the premises on the basis of their logical structure. For example, if a conjunction (say, *A bird eats and a fish swims*) appears as a line in our proof, it follows by the rule of deduction known as *conjunct simplification* that the first conjunct (*A bird eats*) can be inferred. The essence of this rule is that if a sentence of the form *P and Q* is true (where *P and Q* stand for the first and second conjuncts, respectively), then *P* alone must be true. Notice that this procedure does not take into consideration the meaning of any of the content words used in the argument. What the sentences are about is simply not a factor in calculating inferences proof-theoretically. The logical structure of the sentences—in this case, the fact that the argument contains a conjunction—is crucial. Additional rules of deduction pertaining to quantifiers and implication would allow us to analyze and distinguish the arguments in (1a–c) and (2a–c) (see Wall 1973).

A model-theoretic analysis of validity takes the interpretations of linguistic expressions seriously. By assigning set-theoretic interpretations and deriving the truth-conditions of sentences, we can determine the truth or falsity of a given sentence in a given state of affairs. After determining what it takes for a particular sentence to be true, we can then see whether another given sentence would be true in that circumstance. If so, then the first sentence entails the second, and we have determined argument validity model-theoretically. In the case of *A bird eats and a fish flies*, it would be straightforward to show that any state of affairs in which the conjunction is true must involve an eating bird, and that circumstance suffices for the truth of *A bird eats*. This procedure, too, can be formalized and extended to a large fragment of natural language.

Given these two rather different approaches to ascertaining validity, it is interesting to ask which model of deduction provides the more explanatory account of the (real-time) human reasoning process. As we saw in chapter 3, Johnson-Laird (1975) has argued that the model-theoretic approach has greater plausibility in that it yields a better account of which argument forms are more difficult for people to follow.

Now suppose that the model-theoretic system of semantic interpretation sketched earlier turns out to be the best theory of meaning in natural language. The psychologist's problem, then, is to find a way of implementing this theory in an information-processing model. One promising integration of model-theoretic semantics into a theory of real-time language understanding is achieved by the work of Johnson-Laird (1983) and his colleagues on what they call *mental models*. By adopting the mental models approach, one commits oneself to the claim that human information processing involves model construction and that reasoning typically involves more than proof-theoretic deduction. On this view, a person's world is mentally represented in the form of a database, and information is processed by manipulating these internal models.

The models that the mind constructs in the course of understanding a sentence must have the formal features specified in our semantics: the semantic values of the primitives must be of the type that our semantics says they are, and they must compose in the way our semantics says they compose. So, sticking to the simplest account of names and predicates discussed earlier for purposes of illustration, the value of *Churchill* would be an individual in the mental model, and the value of *smokes* in a mental model would be the property of smoking. But these models cannot involve obscure and infinite abstract entities, on pain of losing their plausibility as an account of semantic processing. Appropriate representations of individuals as tokens and of finite sets of individuals as lists are easy to represent in artificial information-processing systems, and presumably in the mind as well. They could include a represented individual called *Churchill* and a representation of a set of individuals called *smokers* (possibly different ones in different possible worlds). For this mental model to represent the proposition expressed by *Churchill smokes*, then, would be for the Churchill individual to be in the set of smokers in the actual world. On this account, real worlds, individuals, and smoking properties do not have to somehow enter our psychology—rather, internally represented data structures that capture the relations specified by our semantic theory will suffice.

In this regard, consider an important feature of our analysis of quantification. We have actually not been uniquely characterizing entities; instead, we have been characterizing classes of entities as specified by their structure and interrelations. For instance, for our semantic purposes, we do not care whether the sentence *A dog died* is made true by the accidental demise of Fido or the deliberate shooting of Scruffy. Any dog and any death thereof will do to make the sentence true. This suggests that in order to construct a mental model that would serve as the semantic representation of a sentence or a longer discourse, like a paragraph, a story, or a conversation, it is not necessary to pick out any particular individuals, properties, worlds, or whatever—just some that are related to one another in the way the text says they are.

Such a semantic processing theory will then have to include descriptions and explanations of at least three important kinds of psychological structures of crucial interest to semantics: a mechanism for representing propositions, a set of semantic model-constructing and -modifying procedures, and the models themselves. Let us examine each of these components in turn, with a view to seeing how the interplay between semantic and psychological theory occurs.

Consider first that we are listeners trying to understand the following discourse:

(40)   A dog died. Churchill smoked. He died, too. Some whales eat.

Our first task is to construct a representation of the sentences we have heard that will enable us to identify their semantic structure—so that we will know what kinds of semantic representations to assign to each one. In the end, the psychologist will have the task of determining exactly how this translation goes, but the semanticist will claim that it should generate something like this (ignoring tense and using the first-order predicate calculus notation):

(41)   a. $(\exists x)[x$ is a dog $\&$ x died$]$
      b. $[$Churchill smoked$]$
      c. $[$Churchill died$]$
      d. $(\exists x)[x$ is a whale $\&$ x eats$]$

That is, semantics can tell psychology what the results of the translation-representation processes involved in understanding should be, so that psychology can set about discovering processes that can perform the required transformations.

Our next task as listeners is to construct a mental model of this discourse. To begin with, one procedure might see (41a), add an entity to the model x, and two sets, {dogs} and {dead things}, and put x into each of them. Another procedure would see the name *Churchill* and add a second entity to the model, called *Churchill*, whereupon another procedure would add him to the already existing set of dead things; still another procedure would construct a new set of smokers with Churchill among its members; and so on until we would have a complete model looking something like this:

{Dead things} $=$ $\{x,$ Churchill, $y, z\}$
{smokers} $=$ $\{$Churchill, $y, w\}$
{dogs} $=$ $\{x,$ Fido, $n\}$
{whales} $=$ $\{a, b, c, z, d, e, f\}$
{eaters} $=$ $\{a, b, c, d,$ Churchill, $x,$ Fido$\}$

Several points about this mental model deserve mention. First, and most important, given the semantic theory we have been exploring, the entire discourse (40) is true on this model. Second, more is represented in this model than is contained in (40) or (41). In part this is forced, because (41d) could not be satisfied without a number of whales and a number of eaters. Some of this information may have been supplied from our own knowledge as listeners. Some may be conjecture, such as the implied starvation of z. Now, semantics can specify what the necessary features of such mental models are and can go a long way toward specifying the general structure of the procedures that construct such models. But detailing exactly what these procedures are, how they are represented, and what triggers them—and specifying what kinds of extra information speakers and hearers put into their models, and under what conditions models are merged, scrapped, and altered—is a task for experimental psychology. It should be clear from this example, however, that this kind of research into semantic information processing would be impossible without the collaboration of semantics and psychology.

Before we leave the topic of mental models, it is worth making an observation about the insight this approach affords into judgments about argument validity. Earlier we noted that semantics must provide a natural account of when the premises of an argument entail its conclusion, and we considered different approaches to this task. To the detriment of our theory, in the discussion of Watson and Holmes we noted certain problems involved in constructing the set of worlds associated with a set of sentences expressing knowledge and beliefs. Often we find that we have constructed a set of worlds in each of which other irrelevant sentences (for example, the logical entailments of the original sentences) are true, distorting our account of propositional attitudes. However, mental models suggest a solution to the dilemma that arises when semantic models confront the logical fallibility of actual human reasoners. Mental models are partial—they represent only a small part of what we take to be ongoing reality at any given moment. This follows from limitations on human memory, attention, and so forth, but perhaps most directly from psychological judgments of relevance. We tend not to model irrelevant matters, even if they happen to be part of the passing scene.

Of course, relevance involves judgment, and we may often disregard facts or connections between facts that are indeed relevant but are judged not to be. Watson and Holmes provide such an example: although a complete formal semantic model would establish the identity of the murderer, Watson's partial model fails to establish all the necessary connections or to consider all the relevant relations between the individuals involved. Viewed from this perspective, semantic models capture the nature of knowledge and the laws of reason in the ideal case, whereas mental models are human approximations to this ideal.

Finally, by developing mental models, we can also account for a rather different sort of error of reasoning that is not directly modeled by our formal semantic theory. Although Watson's mistake was in failing to notice what was there to be noticed, we often err by assuming too much. For example, suppose you are told that these days many Americans are exercising regularly and that many Americans are healthy. The mental model we associate with this proposition needs to establish a set of Americans who exercise and a set of Americans who are healthy. But what is the relationship between those two sets? Many people will mentally construct these sets with the same members, as in this sample mental model,

American (*a*) & Exercising (*a*) & Healthy (*a*)
American (*b*) & Exercising (*b*) & Healthy (*b*)
American (*c*) & Lazy (*c*) & Sickly (*c*)
American (*d*) & Exercising (*d*) & Healthy (*d*)
Albanian (*e*) & Exercising (*e*) & Healthy (*e*)
Albanian (*f*) & Lazy (*f*) & Sickly (*f*)

in effect taking the proposition to imply:

(42)   You will be healthy if and only if you exercise.

In fact, the actual proposition in question does not involve such an implication at all; it has the form of a conjunction, roughly as shown in (43),

(43)   (Many) Americans are exercising and (Many) Americans are healthy.

which does not entitle us to assume any necessary connection between the two sets of Americans. It could as well be satisfied by the following model:

American (a) & Exercising (a) & Healthy (a)
American (b) & Exercising (b) & Sickly (b)
American (c) & Lazy (c) & Healthy (c)
American (d) & Exercising (d) & Healthy (d)
Albanian (e) & Exercising (e) & Sickly (e)
Albanian (f) & Lazy (f) & Healthy (f)

Here again, the discrepancy between a formal semantic theory and our human reasoning behavior can be better understood by investigating how we construct mental models.

As we saw in chapter 3, these types of errors in model construction may also provide the basis for an account of the fallacies of deductive reasoning. For all these reasons, the study of rules of deduction and of model construction from the psychological perspective is a promising and important area in cognitive science.

Finally, let us consider some further connections between semantic theory and research in psychology and AI. Historically, the relationship with AI has taken a number of different shapes as a result of the differing attitudes in the AI community concerning the role of formal semantic theory in a computational model of natural language understanding. In chapter 4 we briefly explored the possibility of incorporating the first-order predicate calculus as a level of representation in an AI system. These implementations of the predicate calculus have not been entirely successful, however, and there is disagreement over the nature of the solution to the problem. Some contend that the logic ought to be developed further, and customized, through the development of *nonstandard* or *deviant* logics, to provide a logic more appropriate to a model of natural language and human reason. This position is really no different from the one we adopted earlier when we were considering the merits of replacing the first-order predicate calculus with an analysis of quantification along the lines suggested by Montague and by Barwise and Cooper. Suppose, for example, we were interested in building a machine that can interpret English sentences, perhaps as a part of a larger task. Such a system might assign a syntactic analysis to its input, translate the syntactic representation into a suitable logical representation, and determine the truth or falsity of the input by comparing the truth-conditions expressed by the logical representation with the current state of affairs in a represented model.

This kind of project combines the syntactic and semantic theories developed by linguists and philosophers in an on-line system. Further potential exists for bringing psychological data concerning processing speed and errors to bear on the development of this research, leading us closer to a computational model of intelligent human behavior.

In addition to the lines of research that have pursued logical-linguistic styles of inquiry, considerable research in AI and psychology has focused on rather different approaches to meaning and understanding. Logical analyses of meaning tend not to provide a complete account of the meaning of the nonlogical (content) words of the language. For example, although a formal semantic theory might represent the semantic value of an intransitive verb as a set of individuals, it does not explain what property an individual must have in order to count as a member of the set in question. Thus, this sort of analysis simply does not provide an account of the meaning of individual words (as opposed to an account of the rules for combining these meanings once they are given).

Researchers in cognitive science have pursued the study of lexical semantics from a variety of perspectives (Putnam 1975; Rosch 1973; Katz and Fodor 1963; Quillian 1968). For example, we saw in chapters 2, 3, and 4 that semantic networks can be used to represent concepts or, roughly equivalently, the meanings of words. Semantic networks are compatible with the approach followed in this chapter because they can be viewed as an alternative representational format for structured logical expressions. Researchers in AI and psychology have been interested in semantic networks not because their expressive power differs from predicate-calculus-like notations but because the explicit representation of associative relations among concepts and propositions can be used to organize long-term memory and to facilitate the retrieval of relevant information from memory during cognitive processing.

In classical systems, propositions that are retrieved from (or activated in) semantic networks can be fed into symbolic reasoning processes that employ either proof-theoretic rules of inference or finite mental models. Shastri's (1992) connectionist implementation of semantic networks, introduced in chapter 3, significantly increases their processing power by allowing inferences that are based directly on concept meaning to be carried out by patterns of activation spreading through the network. The innovation here concerns processing efficiency and the solution of the problem of variable binding in networks. The representations and inferences are straightforwardly equivalent to their counterparts in the predicate calculus, and, therefore, they could be assigned semantic values of the kind considered in this chapter. The general problem of logical deduction, or theorem proving, has also been studied by connectionists (Ballard 1987). In one type of connectionist model, nodes associated with a proposition would be associated with the nodes associated with its entailments. For example, $P\&Q$ would be connected to P and to Q, and activation of the premise would be passed down to activate its conclusions. Many further details, which will not be discussed here, are needed to make such a network work well. The approach must also be considered In light of the arguments by Fodor and Pylyshyn (1988), introduced in chapter 2, that nonsymbolic connectionist networks cannot function as general reasoning systems.

Some recent work on concept representation in the connectionist paradigm bears a more uncertain relationship to the work described in this chapter. Smolensky (1988) and other proponents of distributed representations argue that the momentary representation of a concept or word is the pattern of activation over a large set of semantic microfeatures, each of which participates in the representation of many concepts, and none of which functions singly as the representation of a concept at the symbolic level of analysis. The contextual variability of patterns of activation is a potentially attractive way of handling the problem of the contextual sensitivity of meaning, discussed earlier in this chapter. However, connectionist models with distributed representations typically contain no facilities for explicitly representing structured symbolic expressions, over which the rules of semantic interpretation and the rules of deduction discussed in this chapter are defined. One possible solution to this problem, sketched by Smolensky (1988), is that conceptual meaning is handled by a subsymbolic intuitive processor, whereas the meanings of linguistic expressions are handled by a symbolic, conscious, rule-governed processor. The symbolic processor is a production system that can take inputs from and send outputs to the subsymbolic processor. The proposal of an intuitive, subsymbolic system of meaning is not considered feasible by proponents of the physical symbol system hypothesis, such as Fodor and Pylyshyn (1988), who argue that all thought (including nonverbal thought) involves structured symbolic representations that have a compositional semantics of the type sketched in this chapter. Smolensky's dual system proposal might also be thought to be premature in the sense that it should not be adopted until researchers can fully explore the semantics of distributed representations. It is a matter of further research whether it is better to map vectors of activation onto families of sets or possible worlds or to characterize their semantics entirely in terms of the ability of distributed connectionist networks to map inputs onto appropriate outputs, thus dispensing with traditional semantic values.

Procedural semantics, the final line of inquiry to be considered here, employs procedures in place of semantic values. The fundamental claim of procedural semantics has much in common with some connectionist views. The idea is that knowing a language involves knowing how to respond appropriately to the verbal and nonverbal environment. For example, Winograd's (1972) SHRDLU program answers questions about and acts in a "blocks world" filled with objects of various geometric shapes. The program allows screen representations of blocks to be moved about on command, and it can respond to inquiries about its changing database such as "Which cube is sitting on the table?" or "How many blocks are not in the box?" The semantic analyzer relies on word definitions, information about grammatical structure, contextual information, and deductive procedures. Ultimately, however, "For the computer, the final 'meaning' of a phrase or sentence is an internal program that tells what actions it must take" (Winograd 1974)—moving a block, printing an answer, searching memory, or updating the database, as appropriate.

Although the proposed computational mechanisms are just variants of classical symbolic models, procedural semantics seeks to provide a new paradigm for the study of meaning. The meanings of expressions are treated not in terms of mappings to the world (or possible worlds) but in terms of the actions (internal or external) that they trigger. Like the more radical connectionist approaches to meaning, procedural semantics is highly controversial as a semantic theory (see J. A. Fodor 1978), though less so as a style of semantic processing theory.

Suggested Readings

A summary of Montague's semantic system is presented in "An Overview of Montague Semantics" (Weisler 1991). For a more rigorous introduction to Montague Grammar and formal semantics, see *Introduction to Montague Semantics* (Dowty, Wall, and Peters 1981). A more basic introduction to logic is available in the beginning chapters of Wall's *Introduction to Mathematical Linguistics* (Wall 1973) or in *The Language of First-Order Logic* (including the Macintosh Program Tarski's World) (Barwise and Etchemendy 1990), which also discusses model-theoretic interpretation. *Meaning and Grammar: An Introduction to Semantics* (Chierchia and McConnell-Ginet 1990) discusses recent approaches to the standard problems in the theory of meaning. Many important articles in philosophy of language and semantics are conveniently anthologized. Two such books are *Logic and Philosophy for Linguists: A Book of Readings* (Moravcsik 1974) and *Readings in the Philosophy of Language* (Rosenberg and Travis 1971). For a history of semantics in the early and more recent periods of generative grammar, see *Semantics: Theories of Meaning in Generative Grammar* (J. D. Fodor 1977).

For a broader perspective on work on meaning from a variety of points of view, see *Semantics: An Interdisciplinary Reader in Philosophy, Linguistics, and Psychology* (Steinberg and Jakobovits 1971).

References

Austin, J. L. (1962). *How to do things with words*. Oxford: Clarendon Press.

Ballard, D. H. (1987). Parallel logical inference and energy minimization. Report TR142, Computer Science Department, University of Rochester, Rochester, N.Y.

Barwise, J., and R. Cooper (1981). Generalized quantifiers and natural language. *Linguistics and Philosophy* 4, 159–219.

Barwise, J., and J. Etchemendy (1990). *The language of first-order logic*. Palo Alto, Calif.: Center for the Study of Language and Information.

Barwise, J., and J. Perry (1983). *Situations and attitudes*. Cambridge, Mass.: MIT Press.

Chierchia, G., and S. McConnell-Ginet (1990). *Meaning and grammar: An introduction to semantics*. Cambridge, Mass.: MIT Press.

Cresswell, M. (1985). *The semantics of propositional attitudes*. Cambridge, Mass.: MIT Press.

Dowty, D. (1982). Tenses, time adverbs and compositional semantic theory. *Linguistics and Philosophy* 5, 23–55.

Dowty, D., R. Wall, and S. Peters (1981). *Introduction to Montague semantics*. Dordrecht: Reidel.

Fodor, J. A. (1978). Tom Swift and his procedural grandmother. *Cognition* 6, 229–247.

Fodor, J. A., and Z. W. Pylyshyn (1988). Connectionism and cognitive architecture. In S. Pinker and J. Mehler, eds., *Connections and symbols*. Cambridge, Mass.: MIT Press.

Fodor, J. D. (1977). *Semantics: Theories of meaning in generative grammar*. New York: Thomas Y. Crowell.

Johnson-Laird, P. N. (1975). Models of deduction. In R. Falmagne, ed., *Reasoning: Representation and process*. Hillsdale, N.J.: Erlbaum.

Johnson-Laird, P. N. (1983). *Mental models*. Cambridge, Mass.: Harvard University Press.

Kamp, H. (1984). A theory of truth and semantic representation. In J. Groenendijk, T. Jassen, and M. Stokof, eds., *Truth, interpretation and information*. Dordrecht: Foris.

Katz, J., and J. A. Fodor (1963). The structure of a semantic theory. *Language* 39, 170–210.

Kripke, S. (1980). *Naming and necessity*. Cambridge, Mass.: Harvard University Press.

Montague, R. (1973). The proper treatment of quantification in ordinary English. In R. Thomason, ed., *Formal philosophy*. New Haven, Conn.: Yale University Press.

Moravcsik, J. M. E. (1974). *Logic and philosophy for linguists: A book of readings*. The Hague: Mouton.

Partee, B. (1973). Some structural analogies between tenses and pronouns. *Journal of Philosophy* 70, 601–609.

Partee, B. (1979). Semantics—mathematics or psychology? In R. Bauerle et al., eds., *Semantics from different points of view*. Berlin; Springer-Verlag.

Putnam, H. (1975). *Mind, language, and reality*. Cambridge: Cambridge University Press.

Quillian, M. R. (1968). Semantic memory. In M. Minsky, ed., *Semantic information processing*. Cambridge, Mass.: MIT Press.

Rosch, E. (1973). On the internal structure of perceptual and semantic categories. In T. E. Moore, ed., *Cognition, development and the acquisition of language*. New York: Academic Press.

Rosenberg, J., and C. Travis (1971). *Readings in the philosophy of language*. Englewood Cliffs, N.J.: Prentice-Hall.

Shastri, L., and V. Ajjanagadde (1992). From simple associations to systematic reasoning: A connectionist representation of rules, variables, and dynamic bindings using temporal synchrony. Technical Report: MS-CIS-90-05. Philadelphia, PA: Computer and Information Science Department, University of Pennsylvania.

Smolensky, P. (1988). On the proper treatment of connectionism. *Behavioral and Brain Sciences* 11, 1–74.

Steinberg, D., and L. Jakobovits (1971). *Semantics: An interdisciplinary reader in philosophy, linguistics, and psychology*. Cambridge: Cambridge University Press.

Wall, R. (1973). *Introduction to mathematical linguistics*. Englewood Cliffs, N.J.: Prentice-Hall.

Weisler, S. (1991). An overview of Montague semantics. In J. Garfield and M. Kiteley, eds. *Meaning and truth: The essential readings in modern semantics*. New York: Paragon House.

Winograd, T. (1972). *Understanding natural language*. New York: Academic Press.

Winograd, T. (1974). Artificial intelligence: When will computers understand people? *Psychology Today*, May, 73–79.

Chapter 11

Natural Language Processing

In his now-classic treatise on vision David Marr (1982) argues that any information-processing system must be understood at three levels: (1) as a computational theory, (2) in terms of representation and algorithm, and (3) as a hardware implementation. As characterized in chapter 6, a grammar can be regarded as a computational theory—a precisely defined abstract account of the properties of a language, dedicated to the task of characterizing the set of well-formed utterances for that language. In chapter 7 we addressed the question of the "hardware" implementation of language in the human brain and nervous system. Now we turn our attention to the second of Marr's levels—to an understanding of the mental algorithms that carry out the various tasks of linguistic processing.

Marr (1982, 25) suggests that "since the three levels are only rather loosely related, some phenomena may be explained at only one or two of them." To what degree the three levels interact, and to what degree each level can be understood in terms of the others, is therefore an open and interesting question. Grammars, in the sense of chapter 6, are theories of abstract linguistic competence, but they may or may not provide an appropriate framework for understanding the mental processing of language. In this chapter we will explore a number of accounts of natural language processing (NLP), paying special attention to the role that linguistic grammars play in them. As we will see, some approaches assign a special and privileged role to grammatical information. Others see the grammar as only one of several kinds of information that are brought to bear as we perceive and produce sentences. Still other approaches to NLP make little if any use of the structures and properties of formal grammars as linguists conceive them.

11.1 Preliminaries

As we saw in chapter 6, a language can be regarded as a mapping from some physical form to a representation of meaning. That mapping is characterized by a formal grammar, some of whose properties are universal and some of which are specific to particular languages. One general approach to the problem of natural language processing assumes that the *processor* (a rough-and-ready term for the actual mental representations and algorithms that enable us to produce and interpret linguistic utterances) directly involves the various rules and representations of the grammar. We will refer to this as the *grammatical parsing* view. This term should not be taken to suggest that grammatical knowledge is the only kind of information that is used in language processing, since it is surely the case that every account of NLP will require a significant interface with aspects of general knowledge about the world. But the grammatical parsing view is distinctive in that it ascribes a special, well-defined role to linguistic knowledge—grammatical principles and structures are hypothesized to play a primary (and generally early) role in the processing of language.

By contrast, other cognitive scientists take the position that the mapping between form and meaning is accomplished by a system that uses strongly interacting components of grammatical knowledge along with other kinds of information, especially about the context of discourse and general world knowledge, without according special privilege to the role of grammatical information. On this view, there may be relatively less primary, early recourse to structures or information specific to linguistic grammars (or in some cases, particularly within the connectionist framework, little or none at all). We will refer to this as the *integrated knowledge* view. This position has strong proponents among psycholinguists and also, in a rather different vein, in the AI community. In particular, those in the connectionist camp hold that linguistic properties arise from very general processing mechanisms, and many connectionists maintain that grammars based on principles and rules specific to language are analytic artifacts playing no role in actual mental representation.

The debate about the role of grammars in on-line linguistic processing also raises important questions about the general architecture of the mind. Specifically, we will investigate whether, as many proponents of the grammatical parsing view would have it, grammatical information is *autonomously processed* in an essentially *modular* fashion, that is, insulated and isolated from other kinds of information that may be brought to bear on the task of language processing. The argument for modularity (see Fodor 1983; Garfield 1987) constitutes one of the major themes of research in cognitive science in general. Are human information-processing systems composed of discrete components with special properties, whose representations have little or no access to information in other systems? Or are cognitive systems nonmodular and interactive, giving and taking data from component to component (or, indeed, composed of no specially structured components at all)? Debate about these issues is still active and heated. Although some current work in NLP provides compelling evidence suggesting that the mind may indeed be organized in modular fashion, other research suggests that there may be important interactive components in language processing.

In contrast, it is clear that language processing cannot be explained entirely in terms of grammatical information. Thus, although some workers in NLP may underplay the role of grammar, it is important not to undervalue the significance of general knowledge and contextual information in language understanding.

11.2 On the Role of Grammar in Language Processing

Ungrammaticality

Let us begin by looking at some very simple but real problems in language processing. Consider, for example, how the human language processor might be presumed to deal with a minimal utterance like (1):

(1) Mary snores.

Given what we know about the world (and the meaning of lexical items), we can assign an interpretation to *Mary* (a name designating a female human who can be the actor or agent in an utterance) and one to *snore* (an action requiring an animate agent involving the production of a particular noise during sleep). We can assume that these meanings are combined to provide a full understanding of the utterance—that there is some female human named Mary who makes noise while she sleeps (see chapter 10 for discussion). Next, consider how the language processor will react to (2):

(2) *Snores Mary.

It is clear that (2) is not a sentence of English. By this we mean that native English speakers will reliably reject (2) as well formed even when they have only a rough-and-ready conscious conception of grammaticality. Furthermore, there is evidence suggesting that an English speaker will not process (1) and (2) in the same fashion. Indeed, quick introspection should convince you that (2) is not assigned a normal sentential meaning at all, or, at best, the meaning emerges only after a moment of recognition that the utterance is not "normal" in some sense. There is also experimental evidence that ungrammatical sentences involve longer processing times than grammatical sentences. Flores d'Arcais (1982) found that syntactic ungrammaticality prolonged reading time even when subjects were not aware of the syntactic violation.

What makes (2) difficult to process is that the normal syntactic order of simple English sentences is violated. But it is important to note that since languages do exist where the verb normally precedes the subject (for instance, Tagalog), we cannot assume that the language processor automatically (as a general species characteristic) rejects verb-first utterances as impossible or treats them as intrinsically difficult to process. Rather, we infer from these data that grammaticality supports normal processing and that a determination of ungrammaticality forces the processor into an unusual (and time-consuming) mode.

In a similar vein, consider the two syntactically well formed sentences in (3):

(3) a. Selma disqualified Harry.
     b. Harry disqualified Selma.

An approach based purely on knowledge about the meaning and referents of the words in (3a) and (3b) will not be able to distinguish between their quite distinct meanings. The discourse context might provide enough information to determine the appropriate meanings, but it might not. Imagine a conversation like the one in (4):

(4) Speaker A: You'll never guess who disqualified who in the first round!
     Speaker B: I wasn't there. How could I know?
     Speaker A: Well, I'll tell you ... Selma disqualified Harry.

Who disqualified whom is a function of the order of linguistic elements. Our knowledge about which linguistic element corresponds to which thematic role (actor, agent, patient, and so forth—see chapter 6 for discussion) is not part of our knowledge about things in the world: it is a function of normal syntactic word order, that is, a property of the grammar of the particular language that we speak.

Ambiguity

In the simple cases above, the grammatical utterances each admitted of only a single interpretation. Even those simple cases required us to recruit information about the syntactic structure of the sentence. Utterances that can be interpreted in more than one way provide an additional perspective on the kind of knowledge the processor requires.

Consider, for example, a simple sentence like *Time flies*. Under one interpretation, it has the idiomatic meaning that "time goes by quickly." But it can also be construed as

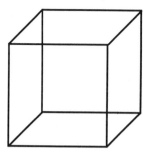

Figure 11.1
A Necker cube

a command to use a stopwatch to measure insect behavior. *Glue sticks* can be a statement about glue's adhesive qualities or a command to use glue to join pieces of wood. As Waltz and Pollack (1985) note, these kinds of sentences have the feel of a linguistic "Necker cube"—a visual illusion in which we perceive a two-dimensional representation of a cube to flip back and forth between two interpretations of its depth characteristics (see figure 11.1). As with the Necker cube, we can "see" both meanings, but not at the same time.

It is not difficult to see how these linguistic ambiguities arise. In the cases discussed above both words can belong to more than one syntactic category. In each case the first word, *time* or *glue*, can be interpreted as a noun, which can serve as the simple subject of the sentence, or as a verb, serving to mark the (subjectless) imperative. The second word, *flies* or *sticks*, can likewise be interpreted as a third-person verb or as a plural noun. Our multiple interpretations of these utterances can be understood quite simply as a function of those alternate categorical properties.

Interestingly, a third interpretation is also possible for each utterance. If we take both words to be nouns, *glue sticks* can be construed as a compound noun meaning "sticks of glue," and *time flies* can be construed (like *dragon flies*) as yet another species of insect. But it is not possible, in either case, to construe both of the words in these utterances as verbs. Why should this be? The answer is straightforward if we assume that the mental language processor is paying attention to the grammar of English. The grammar provides possible structures for the simple declaratives, the imperatives, and the compound nouns—but it does not countenance sequences of verbs. These words can mean something to us, normally, only within the confines of what is grammatically possible (for English).

The above cases strongly suggest that normal interpretation requires at least some purely grammatical information. In other situations where more than a single meaningful interpretation is possible, the roles of grammatical and other types of information may be considerably more complex. Consider, for instance, a sentence like (5), taken from the early work of Winograd (1972), whose SHRDLU program was a pioneering attempt to model natural language processing in the AI framework:

(5)   Put the red cube on the block in the box.

Such a sentence can be read in two ways, as suggested by the alternative bracketings in (6):

(6)   a. Put [the red cube on the block] in [the box].
      b. Put [the red cube] on [the block in the box].

In SHRDLU a highly restricted domain of discourse is established in which a "robot" is presumed to inhabit a "blocks world." In this world variously shaped and colored objects exist in a variety of relationships to one another. The robot is presented with English sentences that refer to the blocks world and is asked to perform manipulations of objects that are consistent with the properties of that world. In this way the robot can be said, in a reasonable sense, to "understand" the sentences that deal with such properties.

Winograd's model presumed a certain degree of syntactic knowledge: for example, the ability to parse an utterance like (5) for the purpose of identifying noun phrases. But, as (6a–b) demonstrate, there is more than one such parsing of (5). It is the common, introspective experience of human language users that, in ordinary discourse, ambiguities of this sort do not seem to interfere with the smooth course of processing; we somehow find a single, appropriate reading of ambiguous sentences, and often we must be led explicitly to recognize the existence of a second interpretation. On a largely grammar-driven view of processing, we might well try to explain this perception by discovering general syntactic principles that favor one reading over another; in a more interactive framework, we might expect to uncover properties of the domain of discourse—the immediate context, and knowledge about the world—that direct the processor to favor some particular reading.

Winograd's solution utilizes such "real-world" knowledge (or "blocks-world" knowledge, in this limited case). The robot proceeds by examining its simulated world and determining whether in that world there exists a unique reference to some configuration of red cubes and boxes. The program determines whether the noun phrase (NP) [red cube] has a referent. If there is a unique referent (only one red cube), the reading in (6b) is invoked, but if the blocks world contains more than one red cube— say, one on a block and one on the table—the program invokes the reading that is most successful in uniquely identifying a referent, given the information in the sentence. In this case it will be the red cube on the block, the reading in (6a). This principle, called the *Principle of Referential Success* by Crain and Steedman (1982) in the context of a model of human language processing, is clearly interactive: it is information about the sentence's meaning and its use, rather than principles operating over its structure, that determines the action of the processor.

Now it may at first blush seem reasonable that a human being, in the blocks world, would follow a similar strategy. It seems right that a human observer who actually perceived a red cube on a block under these circumstances would ultimately hit on reading (6a). If the task can be accomplished without recourse to any additional intermediate syntactic analysis, it would be more computationally efficient to accomplish it without such a step in the process.

Such an assumption may be perfectly appropriate to an enterprise whose goal is to simulate language understanding in a computer: the measure of the program's success is its ability to manipulate its world appropriately, and to do so in a way that places the least burden on the computing device. In the case of human beings, however, there is an additional empirical burden: we cannot simply assume that an approach that is computationally effective for a particular class of contemporary computers is the one that guides human information processing in this domain. The assumption may well be a reasonable default position, in the absence of further evidence. But, as we will now see, there is a body of experimental research that argues against such a view for human language processing.

Garden-Path Effects

Consider the sentence in (7), first discussed by Bever (1970):

(7)   The horse raced past the barn fell.

On first hearing or reading it, native speakers of English typically reject this kind of utterance as ungrammatical. It is a classic example of a *garden-path* sentence in which the listener or reader seems to be "led down a garden path" in assuming that *raced* is the main verb of a simple sentence. Unlike the earlier cases we were considering, this kind of sentence is not ambiguous in the sense of having two overall possible interpretations. Rather, (7) exhibits a kind of temporary or *local* ambiguity that is resolved as processing progresses. Thus, only when it encounters the final verb *fell* does the garden-pathed processor realize that a mistake has been made: (7) is not a grammatical sentence of English under the assumption that the first six words constitute a simple sentence in which the horse was actively racing. The only (grammatical) interpretation is that the horse was being raced (by an unspecified agent). Consequently, (7) can only mean the same as (8):

(8)   The horse that was raced (by someone) past the barn fell.

Moreover, the ambiguity disappears when a different past-participle verb form (like *ridden*) is employed. As the processor proceeds to parse a sentence like *The horse ridden past the barn fell*, it is not garden-pathed because *ridden* cannot be analyzed as the main verb of the sentence whose subject is *the horse*.

A Grammatical Parsing Analysis

Why, then, are we confounded when we try to interpret (7)? Frazier (1987), and others have proposed a processing model that assumes that the speaker initially constructs a syntactic representation of the utterance, quite independently of meaning or context. The model works on input sentences from left to right, assigning each incoming word to some syntactic structure according to the following language-independent principle:

(9)   *Minimal Attachment Principle* (Clifton and Ferreira 1987)
      Each new incoming item is added to the phrase structure representation
      with the least possible number of new syntactic phrase nodes needed
      at the moment of its arrival.

The Minimal Attachment Principle directs the processor to construct the single simplest syntactic constituent that is consistent with incoming data. Assuming the processor is working from left to right, the approach will unfortunately produce an incorrect result in this kind of case: the simplest analysis (part (*b*) of figure 11.2) presumes that there is no embedded sentence (hence, no additional S node) in the subject NP (compare part (*a*)) and goes on to make the incorrect assumption that (7) begins with a simple sentence—only to fail when it comes across *fell*, which cannot be attached to the tree, since there is no phrase structure rule of English that will allow a verb as the final element in a prepositional phrase.

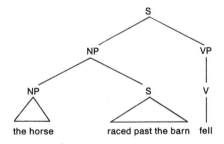

Figure 11.2
Syntactic structure for the well-formed interpretation of (7)

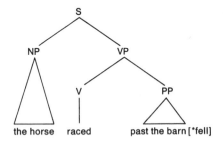

Figure 11.3
Syntactic structure of the "garden-path" interpretation of (7)

Since the structure in figure 11.3 is "minimal" in that it contains just four major category nodes, whereas the first structure (the correct one) contains five nodes, the Minimal Attachment Principle correctly predicts that the processor will incorrectly initially choose the second structure over the first.

We can discern further evidence for a model incorporating the Minimal Attachment Principle by examining another class of structurally ambiguous sentences. Consider a sentence like (10):

> (10)   Al played the records on the stereo.

(10) is normally first understood to mean that Al used the stereo as an instrument to play the records. There is also a second, less likely interpretation, namely, that Al played records that were located on the stereo (say, on its plastic cover).

What determines the preferred "instrumental" reading of (10)? The Minimal Attachment Principle makes just the right prediction. Examine the tree structures in figure 11.4.

Observe that in part (*a*) of figure 11.4, the structure for the instrumental reading, the Prepositional Phrase (PP) *on the stereo* is attached to (and modifies) the Verb Phrase (VP). It is a simple matter to show that the PP is not inside the NP constituent. For instance, it cannot be passivized as a whole with the NP: *The records on the stereo were played by Al* is not a paraphrase of the first interpretation. By contrast, the PP in part (*b*) of figure 11.4, the structure underlying the second interpretation, lies within the (object) NP, and the whole NP is subject to passivization. Indeed, *The records on the stereo were played by Al* is a proper paraphrase of the non-instrumental reading.

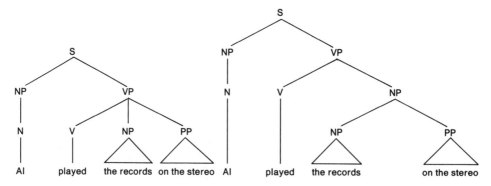

Figure 11.4
Alternative syntactic structures for *Al played the records on the stereo*. (*a*) is the structure for the instrumental reading, and (*b*) is the structure for the noninstrumental reading

Furthermore, the structure in part (*a*) is minimally attached since it contains one node fewer than the structure in part (*b*), and this explains why it corresponds to the preferred first interpretation of the utterance.

The Role of Pragmatics and Discourse

We can also entertain an alternative explanation for the preferred reading based not on a special syntactic parsing strategy like the one embodied in the Minimal Attachment Principle but on the (nonmodular) assumption that nonlinguistic knowledge is involved in the sentence-understanding process simultaneously with the determination of the utterance's grammatical structure. Playing records, we might argue as a matter of our knowledge about such things, is an activity that requires an instrument: we do not simply play records, we play them *on something*. A sentence processor that recruits knowledge about the world as it assigns a syntactic structure would lean toward a structure that is consistent with that knowledge.

It seems, then, that an approach to linguistic processing incorporating pragmatic principles and based on world knowledge may be able to account for the same data as a grammatically based analysis incorporating the Minimal Attachment Principle. How might we choose between these alternatives (with their quite different implications for our understanding of the organization of cognitive processes)?

To adjudicate this question, let us return to the issue of garden-path sentences. It is easy to imagine nonlinguistic information that could help keep the processor off the garden path. Suppose we were to embed the sentence *The horse raced past the barn fell* in a larger discourse like the following: *Two horses were being raced down on the farm. One jockey rode his horse around the pasture. A second was riding near the barn. The horse in the pasture had no trouble. But the horse raced past the barn fell.* Given such a discourse, a great deal of (nonlinguistic) information is available to the processor that might be expected to alleviate the temporary ambiguity in the sentence in question. That is, an interactive processor that simultaneously utilizes linguistic and nonlinguistic knowledge would be expected to avoid garden-pathing in such cases.

Crain and Steedman (1985) adopt a context-dependent view of NLP that, as noted earlier, makes use of mechanisms like the Principle of Referential Success. On a view such as Crain and Steedman's, the complex subjects in classic garden-path sentences like *the man given the book, the horse ridden past the barn,* or *the horse raced past the barn* (in the appropriate sense) have a special pragmatic function, namely, to pick out a unique referent from a set of possible referents in a relevant discourse. The expected role of such descriptions in a discourse containing many horses is to specify a single particular horse. So, *if* the discourse includes a characterization of some set of horses, and the speaker can succeed in picking out a horse that was indeed raced past a barn by someone, *then* a natural interpretation consistent with the Principle of Referential Success will be assigned. However, when a sentence like (7) is presented without any discourse, the listener is led down the garden path since there is no previously established set of relevant horses in the discourse and consequently no reason to expect any distinguishing description of any horse. Thus, the pragmatic function of the complex subject parse is eliminated, and the processor is tricked into trying to find some alternate interpretation. To generalize this position, we would expect that pragmatic and discourse information will typically be useful to the processor in resolving ambiguities and assigning interpretations.

By contrast, a modular, grammatical parsing view predicts that garden-pathing will occur regardless of the discourse context since the processor is presumed to be (at least temporarily) insulated from information outside the syntactic processing module. Ferreira (1985) and Clifton and Ferreira (1987) provide some compelling evidence that information in a discourse does not, in fact, eliminate the processing difficulty that is inherent in garden-path sentences. In Ferreira's experiments subjects are presented temporarily ambiguous garden-path sentences, embedded in contexts where discourse factors ought to be able to play a facilitative role in the processing. Examples are given in (11a–d):

(11) a. John worked as a reporter for a big city newspaper. He sensed that a major story was brewing over the city hall scandal, and he obtained some evidence that he believed pretty much established the mayor's guilt. He went to his editors with a tape and some photos because he needed their approval before he could go ahead with the story.... He ran a tape for one of his editors, and he showed some photos to the other. *The editor played the tape agreed the story was a big one.* The other editor urged John to be cautious.

   b. ... He gave a tape to his editor and told him to listen to it. *The editor played the tape and agreed the story was a big one.* The other editor urged John to be cautious.

   c. ... He brought out a tape for one of his editors and told him to listen carefully to it. *The editor played the tape agreed the story was a big one.* The other editor urged John to be cautious.

   d. ... He brought out a tape for one of his editors and told him to listen carefully to it. *The editor played the tape and agreed the story was a big one.* The other editor urged John to be cautious.

In (11a) the target sentence (italicized) requires a nonminimal syntactic analysis. However, since the discourse context contains two editors who can be distinguished by the description *played the tape*, we might expect a processor that is informed by discourse information at the earliest stages of parsing to avoid going down the garden path. In (11b), the target sentence requires the minimal attachment analysis (and the discourse context that supports this interpretation). Such a sentence should involve little processing difficulty.

In (11c) the target sentence requires nonminimal attachment, but the discourse does not help to cue the grammatical interpretation. Consequently, (11c) should be a difficult sentence to process from both points of view. Finally, the target sentence in (11d) requires the minimal attachment analysis; however, its discourse context might lead the processor to (inappropriately) consider a nonminimally attached structure since it contains a set of editors that could be profitably separated out by the full description that would belong to the complex subject structure [NP the editor played the tape] (recall the Principle of Referential success).

On the grammatical parsing approach, (11a) and (11c) should be more difficult to process than (11b) and (11d), since each requires a nonminimally attached syntactic analysis. But if there is access to discourse information that can guide the syntactic parser, then only (11c) should represent a processing difficulty, since the context seems rich enough to lead the processor to the correct parse in (11a). Furthermore, if discourse information can override the syntactic parser, we might expect (11d) to produce some processing difficulty since the discourse invites an unavailable parse.

Ferreira's subjects were required to read passages like those in (11a–d), and reading times were measured by tracking eye movements and fixation periods. Processing difficulties, whether they arise from constructing a syntactic analysis or a discourse model, would be reflected in longer fixation times. The results of Ferreira's experiment were consistent with the modular syntactic processing view: only the nonminimally attached structures (11a) and (11c) involved a greater processing load (i.e., longer reading times) even when, on the interactive view, the discourse context should have alleviated the difficulty.

Evidence for a Nonmodular Approach

However, other studies suggest that nonlinguistic information does play an important role in language understanding, even at early stages of processing. In a series of experiments Tyler and Marslen-Wilson (1980) presented subjects with sentences like those in (12):

(12)   a. The crowd was waiting eagerly. The young man *grabbed* the guitar
           and ...
       b. The crowd was waiting eagerly. The young man *buried* the guitar
           and ...
       c. The crowd was waiting eagerly. The young man *drank* the guitar
           and ...
       d. The crowd was waiting eagerly. The young man *slept* the guitar
           and ...

The first two utterances, (12a) and (12b), are syntactically normal. But (12b) is pragmatically odd since guitars are not customarily buried on stage. (12c) is semantically ill formed, because the meaning of *drink* normally requires a liquid object. (12d) is deviant at the lexical syntactic level: *slept* is an intransitive verb that cannot take an NP object like *the guitar*. In Tyler and Marslen-Wilson's experiments subjects were asked to press a key when they heard a target word like *guitar*, and their reaction times were measured. The results showed that subjects were slower to press the key in all of the nonnormal conditions than they were in a case like (12a), where no expectations—syntactic, pragmatic, or semantic—were violated. Mean response time for the normal condition (12a) was 241 milliseconds. For the other cases the response times were progressively longer: for the pragmatically unlikely sentence (12b), 268 milliseconds; for the semantic anomaly (12c), 291 milliseconds; and for the syntactically ill formed sentence (12d), 320 milliseconds.

Under the autonomous parsing model, a syntactic analysis is an insulated process that does not directly recruit nonlinguistic information. The long response times in the case of the syntactic ill-formedness described above do suggest that the hearer is indeed trying to assign a syntactic structure to incoming utterances. But the fact that pragmatic implausibility produced a small (but statistically significant) increase in response time can be construed as lending support to a model in which considerations of world knowledge are brought to bear at an extremely early point in processing. Much current research (see, for example, Cowart and Cairns 1987) is devoted to developing a more precise picture of the character and timing of these processes, in an effort to clarify the difficult question of whether syntactic processing is indeed modular and autonomous in character.

11.3 Connectionist Models

In the connectionist paradigm it is assumed that knowledge—be it information about the world, memory, or the representation of linguistic generalizations—resides in the complex patterns of connectivity that can arise in the mind as a consequence of the interaction of myriad very simple processing units. In most connectionist theories, knowledge does not take the form of the kind of abstract rules and higher-order structures that are typical of linguistic theory. Notions like Minimal Attachment, or even phrase structure, may have no independent status in a connectionist model, since whatever knowledge they embody is ultimately built out of simple, relatively homogeneous processing units that, by definition, are not uniquely or modularly dedicated to special tasks like language processing.

Connectionist models have been developed in a number of domains of interest to the student of NLP. For example, such models have been advanced to account for linguistic phenomena of direct relevance to the sentence-processing issues that we discussed earlier. Waltz and Pollack (1985), for example, argue that a form of "semantic" garden-pathing can be insightfully understood within a strong interactive model of processing designed on connectionist principles. They consider sentences like those in (13):

(13)   a. The astronomer married the star.
       b. The sailor ate a submarine.

Each of these sentences is (lexically) ambiguous. But Waltz and Pollack assert that hearers at first generally experience only one reading, indeed, the semantically bizarre interpretation (the astronomer took a celestial body as a spouse and the sailor consumed a boat). It takes some time and thought to recognize that (13a) can mean that the astronomer married a movie celebrity or that (13b) can mean that the sailor ate a sandwich. In a sense, the processor is led down the garden path once again. Once it assigns a semantic interpretation to *sailor* or *astronomer*, it is now *primed* to make further semantic interpretations within the sentence that are in some sense associated with the meaning of that subject NP. But this priming effect confounds the processor, which expects a verb like *eat* to have an edible object.

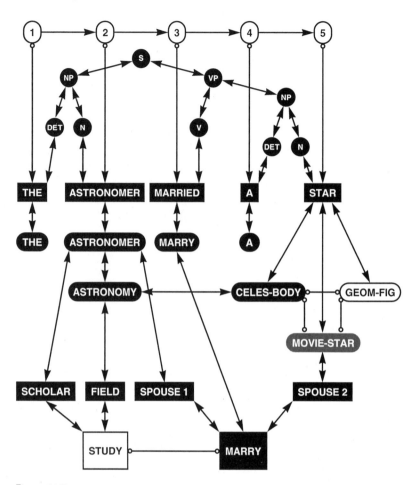

Figure 11.5
A cycle of a connectionist net for the sentence *The astronomer married the star*. (Adapted from Waltz and Pollack 1985.)

Accounts of processing in which each lexical item has a discrete, self-contained meaning are hard pressed to account for this effect. But in a distributed connectionist model of the lexicon, Waltz and Pollack argue, the garden-path effect has a straightforward explanation. The subject NP *sailor* can be presumed to have a strong connection to a set of terms with nautical meanings, including *submarine*, and a much weaker connection to the food terms that include the sandwich meaning of *submarine* (see figure 11.5).

In such a model the activation of *sailor* will produce a high level of activation for the nautical meaning of *submarine*. Indeed, it will do so relatively quickly, accounting for the nature of the initial interpretation. Ultimately, however, the processor will have to deal with the fact that *eat* also expects an edible object, and the activation level of the sandwich meaning of *submarine* will eventually rise, while the processor searches for a connection to a node with foodlike features.

An association-rich distributed model of the lexicon also provides a ready framework in which to make sense of the context effects on processing that have been adduced by Marslen-Wilson, Tyler, and others. If PDP modelers ultimately were also able to account directly for the syntactic effects observed by workers like Frazier, Clifton, and their colleagues, the connectionist paradigm would be a major contender as a broadly empirically adequate model of natural language processing.

11.4 On the Role of Discourse

Although some of the results discussed earlier suggest that contextual information does not necessarily obviate any role for syntactic structure in sentence processing, we have also seen evidence that context and general knowledge play a major part in the task of language understanding. In Ferreira's experiments, for instance, reading time was dependent on linguistic structure and seemed to be unaffected by discourse information. But Ferreira also submitted her subjects to a comprehension task and found that readers retained more information more reliably when the discourse context was biased in favor of the structure of the target sentence. This suggests that special discourse mechanisms may well be operative at some level of language processing that follows the initial parsing stage. It seems entirely plausible, for instance, that some principle like "referential success," in Crain and Steedman's sense, should contribute to the overall coherence of a discourse in a way that enhances general understanding. If the grammatical interpretation of garden-path sentences does indeed presuppose a set of contextually relevant entities in the discourse, and they are not present, we may well expect the processor to have difficulty in recalling and characterizing information about them.

The relationship between grammatical information and other kinds of information relevant to discourse understanding remains a very complex issue. Consider the case of pronominalization, illustrated in the little discourses in (14) and (15):

(14)   Speaker A: What's the matter with Harry?
        Speaker B: John lost *his* umbrella.

(15)   Speaker A: What's the matter with Harry?
        Speaker B: *He* lost John's umbrella.

In each case the language-processing system must assign a referent to the italicized pronoun. What, then, is the role of the discourse context in the process of interpreting the pronouns in these sentences?

Here we might recall Crain and Steedman's Principle of Referential Success, which maintains that "if there is a reading that succeeds in referring to an entity already established in the hearer's mental model of the domain of discourse, then it is favored over one that does not" (Crain and Steedman 1985). In the discourse in (14) Harry is established as the topic of the discourse, and we might suppose that it is the topic that is "established," in Crain and Steedman's sense. Such an analysis would explain why the most likely interpretation of Speaker B's reply takes *his umbrella* to be Harry's umbrella. It is indeed possible to construe (14) to describe a situation where Harry is upset because John has lost his own umbrella; perhaps it was an expensive present from Harry. But this is clearly not the favored reading, as Crain and Steedman would predict.

What then of (15)? Here Harry is once again an entity already established in the hearer's mental model of the discourse, and once again the hearer interprets the pronoun (now *he*) to be coreferential with *Harry*. But this is not simply the favored reading of (15)—it is the only reading that is possible. Pronominalization in English is governed by a purely structural constraint that prevents *he* from being coreferential with *John* within speaker B's reply in (15), regardless of the discourse context. Now, if the language-processing system were not directly guided by properties of grammar, there is no reason why the second reading (albeit less likely in terms of discourse coherence) should be impossible. Indeed, we ought to be able to construct a somewhat richer discourse in which the illegal coreference is rendered plausible. But we cannot.The pronominalization facts in (15) lead us again to the conclusion that special, uniquely grammatical information is operative and imposes strong constraints on processing. Grammatical principles play a powerful initial role in processing, even in contexts beyond the sentence. But the facts in (14) demonstrate that grammatical constraints will not always provide a sufficient basis for understanding.

Moreover, there are types of linguistic representations that involve coreference but do so without pronominal forms of the sort that are subject to the kinds of pronominal constraints we have been discussing. Consider a text like (16):

(16)   Mary couldn't decide whether to buy steak or hamburger. She finally decided to buy the more expensive meat.

Tanenhaus, Carlson, and Seidenberg (1985), to whom this example is due, conducted an experiment demonstrating that speakers expend considerable processing time in assigning an interpretation in the discourse to *the more expensive meat*. When the second sentence involved a contextually neutral statement like *She finally decided to go to another nearby store*, processing time was reduced. Here the interpretation is clearly a function of knowledge about the world: speakers who know that steak costs more than hamburger will understand *the more expensive meat* to refer to steak. Tanenhaus, Carlson, and Seidenberg conclude that this inference from real-world knowledge takes processing time that is not required by the neutral context.

Pragmatics and World Knowledge
Our earlier discussion of structural pronominalization showed that world knowledge alone does not provide a general explanation for the interpretation of reference in discourse. This point can be shown in another way. Labov (1972) cites an argument to the effect that world knowledge is indeed essential to the coherent understanding of discourses like (17):

(17)   Speaker A: Everyone should read the Bible.
       Speaker B: Yes, Deuteronomy is a great book.

Contrast (17) with (18):

(18)   Speaker A: Everyone should read the Bible.
       Speaker B: Yes, *Crime and Punishment* is a great book.

Our knowledge about books and about the Bible (and not properties of grammar or of rules of discourse) might arguably be taken to lead to the judgment that (17) is coherent and (18) is incoherent. But Stubbs (1983) points out that this view is wrong: our understanding of such sentences cannot be said to depend on knowledge about particular facts about the world. He notes that the following kind of discourse is perfectly coherent:

(19) Speaker A: Everyone should read *Wombats Galore*.
      Speaker B: Yes, McQuarrie is a great author.

It does not matter to our understanding of this discourse whether there really is a book called *Wombats Galore* or whether it was indeed written by someone named McQuarrie. Certainly, if these facts are part of our knowledge, we may be able to judge the veracity of the statements or their relevance to one another, and if we know that McQuarrie did not write *Wombats Galore*, we may look for another connection between the two speakers' statements in (19). But in the alternative circumstance in which we know nothing about the authorship of *Wombats Galore*, the processing of such sentences does not appear to be impeded by limitations on our ability to access particular items in our general knowledge representations.

In such cases of limited knowledge, what is at stake is a set of pragmatic rules and conventions that regulate a large part of language understanding. In (19), for instance, we *infer* from the discourse that McQuarrie is the author of a book called *Wombats Galore*. The immediate transition in the discourse from a book title to a person's name leads the processor to conclude that the named person is the writer of (or a person highly relevant to) the book. Why should this be? Grice (1971, 1975) proposes that discourses are guided by a set of *conversational maxims* that require utterances to be *informative, relevant* (to context), and *truthful*. Although Grice was interested in what happens when these maxims are flouted, we will consider what role they can play in guiding discourse processing.

With regard to the discourse in (19), suppose that you are a third party, C, who is interested in the conversation. If Grice's maxims are operative as you try to process the discourse, you will assume that when B refers to McQuarrie, B is providing information. You will assume that this information is relevant to the discourse, and you will assume that B is not inventing the information. Relevance is, of course, a matter of general knowledge as well as of knowledge about the particular discourse, but it is not necessarily a matter of detailed particular knowledge about books, wombats, or someone named McQuarrie. What is required is the general knowledge that people write books. Here, Grice's maxims can be understood to lead the processor to the following reasonable interpretation of the discourse: B is providing information relevant to A's remark, B is not lying, and the pertinent relevance condition is that a person named in relation to a book is likely to be its author. The conclusion is that McQuarrie wrote *Wombats Galore*.

Since Grice's maxims are not binding laws, it may of course be that A was violating one or another of them; and the conversation may need to be interpreted indirectly (see Grice 1971, 1975 for discussion). That is, although Grice's maxims are operative in the processor's normal (default) state, and we ordinarily assume that speakers are providing relevant, true information, in discourse contexts like (20) a nonliteral interpretation is called for:

(20) A family of six is seated at the kitchen table. The stove is burning; everyone feels uncomfortably hot. The mother turns to one child and says "I'm hot." The child says "All right" and proceeds to open the window.

Even though *I'm hot* might literally be interpreted to describe an internal state of the mother or a simple description of the room temperature, in this context it is often taken to be a request (or even a demand). Why should this be so? Since it is irrelevant for speakers simply to declare their internal states, and this irrelevance to the context is readily determined and readily gauged to be purposeful, the listener is led to infer that this utterance must be relevant to the discourse context in some indirect way. In this particular context where all the speakers are affected by the heat, the child takes the utterance to have a pragmatic force that is relevant to their shared information—namely, a request or order to do something that will affect the temperature.

There are, of course, other ways to reduce the heat; for example, turning off the stove, leaving the room to decrease the number of warm bodies, or even (perversely) bringing in large blocks of ice would do the trick. However, the child's understanding of the sentence, and consequent action, is also guided by general plausibility assumptions, by prior experience, and so forth. The point is that the normal default state of the processor must be guided by principles that derive meaning from more than the form of linguistic events.

Speech Acts and Pragmatic Force
Linguistic meaning (discussed in chapter 10) is characterized in terms of structural (grammatical and logical) properties of sentences, perhaps construed in terms of formal logic or a mental model. But the discourse meaning of utterances is not always limited by semantic properties. Sentences as they are actually used also constitute real actions in the external world, and their very use contributes to their meaning (and hence to our understanding of them). They are what writers like Austin (1962) and Searle (1969) call *speech acts*.

The central insight in speech act theory is that sentences can discharge a range of different functions. A speaker who utters a sentence—say, *Mary won the election*—has carried out an *utterance act* simply by virtue of producing the sentence. The speaker might be shouting such a sentence very loudly in a noisy room for the sole purpose of drawing attention or inducing quiet. Utterances can also constitute *propositional acts* that provide information. Indeed, a speaker might shout a sentence like *Mary won the election* with the double intention of drawing attention—as an utterance act—and also of letting it be known that the election results were in—a propositional act.

Speech acts also have a *pragmatic force* with regard to the act potential of the utterance, the speaker's intentions, and the ultimate effect on the hearer. For example, the sentence *I promise you that I will be back at four* itself counts as an act of promising by virtue of the speaker's uttering it in the first person. That is, simply by saying *I promise . . .*, the speaker is actually carrying out the action of promising. This type of speech act in which the utterance automatically constitutes an effective act in the world is typically a consequence of uttering sentences containing so-called *performative verbs* like *promise, report, convince, insist, tell, request,* and *demand;* they can often be identified because they can cooccur with the adverb *hereby*, rendering their performative force apparent. *I hereby report that I have a serious contagious disease* is a performative act since by uttering such a sentence, the speaker is performing the act of reporting.

Utterances may also discharge nonperformative functions that establish different aspects of a speaker's meaning. This level of discourse interpretation, so-called *illocutionary force*, considers the speaker's intention in producing an utterance. For instance, uttering *I have a serious contagious disease* may have the illocutionary force of a threat, a warning, or a plea for pity, depending on what the speaker has in mind. By contrast, the *perlocutionary force* of a speech act constitutes its effect on the hearer: if a speaker utters the sentence *I have a serious contagious disease*, it might variously produce discomfort, concern, or the desire to leave the room. Finally, it should be clear that speech act utterances can simultaneously have multiple pragmatic forces: *I have a serious contagious disease* is at once an utterance act and a propositional act with an illocutionary and a perlocutionary force.

Speech act theory provides a rich framework in which to think about the nature of the language processor working on discourse. Recall the scene in (20). The utterance act *I'm hot* is the speech event that triggers the processor and constitutes its input. In addition, the processor must deal with the utterance act as a propositional act and determine the referents and predications in question. Moreover, it must calculate the illocutionary and/or perlocutionary force of the utterance. It is reasonable to presume that many speech acts of mothers toward children foreground the mother's illocutionary content, and it is clearly the indirect pragmatic force of the mother's utterance that produces the desired perlocutionary response in the child. The task of the child's language processor is to determine the illocutionary force of that utterance that, in turn, determines the perlocutionary force. In its literal meaning, the sentence *I'm hot* is readily construed as a report. But the burden on the processor is to weigh this illocutionary interpretation against others (for example, the likely interpretation as a request or a demand), using Grice's maxims as guidelines. Part of this burden is borne by grammar, inasmuch as many speech acts are simply encoded in particular syntactic forms by means of performative verbs, question and imperative (command) structures, and the like. But as we see in this discussion of indirect commands like *I'm hot*, nongrammatical principles seem to be at work as well.

There have been several attempts to implement computer systems for understanding natural language that recruit discourse and pragmatic insights. A well-known example is the work of Allen (1983), Allen and Perrault (1980), and Cohen, Perrault, and Allen (1982). They have designed a query system, for instance, that models the interaction of a railroad ticket agent and a customer. The system is able to deal appropriately with some of the questions that arise in this situation in normal discourse, by building assumptions about the goals and intentions of the discourse participants into the program.

For example, faced with a query such as *Do you know when the next train leaves for Chicago?*, an adequate model should not respond with a "Yes" or a "No," even though the syntactic form of a "Yes"-"No" question of this sort might elicit such an answer in other circumstances.

Put another way, the linguistic form of the utterance (possibly a politeness convention) is not sufficient by itself to determine how to carry on a conversation. Rather, Allen and his coworkers propose, a language understander must work from a plan—a set of rules that leads from a set of expectations about normal goals to a set of effective actions to achieve those goals.

It is plausible to assume that the customer's intention in a discourse of this sort is to attain specific information about the train—not to determine *whether* the ticket agent knows something, but *what* the agent knows. In terms of one of Grice's postulates, the ticket agent ought to respond in a relevant manner to the inquiry. How does the program know that a "Yes" or "No" answer is, by itself, irrelevant to the conversation? In the model devised by Allen and his coworkers, the customer in this context is presumed to have a starting goal—to get on the train, or to meet someone on it—and the program plans for responses that will advance the attaining of that goal. Simply letting the customer know that the agent is aware of the train schedule, without elaboration, does not make progress toward the goal. But providing relevant information will indeed do so. Knowing the time of departure—already requested, if implicitly—is relevant. So is the place of departure, the train's gate. Even though the customer's utterance makes no mention of the train's location, the model provides that information because it is relevant to an effective plan for attaining a presumed goal.

11.5 More on the Role of General Knowledge

Our investigations thus far have led to the following picture of the human language-processing system. We have seen some evidence for the view that the language processor contains a discrete (modular) grammatical processing subsystem, a parser, that operates in the initial stages of language comprehension to construct purely syntactic representations. But language understanding in discourse also requires pragmatic principles, including those that regulate our use of language in its communicative function. We have also seen a number of cases where nonlinguistic knowledge (neither grammatical nor pragmatic) plays a role in processing. We now look in more detail at the interaction between linguistic information and general knowledge about the world.

Among the researchers in AI who have been predominantly responsible for work in this domain, Schank and his associates are representative (see, e.g., Schank and Abelson 1977, Lehnert 1981). The position they hold is that there is no significant, autonomous syntactic parsing system in processing. This view derives in part from the kind of problems in language understanding that these researchers have concentrated on. They stress that in many narrative accounts of ordinary events, the amount and type of linguistic information underdetermines our capacity to interpret the events. For a typical example, consider the following simple story:

> (21)   A woman walked into a restaurant. The waiter showed her to a table.
> She ordered a rare steak and a bottle of beer. As she left, she smiled
> at the cashier.

This story poses no special difficulties from the standpoint of parsing. There is no structural and little lexical ambiguity, and pronominalization seems to be a simple affair. What is interesting is that the reader can recover information from the story that is not present in any linguistically overt (or recoverable) form. More specifically, nothing is said about chairs, but we infer that the woman sat down on a chair at the table. Nothing is said about the waiter's subsequent behavior, but we assume that he brought the woman her food. Nothing is said about the act of eating itself, but the reader concludes that the woman did indeed eat her steak and drink her beer. The story does not say that she paid her bill, but the reader understands that she did so.

A story-understanding approach holds that our comprehension of this kind of story is dependent on a well-defined knowledge frame, a *script*, that is specific to a particular type of event. Visiting restaurants is a stereotyped activity: we know what to expect as far as physical accoutrements like chairs and tables are concerned; we know that, on ordering food, it normally arrives at the table; we know that restaurant patrons normally eat (at least some of) what they order; and we know that they normally pay their bill when finished. The language processor can be thought of as working interactively with a script of this sort. Where the story fits the characteristics of the conventional script, the processor works as usual; but when elements of the script are not represented by sentences in the story, they are automatically filled in by a script-implementing mechanism that augments the more skeletal linguistic representation.

In early work Schank and his students wrote a Script Applier Mechanism (SAM) program that treated world knowledge about particular situations as stereotyped, self-contained data structures. It is plausible to assume that some elements of script knowledge entail other subscripts. For instance, one might assume that there is a subscript involving payment in commercial establishments that accounts for the inference that the customer paid her bill. But it is also clear that the notion of a fixed script has some severe limitations. Consider a story like (22), cited by Schank (1984, 146):

> (22)   John wanted money. He got a gun and walked into a liquor store. He told the owner he wanted some money. The owner gave John the money and John left.

Here again, the reader understands that John did not intend to purchase anything, that he threatened the owner with the gun, that the owner gave him the money unwillingly, and that John in fact robbed the store. Schank notes that SAM-type models require situation-specific scripts (in this case, some kind of "robbery" script) and observes that, on his account, a speaker would have to know the particular script in order to understand the story. Many speakers, he suggests, will not have had the experience necessary to acquire such a script, yet any competent speaker should be able to understand a story like (22), complete with its inferences. A more adequate model, then, would have to be able to generalize from already acquired scripts to new ones, or to modified versions of original stereotypical scripts. Such a model clearly requires overarching principles of knowledge representation that are far more powerful than the static data structures of local scripts.

Schank and his coworkers have developed a number of elegant programs that attempt to incorporate such principles. For instance, recent programs in this paradigm are able to incorporate new knowledge in ways that break down some of the stereotyped rigidity of the script scheme. But even with a more powerful inference generator and a (limited) capacity for learning, it should be apparent that the model still requires an astronomical number of basic scripts in order to account for the interaction between general knowledge and language understanding. Moreover, as Schank and Birnbaum (1984) suggest, script-based knowledge (whatever its particular character) may not be independent of general memory. They cite Bower, Black, and Turner (1979), who have observed that subjects confuse events that transpire in similar scripts. They also observe that memories of instances when a script is violated often arise on other occasions when an event does not go according to script. For instance, when we read a story about a restaurant customer who fails to pay his bill, we may be reminded of similar anecdotes that inform our understanding of the story. Since violations are, by definition, not "part of the script," these investigators conclude that scripts must be integrated in memory with other information.

To circumvent some of these limitations, other systems have been developed that recruit a more abstract class of knowledge structures. One example is the *thematic affect unit* (TAU) of Dyer and Lehnert (1980). Dyer and Lehnert attempt, among other things, to capture the kind of general commonsense inferential mechanisms that are implicit in everyday adages and proverbs. Thus, on hearing a story about a multimillion-dollar bridge that collapsed because its builders used cheap rivets, the listener may conclude that it would not have done so had the contractor used higher-quality material. "Penny-wise and pound-foolish," one might say. But on hearing another story, this time about an expensive luxury car, replete with other safety devices, whose inexpensive and inadequate seatbelts led to a high fatality rate in accidents, the listener might understand it in the same way. Since the two situations are quite different in their details and vocabulary, what is needed is a higher-order mechanism—a TAU that encodes the planning assumptions of the proverb so that it can apply to a range of relevant stories. Furthermore, Dyer (1981) reports on experimental work suggesting that TAUs may also be real mental organizing principles, aside from their role in facilitating machine understanding of language: in a study by Seifert (1980), subjects grouped stories together that shared a TAU even when their contents were distinct.

11.6 Production

We now turn to the related and important question of language production, the output side of processing. Much of what is known about perception is relevant to production as well. Grammatical knowledge must play an important role in production. Since the vast majority of actual utterances are well-formed but novel sentences, it is reasonable to conclude that speakers are guided by rule, in the sense discussed in chapter 6. Moreover, context, general knowledge, the discourse situation, and the speaker's motivations and dispositions clearly play a very large role in production, since speakers do not produce utterances in a vacuum. Consequently, language generation is thought to be guided by a vast complex of discourse principles, social and sociolinguistic information, general knowledge, and idiosyncratic factors relevant to individual speakers. Still, at this juncture little is understood about the exact processes that use this kind of information in the production of utterances in ordinary life. Certainly, no theoretical model is close to being able to predict the things that speakers will say in a given circumstance. Indeed, this may be as intractable a problem as predicting the behavior of an individual human being or of social groups at large.

Computer Models of Language Production

Despite the overall difficulty of explaining linguistic production, some progress has been made in developing language-generating systems as a practical outgrowth of research in AI. QUALM, for instance, a question-answering system designed by Lehnert (1981), is aimed at enabling a computer program not only to read and understand stories (like SAM) but also to answer questions about them in natural language. Indeed, there is a relatively long history of efforts at making computers "talk," or at least providing the semblance of an active language-producing capacity. The field of natural language generation has received a great deal of attention from computer scientists because, many believe, the ideal form of interaction between humans and computers should be in an ordinary language, avoiding the need to use specialized protocols or artificial languages in communicating with computers and instructing them to perform tasks. Weizenbaum's well-known ELIZA program, developed in the 1970s, is an early example. ELIZA is a simulation of a Rogerian psychotherapist, capable of asking its interlocutors relevant questions and of making prompting remarks that relate to the "patient's" own discourse:

(23)   "Patient": I'm not feeling very happy today.
        ELIZA: Tell me why you're not feeling happy.

As a kind of "parlor game," ELIZA is effective and compelling. For a while, at least, ELIZA's interlocutors are often convinced that they are communicating with a human being. But in most any sustained interaction with ELIZA, it becomes apparent that virtually all of its responses are either "canned" or directly cued by a single word or phrase in the interlocutor's remarks. Furthermore, such systems often have small lexicons restricted to a limited discourse domain, and typically they respond to unknown words with the (all-too-frequent) message *I DON'T UNDERSTAND (word)*. Language-generating systems of this sort were built into popular text-based computer games with the virtue of enabling some natural language interaction between human users and computers. But they are not, on the whole, good models of normal human language production.

More sophisticated language generation models—for instance, the TEXT system of McKeown (1985)—use schemas (scripts) and semantic net representations to provide a knowledge base and establish a coherent discourse context in which sentences (often answers to questions) are produced. As conversations proceed and the set of appropriate responses becomes more varied, TEXT also uses a focusing mechanism to determine the most relevant response. It does this by tracking the syntactic structure of the interlocutor's sentences, looking for clues such as topicalization or passive morphology. The system then limits the choice of response so that it is appropriate to the center of the speaker's attention. Thus, to the question *Do cats hunt birds?* a likely response might be *Yes, because cats are predatory by nature*. But to the question *Are birds hunted by cats?* the answer might well be *Yes, because birds are the natural prey of cats*. The content of these answers would, of course, depend on the particular properties of birds and cats that are included in the knowledge base, and the focusing mechanism depends strongly on a parsing module that can derive focus information from linguistic structure. The latter problem is the target of much current research within linguistic theory; it is an even more complex problem when the input is phonological rather than written (for example, in cases where the focus of attention is defined by acoustic cues such as intonation or loudness). Successfully implemented, this kind of system promises to add significantly to the naturalness of computer-generated conversation.

The KAMP system of Appelt (1985), and related approaches, deal with the problem of language generation from a somewhat different point of view. Implicit in KAMP (Knowledge and Modalities Planner) is the assumption that language generation bears a strong relationship to planning mechanisms in general cognition and action. Plans are processes that define and regulate the order in which a series of actions toward a particular goal are carried out. It is not unreasonable to think of a linguistic discourse (on the part of either participant, acting as speaker or hearer) as a set of plans to request, to order, or to inform. KAMP plans speech acts, rather than actions in the real world. In so doing, it is in part guided by pragmatic constraints of the sort discussed earlier, in that it is designed to generate utterances that are (at least) relevant, truthful, and informative with respect to a given plan. Asked *What time does the train to New Haven leave?*, a speech-act–based system like KAMP will interpret the utterance not only as a question but also as the initial step in a plan to acquire information for travel. In other words, in addition to taking the question to be a request and responding relevantly, it will provide other information that is both true and relevant to a travel plan (for example, timetable information that may contain not only the departure time but also the number of the track on which the train leaves), because such plans require that information as well, at later stages. As a result, the discourse that speech-act–based language generating systems produce can have some of the feel of natural linguistic interaction.

Human Language Production and the Role of Grammar

Of course, it is not enough for a computer to model the discourse conditions of speech, since no language-generating system will "feel natural" unless the utterances that it produces are also grammatical sentences of the language involved. Robots that speak in a mechanical monotone, without stress or intonation contours, do not meet that criterion. Nor do computers that use simplified telegraphic utterances like *File saved* or *Insert disk now*. Nor, for that matter, do systems like ELIZA, which rely on a small set of precompiled syntactic structures and do not recognize infinitely many members of the infinitely large set of sentence structures that characterize any human language. Although (as we have seen) there is much debate about the centrality and even the necessity of linguistic grammars in the perception and processing of language, there is much less doubt that language generation must incorporate a grammar, or some equivalent knowledge system (perhaps a connectionist model), that is also, in principle, fully capable of characterizing the set of grammatical sentences in a given language. However possible it may be to understand language without recourse to grammar, it does not seem possible to constrain language production by meaning or by context in ways that would guarantee linguistically well formed output.

Curiously, perhaps, relatively little scientific attention has been paid to human language production. In part, this may be because the initial stage of production—the generation of the intentions, thoughts, and emotions that are ultimately encoded in language—remains deeply mysterious. But if the input to the production system is opaque to us, the output is readily observable in the form of actual speech. By working backward in a sense, it is still possible to make some important if indirect inferences about the role that grammars and linguistic structures play in the planning and production of speech.

In fact, paradoxically, much of what we know about the production of normal, natural speech derives from the study of abnormal speech—the errors that are commonly produced even by fluent speakers. Although natural speech largely conforms to the generalizations that linguists have discerned, virtually all speakers on occasion exhibit a rich array of dysfluencies and mistakes. These speech errors can offer substantial insight into the representation and organization of linguistic knowledge. First, there is evidence that language production recruits the kind of hierarchical representations that are hypothesized within theories of grammar, at both the phonological and syntactic levels, rather than proceeding in a strictly linear, word-by-word fashion. For example, consider the kind of error that is represented by classical *spoonerisms*, or transpositions of the initial segments of words, as in *queer old dean* for *dear old queen*. While the speaker prepares to initiate the phrase, intending to say the first word, the (/d/-initial) adjective *dear*, the /kw/-initial noun *queen* has already been readied, and the speaker retrieves its initial segments in an anticipatory error. Such errors are quite generally confined to anticipations within a single linguistic constituent, in this case a noun phrase. By the same token, such transpositions can involve phonemes from the same position in the hierarchical syllable structure of the words involved—both /d/

and /kw/ are syllable onsets. Speakers virtually never transpose sounds between a syllable onset and a syllable coda, which would result in *near old queed. Another case is the one cited by Garrett (1988), where a speaker produces the utterance an angwage lacquisition device for a language acquisition device. Here the initial /l/ of language has been transposed into the syllable onset position of acquisition. What is striking about this example is that the phonetic form of the indefinite article (a or an), which depends on whether the following noun begins with a vowel or a consonant, must have been determined after the transposition error was made.

These observations suggest that structures defined by grammars, and rules of grammar, are active, on-line, and central in the planning of production. More specifically, they suggest that there are multiple levels in the production process. Garrett (1975, 1984, 1988) proposes a model with three such levels: a *message level* at which the underlying intention and meaning of the utterance are determined, a *functional level* at which lexical items are chosen and assigned a syntactic structure, and a *positional level* at which the final order and position of elements are fixed. On Garrett's view, it is the positional representation that provides the input to the articulatory mechanisms that generate a phonetic output.

There are also cases in which a lexical item as a whole is subject to production error. We often hear speakers inadvertently replace an intended word with another one to which it is semantically related: *I put the dog out* for *I put the cat out*, and *The moon is shining* for *The sun is shining*. But it is rare indeed to hear speakers erroneously produce sentences like *I ran out of stalagmites* when *I ran out of eggs* was intended. Such errors are consistent with a model of the mental dictionary in which lexical items are organized according to semantic category; it is also compatible with connectionist models of lexical representation where semantic relatedness is captured by assuming node connections with high levels of activation.

Erroneous lexical substitutions may also involve some degree of phonological similarity, in which case they are often called *malapropisms*. Thus, a speaker at a philanthropic dinner was reported to say *Thank you for the lovely recession*, when *Thank you for the lovely reception* was intended. Malapropisms often strike us as amusing, because the word produced in error may share little if any semantic relation to the intended target word and may be strikingly inappropriate. Rather, as Faye and Cutler (1977) observe, malapropisms share segmental, syllabic, and rhythmic properties with the words they replace, and they are also invariably of the same syntactic category. This phenomenon suggests a model of the mental lexicon in which phonological information plays an important role at many levels. Production error creeps in when the section of the lexicon containing the intended word has been correctly accessed, but the retrieval mechanism "slips" and picks up an item whose phonological representation is close to that of the intended word, but not at precisely the right address.

So-called tip-of-the-tongue phenomena suggest a related form of lexical production difficulty. In these cases speakers report knowing a word's meaning but cannot recall its full phonetic form. Nonetheless, the speaker typically has a powerful sense of knowing what the word is, can often identify its initial segment, and can report the correct number of syllables and the word's overall prosodic pattern. The speaker is in the right semantic space in the lexicon, typically knows what syntactic category is involved, and even has access to certain parts of phonological representation, but cannot retrieve information about the complete segmental form of the word.

Taken as a whole, a consideration of errors such as slips of the tongue, lexical substitutions, malapropisms, and tip-of-the-tongue phenomena conveys a picture of production that involves many levels of processing and recruits some rather abstract properties of linguistic representation.

11.7 Conclusion

On the view that we have developed here, natural language processing is a remarkably complex phenomenon. We have examined and found much support for the view that comprehension involves a special, modular parsing system that depends crucially on grammatical representations and operates independently of other components of language processing and of general knowledge. But we have also seen evidence that the pragmatic functions for which sentence structures are used may also play a role in sentence understanding, as well as a (perhaps larger) role in the comprehension of discourses. For instance, the processor must assess the roles of distinct speech act types, in the light of a theory of conversational conventions. We also saw that language understanding in general, even if not the initial stages of processing, depends strongly on interactions with general knowledge about the world. Finally, we examined issues in language production (in computer models as well as in human speakers) that suggest an important role for both grammatical and world knowledge. There may also be a host of other factors, about which we have said very little, that influence language processing. Many other aspects of our mental lives (for instance, our belief systems, humor, empathy, creative drives, and emotional states) are obviously deeply significant in the process of language understanding and production. Still, given current states of knowledge, these issues are not fully understood. One important moral for the student of cognitive science is that the enterprise of explaining these complexly intertwined components could hardly be carried out by workers within a single field. It is only through a synthesis of the efforts of linguists, psychologists, AI researchers, and philosophers that we are beginning to make any real progress in comprehending the mechanisms responsible for the processing and production of natural language.

Suggested Readings

For a broad introduction to issues in language processing, see the general introductory text *Psycholinguistics* (Foss and Hakes 1978). *Computers and Human Language* (Smith 1991) provides an introductory overview of current work on language processing from a computational viewpoint, including recent work on AI. For some examples of the professional literature on parsing with an emphasis on the role of grammar, see *Natural Language Parsing* (Dowty, Karttunen, and Zwicky 1985). *Getting Computers to Talk like You and Me* (Reichman 1985) offers an extensive discussion of the role of discourse and pragmatics in language processing.

References

Allen, J. (1983). Recognizing intentions from natural language utterances. In M. Brady and R. C. Berwick, eds., *Computational models of discourse*. Cambridge, Mass.: MIT Press.

Allen, J., and C. R. Perrault (1980). Analysing intention in utterances. *Artificial Intelligence* 15, 143–178.

Appelt, D. (1985). Planning natural language utterances to satisfy multiple goals. Doctoral dissertation, University of Toronto.

Austin, J. L. (1962). *How to do things with words*. Oxford: Clarendon Press.

Bever, T. G. (1970). The cognitive basis for linguistic structures. In J. R. Hayes, ed., *Cognition and the development of language*. New York: Wiley.

Bower, G., J. Black, and T. Turner (1979). Scripts in memory for text. *Cognitive Psychology* 11, 177–220.

Clifton, C., and F. Ferreira (1987). Modularity in sentence comprehension. In Garfield 1987.

Cohen, P., C. R. Perrault, and J. Allen (1982). Beyond question answering. In W. G. Lehnert and M. H. Ringle, eds., *Strategies for natural language processing*. Hillsdale, N.J.: Erlbaum.

Cowart, W., and H. Cairns (1987). Evidence for an anaphoric mechanism within sentence processing: Some reference relations defy semantic and pragmatic constraints. *Cognition* 15, 318–331.

Crain, S., and M. Steedman (1985). On not being led up the garden path: The use of context by the psychological syntax processor. In Dowty, Karttunen, and Zwicky 1985.

Dowty, D., L. Karttunen, and A. Zwicky, eds. (1985). *Natural language parsing*. Cambridge: Cambridge University Press.

Dyer, M. G. (1981). The role of TAUs in narratives. In *Proceedings of the Third Annual Conference of the Cognitive Science Society*. Berkeley, Calif.

Dyer, M. G., and W. Lehnert (1980). Organization and search processes for narratives. Technical report 175. Computer Science Department, Yale University, New Haven, Conn.

Fay, D., and A. Cutler (1977). Malapropisms and the structure of the mental lexicon. *Linguistic Inquiry* 8, 505–520.

Ferreira, M. F. (1985). The role of context in resolving syntactic ambiguity. Master's thesis, University of Massachusetts at Amherst.

Flores d'Arcais, F. B. (1982). Automatic syntactic computation in sentence comprehension. *Psychological Research* 44, 231–242.

Fodor, J. A. (1983). *The modularity of mind*. Cambridge, Mass.: MIT Press.

Foss, D., and D. Hakes (1978). *Psycholinguistics*. Englewood Cliffs, N.J.: Prentice-Hall.

Frazier, L. (1987). Theories of sentence processing. In Garfield 1987.

Garfield, J. L., ed. (1987). *Modularity in knowledge representation and natural language understanding*. Cambridge, Mass.: MIT Press.

Garrett, M. F. (1975). The analysis of sentence production. In G. H. Bower, ed., *The psychology of learning and motivation*. Vol. 9. New York: Academic Press.

Garrett, M. F. (1984). The organization of processing structure for language production. In D. Caplan, A. Lecours, and A. Smith, eds., *Biological perspectives on language*. Cambridge, Mass.: MIT Press.

Garrett, M. F. (1988). Processes in language production. In F. J. Newmeyer, ed., *Linguistics: The Cambridge survey*. Vol. 3. Cambridge: Cambridge University Press.

Grice, H. P. (1971). Utterer's meaning, sentence-meaning and word-meaning. In J. R. Searle, ed., *Oxford readings in philosophy*. Oxford: Oxford University Press.

Grice, H. P. (1975). Logic and conversation. In P. Cole and J. Morgan, eds., *Syntax and semantics*. New York: Academic Press.

Joshi, A., B. Webber, and I. Sag, eds. (1981). *Elements of discourse understanding*. Cambridge: Cambridge University Press.

Labov, W. (1972). Rules for ritual insults. In W. Labov, ed., *Language in the inner city*. Philadelphia: University of Pennsylvania Press.

Lehnert, W. G. (1981). Human question answering. In Joshi, Webber, and Sag 1981.

Marr, D. (1982). *Vision*. New York: W. H. Freeman.

McKeown, K. R. (1985). *Text generation: Using discourse strategies and focus constraints to generate natural language discourse*. Cambridge: Cambridge University Press.

Reichman, R. (1985). Getting computers to talk like you and me. Cambridge, Mass.: MIT Press.

Schank, R. (1984). *The cognitive computer*. Reading, Mass.: Addison-Wesley.

Schank, R., and R. Abelson (1977). *Scripts, plans, goals and understanding: An inquiry into human knowledge structures*. Hillsdale, N.J.: Erlbaum.

Schank, R., and L. Birnbaum (1984). Memory, meaning and syntax. In T. G. Bever, J. M. Carroll, and L. A. Miller, eds., *Talking minds: The study of language in the cognitive sciences*. Cambridge, Mass.: MIT Press.

Searle, J. R. (1969). *Speech acts*. Cambridge: Cambridge University Press.

Seifert, C. M. (1980). Preliminary experiments on TAUs. Ms., Yale University, New Haven, Conn.

Smith, G. W. (1991). Computers and Human Language. New York: Oxford University Press.

Stubbs, M. (1983). *Discourse analysis*. Chicago: University of Chicago Press.

Tanenhaus, M. K., G. N. Carlson, and M. S. Seidenberg (1985). Do listeners compute linguistic representations? In Dowty, Karttunen, and Zwicky 1985.

Tyler, L. K., and W. D. Marslen-Wilson (1977). The on-line effects of semantic context on syntactic processing. *Journal of Verbal Learning and Verbal Behavior* 16, 683–692.

Tyler, L. K., and W. D. Marslen-Wilson (1980). The temporal structural of spoken language understanding. *Cognition* 8, 1–71.

Waltz, D. L., and J. B. Pollack (1985). Massively parallel parsing: A strongly interactive model of natural language interpretation. *Cognitive Science* 9, 51–74.

Winograd, T. (1972). *Understanding natural language*. New York: Academic Press.

Chapter 12

Vision

12.1 The Problem of Vision

The Input to the Visual System

Vision is possible because the light reflected from physical surfaces is a potential source of information about the physical world. The light entering each eye passes through the *cornea* and *lens*, which focus it into a two-dimensional image on the rear of the eyeball, much like a camera lens focuses an image onto film. The fundamental information-processing task of the human visual system is to extract information about the three-dimensional physical world from this constantly changing pair of two-dimensional images.

Formally, an image is simply a two-dimensional array of values. Each point on the image has a spatial position that can be represented by two coordinate values x and y (the point $(0, 0)$ can be considered the center of the image). The intensity of the light at each point in the image can be represented by $I(x, y)$. Thus, intensity is a function of spatial position. If $I(x, y) = 0$, then no light is present at point (x, y). If $I(x, y) > 0$, then light is present, and increasing values of I represent increasing intensity, or *luminance*.

In the human visual system the initial encoding of the image occurs in the *retina*, a layer of neural cells at the rear of the eyeball. The retina contains a two-dimensional layer of sensory cells, called *rods* and *cones*, which are sensitive to light. Each of these cells is a *transducer* that is capable of generating a neural signal when struck by light. As a first approximation, the activity in the sensory cells can be considered a direct, analog representation of the image currently focused on the cells. That is, at each moment the sensory cells record the value $I(x, y)$ at a very large, but finite, number of points. This approximation helps us focus on the contributions of interdisciplinary vision research, although it disregards a number of fascinating complexities in the responses of the rods and cones to light, which allow the human eye to respond to an enormous range of intensities and to see colors (Cornsweet 1970).

In order to appreciate the staggering capabilities of the human visual system and the problem faced by the researcher who wishes to understand it, the austerity of the image must be appreciated. Although the image in some sense contains the information needed to see objects in space, only intensity values at points are explicitly represented in the image. All other information must be built up by processes that begin their work on these intensity values. Figure 12.1 illustrates this point graphically. Part (*a*) of the figure is a picture. When the picture is delivered to the visual system in the form of reflected light, the visual system performs its information processes, and we see the objects in the picture clearly. Part (*b*) of the figure is a computer printout of the numerical intensity values in a region of the figure. When the picture is delivered in the form of an array of numerical intensity values, it is impossible to immediately

(a)

Figure 12.1
In visual systems an image is initially represented as a two-dimensional array of intensity values. (a) is a photograph of the image of a scene displayed on the monitor screen of a computer. A television camera was focused on the scene, and the output of the camera was converted into an array of intensity values, which were stored in the computer. The computer then converted the intensity array back into a television signal, which was displayed on the monitor and photographed. (b) is a printout of the intensity values in the rectangular region highlighted in the photograph.

discern the content of the picture. Yet intensity values are what visual information processing begins with.

Computer vision systems also take image arrays as their input. The intensity values in figure 12.1 were printed out from an image array stored in a computer's memory. The values in the array were formed by hooking a television camera up to the computer and pointing the camera at the scene pictured in part (a) of the figure. The computer rapidly samples the signal coming out of the camera to form an image array. In this case the array has $512 \times 512 = 262{,}144$ points (sometimes called *pixels* for "picture elements"). Part (a) of the figure is a photograph of a redisplay of the image array on a television screen, showing that a 512×512 array captures enough information for the human visual system to identify objects and perceive their spatial relations. It should be realized, however, that the human retina contains about 126 million sensory cells (about 500 times the number of pixels in the computer image). Furthermore, the human system can continuously process the image registered by these cells rapidly enough to support visual skills such as reading or driving a car. This efficiency is largely due to the parallel structure of the visual system. Until recently, computer vision systems were forced to simulate this parallelism. As a result, computer vision

```
31 30 30 30 30 30 30 30 30 29 30 29 28 28 27 28 27 27 27 27 26 26 25 25 25 25 25 25 24 24 24 24 24 24 24 24 23 23 23 23 23 23
31 30 30 30 29 30 30 30 29 29 29 29 28 27 28 27 27 27 27 26 26 26 26 25 25 25 25 25 24 25 24 24 24 24 23 23 23 23 23 23 23 22
30 30 29 30 29 30 30 29 29 29 28 28 28 27 27 27 27 26 26 25 26 26 25 25 25 24 24 24 24 24 24 23 23 24 23 24 23 23 23 23 22 22
29 30 29 29 29 29 29 29 28 28 27 27 27 27 27 26 26 26 26 25 25 25 25 25 25 24 24 24 24 24 23 23 23 23 23 22 22 22 22 22 22
30 29 29 29 28 28 28 28 28 28 27 28 27 27 26 26 26 26 25 25 25 24 25 24 24 24 24 23 23 23 23 23 23 22 22 22 22 22 21 21 21
29 29 29 29 28 28 28 28 27 27 27 27 26 26 26 25 26 25 25 25 24 24 24 24 23 24 23 23 23 23 22 23 22 22 22 21 21 21 21 21 21
29 28 28 28 28 28 28 27 27 27 27 26 26 26 25 26 25 25 25 25 24 25 23 24 24 24 23 23 23 23 23 22 22 22 21 21 21 21 20 21
29 28 28 28 28 28 28 27 27 27 26 26 26 26 25 25 25 25 24 25 23 24 24 24 23 23 23 23 23 22 22 22 21 21 21 21 20 21 20 20 21
30 28 28 28 28 28 28 27 27 27 26 26 25 25 25 25 24 24 24 23 23 22 23 22 22 22 22 22 22 21 21 21 21 20 20 20
29 29 29 28 28 27 27 28 27 27 27 27 26 26 25 25 25 25 24 24 24 23 24 23 23 23 22 22 22 21 22 21 21 21 21 21 21 21 21
30 29 29 29 28 28 28 27 27 27 27 26 26 26 26 26 25 25 25 25 25 25 24 24 23 23 23 23 23 23 22 22 22 22 22 22 21 21 21 21
30 29 30 29 29 29 28 28 28 27 27 27 27 26 25 25 25 25 25 25 24 24 24 23 24 23 23 23 22 23 23 21 22 21 22 22 21 21 21
30 29 30 30 29 29 29 28 28 28 27 27 27 27 26 26 26 26 26 25 25 24 24 24 24 24 23 23 23 23 23 22 23 22 22 22 22 22 21
30 31 30 30 29 28 29 28 28 28 27 27 27 27 27 26 26 26 26 26 25 25 24 24 24 24 24 24 24 23 23 23 23 23 23 22 22 22 22
30 31 30 30 30 29 30 29 28 29 28 28 27 27 27 27 26 27 26 26 25 25 25 24 24 24 24 24 25 24 24 23 23 23 23 23 23 23 22 22
31 31 30 30 30 29 30 29 29 29 28 28 28 27 28 26 27 26 25 26 25 26 25 25 25 25 25 24 25 24 24 24 24 24 24 24 23 23 23 23 23 22 23 22
31 30 30 30 29 29 29 28 28 28 28 28 27 27 27 26 26 26 26 26 25 25 25 24 24 24 24 24 24 24 23 23 23 23 23 23 22 22
30 30 30 31 29 30 29 28 29 28 28 27 27 26 26 26 26 26 25 25 25 24 24 24 24 24 24 24 23 23 23 23 23 23 22 22 22
30 30 30 29 29 29 28 28 28 27 27 27 27 26 26 26 25 25 25 25 24 24 24 23 24 23 23 24 23 24 24 23 24 22 22 23 22 22 22
30 29 29 29 29 28 28 27 27 27 27 26 26 26 26 25 25 24 24 24 23 23 22 23 22 21 21 22 22 22 22 22 22 22 22 21 21 21
29 29 29 28 28 27 27 27 26 26 25 25 25 25 24 24 24 23 23 22 23 22 23 22 22 21 22 22 22 22 22 22 22 22 22 21 22 22 22 21
29 28 28 27 27 27 27 26 26 25 25 24 24 24 24 23 23 23 22 22 22 21 21 21 21 21 21 21 21 21 21 22 21 21 22 21 22 21 22 21 21
28 27 27 27 27 26 25 25 25 24 24 23 23 23 22 22 22 22 21 21 21 21 21 20 21 20 21 21 21 21 21 21 21 21 21 21 21
27 27 26 26 26 26 25 25 25 24 24 23 24 23 23 22 22 22 22 21 20 20 20 20 19 20 20 20 20 20 20 21 20 20 20 20 20 20 20
26 25 25 26 25 25 24 24 24 24 23 23 23 23 22 22 22 22 21 20 20 20 19 19 19 19 19 19 20 20 19 19 20 19 20 20 19 20 20 19
25 25 25 25 24 24 24 24 23 23 23 23 23 23 22 22 21 21 21 20 20 19 19 18 18 19 19 19 19 20 19 19 20 19 20 19 19 19 19
24 25 24 24 24 24 23 23 23 23 23 23 23 23 22 22 21 21 20 19 20 20 19 19 19 19 19 19 19 20 19 20 19 19 19 19 19 19 19 19
23 23 23 23 23 23 23 23 22 22 23 22 23 22 22 22 21 21 20 19 19 19 19 19 19 19 19 19 19 19 19 19 19 19 19 19 19 19 18
23 23 22 22 22 22 23 21 22 22 22 23 23 22 23 22 21 20 20 20 19 19 19 19 19 19 19 19 19 19 20 20 19 19 19 20 19 19 19
22 22 22 21 21 21 21 21 21 22 22 22 22 22 22 21 21 21 21 20 19 20 19 19 19 18 19 19 19 19 20 19 20 19 20 19 19 19 19 18
21 21 21 21 21 21 21 21 21 22 22 22 22 22 22 22 21 21 20 20 19 20 19 19 19 19 19 19 20 19 20 19 19 20 19 19 19
21 20 21 21 20 21 21 22 22 22 22 22 23 22 22 22 21 20 20 20 20 19 19 19 19 19 19 19 19 20 20 20 20 21 20 20 19 19 19 18
21 20 20 20 20 21 21 21 21 21 22 22 22 22 22 22 21 21 20 20 19 19 19 19 19 19 20 19 20 20 20 20 20 20 20 20 19 19 19
21 20 20 20 20 21 21 21 21 21 22 22 22 22 22 23 22 22 20 20 20 19 19 19 19 19 19 20 20 20 21 20 20 20 20 19 19 19
20 20 20 20 20 20 21 21 21 21 22 22 22 22 22 21 21 20 19 20 19 19 19 19 19 19 19 19 20 20 20 21 20 20 20 20 20 19 19 19
20 20 20 21 21 21 22 22 22 22 23 23 23 22 22 21 21 20 19 20 19 20 19 19 19 20 20 21 21 21 21 21 21 21 21 20 20 20 19 19
                  21 21 21 22 22 23 23 23 23 23 22 21 21 20 20 20 20 19 20 19 20 20 21 21 21 21 21 21 21 21 20 20 20 20 19 19
(b)               21 22 23 23 23 23 24 24 23 23 23 22 21 20 20 20 19 20 19 20 20 20 21 21 21 22 22 22 21 21 20 20 20 20 19 19
                  22 22 24 23 25 24 24 24 23 23 22 22 21 21 21 20 20 21 20 20 21 21 22 22 23 22 22 22 21 21 21 20 20 19 19 19
                  22 23 24 25 25 25 25 24 24 23 23 22 22 21 21 21 21 21 21 21 21 22 23 23 23 23 22 22 21 21 21 21 20 20 20 19
```

Figure 12.1 (cont.)

systems took from minutes to hours to process a single image. Many current computer vision systems now incorporate a significant degree of parallelism at the hardware level, making them more efficient and practical. Our interest in computer vision here, however, is not in its practicality but in its potential to test hypotheses about biological vision.

The Output of the Visual System
Although understanding the output of the visual system in formal terms is the target of ongoing research, our perceptual experience gives us a reasonable initial idea of the cognitive functions that the output must support. We can differentiate the objects in a visual scene. We are aware of their positions in space, their motions, their sizes, their shapes, and their surface textures. We are aware of our movements in space and can guide them so as to regulate speed, reach spatial goals, and avoid collisions. We are able to recognize objects and places that we have seen before. Therefore, the output of the visual system must in some way be storable in memory. We are also able to judge that a novel object is similar to one we have seen before or that it fits a category that has been defined propositionally. Therefore, the output of the system must lend itself to categorization processes and to complex interfacing with other cognitive systems.

12.2 Low-Level Visual Processes

The research problem, then, is to discover information processes that can get from an intensity array $I(x, y)$ to representations that support highly flexible visual cognition and behavior. It is now generally agreed that simple processes working on intensity values cannot recover the output information directly. This conclusion has arisen from computational work on vision as well as from work on the anatomy and physiology of biological visual systems. Computational studies usually divide the problem of vision into a number of somewhat independent subtasks, each of which requires the extraction and refinement of information at several successive levels of analysis. The subtasks can be pursued in parallel, although their outputs are usually assumed to cooperate at various points in the system to settle on some aspect of the developing representation.

Issues in the Theory of Low-Level Vision
Research on low-level vision is concentrated on discovering what information about the world can be initially extracted from the image. An immediate question is whether *bottom-up* processes that take image data as inputs must be guided by *top-down* expectations about what is present in the image. We will begin with the assumption that a great deal of useful information can be extracted from the image by bottom-up processing alone. This view was first developed fully in AI by David Marr (1982) and in psychology by J. J. Gibson (1966), although Gibson did not utilize the computational framework in developing his ideas (Fodor and Pylyshyn 1981). Regardless of its limits, the bottom-up view is an extremely useful heuristic for research on low-level processing, because it forces the researcher to study the information content of images intensively.

Research on low-level vision has been guided by several assumptions. A widely accepted assumption is that early visual computation is highly parallel and local. That is, all areas of the image are worked on simultaneously, and the computations on each point in the image are affected only by computations on immediately adjacent areas and not by computations on distant parts of the image. A strong source of support for this assumption is the anatomical and electrophysiological study of the visual system. The retina and the primary visual cortex seem to be wired up to perform local, parallel computations.

A second assumption is that early visual computation has a modular organization. The image contains several distinct sources of information, and each type of information can be represented independently and at least partially extracted by an independent computational mechanism. For example, there are several sources of information about depth, or the distance of an object from the observer. One source is *stereopsis*. Because the two eyes are located in two different positions in the head, each eye gets a slightly different view of an object. This difference, called the *binocular disparity*, is a source of information about depth, because the amount of disparity is systematically correlated with the distance of the object from the viewer. Computing the disparity values for a pair of images, however, requires matching each point in one image with the corresponding point in the other. There are many potential matches for any one point, and the computation must somehow find the best global set of matches for the whole image. The researcher exploring the bottom-up, modular approach would attempt to develop algorithms that can compute the disparity of each point in the image, without making use of other sources of information, and would attempt to find psychological and physiological evidence that disparity computations are indeed modular in the human visual system.

Another source of information about depth comes from the motion of objects in the world. When an object moves, its image is spatially displaced on the retina. Certain characteristics of the displacement of the image are systematically correlated with depth. To give a simple example, if the image of the object expands, the object is moving toward the viewer, and if the image contracts, the object is moving away from the viewer. To appreciate the fact that this source of information is potentially independent of stereopsis information, note that only one eye is needed to register it. The researcher exploring the bottom-up, modular approach would attempt to develop algorithms that can extract depth information from displacement in the image and to discover psychological and neurophysiological evidence that depth is recovered from displacement information independently from other sources of depth information. If the evidence indicates that the various depth computations are not completely modular, or independent, then the researcher can explore ways of introducing cooperation among the computations so that they mutually constrain each other during computation. In some cases further constraints arising from the top-down flow of high-level information might be hypothesized.

A third assumption guiding research on low-level processes is that the physics of image formation constrains the structure of images in such a way that bottom-up processes can be informative. The low-level processes can take advantage of the fact that the physics of image formation normally ensures certain correlations between properties of the world and properties of the image. To put it another way, the physics prevents the breakdown of these correlations under normal conditions. Suppose we lived in a world where objects regularly expanded and contracted in a smooth manner, rather like balloons that could spontaneously take on and let out air. In such a world optical flow would not be a reliable source of depth information. The expansion of an object's image on the retina would sometimes signal its approach toward the viewer and would sometimes signal that it was taking on air, while remaining stationary. But we do not live in such a world. Few objects in our world undergo frequent, smooth inflation or deflation. Thus, the assumption that optical flow gives reliable information about depth can be built into a visual system. One piece of evidence that the assumption is built into the human visual system comes from an experiment by Ittelson and Kilpatrick (1958) in which human viewers mistook the expansion and contraction of stationary balloons for the approach and retreat of balloons of constant size. An important consequence of the view that the visual system is adapted to physical constraints is that research in vision should in part be a study of these constraints.

Finally, early vision research must be guided by some assumption about what the output of early visual processing is, that is, about what representations it computes. There is less agreement among researchers in this area than in the others. Gibson (1966) assumed that early visual processes are able to determine the *layout of surfaces in three-dimensional space*. Objects are essentially volumes enclosed by two-dimensional surfaces, and the ground is essentially a two-dimensional surface. The notion of surface layout is that the visual system can segregate the points in an image into surfaces. For each point that is a member of a given surface, the system can determine its distance from the viewer and the orientation and curvature of the surface at that point. Thus, early visual processes represent information such as the following: the point at (x, y) on the image represents a point in the world that is forty feet directly ahead lying on a vertical planar surface that is receding to the right. They do not, however, represent more global facts, such as the following: the surface is the right wall of a two-story eighteenth-century New England farmhouse.

Marr's (1982) theory of the *2.5-D sketch* (section 12.3) represents a hypothesis quite similar to Gibson's. However, Marr proposed that early visual processes also compute another representation called the *primal sketch*, which Gibson probably would have argued against. The primal sketch is a representation of local features of an image that are likely to be reliable indicators of physical features of the world, such as elongated, oriented blobs.

Marr's Theory of the Primal Sketch
Cognitive scientists interested in integrating results from psychology, AI, and neuro-physiology have found Marr's (1976, 1982) notion of the *primal sketch* to be one of the most interesting proposals concerning the earliest visual processes. We will use it as our example here. The theory contains several parts, which we will discuss in turn: (1) an account of the way that the physical properties of surfaces and reflected light determine the information in images that can be immediately extracted by low-level processes, (2) a detailed theory of the very earliest visual processes, which compute what is called the *raw primal sketch*, and (3) a theory of grouping processes that operate on the raw primal sketch to produce the *full primal sketch*.

The Information Available for Early Visual Processes   The visible world is composed of physical surfaces. The starting point of the primal sketch theory is that much of the useful information about surfaces is encoded in changes in the intensity of reflected light. For example, imagine two visible surfaces at different orientations that meet in an edge. In nearly all situations the amount of light reaching the eye from one surface will differ from the amount of light reaching the eye from the other. In the image the edge will show up as a line defined by a sudden change in intensity. The idea is that early vision should be organized to detect and explicitly represent such informa-tion-rich changes in intensity.

The task of locating, representing, and interpreting the intensity changes in an image is not simple, however. The straightforward example of two surfaces meeting at an edge is misleading. It is not the case that all the local intensity changes in an image form global lines that signal the boundaries of surfaces in the world. There are several reasons for this.

One factor is that many sudden intensity changes occur within a surface area rather than at its boundaries. That is, surfaces are not uniformly colored. Rather, they often have various kinds of markings or texture. The grain of a wooden surface or the individual stones on a gravel drive will cause many local changes in intensity to show up on an image that do not signal boundaries between the major surfaces in the scene. Thus, the visual system cannot assume that every local intensity change signals an edge.

A further aspect of surface markings is that the physical composition of a surface can cause the local intensity changes to be organized in different ways at different spatial scales. For example, at the smallest scale the individual threads in a herringbone tweed fabric are visible and give rise to local intensity changes in an image of the fabric. At a slightly larger spatial scale the intensity changes are organized into short diagonal line segments, which reflect the way in which threads of different colors are interwoven. At a still larger spatial scale parallel sets of these diagonal lines are organized into vertical stripes. Note, however, that the edge of a vertical stripe is not defined by a continuous change from dark to light. Instead, the edge is defined by the fact that the ends of the parallel diagonal lines are vertically aligned. The human visual system easily registers the organization at the different spatial scales, even though only the smallest scale can be defined directly in terms of intensity changes. The implication is that the theory must allow the local intensity changes that are initially picked up to be reorganized at various spatial scales by more abstract attributes, such as the alignment of terminations.

A second factor is that some important physical processes give rise to gradual changes in intensity rather than to the sudden change typical of two flat surfaces meeting in a sharp edge. Shadows, for example, often have blurry edges that show up in an image as a gradual change in intensity. Another example is the curved surface of a uniformly colored cylinder illuminated from one direction. The intensity of the image of such a surface changes gradually. A system that only detects sharp changes in intensity will miss such gradual changes, which signal important aspects of the physical world such as changes in illumination and surface orientation.

The overall conclusion is that intensity changes in the image are a basic source of information for low-level vision. However, since we do not inhabit a uniformly illuminated world of smooth, flat surfaces that meet each other at crisp edges, our visual systems cannot simply look only for sharp intensity changes and interpret them as surface boundaries. In the actual physical world there are a number of processes that give rise to intensity changes. The visual system must detect both rapid and gradual changes, and it must represent them in a way that allows various interpretations to be made.

Computing Convolutions   By hypothesis, the earliest visual processes locate and represent the intensity changes in the image using local and parallel computations. A local process must be able to determine whether there is an intensity change at a given point in the image by looking only at the immediate (local) spatial neighborhood of that point. The entire image can be processed in parallel if the local process is performed simultaneously on all points in the image.

Digitized images make it easy to think intuitively about local processes for detecting intensity changes. The image is a two-dimensional array of pixels, each of which has an intensity value. To make a local decision about whether there is an intensity change at a particular pixel, we must restrict ourselves to a small window of neighboring pixels. Figure 12.2 illustrates a simple scheme for computing the intensity changes in an image. Part (*a*) shows a small part of the digitized image of a dark vertical bar on a light background. Suppose we wanted to find the points in the image where the intensity value changes in the horizontal direction (note that in this image there are no intensity changes in the vertical direction). A simple way to do this is to take the difference between each adjacent pair of pixel values, by subtracting the left member of the pair from the right. If the two intensity values are equal, the difference will be 0, indicating no change. A negative difference signals a decrease in intensity, and a positive difference signals an increase in intensity.

This computation is conveniently described as the application of a *first-order difference operator* to each pixel in the image. In general, an operator consists of a fixed

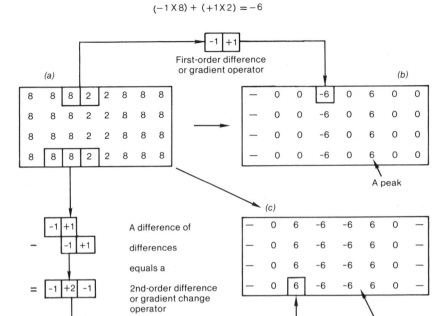

$$(-1 \times 8) + (+1 \times 2) = -6$$

First-order difference
or gradient operator

(a)   (b)

A peak

(c)

A difference of

differences

equals a

2nd-order difference
or gradient change
operator

A zero-crossing

$$(-1 \times 8) + (+2 \times 8) + (-1 \times 2) = 6$$

Figure 12.2
Computing convolutions. (a) shows a small portion of a hypothetical noise-free digitized image of a thin
dark bar ($I = 2$) on a light background ($I = 8$). (b) shows the convolution array that results from applying
a local, first-order operator ($-1, +1$) to the image to find the gradient of intensity in the horizontal
direction. Edges in the image appear as positive and negative peaks in the gradient array. (c) shows the
convolution array that results from applying a second-order operator ($-1, +2, -1$) to the image to find
the change in the intensity gradient. Edges in the image appear as zero-crossings in this array. When the
window of an operator overlaps the edge of the image, its result is shown as undefined ($-$) in (b) and (c).

window, or *mask*, which is placed over the pixel to be processed and some of its
neighbors. Each location in the window is associated with a *weight*. To compute the
value of the operator at a particular location, each intensity value in the window is
multiplied by its associated weight, and the products are added up. Our version of the
first-order difference operator has a two-pixel window with weights of -1 and $+1$.
The $+1$ location in the window is placed over the pixel to be processed and the
weighted sum is computed, giving the difference between the two adjacent intensity
values.

To explicitly represent the results of applying a local operator to each pixel in an
image array, we simply create a new array, replacing each intensity value with the
value of the operator at that point. Part (b) of figure 12.2 shows an array in which the
intensity value at each point has been replaced by the first-order difference at that
point. Such arrays are often called *convolution* arrays because, mathematically, they are
the result of taking the convolution of the intensity function and the operator. Notice
that the difference array contains nonzero values wherever intensity is changing and
zeros where it is not. The nonzero values are a discrete approximation of the slope, or
first partial derivative $\partial I / \partial x$, of the intensity function in the horizontal direction.

Although the first-order difference, or *gradient*, array is able to explicitly represent the edges of the bar in our simple example, it does not do so well in cases where a gradient is spread over a region of space. In this case the gradient array will show many nonzero values, and the transitions between important regions of the image will be signaled by peaks (maxima) and troughs (minima) in these nonzero values. Further operations would have to be performed on the gradient array to find and represent the peaks and troughs. The transitions in the image can be found more easily by computing the gradient of the gradient, using an operator that takes the difference between adjacent first-order differences. Part (c) of figure 12.2 illustrates an operator for such *second-order* differences in the horizontal direction. Peaks and troughs in the gradient show up as *zero-crossings* in the second-order convolution array, which is a finite approximation to the second partial derivative of the intensity function $\partial^2 I/\partial x^2$. The zero-crossings in the second-order array can be found relatively easily by an operator that looks for changes in sign.

Computing convolutions on a digital computer is straightforward. Although parallel machines that can compute convolutions have been developed, convolutions can also be computed point by point on standard serial computers. One can imagine simply moving the operator window along the image array from pixel to pixel and storing each result in a new convolution array. The computation on each pixel value is logically independent of the computations on all the other values, however, so that convolutions can be computed in parallel. Imagine each intensity value in the image array to represent a receptor cell and each value in the convolution array to represent a "convolution output cell." Then each convolution output cell could be wired to its window of receptor cells so as to compute the appropriate operator. For example, a second-order convolution cell would be wired to a window of three receptor cells, receiving a strong excitatory input from the central cell and weak lateral inhibitory input from the two flanking cells. Networks of neurons appear to work in just this way. A slight complication in nerve networks is that neurons cannot have negative firing rates. Therefore, it is necessary to have two arrays of convolution cells, one for the positive values and one for the negative values of the convolution (for details, see Frisby 1980).

Zero-Crossings in Complex Images   The second-order operator of figure 12.2 is not suitable for computing the zero-crossings in real images. It has two problems. First, it detects zero-crossings only in the horizontal direction. Obviously, the important intensity changes in an image can be oriented in any direction. Second, because it has a fixed, small window size, it does not discriminate zero-crossings that arise from sharp intensity changes from those that arise from gradual changes. But we have argued that different physical processes produce intensity changes with different spatial extents. Marr's theory of the primal sketch begins with the basic insight about zero-crossings and reformulates it to address these two problems.

There are two possible approaches to the directionality problem. The first, which has been pursued in a number of computer vision systems, is to have two or more operators, which measure intensity change at two or more orientations (Hanson and Riseman 1978a). This approach has the advantage of explicitly detecting and representing the orientation of a local boundary. Marr and Hildreth (1980) have argued for a second approach, proposing a single operator that is equally sensitive, or *isotropic*, to zero-crossings at all orientations. Although this operator loses orientation information, it appears to be a good model of the earliest processes in biological vision systems. Mathematically, the operator is known as the *Laplacian*, $(\partial^2 I/\partial x^2 + \partial^2 I/\partial y^2)$.

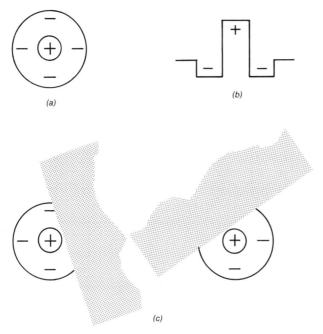

Figure 12.3
Isotropic operators. (*a*) is a diagrammatic representation of the circular window, or receptive field, of an isotropic operator with positively weighted center and negatively weighted surround. (*b*) is a graph of the operator's response profile. (*c*) demonstrates graphically that the operator is isotropic, or insensitive to direction. If two edges of different orientation cover the same amount of positively and negatively weighted area, the operator will give the same response. Thus, the operator cannot signal the orientation of the edge it is responding to.

Intuitively, one can think of creating the isotropic Laplacian operator by spinning the directional second-order operator in figure 12.2 around its center, creating a circular window with positive weights in its central area and negative weights in a surrounding ring. This circularly symmetric operator is illustrated in figure 12.3. Circular operators can be characterized in terms of their weighting profiles, or cross sections. The profile is the sequence of weights along a diameter of the circle. Obviously, for an isotropic operator, the profile will be the same regardless of the orientation of the diameter, so the profile in a sense tells us everything we need to know about the operator. We could list the numerical values of the weights in a profile, but it is often more informative to graph them, as demonstrated in the figure.

Figure 12.3 also graphically illustrates that the circular operator will respond to an intensity change with any orientation. The operator is thus simple computationally, but the directional information it loses must be recovered by later processes. It fits the psychological and physiological data from human and animal vision very well when combined with some further assumptions, which we now consider.

The second problem that the theory must address is that of discriminating between gradual and sudden changes in the gradient. The most straightforward approach to this problem is to apply two or more operators with varying window sizes. The operators we have been considering subtract the weighted sum of the negative pixels from the

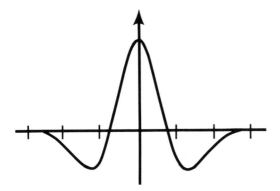

Figure 12.4
The response profile of the Mexican-hat operator, obtained when a profile of the type shown in part (*b*) of figure 12.3 is smoothed with a normal, or Gaussian, function. (Adapted from Marr and Hildreth 1980.)

weighted sum of the positive pixels. As the window size grows, more and more pixels contribute to the sums, and each individual pixel is contributing less and less. Larger operators are essentially averaging over a spatial area, blurring the image. As a result, they will miss highly localized intensity changes by averaging them out, but they will be sensitive to gradual changes that smaller operators can miss.

Marr and Hildreth (1980) have shown that the rectangular weighting profiles that we have been using for illustration cause avoidable errors. They argue that the optimal weighting function for blurring the image is the normal, or Gaussian, function. The profile of the Gaussian is simply the well-known bell-shaped curve of statistics. When the Laplacian is applied to the Gaussian, the smoothly varying profile shown in figure 12.4 is produced. This "Mexican-hat" profile emphasizes the intensity values in the central portions of the positive and negative areas. The result is that for a given window size, more zero-crossings are found, and they are assigned more accurate spatial locations.

The Raw Primal Sketch   The raw primal sketch is a first description of the zero-crossings detected by the operators, or channels, of different sizes. The results from the different operators are compared to sort out zero-crossings that have different physical causes. The sudden intensity change that separates a dark bar will have two zero-crossings in the smallest channel, which may be averaged out in larger channels. A gradual intensity change may not be detected by the smallest channel, but it will show up in two or more larger channels.

Characteristics of the zero-crossings within channels are also explicitly represented. Figure 12.5 shows the zero-crossings that arise from a fairly small channel applied to a natural image. As can be seen in the figure, zero-crossings form closed and continuous tracks. To begin forming the primal sketch, nearby zero-crossings are grouped together into short edge segments. The orientation and contrast of each segment are determined. It is useful to explicitly develop some further descriptive information about these segments, which is illustrated in the figure. When a small set of segments encloses a small area, they are explicitly labeled as a *blob*. Two nearby, parallel segments can be labeled a *bar*. The terminations and sudden discontinuities in lines are also marked. All of these descriptors can be developed by local operations. The raw primal

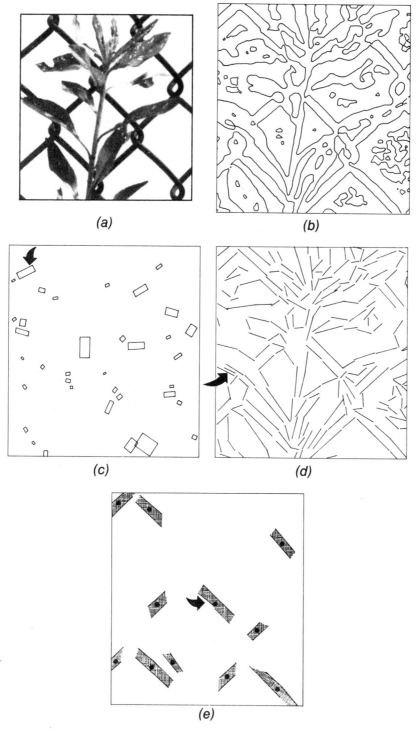

Figure 12.5
The primal sketch. (*a*) A photograph. (*b*) A plot of the zero-crossings detected by a small-sized circular operator with the profile shown in figure 12.4. (*c*), (*d*), and (*e*) are graphic displays of the descriptors built

sketch is a description of the image that is hypothesized to satisfy two criteria. First, it is designed to reflect the physical processes in the visual world that produce intensity changes in the image. Second, it is designed to be a useful description for building up higher-level descriptions of the scene such as surface layout and for recognizing objects.

Psychological Evidence for Channels of Different Sizes   Our everyday perceptual experience does not provide any confirmation of the theory that there are early visual channels with different window sizes. We are directly conscious of the phenomena in the world, such as edges, shadows, and surface curvature, but we are not conscious of the hypothesized processes that detect intensity changes at different scales and combine them in order to make the correct physical interpretations. Nevertheless, it is possible to set up controlled situations, called *psychophysical* experiments, that demonstrate the existence of the channels.

Many of these experiments involve visual stimuli that contain intensity changes in only one direction and at only one spatial scale, or *spatial frequency*. These stimuli are called *sinusoidal gratings*. Figure 12.6 shows pictures of two sinusoidal gratings and plots of their intensity profiles in the horizontal direction. Both intensity profiles are sine waves with the same spatial frequency. That is, the intensity rises and falls at the same rate. However, the two profiles differ in amplitude, or the heights of their peaks and troughs. The difference in amplitude is reflected as a perceived difference in contrast between the two gratings. As the contrast of a grating is reduced, it eventually becomes indistinguishable from a uniform stimulus that has the same average brightness but no spatial variation. The contrast at which a grating becomes just barely visible is called its *contrast threshold*.

Blakemore and Campbell (1969) measured the contrast threshold at various spatial frequencies, producing the *contrast sensitivity* function shown as a solid line in figure 12.7. The contrast sensitivity function plots the observer's sensitivity at each spatial frequency. Sensitivity is simply the inverse of the contrast threshold; that is, the lower the threshold, the higher the sensitivity. Not surprisingly, sensitivity is highest at the spatial frequencies that typically occur in real images and falls off at lower and higher frequencies.

Blakemore and Campbell then tested the hypothesis that the overall contrast sensitivity function results from a combination of several channels, each of which is maximally sensitive to intensity changes at a particular spatial scale defined by a band of spatial frequencies. Their test employed the *adaptation* technique, which rests on the

---

up from the zero-crossings. (c) displays the locations and sizes of the *blobs*. (d) displays the edge segments, and (e) displays the bars. In the primal sketch representation the descriptors actually explicitly encode information that is only implicitly suggested in these graphic displays. Thus, the descriptors, marked with arows in (c), (d), and (e), explicitly represent the following clusters of information:

BLOB	EDGE	BAR
(position 146, 21)	(position 184, 23)	(position 118, 34)
(orientation 105)	(orientation 128)	(orientation 128)
(contrast 76)	(contrast − 25)	(contrast − 25)
(length 16)	(length 25)	(length 25)
(width 6)	(width 4)	(width 4)

(Reprinted with permission from Marr and Hildreth 1980.)

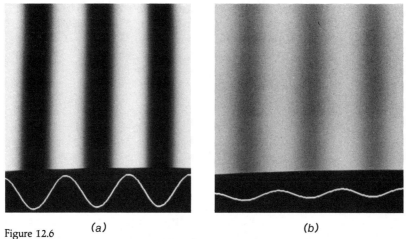

Figure 12.6   *(a)*   *(b)*

Sinusoidal gratings. (*a*) A high-contrast grating produced on a computer graphics system. A plot of the intensity variation is shown below the grating. (*b*) A lower-contrast grating with the same spatial frequency as (*a*). The intensity plot shows that intensity is varying at the same rate but within a smaller range.

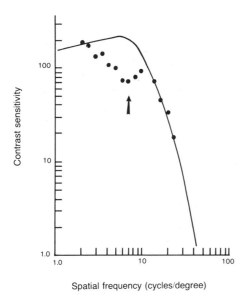

Spatial frequency (cycles/degree)

Figure 12.7

Data from Blakemore and Campbell's adaptation procedure. The solid line shows the contrast sensitivity function for a human subject. The data points show the contrast sensitivity at various spatial frequencies while the subject was adapted to the frequency indicated by the arrow on the graph. (Redrawn with permission from Blakemore and Campbell 1969.)

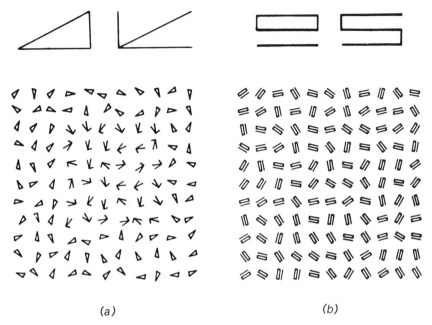

(a)   (b)

Figure 12.8
Two stimulus patterns from Julesz and Bergen's texture discrimination experiments. In their experiments artificial textures are created by repeating simple elements at random orientations. In both of these patterns a square region of texture composed of one element is embedded within a larger region composed of a different element. Enlarged copies of the elements are shown above each pattern. The embedded texture is much easier to discriminate in (a) than in (b). In the laboratory the difference in discriminability can be quantified by analyzing error rates when patterns with and without texture differences are exposed for very brief durations. The superior discriminability of (a) suggests that line terminations are represented in the primal sketch. The two elements used to generate (a) contain the same line lengths and orientations but differ in the number of terminations. The two elements used to generate (b) contain the same line lengths and orientations and also contain the same number of terminations. (Reproduced with permission from Julesz and Bergen 1983.)

following logic. In general, if a neural channel receives prolonged, intense stimulation, its response weakens, and its sensitivity to weak stimulation declines. Therefore, prolonged exposure to a high contrast grating at a particular spatial frequency should reduce sensitivity in the channel that is best tuned to that frequency without reducing sensitivity in channels that are not sensitive to that frequency. The contrast sensitivity function should therefore be reduced at some spatial frequencies and not at others. As can be seen from figure 12.7, the results fit the prediction very nicely. Further psychophysical work supports both the Mexican-hat profile and the hypothesis that there is a relatively small number of zero-crossing detection channels that are tuned to intensity changes at various spatial scales (Wilson 1983; Wilson and Bergen 1979).

Psychophysical evidence also bears on other aspects of raw primal sketch theory. The theory states that the terminations and discontinuities in lines of zero-crossings are explicitly represented. Interesting evidence for this comes from a study by Julesz and Bergen (1983). Part (a) of figure 12.8 demonstrates that textures composed of elements that differ in the number of terminations are easily distinguishable. Part (b) demonstrates that the textures are much more difficult to distinguish if the elements have the same number of terminations. In a controlled laboratory experiment the effect is demonstrated by presenting the patterns for brief durations and asking subjects to judge whether there is a texture difference. Discrimination is reliable for patterns like the ones in part (*a*) when the exposure time is roughly 100 milliseconds. At this duration discrimination of differences like the one in part (*b*) is essentially impossible. There are questions about just what features should be explicitly marked in the primal sketch (Treisman 1985 and Burton and Ruddock 1978 provide examples). It has also been shown that some of the primitive features that have been proposed can be detected by filtering processes that are not dedicated to computing just those features (Bergen and Adelson 1988; Caelli 1985).

Physiological Evidence for the Primal Sketch   Kuffler (1953) demonstrated that the ganglion cells in the cat's retina show the kind of circular receptive fields specified by primal sketch theory. The receptive fields of some cells have excitatory centers and inhibitory surrounds (*on-center* cells), and others have inhibitory centers and excitatory surrounds (*off-center* cells). If a spot of light is projected on the center of the receptive field of an off-center cell, the response rate of the cell is inhibited; that is, it goes below its resting rate.

Later researchers (Rodieck and Stone 1965; Enroth-Cugell and Robson 1966) showed that the receptive fields of ganglion cells have a Mexican-hat response profile. Marr and Ullman (1981) show that the response rates of the cells to various kinds of local intensity change, such as edges and bars, can be precisely predicted by the theory that they compute the isotropic Mexican-hat operator. Since nerve cells cannot have negative firing rates, the on-center cells are hypothesized to carry the positive portion of the Laplacian operator, and the off-center cells the negative.

The next step in the primal sketch computation is the location of the zero-crossings and the explicit representation of local, oriented zero-crossing segments. Marr and Hildreth (1980) present a simple scheme for interconnecting on-center and off-center cells for the detection of oriented zero-crossing segments. Figure 12.9 illustrates the scheme. Zero-crossings can be located by looking for changes in sign in the convolution image. Therefore, in the neural representation, if an on-center and a nearby off-center cell are both firing, then a zero-crossing must occur between them. A cell that detects the zero-crossing can be connected to the on- and off-center cells in such a way that it fires only when both of them fire. This type of connection is called a *logical AND-gate*. If the firing rate of the detector cell reflects the sum of the input rates, then it also signals the contrast of the intensity change.

Hubel and Wiesel (1979) found cells in the visual cortexes of the monkey and cat that respond in exactly the manner required by Marr and Hildreth's model. These *simple cells* respond to local, oriented edge segments within their receptive fields (see chapter 7). Further, Hubel and Wiesel showed that these cells are laid out in a uniform, modular architecture that suggests that they are devoted to the parallel representation of zero-crossing segments and, through their local interactions, to the parallel computation of the various patterns of responding that are required to compute the primal sketch and the further representations of low-level vision.

The retinal image is represented topographically on the visual cortex. That is, the receptive fields of adjacent areas on the cortex are adjacent on the retina. Not surprisingly, given the superior visual acuity in the central area of the retina, larger regions of

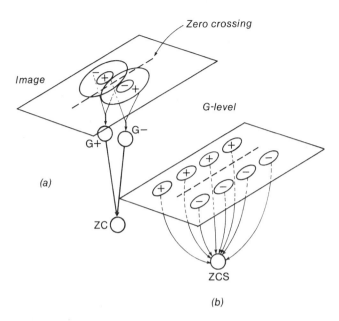

Figure 12.9
A hypothesized physiological mechanism for detecting oriented zero-crossing segments. (*a*) The cells labeled G have circular receptive fields on the image. The receptive fields of the on-center G+ cells have excitatory centers and inhibitory surrounds. The receptive fields of the off-center G− cells have inhibitory centers and excitatory surrounds. The *ganglion* cells in the retina and the cells of the *lateral geniculate nucleus* in the brain have been shown to have these kinds of receptive fields. Two nearby G+ and G− cells drive a cell labeled ZC in such a way that cell ZC fires only if both G+ and G− are firing. The G+ and G− cells will be active simultaneously only if a zero-crossing passes between them. Therefore, the ZC cell functions as a local zero-crossing detector. (*b*) Rows of G cells can be connected to a zero-crossing detector that detects the oriented zero-crossing segments needed for primal sketch computations. The zero-crossing segment detector, ZCS, is connected to parallel rows of G+ and G− cells in such a way that all of the G cells have to be active in order for the ZCS cell to be active. The simultaneous activity of the G cells will occur only when a zero-crossing passes between the two rows of receptive fields on the image. The *simple cells* of the visual cortex in the brain do respond to precisely oriented bars and edges. The figure diagrammatically illustrates the layered organization of early visual computations in the nervous system. A layer of receptor cells that encode intensity values in the image feeds a layer of cells that perform the Mexican-hat operator. This layer of cells in turn feeds a layer of cells that extract primal sketch primitives. (Based on Marr and Hildreth 1980.)

the visual cortex are devoted to it. The visual cortex has a number of horizontal layers that are defined by different types of cells and fibers. For example, the layer commonly labeled 4 contains the simple cells, and the layers labeled 2, 3, 5, and 6 contain the *complex cells*. The visual cortex is organized into vertical columns. If recordings are made from several cells by driving an electrode into the cortex perpendicular to its surface, then all of the cells respond preferentially to the same orientation and to the same eye (called *ocular dominance*).

The orientation and ocular dominance columns are organized into a modular unit called the *hypercolumn* that is regularly repeated over the surface of the visual cortex. Each hypercolumn contains cells that respond to a local region of the image. The cells cover all orientations and respond to both eyes. Figure 12.10 shows in a highly schematic manner how the hypercolumn structure arises from the intersection of *orientation slabs* and *ocular dominance slabs* that run in different directions through the cortex.

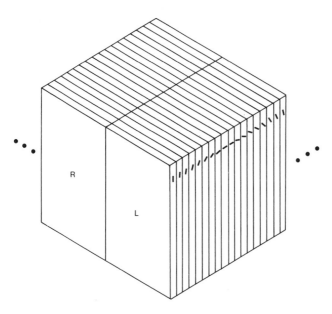

Figure 12.10
The hypercolumn is the basic computational unit of the visual cortex. It is an organized block of cells about a millimeter square that processes a small patch of the input image. It contains a complete set of orientation slabs, which process edges and bars at all orientations in steps of about 10 degrees, and a set of ocular dominance slabs, one of which is preferentially responsive to the right eye and the other to the left eye. Hypercolumns are laid out topographically on the primary visual cortex. That is, adjacent hypercolumns process adjacent areas of the retinal image. (Adapted with permission from Hubel and Wiesel 1979.)

The hypercolumn structure was confirmed by a remarkable radioactive labeling technique (Hubel, Wiesel, and Stryker 1978). An animal is injected with a radioactive form of 2-deoxyglucose, a chemical that is used by the metabolic processes in neurons and that leaves radioactive metabolic products behind in the neurons. The animal is then exposed for 45 minutes to a visual stimulus consisting of stripes in a single orientation. Active neurons take up more of the radioactive substance than inactive neurons and hence become radioactively "labeled." The animal is immediately sacrificed, and its visual cortex is cut into very thin slices that are laid onto radiosensitive photographic plates. When these "autoradiographs" are developed, the orientation slabs show up as dark stripes on horizontal slices of cortex.

The primal sketch theory also requires that zero-crossing segments be detected at different spatial scales, and indeed cortical simple cells are maximally responsive to different spatial frequencies. As in the psychophysical experiments discussed previously, this can be shown by projecting oriented sinusoidal gratings with varying frequencies onto the receptive fields of the cells and recording the responses (Maffei and Fiorentini 1973). There has been some dispute about whether and how variation in spatial scale is incorporated into the hypercolumn, but some autoradiographic evidence suggests that there are also spatial frequency columns within the hypercolumn (Tootell, Silverman, and De Valois 1981; see Maffei and Fiorentini 1977 for conflicting evidence).

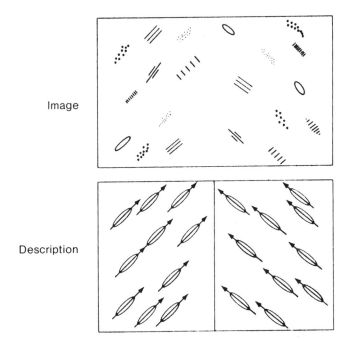

Image

Description

Figure 12.11
Detecting organization in the primal sketch. The visual system readily clusters nearby similar items into
large units. Thus, the dots and line segments in this image are organized into higher-level elongated and
oriented blobs. Nearby blobs with similar shape and orientation are clustered again, and a virtual boundary between the two clusters that divides the image in half can be detected. The lower panel of the figure
is a diagrammatic representation of this final level of organization. (Reprinted with permission from Marr
1982.)

12.3 Intermediate Processes and Representations in Vision

Representing the Organization in the Primal Sketch

So far we have discussed the evidence for the idea that the image is initially processed
in parallel for intensity changes at several spatial scales, and we have looked more
specifically at one computational analysis of this very low level process, Marr's (1982)
theory of the raw primal sketch. A representation of this sort captures the lowest level
of information in the image that is reliably correlated with properties of the physical
surfaces in the real world. The representation is still extremely local and two-dimensional, however. Many researchers believe that further computations are performed on
the primal sketch to detect more global two-dimensional structure or pattern. Marr
used the term *full primal sketch* for a representation that explicitly encodes global
patterns of organization in the primal sketch.

Two related kinds of processing are typically hypothesized to be involved in finding
the organization of the primal sketch: (1) the clustering of locally similar items (bars,
blobs, and so forth) at various scales into higher-order items, and (2) the detection of
boundaries between regions. Boundaries are sometimes marked by a set of edge segments that form a continuous line or contour. Other boundaries are "virtual" boundaries between clusters of items that differ in their properties or parameter values. Figure
12.11 illustrates the two processes schematically. Clusters of similar raw sketch items

form higher-order, oriented, barlike shapes, which are quite easily perceptible. A boundary running vertically down the center of the figure is also perceptible. It is defined by the fact that all the higher-order tokens on the left side of the figure have one orientation, and all the higher-order tokens on the right side of the figure have another. The perception of the boundary requires first that the uniformity of orientation in the two areas be measured, and second that a discontinuity in this measurement between the two areas, which forms the boundary, be detected. Exactly which aspects of this sort of grouping and boundary detection are genuinely part of early vision has not been clearly established. A computational analysis must establish that low-level processes can detect a particular type of organization. Psychophysical and physiological experiments must establish that biological visual systems do in fact make the computation.

Figure 12.12 illustrates two types of visual stimuli that have been utilized in psychophysical experiments. Part (a) of the figure is a *Glass pattern*, which was produced by superimposing two copies of a random dot pattern. In the left panel one copy is rotated slightly, and in the right panel one copy is expanded slightly. Experimental subjects can detect the resulting circular and linear structures in the patterns in extremely brief exposures of less than 80 milliseconds, which is evidence that the structure is recovered by early visual processes. Stevens (1978) argued that such structure can be detected by a local, parallel process that looks at the *virtual lines* that connect points in local neighborhoods. The locally predominant virtual-line orientation predicts the perceived structure of the patterns.

Part (b) of figure 12.12 shows two cases where a boundary between two textured regions can be perceived on the basis of a difference between the two regions in the average value of a parameter. In the left panel the average size of the elements differs. In the right panel the average orientation of the elements differs. Experimental subjects can note a difference of texture and perceive the shape of the boundary in exposures of less than 200 milliseconds. This result suggests that early visual processes represent both the average value of parameters such as size and orientation and the boundaries between regions with differing average values.

The theoretical reason for hypothesizing the existence of computations that detect larger-scale two-dimensional structure is that such organization is very likely to reflect important physical properties of the surfaces in the world. Such things as lines or edges with considerable length, sets of parallel lines or stripes, and regions of similar elements are unlikely to arise as a result of factors such as accidents of illumination and viewpoint, random markings on surfaces, or noise in the imaging process (Witkin and Tenenbaum 1983).

Intrinsic Images

Although a full primal sketch contains a great deal of information that is reliably correlated with properties of the visible three-dimensional world, it does not make any explicit commitments about properties of the world. It explicitly represents only the organization of the intensity changes in the image. For example, suppose that a number of edge segments line up to form a long, continuous contour that is identified in the full primal sketch. Such a contour might represent a marking on the surface of an object, or it might represent the visible boundary of a surface, which separates an object from its background. The primal sketch does not decide between these possibilities; it says only that an important contour that requires interpretation is present. The

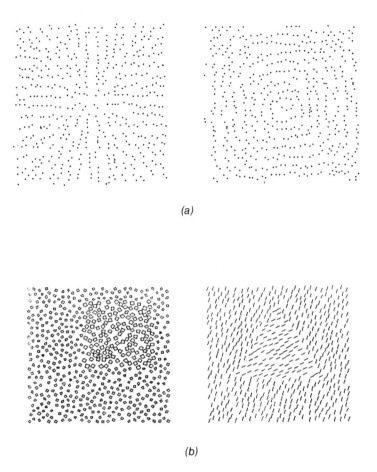

(a)

(b)

Figure 12.12
Evidence for organizational processes. (*a*) The radial and circular organization of these two *Glass patterns* can be rapidly detected. A local process that extracts and organizes virtual lines among primal sketch elements might be responsible for the rapid perception. (*b*) Textural boundaries are perceived when two textures differ in the average value of a parameter. In the left pattern the average size of the elements in the two textures differs, and in the right pattern the average orientation differs. (Part (*a*) reprinted with permission from Stevens 1978, and part (*b*) reprinted with permission from Marr 1982.)

next critical question about visual processing is how to make the transition from low-level, image-based representations to intermediate representations that explicitly encode the intrinsic properties of the scene that gave rise to the image. Such representations have been referred to as *intrinsic* images or representations (Barrow and Tenenbaum 1978).

A representative proposal is Marr's (1982) notion of the *2.5-D sketch*, a representation of visible surfaces in three dimensions. Figure 12.13 illustrates the nature of the 2.5-D sketch. The representation locally encodes the distance and orientation of the visible surfaces. Discontinuities in surface orientation and depth are explicitly represented. Unlike the primal sketch, the 2.5-D sketch assigns portions of the image to surfaces in the world and specifies the distance and orientation of those surfaces relative to the viewer. For various reasons the 2.5-D sketch is not a complete

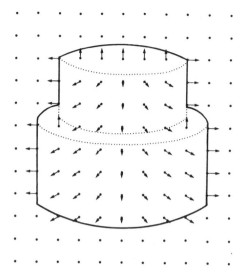

Figure 12.13
A diagrammatic representation of the 2.5-D sketch for a wedding cake suspended in front of a wall. The 2.5-D sketch encodes the orientation relative to the viewer of each small patch of surface. In the diagram the orientation information is symbolized by a small arrow perpendicular to each patch of surface. The arrows for the wall behind the cake appear as dots because they are pointing directly at the viewer. The sketch also encodes points where there are discontinuities; discontinuities in surface orientation are shown as dotted lines in the diagram, and discontinuities in depth between two surface patches are shown as black lines. Finally, the sketch encodes the distance of each patch of surface from the viewer, which is not represented on the diagram. (Reprinted with permission from Marr and Nishihara 1978.)

three-dimensional representation. For example, the surfaces have not been grouped into objects that either are or could be identified.

Something like a 2.5-D or 3-D sketch must be computed by the visual system, because it captures key aspects of our visual awareness and performance. The layout of surfaces in space seems to be naturally available in cognition and behavior, even when no identifiable objects are present in the scene. Such a representation cannot be computed only from a primal sketch representation, however. The computation must draw on a number of different types of information, and it is likely that some types are developed in distinct computational modules. The types of information include stereopsis, motion, surface texture, shape-from-shading, and color. We will discuss visual motion further here as a representative example.

Visual Motion
Under normal conditions the image input to the visual system undergoes constant change over time. Movement of the perceiver's eyes, head, or body causes the entire image to shift on the retina. Movement of an object in the world causes the image of the object to shift on the retina. Our notion of an image as a function specifying intensity at spatial positions, $I(x, y)$, should be augmented to specify intensity at a spatial position at a particular time $I(x, y, t)$. The temporal dimension of the input image poses tremendous problems for visual computation, since a particular point in the image does not necessarily represent the same bit of the world at different moments in time. When motion occurs, the visual system must figure out that at different times,

different parts of the image represent the same part of the world. The problem is compounded by the fact that motion computations must be made extremely rapidly.

Somewhat paradoxically, given that a visual system can cope with visual motion, the temporal dimension of the image is a potentially rich source of information. For example, when the perceiver is moving forward, the rate of expansion in the image specifies the perceiver's velocity, and the direction of motion of a point on the image specifies whether it will pass to the left or the right of, or collide with, the perceiver. In this case a particular kind of visual motion, often called *optical flow*, provides detailed information about motion in the world. In addition, visual motion is a potential source of information about the boundaries and shapes of objects. If an object moves in a plane perpendicular to the line of sight, all points on its image move together. This correlated motion could help the visual system to segregate the object from its background. It can also be shown mathematically that under some conditions visual motion can specify the shape of an object (Ullman 1979).

Psychological Evidence on Visual Motion Perception   Informal observation suggests that the human visual system has a remarkable ability to process and utilize motion information. Consider a pass receiver in football, running at full speed and simultaneously judging the motions of the ball and an approaching defender. Or consider the degree to which our ability to pick out a bird or small animal in foliage is aided by its movement. Psychological experiments confirm and extend this impression. Some of the most striking experiments show that we can indeed recover three-dimensional shape from motion information. In one study Wallach and O'Connell (1953) bent pieces of wire into abstract three-dimensional shapes and mounted them on a rotating turntable. They placed a light behind the rotating shape in such a way that it cast a sharp, ever changing shadow on a screen, which was observed by the subject. The shadow was a two-dimensional image varying in time. All other information that was present when viewing the rotating shape directly had been removed. The subjects perceived the three-dimensional form of the wire shape with no trouble at all; in fact, the perception of three-dimensional form is so strong in this situation that it is impossible to perceive the shadow as a rubbery two-dimensional figure.

Psychological research makes it clear that motion perception is a complex process. Experiments on the minimum conditions for visual motion perception have led to the hypothesis that at least two rather different processes are involved (Braddick 1979; Nakayama 1985). The first process is a short-range process that apparently can register the localized motion of low-level visual information, such as intensity gradients or zero-crossings. Braddick (1974, 1979) studied this process with visual displays that alternated between two square arrays of black and white dots. The two arrays were random and uncorrelated except for a central rectangular patch that was simply shifted horizontally from one array to the other. When viewed alone, each array appeared to be a random arrangement of black and white dots. When the two arrays were alternated in time, subjects clearly perceived a rectangular object moving back and forth. However, a clear perception of the rectangle only occurred when the amount of shift was under 15 minutes of angular displacement, and the time between the two displays was less than 100 milliseconds. These tight constraints on space and time approximate conditions of actual continuous motion across the retina, even though the display is discrete.

The evidence for a second, *long-range* process of motion perception comes from studies of *apparent motion*, which is sometimes called the *phi-phenomenon*. This process can apparently track identifiable higher-level visual elements such as edges or lines over longer time spans and distances. Apparent motion experiments demonstrate this dramatically by alternately flashing two displays that are quite widely separated in space and time. For example, the two frames of display can consist of a single black dot on a white background, with the dot horizontally displaced between the frames. The dot appears to move continuously back and forth even for spatial displacements of many degrees of visual angle and for interframe intervals of 300 milliseconds. The perception of continuous motion in such highly discrete displays suggests that there is a process that detects correspondences between image elements over long ranges of space and time and interprets them in terms of motion in the image and the world. In the stroboscopic apparent motion display the long-range process in a sense "fills in" motion that is not actually present. In the natural world the long-range process does not lead to illusions because there is no natural class of visible objects that jump around discretely in space and that must be discriminated from smoothly moving objects. Given the existence of the long-range process, a nice puzzle is whether and how we in fact know that there are not discretely moving visible objects in the real world that we have never noticed because they appear to move smoothly.

Physiological Evidence on Visual Motion   There is considerable evidence for the existence of specialized neurophysiological circuitry for motion processing. Motion-specific channels or neurons should show signs of adaptation or fatigue with prolonged stimulation, and, indeed, compelling motion aftereffects are easy to produce. The waterfall illusion can be experienced by staring steadily at a waterfall for several minutes and then turning to look at the surrounding stationary scenery. A profoundly ambivalent perception occurs: the scenery appears to be moving upward, and yet it remains in the same place. The illusion can be explained by the existence of a fatigueable physiological channel that is specific to downward motion and separate from other channels that can independently register the spatial position of objects in the scene. The spiral aftereffect can be produced by mounting a painted spiral on a rotating turntable, viewing it for several minutes, and then stopping the turntable. The spiral appears to rotate in the opposite direction. The directional specificity of such effects has been studied quantitatively using contrast thresholds for sinusoidal gratings. Prolonged viewing of a grating moving in a particular direction elevates its contrast threshold relative to the threshold for the same grating moving in the opposite direction (Pantle 1978).

Physiological recordings from single neurons in the visual systems of several species also strongly suggest the existence of specialized motion detection machinery. Many simple and complex cells in the primary visual cortex respond preferentially to stimuli moving in a particular direction (for example, 29 percent of the cells sampled by De Valois, Yund, and Hepler 1982). Thus, if the best stimulus for a cell is a thin vertical line, the cell might respond strongly if the line is moved from left to right across its receptive field and not respond at all if the line is moved from right to left. These cells may be involved in short-range motion perception (Marr and Ullman 1981).

Cells sensitive to visual motion have also been found outside of the visual cortex. For example, a small area on the temporal lobe, called *MT*, contains neurons with large receptive fields that respond preferentially not only to motion in a specific direction but also to a specific velocity (Nakayama 1985). Unlike cortical cells, which have a particular optimal stimulus, these cells respond to a wider variety of stimuli as long as they are moving at the right speed in the right direction. This type of response requires a good deal of computation to separate out speed and direction from other properties of the stimulation, so it is not surprising that the cells occur not in the visual cortex but instead in an area that receives input fibers from the visual cortex.

There is now substantial evidence that MT neurons are output neurons for motion perception. In a series of experiments on monkeys Movshon, Newsome, and several colleagues (Movshon and Newsome 1992) were able to show that MT neurons are both necessary and sufficient for motion discrimination. Part (*a*) of figure 12.14 diagrammatically illustrates the stimuli, which the experimenters displayed on a CRT. A random motion trial consists of a rapid sequence of frames, each containing randomly placed dots. Successive frames are separated by about 50 milliseconds, which is brief enough for short-range motion detection, but there is no correlation in the positions of the dots on successive frames, so no motion is detected. In a 100 percent correlation trial, the initial positions of the dots are random, but successive frames displace all of the dots slightly in the same direction. Such a display produces a strong perception of coherent, continuous motion (although the dots do not in fact move continuously across the screen). In a 50 percent correlation trial, successive frames displace half of the dots in the same direction and put the rest of the dots in random positions. The percentage of correlated dots could be varied throughout the range from 0 to 100 percent. The speed of motion could also be varied by varying the amount of displacement from frame to frame. As shown in part (*b*) of the figure, small lesions to MT produced a dramatic (temporary) decrement in the monkeys' ability to discriminate motion in these displays.

In a second experiment the researchers showed that the responses of MT neurons accurately predicted monkeys' discrimination of the direction of motion. In this experiment an MT neuron was located with electrodes, and its preferred direction of motion was determined through electrophysiological recording during strong motion stimulation. Stimuli with varying directions of motion and varying degrees of correlation were then presented in the portion of the visual field to which the cell responded. Over a large number of neurons in two monkeys, the responses of the neurons were compared with the monkeys' behavioral performance (monkeys chose a direction by moving their eyes toward one of two small lights, one of which was in the true direction of motion). The responses of the neurons predicted the monkeys' choices nearly perfectly.

In a third experiment small populations of about 100 MT neurons were given weak electrical stimulation via an electrode. Since nearby neurons tend to have similar preferred directions, it was likely that the stimulated neurons would be relatively homogeneous in their directional preferences. Stimulation increased the monkeys' tendency to choose the preferred direction. Although the size of the effect varied, probably due to chance variation in the homogeneity of the stimulated populations, the effect was equivalent to adding a fixed amount of correlated motion to the display.

These experiments provide strong evidence that MT is primarily concerned with motion and that it plays a strong role in the discrimination of motion in the image. They are also a powerful demonstration of the modularity of the visual system. The representation provided by MT neurons is probably not the final output representation for motion perception, however. Although MT neurons do encode the rough distance

(a)

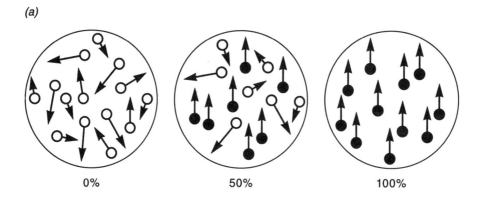

(b)

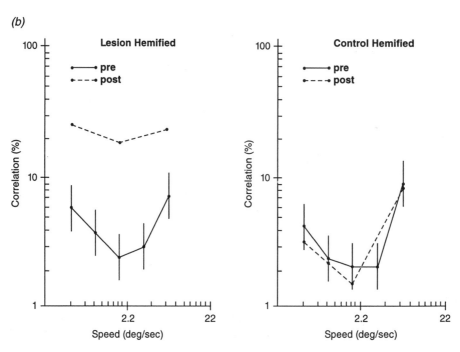

Figure 12.14

Newsome and Paré's (1988) experiment on the necessity of MT signals for motion discrimination. (*a*) Diagrammatic illustration of the stimuli. Arrows represent the direction and extent of motion from frame to frame. Empty circles represent randomly displaced dots. Filled circles represent dots with correlated displacements. See text for further explanation. (*b*) Effect of a small unilateral MT lesion on motion discrimination performance. Each panel plots the threshold of motion detection at various speeds of visual motion. The threshold is expressed as the amount of correlation that must be introduced into the stimulus for motion to be perceived. Since the MT area on the left side of the brain only responds to the right half of the visual field, and vice versa, each animal served as its own post-lesion control. The left panel shows pre- and post-lesion performance when the stimulus is delivered to the visual half-field that stimulates the lesioned MT area. The right panel shows the same data when the stimulus is delivered to the visual half-field that stimulates the unlesioned MT area. Performance in the lesion half-field deteriorated by about a factor of 10. Performance in the control half-field was unaffected. (Adapted with permission from Newsome and Paré 1988.)

between the organism and a region in the image, they do not encode whether the motion in that region of the image is toward or away from the organism (Maunsell and Van Essen 1983). Thus, the neurons encode image motion correlated with slices in depth rather than three-dimensional motion in the world. Local motion in the image is ambiguous with respect to motion in depth, since a particular rate and direction of image motion can be produced by many motion trajectories in depth in the world. The computation of three-dimensional motion requires more integration over time and space than is apparently computed in MT (Saito et al. 1986) and may be enhanced by contributions from other sources of information.

Visual Motion Computations   The computational analysis of visual motion has proven to be difficult. First the two-dimensional motion in the image must be measured, and then it must be interpreted to yield information about the three-dimensional world. Hildreth's (1984a,b) work on the measurement of short-range, or continuous, image motion illustrates some of the complexities of the problem. At an instant in time the motion at a point in the image can be expressed as a vector V, which specifies the velocity and direction of the motion at that point. The computational problem of measuring the motion in the changing image is thus to recover these vectors from the changing intensity values in the image. Formally, the problem is to compute the two-dimensional vector field $V(x, y, t)$ from the changing image $I(x, y, t)$. $V(x, y, t)$ is called the *velocity field*.

Hildreth hypothesizes that the initial local measurements re made on zero-crossings detected by Mexican-hat—type spatial filters. There are two computational arguments for this approach. First, since the zero-crossings are correlated with physical features of the world, the motion measurements will also be correlated with these features. Second, the zero-crossings occur where intensity changes in the image are at a maximum. When these intensity gradients move in the image, they lead to maximum change over time. Thus, measurements at zero-crossings will be the most accurate possible. As we have seen, there is also good physiological evidence that spatial filtering is the first step in the visual process.

Unfortunately, the velocity field cannot be directly recovered from local measurements, because of the *aperture* problem. Suppose that the short-range motion measurements are made by direction-sensitive simple cells in the cortex that respond to the movement of short zero-crossing segments. Each cell is essentially looking through a small window, or aperture, at a local part of a contour. It cannot tell which direction the contour is really moving in. Figure 12.15 shows why this is the case. Each local measurement constrains the vector at that point, but it does not fully specify it. The computation must combine the constraints provided by the local measurements to come up with a full, consistent velocity field.

Attempts to combine the local constraints into a single field run up against a second problem. Many velocity fields are consistent with the local measurements. The constraints provided by the local measurements must be supplemented by some further constraint in order to compute a unique velocity field. One possible approach would be to try to apply constraints from longer-range motion measurements or from other information sources, such as stereopsis or shape. Hildreth, however, explored the possibilities for constraining the computation without using other sources of information in the image. The *smoothness constraint* arises from a basic property of the physical world: the surfaces of objects are smooth relative to their distance from the viewer.

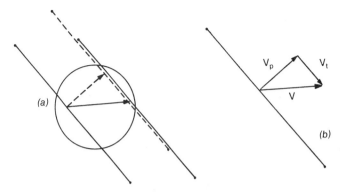

Figure 12.15
The aperture problem. (a) The arrows illustrate two possible movements of a line viewed through a small circular aperture. The dotted vector produces the dotted line, and the solid vector produces the solid line. The two movements produce the same result within the aperture and therefore are indistinguishable to any local process that is restricted to the aperture. (b) The solid vector in (a), symbolized V, can be decomposed into two components. The component V_p is perpendicular to the moving contour (and happens to be identical to the dotted vector in (a)). The component V_t is tangent to the contour. In general, a local operator can only measure the perpendicular component of visual motion. The tangent component must be recovered by integrating a number of local measurements. (Based on Hildreth 1984a.)

Smooth surfaces in motion give rise to smooth velocity fields in the image; that is, the directions and velocities of nearby motion vectors tend to vary continuously. However, there are still many smooth velocity fields that are consistent with any set of local measurements. This led Hildreth to propose the further constraint of choosing the smooth velocity field with the least overall variation. Hildreth proved that under quite general conditions a unique smooth field with minimum variation exists and can be computed from the local measurements.

This version of the smoothness constraint often yields an incorrect velocity field, however. That is, the actual velocity field in the image is different from the smooth field with the least variation. Thus, a perceptual system that utilizes the smoothness constraint will incorrectly perceive the motions and shapes of objects. At this point the theorist has a number of options, which include formulating another constraint or utilizing other sources of information. Hildreth also considered the possibility that the human visual system actually does obey the smoothness constraint, making it susceptible to certain kinds of motion illusions. Computations based on the smoothness constraint agree well with a number of known psychological phenomena in motion perception (Hildreth 1984a,b), predicting both cases of correct and cases of illusory perception. Figure 12.16 illustrates the result for the barber pole illusion. The helical stripe on a barber pole appears to move downward (or upward), although each point on the image of the stripe moves horizontally. The smoothest velocity field for the barber pole stripe turns out to be vertical, predicting the illusion. The perception of the pole is profoundly ambivalent because we simultaneously perceive downward motion and the fixed position of the pole. The perception of the fixed position of the pole and our knowledge that it is merely rotating cannot overcome the perception of vertical movement, however. This suggests that the motion computation involved is primitive and isolated from some of the other sources of information that might inform it.

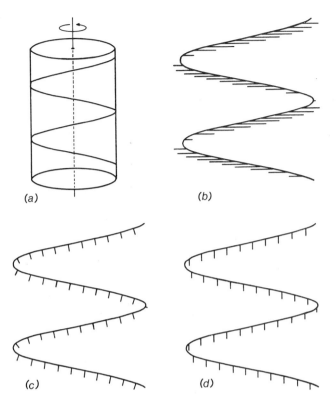

Figure 12.16
The barber pole illusion. (*a*) A rotating, transparent barber pole with a single helical stripe. (*b*) The image of the stripe and the actual velocity field, symbolized by the short line segments attached to various portions of the image. (*c*) The initial perpendicular velocity vectors extracted by local, aperture-restricted measurements. (*d*) The velocity field computed by integrating the local measurements using the least variation constraint. The computed velocity field is incorrect, showing uniform downward motion instead of the horizontal motions in (*b*), but it agrees with our illusory perception. (Reprinted with permission from Hildreth 1984b.)

Neural Network Models of Motion Computation   A number of connectionist and neural network models of visual motion computation have been proposed. Wang, Mathur, and Koch (1990) argue that the activity of direction-selective MT neurons represents the velocity, or optical flow, field. They propose a neural network for computing the optical flow field that incorporates the smoothness constraint. Although the mathematical foundations of the model are too complicated to present here, a block diagram is presented in figure 12.17. The responses of units in the model closely parallel the responses of actual neurons to stimuli, similar to the barber pole, that produce illusory directions of motion. In one such experiment a pattern of vertical stripes moving horizontally is superimposed on a pattern of horizontal stripes moving vertically. Human observers perceive a plaid pattern moving in a diagonal direction, even though all points in the image are moving either horizontally or vertically. The diagonal direction is predicted by the smoothness constraint. Thirty percent of MT neurons and the optical flow units at the top level of the model respond with the perceived diagonal direction. Direction-sensitive neurons in the primary visual cortex and the initial

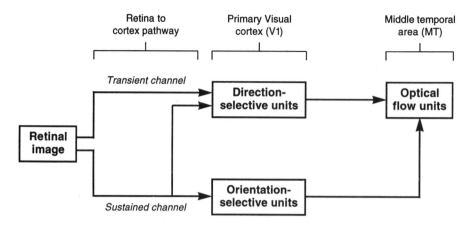

Figure 12.17
A block diagram of Wang, Mathur, and Koch's optical flow model with possible neuronal correspondences. The sustained channel carries the outputs of retinal units that compute the local, circular Mexican-
hat operator discussed earlier in the chapter (see figures 12.3 and 12.4). These units respond to local spatial
variations in intensity that are relatively stable over time. The transient channel carries signals from units
that have the same spatial profiles but that respond only to rapid temporal changes in local contrast. The
orientation-selective units correspond to the cortical simple cells described earlier (figures 12.9 and 12.10).
The model combines the signals in the sustained and transient channels to feed direction-selective cortical
simple cells that are sensitive to oriented edges that are moving in a direction perpendicular to the edge.
Both types of units are common in the primary visual cortex. An optical flow unit represents a particular
spatial location and direction of image motion. For each point in the image there are flow units that
represent a number of different directions of motion. The coding of direction is relatively coarse, and the
optical flow at each point in the image is represented by the population of responses of all the flow
units for that point. Each flow unit receives input from all orientation-selective and direction-selective
units at its spatial location. These inputs tend to force flow cells to respond in terms of the local motion
data that they carry. Each flow unit is also connected to other flow units that encode other directions of
motion and neighboring spatial locations. These lateral interactions adjust the responses of the flow units
so that they yield a smooth flow field in which motion directions in nearby regions are similar. The joint
influence of the lower-level units and the lateral interactions produces a smooth flow field that is reasonably consistent with the lower-level data and that agrees with perceived optical flow for various laboratory displays (see text). (Adapted with permission from Wang, Mathur, and Koch 1990.)

direction-selective units in the model respond only to the horizontal and vertical
directions of the component striped patterns. The model thus makes the case that MT
computes a smoothed velocity field that is not present at lower levels of the visual
pathway.

12.4 High-Level Visual Processes

The Goals of High-Level Processing
High-level visual processes complete the job of delivering a coherent interpretation of
the image. It is assumed that the low-level and intermediate processes make available
a useful, segmented representation of the two- and three-dimensional structure of the
image. The high-level processes must determine what objects are present in the scene
and interpret their interrelations. For example, the intermediate representation of an
outdoor scene might contain a large, greenish, textured blob, connected to a horizontal, greenish, textured surface below it by a brownish, vertically oriented, cylindrical

shape that bifurcates into the blob. High-level processes might interpret these segments as the crown of a tree, a lawn, and the tree's trunk. The high-level processes might also identify several connected rectilinear surfaces as the walls and roof of a house and might confirm that one wall of the house extends behind the crown of the tree. Obviously, the identification of objects and their interrelations provides the interface between vision and general knowledge. For example, identifying a large object in a scene as a house vastly expands the range of potential thoughts and actions bearing on the object. Without the identification the perceiver would be able to approach the house, avoid colliding with it, determine whether its top surfaces were accessible from the branched object next to it, and so on. With the identification an astonishing range of highly detailed information becomes instantly available, which can be used to guide mundane actions such as opening the front door or sophisticated problem-solving processes such as estimating the probable income and political views of the inhabitants. This powerful interface between vision and general knowledge is perhaps the most important thing that distinguishes human vision from the visual capacities of other animals.

An additional, controversial problem concerning high-level vision is the extent to which high-level processes assist the operation of lower-level processes, through the top-down flow of hypotheses about what is present in the image. For example, the identification of the house and tree in the outdoor scene might assist lower-level processes in their segmentation of the area of the image in the region of the tree, making it possible to confirm the hypothesis that a wall of the house extends continuously behind the tree, forming a single surface that is partially occluded and shadowed by the tree. Many computer vision systems make extensive use of this kind of model- or hypothesis-driven top-down processing (Hanson and Riseman 1978b; Binford 1982). Although the role of top-down processing in human vision is hotly debated, we will largely assume that lower-level processes deliver relatively reliable information, allowing us to concentrate on problems that are specific to high-level vision. More specifically, we will concentrate on the problem of identifying individual objects and leave aside the additional problems that arise when trying to arrive at a representation of an entire scene containing multiple objects, supporting or background surfaces, and possibly a horizon or skyline.

The Problems of High-Level Processing
Even if we assume that high-level processes operate on reliable representations, the job of interpretation is formidable. The information in the intermediate representation must somehow be matched to information about the appearance of thousands of objects that is stored in a long-term memory. The intermediate representation is relative to the point of view of the perceiver. It is a *viewer-centered* representation. Much of the information in it is not strictly relevant to the category membership of the objects in the scene. For example, the distance from the viewer and the orientation relative to the viewer of an object's surfaces are not intrinsic characteristics of the object. A refrigerator does not cease to be a refrigerator if it is moved closer to the observer or rotated slightly relative to the observer. Furthermore, in a viewer-centered representation information that is relevant to the identification of an object can be occluded by the object itself or by other objects. Four of the six sides of a refrigerator might be invisible from a particular observation point, and half of one of the visible sides might be occluded by nearby cabinetry.

Much object identification is also more properly characterized as visual categorization. That is, it requires the assignment of a novel object to a category—for example, recognizing that a previously unseen rectangular solid is a refrigerator rather than a telephone booth or a china cabinet. A view of a particular object contains a tremendous amount of visual detail, only some of which is relevant to its category membership. The details of a refrigerator might include the door handle and the color of the door; the handle, which might be partially occluded by a dish towel threaded through it, is relevant to its identity, and the color, which might be highly salient, is not. Somehow, the concrete detail available in intermediate representations must be matched against the necessarily abstract representations of visual categories.

Finally, human object identification is remarkable not only for its flexibility but also for its speed. A typical result from laboratory experiments in psychology is that a photograph of an arbitrary common object with no scenic context can be identified in an exposure of 100 milliseconds or less (Biederman 1985). Given such a brief exposure, a subject can typically speak the name of the object in about 800 milliseconds. Such results confirm the efficiency of low-level visual processes, but they also demonstrate the rapid activation of visual categories in long-term memory by visual input. Biederman (1985) has estimated that the average adult can recognize exemplars from roughly 3,000 basic visual categories, many of which contain several distinct visual types (for example, floor lamps versus table lamps). The recognition of each of these categories is complicated by the factors just mentioned, such as variations in orientation, occlusion, and the abstractness of the categories. A theory of object recognition should give some account of this remarkable efficiency.

Basic Ingredients of High-Level Processing

The central theoretical problem in object recognition, then, is to explain how abstract representations of visual categories in long-term memory (LTM) can be rapidly retrieved, or *indexed*, by the information present in low- or intermediate-level representations of visual input. A proposed LTM representation must express the distinguishing characteristics of visual categories in a vocabulary that is either immediately available or easily computable from intermediate representation. In order to handle the human ability to master new visual categories, the representation must in some sense also be highly general.

A crucial subproblem is to specify how the decomposition of objects into parts figures in the recognition process. Our knowledge of objects intimately depends on our knowledge of their parts, and it seems likely that decomposition into parts plays an important role in the recognition process as well. For example, in cases of partial occlusion the recognition of a part can drive the recognition of the entire object. A slapstick example is recognizing the presence of another person in a room from seeing a pair of feet protruding beneath a curtain. The use of parts also seems likely to be crucial in recognizing deformable or *nonrigid* objects, such as shirts, people, or beer cans. However, parts can be useful in recognition only if they can be at least partially determined on the basis of the intermediate representation prior to identification. That is, the system must be able to carve an object up into its parts before recognizing it. In a sense, this is another aspect of the segmentation problem.

A final problem in object recognition is the representation of shape. Although features such as size, color, and texture play a role in recognition, shape is a critical and often dominant factor. Our ability to easily recognize black-and-white line drawings of common objects provides informal evidence of the central role of shape in recognition. Line drawings lack the rich variation in color, texture, and shading that is present in natural and photographic images, yet in laboratory settings they can be recognized and named with virtually equal speed and accuracy (Biederman 1985). Coming up with a plausible theory of shape representation is a daunting problem for the theorist, however. Shapes seem to have limitless variety and subtlety and to evoke complex esthetic responses. Would any visual theorist dare take on the problem of explaining the painter Georgia O'Keeffe's (1976) mental representation of organic forms, for example? Some researchers have addressed the problem by developing general mathematical descriptions of shape that make no commitments regarding human shape processing (Brady et al. 1985). The mathematical prerequisites for this approach rule out further discussion of it here. Others have restricted themselves to the problem of rapid recognition, arguing that the initial activation of LTM shape descriptions involves a rather qualitative, finite, and coarse encoding (Biederman 1985; Richards and Hoffman 1985). Crudely put, the argument is that recognizing an iris or a pear in one-tenth of a second requires a rough-and-ready form of shape indexing that does not encode the detailed configuration of the particular shape. We will say more about this second approach in the following section.

Theories of Object Recognition

The requirements just discussed suggest the outline of a high-level processor that is capable of recognizing an object in an image. The object as a whole must be segmented from the rest of the image. Here, we assume that lower-level processes accomplish this job. The object must be segmented into parts. The shapes of the parts and their interrelations must then be represented in a way that is suitable for indexing a catalogue of visual categories.

Finding Parts   Hoffman and Richards (1984) have shown that an object can be naturally segmented into parts prior to describing the shapes of the parts. They base their analysis of parts on a powerful geometric regularity called the *transversality principle* that applies when a two-part object is formed by sticking two pieces together. Figure 12.18 illustrates that the joint between the two parts forms a discontinuity that is concave, or pointing into the object. Given this regularity, we can divide the surface of a three-dimensional object into parts by finding contours of concave discontinuity. As the figure illustrates, the joint between two clearly perceivable parts of an object can also be smooth. In such cases the transversality principle fails because there are no discontinuous creases on the object: the entire surface of the object is continuous, or smooth. To cover these cases, Hoffman and Richards develop a generalization of transversality that finds local points where the curvature of the surface has the greatest concavity relative to the surrounding area.

Segmenting an object at the points of maximum local concavity generally accords well with immediate intuitions about the boundaries of parts (aside from some interesting questions about the status of depressions and holes). A more subtle indication of the psychological correctness of the principle is that it predicts the segmentation of well-known reversing figures, some of which are illustrated in figure 12.19.

Assuming the usefulness of the principle of segmenting objects at their concavities, the next question is whether the concavities can be located reliably in low- or intermediate-level visual representations. Hoffman and Richards argue that the three-

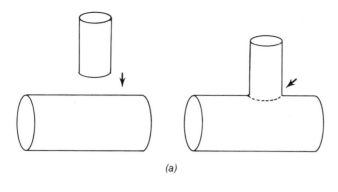

(a)

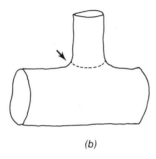

(b)

Figure 12.18
The transversality principle. (a) When one piece of stovepipe is stuck into another one, the joint between the two parts, marked by a dotted line, is a concave crease. In general, such creases identify boundaries between parts. (b) In many cases, such as this tree branch, the boundary between parts is smooth. In these cases the part boundary can be identified with a contour that follows points of maximum concave curvature. (Based on Hoffman and Richards 1984.)

dimensional part boundaries can indeed be recovered from lower-level representations. For example, a concavity on the surface of an object can show up as a concavity in the line that defines the boundary, or silhouette, of the object in the image. Conversely, concavities in the two-dimensional silhouette of an object can be interpreted as cues to the presence of three-dimensional parts. This concavity principle is qualitative in the sense that the presence of a part can be detected over a wide range of orientations.

Hoffman and Richards's work is another example of the search for highly general constraints or uniformities in the physical world that are encoded by the image-formation process. Their generalization of the transversality principle has some very promising properties for the development of a theory of high-level visual processing. Parts can be identified in an intermediate representation that contains only local information about surface curvature. Thus, the description of the global shape of an object or its parts does not have to precede segmentation into parts. Since the procedure finds the same cut points over a range of orientations, it also does not require an intermediate representation that contains highly accurate depth information.

Representing Shape A widely shared approach to shape representation is to decompose the problem of representing the shape of an entire object into the problem of

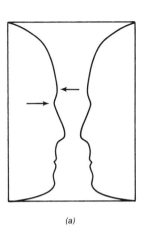 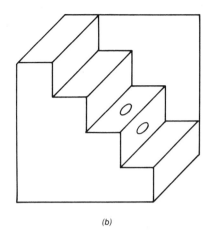

(a)   (b)

Figure 12.19

Hoffman and Richards's segmentation principles help explain the appearance of reversing figures. (a) The reversing goblet can be seen either as a goblet or as two human profiles. Why are the two perceptions so incompatible? One reason is that the segmentation points for the goblet are different from those for the face. The top arrow is a segmentation point for the goblet because it is a local point of maximum concave curvature, where concavity is defined as "pointing into" the figure. When the faces are perceived, the figure shifts to the other side of the contour; concavities become convexities and vice versa. Thus, the upper arrow no longer marks a segmentation point, and the lower arrow marks a new segmentation point. What was a point of convexity on the goblet has become a point of concavity on the face. (b) The reversing staircase can be seen either as a staircase viewed from above or as a staircase viewed from below (for most viewers the below view emerges spontaneously after staring at the figure for a while). In the above view the two dots on the staircase appear to be on the same stair because the edge between them is convex relative to the staircase. In the below view the two dots appear to lie on different stairs because the edge between them is now concave relative to the staircase. (Adapted from Hoffman and Richards 1984.)

representing the shapes of its parts and then representing the spatial relations of the parts. If an object is segmented at concavities, then there is a limit to the complexity of the shape of a single part. It is still a formidable problem to develop a plausible representation for simple parts and test it for psychological validity.

Researchers have typically argued against detailed templates for shape and in favor of descriptions built from some finite primitive vocabulary that allows the basic form of a part to be compactly described. A number of plausible systems of shape description have been investigated. We will discuss the technique of *generalized cylinders* (or *cones*), which has played a key role in several theories of shape. The concept is illustrated in figure 12.20. We can think of a cylinder as generated by moving a circle along a straight line that is perpendicular to its center. We can then generalize this notion in various ways: we can move any two-dimensional shape along an axis; we can allow the shape to expand or contract; we can allow the axis to be curved. Clearly, the representation of an object as a generalized cylinder can be quite compact, consisting of descriptions of its cross-sectional shape, the undulations of its axis, and the rate of expansion and contraction of the cross section. The representational problem is further simplified if we restrict ourselves to describing parts, because a complex generalized cylinder will generally have local concavities that trigger segmentation into parts. For example, although the wineglass in the figure is a single, rather complex generalized

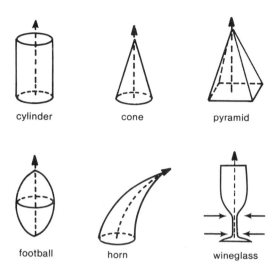

cylinder   cone   pyramid

football   horn   wineglass

Figure 12.20
Generalized cylinders. In each object the dashed line represents the central axis of the object. The objects can be described in terms of the movement of a cross-sectional shape along an axis. Cylinder: a circle moves along a straight axis. Cone: a circle contracts as it moves along a straight axis. Pyramid: a square contracts as it moves along a straight axis. American football: a circle expands and then contracts as it moves along a straight axis. Horn: a circle contracts as it moves along a curved axis. Wineglass: a circle contracts and then expands, creating concave segmentation points marked by arrows.

cylinder, it can be segmented into a bowl, a stem, and a base, each of which has a simple description. An important research question, of course, is just how adequate the generalized cylinder representation is for the range of objects that the human visual system can deal with.

Assuming that generalized cylinders are used to represent parts, the next question is whether the correct representation of a part can be derived from its more primitive and local representation in the low- or intermediate-level data. Marr (1977) and Biederman (1985) have argued that the information available at lower levels can drive the construction of generalized cylinder representations quite naturally. Biederman, for example, proposes that a low- or intermediate-level representation that has been segmented for parts allows the efficient identification of four parameters for generalized cylinders, where each parameter can take on only two or three qualitative values. His scheme is given in table 12.1.

Biederman argues that each of the parameter values is reflected in a regularity in lower-level representations. For example, a curved contour in the image always arises from a curved three-dimensional contour. A straight contour typically arises from a straight three-dimensional contour (with the exception of rare views of curved contours where the curvature lies strictly in a plane that contains the line of sight). Thus, the two parameters that involve a qualitative distinction between straightness and curvature can be identified with high reliability from lower-level representations. Their identification is also not very sensitive to shifts in viewpoint. Similar, though somewhat more complex, arguments can be made concerning the symmetry and constancy of cross-section parameters.

Table 12.1
The four shape parameters in Biederman's (1985) theory of rapid object identification

Parameter	Possible values	Example
Edges of cross section	Straight	Rectangle
	Curved	Circle
Symmetry of cross section	Shape unchanged by rotation or reflection	Circle, square
	Shape unchanged by reflection	Ellipse, rectangle
	Asymmetrical	Triangle with three unequal sides
Size change of cross section	Constant	Cylinder
	Expands	Cone
	Expands and contracts	Football
Curvature of axis	Straight	Cone
	Curved	Horn

In principle, this simplified set of parameters is rich enough to support rapid object recognition. Since the value of each parameter can combine with any of the values of the other parameters, Biederman's scheme generates 36 types of parts ($2 \times 3 \times 3 \times 2$). If we assume that objects typically have two or more parts and that the parts can be joined in two or more ways, a space of several million potential objects is generated. A number of other approaches to shape recognition have a similar thrust, for example, those of Marr and Nishihara (1978) and Richards and Hoffman (1985).

The importance of the segmentation process is suggested by one of Biederman's (1985) psychological experiments. Line drawings of common objects were degraded in two ways by deleting parts of their contours. Nonrecoverable deletions were performed by deleting the concavities that specify the segmentation of the object into its parts. Enough of the region of the concavity was deleted that the contours could not be recovered by extending what remained into the deleted area. Recoverable deletions were made by deleting an equal amount of contour in places that did not destroy the segmentation. When subjects tried to identify the objects after brief exposures ranging from 100 milliseconds to 5 seconds, the recoverable pictures proved to be much more identifiable than the nonrecoverable pictures. This result demonstrates the high information value of regions of concavity and by inference their use in segmentation.

Representing the Entire Object   A theory of object representation must specify not only a vocabulary of parts but also a method of describing the arrangements of parts into entire objects. This is one of the most difficult problems in high-level vision. Many researchers have argued that the parts of an object ought to be given a *hierarchical* representation in which some parts are represented relative to or as part of other parts (Marr and Nishihara 1978). For example, an arm can be thought of as a single part of the human body. It can also be broken down into three parts: the upper arm, the forearm, and the hand. The hand can be further broken down into fingers, and so on.

Hierarchical representations, in which the object is broken down into parts that are in turn broken down into parts, have various theoretical advantages. They capture naturally the varying sizes, or spatial scales, of parts, which potentially allows a part to be identified from a crude large-scale description without reference to its subparts.

Thus, an arm could be identified simply as an elongated cylinder without requiring full segmentation of the hand and fingers. Similarly, a finger could be identified as a smaller-scale elongated cylinder, ignoring a wart that was segmented as a part but is irrelevant to identification. Hierarchical representation can also help solve the problem of representing variation in how the parts of an object are arranged. A finger, for example, can have many different spatial relations to the rest of the body, caused by arm, hand, and finger movement. Clearly, the range of finger positions should be described relative to the hand and not relative to the arm or to the entire body (since on occasion the tip of the right little finger will appear, for example, stuck into the left ear).

If the parts of an object are represented as generalized cylinders, then much of the information about the spatial arrangement of the parts can be captured by describing how the axes of the cylinders are interrelated (Marr and Nishihara 1978). Thus, we can represent the axis of a foot relative to the axis of a leg: the end of the foot axis begins roughly at the end of the leg axis; it is oriented at roughly right angles to the leg axis; it points in a forward direction; under normal conditions it can rotate to a specified range of positions that combine side-to-side and upward-downward movement. In this kind of representation the position of the axis of every subpart is described relative to the axis of its immediate superordinate part. The ultimate reference axis is the overall axis of the biggest part or the entire object. The major axis for the human body would be the axis of the torso. Such representations are genuinely object centered because they make no reference to the viewpoint on the object in an image; that is, the major axis is not required to be positioned in any specified way relative to the image coordinates. The human body would be accorded the same description in front view and three-quarter view, for example. Such representations are also called *canonical* because a single LTM description characterizes the object regardless of viewpoint.

A hierarchical representation that is organized around a qualitative description of parts and their relations is clearly closely related to forms of knowledge representation that have been hypothesized for nonvisual concepts. It is a schema or frame for representing visual information. At this level of encoding, visual and nonvisual knowledge are in a similar enough format to interact easily, and many of the general techniques developed for nonvisual knowledge can be applied in the visual domain. We can make use of pointers to other frames, default values, ranges of values, and exception handling. In fact, we innocently used examples of visual knowledge in earlier chapters without exploring all of the complexities involved. If our frame for a bactrian camel specifies two humps, we now know something about how to describe the humps in a way that is useful to high-level visual processing: they may be described as generalized cylinders with a certain parametric description, and their axes have a specified spatial relation to the axis of the camel's body. Furthermore, we now have a better idea how the humps might be identified in the image, beginning with low-level processes that find the local intensity changes that mark their boundaries and continuing on to a high-level process that segments them from the rest of the camel.

The Retrieval Process   Let us finally consider the remaining problems that must be overcome by a process that can retrieve an object-centered representation from a large LTM catalogue on the basis of lower-level information. An object-centered representation must be built from the lower-level information. The LTM catalogue must then be searched for possible matches. We can imagine this being a one-step process or a cooperative process in which partial descriptions activate possible matches that guide the refinement of the description.

One problem that can arise in building a high-level description is that the viewpoint on the object may distort some of the needed parameters beyond rapid recovery. For example, the axis of a generalized cylinder is severely distorted in the image if it is nearly aligned with the line of sight. It may be difficult to recover it, even qualitatively. A second problem is that one or more parts may be partly or completely occluded in the image. Figure 12.21 suggests that the high-level processes in the human visual system are affected by these factors. An upright wineglass with its major axis fairly perpendicular to the line of sight seems more familiar and easier to identify than foreshortened and occluded views.

Psychological experiments confirm this impression. Palmer, Rosch, and Chase (1981) photographed a set of common objects from twelve different viewpoints. One group of subjects rated each viewpoint of each object for typicality or familiarity. Another group of subjects had to name the photographs in a rapid identification task in which their naming response times were recorded. The typicality ratings of the viewpoints predicted the response times very well. It is important to note that this experiment also

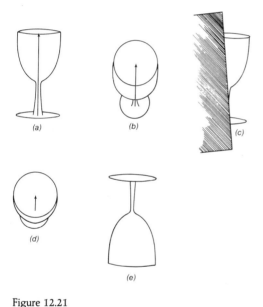

Figure 12.21
Some distortions that can interfere with rapid object identification. (a) An ideal view of a wineglass. The parts and their segmentation points are visible. The major axis of the shape, shown by the arrow, is roughly perpendicular to the line of sight, allowing easy recovery of a generalized cylinder description. (b) A foreshortened view of the wineglass. One of the segmentation points is completely occluded and the image of the major axis of the glass is much shorter than the actual axis in three-dimensional space. (c) The wineglass is occluded by another surface, making it difficult to find and describe all of the parts. (d) A radically foreshortened view. The stem is completely occluded by the glass itself, and the major axis is severely distorted. (e) An inverted view. Inversion can lead to misdescription because the identification process tends to assume that objects appear in standard vertical orientations. That is, the top of the object defined in terms of the current viewpoint is assumed to correspond to the top of the object defined in terms of object-centered coordinates. In this case what is actually the base of the glass might be mis-described as its top.

confirms that human high-level visual processes can cope with unusual views, although at reduced efficiency.

An atypical or nonpreferred view might slow the identification process down in several ways. Because of occlusion or severe foreshortening, only a few of the parts of the object might be describable. Retrieval on the basis of a few parts might be slower than when more parts are present. For example, Palmer, Rosch, and Chase's rear view of a horse completely obscures the axis of the torso, one of the front legs, and the face. However, the neck, the tail, and three of the legs (although not their positioning on the torso) are clearly visible. It might take longer for this reduced description to activate the LTM representation of a horse. The activation might also be so weak that the high-level processes might refine the description of the image on the basis of the horse hypothesis in order to check its correctness. The refinement process might notice the ears, which are barely visible, or it might check to make sure that the positions of the legs in the image are consistent with the LTM model under foreshortening.

Human high-level visual processes also seem to have some special properties that reflect our ecological niche and possibly some neurophysiological design compromises. One property is the pervasiveness of the gravitationally defined upward direction in visual processing (Shepard and Hurwitz 1984). The up-down direction in the environment is sometimes assigned by default as the major axis of an object in the image, and the upward direction is assigned by default as indicating the head or top of the object (Rock 1973). The inverted wineglass in figure 12.20 is a weak case of this phenomenon, which does not interfere very strongly with identification. To appreciate the point better, notice that it is relatively easy to see the inverted wineglass as a flask with a plate resting on its top, whereas it is somewhat more difficult to see an upright wineglass as an inverted flask resting on a plate. It seems that many LTM representations specify that the major axis of the object has a specific orientation with respect to gravity. Unexpected orientations can slow down or introduce errors into the identification process.

The remarkable but very slow-acting process of mental rotation, which was described in chapter 2, is sometimes required to construct complex descriptions of disoriented objects before they can be matched to representations in memory. Mental rotation is not required to identify an inverted wineglass because the axes of its three parts are simply connected end to end and the entire object has a high degree of symmetry. Objects with left-right asymmetry and more complex descriptions, however, often cannot be matched without mental rotation. As stated in chapter 2, there is some evidence that such fine-grained matches are not even performed directly on schematic descriptions. Instead, it appears that the schemas must be read into a special visual buffer that represents the object from a viewpoint and thus has many of the properties of a "high-level" but still viewer-centered representation.

Alternative Approaches to Object Recognition   The approach to object recognition developed above was motivated in part by the recognition that the many possible views of any reasonably complex object will produce a wide range of low-level descriptions that have little in common with each other. Thus, the LTM representation could not be an image-centered or viewer-centered template of low-level information (intensity values, contours, or the like) that could be matched directly against the image (after some repositioning and size scaling) in recognition. In support of this intuition, template-matching approaches had an early history of limited success in computer vision.

By breaking up the image of an object into natural parts, classifying the parts in terms of orientation-independent properties, and describing the structural relations of the parts, the recognition-by-components scheme described above, and similar schemes, attempt to overcome the challenges to object recognition.

More recently, an alternative method of object recognition, called the *alignment* approach (Ullman 1989), has been shown to have much of the required flexibility as well as some unique strengths. The alignment approach was motivated in part by some potential difficulties with the use of simple parts and relations for object recognition. One problem is the crudeness of the part descriptions. Parts with different appearances will often be assigned the same shape description if we are limited to the parameters in table 12.1. The same description, for example, might be given to two rather different wineglasses, the one in figure 12.21 and another with a shorter stem and wider bowl of the same height. A second problem is that some three-dimensional objects are difficult to break into the appropriate kinds of parts (Ullman gives the example of a shoe).

In the simplest version of the alignment method the long-term representation, or model, of an object is a pictorial view, which represents the contours of the object from a point of view. Three alignment points are also associated with the object. These points are located at easily identifiable positions, such as concavities or curvature maxima. When a novel object is presented, a model can be matched against it in a three-stage process. First, three corresponding alignment points are found on the image. Second, the model and the image are aligned by mapping the points in the model onto the points in the image. The mathematical relationship between the two sets of points uniquely determines how much the model would have to be rescaled in size and rotated in order to match the image. The reason for this is that there are geometrically determined limits to the manner in which the spatial relations among the alignment points in the image can change with changing views. In the third step the alignment points in the image are brought into registration with the alignment points on the rescaled and rotated model, and the degree of match between the entire image and the entire model is calculated by measuring how closely their contours agree. If the image is indeed an image of the modeled object, the geometry of the method guarantees a close match.

This version of the method cannot cope with many problems discussed above, but Ullman has proposed various plausible extensions, including the use of more alignment points, the use of multiple model views of an object, and combining the approach with the use of descriptions. He also argues that the alignment process is as feasible computationally as processes that use parts and relations. Computer implementations of the method have been successful in restricted visual domains.

There is some evidence from human object recognition that is consistent with the alignment theory. Sensitivity of object recognition to variations in size and orientation, for example, could reflect an alignment stage. On the other hand, Biederman's approach also predicts many of these effects, and it handles effects that pose some difficulty for the alignment theory (Hummel and Biederman 1992). For example, the degree of match in the alignment method is measured along all of an object's contours, regardless of the object's description in terms of parts. But, as was pointed out above, human recognition is differentially affected by nonrecoverable as opposed to recoverable contour deletions.

12.5 The Architecture of Visual Computation

We have focused on a few of the tasks of vision, for example, the extraction of contour, textural grouping, the extraction of motion, finding parts, and describing objects. There are a number of other tasks that we have not had the time to address in detail, such as the perception of color and brightness, the perception of shape from shading, and the perception of depth. A crucial additional issue in the computational study of vision, however, is how the many tasks of vision, at both the lower and the higher levels, are integrated into a functioning system. There are questions about how independently each of the tasks of vision is carried out, about the points at which they should influence each other, and about how they are brought together to produce the final outputs of the system. Addressing these questions tends to raise the issue of how visual computation is actually implemented in neural circuitry. We can approach them by looking further at what is actually known about visual anatomy and physiology and by looking at connectionist models that tackle some of the larger problems of vision.

Vision and the Brain

We have seen that the computation of each type of information tends to be intensely parallel. In low-level visual processes, for example, the same computation is performed on all of the (overlapping) local areas of the entire image. Such computations are intrinsically parallel in the sense that the computation in each local area is independent of the results in all of the other areas. All of the local computations can proceed simultaneously. In the case of contour extraction and motion detection we saw that biological vision systems do indeed compute in parallel. On a larger scale, from figure 7.10, we have the general notion that biological sensory pathways are organized into parallel pathways, each of which has hierarchical structure as well. Computationally, vision is well suited to this organization because there are a number of different types of information that can be extracted from images independently (color, depth, contour, etc.) and because the overall problem is complicated enough that information has to be refined and combined through a number of stages in order to compute the desired outputs.

The Primate Visual Pathway   There is considerable evidence that at the higher levels visual computation is organized into two main components, a *what* system, concerned mainly with identifying or categorizing the objects in the visual field, and a *where* system, concerned with locations of objects and surfaces in the visual field. At the output level, the what system is associated with the inferior temporal lobe, and the where system is associated with the parietal lobe (see figure 7.3 and associated text). Although the two systems must interact in order to bind object identities to positions in space, they operate with considerable integrity. For example, Ungerlieder and Mishkin (1982) trained monkeys to associate food either with a shape on the cover of a container or with the spatial location of the container. Monkeys with parietal lesions could perform the shape task, but their performance on the spatial location task was severely impaired. Monkeys with temporal lesions could perform the spatial location task but were severely impaired on the shape task. Recordings from single cells in the two regions confirm this picture. Temporal cells have large receptive fields that include the central portion of the retina (fovea), and some of them respond to specific shapes, such as faces or hands (Desimone 1991). Parietal cells are sensitive to spatial properties of visual stimulation. For example, the direction of gaze modulates the responses of some cells that have localized receptive fields on the retinal image (Andersen, Essick, and Siegel 1985). Such cells are probably involved in the transformation from image-based spatial representation to head-based spatial representation that must be accomplished by the visual system. This transformation is necessary because the system ultimately must compute where things are in the world as opposed to where they are on the image. The correlation between image position and world position changes with eye movement. Zipser and Andersen (1988) have developed a connectionist model in which hidden units learn to compute the transformation between the two coordinate systems.

The functional significance of the what-where separation is probably the natural distinction between the identity of an object and its position. Generally, spatial position relative to viewpoint is not correlated with object identity, since objects occur at various distances and angles of view. It would be inefficient and perhaps impossible to wire up a cortical map in such a way that a full set of object-recognition machinery was present at every location in the map. It makes more sense to have a single system for object recognition and the ability to dynamically bind current objects to spatial positions. A mechanism of visual attention is also required to restrict object-recognition machinery to a single object at a given moment, as well as a way of computing a map of three-dimensional visual space that is independent of prior object recognition.

The various kinds of information available to low-level vision must be computed and delivered appropriately to the what and where systems. The principal known anatomical pathways from retina to inferotemporal and parietal cortex are shown schematically in figure 12.22. As we saw in chapter 7, the segregation of visual processing into parallel streams, or systems, begins with the ganglion cells on the retina (figure 12.9). There are two types of ganglion cells, distinguished by the sizes of their cell bodies, the shapes of their dendritic trees, and their response properties. The small P-cells project to the parvocellular layers of the lateral geniculate nucleus (LGN) of the thalamus (figure 7.3), and the large M-cells project to the magnocellular layers. In the primary visual cortex (V1) the magnocellular (M) stream is maintained, and the P stream divides into two separate streams, the parvo-interblob (PI) and the parvo-blob (PB). The three streams are maintained, with various cross-connections, through further processing in various cortical areas until they finally feed the output systems.

The relationships between the tripartite anatomy and computational function are complex and far from fully understood (DeYoe and Van Essen 1988; Livingstone and Hubel 1988). The complicated relationships begin with the primitive distinction between M and P cells in the retina and LGN. The two types of cells are specialized for the detection of different types of primitive image information. The parvo cells in the LGN have small receptive fields, making them sensitive to local contrast; they respond slowly but give sustained responses; they operate at high contrast; and they have wavelength preferences. The response properties of magno cells are complementary. They have large receptive fields, making them sensitive to area contrast; they respond quickly and transiently (that is, their response to a stimulus dies out very rapidly); they operate at very low contrasts; they are not wavelength selective. Since both types of cells exist in both eyes, binocular disparity information can be computed in processing streams that derive from both channels as well. The high spatial resolving power and wavelength selectivity of the parvo LGN cells suggest that the P stream of processing will be heavily concerned with the perception of shape and color. The transient properties and high sensitivity of the magno LGN cells suggests that the M stream of

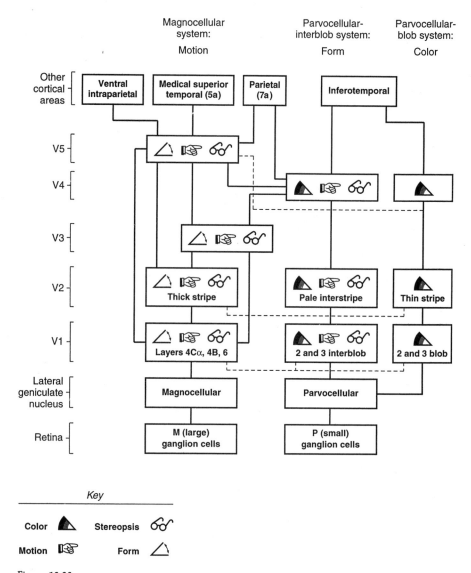

Figure 12.22
Schematic diagram of the primate visual pathway. V1 through V5 are areas of the visual cortex. Layers refer to the fact that the cortex is made up of distinct layers of cells. Blobs and stripes refer to the microscopic appearance of areas of the cortex after staining. Solid lines represent extensive connections. Although the discussion emphasizes the flow of information from lower to higher levels of representation, there are extensive backward connections in most cases. Dotted lines represent possible connections. (Adapted with permission from DeYoe and Van Essen 1988 and from Kandel 1991).

processing will be heavily concerned with motion computations. These expectations have largely been borne out, with a number of complications.

The PB stream, which arises from parvocellular inputs, appears to be dedicated to color perception. Cells in this pathway tend to show wavelength selectivity but not other kinds of selectivity, for example, for motion or orientation. The hierarchical stages of the pathway are probably in part required for color constancy computations. The spectral composition of the light reflected from a surface varies with the spectral composition of the illuminating light. By and large, we see a particular surface as having a constant color under changing illumination. Somehow the visual system manages to compensate for the effects of the illumination. The responses of PB cells in the primary visual cortex, however, are not color constant. The constancy must arise at a later stage (perhaps in V4) via spatial interactions across the image.

The PI pathway is a major input to the inferotemporal cortex. PI cells tend to be orientation sensitive and to have high acuity. These facts suggest that the stream's primary job is the analysis of shape via contour. The presence of wavelength sensitivity in PI processing is probably due to the usefulness of color contrasts (in addition to intensity contrasts) in contour detection. Color differences in this channel may constitute what DeYoe and Van Essen (1988) call a concealed cue to form. That is, the wavelength information is contributing to form perception rather than to color perception. Binocular-disparity, or stereopsis, information may also be present in the PI pathway in part because of its usefulness in shape perception. Stereoscopic information can specify that different parts of an object are at different distances from the perceiver and thus help to contribute the third dimension to the perception of a shape. The connection from the PI stream to the parietal cortex probably reflects the potential PI contributions to space perception. Stereo information from a high-acuity channel and perspective cues from contour information could contribute to space perception.

The multiple connections of the M pathway to area MT are not surprising, given the evidence, discussed above, that it is concerned with motion computations. The presence of stereo selectivity in the M stream probably reflects the need to ultimately compute motion in depth (although it appears that MT does not fully accomplish this). The presence of orientation information may reflect the usefulness of local contrast information in motion tracking, as well as the need to compute the motion of entire contours as opposed to localized spots. The connection from the PI system to the M system confirms Wang, Mathur, and Koch's theory (figure 12.17) that sustained contour information is needed to constrain the velocity-field smoothing computations within MT. Signals from the M to the PI pathway also make sense, because information about the shape of an object can be recovered from its motion.

Limits to Parallelism in Vision Figure 12.22 suggests a complete parallelism in the visual pathway, but detailed shape analysis and object recognition cannot be done in parallel across the visual field. In part this is because of the independence of the inferotemporal shape analysis system from spatial position, noted above, and in part it is because of an unequal division of resources between the central region of the image and the periphery, which extends from the retina through the visual cortex. Many of the ganglion cells in the central, foveal portion of the retina have very small receptive fields, making their outputs suitable for detailed pattern analysis. The ganglion cells in the periphery have larger receptive fields. The peripheral retina is essentially specialized for a rougher take on the image. Eye movements, which are often cued by motion in the periphery, function to bring regions of the visual field to the center of the retinal image, initiating more detailed processing, particularly high-resolution pattern processing. The central portion of the retina, which is only about 2.5 degrees in diameter, projects to about 25 percent of the primary visual cortex (De Valois and De Valois 1990). Full visual analysis of a scene requires a series of eye movements and fixations, allowing different regions of the scene to enter the limited window of maximum-quality visual computation.

One aspect of visual attention, then, is voluntary eye movements. There also seems to be an additional internal attentional mechanism that is required to process objects. There is evidence of various kinds that the extraordinary parallelism of the visual system breaks down at about the point where the various sources of information available in a region of the image have to be bound together into a representation of an object. Treisman (1985) found evidence of *illusory conjunctions* of simple visual features in preattentive vision. For example, in a briefly exposed array of several letters of different colors a subject will often report letter-color combinations that were not present in the display. If the subject has to locate a letter of a particular color (e.g., a green *T*) in a field of distractors (red *T*s and green *S*s), response time rises with the number of distractors present, indicating that the subject has to make an attention-demanding serial search for the target conjunction. Targets that are distinguished by a single low-level feature (e.g., a green *T* among red *T*s) seem to "pop out," however; response time stays constant with increasing numbers of distractors. In this case the search is done in parallel, reflecting the parallel organization of lower-level vision. In addition to feature binding, visual attention appears to be required for other relatively simple visual tasks, such as deciding whether one object is inside or outside the boundaries of another. Ullman (1984) calls the required processes *visual routines*. The neural locus of visual attention is unknown (Crick and Koch 1990 explores the issue).

Treisman (1992) and others (e.g., Feldman 1985) have pointed out that the phenomena of visual attention and eye movements require the existence of a scene buffer of some sort that can hold the representation of a scene as it is built up. For example, there must be a temporary representation of the current occurrence of an object (an object token) in addition to its long-term representation, which is used for object recognition. The neural mechanisms involved are again unknown, although the need for temporary object tokens suggests that the inferotemporal area should not be looked upon as merely a repository of visual category information.

Connectionist Approaches to Vision

It is important to realize that the anatomical connections and neuronal response selectivities discussed above fall far short of providing a complete theory of the neural architecture of vision. Even at low levels of the system, and increasingly at higher levels, very little is known about how the neural representation at a given level is actually computed by neural circuitry, or, in many cases, even about just what the neural representation is. The increasingly detailed knowledge of anatomical connections and cell response properties, however, provides a fertile ground for connectionist modeling. The known neurophysiological details can be used to constrain connectionist models, and the models can be used to guide further research into neural computation. The models of Wang, Mathur, and Koch (1990) and of Zipser and Andersen (1988), mentioned above, are both cases where knowledge of the inputs and outputs of a neural system were used successfully to constrain the development of a neural network model.

Another instructive example is Lehky and Sejnowski's (1990) model of shape from shading. The problem of shape from shading is to compute information about the three-dimensional shape of an object's surfaces from the shading of the surfaces. The input units to the model had standard Mexican-hat receptive fields on the image. The output units coded the orientation and curvature of the surfaces depicted in the input image. A hidden layer of units was trained with the backpropagation algorithm to compute the mapping from the input units to the shape units. Surprisingly, with training, the hidden units developed response properties that were similar to those of cortical simple cells. That is, they responded maximally to oriented local edges or bars. One lesson that the researchers drew from the model was that the computational function of a population of neurons cannot always be deduced directly from the neuronal response properties. It is usually assumed that the cortical simple cells are engaged in the computation of contours, since they respond to oriented edges. Yet the model demonstrated that such cells can compute shape from shading (under the conditions used in the simulation).

The connectionist literature contains many ideas about how different types of lower-level information can interact in the computation of higher-level information. In some cases a constraint relationship exists between two types of information that can be computed independently. One example is that information about the edge of a surface coming from edge computation can constrain the computation of surface orientation from shading. Although this constraint is rather mathematical in the general case, Barrow and Tenenbaum (1981) present a simple demonstration of a special case, shown in figure 12.23. When the edge of a surface is qualitatively inconsistent with its shading, the curvature due to shading is not perceived. This kind of constraint could be implemented by connections between a primal sketch subsystem and a shape-from-shading subsystem.

In other cases local representations must be aggregated to explicitly code more global segments. Here, units representing the more global segments must be excited or inhibited by units representing relevant lower-level local features. One simple example is the use of connections to find long, straight lines from a raw primal sketch that contains only short, local line segments. Figure 12.24 shows that a line can be represented as a pair of values: a distance from the origin and an orientation. We can

(a)   (b)

Figure 12.23
An example of the interaction of intrinsic image computations. The shading in both (a) and (b) indicates curvature around a vertical axis. The outline in (a) is consistent with this curvature. The outline in (b) indicates curvature around a horizontal axis and thus is inconsistent with the shading. In this case the outline information dominates the perception, and the inconsistent shading information seems to be suppressed. (Adapted from Barrow and Tenenbaum 1981.)

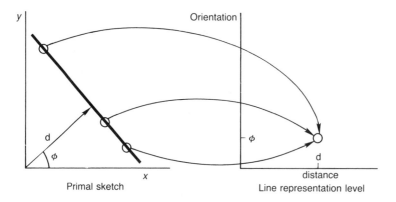

Figure 12.24
An example of how connections can be used to achieve global segmentations from local features. In this case the local oriented edge segments found by primal sketch computations must be grouped into the lines that they are part of. At the line representation level there is a unit for each possible global line. The circle on the line representation graph represents such a unit. A line in the image can be described by two parameters: a distance from the origin, and an angle that the distance vector makes with the x-axis. Thus, each line representation unit represents a potential line in the image with a particular distance from the origin and orientation. Connections between primal sketch units and line units can be made in such a way that each primal sketch unit is connected to the line units that it is consistent with. The connections between three primal sketch units and the consistent line unit are shown in the figure. When a line is present in an image, it activates many edge-segment units at the primal sketch level, which in turn activate a single global line unit at the line representation level. (Redrawn with permission from Ballard 1984.)

postulate a level of representation in which there is a unit for each possible combination of distance and orientation. In the raw primal sketch a line segment is represented by its (x, y) location and orientation. We have already postulated a level of representation at which there is a separate unit for every combination of location and local orientation. In fact, the simple cortical cells seem to be precisely such a representation. Now, we can imagine excitatory connections between each local segment unit and the global line units with which it is consistent. A global line unit will become highly activated only if it is "voted for" by many local segments.

Grossberg and his colleagues (Grossberg and Mingolla 1985 is a representative paper) have developed a network model of vision that stresses the interplay between a *boundary contour system* (BCS) and a *featural filling-in system* (FCS). The BCS develops contour information in much the way we have described, although it contains interesting mechanisms for extending and completing contours. The FCS tends to spread features, such as color, but the spreading is stopped at boundaries by inhibitory connections from the BCS. The model explains a number of counterintuitive phenomena in contour, texture, and color perception.

The applicability of connectionist ideas should extend to high-level vision. Within the focus of visual attention, for example, the recognition of simple objects takes under a second and is therefore subject to the hundred-step rule (see chapter 2). Any well-developed theory of object recognition poses significant challenges for connectionist modeling, however. As we saw above, Biederman's theory of object recognition, for example, requires quite a bit of structural description. The features of each of the parts of an object, called *geons*, must be in a particular arrangement (e.g., circular cross section, parallel sides), and the geons themselves must be in a particular spatial arrangement (in a wineglass the base is attached to the stem, which is attached to the bowl).

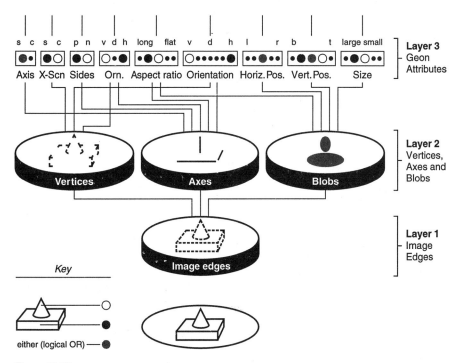

Figure 12.25

An overview of the first three layers of Hummel and Biederman's model, indicating the representation activated at each layer by the image in the key. In layer 3 large dots indicate active units, and small dots inactive units. Units in layer 1 represent local edge segments. Units in layer 2 represent vertices, axes, and blobs (enclosed areas) defined by conjunctions of edges in Layer 1. Layer 3 represents the geons in the image in terms of their defining dimensions: axis shape, straight (s) or curved (c); cross-section shape, straight or curved; whether the sides are parallel (p) or nonparallel (n); coarse orientation, vertical (v), diagonal (d), or horizontal (h); aspect ratio, elongated (long) to flattened (flat); fine orientation, vertical, diagonal to the left, diagonal to the right, or horizontal in one of four possible orientations in depth; horizontal position in the visual field, left (l) to right (r); vertical position in the visual field, bottom (b) to top (t); size, small (near 0 percent of the visual field) to large (near 100 percent of the visual field). Note that a particular geon attribute can be excited by more than one geon in the input; for example, both geons in the input shown (cone and brick) have straight cross sections. (Adapted with permission from Hummel and Biederman 1992.)

We saw in chapters 2 and 3 that structured representations can be difficult to encode in connectionist networks. Biederman's object descriptions pose a severe version of the binding problem, introduced in section 3.3. The features of each geon in an object must be properly bound together, and all the geons must then be properly bound to each other. However, Hummel and Biederman (1992) have developed a connectionist model for the recognition-by-components theory. Like Shastri and Ajjanagadde (1992), they solve the binding problem via the synchronous firing of nodes (see figure 3.5 and the accompanying discussion). Throughout the model, units representing items that are bound together fire in phase.

The input units to the network encode local edge information, and the output units represent object identities. The computation breaks down into two rough stages: finding the geons and finding their relations. The first three layers of the model are diagrammed in figure 12.25. There are appropriate excitatory and inhibitory

(a)

L
Two legs, either straight or curved

Fork
Three legs, no angles greater than 180°

Arrow
Three legs, one angle greater than 180°

Tangent-Y
Three legs, two (including the inner leg)
curved, one angle greater than 180°

(b)

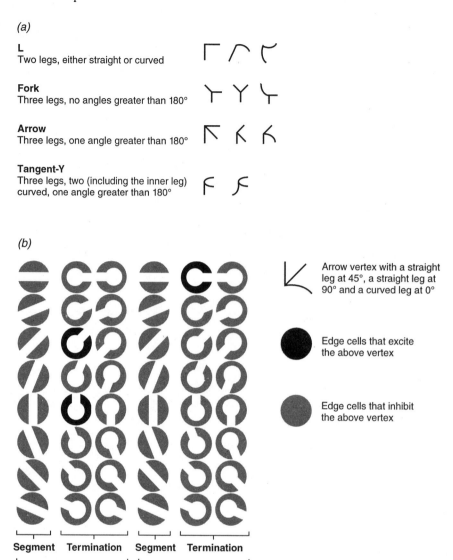

Arrow vertex with a straight
leg at 45°, a straight leg at
90° and a curved leg at 0°

Edge cells that excite
the above vertex

Edge cells that inhibit
the above vertex

Segment   Termination   Segment   Termination

Straight   Curved

Figure 12.26
Connections between layer 1 and layer 2 of Hummel and Biederman's model. (*a*) The types of vertices
detected in layer 2. (*b*) An illustration of the mapping from the edge units at a given image location in
layer 1 to a vertex unit in the corresponding location in layer 2. At each image location in layer 1 there
is a full complement of units that detect local edge types. Segment units detect straight or curved oriented
edges that run through the entire receptive field. Termination units detect straight or curved oriented
edges that terminate within the receptive field. At each image location in layer 2 there is a unit for each
type of vertex at each orientation. Detecting a vertex of a particular type and orientation at a particular
location is a matter of detecting a conjunction of appropriate edge terminations. Thus, as shown, each
vertex unit receives excitatory connections from its constituent termination units in layer 1 and inhibitory
input from inconsistent edge units in layer 1. (Adapted with permission from Hummel and Biederman
1992.)

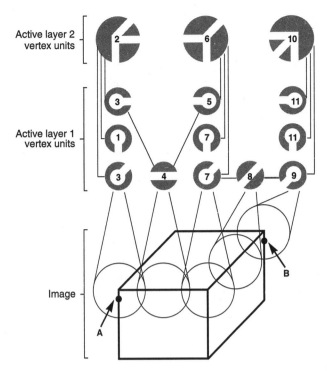

Figure 12.27
An example of how features are grouped into geons using chains of fast enabling links (FEL chains). The circles on the image illustrate the area of the image represented by Layer 1 cells responding to that portion of the image. For example, the units labeled 1 and 3 respond to the front, upper, left vertex of the brick. The connections between units shown are FELs. The numbers in the units represent steps in the FEL chain originating at point A and terminating at point B on the brick. When unit 1, representing point A, fires, it causes unit 2 to fire in synchrony via a FEL signal. This event causes cells labeled 3 to fire, and so on until the process reaches point B (unit 11). Because of the properties of FEL signals, all units are then firing in synchrony.

connections between edge units in layer 1 and the vertex, axis, and blob units in layer 2. Figure 12.26 illustrates how edge units are connected to vertex units. Layer 3 is not an image map. There is one unit for each geon feature, a total of fifty-eight. Units in layer 2 excite consistent geon features in layer 3. For example, fork and arrow vertex units in layer 2 excite the straight cross-section unit in layer 3. Curved-L and tangent-Y vertex units excite the curved cross-section unit in layer 3. Within layer 3 there are inhibitory connections between inconsistent geon features. For example, the straight and curved cross-section units inhibit each other.

The model as so far described does not solve the binding problem. For example, there is no representation of which vertices are grouped into the same geon. In figure 12.25 six L-vertex units will fire in layer 2, but there is no representation of the fact that three of them belong to the cone and three to the brick. The binding problem is solved by a mechanism that causes the vertex, axis, and blob units belonging to the same geon to fire in synchrony. Different geons are randomly assigned to different phases. For example, in figure 12.25 the layer 2 units belonging to the cone will fire together in one phase, and the units belonging to the brick will fire together in a different phase. Geon attribute units in layer 3 fire in phase with the geons they belong to.

Synchronous firing is achieved in Hummel and Biederman's model using a second kind of connection, called the *fast enabling link* (FEL). FELs are independent of standard connections. If two units are active and share a FEL, they fire in synchrony. Transmission along FELs is assumed to be fast enough that if a chain of active units is connected by FELs (a FEL chain), all the units fire in synchrony. Binding via FEL chains is illustrated in figure 12.27. A similar strategy of synchronous firing is also used higher in the network to represent the structural relations of the geons.

In many respects Hummel and Biederman's model and their computer simulations of it are highly oversimplified. The model has an impoverished vocabulary of geons and relations. Its only input is a clean representation of local edge information. Naturalistic visual input is noisier but includes many more sources of information. The FEL mechanism also has no known neurophysiological substrate. Nevertheless, the model illustrates that a connectionist approach to complex object recognition is feasible.

Research on vision is one of the most exciting areas of cognitive science because knowledge of the inputs, outputs, and neural hardware of the visual system has advanced to the point where detailed computational models with considerable neural plausibility can be developed.

Suggested Readings

Seeing: Illusion, Brain, and Mind (Frisby 1980) is an introductory, but very rigorous, treatment of some of the main ideas in this chapter. *Vision: A Computational Investigation into the Human Representation and Processing of Visual Information* (Marr 1982) is a classic because of its clear and detailed development of the cognitive science perspective. Although some of Marr's specific theories are losing influence, the book continues to repay careful reading for its philosophical perspective and its integration of the methods of AI, psychology, and neuroscience. *Perception* (Sekuler and Blake 1990) covers many topics in the psychology and physiology of vision and the other senses that could not be included in this chapter. *The Computational Brain* (Churchland and Sejnowski 1992) introduces the connectionist approach to vision.

References

Andersen, R. A., G. K. Essick, and R. M. Siegel (1985). Encoding of spatial location by posterior parietal neurons. *Science, 230,* 456–458.

Ballard, D. H. (1984). Parameter nets. *Artificial Intelligence 22,* 235–267.

Barrow, H. G., and J. M. Tenenbaum (1978). Recovering intrinsic scene characteristics from images. In A. R. Hanson and E. M. Riseman, eds., *Computer vision systems.* New York: Academic Press.

Barrow, H. G., and J. M. Tenenbaum (1981). Interpreting line drawings as three-dimensional surfaces. *Artificial Intelligence 17,* 75–116.

Bergen, J. R., and E. H. Adelson (1988). Early vision and texture perception. *Nature 333,* 363–364.

Biederman, I. (1985). Human image understanding: Recent research and a theory. *Computer Vision, Graphics, and Image Processing 32,* 29–73.

Binford, T. (1982). Survey of model based image analysis systems. *International Journal of Robotics Research 1,* 18–64.

Blakemore, C., and F. W. Campbell (1969). On the existence of neurones in the human visual system selectively sensitive to the orientation and size of retinal images. *Journal of Physiology 203,* 237–260.

Braddick, O. J. (1974). A short-range process in apparent motion. *Vision Research 14,* 519–527.

Braddick, O. J. (1979). Low-level and high-level processes in apparent motion. *Philosophical Transactions of the Royal Society of London* B 290, 137–151.

Brady, M., J. Ponce, A. Yuille, and H. Asada (1985). Describing surfaces. *Computer Vision, Graphics, and Image Processing* 32, 1–28.

Burton, G. J., and K. H. Ruddock (1978). Visual adaptation to patterns containing two-dimensional spatial structure. *Vision Research* 18, 93–99.

Caelli, T. (1985). Three processing characteristics of visual texture segmentation. *Spatial Vision* 1, 19–30.

Churchland, P. S., and T. J. Sejnowski (1992). *The computational brain*. Cambridge, Mass.: MIT Press.

Cornsweet, T. N. (1970). *Visual perception*. New York: Academic Press.

Crick, F., and C. Koch (1990). Towards a neurobiological theory of consciousness. *Seminars in the Neurosciences* 2, 263–275.

Desimone, R. (1991). Face-selective cells in the temporal cortex of monkeys. *Journal of Cognitive Neuroscience* 3, 1–24.

De Valois, R. L., and K. K. De Valois (1990). *Spatial vision*. New York: Oxford University Press.

De Valois, R. L., E. W. Yund, and N. Hepler (1982). The orientation and direction selectivity of cells in macaque visual cortex. *Vision Research* 22, 531–544.

DeYoe, E. A., and D. C. Van Essen (1988). Concurrent processing streams in monkey visual cortex. *Trends in Neurosciences* 11 (5), 219–226.

Enroth-Cugell, C., and D. Robson (1966). The contrast sensitivity of retinal ganglion cells of the cat. *Journal of Physiology (London)* 187, 517–522.

Feldman, J. A. (1985). Four frames suffice: A provisional model of vision and space. *Behavioral and Brain Sciences* 8, 265–289.

Fodor, J. A., and Z. W. Pylyshyn (1981). How direct is visual perception? Some reflections on Gibson's "ecological approach." *Cognition* 9, 139–196.

Frisby, J. P. (1980). *Seeing: Illusion, brain, and mind*. New York: Oxford University Press.

Gibson, J. J. (1966). *The senses considered as perceptual systems*. Boston: Houghton Mifflin.

Grossberg, S., and E. Mingolla (1985). Neural dynamics of perceptual grouping: Texture, boundaries, and emergent segmentations. *Perception and Psychophysics*, 38, 141–171.

Hanson, A. R., and E. M. Riseman (1978a). Segmentation of natural scenes. In A. R. Hanson and E. M. Riseman, eds., *Computer vision systems*. New York: Academic Press.

Hanson, A. R., and E. M. Riseman (1978b). VISIONS: A computer system for interpreting scenes. In A. R. Hanson and E. M. Riseman, eds., *Computer vision systems*. New York: Academic Press.

Hildreth, E. C. (1984a). Computations underlying the measurement of visual motion. *Artificial Intelligence* 23, 309–354.

Hildreth, E. C. (1984b). The computation of the velocity field. *Proceedings of the Royal Society of London* B 221, 189–220.

Hoffman, D. D., and W. A. Richards (1984). Parts of recognition. *Cognition* 18, 65–96.

Hubel, D. H., and T. N. Wiesel (1979). Brain mechanisms of vision. In *The brain: A Scientific American book*. New York: W. H. Freeman.

Hubel, D. H., T. N. Wiesel, and M. P. Stryker (1978). Anatomical demonstration of orientation columns in macaque monkey. *Journal of Comparative Neurology* 177, 361–379.

Hummel, J. E., and I. Biederman (1992). Dynamic binding in a neural network for shape recognition. *Psychological Review*, 99, 480–517.

Ittelson, W. H., and F. P. Kilpatrick (1958). Experiments in perception. In D. C. Beardslee and M. Wertheimer, eds., *Readings in perception*. Princeton, N.J.: Van Nostrand.

Julesz, B., and J. R. Bergen (1983). Textons, the fundamental elements in preattentive vision and perception of textures. *Bell System Technical Journal* 62, 1619–1645.

Kandel, E. R. (1991). Perception of motion, depth, and form. In E. R. Kandel, J. H. Schwartz, and T. M. Jessell, eds., *Principles of neural science*. 3rd ed. Norwalk, Conn.: Appleton and Lange.

Kuffler, S. W. (1953). Discharge patterns and functional organization of the mammalian retina. *Journal of Neurophysiology* 16, 37–68.

Lehky, S. R., and T. J. Sejnowski (1990). Neural network model of visual cortex for determining surface curvature from images of shaded surfaces. *Proceedings of the Royal Society of London*, B 240, 251–278.

Livingstone, M., and D. Hubel (1988). Segregation of form, color, movement, and depth: Anatomy, physiology, and perception. *Science* 240, 740–749.

Maffei, L., and A. Fiorentini (1973). The visual cortex as a spatial frequency analyzer. *Vision Research* 13, 1255–1267.

Maffei, L., and A. Fiorentini (1977). Spatial frequency rows in the striate visual cortex. *Vision Research* 17, 257–264.

Marr, D. (1976). Early processing of visual information. *Philosophical Transactions of the Royal Society of London* B 275, 483–524.

Marr, D. (1977). Analysis of occluding contour. *Proceedings of the Royal Society of London* B 197, 441–475.

Marr, D. (1982). *Vision: A computational investigation into the human representation and processing of visual information.* New York: W. H. Freeman.

Marr, D., and E. Hildreth (1980). Theory of edge detection. *Proceedings of the Royal Society of London* B 207, 187–217.

Marr, D., and H. K. Nishihara (1978). Representation and recognition of the spatial organization of three-dimensional shapes. *Proceedings of the Royal Society of London* B 200, 269–294.

Marr, D., and S. Ullman (1981). Directional selectivity and its use in early visual processing. *Proceedings of the Royal Society of London* B 211, 151–180.

Maunsell, J. H. R., and D. van Essen (1983). Functional properties of neurons in middle temporal visual area of the macaque monkey: II. Binocular interactions and sensitivity to binocular disparity. *Journal of Neurophysiology* 49, 1148–1167.

Movshon, J. A., and W. T. Newsome (1992). Neural foundations of motion perception. *Current Directions in Psychological Science* 1 (1), 35–39.

Nakayama, K. (1985). Biological image motion processing: A review. *Vision Research* 25, 625–660.

Newsome, W. T., and E. B. Paré (1988). A selective impairment of motion perception following lesions of the middle temporal visual area (MT). *Journal of Neuroscience* 8, 2201–2211.

O'Keeffe, G. (1976). *Georgia O'Keeffe.* New York: Viking Press.

Palmer, S. E., E. Rosch, and P. Chase (1981). Canonical perspective and the perception of objects. In J. Long and A. Baddeley, eds., *Attention and performance IX.* Hillsdale, N.J.: Erlbaum.

Pantle, A. (1978). Temporal frequency response characteristics of motion channels measured with three different psychophysical techniques. *Perception and Psychophysics* 24, 285–294.

Richards, W., and D. D. Hoffman (1985). Codon constraints on closed 2D shapes. *Computer Vision, Graphics, and Image Processing* 32, 265–281.

Rock, I. (1973). *Orientation and form.* New York: Academic Press.

Rodieck, R. W., and J. Stone (1965). Analysis of receptive fields of cat retinal ganglion cells. *Journal of Neurophysiology* 28, 833–849.

Saito, H., M. Yukie, K. Tanaka, K. Hibosaka, Y. Fukuda, and E. Iwai (1986). Integration of direction signals of image motion in the superior sulcus of the macaque monkey. *Journal of Neuroscience,* 6, 145–157.

Sekuler, R., and R. Blake (1990). *Perception.* 2nd ed. New York: Alfred Knopf.

Shastri, L., and V. Ajjanagadde (1992). From simple associations to systematic reasoning: A connectionist representation of rules, variables, and dynamic bindings using temporal synchrony. Technical report MS-CIS-90-05, Computer and Information Science Department, University of Pennsylvania, Philadelphia, Penn.

Shepard, R. N., and S. Hurwitz (1984). Upward direction, mental rotation, and discrimination of left and right turns in maps. *Cognition* 18, 161–193.

Stevens, K. A. (1978). Computation of locally parallel structure. *Biological Cybernetics* 29, 19–28.

Tootell, R. B., M. S. Silverman, and R. L. De Valois (1981). Spatial frequency columns in primary visual cortex. *Science* 214, 813–815.

Treisman, A. (1985). Preattentive processing in vision. *Computer Vision, Graphics, and Image Processing* 31, 156–177.

Treisman, A. (1992). Perceiving and re-perceiving objects. *American Psychologist* 47, 862–875.

Ullman, S. (1979). *The interpretation of visual motion.* Cambridge, Mass.: MIT Press.

Ullman, S. (1984). Visual routines. *Cognition* 18, 97–159.

Ullman, S. (1989). Aligning pictorial descriptions: An approach to object recognition. *Cognition* 32, 193–254.

Ungerlieder, L. G., and M. Mishkin (1982). Two cortical visual systems. In D. J. Ingle, M. A. Goodale, and R. J. W. Mansfield, eds., *Analysis of visual behavior.* Cambridge, Mass.; MIT Press.

Wallach, H., and D. N. O'Connell (1953). The kinetic depth effect. *Journal of Experimental Psychology* 45, 205–217.

Wang, H. T., B. Mathur, and K. Koch (1990). I thought I saw it move: Computing optical flow in the primate visual system. In M. A. Gluck and D. E. Rumelhart, eds., *Neuroscience and connectionist theory*. Hillsdale, N.J.: Erlbaum.

Wilson, H. R. (1983). Psychophysical evidence for spatial channels. In O. J. Braddick and A. C. Sleigh, eds., *Physical and biological processing of images*. New York: Springer-Verlag.

Wilson, H. R., and J. R. Bergen (1979). A four mechanism model for threshold spatial vision. *Vision Research 19*, 19–32.

Witkin, A. P., and J. M. Tenenbaum (1983). On the role of structure in vision. In J. Beck, B. Hope, and A. Rosenfeld, eds., *Human and machine vision*. New York: Academic Press.

Zipser, D., and R. A. Andersen (1988). A back-propagation programmed network that simulates response properties of a subset of posterior parietal neurons. *Nature 331*, 679–684.

Index